A Professional Approach

Microsoft® Office
Excel®

Comprehensive

2003

Kathleen Stewart

McGraw Hill **Technology Education**

Boston Burr Ridge, IL Dubuque, IA Emeryville, CA Madison, WI New York San Francisco St. Louis
Bangkok Bogotá Caracas Kuala Lumpur Lisbon London Madrid Mexico City
Milan Montreal New Delhi Santiago Seoul Singapore Sydney Taipei Toronto

 **Technology Education**

1333 Burr Ridge Parkway
Burr Ridge, Illinois 60527
U.S.A.

Microsoft® Office Excel® 2003: A Professional Approach, Comprehensive
Student Edition

Copyright © 2005 by The McGraw-Hill Companies, Inc. All rights reserved. No part of this publication may be reproduced or distributed in any form or by any means, or stored in a database or retrieval system, without the prior written consent of The McGraw-Hill Companies, Inc., including, but not limited to, in any network or other electronic storage or transmission, or broadcast for distance learning.

For information on translations or book distributors outside the U.S.A., please see the International Contact Information page immediately following the index of this book. Some ancillaries, including electronic and print components, may not be available to customers outside the United States.

6 7 8 9 0 QPD QPD 0 1 9 8 7
ISBN: 978-0-07-225449-5
MHID: 0-07-225449-1

Sponsoring Editor
Gareth Hancock

Developmental Editor
Lisa Chin-Johnson

Senior Project Editor
Betsy Manini

Technical Editors
XinGuo Zhu, Darren Choong, EK Choong

Copy Editor
Bob Campbell

Proofreader
Stefany Otis

Indexer
Valerie Perry

Composition
Carie Abrew, Tabitha M. Cagan

Illustrators
Kathleen Edwards, Melinda Lytle

Interior Design
Leggitt Associates, Creative Ink, Inc.,
Peter F. Hancik

This book was composed with Corel VENTURA™ Publisher.

www.mhteched.com

Contents

UNIT 1   INTRODUCTION TO EXCEL

UNIT 2   WORKING WITH FORMULAS AND FUNCTIONS

UNIT 3   ENHANCING WORKSHEET APPEARANCE

UNIT 4   IMPROVING USES OF WORKSHEET DATA

UNIT 5   INCREASING PRODUCTIVITY

UNIT 6 USING ANALYSIS, LINKING, AND WORKGROUP FEATURES

UNIT 7   USING DATA AND LIST FEATURES

What does this logo mean?

It means this courseware has been approved by the Microsoft® Office Specialist Program to be among the finest available for learning *Microsoft® Office Excel® 2003*. It also means that upon completion of this courseware, you may be prepared to take an exam for Microsoft Office Specialist qualification.

What Is a Microsoft Office Specialist?

A Microsoft Office Specialist is an individual who has passed exams for certifying his or her skills in one or more of the Microsoft Office desktop applications such as Microsoft Word, Microsoft Excel, Microsoft PowerPoint, Microsoft Outlook, Microsoft Access, or Microsoft Project. The Microsoft Office Specialist Program typically offers certification exams at the "Specialist" and "Expert" skill levels.* The Microsoft Office Specialist Program is the only program in the world approved by Microsoft for testing proficiency in Microsoft Office desktop applications and Microsoft Project. This testing program can be a valuable asset in any job search or career advancement.

More Information:

To learn more about becoming a Microsoft Office Specialist, visit www.microsoft.com/officespecialist. To learn about other Microsoft Office Specialist approved courseware from McGraw-Hill/Technology Education, visit http://www.mhteched.com.

Preface

Microsoft® Office Excel® 2003: A Professional Approach, Comprehensive Student Edition is written to help you master Microsoft Excel for Windows. The text takes you step-by-step through the Excel features that you're likely to use in both your personal and business life.

Case Study

Learning about the features of Excel is one thing, but applying what you learn is another. That's why a Case Study runs through the text. The Case Study offers the opportunity to learn Excel in a realistic business context. Take the time to read the Case Study about Klassy Kow Ice Cream, Inc., a fictional business located in San Francisco, California. All the documents for this course involve Klassy Kow Ice Cream, Inc.

Organization of the Text

The text includes seven units. Each unit is divided into smaller lessons. There are 24 lessons, each building on previously learned procedures. This building-block approach, together with the Case Study and the features listed below, enable you to maximize the learning process.

Features of the Text

- ☑ *Objectives* are listed for each lesson
- ☑ Required skills for the *Microsoft Office Specialist and Expert Certification Exams* are listed for each lesson
- ☑ The *estimated time* required to complete each lesson (up to the "Using Online Help") is stated
- ☑ Within a lesson, each *heading* corresponds to an objective
- ☑ Easy-to-follow *exercises* emphasize "learning by doing"
- ☑ *Key terms* are italicized and defined as they are encountered
- ☑ Extensive *graphics* display screen contents
- ☑ *Toolbar buttons* and *keyboard keys* are shown in the text when used
- ☑ *Large toolbar buttons in the margins* provide easy-to-see references
- ☑ Lessons contain important *Notes*, useful *Tips*, and helpful *Reviews*
- ☑ *Using Online Help* introduces you to a Help topic related to lesson content
- ☑ A *Lesson Summary* reviews the important concepts taught in the lesson
- ☑ A *Command Summary* lists the commands taught in the lesson
- ☑ *Concepts Review* includes true/false, short answer, and critical thinking questions that focus on lesson content
- ☑ *Skills Review* provides skill reinforcement for each lesson
- ☑ *Lesson Applications* ask you to apply your skills in a more challenging way
- ☑ *On Your Own* exercises let you apply your skills creatively
- ☑ *Unit Applications* give you the opportunity to use the skills you learn in a unit
- ☑ Also included are an *Appendix* of Microsoft Office Specialist standards, a *Glossary*, and an *Index*

Microsoft Office Specialist Certification Program

The Microsoft Office Specialist certification program offers certification at two skill levels—"Specialist" and "Expert." This certification can be a valuable asset in any job search. For more information about this Microsoft program, go to www.microsoft.com/officespecialist. For a complete listing of the skills for the Excel 2003 "Specialist" and "Expert" certification exams (and a correlation to the lessons in the text), see the Appendix: "Microsoft Office Specialist and Expert Certification."

Conventions Used in the Text

This text uses a number of conventions to help you learn the program and save your work.

- ☑ Text to key appears either in **boldface** or as a separate figure.

- ☑ Filenames appear in **boldface**.

- ☑ Options that you choose from menus and dialog boxes appear in a font that is similar to the on-screen font; for example, "Choose Print from the File menu." (The underline means you can press Alt and key the letter to choose the option.)

- ☑ You're asked to save each document with your initials followed by the exercise name. For example, an exercise might end with this instruction: "Save the workbook as *[your initials]*5-12." Documents are saved in folders for each lesson.

If You Are Unfamiliar with Windows

If you're unfamiliar with Windows, review the "Windows Tutorial" on the Professional Approach Student web site at www.mhteched.com/pas before beginning Lesson 1. This tutorial provides a basic overview of the program and shows you how to use the mouse. You might also want to review "File Management" (also on the Professional Approach Student web site) to get more comfortable using files and folders.

Screen Differences

As you practice each concept, illustrations of the screens help you follow the instructions. Don't worry if your screen is different from the illustration. These differences are due to variations in system and computer configurations.

Acknowledgments

We thank the technical editors and reviewers of this text for their valuable assistance: XinGuo Zhu; Rajiv Malkan, Montgomery College, TX; Darren Choong; EK Choong; Susan Olson, Northwest Technical College, East Grand Forks, MN; John Walker, Doña Ana Community College, Las Cruces, NM; Mary Davey, Computer Learning Network, Camp Hill, PA.

Installation Requirements

You'll need Microsoft Excel 2003 to work through this textbook. Excel needs to be installed on the computer's hard drive or on a network. Use the following checklist to evaluate installation requirements.

Hardware

- ☑ Computer with 233 MHz or higher processor and at least 128MB of RAM
- ☑ CD-ROM drive and other external media (3.5-inch high-density floppy, ZIP, etc.)
- ☑ 400MB or more of hard disk space for a "Typical" Office installation
- ☑ Super VGA (800 × 600) or higher-resolution video monitor
- ☑ Printer (laser or ink-jet recommended)
- ☑ Mouse
- ☑ Modem or other Internet connection (required for Using Online Help and Web-based exercises)

Software

- ☑ Excel 2003 (from Microsoft Office System 2003)
- ☑ Windows 2000 with Service Pack 3 or later, or Windows XP or later operating system
- ☑ Browser with dial-up or broadband Internet access

Internet Access

Access to the Internet is required for most of the Using Online Help exercises and Web-related exercises. Many of the help features are only available online. Microsoft Office Online is also a valuable resource for additional clip art, photographs, templates, and other Excel resources.

Installing New Features

Some lessons take advantage of Excel or Office features that may require installation or copying of files. The following table lists those features, explains their use, and how to install/use a feature.

LESSON	FEATURE	USE	HOW TO INSTALL
5, 6, 7, 10, 14, 16, and 18	Worksheet templates on CD	Build a new workbook based on template.	Copy files from CD to C:\Documents and Settings\User\Application Data\Microsoft\Templates for files to appear in the General tab of Templates dialog box.
5, 11, 14, Unit 4, 15, 16, and 17	Clip Art, additional	Use clip art related to the case.	Copy files to any usable folder, or insert directly from CD.
14	Excel templates (Spreadsheet Solutions)	Build a new workbook based on template.	Part of typical installation; files are in C:\Program Files\Office 11\Templates\1033.
10	Comments	Add an annotation/comment to a worksheet cell.	Tools, Options, View. Verify that comment indicator only will display.
9–24	Internet functionality	Use Online Help, use Online Template Gallery, use additional research tools, view Web pages.	Specific to classroom.
11	Language tools	Use thesaurus and translation tools in Research task pane.	Install when prompted at first use. May require installation CD.
17	Visual Basic Editor	View, edit, and save macros.	Part of a typical installation for Office 2003 Professional. Install if/when prompted. May require installation CD.
18	Digital Certificate for VBA Projects	Create a digital certificate for a workbook.	Part of a typical installation for Office 2003 Professional. Listed with Microsoft Office Tools. Install if/when prompted. May require installation CD.
19	Goal Seek	Perform what-if analysis.	Part of a typical installation for Office 2003 Professional. Install if/when prompted. May require installation CD.
19	Solver	Perform what-if analysis.	Choose Tools, Add-Ins, and Solver Add-In. Click OK.
22	XML functionality	View, edit, and save XML files.	Part of a typical installation for Office 2003 Professional. Install if/when prompted. May require installation CD.
22	MS Query	Import a database file.	Part of a typical installation for Office 2003 Professional. Install if/when prompted. May require installation CD.
22, 23	Microsoft Word	Open word processing files.	Included with all versions of Office 2003. Install from Control Panel or installation CD.
22, 23	Notepad or WordPad	Open text files.	Part of typical Windows installation. Install from Control Panel or installation CD.
23, 24	Office Web Components and Internet Explorer	Publish a PivotTable List and an interactive workbook.	Part of a typical installation for Office 2003 Professional. Install if/when prompted. May require installation CD.

CASE STUDY

Klassy Kow ICE CREAM, Inc.

There's more to learning a spreadsheet program like Microsoft Office Excel than simply keying data. You need to know how to use Excel in a real-world situation. That's why all the lessons in this book relate to everyday business tasks.

As you work through the lessons, imagine yourself working as an intern for Klassy Kow Ice Cream, Inc., a fictional San Francisco business that manufactures and sells ice cream.

Klassy Kow Ice Cream, Inc.

Klassy Kow Ice Cream, Inc., was formed in 1985 by Conrad Steele shortly after the death of his father. Since 1967, Conrad's father and mother had been dairy farmers in Klamath Falls, Oregon. As an addition to their farm, Archibald and Henrietta Steele opened a small ice cream shop. They made their own ice cream from fresh cream, eggs, and butter—starting simply with vanilla, chocolate, and strawberry flavors. They also sold cones, sundaes, shakes, and malts.

As word spread about their delicious ice cream, Archie and Henrietta's business blossomed from a seasonal shop to a year-round one. Eventually, the Steeles' expanded the number of flavors and started to offer hand-packed ice cream pies and cakes. They also started to sell to small supermarkets in southern Oregon under the "Klassy Kow" name, allowing their many customers to buy half-gallons at their favorite supermarket.

The business continued to expand and soon reached into supermarkets in the Pacific Northwest. Archibald and Henrietta opened new ice cream shops in Medford, Oregon, and in Eureka and Red Bluff, California.

After Archibald Steele died, Conrad and his mother sold the dairy farm but kept the ice cream shops. They continue to buy ice cream from the new owners (the Klamath Farm) and have expanded the ice cream business to include 33 franchised ice cream shops in the West.

In 1998, with Klassy Kow continuing to grow steadily, Conrad decided to move the corporate headquarters to San Francisco, California. His mother, Henrietta, is retired and still lives in Klamath Falls. She continues to help create and test new flavors for the Klamath Farm.

The company now has over 200 employees, but the number of employees in the San Francisco office is surprisingly small. Most of the employees work in the ice cream shops scat-

FIGURE CS-1   Sales area for Klassy Kow Ice Cream, Inc.

tered across Washington, Oregon, Nevada, and northern California. Figure CS-1 shows the general area in which Klassy Kow Ice Cream Shops are located. Some of the more important employees from the San Francisco office are shown in Figure CS-2. It might be helpful to associate the pictures of the employees with their names as you work in the course. Pay particular attention to each person's area of responsibility.

Conrad Steele, who is now president and chief executive officer of Klassy Kow, is responsible for the general operation of the company. He says, "I love to see the big smiles on the customers' faces after the first lick. It makes it all worth it."

Conrad visits many of the ice cream shops and likes to keep in touch with customers. He visits Klamath Farms at least four times a year to keep in contact with his major supplier.

All the worksheets, documents, and graphics you will use in this course relate to Klassy Kow Ice Cream, Inc. As you work with the worksheets in the text, take the time to notice the following things:

- The types of worksheets needed in a small business to carry on day-to-day business.
- The formatting of worksheets. Real businesses don't always pay much attention to formatting internal worksheets. However, they do focus on formatting worksheets that the customer will see.
- The types of business activities required by a company such as Klassy Kow. For example, it must deal with employees, internal accounting, and suppliers.

As you use this text and become more experienced with Microsoft Office Excel, you will also gain expertise in creating, editing, and formatting the sort of worksheets generated in a real-life business environment.

FIGURE CS-2 Key employees

| **CONRAD STEELE** | **JUAN SANTE** | **KEIKO SUMARA** | **ROBIN MCDONALD** |
| President and Chief Executive Officer | Vice President, Financial Operations | Sales and Marketing Manager | Director of Human Resources |

Klassy Kow Ice Cream, Inc.

Products

Sugar Cones
Waffle Cones
Ice Cream
Frozen Yogurt
Shakes
Malteds
Ice Cream Sodas
Ice Cream Sundaes
Ice Cream Cakes
Ice Cream Pies
Ice Cream Sandwiches
Coffee
Soda

Klassy Kow Klassics

Kowabunga
(An ice cream freeze, in several flavors)
KowOwow
(A cow-shaped ice cream bar)

Introduction to Excel

Getting Started with Excel

After completing this lesson, you will be able to:

1. **Start Excel.**
2. **Navigate in a workbook.**
3. **Open an existing workbook.**
4. **Edit a worksheet.**
5. **Manage files.**
6. **Print Excel files.**

 Estimated Time: 1 hour

Microsoft Excel is *electronic spreadsheet software.* You can use Excel to create professional reports that perform business or personal calculations, display financial or scientific calculations, complete list management tasks, and show charts. Excel is powerful but easy to use. You'll become a productive Excel user as soon as you learn the basics.

Starting Excel

There are several ways to start Excel, depending on how your software is installed. For example, you can use the Start button on the Windows taskbar, usually located in the bottom-left corner of the screen, to choose Excel from the list of available applications. There may be an Excel shortcut icon on the desktop that you can double-click to start Excel.

NOTE: Windows provides many ways to start applications. If you have problems, ask your instructor for help. If you are unfamiliar with Windows, see "Windows Tutorial" available at www.mhteched.com/pas for online help.

EXERCISE 1-1 Start Excel

When the instructions tell you to "click" a menu option or a toolbar button, use the left mouse button. Use the left mouse button to carry out commands unless you are told explicitly to use the right mouse button.

1. Turn on your computer. Windows loads.
2. Click the Start button 🏁 *start* on the taskbar and point to All Programs.
3. On the All Programs submenu, click Microsoft Office Excel 2003. The program is loaded and a blank Excel workbook opens.

EXERCISE 1-2 Identify Parts of the Excel Screen

Excel opens showing a blank workbook, the menu bar, the Standard toolbar, the Formatting toolbar, and the Getting Started task pane (see Figure 1-1). New workbooks are numbered and named Book1, Book2, and so on during each work session.

FIGURE 1-1
Excel screen

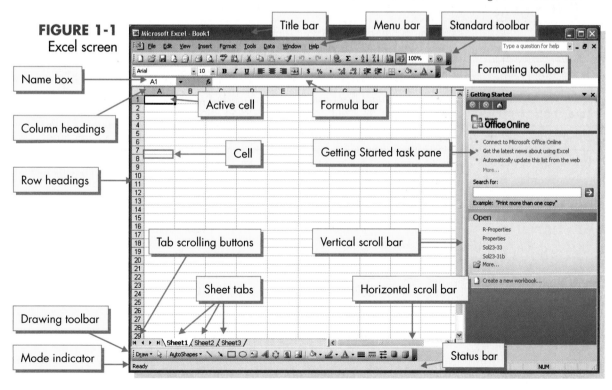

Depending on your screen, the Standard and Formatting toolbars appear on one or two rows.

NOTE: If you do not see the Getting Started task pane, choose Tas**k** Pane from the **V**iew menu. The filenames in your task pane are the most recently used documents at your computer. Your computer may not initially show the Drawing toolbar.

TABLE 1-1 Parts of the Excel Screen

PART OF SCREEN	PURPOSE
Title bar	Contains the program name and the name of the workbook.
Menu bar	Displays the names of menus used to perform various tasks.
Standard toolbar	A row of buttons used to execute commands with the mouse.
Formatting toolbar	A row of buttons used to apply font, size, style, color, and number formats with the mouse.
Name box	A drop-down list that shows the address of the active cell. You can also use it to move the pointer to a specific location.
Formula bar	Displays the contents of the active cell. You can also enter text, numbers, or formulas in the formula bar.
Column headings	Alphabetic characters across the top of the worksheet that identify columns.
Row headings	Numbers down the left side of the worksheet that identify rows.
Active cell	The cell outlined in a heavy black border. It is ready to accept new data, a formula, or for you to edit its current contents.
Status bar	Displays information about the current task and shows the current mode of operation.
Scroll bars	Used to move different parts of the screen into view.
Sheet tabs	Indicators at the bottom of the worksheet to identify sheets in the workbook.
Tab scrolling buttons	Navigation buttons to scroll through worksheet tabs.

NOTE: The first two steps in this exercise organize the Standard and Formatting toolbars on separate rows. If your toolbars are already in two rows (as shown in Figure 1-2), start with step 3.

1. Click the Toolbar Options button 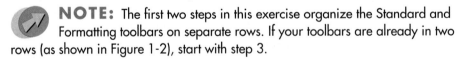 on either the Standard or Formatting toolbar. The shortcut menu shows S**h**ow Buttons on Two Rows if your toolbars are on one row.

FIGURE 1-2
Showing toolbars
on two rows

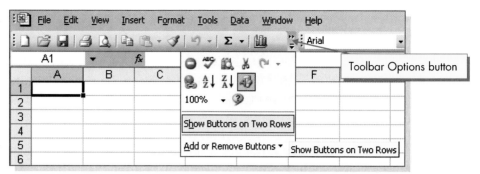

2. Click S̲how Buttons on Two Rows. The toolbars are rearranged, one on top of the other, so that you can see more buttons at once.

3. Click V̲iew on the menu bar. If the menu is not expanded to show all the choices, click the down-pointing arrows at the bottom of the menu. These are the Expand arrows. The menu expands.

4. Move the pointer to F̲ull Screen and click. The Full Screen view shows the menu bar, row and column headings, and the Full Screen floating toolbar.

5. Click C̲lose Full Screen on the floating toolbar.

6. Position the pointer over the New button on the Standard toolbar, but do not click. A *ScreenTip* (a box with the button name) appears below the button.

> **NOTE:** You might notice a floating Language toolbar on your screen. This toolbar, which appears only if your computer is set up with a microphone, can be used for speech recognition. You can use speech recognition for menu commands, toolbar buttons, and text entry. For more information, you can go online to www.mhteched.com/pas.

Navigating in a Workbook

A *workbook* is the file Excel creates to store your data. When you look at the screen, you are viewing a worksheet. A *worksheet* is an individual page or tab in the workbook. A new workbook opens with three blank worksheets. You can insert or delete worksheets in the workbook. A workbook can have from 1 to 255 worksheets.

> **NOTE:** The workbooks you create and use in this course relate to the Case Study (see pages 1–4) about Klassy Kow Ice Cream, Inc., a fictional ice cream company.

A worksheet has a grid that defines *rows* and *columns*. The rows are numbered and reach row 65,536. There are 256 columns, lettered from A to Z, then AA to AZ, BA to BZ, and so on, up to column IV.

The intersection of a row and a column forms a rectangle known as a *cell*. You enter a piece of information (text, a number, or a formula) in a cell. Cells have *cell addresses* or *cell references*, which identify where the cell is located on the worksheet. Cell B2, for example, is the cell in column B, row 2.

NOTE: When you give a cell address, the column letter always comes first.

The *active cell* is the cell that appears outlined with a thick border on the worksheet. It is ready to accept data or a formula, or if it already contains data or a formula, it is ready to be modified. It is the cell in which you are currently working. When you open a new workbook, the active cell is cell A1, the top-left cell in the worksheet. Cell A1 is referred to as *"Home."*

The mouse pointer displays as a thick white cross when you move it across cells in the worksheet. When you point at one of the worksheet tabs or a menu or toolbar item, it turns into a white arrow.

TABLE 1-2 Navigation Commands in a Workbook

PRESS	TO DO THIS
Ctrl + Home	Move to the beginning of the worksheet.
Ctrl + End	Move to the last used cell on the worksheet.
Home	Move to the beginning of the current row.
Page Up	Move up one screen.
Page Down	Move down one screen.
Alt + Page Up	Move one screen to the left.
Alt + Page Down	Move one screen to the right.
↑, ↓, ←, →	Move one cell up, down, left, or right.
Ctrl + arrow key	Move to the edge of a group of cells with data.
F5 or Ctrl + G	Open the Go To dialog box.
Click	Move to the cell that is clicked.
Tab	Move to the next cell in a left-to-right sequence.
Shift + Tab	Move to the previous cell in a right-to-left sequence.
Ctrl + Backspace	Move to the active cell when it has scrolled out of view.
Ctrl + Page Up	Move to the previous worksheet.
Ctrl + Page Down	Move to the next worksheet.

EXERCISE `1-3` **Move Between Worksheets**

A new workbook has three worksheets named Sheet1, Sheet2, and Sheet3. The Sheet1 worksheet is displayed when a new workbook is opened.

1. Click the Sheet2 tab. You can tell which sheet is active because its tab is colored white and the worksheet name appears in boldface on the tab. The other tabs are colored gray.

 NOTE: Cell A1 is the active cell on all three worksheets in a new workbook.

2. Click the Sheet3 tab. All three sheets are empty.

3. Press Ctrl+Page Up. This shortcut moves to the previous worksheet, Sheet2, in this case.

 NOTE: When keyboard combinations (such as Ctrl+Page Up) are shown in this text, hold down the first key without releasing it and press the second key. Release the second key and then release the first key.

4. Press Ctrl+Page Down. This command moves to the next worksheet, Sheet3.

5. Click the Sheet1 tab to return to Sheet1.

EXERCISE | **1-4** | **Go to a Specific Cell**

When you move the mouse pointer to a cell and click, the cell you clicked becomes the active cell. It is outlined with a black border, and you can see the cell address in the *Name box*. The Name box is the text box with a drop-down arrow at the left edge of the formula bar. You can also determine the cell address by the orange-shaded column and row headings.

1. Move the mouse pointer to cell D4 and click. Cell D4 is the active cell, and its address appears in the Name box. The column D and row 4 headings are shaded.

FIGURE 1-3
Active cell showing
a thick border

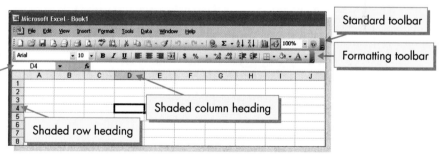

2. Press Ctrl+Home. This shortcut makes cell A1 the active cell.

3. Press Ctrl+G to open the Go To dialog box.

 TIP: As an alternative, open the Go To dialog box by choosing the Go To command on the Edit menu or by pressing the F5 key.

4. Key **b19** in the Reference box and press (Enter). Cell B19 becomes the active cell, and its address is shown in the Name box.

FIGURE 1-4
Go To dialog box

5. Press (Ctrl)+(G) or (F5) to open the Go To command. Recently used cell addresses are listed in the Go to list in the Go To dialog box.

6. Key **c2** and click OK.

7. Click the arrow next to the Name box. The current cell address is highlighted.

8. Key **a8** and press (Enter).

FIGURE 1-5
Using the
Name box

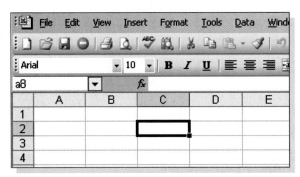

9. Press (Ctrl)+(Home) to return to cell A1.

EXERCISE **1-5** **Scroll Through a Worksheet**

When you scroll through a worksheet, the location of the active cell does not change. Instead, the worksheet moves on the screen so that you can see different columns or rows. The number of rows and columns you see at once depends on your monitor's resolution and the Zoom size in Excel.

FIGURE 1-6
Using scroll bars

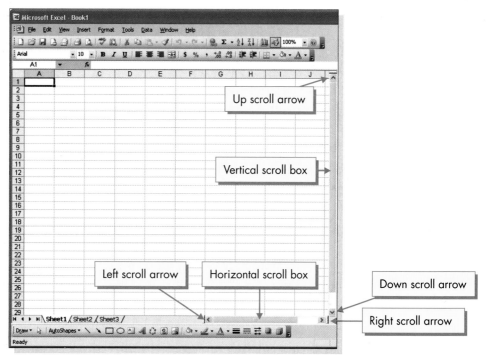

TABLE 1-3

Scrolling Through a Worksheet

TO MOVE THE VIEW	DO THIS
One row up	Click the up scroll arrow.
One row down	Click the down scroll arrow.
Up one screen	Click the scroll bar above the scroll box.
Down one screen	Click the scroll bar below the scroll box.
To any relative position	Drag the scroll bar up or down.
One column to the right	Click the right scroll arrow.
One column to the left	Click the left scroll arrow.

1. On the vertical scroll bar, click below the scroll box. The worksheet has been repositioned so that you see the next group of about 20–30 rows.

2. Click above the vertical scroll box. The worksheet has scrolled up to the top row.

3. Click the right scroll arrow on the horizontal scroll bar once. The worksheet scrolls one column to the right.

4. Click the left scroll arrow once to bring the column back into view.

5. Click the down scroll arrow on the vertical scroll bar twice.

 NOTE: You cannot see the active cell (cell A1) during your scrolling.

6. Drag the scroll box to the top of the vertical scroll bar. Notice that in all this scrolling, the active cell has not changed from cell A1.

EXERCISE 1-6 Change the Zoom Size

The *Zoom size* controls how much of the worksheet you see on the screen. You can set the Zoom size to see more or less on the screen so you won't need to scroll as much. The 100% Zoom size shows the data close to print size.

1. Click the down arrow next to the Zoom box on the Standard toolbar. The Zoom submenu opens.

2. Click 75%. The worksheet is reduced so that you can see more columns and rows.

FIGURE 1-7
Changing the
Zoom size

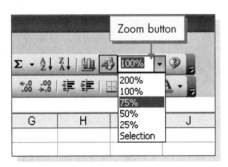

3. From the <u>V</u>iew menu, choose <u>Z</u>oom. The Zoom dialog box opens.

4. Click the 20<u>0</u>% Magnification button in the Zoom dialog box. Click OK. The worksheet is made larger, but you see less.

 TIP: It is faster for most people to change views by using the Zoom box on the Standard toolbar.

5. Click the arrow next to the Zoom box. Key **85**. You do not need to key the percent sign.

6. Press (Enter). You can enter any size, or choose from the list.

7. Click the arrow next to the Zoom box. Choose 100%.

EXERCISE   1-7   Close a Workbook

After you finish working with a workbook, you usually save your work and close the workbook. You can close a workbook in several ways.

- Click the Close Window button ⊠ on the right side of the menu bar.

FIGURE 1-8
Close Window
button

- Click the Control icon for the workbook. The Control icon for the workbook appears to the left of the word <u>F</u>ile on the menu bar. Choose <u>C</u>lose from the Control menu.
- Click the <u>F</u>ile menu and choose <u>C</u>lose.
- Use keyboard shortcuts. Ctrl+W or Ctrl+F4 closes a workbook.
1. Click the Close Window button ⊠. The workbook closes, and a blank gray screen appears. If you have made a change to the workbook, a dialog box asks if you want to save the changes.
2. Click <u>N</u>o if this dialog box opens.

Opening an Existing Workbook

You will often open workbooks that have already been created. There are several ways to open an existing workbook.

- Click the Open button 📂 on the Standard toolbar.
- Use the keyboard shortcut Ctrl+O.
- Click the filename (or More) in the <u>O</u>pen section of the Getting Started task pane.
- From the <u>F</u>ile menu, choose the <u>O</u>pen command.
- Navigate through the folders in Windows Explorer or My Computer to find your workbook and double-click its filename or icon.

EXERCISE   1-8   Open a Workbook

1. Click the Open button 📂. The Look <u>i</u>n text box shows the most recently used folder.

2. Click the down arrow next to the Look in box. Choose the appropriate drive/folder according to your instructor's directions. The workbooks for this lesson appear in the list box.

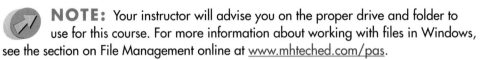 **NOTE:** Your instructor will advise you on the proper drive and folder to use for this course. For more information about working with files in Windows, see the section on File Management online at www.mhteched.com/pas.

 3. Click the arrow next to the Views button ⊞. A list of View options appears.

4. Choose List to see a list of the filenames.

5. Click the arrow next to the Views button ⊞ again. This time, choose Preview to see a preview of the workbook.

NOTE: Not all workbooks have a preview; it depends on file property settings at the time a workbook is saved. You will learn about file properties in Lesson 14.

FIGURE 1-9
Open dialog box

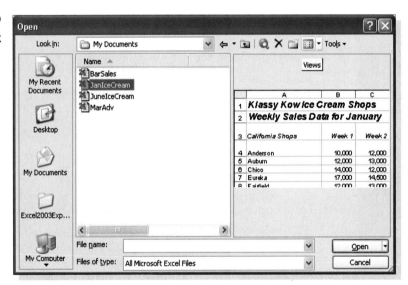

6. Find **JanIceCream**. Double-click the filename. The workbook opens and the Getting Started task pane closes.

NOTE: The workbooks in this course relate to the Case Study about Klassy Kow Ice Cream, Inc., a fictional manufacturer of ice cream (see pages 1 through 4).

TABLE 1-4   Open Dialog Box Buttons

BUTTON	ACTION
My Recent Documents	Lists the most recently opened files and folders.
Desktop	Lists items on your computer's desktop.
My Documents	Opens a Windows folder for storing your documents.
My Computer	Lists drives available on your computer.
My Network Places	Lists folders and files you can use on network drives and Web servers.
Back	Moves to the last most recently used folder.
Up One Level	Moves up one level in the hierarchy of folders or drives on your computer or other computers in your network.
Search the Web	Opens the Search page of your Internet browser so that you can start a Web search for information.
Delete	Deletes the selected files or folders.
Create New Folder	Creates a new folder for storing your work.
Views	Lists options for showing file information in the dialog box.
Tools	Lists options for working with files including Search and Print.

Editing a Worksheet

The JanIceCream workbook has three worksheets. The sheets have been renamed WeeklySales, Owners, and Chart to better indicate what is on the sheet. For instance, the WeeklySales sheet shows sales for each city in each of the four weeks in January.

Worksheet cells contain text, numbers, or formulas. A formula calculates an arithmetic result. By simply viewing the worksheet, you might not know if the cell contains a number or a formula. However, you can determine a cell's content by checking the formula bar. You can also use the formula bar to change the contents of cells.

EXERCISE   **1-9**   **View Worksheets and Cell Contents**

1. Click the Owners tab. The Owners worksheet shows the name of each shop owner.

2. Click the Chart tab. The Chart tab has a bar chart showing January sales data for each store.

3. Press [Ctrl]+[Page Up]. This moves to the Owners worksheet.

4. Press [Ctrl]+[Page Down]. The active tab is the Chart sheet.

5. Click the WeeklySales tab.

 TIP: If you do not see column F and row 19, set your Zoom size so that you can see columns A through F and up to row 19.

6. Press [F5] to open the Go To dialog box.

7. Key **a5** and press [Enter]. The active cell is changed to cell A5. This cell contains the name of a city (Auburn) which you can see in the formula bar and on the worksheet.

FIGURE 1-10
Cell contents and the formula bar

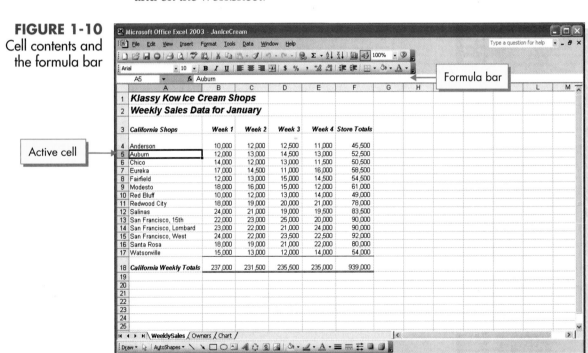

8. Press [F5], key **c10**, and press [Enter]. Cell C10 contains a number. In the formula bar, the number does not show the comma.

9. Press [F5], key **f17**, and press [Enter]. Cell F17 contains a formula, which you can see in the formula bar. Formulas calculate a number.

EXERCISE **1-10** **Replace Cell Contents**

When the workbook is in Ready mode, you can edit or replace the contents of a cell. To replace a cell's contents, make it the active cell, key the new data, and press Enter. You can also click the Enter button ✓ in the formula bar or press any arrow key on the keyboard to complete the replacement.

If you replace a number used in a formula, the result of the formula automatically recalculates when you complete your change.

1. Click cell B5 to make it the active cell.

2. Key **20000** without a comma. As you key the number, it appears in the cell and in the formula bar. The status bar shows Enter to indicate that you are in Enter mode.

FIGURE 1-11
Replacing cell
contents

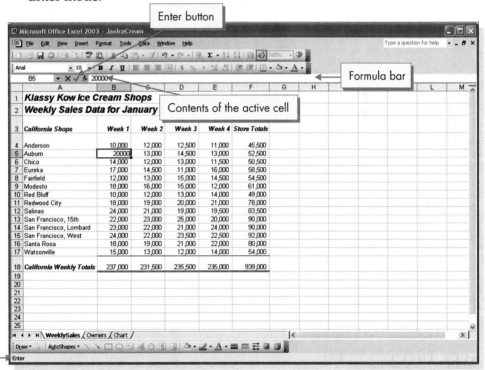

3. Press Enter. Excel inserts a comma, and the next cell in column B is active. The "Store Total" (cell F5) and the "California Weekly Totals" amounts (in cells B18 and F18) are recalculated. The worksheet returns to Ready mode.

 TIP: The commas are part of the cell format in this worksheet.

 4. Press ↑ to move to cell B5. Key **10000** without a comma. Click the Enter button ✓ in the formula bar. Notice that when you use the Enter button ✓, the pointer stays in cell B5.

5. Click the Chart tab. Notice the length of the Auburn bar, showing sales just over $50,000.

6. Click the WeeklySales tab.

7. In cell B5, key **0**, and press ⊕. A zero appears as a short dash in this worksheet.

8. Click the Chart tab. The chart on this worksheet is based on the data in the WeeklySales worksheet. Now that you have reduced sales, the Auburn bar is shorter.

9. Click the WeeklySales tab and key **10000** in cell B5. Press ⊕.

EXERCISE **1-11** **Edit Cell Contents**

If a cell contains a long or complicated entry, you can edit it rather than rekeying the entire entry. Edit mode starts when you:

- Double-click the cell.
- Click the cell and press F2.
- Click the cell and then click anywhere in the formula bar.

TABLE 1-5 **Keyboard Shortcuts in Edit Mode**

KEY	TO DO THIS
Enter	Complete the edit and return to Ready mode.
Esc	Cancel the edit and restore the existing data.
Home	Move the insertion point to the beginning of the data.
End	Move the insertion point to the end of the data.
Delete	Delete one character to the right of the insertion point.
Ctrl + Delete	Delete everything from the insertion point to the end of the line.
Backspace	Delete one character to the left of the insertion point.
← or →	Move the insertion point one character left or right.
Ctrl + ←	Move the insertion point one word left.
Ctrl + →	Move the insertion point one word right.

1. Click cell A2. The text in cell A2 is long, and its display overlaps into columns B and C.

2. Press F2. Edit mode is shown in the status bar. An insertion point appears in the cell at the end of the text.

3. Double-click "Data" in the cell.

TIP: Double-clicking highlights or selects a word in all of the Office applications.

4. Key **Information**. It replaces the word "Data."

FIGURE 1-12
Using Edit mode

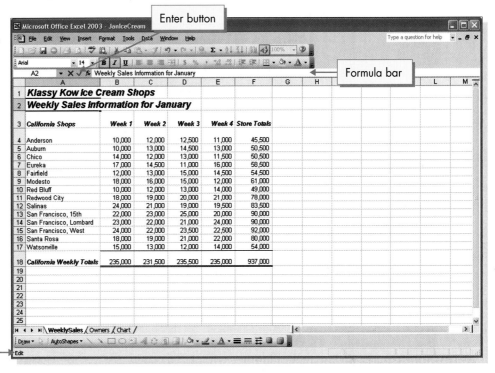

5. Press Enter to complete the edit. Pressing Enter does not start a new line in the cell when the worksheet is in Edit mode.

6. Double-click cell A3. This starts Edit mode, and an insertion point appears in the cell.

7. In the cell, click to the left of the "S" in "Shops."

8. Key **Retail** and press Spacebar. Press Enter.

9. Click cell F1. There is nothing in this cell.

10. Key your first name, a space, and your last name in the cell. Press Enter. If your name is longer than column F, part of its display might overlap into column G and even into column H.

EXERCISE **1-12** **Clear Cell Contents**

When you clear the contents of a cell, you delete the text, number, or formula in that cell.

1. Click cell B5. Press [Delete]. The number is deleted, and Excel recalculates the formula results in cells F5, B18, and F18.

 NOTE: A green triangle may appear in the corners of cells F5 and B19 to indicate that a formula error has occurred. Ignore them for now.

2. Press [→] to move the pointer to cell C5.

3. From the Edit menu, choose Clear and then Contents. The number is deleted, and the formula is recalculated again.

EXERCISE **1-13** **Use Undo and Redo**

The Undo command reverses the last action you performed in the worksheet. For example, if you delete the contents of a cell, the Undo command restores what you deleted. The Redo command reverses the action of the Undo command. It "undoes" your Undo.

To use the Undo command, you can:

- Click the Undo button [⤺ ▾] on the Standard toolbar.
- Press [Ctrl]+[Z].
- From the Edit menu, choose Undo.

To use the Redo command, you can:

- Click the Redo button [⤻ ▾] on the Standard toolbar.
- Press [Ctrl]+[Y].
- From the Edit menu, choose Redo.

Excel keeps a history or list of your editing commands, and you can undo or redo several at once.

1. Click the Undo button [⤺ ▾]. The number in cell C5 is restored.

2. Click the Redo button [⤻ ▾]. The number is cleared again.

3. Click cell A8 and key **Gotham**. Press [Enter].

4. In cell A9 key **Los Angeles** and press [Enter].

5. Click the arrow next to the Undo button [⤺ ▾] to display the history list.

6. Move the mouse to highlight the top two actions and click. The last two changes are undone, and the original city names are restored.

FIGURE 1-13
Undoing
multiple edits

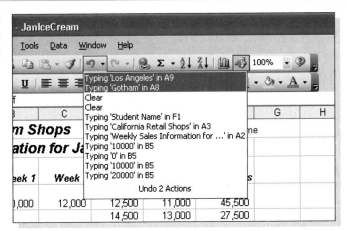

 NOTE: Depending on the actions that have been undone and redone on your computer, your list might be different from the one shown in Figure 1-13.

7. Click the arrow next to the Redo button to display the history list.

8. Move the mouse to highlight the top two actions and click. The names you keyed are restored.

9. Press `Ctrl`+`Home` to place the pointer in cell A1.

 TIP: If you place the pointer in cell A1 when you save a workbook, cell A1 is the active cell the next time you open the workbook.

Managing Files

Workbook files are usually stored in folders. A *folder* is a location on a disk, net-work, floppy, or CD drive. Folders are organized in a structure like a family tree. The top level of the hierarchy is a letter such as A, B, or C to represent your disk drive, other disk drives, or other storage devices. Under each drive letter, you can create folders to help you organize and manage your work.

For your work in this text, you will save your files in a folder you create for each lesson.

EXERCISE   **1-14**   **Create a New Folder and Use Save As**

1. Open the File menu and choose Save As. You will save **JanIceCream** with a new filename in a lesson folder you will create.

NOTE: Ask your instructor where to save lesson folders for this course.

2. Choose the appropriate drive and folder location from the Save in drop-down list.

3. Click the Create New Folder button 📁. The New Folder dialog box opens.

4. In the Name box, key *[your initials]***Lesson1**. Click OK. Your new folder's name now appears in the Save in box.

5. In the File name box, make sure the filename **Copy of JanIceCream** (or **JanIceCream**) is highlighted or selected. If it is not highlighted, triple-click it.

NOTE: JanIceCream is a "read-only file" if you opened it from the CD or if your instructor set it as read-only. This means you cannot save it with the same filename. Excel supplies a name that includes the original filename preceded by "Copy of."

FIGURE 1-14
Save As dialog box

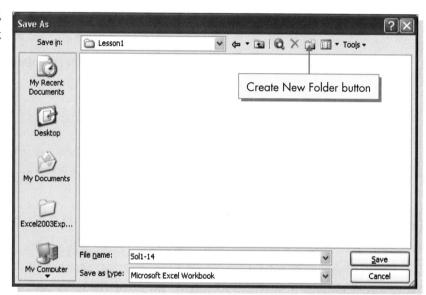

NOTE: Excel automatically assigns the **.xls** extension to files you save, but if your computer uses default Windows settings, you will not see filename extensions.

6. Key *[your initials]***1-14** and click Save. Your new filename now appears in the title bar.

Printing Excel Files

You can use any of these methods to print a worksheet:

- Click the Print button 🖨 on the Standard toolbar.
- Click Print while in Print Preview.

- From the File menu, choose Print.
- Press Ctrl+P.

Clicking the Print button ⊟ on the Standard toolbar sends the worksheet to the printer, using Excel's default print settings. The other methods open the Print dialog box, where you can change printing options.

EXERCISE **1-15** **Preview a Worksheet**

You should preview your work before sending it to the printer. The Print Preview command allows you to see the worksheet as it will print.

1. Click the Print Preview button ⌕. The worksheet is shown in a reduced size so that you can see the entire page.

FIGURE 1-15
Worksheet in
Print Preview

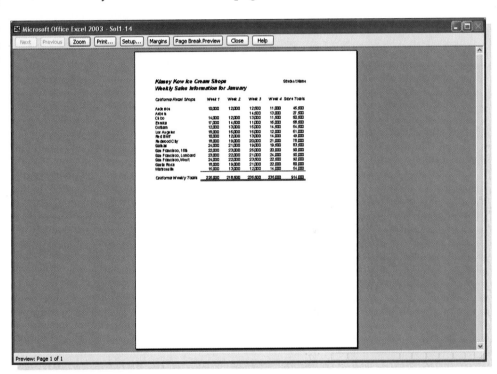

2. Move the mouse pointer near the main title. The mouse pointer appears as a small magnifying glass icon.
3. Click the mouse button while pointing at the main title. The worksheet changes to a larger size, close to the actual print size.
4. The mouse pointer appears as a white solid arrow. Click anywhere to return to a reduced size.

NOTE: Changing the size in the Print Preview window is called zooming in and out.

5. Zoom in on the "California Weekly Totals" row. Click anywhere to zoom out.
6. Click Print. The preview window closes, and the Print dialog box displays your workstation's default printer and settings.
7. Click OK. A printer icon appears on the taskbar as the worksheet is sent to the printer. Only the WeeklySales worksheet is printed.

EXERCISE 1-16 Print a Workbook

You can print all three sheets in the workbook with one command. To print the entire workbook, you must use the Print dialog box.

1. Press Ctrl + P. The Print dialog box opens with your default settings.

FIGURE 1-16
Print dialog box

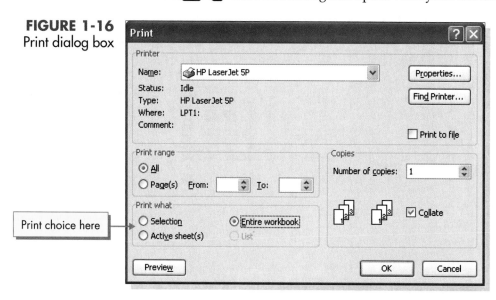

Print choice here

2. In the Print what section, click the option button for Entire workbook.
3. Click Preview. The reduced size shows the first page, the WeeklySales sheet. The status bar shows that this is page 1 of 3.
4. Press Page Down. This is the second sheet, the Owners worksheet.
5. Press Page Down. This is the Chart sheet. It is set to print in a landscape orientation.
6. Click Previous two times to return to the first sheet.
7. Click Print. All three sheets are sent to the printer and Print Preview closes.

EXERCISE **1-17** **Exit Excel**

You can exit Excel and close the workbook at the same time. If you give the command to exit Excel, you will see a reminder to save the workbook if you have not yet done so.

There are four ways to close a workbook and exit Excel:

- Use the Close Window button ✗ to close the workbook or the Close button ✗ to close Excel. (The close buttons are in the upper-right corner of the document and application windows.)
- Use the keyboard shortcut Alt + F4 to exit Excel.
- From the File menu, choose Close (to close the workbook) or Exit (to close Excel).
- Use the Control icons in the upper-left corner of the window. The Excel Control icon is next to the application name in the title bar.

FIGURE 1-17
Control menus

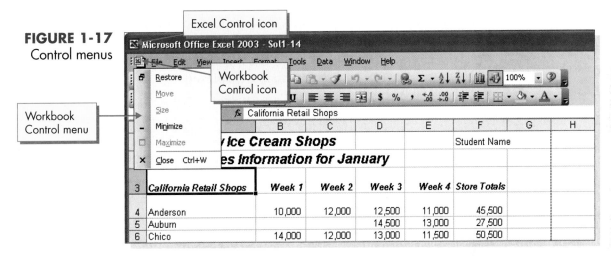

1. Click the Close Window button ✗ to close the workbook. Do not save changes if asked.
2. Click the Close button ✗ to exit Excel.

USING ONLINE HELP

Online Help is available both at your computer and on the Microsoft Office Web site. An easy way to use Help at your computer is to type a question in the Ask a Question box at the top right of the screen.

Get acquainted with using Help:

1. Start Excel and locate the Type a question for help box in the upper-right corner of the screen.

2. Click the box, key **get help** and press Enter.

3. From the list of topics in the Search Results task pane, find and click About getting help while you work.

4. In the Help dialog box, click each of the topics shown in blue text (or click Show All in the upper-right corner of the Help screen) to review the information.

5. Close the Help window and close the Search Results task pane.

LESSON Summary

➤ There are different ways to start Excel, depending on your computer and its settings.

➤ Excel opens with a blank workbook. The menu bar is across the top. When you click a menu name, a list of commands is displayed.

➤ The Standard and Formatting toolbars can be set to show on one or two rows.

➤ A new workbook opens with three worksheets. A worksheet is an individual tab in the workbook.

➤ Press Ctrl+Page Up and Ctrl+Page Down to move between worksheets in a workbook.

➤ Worksheets are divided into cells, which are the intersections of rows and columns. The location of the cell is its address (also called its cell reference).

➤ Move the pointer to a specific cell with the Go To command or by clicking the cell.

➤ The active cell is outlined with a black border. It is ready to accept new data or a formula or be edited.

➤ The Name box shows the address of the active cell. You can also use it to change the active cell.

➤ If you use the scroll box or arrows to reposition the worksheet on the screen, the active cell does not change.

➤ The Zoom size controls how much of the worksheet you can see at once.

➤ Replace any entry in a cell by clicking the cell and keying new data. Edit long or complicated cell data rather than rekeying it.

➤ The Undo button and the Redo button both have history arrows so that you can undo or redo multiple commands at once.

➤ Preview your worksheet or the entire workbook before printing it. To preview and print all the worksheets in a workbook, choose File, Print. Then choose Entire workbook.

LESSON 1　Command Summary

FEATURE	BUTTON	MENU	KEYBOARD
Clear cell contents		Edit, Clear, Contents	Delete
Close a document	✗	File, Close	Ctrl+W or Ctrl+F4
Exit Excel	✗	File, Exit	Alt+F4
Full Screen		View, Full Screen	
Go To		Edit, Go To	Ctrl+G or F5
Open a workbook		File, Open	Ctrl+O
Print		File, Print	Ctrl+P
Print Preview		File, Print Preview	
Redo		Edit, Redo	Ctrl+Y
Save As		File, Save As	F12
Undo		Edit, Undo	Ctrl+Z
Zoom	100%	View, Zoom	

Concepts Review

Each of the following statements is either true or false. Indicate your choice by circling T or F.

T (F)   **1.** A worksheet contains at least one workbook.

(T) F   **2.** The Name box shows the address of the active cell.

T (F)   **3.** The Zoom size for a particular screen is permanent.

T (F)   **4.** You can use the scroll bars to move the pointer to a specific cell.

(T) F   **5.** You can replace a cell's contents by clicking the cell and keying new data.

T (F)   **6.** You must use Windows Explorer to create a new folder.

(T) F   **7.** Edit mode starts when you press F2.

T (F)   **8.** If you click the Print button 🖨, all worksheets in a workbook are printed.

Write the correct answer in the space provided.

1. What is the name for the cell with the heavy black border that is ready to accept new data or a formula or for you to edit?

Active cell

2. Give an example of a cell address for a title somewhere in the first column of a worksheet.

_A 12_

3. What is one keyboard shortcut for the Go To command?

_F5_

4. What command enables you to use a different filename for a workbook?

5. What is the keyboard shortcut to move the pointer to cell A1?

Ctrl + home

6. Which part of the Excel screen shows the contents of the active cell?

   Formula bar

7. How do you print all three sheets in a workbook with one command?

   Click the option button for Entire workbook in the
   print what

8. What do you use to reposition the worksheet on the screen without changing the location of the active cell?

CRITICAL THINKING

Answer these questions on a separate page. There are no right or wrong answers. Support your answers with examples from your own experience, if possible.

1. You can replace or edit cell contents. Discuss when you might use each procedure.

2. Why should you use folders for organizing your files? Give examples of folder names that might be used in a real estate office.

Skills Review

EXERCISE 1-18

Start Excel. Navigate through a blank worksheet.

NOTE: Number and write your answers to questions in the Skills Review exercises on a piece of paper to hand in. Include your name, the date, the exercise number, and the question number.

1. Start Excel by following these steps:

   a. Click Start on the Windows taskbar.
   b. Point to Programs and choose Microsoft Office Excel 2003.

2. Navigate through a worksheet by following these steps:

   NOTE: Number and write your answers to questions in the Skills Review exercises on a piece of paper to hand in. Include your name, the date, the exercise number, and the question number.

   a. Click the Maximize button 🔲 to maximize the workbook.
   b. Press (Ctrl)+(Page Down) two times. Which sheet is active?
   c. Drag the scroll box on the vertical scroll bar to the bottom of the scroll bar. What is the last row shown on the worksheet?

d. Press Ctrl+PageUp two times. Which sheet is active?

e. Press F5 and key **a35**. Press Enter. What appears in the Name box?

f. Press Tab. What is the active cell?

g. Press Shift+Tab. What is the active cell?

h. Press Ctrl+Home. What is the active cell?

i. Press Ctrl+End. What is the active cell?

 NOTE: When there is no data on a worksheet, Ctrl+End goes to cell A1.

 j. Click the Close Window button ☒. Do not save the workbook if a message box appears.

EXERCISE 1-19

Open a workbook. Edit a worksheet.

1. Open a workbook by following these steps:

 a. Click the Open button 🖼.

b. Click the down arrow with the Look in box.

c. Choose the drive according to your instructor's directions.

d. Find **MarAdv** and double-click it.

2. Edit a worksheet by following these steps:

 NOTE: Number and write your answers to questions in the Skills Review exercises on a piece of paper to hand in. Include your name, the date, the exercise number, and the question number.

a. Press F5, key **b4**, and press Enter.

b. Key **2000** and press Enter. What is the new total for the Aberdeen store?

c. Click cell D10 and press Delete. What is the California total for this week?

 d. Click the arrow next to the Undo button 🔙. What are the first two tasks listed?

e. Press Esc.

f. Click the Close Window button ☒. Choose No to discard your changes.

EXERCISE 1-20

Edit a workbook. Manage files.

1. Open **MarAdv**.

2. Edit a workbook by following these steps:

NOTE: Number and write your answers to questions in the Skills Review exercises on a piece of paper to hand in. Include your name, the date, the exercise number, and the question number.

    a. Click cell A2 and press F2. What is the current mode for your worksheet?

    b. Double-click "March" and key **April**. Press Enter. What is the active cell?

    c. Double-click cell A11. How can you select or highlight the word "California?"

    d. Delete "California." Also delete the space before the "W."

    e. What key will finish your editing?

3. Manage files by following these steps:

    a. Choose File, Save As. What folder appears in the Save in text box?

    b. Set the folder to *[your initials]***Lesson1**. On what drive is this folder located?

    c. In the File name box, make sure the original name is highlighted or selected. If it is not, triple-click the filename.

    d. Key *[your initials]***1-20** and press Enter.

    e. What filename appears in the title bar?

 4. Click the Close Window button ⊠.

EXERCISE 1-21

Edit cells. Print a worksheet.

1. Open **MarAdv**.

2. Press F12. Set the Save in folder to *[your initials]***Lesson1**.

 TIP: F12 is the keyboard shortcut for File, Save As.

3. In the File name box, key *[your initials]***1-21** and press Enter.

4. Edit cells by following these steps:

    a. Click cell A2 and press F2.

    b. Double-click "March" and key **May**. Press Enter.

    c. Double-click cell A11. Double-click "California."

    d. Key **Washington** and press Enter.

    e. Click cell F1. Key your first and your last name and press Enter.

5. Print a worksheet by following these steps:

     a. Click the Print Preview button 🔍.

    b. Point near the main title and click.

    c. Point anywhere and click again.

    d. Click Print.

    e. Click OK.

 6. Click the Close Window button ⊠.

7. Choose No if asked to save changes.

Lesson Applications

Open a workbook. Edit and print a worksheet.

1. Open **JanIceCream**.

 REVIEW: Set the Zoom size so you can see as much of the data as possible.

2. Edit cell A2 to show the current month.

 TIP: You do not need to key the commas in this worksheet. They are part of the formatting.

3. Change the first week total for Modesto to **15500**.

4. Key your first and your last name in cell A20. Press [Ctrl]+[Home].

5. Save the workbook as *[your initials]***1-22** in your Lesson 1 folder.

6. Preview the worksheet and print it.

7. Close the workbook.

Open a workbook. Edit a worksheet. Print a worksheet.

1. Open **BarSales**.

2. Change cell A3 to show **2003-2005**.

3. Change the fourth quarter amount for 2003 to **55000**.

 NOTE: Numbers align at the right edge of a cell; text aligns at the left edge unless you change its alignment. You may see green triangles in cells B10 and C10 to mark potential formula errors. You learn about them soon.

4. Key your first and your last name in cell A12. Press [Ctrl]+[Home].

 TIP: The keyboard shortcut for the Save As command is [F12] in most Windows applications.

5. Save the workbook as *[your initials]***1-23** in your Lesson 1 folder.

6. Preview the worksheet and print it.

7. Close the workbook.

EXERCISE 1-24

Open and edit a workbook. Print a workbook.

1. Open **JuneIceCream**.
2. In cell F1 on the WeeklySales sheet, key your first and last name. Press Ctrl + Home.

 TIP: It is good practice to position the pointer at cell A1 before saving so the worksheet opens with that cell as the active cell.

3. In cell B18 on the Owners sheet, key your first and last name. Press Ctrl + Home.
4. Press Ctrl + P and select the option to print the entire workbook.
5. Preview the workbook before printing it. Print all the sheets.
6. Save the workbook as *[your initials]*1-24 in your Lesson 1 folder.
7. Close the workbook.

EXERCISE 1-25 *Challenge Yourself*

Open a workbook. Edit worksheets. Print a workbook.

1. Open **JanIceCream**.
2. On the WeeklySales sheet, change the values for the first week as shown here.

 TIP: Start in cell B4 and press Enter to key the values down a column.

FIGURE 1-18

	A	B
4	Anderson	12000
5	Auburn	14000
6	Chico	12000
7	Eureka	18000
8	Fairfield	15000
9	Modesto	16000
10	Red Bluff	11000
11	Redwood City	16000

continues

FIGURE 1-18   *continued*

	A	B
12	Salinas	26000
13	San Francisco, 15th	24000
14	San Francisco, Lombard	24000
15	San Francisco, West	*[Do not change]*
16	Santa Rosa	19000
17	Watsonville	16000

3. In cell E1, key **Prepared by** *[your first and last name]*. Press `Ctrl`+`Home`.

4. On the Owners sheet, key your first and last name in cell C1. Press `Ctrl`+`Home`.

5. Save the workbook as *[your initials]***1-25** in your Lesson 1 folder.

 REVIEW: Choose File, Print to print the entire workbook.

6. Preview and print the entire workbook, including the chart.

 NOTE: If you use a black-and-white printer, the chart uses shades of gray for the bars.

7. Close the workbook.

On Your Own

In these exercises you work on your own, as you would in a real-life work environment. Use the skills you've learned to accomplish the task—and be creative.

EXERCISE 1-26
Open **JuneIceCream**. On the WeeklySales sheet, practice each of the navigation shortcuts in Table 1-2. On the Owners sheet, change each owner's name to someone you know. Include your own name as one of the owners. Print this worksheet. Save the workbook as *[your initials]***1-26** in your Lesson 1 folder. Close the workbook.

EXERCISE 1-27

Open **MarAdv**. Change the month to this month. Using the Internet or a map, change each city to a different city in your state. Change the titles to specify your state, too. Key your first and last name in cell A14. Save the workbook as *[your initials]*1-27 in your Lesson 1 folder and print it.

EXERCISE 1-28

In the Open dialog box, set the Views to show Preview. Then select and highlight the filename of each of the workbooks you used in this lesson (**BarSales**, **JanIceCream**, **JuneIceCream**, and **MarAdv**). Which of these files does not have a preview? In the Excel Help system, look up how to save a file with a preview. On a piece of paper, write in your own words what you should do to save a file with a preview. Include your first and last name, the exercise number, and the date.

Creating a Workbook

OBJECTIVES

After completing this lesson, you will be able to:

1. Enter labels.
2. Change the font.
3. Select cell ranges.
4. Modify column width and row height.
5. Enter values and dates.
6. Save a workbook.
7. Enter basic formulas.

 Estimated Time: 1½ hours

MICROSOFT OFFICE SPECIALIST ACTIVITIES

In this lesson:
XL03S-1-1
XL03S-2-3
XL03S-2-4
XL03S-3-1
XL03S-3-3
XL03S-3-4
XL03S-5-2
XL03S-5-10

See Appendix.

When you create a new workbook, you start with three blank worksheets. You can key text, numbers, or formulas in any cell in any of the worksheets. Although Excel applies some automatic styles or formats as you enter data, you can change the font and font size, adjust the width and height of columns, add colors, and more.

Entering Labels

If you key data that begins with a letter, Excel recognizes it as a *label*. Labels are aligned at the left edge of the cell and are not used in calculations.

EXERCISE   **2-1**   **Enter Labels in a Worksheet**

As you key data, it appears in the active cell and in the formula bar. If you change your mind or make an error, press Esc to start over. You can also press Backspace to edit the entry.

There are several ways you can complete an entry.

TABLE 2-1   **Ways to Complete a Cell Entry**

KEY OR BUTTON	RESULT
Press Enter	Completes entry and moves the pointer to the cell below.
Press TAB	Completes entry and moves the pointer to the cell to the right.
Press SHIFT + Tab	Completes entry and moves the pointer to the cell to the left.
Press an arrow key	Completes entry and moves the pointer one cell in the direction of the arrow.
Click another cell	Completes entry and moves the pointer to the clicked cell.
Click the Enter button	Completes entry and leaves the pointer in the current cell.

1. Start Excel. A blank workbook opens with the Getting Started task pane at the right. Cell A1 on Sheet1 is active.

 NOTE: The first new workbook in a work session is named Book1 until you save it with another name. The next new workbook is Book2, and so on.

2. Click the Close Window button ✖ in the Getting Started task pane. This gives you more room to work on the sheet.

 REVIEW: You can reopen the task pane by pressing Ctrl + F1 or by choosing View, Task Pane.

3. In cell A1, key **Klassy Kow Sa** to start a label. The worksheet is in Enter mode, shown in the status bar. The label appears in the formula bar and in the cell.

4. Press Backspace to delete **Sa**.

  5. Key **Promotions**. Notice that an Enter button ✔ and a Cancel button ✖ appear in the formula bar when you are in Enter mode.

FIGURE 2-1
Label appearing
in the formula
bar and the cell

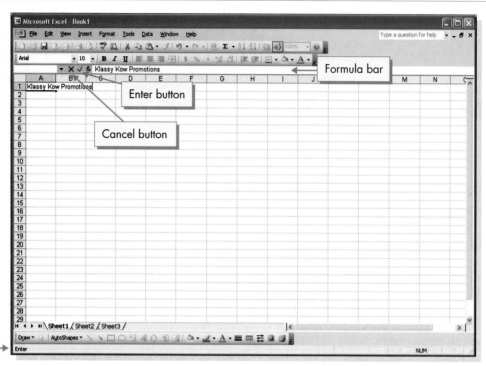

Formula bar

Enter button

Cancel button

Mode indicator

6. Press Enter. The label is completed in cell A1, and the pointer moves to cell A2. The label is longer than column A, so its appearance spills into columns B and C.

7. In cell A2, key **Market** to start a label. Press Esc to delete your entry. You can use Esc to delete an entry if you haven't yet pressed Enter or moved away from the cell.

 REVIEW: If you pressed Enter or moved away from the cell and need to edit it, click the cell. Key the new data and press Enter.

8. Key **Company Plan** and click the Enter button ✓ in the formula bar. The label's appearance spills into cell B2.

9. Click cell A3 to make it active.

10. Key **Name** and press →. The pointer is now in cell B3.

11. Key **Starting Date** and press →. The label is too long for column B and spills into column C.

12. Key **Ending Date** in cell C3 and press →. The label cuts off the label from column B and spills into cell D3. You will fix these problems soon.

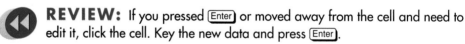 **NOTE:** Text display can spill into adjacent cells only if they are empty.

13. Key **Price** and press →. Key **Special Price** in cell E3 and press Enter. This label is not cut off, because there is nothing in the cell to the right.

14. Key the following labels in column A, starting in cell A4. Press (Enter) after each.

Berry Kowabunga
Easter Bunny Pie
Triple-Scoop Cone
24 oz. Shake

Changing the Font

The default font for data keyed in a new workbook is 10-point Arial. You can change the font style and size by using the Formatting toolbar or the Format Cells dialog box. If you choose a larger font size, the height of the row is automatically made taller to fit the font.

EXERCISE   2-2   Change the Font, Font Size, and Style

1. Click cell A1.

2. Click the down arrow next to the Font box on the Formatting toolbar. A drop-down list appears, showing font names for your computer.

FIGURE 2-2
Choosing a font

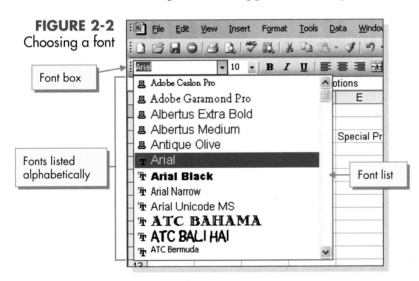

Font box

Fonts listed
alphabetically

Font list

3. Key **t** to move to the font names starting with "T."

4. Choose Times New Roman.

 NOTE: You can also scroll in the Font list to a new font.

5. Click the drop-down arrow next to the Font Size box on the Formatting toolbar. Choose 16. The label spills into column D. Notice that row 1 is taller than the other rows to accommodate the larger font size.

 TIP: You can key a font size that is not in the list.

FIGURE 2-3
Choosing a font

Font Size list

EXERCISE | **2-3** | **Use the Format Painter**

With the Format Painter, you can copy cell formats from one cell to another. This is often faster than applying formats individually.

 To use the Format Painter, make the cell with formatting the active cell. Then click the Format Painter button . While the pointer is a white cross with a small paintbrush, click the cell to be formatted.

1. Make sure cell A1 is the active cell.

2. Click the Format Painter button . Cell A1 shows a moving marquee, and the pointer is a thick white cross with a paintbrush.

FIGURE 2-4
Using the
Format Painter

Moving marquee

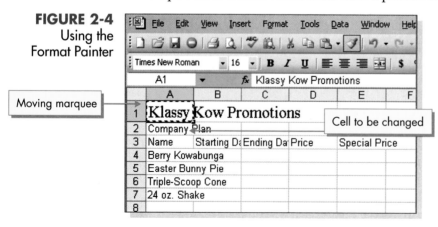

3. Click cell A2. The font and size are copied, and row 2 is made taller. The Format Painter command is canceled.

4. Make sure cell A2 is now the active cell.

5. Double-click the Format Painter button 🖌. This locks the painter on so that you can format more than one cell.

6. Click cell A3 to copy the format. Then click cell B3 to copy the format again.

7. Click the Format Painter button 🖌 to cancel the command.

8. Click the arrow next to the Undo button 🔄 ▾. Excel shows Format Painter as Paste Special in the Undo history list.

9. Undo the last two Paste Special commands. These are your last two uses of the Format Painter. The labels in row 3 return to the default font and font size (10-point Arial).

10. Press Esc to cancel the marquee.

Selecting Cell Ranges

A *range* is a group of cells that forms a rectangle on the screen. In many cases, you want to work with a range of cells. For example, you might need to format all the cells in rows 3 through 7.

When a range is active, it is highlighted on the screen. Like an individual cell, a range has an address. A *range address* is the upper-left cell address and the lower-right cell address, separated by a colon.

TABLE 2-2   **Examples of Range Addresses**

RANGE ADDRESS	CELLS IN THE RANGE
A1:B3	6 cells on 3 rows and in 2 columns
B1:B100	100 cells, all in column B
C3:C13	11 cells, starting at cell C3, all in column C
D4:F12	27 cells on 9 rows and in 3 columns
A1:IV1	256 cells, or the entire row 1

EXERCISE 2-4 **Select Ranges with the Mouse**

When you start to select a range of cells, you will see a thick white, cross-shaped pointer. This is called the *selection pointer,* because it is used to select ranges of cells on the worksheet.

There are several ways to select a range of cells by using the mouse:

- Drag across adjacent cells to select the range.
- Click the first cell in the range. Hold down (Shift) and click the last cell in the range.
- Click a column heading letter to select a column or click a row heading number to select a row.
- Drag across adjacent column heading letters or row heading numbers to select multiple columns or rows.
- Click the Select All button (see Figure 2-5) to select the entire worksheet.

1. Click cell A3 to make it active.

2. While you see the thick white, cross-shaped pointer, click and drag to the right to cell E3.

 TIP: If you do not select the correct cells, click cell A3 and try again.

3. Release the mouse button. Cells A3 through E3 are selected. The Name box shows the first cell in the range. The first cell appears white, and the remaining cells are light blue-gray or purple.

FIGURE 2-5
Selecting a
range of cells

4. Click the Bold button . All the cells in the selected range are now bold.

B

 TIP: You can also apply bold by using the keystroke combination (Ctrl)+(B). You can apply italic by using (Ctrl)+(I).

5. Click cell A1. This makes cell A1 active and deselects the range. The range is no longer highlighted.

6. Click cell A1 and drag to cell F1. Do not release the mouse button.

7. Drag down to cell F3 and then release the mouse button. The selected range is A1:F3.

 TIP: If you select the wrong range of cells, click cell A1 and try again.

8. Click cell A1 to deselect the range and make cell A1 active again.

9. Point to the row 1 heading. The pointer changes shape and is a solid black arrow. The pointer shows a different shape when you point at a row or column heading.

10. Click the row 1 heading to select the row.

11. Click cell B2. The range is deselected. You can click any cell to deselect a range.

12. Point to the row 1 heading. Click and drag down through the row headings from row 1 to row 5.

13. Release the mouse button. Five rows are now selected.

14. Click any cell to deselect the rows.

15. Click the column A heading. This selects the column.

16. Click any cell to deselect the column.

17. Click the column B heading and drag to the column G heading. This selects a range that includes all the cells in columns B through G.

18. Click cell B5. Hold down [Shift] and click cell E18. This is another way to select a range. This range is B5:E18.

EXERCISE   **2-5**   **Select Ranges with Keyboard Shortcuts**

You can select a range of cells by using keyboard shortcuts. These shortcuts work in many other Windows programs (particularly Office programs) for selecting data.

TABLE 2-3   Keyboard Shortcuts to Select Cell Ranges

KEYSTROKE	TO DO THIS
[Shift]+arrow key	Select from the active cell, moving in the direction of the arrow.
[Ctrl]+[Spacebar]	Select the current column.

continues

TABLE 2-3 Keyboard Shortcuts to Select Cell Ranges *continued*

KEYSTROKE	TO DO THIS
Shift + Spacebar	Select the current row.
F8	Start Extend Selection mode.
Esc	End Extend Selection mode.
F8 + arrow key	Extend selection from active cell in the direction of the arrow.
Shift + Page Up	Extend selection from active cell up one screen in the same column.
Shift + Page Down	Extend selection from active cell down one screen in the same column.
Ctrl + Shift + Home	Extend selection from active cell to beginning of data.
Ctrl + Shift + End	Extend selection from active cell to end of data.

 NOTE: Ctrl + A selects every available cell on a worksheet—all 65,536 rows and all 256 columns.

1. Click cell A3. Hold down Shift and press → four times. The range is A3:E3.

2. Click the down arrow next to the Font box. Key **t** and choose Times New Roman (or scroll to the font).

3. Click the down arrow next to the Font Size box. Choose 12.

4. Hold down Shift and press ↓ to reach row 15. The range is extended to A3:E15.

5. Click cell A3 to deselect the range.

6. Press F8. This starts Extend Selection mode. Notice that EXT appears at the right in the status bar.

7. Press → four times. Press ↓ to reach row 15. The range A3:E15 is selected again.

 TIP: If you go too far, press ↑ to reach row 15.

8. Press Esc to cancel Extend Selection mode.

9. Click cell A4. Hold down Shift and click E15. This is another way to select the range.

10. Hold down Ctrl. Click cell A17 and drag across to cell E17. Now two different-sized ranges that are not next to each other are selected at the same time.

FIGURE 2-6
Selecting two
ranges

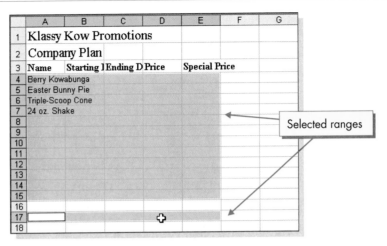

Selected ranges

11. Click cell A4. Hold down (Shift) and click cell A7.

12. Change the font to 12-point Times New Roman.

13. Press (Ctrl)+(Home).

Modifying Column Width and Row Height

Excel makes all columns 8.43 spaces (64 pixels) wide in a new workbook. Many labels do not fit in a column this wide. If the column on the right is empty, the label spills into it so that you can still see the label on the screen. However, if the column on the right is not empty, you can widen the column so that the label is not cut off.

Rows in a new workbook are 12.75 points (17 pixels) high to fit the default 10-point Arial font. Although Excel resizes the height of the row for some changes you make, there are times when Excel does not resize the row height and you need to do it.

Here are the ways you can resize column widths and row heights:

- Drag a column or row border to a different size.
- Double-click a column's right border to AutoFit the column. *AutoFit* means the column is widened to fit the longest entry in the column.
- Double-click a row's bottom border to AutoFit the row height. A row is AutoFitted to fit the largest font size.
- Open the Format menu, and choose Row and then Height or Column and then Width.

When you use the mouse to change the row height or column width, you will see the size in a ScreenTip. For rows, the height is shown in points (as it is for fonts) as well as in pixels. For columns, the width is shown in character space and in pixels. A *pixel* is a screen dot, a single point of color on the screen. A *character space* is the average width of a numeric character in the standard font used in the worksheet.

If you use the menu to change the column width or row height, you must key the entry by using points or character spaces, not pixels.

EXERCISE **2-6** **Modify Column Width**

Now use the methods just described to modify column width.

1. Place the pointer on the vertical border between the column headings for columns A and B. The pointer changes to a two-pointed arrow with a wide vertical bar.

2. Drag the pointer to the right until the ScreenTip shows 17.86 (130 pixels). At this width, the column should be wide enough for the longest promotion item.

FIGURE 2-7
Resizing columns

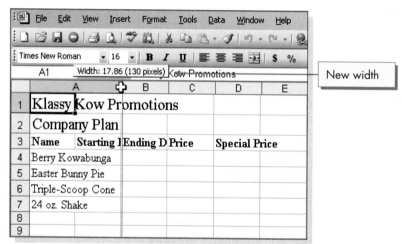

3. Place the pointer between the column headings for columns B and C. Double-click. Excel AutoFits column B to fit the label.

4. Double-click the border between the column headings for columns C and D. Excel AutoFits column C.

 NOTE: If you change data in a column that you've AutoFitted, the column does not automatically AutoFit for the new entry.

5. Click anywhere in column D.

6. Open the Format menu. Choose Column and then Width. The Column Width dialog box opens.

7. Key **10** and press Enter. The column width is changed to 10 spaces.

 TIP: Be careful about AutoFitting columns that include worksheet titles in rows 1 and 2. Excel will AutoFit the column to include the long worksheet titles.

8. Double-click the border between the column headings for columns E and F to AutoFit column E.

EXERCISE **2-7** Modify Row Height

Now you will use different methods for modifying row height.

1. Place the pointer on the horizontal border between the headings for rows 3 and 4. The pointer turns into a two-pointed arrow.

2. Drag down until the ScreenTip shows 22.50 (30 pixels).

FIGURE 2-8
Resizing rows

New height

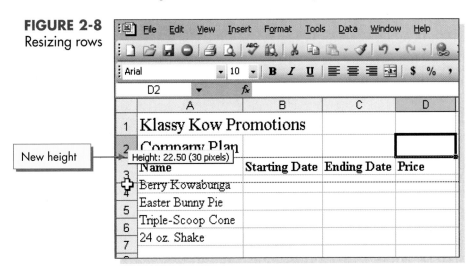

3. Click anywhere in row 4.

4. Open the Format menu and choose Row and then Height. The Row Height dialog box opens.

5. Key **22.5** and press (Enter). The row is 22.5 points high.

Entering Values and Dates

When you key an entry that starts with a number or an arithmetic symbol, Excel assumes it is a *value.* A value is right-aligned in the cell and is included in calculations. Arithmetic symbols include =, –, and +.

 TIP: You can format a number as a label by keying an apostrophe before the number. The number is then not used in calculations.

EXERCISE 2-8 Enter Dates and Values

Excel recognizes dates if you key them in a typical date style. For example, if you key "1/1/05," Excel formats it as a date. Dates have special formats and can be used in date arithmetic.

1. Click cell B4.
2. Key **12/1/05** and press Enter. Excel recognizes a date and shows four digits for the year.
3. Continue keying the following dates in column B. Press Enter after each one:
   3/15/05
   8/1/05
   10/15/05
4. Key these dates in cells C4:C7:
   12/31/05
   4/15/05
   8/31/05
   11/15/05
5. Key the following prices in the "Price" and "Special Price" columns. Figure 2-10 shows the worksheet thus far.

FIGURE 2-9

	D	E
4	2.59	2.19
5	12.99	10.99
6	2.39	2.09
7	2.69	2.29

FIGURE 2-10
Worksheet data
entry completed

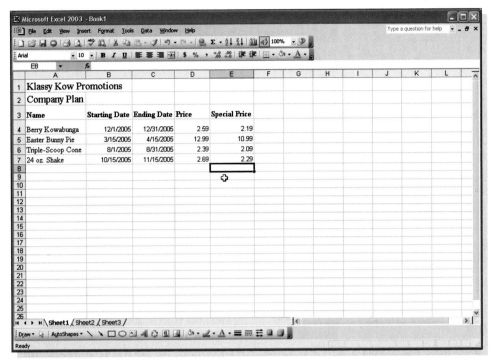

EXERCISE   **2-9**   **Apply Number Formats from the Toolbar**

When you first key a value, it is formatted in a "General" style. This style shows
only the digits in the number and no commas. If the value has a decimal point, it is
shown with as many places after the decimal point as you key.

To increase the readability of your worksheet, you can apply common formats
by using the Formatting toolbar. You first select the range of cells to be formatted
and then click a button in the toolbar.

1. Click cell D4. Drag to select cells D4:E7.

2. Click the Currency Style button $ on the Formatting toolbar. The cells in the
range are reformatted to show a dollar sign and two decimal places.

EXERCISE   **2-10**   **Apply Date Formats from the Dialog Box**

Excel includes many date formats in the Format Cells dialog box. You can open
the Format Cells dialog box for the active cell or the active range by:

● Pressing Ctrl+1.
● Right-clicking the cell or range and choosing Format Cells from the
shortcut menu.
● Opening the Format menu and choosing Cells.

1. Click cell B4. Click and drag to select cells B4:C7.
2. Point at any of the selected cells and right-click. A shortcut menu opens.
3. Choose Format Cells. The Format Cells dialog box opens.
4. Click the Number tab.
5. Click Date in the Category list on the left. Many preset date formats are displayed in the Type box on the right.
6. Click a Type that shows the date first, a hyphen, an abbreviation for the month, another hyphen, and a two-digit year (example "14-Mar-01") and click OK. All of the dates are reformatted.

FIGURE 2-11
Choosing a date
format

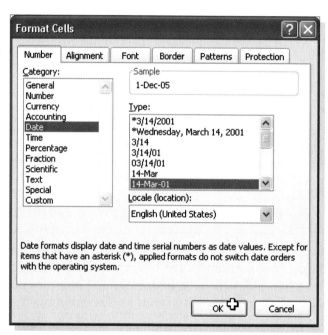

NOTE: Two-digit years between 00 and 29 are shown as the twenty-first century (2000, 2001, 2015). Two-digit years between 30 and 99 are shown as the twentieth century (examples 1930, 1950, and 1999).

EXERCISE **2-11** **Change the Font Color**

In addition to changing the font, size, and style, you can set a new color for data in a workbook. You can change the font color for a selected cell or range by:

● Clicking the Font Color button [A ▾] in the Formatting toolbar.
● Opening the Format Cells dialog box and choosing the Font tab.

1. Select cells E4:E7 (the column with special prices).

2. Click the Font Color button A ▾. The color shown on the button is applied to the selected range.

3. Click the arrow next to the Font Color button A ▾. A color palette opens, showing color swatches for the available colors.

> **TIP:** The color swatches in the palette have ScreenTips indicating the color's name.

4. Click "Green" in the fourth column, second row. The palette closes, and the color is applied to the selected range.

5. Select cells A1:A2.

> **TIP:** After you change the color of a selected range, deselecting the range or selecting another column enables you to see the color you applied without any highlighting.

6. Press Ctrl+1 and click the Font tab.

7. Click the drop-down arrow for Color. Choose Dark Purple (in the second row from the bottom, fifth column) and click OK.

FIGURE 2-12
Changing the color
from the Format
Cells dialog box

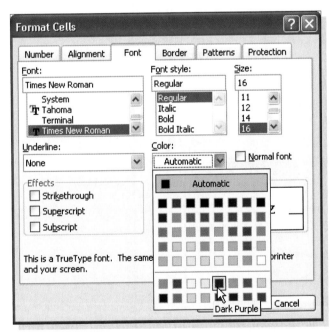

EXERCISE **2-12** Rename a Worksheet and Change the Tab Color

You can rename a worksheet with a more descriptive name to help you and others remember the worksheet's purpose. Worksheet names can be up to 31 characters. You can use spaces in the name of a worksheet tab.

1. Double-click the worksheet tab for Sheet1. The tab name is selected.
2. Key **Promos** and press Enter.
3. Double-click Sheet2 and name it **Plans**. The Plans sheet is empty.

 TIP: Another way to rename a worksheet tab is to right-click the tab and choose Rename.

4. Right-click the Promos tab and choose Tab Color. The Format Tab Color dialog box opens with a palette of colors.
5. Choose the yellow color in the third column, fifth row as the tab color. Click OK. It is difficult to see the color when the tab is selected.

FIGURE 2-13
Changing the tab color

3	Name	Starting Date	Ending Date
4	Berry Kowabunga	1-Dec-05	31-Dec-05
5	Easter Bunny Pie	15-Mar-05	15-Apr-05
6	Triple-Scoop Cone	1-Aug-05	31-Aug-05
7	24 oz. Shake	15-Oct-05	15-Nov-05
8			
9			
10			
11			
12			
13			
14			
15			
16			
17			

Format Tab Color

Tab Color

No Color

OK   Cancel

Ready

6. Click the Plans tab. Now you can see the color of the Promos tab better, because it's no longer selected.
7. Click the Promos tab again to make it the active sheet.

Saving a Workbook

When you create a new workbook or make changes to an existing one, you must save the workbook to keep your changes. Until you save your changes, your work can be lost if there is a power failure or computer problem.

To save a workbook, you must first give it a filename. A *filename* is the file identifier you see in the Open dialog box, My Computer, or Windows Explorer. When you name a file in Windows, you can use up to 255 characters. Included in those 255 characters are the drive and folder names, so the actual filename is really limited to fewer than 255 characters. Generally, it is a good idea to keep filenames as short as possible.

You can use uppercase or lowercase letters, or a combination of both, for filenames. Windows is case-aware, which means it does recognize uppercase and lowercase that you key. However, it is not case-sensitive, so it does not distinguish between "BOOK1" and "book1." You can use spaces in a filename, but you cannot use the following characters: \ ? : * " < > |

Filenames are followed by a period and a three-letter extension, supplied automatically by the software. Excel workbooks have the extension ".xls." Extensions identify the type of file.

For a new workbook, you can use either the Save or the Save As command to save and name the workbook. When you make changes to an existing workbook and want to save it with the same filename, use Save. If you want to save a workbook with a different filename, use Save As.

Excel saves workbooks in the current drive or folder unless you specify a different location. You can easily navigate to the appropriate location in the Save dialog box.

Throughout the exercises in this book, filenames consist of two parts:

- *[your initials]*, which might be your initials or an identifier your instructor asks you to use, such as **kms**
- The number of the exercise, such as **2-13**

 NOTE: You may not see filename extensions if your Folder Options are set to hide them.

EXERCISE 2-13 **Save a Workbook**

Depending on how difficult it would be to redo the work, you should probably save your file every fifteen minutes to a half hour.

1. Click cell A1.

> **TIP:** Wherever the pointer is when you save a workbook is where it appears the next time you open the workbook. Many people prefer to make A1 the active cell before saving/closing the workbook.

2. Click the Save button .

3. Choose the appropriate drive and folder location from the Save in drop-down list.

> **NOTE:** Your instructor will tell you what drive/folder to use to save your workbooks.

4. Click the Create New Folder button.

5. In the Name box, key *[your initials]***Lesson2**. Click OK. The location is updated to your folder.

6. In the File name box, key *[your initials]***2-13**.

7. Click Save. The title bar shows the new filename.

FIGURE 2-14
Saving a new
workbook

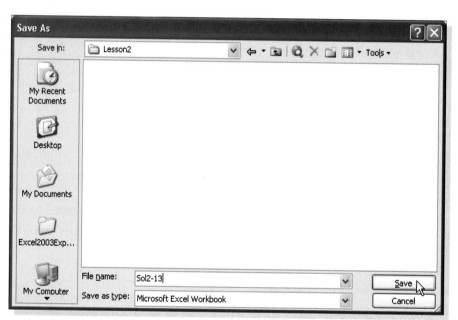

Entering Basic Formulas

A *formula* is an equation that performs a calculation on values in your worksheet and displays an answer. You key a formula in a cell. After you press a completion key, the formula results appear in the cell. The formula itself is visible in the formula bar.

Formulas are one of the main reasons for using Excel, because a formula performs calculations for you. If you later change any of the numbers used for the calculations, Excel quickly recalculates the formula to show a revised answer.

Formulas begin with an = sign as an identifier. After the = sign, you enter the address of the cells you want to add, subtract, multiply, or divide. Then you use *arithmetic operators* in the ten-key pad or across the top of the keyboard to complete the calculation. You probably recognize all of the arithmetic operators shown in Table 2-4, with the possible exception of "exponentiation." The *exponentiation* operator raises a number to a power. For example, 3^2 represents 3 to the second power, or 3^2, which means 3×3 or 9.

TABLE 2-4   **Arithmetic Operators**

KEY OR SYMBOL	OPERATION
^	Exponentiation
*	Multiplication
/	Division
+	Addition
–	Subtraction

NOTE: Arithmetic operators in a formula are calculated in a specific order: first, exponentiation; second, multiplication and division; and finally, addition and subtraction. You will learn about this order in Lesson 5.

EXERCISE   **2-14**   **Key a Basic Formula**

In your workbook, you can calculate the difference between the regular price and the special promotion price. This is a simple subtraction formula. You will be working in column F. If you cannot see column F, set your Zoom size to a smaller size so you can see it.

1. Click cell F3. Key **Difference** and press Enter. The label is automatically formatted with the same style as the other labels in the row.

   NOTE: If three or more columns to the immediate left of the cell in which you enter data are already formatted, Excel applies the same format to the cell in which you are entering data.

2. Double-click the border between the column headings for columns F and G to AutoFit column F.

3. Key **=d4-e4** in cell F4. The formula appears in the cell and in the formula bar. The cells used in the formula are outlined in colors that match the colors of the formula in the cell.

FIGURE 2-15
Keying a formula

Formula bar

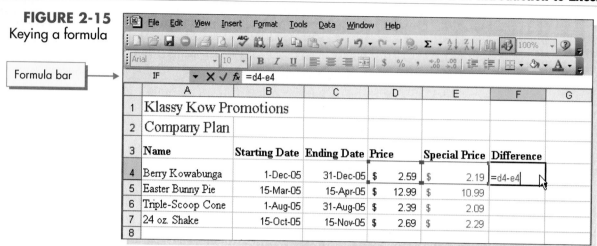

4. Press (Enter). The difference in price is 40 cents. It is shown in the same format ("Currency") as the cells used in the formula.

5. Press (↑) to return to cell F4. Notice that the formula bar shows the formula, but the cell shows the result of the formula.

 NOTE: After you complete a formula, Excel capitalizes cell references.

EXERCISE 2-15 Enter a Basic Formula by Pointing

You can use the mouse to point to cells used in the formula. This increases accuracy, because you don't have to worry about keying the wrong cell address.

1. Click cell F5. Key = to start the formula.

2. Click cell D5. The address appears in cell F5 and in the formula bar. Cell D5 has a moving marquee.

3. Key – to subtract the next cell.

4. Click cell E5. It is placed in the formula after the minus sign and now has the moving marquee.

5. Click the Enter button ✓ in the formula bar. The difference of $2 is calculated.

FIGURE 2-16
Entering a formula
by pointing

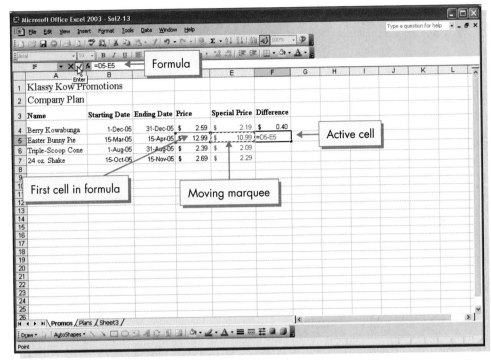

EXERCISE **2-16** **Copy a Basic Formula by Using the Copy and Paste Buttons**

The formula in cell F5 is the same as the one in cell F4 except for the row references. The formula is relative to its location on the worksheet. When you copy a formula with row or cell references, Excel usually makes this adjustment automatically.

1. Click cell F5. Click the Copy button [icon]. The cell now has a moving marquee. The status bar tells you to select the destination for the copy.

2. Click cell F6 and drag to select the range F6:F7.

3. Click the Paste button [icon]. The formula is copied to both cells in the range. The Paste Options button [icon] appears just below the pasted data.

4. Place the pointer on the Paste Options button [icon]. A down arrow appears next to the button. Click the down arrow; options for copying the data are listed.

5. Click Keep Source Formatting to format the copied results in the same style as the original.

FIGURE 2-17
Copying a formula

	C	D	E	F	G	H	I	J
Ending Date	Price		Special Price	Difference				
31-Dec-05	$	2.59	$	2.19	$	0.40			
15-Apr-05	$	12.99	$	10.99	$	2.00			
31-Aug-05	$	2.39	$	2.09	$	0.30			
15-Nov-05	$	2.69	$	2.29	$	0.40			

- ⦿ Keep Source Formatting
- ○ Match Destination Formatting
- ○ Values Only
- ○ Values and Number Formatting
- ○ Values and Source Formatting
- ○ Keep Source Column Widths
- ○ Formatting Only
- ○ Link Cells

6. Press [Esc] to cancel the moving marquee and finish the Paste command.

NOTE: You can press [Enter] to complete a Copy or Paste command. This automatically cancels the moving marquee.

7. Click cell F6 and review the formula in the cell. Notice that Excel has automatically adjusted the formula to take into account the relative position of the cell.

8. Click cell F7. Review the formula. Excel has adjusted it as well.

EXERCISE **2-17** **Use AutoSum, Average, and Max**

Some calculations are so common in business and personal use that Excel includes them as functions. A *function* is a built-in formula in Excel. An example of a function is "SUM," in which Excel automatically totals a column or row. A function starts with =, just like a formula. Excel has several "auto" functions, available in the Standard toolbar.

1. Click cell F8. Click the AutoSum button ⟨Σ ▾⟩ in the Standard toolbar. A formula is placed in the cell, with the word "SUM" followed by the range that will be summed. A moving marquee surrounds cells that will be summed.

FIGURE 2-18
Using AutoSum

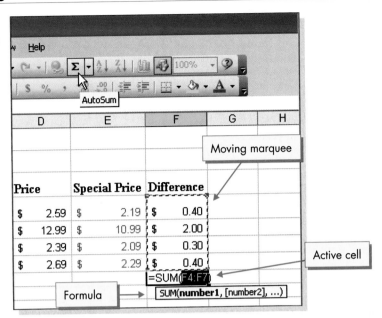

2. Press Enter. The formula is completed.

3. Click cell F8. Notice that the formula includes the function name SUM and the range in parentheses.

4. Click cell D8.

5. Click the down arrow next to the AutoSum button Σ▾ on the standard toolbar.

6. Choose Average. The AVERAGE function now appears in the formula bar and in the active cell. A moving marquee surrounds the cells in the range.

7. Press Enter to complete the function. Then click cell D8 again. Notice that now the formula includes the function name AVERAGE and the range of cells that is averaged.

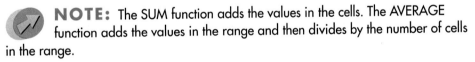

NOTE: The SUM function adds the values in the cells. The AVERAGE function adds the values in the range and then divides by the number of cells in the range.

8. Click cell D9. Click the arrow next to the AutoSum button Σ▾.

9. Choose Max. A moving marquee surrounds the cells that will be used by the MAX function. The MAX function is used to determine the largest value in a range.

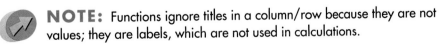

NOTE: Functions ignore titles in a column/row because they are not values; they are labels, which are not used in calculations.

10. Click cell D4 and drag to select the range D4:D7. Don't include cell D8 in this function, because it is the average you just calculated.

11. Press Enter.

12. Click cell D9 again. The result of the formula shows the highest price in the column.

EXERCISE | **2-18** | **Check Results with AutoCalculate**

The feature called *AutoCalculate* displays formula results in the status bar for a selected range. AutoCalculate can display sums, averages, counts, maximums, or minimums. You set the AutoCalculate feature by right-clicking in the status bar.

1. Right-click the status bar. Choose Sum from the shortcut menu.

2. Select the range F4:F7. AutoCalculate shows the sum in the status bar.

FIGURE 2-19
Using AutoCalculate

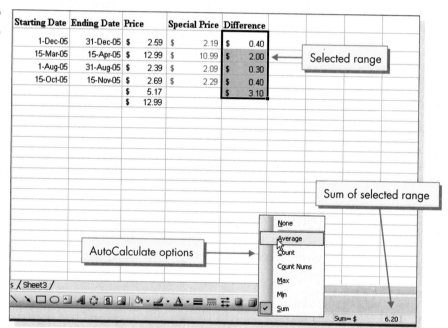

3. Right-click the status bar and choose Average. The average of the cells in the range appears in the status bar.

4. Select the range D4:D7. AutoCalculate shows the average of these cells (the same result as from your formula in cell D8).

5. Select the range E4:E7.

6. Right-click the status bar and choose Max. The highest price is shown in the status bar.

7. Select cells A4:A7. Right-click the status bar and choose Count. The COUNT function counts how many cells contain data.

8. Key your first and last name in cell A9.

9. Press F12 and save the workbook as *[your initials]*2-18 in your Lesson 2 folder.

10. Preview and print your worksheet.

 NOTE: If you print to a black-and-white printer, the colors will appear as shades of gray.

11. Click the Close Window button ☒ to close the workbook.

USING ONLINE HELP

Building basic formulas is an important skill. You will use it as the basis for becoming a proficient Excel user. Learn more about Excel formulas by asking a question.

Look up formulas by asking a question:

1. Start Excel if it's not open, and close the Getting Started task pane.

2. Click in the Type a question for help box, key **create formula**, and press Enter.

3. In the list of topics in the Search Results task pane, click the topic Create a formula.

4. Click Show All at the top right of the window. Read the Help information about different types of formulas.

5. When you finish investigating formulas, close the Help window and the Search Results task pane.

LESSON 2 Summary

➤ In a blank workbook, you can key values, labels, dates, or formulas. Excel recognizes data by the first character you key in the cell.

➤ Labels are aligned at the left edge of a cell. If they are longer than the column width, they spill into the next column if it is empty. Otherwise, they appear cut off on the screen.

➤ To complete a cell entry, press Enter, Tab, or any arrow key or click another cell. You can also click the Enter button ☑ in the formula bar.

➤ The default font for data is 10-point Arial. You can change the font, the font size, the color, and the style.

➤ Use the Format Painter to copy formats from one cell to other cells.

➤ Many commands require that you first select a range of cells. You select a range of cells by using the mouse or keyboard shortcuts.

➤ The default row height matches the default font size. The row height adjusts if you choose a larger font. The default column width is 8.43 character spaces. It does not adjust when you use a larger font or if you key long data.

➤ Common formats, such as "Currency," can be applied to cells from the Formatting toolbar. Many other formats are available in the Format Cells dialog box.

➤ It's usually a good idea to change the default worksheet tab name to a more descriptive name. You can also change the worksheet tab color for visual cues.

➤ You must save a new workbook to keep your work. For a new workbook, you can use the Save or the Save As command.

➤ To create a formula in a cell, you can key it or you can construct it by pointing to the cells used in the formula. All formulas begin with the = symbol.

➤ When you copy a formula, Excel adjusts it to match the row or column where the copy is located.

➤ Excel has functions for common calculations such as Sum, Average, Max, Min, and Count.

➤ You can see results for some functions without keying a formula if you use AutoCalculate.

LESSON 2   Command Summary

FEATURE	BUTTON	MENU	KEYBOARD
AutoSum	Σ ▾		
Column Width		Format, Column, Width	
Copy	📋	Edit, Copy	Ctrl + C
Currency Style	$	Format, Cells	Ctrl + 1
Font Color	A ▾	Format, Cells	Ctrl + 1
Font	Arial ▾	Format, Cells	Ctrl + 1
Font Size	10 ▾	Format, Cells	Ctrl + 1
Format Painter	🖌	Edit, Paste Special	

continues

LESSON 2 Command Summary *continued*

FEATURE	BUTTON	MENU	KEYBOARD
New Workbook		File, New	Ctrl+N
Paste		Edit, Paste	Ctrl+V
Rename sheet		Format, Sheet, Rename	
Row Height		Format, Row, Height	
Save		File, Save	Ctrl+S
Tab color		Format, Sheet, Tab Color	

Concepts Review

TRUE/FALSE QUESTIONS

Each of the following statements is either true or false. Indicate your choice by circling T or F.

T F   **1.** If you key **ABC Company** in a cell, Excel will recognize it as a label.

T F   **2.** When text is too long for the column, it spills to the next row.

T F   **3.** A range is a rectangular group of cells.

T F   **4.** Formulas must be keyed in the formula bar.

T F   **5.** Common format styles are shown as buttons on the Standard toolbar.

T F   **6.** The AutoSum button uses the SUM function.

T F   **7.** AutoCalculate and AutoSum both display the results in a worksheet cell.

T F   **8.** If you copy a formula from one cell to another, Excel changes it to match the new row and column.

SHORT ANSWER QUESTIONS

Write the correct answer in the space provided.

1. What symbol is used to start a formula?

_____

2. Describe how to rename a worksheet tab.

_____

3. What keyboard shortcut opens the Format Cells dialog box?

_____

4. If the pointer is in cell B3 as you key a label and you want to key a label in cell C3, what key can you press to go directly to cell C3?

_____

5. Give an example of a range address.

_____

6. What function key starts Extend Selection mode?

_____

7. How can you AutoFit a column to the longest text in it?

_____

8. List three arithmetic operators that might be used in a formula.

_____

CRITICAL THINKING

Answer these questions on a separate page. There are no right or wrong answers. Support your answers with examples from your own experience, if possible.

1. A workbook starts with three separate sheets. Give examples of how you might use different sheets in the same workbook if you worked in an accounting office.

2. Why does Excel have different data types such as values, labels, and dates? What are some of the differences among these types?

Skills Review

EXERCISE 2-19

Enter labels. Change the font. Save the workbook.

1. Create a workbook and enter labels by following these steps:

   a. Click the New button 🗋.
   b. Key the labels shown in Figure 2-20 on the next page.

   ◀◀ **REVIEW:** Press [Backspace] to correct errors in a cell as you are keying, or press [Esc] to start over. Remember that labels in some cells might spill over to other cells.

2. Change the font by following these steps.

   a. Click cell A1 and click the down arrow next to the Font box.
   b. Key **t** and choose Times New Roman (or scroll to the font).
   c. Click the down arrow next to the Font Size box. Choose 18.
   d. Click cell A2 and click the down arrow next to the Font box. Make this cell 14-point Times New Roman.

3. Key your first and last name in cell A9. Press [Ctrl]+[Home].

FIGURE 2-20

	A	B	C	D	E
1	Klassy Kow Ice Cream				
2	Ice Cream Pie Sales Sales for September				
3		1st Qtr	2nd Qtr	3rd Qtr	4th Qtr
4	Chocolate				
5	Vanilla				
6	Strawberry				
7	Turtle				

4. Save the workbook as *[your initials]*2-19 in your Lesson 2 folder.

5. Click the Print Preview button. Check your work in a reduced and normal size.

6. Click Print in the preview window. Then click OK to print the worksheet.

7. Close the workbook.

EXERCISE 2-20

Select cell ranges. Change the font. Save the workbook.

1. Open **CakeSales**.

2. Press F12 and save the workbook as *[your initials]*2-20 in your Lesson 2 folder.

3. Select cell ranges by following these steps:

   a. Click cell A1 and drag to select cells A1:A2.

   b. Click the down arrow next to the Font box and choose Times New Roman.

   c. Click the down arrow next to the Font Size box and choose 16.

   d. Click cell B3 and press F8 to start Extend Selection mode.

   e. Press the right arrow three times.

   f. Click the Bold button.

   g. Click cell A4.

   h. Press F8 to turn Extend Selection on again.

   i. Press Ctrl+↓. Press Ctrl+→. Change the size to 11.

4. Key your first and last name in cell A9. Press Ctrl+Home.

 5. Click the Print button 🖨. This worksheet prints with row and column headings.

6. Close the workbook and click Yes to resave it with your changes.

EXERCISE 2-21

Change the column width. Set the row height. Enter and format values and dates. Save a workbook.

1. Open **PromoPlans**. Press F12 and save the workbook as *[your initials]*2-21 in your Lesson 2 folder.

2. Change the column width by following these steps:

   a. Place the pointer on the border between the column headings for columns A and B.
   b. Drag the pointer to the right to 17.86 (130 pixels).
   c. Double-click the border between the headings for columns C and D to AutoFit column C.

3. AutoFit columns D, E, and F.

4. Change the row height by following these steps:

   a. Click the row heading for row 3.
   b. Drag to select rows 3 and 4.
   c. Drag the bottom border for row 4 to 22.50 (30 pixels).

5. Enter the values and dates shown in Figure 2-21.

FIGURE 2-21

	B	C	D	E	F
4	3/3/05	4/15/05	2.19	2500	3500
5	9/1/05	9/30/05	8.29	950	1800
6	1/15/05	1/31/05	2.99	4000	4700
7	5/1/05	5/31/05	1.99	3500	3900

6. Format values and set font colors by following these steps:

   a. Select the range E4:F7. Press Ctrl+1.
   b. Click the Number tab. Choose Number in the Category list.
   c. Click the down scroll arrow for Decimal places to reach 0.
   d. Click the Use 1000 Separator (,) box to select it and then click OK.

NOTE: The thousands separator is a comma.

 e. Select the range D4:D7. Click the Currency Style button $.

f. With the range D4:D7 still selected, hold down Ctrl and drag to select the range F4:F7.

 g. Click the down arrow next to the Font Color button A ▾. Choose Blue in the second row of colors.

7. Key your first and last name in cell A9 and press Ctrl+Home.

8. Double-click the Sheet1 tab and key **PricePromos**. Press Enter.

9. Right-click the PricePromos **tab** and choose Tab Color. Choose the same blue in the second row of colors. Click OK.

 10. Save the workbook by clicking the Save button . The workbook is saved with the same name.

11. Preview and print your workbook.

12. Close the workbook.

EXERCISE 2-22

Create and save a new workbook. Enter labels and values. Enter and copy formulas.

1. Create and save a new workbook by following these steps:

 a. Click the New button .

b. Double-click the Sheet1 tab. Key **MediaPlans** and press Enter.

c. Right-click the MediaPlans **tab** and choose Tab Color. Choose a light color and click OK.

 d. Click the Save button .

e. For the Save in folder, choose your Lesson 2 folder.

f. Key *[your initials]***2-22** in the File name box.

g. Click Save.

2. Enter labels and values by following these steps:

 TIP: You can set the font, size, and style before keying data.

a. In cell A1, set the font for 16-point Arial.

b. Key **Klassy Kow Media Schedule** and press Enter.

c. Select the range A2:D2 and set the font to 12-point Arial bold.

d. In cell A2, key **Media** and press →.

e. In cell B2, key **Frequency** and press →.

f. In cell C2, key **Cost per Ad** and press →.

g. In cell D2, key **Total** and press Enter.

h. Click the column B heading and drag to select columns B through D.

> *i.* Double-click the border between the column headings for columns D and
> E to AutoFit the selected columns.
> *j.* Place the pointer on the border between the column headings for
> columns A and B. Drag the pointer to the right to 15.00 (110 pixels).

 REVIEW: If you AutoFit column A when it contains a long label in cell
A1, the column will be sized to accommodate that label.

> *k.* Key the remaining labels and values shown in Figure 2-22.

FIGURE 2-22

	A	B	C
3	KOW Radio	15	150
4	Channel 3 Cable	10	125
5	Star Newspaper	4	105
6	Clipper Mailer	1	75

> *l.* Click the row heading for row 2. Drag to select rows 2 and 3. Drag the
> bottom border for row 3 to 22.50 (30 pixels).

3. Enter a formula by following these steps:

> *a.* Click cell D3. Key = to start the formula.
> *b.* Click cell B3. This is the first cell used by the formula.
> *c.* Key * to multiply the next cell.
> *d.* Click cell C3. This is the second cell used in the formula.
> *e.* Press (Enter). The result of the formula is shown in cell D3.

4. Copy a formula by following these steps:

> *a.* Click cell D3 and click the Copy button ⌨. You are copying this formula.
> *b.* Click cell D4 and drag to select cells D4:D6. You are copying the formula
> to this range.
> *c.* Press (Enter) to complete the copy.

5. Select cells C3:D6. Click the Currency Style button $.

6. Key your first and last name in cell A9.

7. Press (Ctrl)+(Home) to return to cell A1.

8. Click the Save button 💾.

9. Preview and print your workbook.

10. Close the workbook.

Lesson Applications

EXERCISE 2-23

Enter and format labels and values. Enter and copy a formula.

1. Create a new workbook. Save it as *[your initials]*2-23 in your Lesson 2 folder.
2. Key the following labels in the specified cells:
   - **A1** **Klassy Kow Ice Cream**
   - **A2** **Ice Cream Pie Sales**
   - **A3** **March 31,** *[and the current year]*
3. Select all three cells and make them 16-point Times New Roman.
4. Format the date to show the month spelled out, the date, a comma, and four digits for the year.

 REVIEW: Press Ctrl+1 to format the date.

5. Make column A 20.71(150 pixels) wide.
6. Key the labels and values shown in Figure 2-23.

FIGURE 2-23

	A	B	C	D	E	F
4		Week 1	Week 2	Week 3	Week 4	Total
5	Turtle Candy	10	3	5	8	
6	Rainbow	4	7	6	2	
7	Neapolitan	2	0	3	0	
8	Cookie Crunch	3	5	2	0	

7. Make the labels in row 4 bold.
8. Change the height of row 4 to 22.50 (30 pixels).
9. Click cell F5 and use AutoSum button .
10. Copy the formula in cell F5 to cells F6:F8.
11. Change the height of row 5 to 22.50 (30 pixels).
12. Key your first and last name in cell A10.

13. Return the pointer to cell A1.

14. Preview and print the worksheet. Save and close the workbook.

EXERCISE 2-24

Format and key a label. Enter and copy a formula. Use AutoSum. Rename a worksheet.

1. Open **PieSales**. In cell A9, set the font to 12-point Times New Roman, bold. Then key **Quarter Total**.

2. In cell B9, key =.

3. Create an addition formula that adds cells B5 through B8. Use the mouse to construct the formula.

 NOTE: If you accidentally key an addition symbol (+) at the end of a formula, Excel notes the error and can correct it. Read the message box and click Yes.

4. Copy the formula to the range C9:E9.

5. Change the font for cells B9:E9 to 12-point Times New Roman, bold.

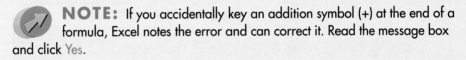 **NOTE:** When you select more than one cell and use AutoSum, there is no moving marquee and you do not need to press Enter.

6. Select cells F5:F9 and click the AutoSum Σ ▾ button.

7. Use the Format Painter to copy the format from cell B9 to the range F5:F9.

8. Use the Format Cells dialog box to format the range B5:F9 to use a Number format with no decimals and the thousands separator.

9. In cell F4, key **Year Totals**. Excel formats this automatically.

10. Rename the worksheet **Pies**. Choose a color for the tab.

11. Key your first and last name in cell A10.

12. Preview and print the worksheet.

13. Make A1 the active cell, save the workbook as *[your initials]*2-24 in your Lesson 2 folder, and close it.

EXERCISE 2-25

Change the font. Modify column width and row height. Enter and copy a formula. Rename a worksheet.

1. Open **MediaPlans**. Save it in your Lesson 2 folder as *[your initials]*2-25.

2. Make the labels in row 2 bold.

3. Widen column A to show the data.

4. In cell E3, create a formula that multiplies "# of Times Run" by "Individual Cost." Copy the formula to all appropriate cells.

 TIP: If you copy a formula to the wrong cell, delete the cell contents.

5. Use AutoSum in cell E9.

6. Make sure the font for formula results match the font of other values in the worksheet.

7. Set a row height of 18.75 (25 pixels) for rows 3 through 8.

8. Rename the sheet **MediaPlans**.

9. Key your first and last name in cell A10.

10. Preview and print the worksheet.

11. Return the pointer to cell A1. Save and close the workbook.

EXERCISE 2-26   *Challenge Yourself*

Create a workbook. Enter and format labels and values. Enter formulas.

1. Create a new workbook.

2. Rename Sheet1 as **DailySales**. Choose a tab color.

3. Save the workbook as *[your initials]***2-26** in your Lesson 2 folder.

4. Format the range A1:A2 as 16-point Times New Roman.

5. Key the following labels in the specified cells:
   - **A1   Klassy Kow Ice Cream Shops**
   - **A2   Daily Double Scoop Sales in** *[your home city]*
   - **B3   Friday**
   - **C3   Saturday**
   - **D3   Sunday**

6. Make all the labels in row 3 12-point Times New Roman, bold.

7. Change the height of row 3 to 36 pixels.

8. Format the range A4:D8 as 12-point Times New Roman.

9. In cells A4 through A8, key the names of five different flavors of ice cream, one in each cell. Manually size the column to fit the longest flavor.

NOTE: If you type a flavor name that begins with a *k, d,* or the same letter as one of your other flavors, you might see an AutoComplete ScreenTip. Ignore it and continue typing.

10. In cells B4:D8, key values to indicate how many double-scoop cones were sold on each day.

11. Format the values so that they appear without decimals and with a thousands separator (a comma).

12. Add the label **Flavor Totals** in cell E3.

13. Add the label **Totals** in cell A9. Set the row height for row 9 to 24 pixels.

14. Use AutoSum to add the values for each flavor and for each day. Include a grand total for all flavors on all days, too. Format the results so that they appear without decimals and a thousands separator (comma). Check that all values use the same font and size.

15. Key your first and last name in cell A12.

16. Return the pointer to cell A1. Preview and print the worksheet.

17. Save the workbook as *[your initials]*2-26 in your Lesson 2 folder and close it.

On Your Own

In these exercises you work on your own, as you would in a real-life work environment. Use the skills you've learned to accomplish the task—and be creative.

EXERCISE 2-27
Open **MediaPlans**. Change the names in column A to the names of radio stations, TV stations, newspapers, or magazines in your city. Call each medium and ask the cost of a popular ad on a weekday. Change the costs in the worksheet. Add your name and the exercise number to the worksheet. Save it as *[your initials]*2-27 in your Lesson 2 folder. Print the worksheet and close it.

EXERCISE 2-28
Sketch on paper a workbook that shows the names of five people in your class or with whom you work. List each person's city, phone number (with area code in parentheses), and birthday. Include a main title and titles for the columns.

Create a workbook based on your sketch. Format it attractively. Add your name and the exercise number to the worksheet. Save it as *[your initials]*2-28 in your Lesson 2 folder. Print the worksheet and close it.

EXERCISE 2-29
Look through a print or Internet catalog and list five products you would like to purchase. Make sure one of the products is small enough that you will want to purchase several of them.

In a new workbook, list the product name, the store or Web site, and the price for each product. Add a quantity column to show how many of each item you would purchase. Create a formula to show what it would cost to buy your items (do not include such things as sales tax or shipping charges). Add your name and the exercise number to the worksheet. Save it as *[your initials]*2-29 in your Lesson 2 folder. Print the worksheet and close it.

Using Editing and Formatting Tools

OBJECTIVES

After completing this lesson, you will be able to:

1. Use AutoCorrect.
2. Look at Trace Error options.
3. Use Spelling.
4. Use Find and Replace.
5. Use series and AutoFill.
6. Apply AutoFormats.
7. Change the page setup.

MICROSOFT OFFICE SPECIALIST ACTIVITIES

In this lesson:
XL03S-1-1
XL03S-1-2
XL03S-3-1
XL03S-5-7
XL03S-5-8

See Appendix.

 Estimated Time: 1½ hours

Excel has several tools to help you make your workbooks accurate and easy to use. Excel finds and flags common formula errors. It has electronic dictionaries that can correct common spelling errors as you type. Other tools enable you to quickly find and replace data and to fill in data automatically.

Using AutoCorrect

The *AutoCorrect* feature makes spelling corrections for you as you type. It recognizes common errors such as "teh," which it corrects to "the." It capitalizes the days of the week and the months and corrects some capitalization errors, such as THis. You can also set it to help you enter routine data more efficiently.

EXERCISE **3-1** **Use AutoCorrect to Correct Errors**

The **KowaSales** worksheet compares sales of the Kowabunga ice cream novelty, which is available in several flavors, over a period of three years. For the years 2004 and 2005, a percentage increase is computed.

 NOTE: As you key the labels for this exercise, be sure to key the errors that are shown.

1. Open **KowaSales**.
2. In cell A1, key **KLassy KOw** and press (Spacebar). The two incorrect uppercase letters are corrected automatically. Notice that the font and size were already set for cell A1.
3. Key **Ice Cream Shops** to complete the label. Press (Enter).
4. Key **saturday** and press (Enter). As you can see, AutoCorrect capitalizes the days of the week.
5. In cell A3, change the font to 9-point Arial.
6. Key **teh shop tracked olny saturday sales.** Press (Enter). Many common errors are corrected as soon as you press (Spacebar), but not all errors are found by AutoCorrect. The word "only" has not been corrected, nor was "the" capitalized. Leave these errors for now.

EXERCISE **3-2** **Set AutoCorrect Options**

If you key "acn," AutoCorrect changes your typing to "can." If "ACN" were the initials of an employee or a company, you would want to delete this correction from AutoCorrect. You can also add new corrections to AutoCorrect.

1. Choose Tools, and then choose AutoCorrect Options. The errors and corrections in AutoCorrect are listed in alphabetical order.
2. In the Replace box, key **kk**. Press (Tab).

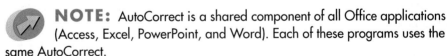 **NOTE:** AutoCorrect is a shared component of all Office applications (Access, Excel, PowerPoint, and Word). Each of these programs uses the same AutoCorrect.

3. In the With box, key **Klassy Kow**. Click Add to add this entry to the AutoCorrect list. Click OK.

FIGURE 3-1
AutoCorrect
dialog box

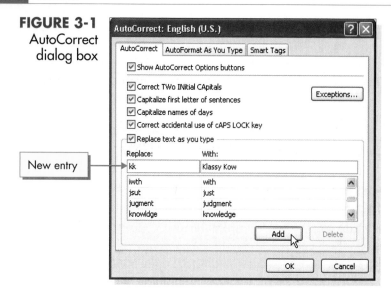

New entry

4. Click cell F3, key **kk**, and press (Spacebar). The initials are changed to "Klassy Kow."

5. Key **Marketing Department** to finish the label. Press (Enter).

6. Choose Tools, and then choose AutoCorrect Options.

7. In the Replace box, key **kk** to move to the "Klassy Kow" entry in the list.

8. Click Delete to remove the entry. Click OK.

9. Click cell F4, key **kk**, and press (Enter). The initials are not changed, because the entry has now been removed from AutoCorrect.

10. Delete the characters in cell F4.

11. Press (Ctrl)+(Home) to return to cell A1.

 NOTE: You have been instructed to delete the "Klassy Kow" AutoCorrect entry so other students in other classes can use your computer without having this entry already listed among the AutoCorrect entries.

Looking at Trace Error Options

Excel automatically alerts you to problems with formulas by showing an error indicator and an Error Checking Options button. The error indicator is a small green triangle in the top-left corner of the cell. The Error Checking button is a small exclamation point within a diamond. It appears when you click the cell with the error indicator. When an error indicator warns of a potential error, you can review the type of error, fix it, or ignore the error.

 NOTE: The Error Checking Options button is also called the Trace Error button ▣.

EXERCISE 3-3 Review Error Checking Options

Cells B11:D11 display small triangles in the top-left corner, signaling a potential error.

1. Click cell B11. The Trace Error button appears to the left of the cell.
2. Position the mouse pointer on the Trace Error button to see a ScreenTip.
3. Click the down arrow next to the button. Its shortcut menu opens. The first line in the menu explains the error, that the formula omits adjacent cells. Excel assumes that a SUM formula in cell B11 would sum the cells directly above, cells B6:B10. However, the formula is correct because the year in cell B6 should not be included in the formula.

FIGURE 3-2
Trace Error button

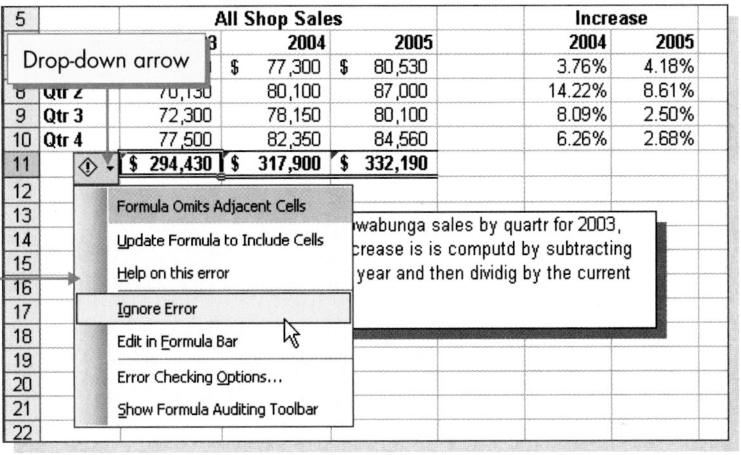

4. Choose Ignore Error. The small triangle is removed.
5. Click cell C11 and drag to select the range C11:D11. The formulas in these cells are also correct.
6. Position the mouse pointer on the Trace Error button and click the down arrow.
7. Choose Ignore Error. Press Ctrl+Home to return to cell A1.

Using Spelling

AutoCorrect finds errors that are considered common typographical mistakes. Excel's Spelling feature does a thorough job of scanning the worksheet and finding words that do not match entries in its dictionaries. It also finds repeated words. The Spelling dialog box provides options for handling errors. These options are described in Table 3-1.

TABLE 3-1 Spell-Check Dialog Box Options

BUTTON	ACTION
Ignore Once	Do not change the spelling of this occurrence of the word. If it is a repeated word, do not delete one of the words.
Ignore All	Do not change the spelling of any occurrences of the word. If it is a repeated word, do not delete the double word.
Add to Dictionary	Add this word to the dictionary so that Excel will not regard it as misspelled.
Change	Replace the current spelling with the highlighted alternative in the Change To box.
Delete	Appears only for repeated words. Click to delete one occurrence of the word.
Change All	Replace the current spelling with the highlighted alternative every time this misspelling occurs.
AutoCorrect	Add the misspelled word with its correction to the AutoCorrect list.
Undo Last	Reverse/undo the last spelling correction.
Options	Offers choices for changing the dictionary language, ignoring uppercase and words with numbers, and ignoring Internet addresses.

E X E R C I S E   **3-4**   **Spell-Check a Worksheet**

Excel starts spell-checking at the active cell and checks to the end of the worksheet. When the spell-checker reaches the end of the worksheet, a dialog box opens, asking if you want to continue spell-checking from the beginning of the worksheet.

The **KowaSales** worksheet has a text box that starts near row 13 with several spelling errors. (A text box is used for special text displays and notations. You will learn how to create them in a later lesson. If you accidentally click the text box in this lesson, click any cell away from the box to continue working.)

 TIP: You can select a range of cells and then click the Spelling button 🏷 to spell-check only that range.

1. Click the Spelling button 🏷. Excel finds "worksheet" in the text box. It offers two suggestions for the correct spelling.
2. Click worksheet in the Suggestions list.

FIGURE 3-3
Spelling dialog box

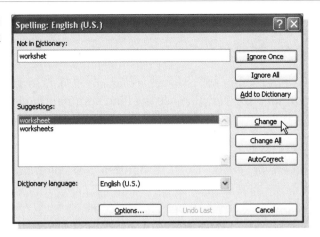

3. Click Change. The correction is made, but you will not see it until you close the Spelling dialog box. Notice that the next error is "Kowabunga." This spelling is not an error; it is correct.

 TIP: You can move the Spelling dialog box by dragging its title bar.

4. Click Ignore All. Excel will ignore any more occurrences of "Kowabunga" in this worksheet. The word "quartr" appears next in the text box.

5. Double-click quarter in the Suggestions list. A double-click is the same as clicking the word and then clicking Change. The next error is a Repeated Word, two occurrences of the word "is."

6. Click Delete to remove one occurrence of the word.

7. Choose the correct alternative for "computd" and click Change.

8. Correct "dividng."

9. "Klassy" is correct, so ignore all occurrences of it. "Kow" is correct, too.

10. Correct any other errors Excel finds. When Spelling is complete, a message box tells you that the spell check is complete.

11. Click OK.

12. Click cell A3. Notice that Excel did not find the capitalization error in cell A3.

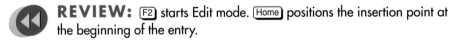 **REVIEW:** F2 starts Edit mode. Home positions the insertion point at the beginning of the entry.

13. Start Edit mode and press Home.

14. Change "the" to "The." Press Enter.

Using Find and Replace

You use the Find command to locate a *character string*, a sequence of letters, numbers, or symbols. You can also use the Find command to locate formats, such as everything in the worksheet that is bold.

You can use wildcards in a Find command when you are not sure about spelling or want to find a group of data. A *wildcard* is a character that represents one or more numbers or letters. Excel recognizes two common wildcard characters. They are:

- * Represents any number of characters
- ? Represents a single character

The character string "mar*" would find everything in the worksheet that starts with the characters "mar" followed by any number of letters or values. This would include "March," "Mar2003," and "Marketing." The character string "?n" would locate all entries that start with a single character followed by an "n." Examples are "in," "2n," and "on."

There are two ways to start the Find command:

- Press Ctrl+F.
- Open the Edit menu and choose Find.

 NOTE: You can add Find/Replace as a button to one of your toolbars.

The Replace command typically locates occurrences of a character string and substitutes a replacement string. A *replacement string* is a sequence of characters that is exchanged for existing data. The Replace command can also search for a format, replacing it with another format.

There are two ways to start the Replace command:

- Press Ctrl+H.
- Open the Edit menu and choose Replace.

Find and Replace share a dialog box, so you can actually use any of these four methods to start either command.

EXERCISE   3-5   Find Data

In the Find and Replace dialog box, you can choose whether to search the worksheet or the workbook. You can search by column or row. If you know that the name you are looking for is in either column A or B, it is faster to search by column. You can also choose to search formulas or values in addition to labels. Other options let you match the capitalization or the entire cell contents. The Find command searches only worksheet cells. It does not search objects that might be embedded within a worksheet (such as the text box in **KowaSales**).

In Find and Replace character strings, do not include format symbols such as the dollar sign and the comma. These are inserted as part of the formatting of a worksheet and are not really worksheet data.

1. Press Ctrl+Home to make cell A1 active.

2. Press Ctrl+F. The Find and Replace dialog box opens. Notice that each command has a separate tab.

3. Key **2004** in the Find what box.

4. Click Find All. The dialog box expands to list information about two cells that include this string of numbers. The first occurrence is highlighted in the worksheet and the list.

FIGURE 3-4
Find and Replace
dialog box,
Find tab

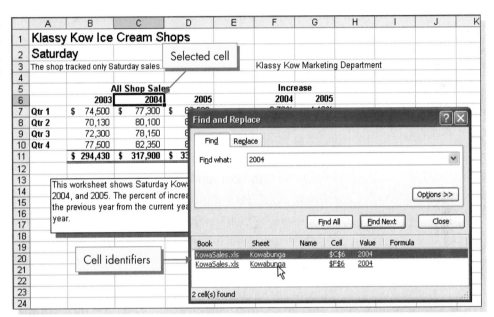

 TIP: You can expand the Find dialog box by dragging one of its corners.

5. Click the second cell identifier in the Find tab. The pointer moves to that cell in the worksheet.

6. Double-click "2004" in the Find what box and key **qtr**. Character strings you key in the Find what box are not case-sensitive unless you turn on the Match case option.

7. Click the Options >> button. The dialog box expands to show you additional settings.

NOTE: If the dialog box shows Options <<, it is expanded.

8. Click the arrow next to the Within box. You can find data within the active sheet or the entire workbook.

9. Choose Sheet, if it is not already selected.

10. Click the arrow next to the Search box. For many worksheets, you might not see much difference in speed if you search by columns or by rows.

11. Choose By Rows, if it is not already selected.

12. Click the arrow next to the Look in box. Excel ignores character strings within values and comments unless you specify that these should be included. (A comment is a message box you attach to a cell.)

13. Choose Formulas, if it is not already selected.

14. Click Find All. Four cells include this character string.

EXERCISE 3-6 Use Wildcards

Now you will use wildcards with the Find and Replace commands.

1. Double-click "qtr" in the Find what box and key *500. This character string is used to find all cells with an entry that ends in "500" preceded by any amount of letters or numbers.

2. Click Find All. Two values in the worksheet match this character string.

3. Double-click "*500" in the Find what box and key o* (lowercase letter "O," not zero, and an asterisk). This character string is used to find all cells with an entry that includes the letter "o" followed by any number of other characters.

4. Click Find All. There are several cells with such entries.

5. Double-click "o*" in the Find what box and key ????0 (four question marks and a zero). This character string is used to find cell contents that end in 0, preceded by at least four characters.

6. Click Find All. There are 17 cells in the list. Some of the cells have formulas with a zero.

7. Click to place a check mark with Match entire cell contents. Click Find All. Now only 12 cells are listed. These cells all have exactly four characters/ values in front of the zero; the comma and the dollar sign are not counted as characters.

8. Click Close to close the Find and Replace dialog box.

EXERCISE   3-7   Replace Data

You can replace a character string one occurrence at a time or all at once. Some-times replacing them all at once can be a problem, because you might locate some character strings you didn't anticipate.

1. Press [Ctrl]+[Home] to make cell A1 active.
2. Press [Ctrl]+[H]. The same Find and Replace dialog box opens, this time with the Replace tab active. Excel remembers your most recent Find character string.
3. Double-click "????0" in the Find what box and key **2004**.
4. Click in the Replace with box and key **2006**. This will change occurrences of "2004" to "2006."
5. Click Find Next to locate the first occurrence of "2004."

FIGURE 3-5
Find and Replace
dialog box,
Replace tab

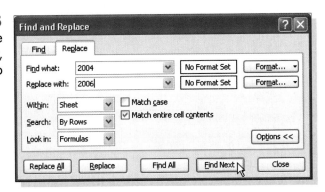

6. Click Replace to change "2004" to "2006." Excel locates the next occurrence.
7. Click Replace. Excel doesn't locate any more occurrences of "2004."

EXERCISE   3-8   Replace a Function in a Formula

1. Double-click "2004" in the Find what box and key **sum**.
2. Turn off Match entire cell contents.
3. Click Find All. Excel locates three cells with the SUM function.
4. Double-click "2006" in the Replace with box and key **avg**. Suppose you want to change the function in these three cells from SUM to AVERAGE, but you incorrectly key **avg**.
5. Click Replace. The first occurrence is replaced. Excel notifies you that this is incorrect spelling for the AVERAGE function. The cell shows #NAME?, a type of error.

6. Click Replace All. Two more replacements are made. This is an example of what could happen if you replace all instances with a new character string that contains an error.

7. Click OK. Because you misspelled "average," all the cells affected by the replacement show an error message.

8. Click Close to close the Find and Replace dialog box. You will correct the errors in the next exercise.

EXERCISE **3-9** **Correct Errors with Replace**

Now you can use Find and Replace to correct the spelling of "average."

1. Click cell B11. Position the pointer on the Trace Error button ⬇.

2. Click the arrow next to the button. This is an "Invalid Name Error." The name of the function is "average," not "avg."

FIGURE 3-6
Error messages

3	The shop tracked only S					Klassy Kow Marketing
4						
5		**All Shop Sales**			**Increase**	
6		**2003**	**2006**	**2005**	**2006**	**2005**
7	Qtr 1	$ 74,500	$ 77,300	$ 80,530	3.76%	4.18%
8	Qtr 2	70,130	80,100	87,000	14.22%	8.61%
9	Qtr 3	72,300	78,150	80,100	8.09%	2.50%
10	Qtr 4	77,500	82,350	84,560	6.26%	2.68%
11	⬇ ▾	#NAME?	#NAME?	#NAME?		
12		Invalid Name Error				
13						
14		Help on this error	Kowabunga sales by quarter for 2003,			
15			crease is computed by subtracting			
16		Show Calculation Steps...	year and then dividing by the current			
17		Ignore Error				
18		Edit in Formula Bar				
19						
20		Error Checking Options...				
21		Show Formula Auditing Toolbar				
22						

3. Click cell B11 to close the shortcut menu.

4. Press Ctrl + H.

5. Double-click in the Find what box and key **avg**.

6. Press Tab. In the Replace with box, key **average**.

7. Click Find All. All the cells with the misspelled function are listed.

8. Click Replace All. The replacements are made.

9. Click OK and then click Close. Another Trace Error button ⬇ has appeared. The AVERAGE function assumes that all the cells immediately above the

cell containing the function are included in the range. That's not true in this case.

10. Click cell B11 and drag to select the range B11:D11.
11. Position the mouse pointer on the Trace Error button ⬇. A down arrow appears next to the button. Click the arrow next to the button.
12. Choose Ignore Error.

EXERCISE **3-10** **Find and Replace Formats**

In addition to finding or replacing characters, you can locate formats and change them. For example, you can find the labels and values that are bold 10-point Arial and change them to bold italic. When you replace formats, you should not show any text or numbers in the Find what or Replace with boxes.

1. Press Ctrl+Home to make cell A1 active.
2. Press Ctrl+H.
3. Double-click in the Find what box and press Delete. The box is empty.
4. Double-click in the Replace with box and press Delete.
5. Click the arrow next to Format to the right of the Find what box.
6. Click Choose Format From Cell. The dialog box closes, and the pointer shows the selection pointer with an eyedropper.
7. Click cell B6. The dialog box expands. The format from cell B6 is shown in the Preview area for Find what.
8. Click the arrow next to Format to the right of the Replace with box.
9. Choose Format. The Replace Format dialog box opens.
10. Click the Font tab. In the Font list, choose Arial.
11. In the Font style list, choose Bold Italic. In the Size list, choose 10.
12. Click OK. The previews show what will be found and how it will be replaced.

FIGURE 3-7
Replacing formats

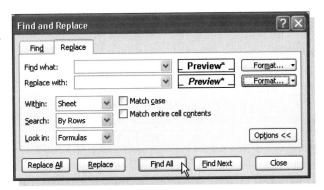

13. Click Find All. The cells with 10-point Arial bold are listed.
14. Click Replace All. The replacements are made.
15. Click OK and then click Close. Two labels were not replaced (cells B5 and F5), because they include a centering command in addition to 10-point Arial bold. Notice also that no values were changed (row 11); they include the Currency format.

 NOTE: You can click the Close button ☒ to close the Find and Replace dialog box.

EXERCISE   3-11   Reset Find and Replace Formats

After replacing formats, it is a good idea to remove those settings. If you don't, they are in effect the next time you use Find and Replace and could affect your results.

1. Press Ctrl+H.
2. Click the arrow next to Format for the Find what box.
3. Click Clear Find Format. The area shows No Format Set.
4. Click the arrow next to Format for the Replace with box.
5. Click Clear Replace Format.
6. Click Close.

Using Series and AutoFill

A *series* is a list of labels, numbers, dates, or times that follows a pattern. The days of the week are a series that repeats every seven days. Months repeat their pattern every twelve months. These are common series that Excel recognizes if you key a label in the series.

You can create your own series by keying two values or labels to set an interval or pattern. The *interval* is the number of steps between numbers or labels. For example, the series "1, 3, 5, 7" uses an interval of two because each number is increased by 2 to determine the next number. The series "Qtr 1, Qtr 2, Qtr 3" uses an interval of one.

EXERCISE   3-12   Create Month and Week Series

The easiest way to create a series is by using the *AutoFill command,* which copies and extends data from a cell or range of cells to adjacent cells. The AutoFill command uses the *Fill handle,* a small rectangle at the lower-right corner of a cell or range.

1. Press Ctrl + G. The Go To dialog box opens.

2. Key **a25** and press Enter. The insertion point is in cell A25.

3. Key **January** and press Enter.

 TIP: AutoFill works only if you spell the first entry correctly.

4. Click cell A25. Click the Down scroll arrow on the vertical scroll bar several times until you can see rows 25 through 36 on your worksheet.

5. Place the pointer on the Fill handle for cell A25. The pointer changes to a solid black cross.

6. Drag down to cell A36. As you drag, a ScreenTip shows each month as it is filled in.

FIGURE 3-8
Creating a
month series

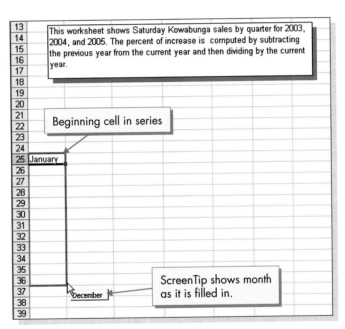

This worksheet shows Saturday Kowabunga sales by quarter for 2003, 2004, and 2005. The percent of increase is computed by subtracting the previous year from the current year and then dividing by the current year.

Beginning cell in series

ScreenTip shows month as it is filled in.

7. Release the mouse button. The series is filled with the remaining months. The AutoFill Options button also appears just below your filled selection. It includes options for filling data.

8. Click the arrow with the AutoFill Options button.

9. Choose Fill Series for just a regular AutoFill task.

10. Click cell B24. Key **Week 1** and press Enter.

11. Click cell B24 and place the mouse pointer on its Fill handle.

12. Drag right to cell E24. Release the mouse button. The series is filled with additional weeks.

EXERCISE 3-13 Create a Number Series

To establish a value series, first key two values in the series. Then select both cells and drag the Fill handle. If you drag the Fill handle too far, just drag it back to where you wanted to finish.

1. Click cell B25. Key **5** and press (Enter).

2. Key **10** in cell B26. This sets a pattern with an interval of 5, increasing each value by 5.

3. Click cell B25 and drag to select cell B26. There is one Fill handle for the range.

4. Place the pointer on the Fill handle for cell B26.

5. Drag down to B36 and release the mouse button. The series is filled in, and the range is selected.

EXERCISE 3-14 Copy Data with the Fill Handle

When there is no apparent pattern in the range, the Fill handle copies data rather than creating a series.

1. The series you just filled in should still be selected. The Fill handle for the range is located in cell B36. Place the mouse pointer on the Fill handle.

2. Drag right to column E and release the mouse button. The range is copied, because no pattern was set for going from one column to the next.

FIGURE 3-9
Using the Fill
pointer to copy

		Copied range			
23					
24		Week 1	Week 2	Week 3	Week 4
25	January	5	5	5	5
26	February	10	10	10	10
27	March	15	15	15	15
28	April	20	20	20	20
29	May	25	25	25	25
30	June	30	30	30	30
31	July	35	35	35	35
32	August	40	40	40	40
33	Septembe	45	45	45	45
34	October	50	50	50	50
35	November	55	55	55	55
36	Decembe	60	60	60	60
37					
38					Auto Fill Options
39					

3. Make column A 10.71 (80 pixels) wide.

EXERCISE 3-15 Copy a Formula with the Fill Handle

You can also use the Fill handle to copy a formula.

1. Click cell F25.
2. Click the AutoSum button . The SUM function is displayed, with the range to be summed shown as B25:E25.
3. Press Enter. The formula is completed.
4. Click cell F25 and look at the formula bar. You can copy this formula to the rest of the rows by using the Fill handle.
5. Place the pointer on the Fill handle.
6. Drag down to cell F36 and release the mouse. Excel copies the formula, and the AutoFill Options button appears.
7. Move the mouse pointer to the arrow next to the button and click. The options determine how AutoFill completes the task. You do not need to make a change.
8. Click cell F26. The copied formula is relative to where it is on the worksheet, just as when you use Copy and Paste.

Applying AutoFormats

An *AutoFormat* is a built-in set of formatting instructions that applies fonts, colors, borders, and other formatting features to a range of cells. It enables you to quickly change the appearance of your work.

EXERCISE 3-16 Apply an AutoFormat

If you place the pointer anywhere in a range of cells, an AutoFormat is applied to that entire range.

1. Click cell B24.
2. From the Format menu, choose AutoFormat. The AutoFormat dialog box shows a sample of several Excel AutoFormats. Notice that the range A24:F36 is selected on your worksheet.
3. Scroll to find Colorful 2 in the AutoFormat list and click the sample. It is outlined with a border to indicate that it is the active AutoFormat.
4. Click OK. Excel applies the "Colorful 2" AutoFormat to the selected range. The colors, fonts, borders, and shading for the range are reformatted.

FIGURE 3-10
AutoFormat
dialog box

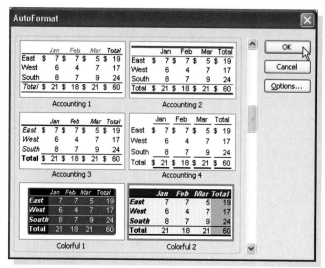

5. Press Ctrl + Home to make cell A1 active. In reformatting the bottom part of your worksheet, you now have a problem with the top part.

6. Click cell B7. This cell and others show several # symbols; however, the formula bar still shows the correct value for cell B7. The # symbol indicates that the value in the cell is too wide for the column. The "Colorful 2" AutoFormat adjusted the column widths, making them too narrow for the top of the worksheet.

FIGURE 3-11
Columns not wide
enough for
existing values

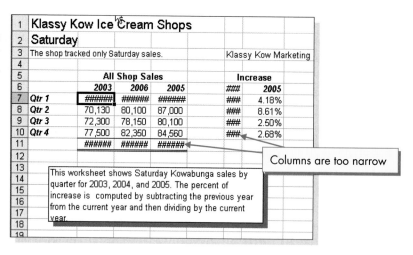

7. AutoFit column B.

8. AutoFit all the columns that show the # symbol. Notice that column F AutoFits to the label in F3. This is much wider than necessary.

9. Change the width of column F to 13.57 (100 pixels).

EXERCISE **3-17** **Change AutoFormat Options**

You can change AutoFormat options. For example, you can keep your own for-matting selections for the font but allow the AutoFormat to change the borders, column width, and row heights.

1. Click cell B24. Notice that the font for the labels is white bold italic. This is the setting for the "Colorful 2" AutoFormat.
2. Click cell A5 and drag to select cells A5:D11.
3. Choose Format and then AutoFormat. Click Colorful 2.
4. Click Options. The dialog box expands to show the options you can set for this AutoFormat.
5. Click the Font box to remove the check mark.

FIGURE 3-12
AutoFormat Options

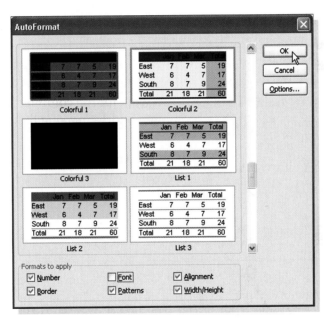

6. Click OK. "Colorful 2" is applied, but now without the white bold italic font.
7. Press Ctrl + Home to make cell A1 active.
8. Set column A again to 10.71 (80 pixels) wide.

EXERCISE **3-18** **Print a Selection**

In the current worksheet, you might want to print only the monthly data at the bottom. To print a portion of a worksheet, select the range of cells you want to print. Open the Print dialog box and choose Selection.

1. Go to cell A23 and key your first and last name. Press `Enter`.
2. Select the range A23:F36 as the range to be printed.
3. Press `Ctrl`+`P`.
4. Choose Selection in the Print what area.
5. Click Preview. The Print Preview shows the selected range that will be printed.
6. Click Print. Only the range you specified is printed.
7. Save the workbook as *[your initials]*3-18 in a new folder for Lesson 3.

Changing the Page Setup

In addition to printing a portion of a worksheet, you have several options for setting how Excel prints your worksheet. From the Page Setup dialog box, you can:

- Create headers and footers
- Change margins or center the worksheet
- Change the page orientation
- Scale the worksheet to fit the page or print larger than the page
- Print gridlines and row or column headings
- Change the page order

In this lesson, you will create a header and a footer, display row and column headings, and change the margins. You will use the other print options in other lessons.

EXERCISE **3-19** **Set Headers and Footers**

Headers and footers can be used to display a company name, a department, the date, or even a company's logo. A *header* prints at the top of each page in a worksheet. A *footer* prints at the bottom of each page. Excel has preset headers and footers, and you can create your own.

A header or footer can have up to three sections. The left section prints at the left margin. The center section prints at the horizontal center of the page. The right section aligns at the right margin.

You can create headers and footers by:

- Opening the View menu and choosing Header and Footer.
- Opening the File menu, choosing Page Setup, and clicking the Header/Footer tab.
- Clicking Setup in the Print Preview window and clicking the Header/Footer tab.

1. With *[your initials]***3-18** open, press Ctrl + Home to make cell A1 the active cell.

2. Click the Print Preview button .

3. Click Setup (at the top of the Print Preview window). The Page Setup dialog box opens.

4. Click the Header/Footer tab. You can create a header, a footer, or both.

5. Click the arrow at the right of the Header box. Several preset headers are listed. Sections are separated by commas. If you choose a single item, it prints in the center section. Two items print in the center and at the right margin. Three items print at the left margin, in the center, and at the right margin.

 NOTE: The same preset items are available for footers and headers.

6. Find and click the first occurrence of your filename. The Header preview box shows the new header.

FIGURE 3-13
Page Setup
dialog box

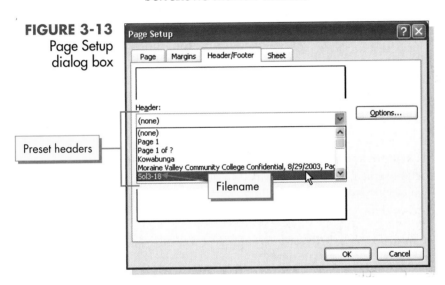

7. Click Custom Footer. The Footer dialog box shows the three sections and buttons for preset items. The insertion point is in the Left section.

 NOTE: The buttons in the Custom Footer dialog box offer the same information you saw listed in the preset Header text box list.

8. Key your first and last name.

9. Click in the Center section. The insertion point is now in the Center section.

 10. Click the Filename button . The code for displaying the filename is &[File]. You can click the button to insert the code or key it.

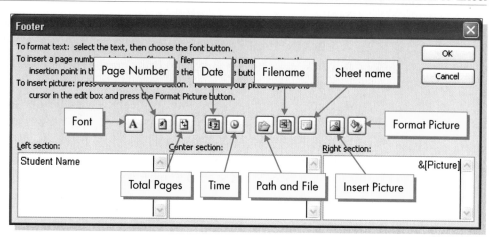

FIGURE 3-14
Adding a
custom footer

11. Press Tab. The insertion point is at the right edge of the Right section.

12. Click the Date button 🗓. The code for displaying the current date is &[Date].

13. Click OK in the Footer dialog box. Your custom footer appears in the Footer preview box.

EXERCISE 3-20 Print Gridlines and Row and Column Headings

Gridlines and row and column headings are visible while you work on a worksheet; however, they do not print as a default. You can turn them on to print. Printing a worksheet with the gridlines and row and column headings makes it easy to locate data or to re-create a worksheet, if needed.

1. With *[your initials]*3-18 and its Page Setup dialog box open, click the Sheet tab.

2. In the Print section, click to place a check mark in the Gridlines box.

3. Click to place a check mark in the Row and column headings box.

4. Click OK. Excel returns you to the Print Preview window.

EXERCISE 3-21 Change Page Margins and Column Widths in Print Preview

Excel has default left and right margins of 0.75 inch for a new worksheet. The top and bottom margins are both 1 inch. The header and footer are preset to print 0.5 inch from the top and bottom of the page.

You can change the margins and the column widths in the Print Preview window by dragging a marker. A *marker* is a small black rectangle at the location for the margin or the right edge of a column. As you drag a marker, the margin setting or column width is shown in inches or character spaces in the status bar.

1. Click <u>M</u>argins (at the top of the Print Preview window). Margin and column markers appear as small black rectangles at the edges of the page.

> **NOTE:** If Excel already displays your margin and column markers, do not click <u>M</u>argins.

2. Place the mouse pointer over the left margin marker. It changes to a two-pointed arrow.

3. Click and drag right to set a left margin of about 1.00. Watch the status bar for the setting as you drag. Your margin setting does not need to be exact.

FIGURE 3-15
Changing page margins in Print Preview

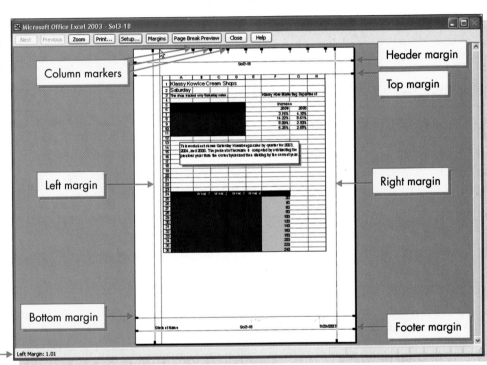

Status bar indicates setting

4. Place the mouse pointer over the right margin marker. Click and drag left to reach about 1.00.

5. Place the pointer on the column marker between columns A and B. Drag right to make column A wider, about 11. The width is shown in the status bar.

6. Make column F slightly less wide.

7. Click <u>C</u>lose to close the Print Preview window.

8. Press F12 and save the workbook as *[your initials]*3-21 in your Lesson 3 folder.

9. Click the Print button 🖫. Close the workbook.

USING ONLINE HELP

Series and AutoFill are time-saving features of Excel. They enable you to work more quickly and more accurately. Read more about series and the AutoFill command by asking a question.

Look up AutoFill and series by asking a question:

1. Start Excel and close the Getting Started task pane.
2. Click in the Type a question for help box. Key **autofill** and press ⌑Enter⌑.
3. In the Search Results task pane, click the topic About filling in data based on adjacent cells. Read the help information.
4. Close the Help window. Close the Search Results task pane.

LESSON 3   Summary

➤ AutoCorrect corrects common typing errors as you work. You can add your own entries or delete existing ones.

➤ The Spelling command spell-checks a worksheet by comparing labels to dictionary entries. Options let you decide if and how to make the correction.

➤ The Find command locates and lists all occurrences of data that match your Find what character string. You can use wildcards in the character string.

➤ The Replace command locates and substitutes new data for existing data. You can complete the changes one at a time or all at once.

➤ Excel displays options buttons for some commands and formula errors. You can look at the message for the button, make a change, or ignore it.

➤ All cells have a Fill handle that can be used for filling in a series or for copying data.

➤ Excel recognizes common series for the days of the week, the months of the week, and patterns such as "Week 1," "Week 2," and so on.

➤ You can create your own series with any interval by keying at least two cells that define the pattern.

➤ AutoFormats apply colors, fonts, and other formatting options to a range.

➤ The Page Setup dialog box includes many options for controlling how your worksheet prints.

LESSON 3   Command Summary

FEATURE	BUTTON	MENU	KEYBOARD
Spelling		Tools, Spelling	F7
Find		Edit, Find	Ctrl + F
Replace		Edit, Replace	Ctrl + H
AutoFormat		Format, AutoFormat	
Page Setup		File, Page Setup	
Margins		File, Page Setup	
Gridlines		File, Page Setup	
Row/column headings		File, Page Setup	
Column width		Format, Column, Width	
Header/Footer		View, Header/Footer	
AutoFill/Series		Edit, Fill, Series	
Print selection		File, Print	

Concepts Review

TRUE/FALSE QUESTIONS

Each of the following statements is either true or false. Indicate your choice by circling T or F.

T F **1.** If you key **THe** as part of a label, AutoCorrect will automatically fix the capitalization error.

T **F** **2.** The Spelling command completes columns of month or day names.

T F **3.** You can use a wildcard character in the Find command.

T F **4.** The Replace command can be used to locate and change the font or the font style.

T F **5.** Options buttons are screen messages that tell you what command to choose next.

T **F** **6.** The Fill handle displays a small hollow circle.

T F **7.** A series is a list with a recognizable pattern.

T F **8.** The option to print a selected range is in the Page Setup dialog box.

SHORT ANSWER QUESTIONS

Write the correct answer in the space provided.

1. What wildcards does Excel use?

*, ?, #

2. What feature enables you to automatically complete a list of twelve months after you key one month?

Autofill

3. What keyboard shortcut opens the Replace dialog box?

Ctrl + H

4. How can you use part of the formatting choices from an AutoFormat?

5. Name the three sections available for a footer.

_____

6. In Print Preview, how can you tell Excel to print row and column headings?

_____

7. In the Print Preview window, what do you use to display markers on screen for the margins and columns?

_____

8. What does Excel display when it finds a formula error or after you use the AutoFill command?

_____

CRITICAL THINKING

Answer these questions on a separate page. There are no right or wrong answers. Support your answers with examples from your own experience, if possible.

1. Find and Replace are powerful commands. Give an example of when they could be timesavers. Think of times when they might create problems.

2. You can copy a formula with the Copy and Paste buttons (as you did in Lesson 2) or with the Fill handle. Which do you prefer and why? When wouldn't it be a good idea to use the Fill handle to copy a formula?

Skills Review

EXERCISE 3-22

Use AutoCorrect. Look at Trace Error options. Spell-check a worksheet.

1. Open **ExpWA**. Press [F12] and save the workbook as *[your initials]*3-22 in your Lesson 3 folder.

2. Use AutoCorrect by following these steps:

    a. Click cell A2.

 NOTE: Key the cell entries with the errors as shown.

    b. Key **Marketing adn Promotions** and press [Enter].
    c. Click cell A14.

> *d.* Key **Thsi workshet was prepared by STudent** *[your last name]* **on monday.** Press (Enter).

3. Change the width of column A to 23.57 (170 pixels). Change the height of row 3 to 22.50 (30 pixels). Make row 11 the same height.

4. Press (Ctrl)+(Home) to make cell A1 active.

5. Click the Save button 🖫.

6. Review Trace Error options by following these steps:

> *a.* Click cell B11. Position the mouse pointer on the Trace Error ⬙ button and click its arrow. This formula is missing a cell.
> *b.* Choose Update Formula to Include Cells.
> *c.* Click cell F6 and display the Trace Error button ⬙ shortcut menu. This formula is not the same as others in the column.
> *d.* Choose Copy Formula from Above.

7. Spell-check a worksheet by following these steps.

> *a.* Press (Ctrl)+(Home). Click the Spelling button ⚏.
> *b.* What is the first misspelled word? What will you do about it?

> **NOTE:** Write your answers to questions in this exercise on a piece of paper. Include your name, the date, the exercise number, and the question number.

> *c.* Take the action you described in the previous step.
> *d.* On your answer sheet, list all the errors Excel finds and the steps you take to correct each one. In your opinion, did Excel miss any errors?

8. Press (Ctrl)+(Home) to make cell A1 active.

9. Click the Print Preview button 🔍. Preview your worksheet in a reduced and in a normal size.

10. Print the worksheet. Save and close the workbook.

EXERCISE 3-23

Use Find. Use Replace.

1. Open **MayPromo**. Save it as *[your initials]***3-23** in your Lesson 3 folder.

2. Use Find by following these steps:

> *a.* Press (Ctrl)+(F).
> *b.* Key **ee** in the Find what box.
> *c.* Click Find All. How many cells include this character string?

> **NOTE:** Write your answers to questions in this exercise on a piece of paper. Include your name, the date, the exercise number, and the question number.

> **d.** Double-click "ee" in the Find what box and key **100**.
> **e.** Click Find All. How many cells include this character string?

3. Use Replace by following these steps:
> **a.** Click the Replace tab.
> **b.** Key **200** in the Replace with box.
> **c.** Click Replace to change the first occurrence.
> **d.** Click Replace to change the second occurrence.

 REVIEW: Move the dialog box if you cannot see the affected cells.

> **e.** Click Find Next to skip the third occurrence.
> **f.** Click the Close button .

 4. Key your first and last name in cell A13. Change the tab name to **MayExp**.

5. Press [Ctrl]+[Home] to make cell A1 active.

6. Click the Print Preview button. Preview and print the worksheet.

7. Save and close the workbook.

EXERCISE 3-24

Create a day series. Create a label series. Use AutoFill to copy values.

1. Create a new workbook. Save it as *[your initials]*3-24 in your Lesson 3 folder.

2. Key **Klassy Kow Ice Cream Shops** in cell A1. Format it as 18-point Arial.

3. Use 12-point Arial in cell A2 and key **Summary prepared by** *[your first and last name]*.

4. Create a day series by following these steps:
> **a.** Click cell B3 and key **monday**. Press [→].

 REVIEW: AutoCorrect capitalizes the names of the days of the week.

> **b.** Key **wednesday** in cell C3 and press [←].
> **c.** Select cells B3:C3. Place the pointer on the Fill handle.
> **d.** Drag right far enough to build a series ending with "Sunday."

5. Change the height of row 3 to 22.50 (30 pixels).

 REVIEW: If you use Format, Row, Height, use points (not pixels).

6. Create a label series by following these steps:
> **a.** Click cell A4 and key **Week 1**.
> **b.** Click cell A4 and place the pointer on the Fill handle.
> **c.** Drag down far enough to build a series ending with "Week 4."

7. Make the range A4:A7 bold.

8. Use the Fill handle to copy values by following these steps:

   a. Click cell B4 and key **10**. Press →.
   b. In cells C4:E4, key **20**, **40**, and **30**.
   c. Select cells B4:E4. Place the mouse pointer on the Fill handle for the range.
   d. Drag down to reach row 7.

 9. Select cells B8:E8. Click the AutoSum button Σ ▾.

10. Change the height of row 8 to 18.75 (25 pixels). Change the width of column C to 10.00 (75 pixels).

11. Press Ctrl+Home to make cell A1 active.

 12. Click the Save button 🖫.

13. Preview and print the worksheet, and then close the workbook.

EXERCISE 3-25

Apply an AutoFormat. Create a footer. Turn off gridlines and row and column headings.

1. Open **CakeSales**.

2. Save the workbook as *[your initials]*3-25 in your Lesson 3 folder.

3. Apply an AutoFormat by following these steps:

   a. Open the Format menu and choose AutoFormat.
   b. Choose Simple and click OK.

4. Create a footer by following these steps:

    a. Click the Print Preview button 🔍.
   b. Click Setup.
   c. Click the Header/Footer tab.
    d. Click Custom Footer. Key your first and last name.
   e. Click in the Center section. Click the Filename button 🖳.
    f. Click in the Right section. Click the Date button 📅.
   g. Click OK.

5. Turn off gridlines and row and column headings by following these steps:

   a. Click the Sheet tab.
   b. In the Print section, click to remove the check mark in the Gridlines box.
   c. Click to remove the check mark in the Row and column headings box.
   d. Click OK.

6. Print the worksheet.

7. Save and close the workbook.

Lesson Applications

Use Find and Replace. Create a footer. Change the left margin.

1. Open **MayPromo**. Save it as *[your initials]*3-26 in your Lesson 3 folder.

2. Replace all occurrences of "california" with **Washington**.

    NOTE: You do not need to key uppercase characters in a Find character string, but you should key them in the Replace character string.

3. Change the worksheet tab name to **MayExpense** and choose a tab color.

4. Change the width of column A to 24.29 (175 pixels).

5. Find and correct errors flagged in the worksheet.

6. Create a footer that shows your name in the left section.

7. In the footer's center section, click the Tab Name button 🔲. Add the date to the right section.

8. Change the left margin to about 1.25 in Print Preview.

    TIP: You can drag the left margin marker at the top or the bottom of the Print Preview window.

9. Preview and print the worksheet, and then save and close the workbook.

Create series. Apply an AutoFormat. Set AutoFormat options.

1. Create a new workbook. Save it as *[your initials]*3-27 in your Lesson 3 folder.

2. Key **Klassy Kow Specials** in cell A1. In cell A2, key **Price Promotions**.

3. In cell B3, key **Regular Price**. In cell C3, key **Special Price**. In cell D3, key **Savings**. AutoFit each column to show the label.

4. In cell A4, key **Ice Cream Cakes**.

    REVIEW: Press [Ctrl]+[1] to format the date.

5. In cell A5, key **January 1, 200x** (using next year in place of the "x"). Key **February 1, 200x** in cell A6, with the same year. Select both cells and format

the date to spell out the month and show the date, a comma, and a four-digit year.

6. Select cells A5:A6 if they are not already selected, and use the Fill handle for the range to extend the dates to May 1 of the same year.

7. Select cells B5:D9 and format them for Currency Style.

8. Key **12.5** in cell B5. Use the Fill handle to copy this value to the range B6:B9.

9. Key the following special prices:

   - January   **9.99**
   - February   **11.25**
   - March   **10.50**
   - April   **10.99**
   - May   **9.99**

10. In cell D5, key =. Click cell B5 and then key − for subtraction. Click cell C5 and press (Enter). This formula computes the difference between the regular price and the special price.

11. Use the Fill handle for cell D5 to copy the formula to cells D6:D9.

12. Press (Ctrl)+(Home) to make cell A1 active.

13. Rename the worksheet tab as **Cakes** and choose a tab color.

14. Use the Accounting 2 AutoFormat, but turn off the option for Number.

 TIP: If you don't turn off the Number option, you will need to format the date and currency numbers again.

15. Add a custom header to show your name at the left, the tab name in the center, and the filename at the right.

16. Preview and print the worksheet, and then save and close the workbook.

EXERCISE 3-28

Spell-check a worksheet.

1. Open **OrderSheet**. Spell-check the worksheet and correct all misspelled words.

 NOTE: The correct spelling of Klassy Kow's flavor is "Bubble Gum Goo."

2. In cell F3, key today's date in this format: mm/dd/yy.

3. In cell F4, key *[your last name]*'s **Supermarket**.

4. Key the following quantities for each ice cream flavor. Not all flavors are being ordered. No quantity appears for flavors that are not being ordered.

- Vanilla   25
- Chocolate   25
- Strawberry   20
- Butter Pecan   10
- French Vanilla   10
- Chocolate Chip   10
- Chocolate Mint Melody   10
- Peppermint Candy   10
- Raspberry Swirl   15
- Purple Kow   12

The flavors in Rows 17–24 are not being ordered.

- Apple Pie   5
- Rum Raisin   5
- Blueberry   5
- New York Cherry   5

5. Paint the format from cell E28 to cell E32.

6. Press Ctrl + Home to make cell A1 active.

7. Save the workbook as *[your initials]*3-28 in your Lesson 3 folder.

8. Preview and print the worksheet, and then close the workbook.

EXERCISE 3-29 *Challenge Yourself*

Use AutoCorrect. Create day series. AutoFill values. Apply an AutoFormat. Create a footer. Change the margins.

1. Create a new workbook. Rename Sheet1 as **ShakeSales**. Save the workbook as *[your initials]*3-29 in your Lesson 3 folder.

2. Key **Klassy Kow Ice Cream Shops** in cell A1. Key **Daily Shake Sales in** *[your home city]* in cell A2.

3. Key **Chocolate** in cell B3. Key **Vanilla** in cell C3.

4. Key **Monday** in cell A4. Fill in the days of the week up to and including "Sunday" in column A.

5. Key **4** in cell B4. Key **8** in cell B5. Extend this series down column B to fill in values up to "Sunday." Copy the entire range of values to the "Vanilla" column.

6. Use AutoSum to total the values for each flavor.

7. Apply the Classic 1 AutoFormat.

8. Change the width of column A to 16.43 (120 pixels). Set the row heights for rows 1 through 3 to be more than the other rows.

9. Change the left and top margins to 2.00 (or as close to 2 inches as you can get on your computer).

10. Add a custom footer with your name at the left, the filename in the center, and the date at the right.

11. Press Ctrl + Home to make cell A1 active.

12. Preview, print, and save the worksheet, and then close the workbook.

On Your Own

In these exercises you work on your own, as you would in a real-life work environment. Use the skills you've learned to accomplish the task—and be creative.

EXERCISE 3-30

Open **PieSales**. Change the date in cell A3 to today's date. One at a time, apply six of the AutoFormats to the worksheet. Record which one you like best, and then apply it again. Create a custom footer with your name in the left section, the name of the AutoFormat in the center, and the date at the right. Save the worksheet as *[your initials]*3-30 in your Lesson 3 folder. Preview and print it, and then close the workbook.

EXERCISE 3-31

Create a new workbook and save it as *[your initials]*3-31 in your Lesson 3 folder. In cell A1, key the label **Using AutoFill and Series**. Format it with an 18-point font.

Build a 15-month series in column A, using a 3-month interval. Build a 15-day series in column B, using an every-other-day interval. In row 20, build a 10-year series, using a 4-year interval. In row 22, build a 10-value series starting at 2 and using an interval of 2. In cell A24, key today's date. In cell A25, key the date one week from today. Build a 12-date series in column A, using cells A24:A25 to start the series.

Add your name, the filename, and the date in a custom header. Preview and print the worksheet, and then close the workbook.

EXERCISE 3-32

Use the Internet or printed maps to determine the approximate mileage between your city and five major cities in your part of the country. Determine approximate driving time to drive to each city from your city. Create a workbook that shows this information in an easy-to-read layout. Include a main title and column titles. Apply an AutoFormat to your worksheet and spell-check it. Add your name, the filename, and the date in a custom header. Save the workbook as *[your initials]*3-32 in your Lesson 3 folder. Preview and print the worksheet, and then close the workbook.

Working with Cells, Columns, Rows, and Sheets

MICROSOFT OFFICE SPECIALIST ACTIVITIES

In this lesson:
XL03S-1-1
XL03S-3-1
XL03S-3-3
XL03S-5-2
XL03S-5-4
XL03S-5-6

See Appendix.

OBJECTIVES

After completing this lesson, you will be able to:

1. **Insert and delete worksheets.**
2. **Insert and delete cells.**
3. **Add labels by using AutoComplete and Pick From List.**
4. **Copy, cut, and paste cell contents.**
5. **Work with columns and rows.**
6. **Work with cell alignment.**
7. **Use Merge and Center.**
8. **Apply borders and shading.**

 Estimated Time: 1¼ hours

You can modify a workbook or worksheet in many ways. You can add or delete worksheets if you need more or fewer sheets than the usual three. You can insert or delete cells, columns, or rows in a worksheet if you find you forgot data and need to make room for it. This lesson focuses on modifying worksheets and enhancing them with additional formatting.

Inserting and Deleting Worksheets

A new workbook opens with three blank sheets, enabling you to separate parts of your work. You can insert and delete sheets as needed.

You insert a new worksheet when you:

- Press Shift + F11.
- Open the Insert menu and choose Worksheet.
- Right-click the worksheet tab and choose Insert.

You delete a worksheet when you:

- Open the Edit menu and choose Delete Sheet.
- Right-click the worksheet tab and choose Delete.

EXERCISE   4-1   Insert Worksheets

When you insert a new worksheet, it is placed to the left of the active sheet. Excel names new sheets starting with the next number in sequence. For example, if the worksheet already has Sheet1, Sheet2, and Sheet3, a new sheet would be named Sheet4.

1. Open **AcctRec**. This workbook has one worksheet named AR2004 for "Accounts Receivable" in 2004. Notice that there is no Sheet1.

2. Press Shift + F11. A new worksheet named Sheet1 is placed in front of the AR sheet.

3. Double-click the Sheet1 worksheet tab.

4. Key **SalesReps** and press Enter. The worksheet tab is renamed.

5. Right-click the SalesReps tab. A shortcut menu opens.

6. Choose Insert. The Insert dialog box opens.

7. Click the General tab, if it is not already open. This tab shows the types of objects you can insert in your workbook.

FIGURE 4-1
Insert Worksheet
dialog box

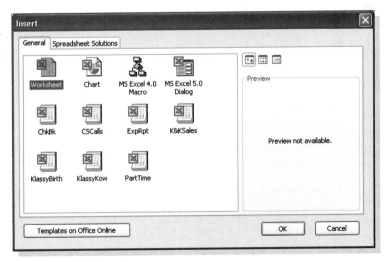

8. Click Worksheet and then click OK. Sheet2 is placed before the SalesReps worksheet.

EXERCISE **4-2** **Move and Delete Worksheets**

You can rearrange worksheet tabs to place them in a different order. Additionally, when you don't need all the sheets in a workbook, you should delete them to conserve file space. You cannot delete a sheet, however, if it is the only one in the workbook.

1. Click the AR2004 tab. It becomes active and appears on top of the other sheets.
2. Point at the tab to display a white arrow pointer.
3. Click and drag the tab to the left of Sheet2. As you drag, you see a small sheet icon and a triangle that marks the new position of the sheet.
4. Release the mouse button. The AR2004 sheet is now the leftmost tab.
5. Right-click the Sheet2 tab. The sheet becomes the active sheet and a shortcut menu opens.
6. Choose Delete. The sheet is deleted, and the SalesReps worksheet is active.

 TIP: You can also move a sheet by right-clicking the tab and choosing Move or Copy from the shortcut menu.

Inserting and Deleting Cells

If you have forgotten a column or row entry, you can insert a cell to make room for the missing data. You might also sometimes find extra entries in a column or row and need to delete cells. When you insert or delete cells, you decide if existing cells should move up, down, left, or right.

EXERCISE **4-3** **Insert Cells**

When you insert or delete cells, you affect the entire worksheet, not just the column or row where you are working. You can accidentally rearrange data if you don't watch the entire sheet.

1. Click the AR2004 tab in **AcctRec**. Set the Zoom size so that you can see columns A through H.
2. Click cell B8.

NOTE: If you use a laptop computer that does not have a numeric keypad, press Ctrl + Shift + +, using the + in the top row of keys.

3. Press Ctrl + + in the numeric keypad. (The *numeric keypad* is the set of number and symbol keys at the right side of the keyboard.) An Insert dialog box opens with choices about what happens after the cell is inserted.

FIGURE 4-2
Insert dialog box

4. Choose Shift cells down if it's not already selected and click OK. A blank cell is inserted. The cells originally in cells B8:B15 have moved down to cells B9:B16. The data in the other columns did not shift.

5. Click cell C12. This reference number and related paid date are in the wrong columns.

6. Right-click cell C12 and choose Insert.

7. Choose Shift cells right and click OK. All the cells in the worksheet shift to the right, including those in column H and beyond.

FIGURE 4-3
One cell inserted, with other cells shifted right

	A	B	C	D	E	F	G	H	I	J
1	Date	Account Name	Amount Due	Reference No.	Date Paid			Account Name	Sales Representative	YTD Sales
2	1/1/2004	Regan Supermarke	4501.26	20101	2/1/2004			Regan Supermarkets	José Garcia	11321
3	1/7/2004	Southwest Office	345	20107	3/1/2004			Southwest Office	Gary Johnson	9875
4	2/5/2004	Stop and Shop	1000.55	20205	2/26/2004			Stop and Shop	Kathleen D'Alvia	4533
5	2/15/2004	Corner Store	541.32	20215	3/15/2004			Corner Store	Lisa Watson	7566
6	4/2/2004	SafeTop Stores	15245.78	20402	4/30/2004			SafeTop Stores		14500
7	4/15/2004		12567	20415	5/15/2004					12375
8	5/8/2004		3677.87	20508	6/8/2004			International Groceries		8655
9	5/24/2004	International Groce	5590	20524	6/24/2004					7544
10	6/18/2004	Tom's Foods	25125.24	20601	7/18/2004					11900
11	6/23/2004	Regan Supermarke	15200.35	20612	7/30/2004				Tom's Foods	10555
12	7/6/2004			20618	8/2/2004					
13	8/14/2004		11245.56	20623	9/14/2004			Dominic's Foods		9877
14	8/24/2004		8750	20706	9/30/2004			Diamond Food Stores		13000
15	9/7/2004	South Island Foods		20814	9/30/2004			Bryce Groceries		
16	9/23/2004	Fresh Foods		20824	10/23/2004			South Island Foods		
17								Fresh Foods		
18										
19										
20										
21										

Cell inserted here

Cell shifted right

EXERCISE **4-4** **Delete Cells**

When you delete cells, watch the entire worksheet for changes.

1. Scroll the worksheet so that you can see columns D through I. Adjust your Zoom size again if you can't see all the columns at the same time.

2. Click cell H7.

3. Press Ctrl + – in the numeric keypad. The Delete dialog box opens.

4. Choose Shift cells up, and click OK. This creates a problem. There is no room to move "Tom's Foods" to column H.

 5. Click the Undo button .

6. Click cell H12. This is an extra cell.

7. Press Ctrl+⌐ on the numeric keypad.

8. Choose Shift cells left and click OK. Only the cells in columns H and beyond are shifted.

9. Now right-click cell H7 and choose Delete.

10. Choose Shift cells up, if it's not already selected, and click OK.

11. Select cells H8:H10. Right-click any cell in the range.

12. Choose Delete and Shift cells up. Click OK.

13. Press Ctrl+Home.

Adding Labels with AutoComplete and Pick From List

Labels for frequent customers, standard suppliers, or cities might be repeated many times in a column. Excel has two features that make it easy to enter duplicate labels in a column. Both features use text already in the column.

- *AutoComplete* displays a suggested label after you key the first character(s) in a cell. This method is helpful when most labels don't start with the same character(s).

- *Pick From List* displays a list of all labels already in the column. You then choose a label from the list. This method is helpful when you are not sure how to spell the label or when several labels start with the same character(s).

EXERCISE 4-5 **Use AutoComplete**

When you key a new label, Excel scans the column for the same initial characters. In the cell, it displays a suggested entry that starts with the same letter. If the suggestion is correct, press Enter. If the suggested label is not what you want, ignore it and continue to key the correct label. You may need to key a few characters before Excel makes the correct suggestion.

1. Click cell B7.

 TIP: AutoComplete is not case-sensitive. You can key lower- or uppercase letters to see a suggested label.

2. Key **r** to see an AutoComplete suggestion. In this case, Excel's suggestion is correct.

FIGURE 4-4
An AutoComplete
suggestion

	A	B	C	D	E	F
1	*Date*	*Account Name*	*Amount Due*	*Reference No.*	*Date Paid*	
2	1/1/2004	Regan Supermarke	4501.26	20101	2/1/2004	
3	1/7/2004	Southwest Office	345	20107	3/1/2004	
4	2/5/2004	Stop and Shop	1000.55	20205	2/26/2004	
5	2/15/2004	Corner Store	541.32	20215	3/15/2004	
6	4/2/2004	SafeTop Stores	15245.78	20402	4/30/2004	
7	4/15/2004	regan Supermarkets		20415	5/15/2004	
8	5/8/2004		3677.87	20508	6/8/2004	
9	5/24/2004	International Groce	5590	20524	6/24/2004	
10	6/18/2004	Tom's Foods	25125.24	20601	7/18/2004	
11	6/23/2004	Regan Supermarke	15200.35	20612	7/30/2004	
12	7/6/2004			20618	8/2/2004	

3. Press (Enter). The label is entered.

4. Key **s** in cell B8. No suggestion is made, because several labels in the column start with "s." Excel needs more information.

5. Key **t** to see a suggestion for "Stop and Shop."

6. Press (Enter).

7. Click cell B12 and key **south**. Excel has still not found a match.

8. Press (Spacebar). It now suggests "South Island Foods." That's the correct choice.

9. Press (Enter).

10. Key **PDQ Shop** in cell B13 and press (Enter). No suggestion is made, because no existing label starts with "p."

11. Click cell C15 and key **87**. Excel does not make AutoComplete suggestions for values.

12. Press (Esc).

EXERCISE   4-6   Use Pick From List

The Pick From List option appears on the shortcut menu when you right-click a cell in a column containing labels.

1. Right-click cell I6. A shortcut menu appears.

2. Choose Pick From List from the shortcut menu. Excel displays a list of labels already in column I.

3. Click José Garcia. (See Figure 4-5 on the next page.)

4. Right-click cell I7. Choose Pick From List.

5. Click Lisa Watson.

6. Right-click cell B14. Choose Pick From List. The list is longer and includes a scroll bar.

FIGURE 4-5
Using Pick From List

	G	H	I	J
		Account Name	*Sales Representative*	*YTD Sale*
		Regan Supermarkets	José Garcia	11321
		Southwest Office	Gary Johnson	9875
		Stop and Shop	Kathleen D'Alvia	4533
		Corner Store	Lisa Watson	7566
		SafeTop Stores		14500
		International Groceries	Gary Johnson	12375
		Tom's Foods	José Garcia / Kathleen D'Alvia	8655
		Dominic's Foods	Lisa Watson	7544
		Diamond Food Stores		11900
		Bryce Groceries		10555
		South Island Foods		5600
		Fresh Foods		9877
				13000

7. Find and click Tom's Foods.

8. Right-click cell C15. Choose Pic_k From List. Excel does not display a list for values.

9. Press (Esc).

Copying, Cutting, and Pasting Cell Contents

You can copy, cut, and paste cell contents to speed data entry or to make changes in a worksheet. When you copy or cut a cell or range of cells, a duplicate of the data is placed on the *Windows Clipboard.* This is a temporary memory area used to keep data you have copied or cut.

Data that is cut can be pasted once. Data that is copied can be pasted many times and in many locations. Copied data stays on the Windows Clipboard until you copy or cut another cell or range. Then that data replaces the data on the Clipboard.

The Cut command and the Paste command are used to move labels and values from one cell to another. To use cut and paste, you first select the cells you want to cut, and then you can:

- Click the Cut button ✄. Position the pointer at the new location and then click the Paste button 📋 ▾ or press (Enter).
- Press (Ctrl)+(X). Position the pointer at the new location and press (Ctrl)+(V).
- From the Edit menu, choose Cut. Position the pointer at the new location, open the Edit menu, and choose Paste.
- Right-click the selected cells. Choose Cut from the shortcut menu. Position the pointer at the new location, right-click, and choose Paste from the shortcut menu.
- Select the cell or range. Drag it to a new location.

The Copy and Paste commands make a duplicate of the data in another location. To use copy and paste, you first select the cells you want to copy, and then you can:

- Click the Copy button 📋. Position the pointer at the new location and then click the Paste button 📋 ▾ or press Enter.
- Press Ctrl+C. Position the pointer at the new location and press Ctrl+V.
- From the Edit menu, choose Copy. Position the pointer at the new location, open the Edit menu, and choose Paste.
- Right-click the selected cells. Choose Copy from the shortcut menu. Position the pointer at the new location, right-click, and choose Paste.
- Select the cell or range. While holding down the Ctrl key, drag it to a new location.

EXERCISE **4-7** **Cut and Paste Cell Contents**

When you paste cells that have been cut, the cut data replaces existing data unless you tell Excel to insert the cut data.

1. Click cell C14. Click the Cut button ✂. A moving marquee surrounds the cell.

2. Click cell C12 and then click the Paste button 📋 ▾. The data is removed from cell C14 and pasted in C12. The marquee is canceled.

3. Select cells B15:B16. Press Ctrl+X. The range displays the moving marquee. (The Office Clipboard task pane may open; you will work with it later in this lesson.)

4. Click cell B17 and press Enter.

FIGURE 4-6
Cutting cell contents

	A	B	C	D	E
1	*Date*	*Account Name*	*Amount Due*	*Reference No.*	*Date Paid*
2	1/1/2004	Regan Supermarke	4501.26	20101	2/1/2004
3	1/7/2004	Southwest Office	345	20107	3/1/2004
4	2/5/2004	Stop and Shop	1000.55	20205	2/26/2004
5	2/15/2004	Corner Store	541.32	20215	3/15/2004
6	4/2/2004	SafeTop Stores	15245.78	20402	4/30/2004
7	4/15/2004	Regan Supermarke	12567	20415	5/15/2004
8	5/8/2004	Stop and Shop	3677.87	20508	6/8/2004
9	5/24/2004	International Groce	5590	20524	6/24/2004
10	6/18/2004	Tom's Foods	25125.24	20601	7/18/2004
11	6/23/2004	Regan Supermarke	15200.35	20612	7/30/2004
12	7/6/2004	South Island Foods	8750	20618	8/2/2004
13	8/14/2004	PDQ Shop	11245.56	20623	9/14/2004
14	8/24/2004	Tom's Foods		20706	9/30/2004
15	9/7/2004	South Island Foods		20814	9/30/2004
16	9/23/2004	Fresh Foods		20824	10/23/2004
17					
18					

5. Click the Cut button ⬚. The range displays a moving marquee.

6. Right-click cell B14. A regular Paste would replace the existing entry.

7. Choose Insert Cut Cells. The cells that had been cut are inserted into the column.

 NOTE: Close the Clipboard task pane if it is open.

EXERCISE | 4-8 | Copy and Paste Cell Contents

The Paste Options button ⬚ appears just below a pasted selection. When you click it, you see a list of options that establish how the selection is pasted.

1. Click cell B1 and click the Copy button ⬚. The cell is surrounded by the moving marquee.

2. Click cell B13 and click the Paste button ⬚. The label is pasted, the original data is removed, and the Paste Options button ⬚ appears.

3. Rest the mouse pointer on the Paste Options button ⬚. Click its arrow.

4. Choose Formatting Only. This option copies only the formatting; it does not copy the actual label.

FIGURE 4-7
Pasting over
existing data

	A	B	C	D	E
1	*Date*	*Account Name*	*Amount Due*	*Reference No.*	*Date Paid*
2	1/1/2004	Regan Supermarke	4501.26	20101	2/1/2004
3	1/7/2004	Southwest Office	345	20107	3/1/2004
4	2/5/2004	Stop and Shop	1000.55	20205	2/26/2004
5	2/15/2004	Corner Store	541.32	20215	3/15/2004
6	4/2/2004	SafeTop Stores	15245.78	20402	4/30/2004
7	4/15/2004	Regan Supermarke	12567	20415	5/15/2004
8	5/8/2004	Stop and Shop	3677.87	20508	6/8/2004
9	5/24/2004	International Groce	Paste Options button	20524	6/24/2004
10	6/18/2004	Tom's Foods		20601	7/18/2004
11	6/23/2004	Regan Supermarke	15200.35	20612	7/30/2004
12	7/6/2004	South Island Foods	8750	20618	8/2/2004
13	8/14/2004	*Account Name*	11245.56	20623	9/14/2004
14	8/24/2004	South Island Foods		20706	9/30/2004
15	9/7/2004	Fresh Foods		20814	9/30/2004
16	9/23/2004	Tom's Foods			10/23/2004
17					
18					
19					
20					
21					
22					
23					
24					

Paste Options menu:
- ● Keep Source Formatting
- ○ Match Destination Formatting
- ○ Values and Number Formatting
- ○ Keep Source Column Widths
- ○ Formatting Only
- ○ Link Cells

TIP: The marquee is not automatically canceled after you click the Paste button . This enables you to paste the data again in a different location.

5. Click the Undo Button 🔄. Press Esc.

6. Click cell I2 and drag to select the range I2:I7.

7. Press Ctrl+C. Excel displays a marquee around the range.

8. Click cell I8. You only need to click in the first cell for the copy.

9. Press Ctrl+V. The range of names is duplicated, and the marquee is still shown. The Paste Options button 📋▾ appears again.

10. Click cell I14. Press Ctrl+V to paste the data again.

11. Press Esc to cancel the marquee.

12. Select the range C8:C10 and press Ctrl+C to copy the range.

REVIEW: Copied cells replace existing data unless you choose the option to insert them.

13. Right-click cell C11.

14. Choose Insert Copied Cells. The Insert Paste dialog box opens.

15. Choose Shift cells down. Click OK. The copied cells are inserted and the existing cells are shifted down in the column.

16. Press Esc to cancel the marquee.

EXERCISE **4-9** **Use Drag and Drop**

Use the drag-and-drop method to cut or copy data when you can see the original copy and where you want to paste the data at the same time. The *drag-and-drop pointer* is a four-pointed arrow that is visible when you point at the border or edge of a cell or range.

1. Select cell C16. Place the pointer at the top or bottom edge of the cell. The drag-and-drop pointer appears.

2. Hold down the mouse button and drag to cell C17. A ScreenTip identifies the cell. You can also see a ghost highlight that shows where the cell will be placed. (See Figure 4-8 on the next page.)

3. Release the mouse button. You have used the drag-and-drop method to perform a cut and paste.

4. Place the pointer at the top or bottom edge of cell C17 to display the drag-and-drop pointer.

5. Hold down Ctrl. You will see a tiny plus sign (+) next to the drag-and-drop pointer to signify this will be a copy and paste. Do not release Ctrl.

FIGURE 4-8
Using drag and
drop to cut
and paste

	A	B	C	D	E	F
1	Date	Account Name	Amount Due	Reference No.	Date Paid	
2	1/1/2004	Regan Supermarke	4501.26	20101	2/1/2004	
3	1/7/2004	Southwest Office	345	20107	3/1/2004	
4	2/5/2004	Stop and Shop	1000.55	20205	2/26/2004	
5	2/15/2004	Corner Store	541.32	20215	3/15/2004	
6	4/2/2004	SafeTop Stores	15245.78	20402	4/30/2004	
7	4/15/2004	Regan Supermarke	12567	20415	5/15/2004	
8	5/8/2004	Stop and Shop	3677.87	20508	6/8/2004	
9	5/24/2004	International Groce	5590	20524	6/24/2004	
10	6/18/2004	Tom's Foods	25125.24	20601	7/18/2004	
11	6/23/2004	Regan Supermarke	3677.87	20612	7/30/2004	
12	7/6/2004	South Island Foods	5590	20618	8/2/2004	
13	8/14/2004	PDQ Shop	25125.24			
14	8/24/2004	South Island Foods	15200.35			
15	9/7/2004	Fresh Foods	8750	20814	9/30/2004	
16	9/23/2004	Tom's Foods	11245.56	20824	10/23/2004	
17						
18						
19			C17			
20						
21						
22						

Ghost highlight

ScreenTip

6. Click and drag to cell C16. Release the mouse button first and then release Ctrl. You have used the drag-and-drop method to perform a copy and paste.

7. Select cells B6:B7. Place the pointer at the top or bottom edge of the range to display the drag-and-drop pointer.

8. Hold down the Ctrl key to display the plus sign (+). Do not release the Ctrl key.

9. Click and drag down to cells B17:B18. Release the mouse button and then Ctrl. Both labels are copied.

EXERCISE 4-10 Use the Office Clipboard

The *Office Clipboard* is a temporary memory area that can hold up to 24 copied items. It is separate from the Windows Clipboard. The Office Clipboard is available when any of the Office applications (Excel, Access, Word, or PowerPoint) is running. It is shared among all these programs, so something you copy in Excel can be pasted in Word.

1. Choose <u>V</u>iew, Tas<u>k</u> Pane. Click the down arrow to display the other task panes choices and choose Clipboard.

 NOTE: If your Clear All button 🗙 Clear All is grayed out or dimmed, you have nothing on the Clipboard and can continue.

2. Click the Clear All button 🗙 Clear All in the task pane.

3. Select the range A4:E4 and click the Copy button. An Excel icon and the data appear in the task pane.

4. Select the range A6:A7 and click the Copy button. Another icon and data appear in the pane, above the first icon.

5. Select the range A8:E8 and click the Copy button. Three items have been copied and are on the Office Clipboard.

6. Press (Esc). The marquee is removed.

7. Click cell A17. Click the second item in the task pane to paste two dates to the active cell.

FIGURE 4-9
Using the Clipboard
task pane

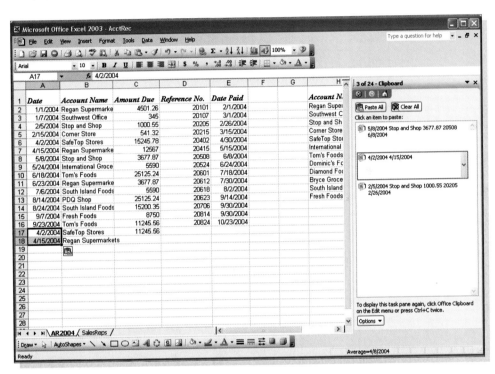

8. Click cell A19. Click the third item in the task pane to paste it.

9. Repeat these steps to paste the first item, beginning in cell A20.

10. Click the Clear All button in the task pane and then close it.

Working with Columns and Rows

Inserted or deleted rows and columns extend across the entire worksheet. If you have used different parts of the worksheet for various types of data, you could interrupt data on the sheet that is not immediately visible.

EXERCISE 4-11 Insert Rows

If you insert a column or row, check for formulas that might be affected by the insertion. Excel updates formulas to include an inserted row or column if it falls within the original range used in the formula.

1. From the Tools menu, choose Options. Click the Error Checking tab.

2. Click to place a check mark for Formulas referring to empty cells. Click OK.

3. Click cell C18 and key **345.7** to fill in the cell.

4. Click cell C21, click the AutoSum button Σ ▾, and press Enter.

5. Click cell C21 again and look at the formula. The SUM function sums the range C2:C20.

6. Click cell J20 and click the AutoSum button Σ ▾. Press Enter.

7. Click cell J20. Position the mouse pointer on the Trace Error button ◈. Click its arrow. The formula refers to empty cells.

8. Press Esc after you view the cause of the error.

9. Click cell A12. Press Ctrl + + in the numeric keypad. The Insert dialog box opens.

10. Choose Entire row and click OK. A new row is inserted, and the existing rows shift down. Notice that the new row spans the worksheet and interrupts the names and counts in columns H and J.

FIGURE 4-10
Row inserted

	A	B	C	D	E	F	G	H	I	J
1	*Date*	*Account Name*	*Amount Due*	*Reference No.*	*Date Paid*			*Account Name*	*Sales Representative*	*YTD Sales*
2	1/1/2004	Regan Supermarke	4501.26	20101	2/1/2004			Regan Supermarkets	José Garcia	11321
3	1/7/2004	Southwest Office	345	20107	3/1/2004			Southwest Office	Gary Johnson	9875
4	2/5/2004	Stop and Shop	1000.55	20205	2/26/2004			Stop and Shop	Kathleen D'Alvia	4533
5	2/15/2004	Corner Store	541.32	20215	3/15/2004			Corner Store	Lisa Watson	7566
6	4/2/2004	SafeTop Stores	15245.78	20402	4/30/2004			SafeTop Stores	José Garcia	14500
7	4/15/2004	Regan Supermarke	12567	20415	5/15/2004			International Groceries	Lisa Watson	12375
8	5/8/2004	Stop and Shop	3677.87	20508	6/8/2004			Tom's Foods	José Garcia	8655
9	5/24/2004	International Groce	5590	20524	6/24/2004			Dominic's Foods	Gary Johnson	7544
10	6/18/2004	Tom's Foods	25125.24	20601	7/18/2004			Diamond Food Stores	Kathleen D'Alvia	11900
11	6/23/2004	Regan Supermarke	3677.87					Bryce Groceries	Lisa Watson	10555
12				Interrupted data						
13	7/6/2004	uth Island Foods	5590					South Island Foods	José Garcia	5600
14	8/14/2004	PDQ Shop	25125.24					Fresh Foods	Lisa Watson	9877
15	8/24/2004	South Island Foods	15200.35	20706	9/30/2004				José Garcia	13000
16	9/7/2004	Fresh Foods	8750	20814	9/30/2004				Gary Johnson	
17	9/23/2004	Tom's Foods	11245.56	20824	10/23/2004				Kathleen D'Alvia	
18	4/2/2004	SafeTop Stores	11245.56						Lisa Watson	
19	4/15/2004	Regan Supermarke	345.7						José Garcia	
20	2/5/2004	Stop and Shop	1000.55	20205	2/26/2004				Lisa Watson	
21	5/8/2004	Stop and Shop	3677.87	20508	6/8/2004					127301
22			154452.72							
23										

11. Click cell C22. The formula has been updated to include rows 2 through 21 and now refers to empty cells.

12. Click the row heading for row 15.

13. With the black right-arrow pointer, drag to select the row headings for rows 15 through 17. Three rows are selected or highlighted.

14. Right-click any of the selected row headings. The shortcut menu opens.

15. Choose Insert. Three rows are inserted, because you selected three rows before giving the Insert command.

FIGURE 4-11
Inserting three
rows at once

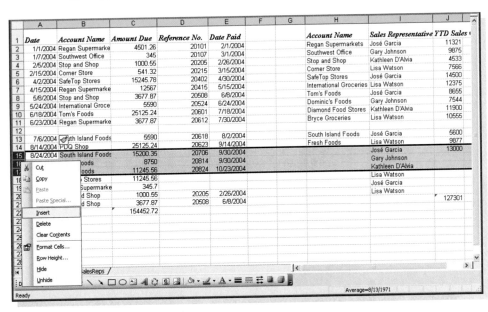

EXERCISE **4-12** **Delete Rows**

1. Click cell A12 and press Ctrl + –. The Delete dialog box opens.

   NOTE: You can use the – in the numeric keypad or in the top row of keys to delete cells.

2. Choose Entire row and click OK. The row is deleted.

3. Select the range A6:E7.

4. Drag the range to the location A14:E15 and drop it.

5. Click the row heading for row 6. Drag to select the row headings for rows 6 and 7.

6. Right-click one of the selected row headings. Choose Delete. Two rows are deleted. Some account names are missing from column H.

7. Click anywhere in row 14. Choose Delete from the Edit menu.

8. Choose Entire row and click OK.

9. Click cell C21. Through all the adjusting, the formula has been updated to sum the correct rows.

EXERCISE 4-13 Insert and Delete Columns

When you insert a column, it extends as far down as row 65,536.

1. Right-click the column D heading. The column is selected and the shortcut menu opens.

2. Choose <u>I</u>nsert. One column is inserted, and the existing columns move right.

 NOTE: When you choose <u>I</u>nsert or <u>D</u>elete from the shortcut menu, the dialog box does not open.

3. Key **Discount** in cell D1 and press (Enter). Excel uses the same format in this column as in the three columns with formatted labels that precede it.

4. Click anywhere in column G. Press (Ctrl)+(-).

5. Choose Entire <u>c</u>olumn and click OK. Column G is deleted, and the other columns move left to fill the space.

EXERCISE 4-14 Hide and Unhide Columns and Rows

Since you have not filled in discount amounts, you can temporarily hide the column. In that way, your worksheet does not print with an empty column, and the column does not take up space. You can hide columns or rows that include data you need for your file but don't really need to see or print. Even though a row or column is hidden, its values are used in calculations.

You can see when columns or rows are hidden, because their column or row headings are also hidden.

1. Right-click the column heading for column D to select the column.

2. Choose <u>H</u>ide from the shortcut menu. Column D is hidden.

3. Drag across the row headings for rows 12 through 14.

4. Open the F<u>o</u>rmat menu and choose <u>R</u>ow and <u>H</u>ide.

5. Click cell C21. Notice that the formula still sums all the rows, even though three are hidden from view.

6. Drag across the column headings for columns C through E. Column D is hidden between these two columns.

7. Point at the column heading for either column and right-click. Choose <u>U</u>nhide from the shortcut menu.

 NOTE: To unhide a column or row, select the rows or columns on both sides of the hidden rows or columns.

8. Drag across the headings for rows 11 through 15. Rows 12 through 14 are hidden between these rows.

9. From the Format menu, choose Row and Unhide. Rows 12 through 14 are now visible.

10. Press [Ctrl]+[Home] to make cell A1 active.

EXERCISE **4-15** *Freeze and Unfreeze Rows and Columns*

In large worksheets, seeing two related columns or rows on-screen at the same time can be difficult if they are not next to each other. You can keep data in view by freezing one of the columns or rows.

1. Click in the Zoom box and key **130**.

2. Press [Enter]. This enlarges the display. Now you probably cannot see all the rows. (Use a higher Zoom setting if you still see all the rows.)

3. Click cell A2.

4. From the Window menu, choose Freeze Panes. A solid horizontal line identifies where the row(s) are locked in position, between rows 1 and 2.

5. Press the [↓] to reach Row 30. The labels in row 1 do not scroll out of view.

6. Press [Ctrl]+[Home]. The pointer returns to the first unfrozen cell (cell A2).

7. From the Window menu, choose Unfreeze Panes.

8. Click cell C1. From the Window menu, choose Freeze Panes. The solid line is vertical to show that columns A and B are frozen.

9. Press [→] to reach column K. Columns A and B do not scroll.

10. Press [Ctrl]+[Home]. The pointer returns to the first unfrozen cell.

TIP: To freeze a column, click the column letter or the cell in row 1 to the immediate right of the last column to be frozen. To freeze a row, click the row number or the cell in column A immediately below the last row to be frozen.

11. From the Window, choose Unfreeze Panes.

12. Click the arrow next to the Zoom button. Choose 100%.

13. Press [Ctrl]+[Home]. Save the workbook as *[your initials]*4-15 in a new folder for Lesson 4.

Working with Cell Alignment

Cell alignment establishes how the contents of a cell are positioned in the cell. Cell contents can be aligned both horizontally and vertically.

TABLE 4-1   Horizontal Alignment Options

SETTING	RESULT
General	Aligns numbers and dates on the right, text on the left, and center aligns error and logical values.
Left (Indent)	Aligns cell contents on the left of the cell indented by the number of spaces entered in the Indent box.
Center	Aligns contents in the middle of the cell.
Right (Indent)	Aligns cell contents on the right side of the cell indented by the number of spaces entered in the Indent box.
Fill	Repeats the cell contents until the cell's width is filled.
Justify	Spreads the text to the left and right edges of the cell. This works only for wrapped text that is more than one line.
Center across selection	Places the text in the middle of a selected range of columns.

If a label is too wide for a cell, it spills into the cell to the right if that cell is empty. If the adjacent cell is not empty, the label is partially visible.

TABLE 4-2   Vertical Alignment Options

SETTING	RESULT
Top	Aligns cell contents at the top of the cell.
Center	Aligns cell contents in the vertical middle of the cell.
Bottom	Aligns cell contents at the bottom of the cell.
Justify	Spreads text to fill to the top and bottom edges of the cell. This works only for wrapped text that is more than one line.
Distributed	Positions text at an equal distance from the top and bottom edges.

EXERCISE   4-16   **Change the Horizontal Alignment**

The Formatting toolbar contains three Alignment buttons: the Align Left button, the Center button, and the Align Right button.

1. Click cell A1. This label is left-aligned, but the dates in the column are right-aligned for a slightly off-balance look.

2. Click the Align Right button ▤. The label is now aligned at the right edge of the cell and balances the dates better.

3. Double-click the border between the column headings for columns B and C. The column title and the entries are left-aligned labels.

4. Click cell B1 and click the Center button ☰. Column titles are often centered over labels.

5. Click cell C1. Click the Align Right button ☰. Now the label better aligns with the values in the column.

E X E R C I S E **4-17** **Use Center Across Selection**

The Center Across Selection command allows you to horizontally center multiple rows of cells across a part of the worksheet.

1. Point at the row 1 heading and drag to select rows 1 and 2.

2. Right-click either the row 1 or row 2 heading and choose Insert. Two rows are inserted.

3. In cell A1, key **Klassy Kow Accounts Receivable** and press Enter.

4. Format cell A1 as 16-point Times New Roman.

5. In cell A2, key **Commercial Accounts** and press Enter.

6. Format cell A2 as 14-point Times New Roman.

7. Select the range A2:F2. You want to center both titles over this part of the worksheet.

8. Right-click a cell in the range and choose Format Cells. The Format Cells dialog box opens.

9. Click the Alignment tab.

10. Click the arrow for the Horizontal box to display the options.

FIGURE 4-12
Alignment tab in
the Format Cells
dialog box

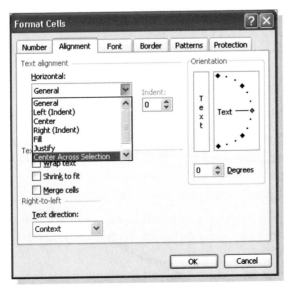

11. Choose Center Across Selection. Click OK. The labels are centered over the columns you selected.

EXERCISE 4-18 Change the Vertical Alignment

1. Change row 1 to 37.50 (50 pixels) high. You can see that the label is at the bottom of the cells.

2. Click cell A1. Press Ctrl+1 to open the Format Cells dialog box.

3. On the Alignment tab, click the arrow for the Vertical box.

4. Choose Center and then click OK. The label is centered in the row.

EXERCISE 4-19 Wrap Text and Change Indents

If a label has more than one word and is rather long, you can turn on the Wrap Text setting. This allows the label to split into more than one line in the cell so that the column doesn't have to be so wide. (It will, of course, take up more vertical space.)

Another way to improve the appearance of your worksheets is by adding an indent to labels. This moves them away from the left edge of the cell.

1. Change column E to 10.71 (80 pixels) wide. Notice that this is wide enough for the data, but not wide enough for the label.

2. Click cell E3 and press Ctrl+1.

3. On the Alignment tab, click to place a check mark for Wrap text in the Text control section.

4. Click OK. The label splits into two lines, but now the row isn't high enough.

5. Change row 3 to 30.00 (40 pixels) high.

6. Click the Center button ≡. The wrapped label looks better centered.

7. Click cell B3.

8. Press F8 to start Extend Selection mode.

9. Press Ctrl+↓. This selects cells with data in the column.

10. Press Ctrl+1.

11. On the Alignment tab, click the arrow for the Horizontal box.

12. Choose Left (Indent).

13. Click the up arrow for Indent to change it to 1.

14. Click OK. The labels are now indented one space from the left edge of the cell, leaving some space between them and the right-aligned dates in column A.

15. Double-click the border between the column headings for columns B and C.

Using Merge and Center

You can merge cells to combine a range of cells into one cell that occupies the same amount of space. You can merge any number of columns and rows to create special effects and alignment settings. The range of cells to merge should be empty except for the top-left cell.

EXERCISE 4-20 **Use Merge and Center**

1. Select the range H1:J22 and click the Cut button .
2. Click the SalesReps worksheet tab and then press (Enter). This data is now on its own sheet.
3. Double-click the border between each set of columns to AutoFit each one.
4. Select the range B16:C22 and press (Delete).
5. Click cell A1 and key **Supermarket Sales Associates**. Press (Enter).
6. Click cell A1 and drag to select the range A1:C1.

7. Click the Merge and Center button ▦. The three cells are now one, and the label is centered.

   NOTE: You can unmerge cells by clicking the Merge and Center button ▦ to turn off the command.

8. Right-click the row 2 heading and choose Delete.
9. Click cell C2 and point at an edge to show the drag-and-drop pointer.
10. Click and drag the cell to cell D3.
11. Click cell D3 and drag to select cells D3:D12.
12. Click the Merge and Center button ▦. The cells are one cell that occupies the same amount of space, and the label is horizontally centered at the bottom.

EXERCISE 4-21 **Change Cell Orientation**

The label in the merged cell D3 is displayed horizontally like the rest of your data. Because the cells were merged vertically, you should change the text's rotation to match.

1. Right-click cell D3 and choose Format Cells.
2. On the Alignment tab, click the red diamond in the Orientation box.

3. Drag the red diamond down to show –90 degrees (that's "minus 90 degrees"). Click OK. The text is rotated –90 degrees. Now you should change the vertical centering as well.

FIGURE 4-13
Rotating text
–90 degrees

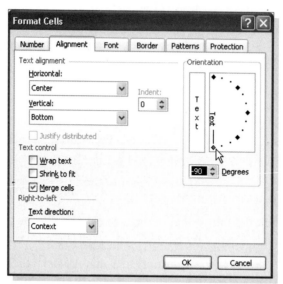

TIP: You can key the degree of rotation in the text box below the graphic.

4. Press Ctrl+1. You are going to adjust the vertical centering now.
5. On the Alignment tab, click the arrow next to the Vertical box.
6. Choose Center and click OK.
7. Change column C to 11.43 (85 pixels) wide.
8. Make cell A1 14-point Times New Roman.

Applying Borders and Shading

A *border* is a line around a cell or a range of cells. You can use borders to draw attention to a part of a worksheet, to show totals, or simply to group information in your worksheet.

Shading is the background pattern or color for a cell or a range of cells. You can use shading in much the same way as a border—to group information on the worksheet or to add emphasis.

EXERCISE **4-22** **Apply Cell Borders Using the Borders Button**

Cells share borders, so adding a border to the bottom of cell A1 has the same effect as adding a border to the top of cell A2.

Excel provides two methods to apply a border to a cell or a range of cells:

- Use the Borders button .
- Use the Format Cells dialog box.

1. Click cell C12.
2. Click the Borders button . Notice that the current border style (a single-line bottom border) is shown on the button. This is the border style that Excel applies to cell C12.
3. Click cell C14 to see the border better. Notice that the border fills the width of the cell.
4. Select cell C13 and click the AutoSum button Σ ▾. Press Enter.
5. Click cell C13 and then click the arrow next to the Borders button ▦ ▾. Excel shows 12 border styles, each with a descriptive ScreenTip.

FIGURE 4-14
Borders palette

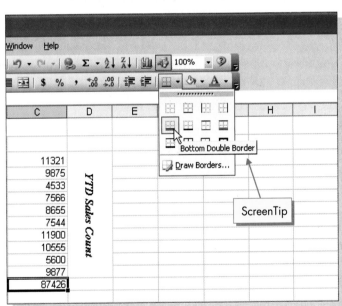

6. Click Bottom Double Border.

 TIP: Totals in accounting and other financial reports are often shown with a single border above and a double border below.

7. Click cell B13 to see the border. Notice that the Borders button ▦ ▾ shows the last-used style.

EXERCISE **4-23** **Apply Borders Using the Dialog Box**

The Format Cells dialog box provides a bit more flexibility in defining borders.

1. Click the AR2004 worksheet tab and then press F5. Key **c23** and press Enter.
2. Press Ctrl + 1.
3. Click the Border tab. There are presets for None, an Outline, or Inside.

 TIP: Inside borders can be applied to multiple cells, not to a single cell.

4. Click Outline. The Border buttons around the preview show which borders are available for an outline border.
5. Click None to remove the border.
6. Click the down arrow for the Color box. Choose "Red" in the first column, third row.

 NOTE: You must choose the Color and Style of a line before choosing the style of border in the Format Cells dialog box.

7. In the Style box, choose a single line (first column, last line).
8. In the Text preview area, click where the top border will be located. A preview of the red single-line border is shown.

FIGURE 4-15
Border tab in the
Format Cells
dialog box

Preset buttons

Click here to place
a top border.

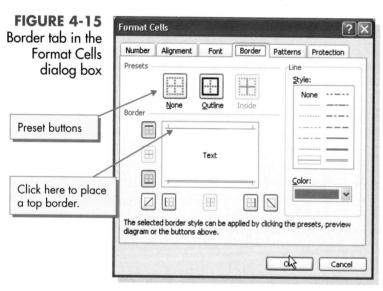

9. In the Style box, choose a double line (second column, last line).

 NOTE: Click in the Text preview to turn the borders on and off.

10. In the Text preview area, click where the bottom border will be located.

11. Click OK.

12. Deselect the cell in the worksheet so that you can see the borders you have created.

E X E R C I S E **4-24** **Draw Cell Borders**

You can draw your own borders around a cell or range of cells. Excel follows the cell edges so that your lines are straight. If you are accustomed to drawing in other programs, this can be quick and easy.

1. Click the down arrow next to the Borders button ⊞▾.

2. Choose Draw Borders. The Borders toolbar opens. The pointer is a pencil shape.

FIGURE 4-16
Borders toolbar

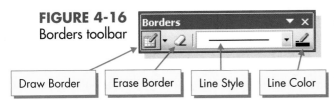

3. Click the top-left corner of cell A1 with the Pencil pointer. Drag to the bottom-right corner of cell F2.

4. Release the mouse button. The border is completed.

 5. Click the Erase Border button 🖉. The pointer changes to an eraser shape.

6. Click cell A1, drag to cell F2, and then release the mouse button. The border is removed.

 7. Click the Draw Border button 🖉▾.

8. Click the arrow next to the Line Style button ▤. A palette of line styles opens.

 9. Choose one of the dashed or dotted styles.

10. Click the Line Color button 🖋.

11. Choose a color from the palette.

12. Draw a border around the range A1:F2.

TIP: You can open the Borders toolbar by choosing View, Toolbars. You can also right-click any toolbar and turn it on from the shortcut menu.

 13. Click the Close button ✕ on the Borders toolbar.

 14. Click the Print Preview button 🔍. If you do not see the entire border, zoom in.

REVIEW: Borders will appear in a shade of gray if your default printer is a black-and-white printer.

15. Close print preview.

EXERCISE 4-25 **Apply Shading**

The background of a cell or a range of cells can be filled or shaded with a solid color or a pattern.

Excel provides two methods for applying shading to a cell or a range of cells:

- Use the Fill Color button .
- Use the Format Cells dialog box.

1. Click the SalesReps worksheet tab.
2. Select the range A3:C3. Click the Fill Color button . Excel applies the color shown beneath the paint bucket icon.
3. Click in row 5 to see the shading.
4. Click the Undo button. The shading is removed, and the range is still selected.
5. Click the arrow next to the Fill Color button. The color palette opens.
6. Choose Gray-25% in the last column, second row from the bottom.
7. Select the range A5:C5. Press Ctrl+1 and click the Patterns tab.
8. For the Cell shading Color, choose Gray-25% in the last column, in the second row from the bottom. Click OK. The pattern is solid.

9. Double-click the Format Painter button. This locks the painter on.
10. Select the range A7:C7. Then select the range A9:C9, followed by A11:C11. Each range you select receives the shading.
11. Click the Format Painter button to turn it off.

EXERCISE 4-26 **Use a Pattern**

A pattern might be dots or crisscrossed lines. Patterns are acceptable for cells that do not contain data or for cells with minimal data. They can make it difficult to read text or values in the cell.

1. Click cell D3 and press Ctrl+1.
2. Click the Patterns tab. For the Cell shading Color, choose Gray-25% in the second row from the bottom.
3. Click the arrow for the Pattern box. The patterns include dots, stripes, and crosshatches.
4. Choose 12.5% Gray in the first row of pattern tiles, the second from the right. This is a dotted pattern. (See Figure 4-17 on the next page.)
5. Click OK.

TIP: Many patterns make it difficult to read data in the cell.

FIGURE 4-17
Changing the
pattern

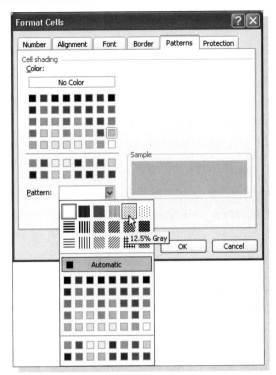

EXERCISE 4-27 Complete the Number Formatting

The Comma Style button inserts commas and two decimal places in a value. If you want one or no decimal places, you can use the Decrease Decimal button to remove positions one at a time.

You can build your own formats by using the Format Cells dialog box. For example, you can create a format that shows a *leading zero*, which is a zero (0) as the first digit in a number, typically a decimal number (example "0.59"). Normally, Excel does not show a leading zero because it has no value.

1. Select the range C3:C13. Click the Comma Style button . Commas and two decimal places are added to the values.
2. Click the Decrease Decimal button . One decimal position is removed.
3. Click the Decrease Decimal button again. The values still have the commas, but no decimals.
4. Click the AR2004 worksheet tab.
5. Click cell C4. Hold down Ctrl and click cell C23.
6. Press Ctrl+1. Click the Number tab.
7. Choose Accounting in the Category list. A sample is displayed in the dialog box.

8. Click OK. This format aligns the currency symbol at the left edge of the cell.

9. Select the range C5:C22. Click the Comma Style button.

10. Select the range E4:E22.

11. Press Ctrl+1 and click the Number tab.

12. Choose Custom in the Category list. Click 0 in the Type list. The zero appears in the entry box under Type.

13. Click after the 0 in the box and key **00000** to show six zeros. Zero **(0)** means that a digit is required. This format requires that the entry be six digits. If the value uses only five digits, Excel inserts a zero in the first position.

FIGURE 4-18
Custom format for
the Reference
numbers

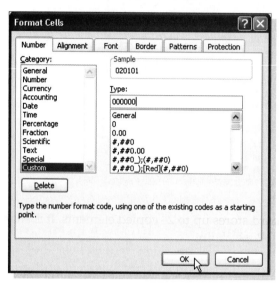

14. Click OK.

15. Key your first and last name in cell A24. Print the worksheet.

16. Key your first and last name in cell A14 on the SalesReps worksheet. Print the worksheet.

17. Press Ctrl+Home to make cell A1 active.

18. Save the workbook as *[your initials]*4-27 in your Lesson 4 folder and then close it.

USING ONLINE HELP

In addition to freezing parts of the worksheet on the screen, you can split the worksheet into more than one window or pane.

Explore how to split panes:

1. Start Excel and close the Getting Started task pane.

2. Click in the Type a question for help box and key **split panes**. Press Enter.
3. Click the topic View two parts of a sheet by splitting or freezing panes in the Search Results task pane.
4. Click Show All in the top-right corner of the Help window. Read the information.
5. Close the Help window. Close the Search Results dialog box.

LESSON 4 Summary

➤ You can insert, delete, move, and rename worksheets in a workbook.

➤ Insert or delete cells when you need more space for missing data or have blank rows or columns in a worksheet.

➤ The AutoComplete feature makes suggestions when you key a label that begins with the same characters as labels already in the column.

➤ The Pick From List feature displays a list of all labels already in the current column.

➤ When you cut or copy data, it is placed on the Windows Clipboard and the Office Clipboard. Copied data can be pasted more than once.

➤ The Office Clipboard stores up to 24 copied elements. It is shared among Word, Excel, Access, and PowerPoint.

➤ When you delete or insert a row or column, it is inserted across the entire worksheet. Be careful about data that is on the sheet but out of view.

➤ Change the cell alignment to make data easier to read and more professional looking. There are several horizontal and vertical alignment choices.

➤ Text can be wrapped, indented, or rotated.

➤ The Merge and Center command combines a range of cells into one cell.

➤ Borders outline a cell or range of cells with a variety of line styles and colors.

➤ Shading is the background pattern or color for a cell or range of cells.

LESSON 4   Command Summary

FEATURE	BUTTON	MENU	KEYBOARD
Align Left		Format, Cells	Ctrl + 1
Align Right		Format, Cells	Ctrl + 1

continues

LESSON 4   Command Summary   *continued*

FEATURE	BUTTON	MENU	KEYBOARD
Border		Format, Cells	Ctrl+1
Center		Format, Cells	Ctrl+1
Center across selection		Format, Cells	Ctrl+1
Comma Style		Format, Cells	Ctrl+1
Copy		Edit, Copy	Ctrl+C
Cut		Edit, Cut	Ctrl+X
Decrease Decimal		Format, Cells	Ctrl+1
Delete cell, row, column		Edit, Delete	Ctrl+-
Freeze rows/columns		Window, Freeze Panes	
Hide/unhide column		Format, Column, Hide/Unhide	
Hide/unhide row		Format, Row, Hide/Unhide	
Indent text		Format, Cells	Ctrl+1
Insert cell, row, column		Insert, Cells	Ctrl++
Merge and Center		Format, Cells	
Text orientation		Format, Cells	Ctrl+1
Paste		Edit, Paste	Ctrl+V
Shading		Format, Cells	Ctrl+1
Unfreeze rows/columns		Window, Unfreeze Panes	
Wrap text		Format, Cells	Ctrl+1

Concepts Review

TRUE/FALSE QUESTIONS

Each of the following statements is either true or false. Indicate your choice by circling T or F.

T   F   **1.** Inserted cells do not affect the position of existing cells.

T   F   **2.** A column is hidden when it is frozen.

T   F   **3.** Freezing rows and columns locks them in position on the screen.

T   F   **4.** AutoComplete fills in formulas and cell addresses.

T   F   **5.** You can set both horizontal and vertical cell alignment.

T   F   **6.** Shading creates a shadow effect around cell borders.

T   F   **7.** The Merge and Center command works for one row or one column at a time.

T   F   **8.** The Windows Clipboard and the Office Clipboard both store 12 items of cut or copied data.

SHORT ANSWER QUESTIONS

Write the correct answer in the space provided.

1. What two commands help you enter labels in columns that already have many labels?

_____

2. If you want to repeat a lengthy label several times throughout a worksheet, would you cut it or copy it?

_____

3. What does the term "drag and drop" mean?

_____

4. What is the default alignment for values and dates in a cell?

_____

5. What command will lock rows or columns in position on the screen?

_____

6. What command combines several cells into one cell occupying the same screen space?

_____

7. How can you format a number to show leading zeros?

_____

8. What alignment option allows a label to split within a cell?

_____

CRITICAL THINKING

Answer these questions on a separate page. There are no right or wrong answers. Support your answers with examples from your own experience, if possible.

1. When you delete a row or a column, it is deleted across the entire worksheet. What problems could result from this?
2. AutoComplete and Pick From List are handy and easy to use. What are the advantages of each? What are the disadvantages of each?

Skills Review

EXERCISE 4-28

Insert and delete worksheets. Insert and delete cells. Add data with AutoComplete and Pick From List.

1. Open **Personnel**. Save it as *[your initials]*4-28 in your Lesson 4 folder.

 NOTE: Column C has e-mail addresses. If you click an e-mail address, Excel launches your e-mail service and adds the address to the recipient list.

2. Rename Sheet1 as **Employees**. Choose a tab color.
3. Insert and delete worksheets by following these steps:
   a. Right-click Sheet2 and choose Delete.
   b. Repeat these steps to delete Sheet3.
   c. Press Shift + F11.
   d. Name the new sheet **Interviews**.
   e. Point at the Employees worksheet tab.
   f. Drag it to the left of the Interviews tab.
4. Insert and delete cells by following these steps:
   a. Right-click cell E13 and choose Insert.

   b. Choose Shift cells <u>d</u>own and click OK.

   c. Key **5/29/78** in cell E13.

   d. Select cells F13:F14. Press Ctrl+-.

   e. Choose Shift cells <u>u</u>p and click OK.

 5. Add data with AutoComplete by following these steps:

   a. Click cell A16 and key **Biesterfield**. Press Tab.

   b. Key **ka** and press →.

 6. Key **kbiesterfield@kkic.net** and press →.

 7. Key today's date in cell D16.

 8. Add data with Pic<u>k</u> From List by following these steps:

   a. Right-click cell F16 and choose Pic<u>k</u> From List.

   b. Choose Human Resources.

   c. Right-click cell G16 and choose Pic<u>k</u> From List.

   d. Choose Klamath Falls.

   e. Right-click cell F14 and choose Pic<u>k</u> From List.

   f. Choose Finance.

   g. Right-click cell F15, Pic<u>k</u> From List, and then choose Marketing.

 9. Widen column C to display all the cell contents. Change columns A and B to 10.71 (80 pixels) wide.

 10. Press Ctrl+Home to make cell A1 active.

 11. Click the Print Preview button and click <u>S</u>etup. Create a custom footer with your first and last name in the <u>L</u>eft section, the filename in the <u>C</u>enter section, and the date in the <u>R</u>ight section. Close the Page Setup dialog box.

 12. Click <u>M</u>argins in Print Preview. Drag the left margin marker to .40 inches or slightly less. Do the same for the right margin marker. AutoFit columns, if needed, to fit the worksheet on one page.

 13. Print the worksheet, and then save and close the workbook.

EXERCISE 4-29

Copy and paste cell contents. Insert and delete columns and rows.

 1. Open **Personnel**. Save the workbook as *[your initials]*4-29 in your Lesson 4 folder.

 2. Click cell A16 and key **McTavish**. Ignore the AutoComplete suggestion. Press Tab.

   REVIEW: You can press Tab or → to enter data in a row.

 3. Key **Diane** and press Tab. Key **dmctavish@kkic.net** and press Tab.

4. Copy and paste cell contents by following these steps:

   a. Click cell D8 and click the Copy button .
   b. Click cell D16 and press Enter.
   c. Click cell E15 and display the drag-and-drop pointer.
   d. Hold down Ctrl and drag a copy to cell E16.
   e. Click cell F7 and press Ctrl+C.

    TIP: You can close the Clipboard task pane for more screen space.

   f. Click cell F16 and press Ctrl+V. Press Esc.
   g. Copy any city from a cell in column G to cell G16.

    NOTE: If you paste copied cells where there is existing data, the copy replaces the existing data.

5. Insert columns by following these steps:

   a. Right-click anywhere in column A. Choose Insert.
   b. Choose Entire column and click OK.

6. Key **Emp #** in cell A2. Copy the format from cell B2 to cell A2.

    REVIEW: Use the Format Painter to copy the font, size, and style.

7. In cell A3, key **1** and press Enter. In cell A4, key **2** and press Enter. Select cells A3:A4 and use the Fill handle to fill in values down to cell A16.

8. Drag the label in cell B1 and drop it in cell A1.

9. Delete columns and insert rows by following these steps:

   a. Right-click the column D heading and choose Delete.
   b. Right-click the row 2 heading and choose Insert.

10. In cell A2, key **January 200X** using the current year. Press Enter. Press Ctrl+Home.

     NOTE: The date is formatted in a default style for your computer.

11. Create a custom footer with your first and last name in the Left section, the filename in the Center section, and the date in the Right section. Close the Page Setup dialog box.

12. Click the Margins. Set the left margin to .50 inches. Do the same for the right margin.

13. Print the worksheet. Save and close the workbook.

E X E R C I S E   4 - 3 0

Use cell alignment options. Rotate cell contents. Use Merge and Center.

1. Open **EmpNo**. Save it as *[your initials]*4-30 in your Lesson 4 folder.

2. Use cell alignment options by following these steps:

   a. Click cell D2. Hold down Ctrl and click cell G2.

    REVIEW: Use the Ctrl key to select nonadjacent cells.

   b. Click the Center button ▤. Both cells are center-aligned.

   c. Click cell A2 and press Ctrl+1.

   d. Click the Alignment tab. In the Text control section, click to place a check mark in the Wrap text box. Click OK.

   e. Click the Center button ▤.

3. Change column A to 10.71 (80 pixels) wide. Change row 2 to 30.00 (40.00 pixels) high.

4. Rotate text by following these steps:

   a. Select the range A2:G2 and press Ctrl+1.

   b. Click the Alignment tab.

   c. Click the red diamond in the Orientation box. Drag the diamond up to reach 45 degrees. Click OK.

5. Change row 2 to 60.00 (80 pixels) high.

6. Drag across the column headings for columns E and F. Right-click either heading and delete the columns.

7. Use Merge and Center by following these steps:

   a. Select the range A1:E1.

   b. Click the Merge and Center button ▦.

8. Delete Sheet2 and Sheet3. Rename Sheet1 as **Personnel** and choose a tab color.

9. Create a custom footer with your first and last name in the Left section, the tab name in the Center section, and the date in the Right section.

10. Print the worksheet. Save and close the workbook.

E X E R C I S E   4 - 3 1

Apply borders and shading.

1. Create a new workbook and save it as *[your initials]*4-31 in your Lesson 4 folder.

2. Key **Klassy Kow Ice Cream Shops** in cell A1 and make it 16-point Arial. Key **Intern Interviews** in cell A2 and format it as 12-point Arial bold.

3. Key the labels, dates, and times shown in Figure 4-19 to complete the worksheet. Use the default date and time formats for your computer.

FIGURE 4-19

	A	B	C
3	Name	Date	Time
4	Jonathan Aria	May 24	9 am
5	Christophe Kryztish	June 5	11 am
6	Melinda Dapoulas	June 5	2 pm
7	Pamela Dryzski	June 8	10 am
8	Yoshima Sato	June 9	10 am

4. Make the labels in row 3 bold and make the row 22.50 (30 pixels) high.

5. Change column A to 17.14 (125 pixels) wide. Change both columns B and C to 11.43 (85 pixels) wide.

6. Center cells across a selection by following these steps:

   a. Select the range A1:C2.
   b. Press Ctrl+1 and click the Alignment tab.
   c. Click the Horizontal box arrow and choose Center Across Selection. Click OK.

7. Apply borders and shading by following these steps:

   a. Select the range A1:C3.
   b. Click the down arrow next to the Borders button ⊞▾.
   c. Choose Top and Bottom Border in the second row.
   d. Select the range A4:C4.
   e. Click the down arrow next to the Fill Color button ⬥▾.
   f. Choose Gray-25% in the second row from the bottom.
   g. Double-click the Format Painter button ⌗.
   h. Paint the shading across the range A6:C6 and A8:C8. Press Esc to unlock the Format Painter.

8. Delete Sheet2 and Sheet3. Rename Sheet1 as **Interviews** and choose a tab color.

9. Press Ctrl+Home to make cell A1 active.

10. Create a custom footer with your first and last name in the Left section, the tab name in the Center section, and the date in the Right section.

11. Print the worksheet. Save and close the workbook.

Lesson Applications

EXERCISE 4-32

Cut and paste rows. Copy and paste labels.

1. Open **KowOwow** and save it as *[your initials]***4-32** in your Lesson 4 folder.
2. On the Oregon sheet, cut the "Ashland" row. Right-click the "Eugene" row and choose Insert Cut Cells.
3. Cut the "Medford" row and insert it at the "Roseburg" row.
4. Select the range A5:A10. Display the drag-and-drop pointer and hold down the Ctrl key. Drag a copy to the range A13:A18.
5. Key the following values for 2005:

FIGURE 4-20

	Chocolate	Vanilla
2005		
Ashland	22000	21000
Eugene	27000	28000
Klamath Falls	20000	18000
Medford	18000	16000
Roseburg	17000	15000

6. Select the range D5:D9 and click the AutoSum button . Do the same for the range B10:D10.

7. Select the range B5:D10. Click the Comma Style button ⌐. Click the Decrease Decimal button ⌐ two times.
8. On the California sheet, copy the range A5:A19 to A22:A36.
9. Use AutoSum to determine the totals for 2005.
10. Format the range B5:D19 to show commas, no decimals, and no currency symbols.

REVIEW: You must open the Print dialog box to print/preview the entire workbook. Press Page Up or Page Down to move between pages.

11. Preview the California sheet. Add a custom footer with your first and last name at the left, the tab name in the center, and the filename at the right.

12. Preview the Oregon sheet and add the same footer.

13. Print the entire workbook. Save and close it.

EXERCISE 4-33

Insert worksheets. Move worksheets. Copy labels.

1. Open **EstKowO** and save it as *[your initials]*4-33 in your Lesson 4 folder.

2. Insert two new worksheets and name them **Nevada** and **Washington**.

3. Arrange the worksheets so that they are in alphabetical order, going from left to right.

4. Select the range A1:D4 on the California sheet. Click the Copy button . Go to the Nevada sheet and paste the cells. Go to the Washington sheet and paste the cells again. Cancel the Paste command.

5. On the Nevada sheet, change column A to 21.57 (156 pixels) wide. Change columns B, C, and D each to 10.00 (75 pixels) wide. Make the same changes on the Washington sheet.

6. Preview the Nevada sheet. Add a custom footer with your first and last name at the left, the tab name in the center, and the filename at the right. Print the sheet.

7. Preview the Washington sheet and add the same footer. Print the sheet.

8. Save and close the workbook.

EXERCISE 4-34

Work with cell alignment options. Cut and paste cells. Apply borders.

1. Open **EstKowO** and save it as *[your initials]*4-34 in your Lesson 4 folder.

2. Select the range B5:D5. Hold down Ctrl and select the range B10:D10. While holding down the Ctrl key, add the ranges B13:D13 and B18:D18. Click the Currency Style button $.

3. Click the Decrease Decimal button two times.

> ✦ **TIP:** A column filled with # symbols means the column is not wide enough.

4. Cut row 4 and insert it at row 3. Select the range A3:D3 and open the Format Cells dialog box. Choose Center Across Selection from the Horizontal alignment choices. Center cells A12:D12 across the selection also. Do the same for cells A1:D2.

5. Select the range B4:D4 and click the Center button .

6. Select the ranges B10:D10 and B18:D18. Apply a Top and Double Bottom border.

7. Preview the worksheet. Change the left margin to 2.00 inches.

8. Add a custom footer with your first and last name at the left, the filename in the center, and the date at the right. Print the sheet.

9. Save and close the workbook.

EXERCISE 4-35   ✚   *Challenge Yourself*

Cut and paste rows. Change cell alignment.

1. Open **CakeSales** and save it as *[your initials]*4-35 in your Lesson 4 folder.

2. Cut and insert the rows to arrange the flavors in alphabetical order.

3. Apply the Accounting 1 AutoFormat. Change the alignment for cells A1:A2 to left and then center the cells across the range A1:E2.

4. Use AutoSum in cells B8:E8.

5. Add a custom footer with your first and last name at the left, the filename in the center, and the date at the right. Turn off the gridlines and row and column headings.

6. Print the worksheet. Save and close the workbook.

On Your Own

In these exercises you work on your own, as you would in a real-life work environment. Use the skills you've learned to accomplish the task—and be creative.

EXERCISE 4-36

Create a new workbook and save it as *[your initials]*4-36 in your Lesson 4 folder. Key the names of eight people in your class, relatives, or coworkers. List each person's city, state, and favorite food. Use AutoComplete or Pick From List to enter data. Include a main title and titles for the columns. You may need to insert rows if you did not leave room for titles. Apply shading to the worksheet to enhance its readability. Add the usual footer with your name, the filename, and the date. Print the worksheet, save the workbook, and close it.

EXERCISE 4-37

Create a new workbook and save it as *[your initials]*4-37 in your Lesson 4 folder. In cell A1, key **Restaurants and Fast Food Shops**. Enter three column titles to list the names of restaurants or fast food shops in your city, their phone numbers, and their cuisine ("Italian," "Seafood," and so on). Key the names of ten restaurants or fast food shops (use the phone book or Internet to find names). Use AutoComplete for the cuisine type when possible. Apply borders and shading or use Merge and Center to format your work. Add the usual footer. Print the worksheet. Save and close the workbook.

EXERCISE 4-38
Create a new workbook with a variety of labels and values to experiment with alignment options. For example, you might key **This is wrapped text** and then apply that setting to the cell to illustrate it. Experiment with settings you did not use in this lesson. Add the usual footer. Save the worksheet as *[your initials]*4-38 in your Lesson 4 folder. Print and close it.

Unit 1 Applications

UNIT APPLICATION 1-1

Open a workbook. Rename and delete sheets. Spell-check a worksheet. Use Find and Replace. Use Center Across Selection. Apply shading and borders.

Klassy Kow Ice Cream keeps a statement of assets that lists all valuable items, including cash, equipment, and supplies. You have been asked to make changes to the data, add a formula, and format the worksheet.

1. Open **Assets**. Rename Sheet1 as **Assets** and choose 25% gray as a tab color. Delete Sheet2 and Sheet3. Save the workbook as *[your initials]***u1-1** in a Unit 1 folder.

2. Widen column B to show its longest label.

3. Format the range C4:C13 as Comma style with no decimals.

4. Use the Find and Replace command to change the occurrences of "valuables" to "assets."

5. Spell-check the worksheet.

6. Use AutoSum in cell C8 to determine the value of the current assets.

7. In cell C12, create a formula to subtract depreciation from the property, plant, and equipment amount.

   ⏪ **REVIEW:** All formulas begin with =. Point and click to enter a cell address in a formula.

8. Key a formula in cell C13 to add cells C8 and C12.

9. Format cells C4, C8, C10, and C13 as Currency with no decimals.

   ⏪ **REVIEW:** Select cells that are not next to each other by holding down Ctrl.

10. Apply top and double bottom borders to cells C8 and C13.

11. Press Ctrl + Home.

12. Add a footer with your name at the left, the filename and the tab name in the center separated by a space, and the date at the right.

13. Print the worksheet. Save and close the workbook.

UNIT APPLICATION 1-2

Create and print a worksheet. Enter and format values and labels. Cut and paste cells.
Enter formulas. Insert rows.

An income statement shows revenues (money from sales), expenses, and net income (money from sales minus expenses). Klassy Kow Ice Cream prepares an income statement every month. You have been asked to prepare and format this month's statement.

1. Create a new workbook. Rename Sheet1 as **IncStatement**. Delete Sheet2 and Sheet3. Save the workbook as *[your initials]***u1-2** in your Unit 1 folder.
2. In the range A1:B11, key the data shown in Figure U1-1.

FIGURE U1-1

	A	B
1	Revenue	1500000
2	Cost of goods sold	975000
3	Sales expenses	57000
4	Administrative expense	50000
5	Depreciation	8000
6	Other expenses	2500
7	Total operating expenses	
8	Earnings before interest and taxes	
9	Interest expense	10000
10	Income taxes	150000
11	Net income	

3. Make column A wide enough for its longest label.
4. Move the contents of cell B1 to cell C1.

5. Click the AutoSum button in cell C7. Do not accept the highlighted range, but drag to select cells B2:B6.

6. In cell C8, key = and then click cell C1. Key – for subtraction and click cell C7. Press Enter. This formula subtracts expenses from revenue.

7. In cell C11, key = and then click cell C8. Key – and click cell B9. Key – again and click cell B10. Press Enter. This formula subtracts interest and income taxes from earnings.

8. Select and format all values as Comma with no decimals. Then select cells C1, C7:C8, and C11 and format them as Currency with no decimals.

> **NOTE:** The Insert Options button will appear when you insert rows, but you can ignore it.

9. Select rows 1 and 2 and insert two rows. Format cells A1 and A2 as 16-point Times New Roman. Key **Klassy Kow Ice Cream Shops** in cell A1. Using the current month, key *[This Month]* **Income Statement** in cell A2. Change row 3 to 30 points (40 pixels) high.

10. Apply a single-line bottom border to cells B8, B12, C9, and C12. Select cells A1:C2 and center them across the selection.

11. Press Ctrl + Home.

12. Add a footer with your name at the left, the filename and the tab name in the center separated by a space, and the date at the right. Change the left margin to about 1.75 inches.

13. Print the worksheet. Save and close the workbook.

UNIT APPLICATION 1-3

Create and print a workbook. Use AutoFill and AutoSum. Enter, copy, and edit data. Format cells.

Klassy Kow Ice Cream prepares a workbook each week for sales in each state. Each workbook includes a sheet for the sales and a sheet listing the shops' owners. You will start with the shops in Oregon.

1. Create a new workbook. Rename Sheet1 **WeeklySales**. Rename Sheet2 **Owners**. Delete Sheet3. Save the workbook as *[your initials]***u1-3** in your Unit 1 folder.

2. On the WeeklySales sheet, format cells A1:A2 as 16-point Times New Roman. Key **Klassy Kow Ice Cream Shops** in cell A1. Using the current month, key **Weekly Sales Data for [*This Month*]** in cell A2.

3. Select the range A3:F3 and make it 10-point Arial bold. Make row 3 about twice its current height. In cell A3, key **Oregon Shops**.

4. In cell B3, key **Week 1**. Use the Fill handle to add Weeks 2, 3, and 4 in the range B3:E3. Center the labels in cells B3:E3. Widen column A to show the label in row 3. Center cells A1:A2 across columns A:E.

5. Starting in cell A4, key the locations of the shops and the weekly sales data as shown in Figure U1-2.

FIGURE U1-2

	A	B	C	D	E
4	Ashland	10000	9500	9900	11000
5	Eugene	18000	21000	19000	22000
6	Klamath Falls	20000	22000	17000	18500
7	Medford	12500	14000	18500	16000
8	Roseburg	12000	10500	11000	12000

6. Format the values as Comma style, with no decimals.

7. In cell F3, key the label **Shop Total**. Select cells F4:F8 and click the AutoSum button . Make sure the values are Comma style, with no decimals.

8. In cell A9, key the label **Weekly Total**. Match its format to the label in cell A3. Use AutoSum to show a total in cells B9:F9. Make sure all data is visible, and make row 9 the same height as row 3.

9. Press Ctrl+Home. Click the Copy button 📋. Go to the Owners sheet and paste in cell A1. Change the alignment to left.

10. Edit the label to show **Klassy Kow Ice Cream Shop Owners**.

REVIEW: Start Edit mode by pressing F2.

11. Select cells A3:A8 on the WeeklySales sheet. Copy these cells to the Owners sheet, beginning in cell A2.

12. Change row 2 on the Owners sheet to 30.00 (40 pixels) high. Change column A to 17.14 (125 pixels) wide.

13. In cell B2, key **Owner(s)**. Copy the format from cell A2.

14. Key the names shown in Figure U1-3. Widen column B to show the longest name.

FIGURE U1-3

Oregon Shops	Owener(s)	
Ashland	Heinrich Kraus	
Eugene	*[Key your first and last name]*	
Klamath Falls	Glenn Ladewig	
Medford	Nassar Eassa	
Roseburg	Tim Sumata	

15. Open the Print dialog box to preview the entire workbook. On the first page, add a footer to show your name at the left, the filename in the center, and the date at the right. Print the workbook.

16. Save and close the workbook.

UNIT APPLICATION 1-4 *Using The Internet*

Use your browser and your favorite search engine to search online bookstores for book and video titles about Excel. Make a list of five titles, including the authors, the publishers, and the prices. Indicate whether the item is a book or other media. Look for information about shipping charges.

Prepare a worksheet that lists the title, the media, the author, the publisher, and the price, using five columns. In a sixth column, enter an amount for a shipping charge, using a different value for each item. In the seventh column, use a formula to determine the total cost for buying the item.

Add an appropriate title (insert rows if you did not leave room). Apply an AutoFormat. Add the standard footer (be sure to include your name). Save your workbook as *[your initials]***u1-4** in your Unit 1 folder and print your worksheet. Close the workbook.

Working with Formulas and Functions

Working with Simple Formulas

OBJECTIVES

After completing this lesson, you will be able to:

MICROSOFT OFFICE
SPECIALIST
ACTIVITIES

In this lesson:
XLO3S-2-3
XLO3S-3-1
XLO3S-3-4
XLO3S-5-1
XLO3S-5-7
XLO3S-5-8

See Appendix.

1. Use a template to create a workbook.
2. Build addition and subtraction formulas.
3. Build multiplication and division formulas.
4. Use order of precedence in a formula.
5. Use relative, absolute, and mixed references.
6. Refine format and print options.

 Estimated Time: 1½ hours

In this lesson, you spend time building formulas, using each of the common business arithmetic operations (addition, subtraction, multiplication, and division). In the process of learning more about formulas, you will review the mathematical order of precedence. This determines how Excel completes a series of calculations.

You have seen how Excel updates a reference in a formula relative to its position when it is copied to a new location. In this lesson you explore other types of references.

 NOTE: The workbooks you create and use in this course relate to the Case Study (see pages 1–4) about Klassy Kow Ice Cream, Inc., a fictional ice cream company.

Using a Template to Create a Workbook

A *template* is a model or sample workbook that can include font types and styles, alignment settings, borders, labels, values, and formulas. A template is useful as the basis for a workbook that is the same each week or month but with different data. For example, you might key an income statement every month that is the same except for the amounts.

You can use a template as the model for a workbook by:

- Choosing On my computer in the Templates section of the New Workbook task pane.
- Choosing the template name in the Recently used templates section of the New Workbook task pane.

Templates are automatically saved with an **.xlt** filename extension. This is different from a workbook's **.xls** extension. Templates are also automatically saved in a Templates folder for your computer. Templates must be in the Templates folder if you want the templates to be listed in the Templates dialog box.

 NOTE: You must copy the templates from the CD to the folder Documents and Settings\UserName\Application Data\Microsoft\Templates. Check with your instructor if you need help locating the templates used in this lesson.

EXERCISE   **5-1**   **Create a Workbook from a Template**

When you create a new workbook from a template, a copy of the template opens as a new workbook. The workbook has the same name as the template, followed by a number.

1. Choose File, New. The New Workbook task pane opens.
2. Click On my computer in the Templates section of the task pane. The Templates dialog box opens with tabs for two groups of templates.
3. Find the template **KlassyKow**.
4. Click **KlassyKow** and then click OK. A new workbook opens with labels, values, and a picture. The title bar shows the template name with a number, probably 1.

 TIP: Excel includes several professionally designed templates. You can download other Excel templates from Microsoft's Web site.

FIGURE 5-1
Templates
dialog box

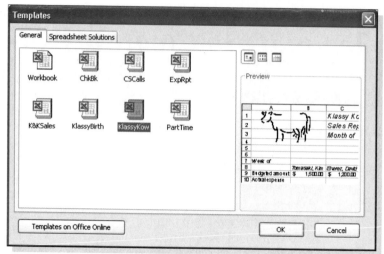

Building Addition and Subtraction Formulas

Simple addition formulas total or sum cells using the plus sign (+). Subtraction formulas compute the difference between cells using the minus sign (–).

 TIP: When cells are next to each other in a row or a column, it is usually faster to use AutoSum than to key a formula for addition.

EXERCISE 5-2 **Create and Copy Addition Formulas**

This worksheet tracks monthly expenses of sales representatives. The budgeted amounts for each week need to be added, as well as the expenses for each week. (The expenses are entered each week, because they change from week to week.)

You start by keying a formula to determine the total budgeted amount for the month for each salesperson.

1. Choose Tools and Options. Click the Error Checking tab.
2. If necessary, click to place a check mark for Formulas referring to empty cells. Click OK.
3. Set the Zoom size so that you can see rows 1 through 30. Then click cell B28.
4. Press = to start a formula.
5. Click cell B9, the budget amount for the first week for Kim Tomasaki. A marquee appears around the cell, and it is outlined in a color.
6. Key + and click cell B14, the second week budget amount.

TIP: You can use ⊞ on the numeric keypad or at the top of the keyboard to key the plus symbol in a formula.

7. Key + and click cell B19, the third week.

8. Key + and click cell B24, the fourth week. This is the addition formula to determine the total budgeted amount for the month for this salesperson.

FIGURE 5-2
Entering an
addition formula

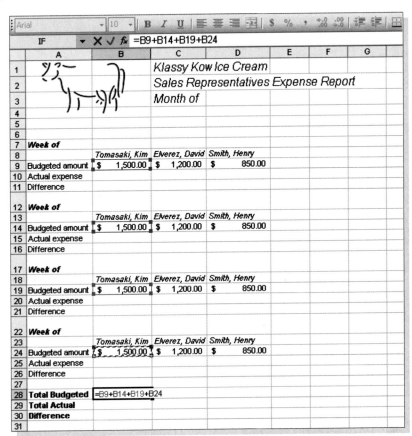

9. Press Enter.

 REVIEW: You can click the Enter button ☑ in the formula bar to finish a formula.

10. In cell B29, key = to start the formula.

11. Click cell B10, the cell where the first week's actual amount will be keyed.

 REVIEW: You can include empty cells in a formula.

12. Key + and click cell B15, the second week.

13. Key + and click cell B20, and then key + and click cell B25.

14. Key + again to make a deliberate error.

15. Press (Enter). The last plus sign is not necessary, and Excel proposes a correction, eliminating the extra + sign.

FIGURE 5-3
Error message box
about incorrect
formula

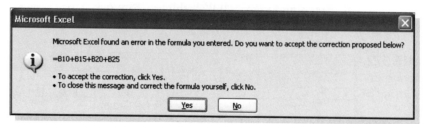

16. Choose Yes. This worksheet displays a single dash to indicate zero, and the cell shows a small green triangle indicating an error.

17. Click cell B29 and position the mouse pointer on the Trace Error button .

18. Click the arrow next to the Trace Error button to see that the formula refers to empty cells.

19. Choose Ignore Error.

20. Select cells B28:B29. Position the mouse pointer on the Fill handle for the range.

21. Drag the Fill handle to cell D29 to copy the formulas. The AutoFill Options button appears just below the filled range. Results appear in row 28, and green triangles mark errors in cells B29:D29.

22. Click cell C29.

23. Individually select each cell with an error, click the arrow next to the Trace Error button , and ignore the error.

E X E R C I S E   5-3   Create and Copy Subtraction Formulas

This worksheet computes the difference by subtracting the actual amount from the budgeted amount. You can use ⊟ on the numeric keypad or at the top of the keyboard.

1. Click cell B30 and key = to start a formula.

2. Click cell B28, the budget total.

NOTE: Because there are no actual values, the difference is the same as the budget total.

3. Key – and click cell B29, the actual total. Press (Enter).

4. Use the Fill handle to copy cell B30 to cells C30:D30.

5. Click cell B11. Key = and click cell B9, the budgeted amount for the week.

6. Key – and click cell B10, the actual amount for the week. Press (Enter).

7. Use the Fill handle to copy cell B11 to cells C11:D11. The AutoFill options button appears, as well as green triangles to mark potential errors.

 NOTE: Error triangles do not print and have no other effect on your worksheet, so you can ignore them when you know that nothing is wrong.

8. Click the Copy button 🗎.
9. Click cell B16 and click the Paste button 🗎▾.
10. Click cell B21 and click the Paste button 🗎▾. Paste again in cell B26.
11. Press (Esc) to cancel the marquee. The differences are the same as the budget amounts, because no actual expenses are shown yet.

Building Multiplication and Division Formulas

Multiplication formulas use an asterisk (*). You might use a multiplication formula to determine an employee's weekly wages by multiplying hours worked by the rate of pay.

A division formula uses a slash (/). Division formulas can be used to determine percentages, averages, individual prices, and more.

The result of a multiplication or division formula is formatted with decimals if the result is not a whole number. A *whole number* is a value without a fraction or decimal.

EXERCISE **5-4** **Create Multiplication Formulas**

Klassy Kow projects that its salespeople will spend 10 percent more money next year than this year. You can multiply the current total amounts by 10 percent to determine next year's increases. When you multiply by a percent, you can key the actual percent with the percent sign (%). If you do not key the percent sign, you must key the decimal equivalent of the percent value.

 TIP: Convert a percent to its decimal equivalent by dividing the percent amount by 100. For example, 89% is 89/100 or 0.89.

1. Select cells A28:A29. Display the drag-and-drop pointer, hold down (Ctrl), and drag the cells to cell A32.

 REVIEW: Display the drag-and-drop pointer by pointing at the top or bottom edge of a selection.

2. Click cell A32 and press (F2).
3. Press (Home) and key **Increased**.

4. Delete **Total** and press Enter.

5. Edit cell A33 to show **Increased Actual**.

6. Widen column A to fit these labels.

7. Click cell B32 and key =.

8. Click cell B28, key *, and then key **10%**. Press Enter. This amount is the increase in dollars, not a new total amount.

EXERCISE | **5-5** | **Edit a Formula in the Formula Bar**

A percent of increase determines how much more money will be needed. To determine what the new total will be, you need to multiply by 110%, because 110% is the current amount (100%) plus the expected increase (10%).

1. Click cell B32 and click in the formula bar. A text insertion point appears, and the cell used in the formula is outlined in color.

2. Click between the 1 and the 0 in the formula bar.

3. Key **1** to change the percent to 110%.

4. Press Enter. The new total is calculated.

FIGURE 5-4
Editing a formula
in the formula bar

	A	B	C	D	E
	IF ▾ X✓ ƒx	=B28*11⟩% ← Formula bar			
5		Enter			
6					
7	*Week of*				
8		Tomasaki, Kim	Elverez, David	Smith, Henry	
9	Budgeted amount	$ 1,500.00	$ 1,200.00	$ 850.00	
10	Actual expense				
11	Difference	1,500.00	1,200.00	850.00	
12	*Week of*				
13		Tomasaki, Kim	Elverez, David	Smith, Henry	
14	Budgeted amount	$ 1,500.00	$ 1,200.00	$ 850.00	
15	Actual expense				
16	Difference	1,500.00	1,200.00	850.00	
17	*Week of*				
18		Tomasaki, Kim	Elverez, David	Smith, Henry	
19	Budgeted amount	$ 1,500.00	$ 1,200.00	$ 850.00	
20	Actual expense				
21	Difference	1,500.00	1,200.00	850.00	
22	*Week of*				
23		Tomasaki, Kim	Elverez, David	Smith, Henry	
24	Budgeted amount	$ 1,500.00	$ 1,200.00	$ 850.00	
25	Actual expense				
26	Difference	1,500.00	1,200.00	850.00	
27					
28	**Total Budgeted**	$ 6,000.00	$ 4,800.00	$ 3,400.00	
29	**Total Actual**	-	-	-	
30	**Difference**	$ 6,000.00	$ 4,800.00	$ 3,400.00	
31					
32	Increased Budgeted	=B28*110%			
33	Increased Actual				
34					

   5. Copy cell B32 to cells C32:D32.
   6. Copy cells B32:D32 to cells B33:D33. This applies the same increase to the actual amounts, but they are zero at this point.

EXERCISE   5-6   Create Division Formulas

The actual expenses are keyed each month after the sales reps submit their re-ports. If you select a range before keying data, you can press the (Enter) key to move from one cell to the next in top-to-bottom, left-to-right order.

   1. Select cells B10:D10.

 NOTE: The template includes formatting for cells B10:D10.

   2. Key **1000** and press (Enter).
   3. Key **950** and press (Enter).
   4. Key **725** and press (Enter). As you fill in the amounts, the difference is calculated.
   5. Select cells B15:D15 and key these values:
      1300   1250   925
   6. Key these values in cells B20:D20 and cells B25:C25. The totals are calculated in rows 28 and 29 as you key the values.
      900   850   625
      1000   750   575
   7. Click cell B31 and key = to start a formula.
   8. Click cell B29 and key / for division. Dividing the actual amount by the budget amount determines the percent of actual expenses in relation to the budget amount.
   9. Click cell B28 and press (Enter). The result is formatted as a decimal, not a percent.

EXERCISE   5-7   Apply the Percent Style and Increase Decimal Positions

Excel converts a decimal to a percent when you apply the Percent Style. It does this by multiplying the decimal value by 100. For example, 0.7 is 0.7*100 or 70%. You can apply the Percent Style by:

   • Clicking the Percent Style button % on the Formatting toolbar.
   • Choosing Percentage from the Category list in the Format Cells dialog box.

1. Click cell B31 and click the Percent Style button %. The percent symbol is added, and the value is converted.

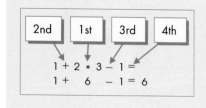

2. Click the Increase Decimal button 🔾 two times. A decimal position is added with each click.

3. Use the Fill handle to copy the formula in cell B31 to cells C31:D31.

4. In cell A31, key **Actual as % of Budget**. Because three rows precede this row, the format of those rows is applied.

5. Widen column A to show this label. Press Ctrl + Home.

6. Press F12 and save the workbook as *[your initials]5-7* in a new folder for Lesson 5. The title bar now shows your filename.

7. Print the worksheet. Close the workbook.

Using Order of Precedence in a Formula

Excel follows basic mathematical rules when it calculates a formula. These rules include an *order of precedence*, sometimes called *order of operation* or *math hierarchy*. The order of precedence determines what portion of a formula is calculated first. Generally, a formula is calculated from left to right, but some arithmetic operators take priority over others. For example, if you key a formula with both a multiplication symbol (*) and an addition symbol (+), Excel calculates the multiplication operation first even if it is the second symbol as you move from left to right. You can override the order of precedence by enclosing parts of the formula within parentheses.

When two operators have the same order of precedence—for example, multiplication and division—you perform the operations from left to right (see Table 5-1).

Figure 5-5 shows three formulas with the same values and the same operators. The results differ, depending on the placement of the parentheses.

FIGURE 5-5 Parentheses change the order of operations

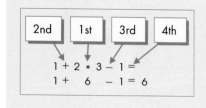
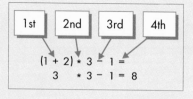
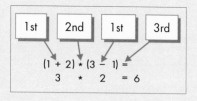

TABLE 5-1   Operator Precedence in Excel

OPERATOR	PRECEDENCE	DESCRIPTION
^	1st	Exponentiation
*	2nd	Multiplication
/	2nd	Division
+	3rd	Addition
–	3rd	Subtraction
&	4th	Concatenation (symbol used to join text strings)
=	5th	Equal to
<	5th	Less than
>	5th	Greater than

> **TIP:** Using the first letter for each description in this table, you can memorize the order of precedence for parentheses and the first five operators: "Please excuse my dear Aunt Sally" (parentheses, exponentiation, multiplication, division, addition, and subtraction).

EXERCISE   **5-8**   **Compare Formulas**

In this worksheet, you calculate the dollar value of all beverages sold. You need to total the items for each state and multiply by the price. As part of the learning process, you first key the formula with an error and then fix it.

1. Open **DrinkSize**.
2. Click cell B11 and key =.
3. Click cell B5, the price for a 16 oz. soda.
4. Key * to multiply the price by the number sold.
5. Select cell C5 and key +. Click cell D5 and key +. Click cell E5 and key +. Click cell F5. This part of the formula adds the items from each state.
6. Press Enter. The result looks OK, but it is wrong.
7. Click cell B11. The formula includes a multiplication symbol, so cell B5 is multiplied by cell C5. Then the other cells are added to the result of that multiplication.
8. Right-click the AutoCalculate area and choose Sum.

 REVIEW: AutoCalculate results are visible in the status bar.

9. Select cells C5:F5. Check the AutoCalculate area for the sum of the selected cells. The total quantity sold is 30,000.

10. Click cell D11 and key = to start a formula. You are temporarily using an empty cell to calculate the correct amount.

11. Click cell B5, key ***30000**, and press ⏎Enter. This is the correct amount— the total number sold (30,000) multiplied by the price.

12. Delete the contents of cell D11.

EXERCISE   **5-9**   **Revise a Formula in the Worksheet**

---

1. Double-click cell B11 to start Edit mode. The formula is in the cell and in the formula bar. The referenced cells are outlined in color.

2. In the worksheet cell, click in front of or to the left of C5.

3. Key a left parenthesis (in front of C5.

4. Press ⏎End. The insertion point moves to the end of the formula.

5. Key a right parenthesis).

6. Press ⏎Enter. These parentheses force the additions to be calculated first. That result is multiplied by cell B5.

FIGURE 5-6
Changing the order of precedence

	Arial		10	B *I* U	≣ ≣ ≣	$ %				
	IF	▾ ✗ ✓ ƒx =B5*(C5+D5+E5+F5)								

	A	B	C	D	E	F	G
1	Klassy Kow Ice Cream Shops						
2	Comparison of Drink Sizes Sold						
3	Count of Items for June						
4		Price	California	Washington	Oregon	Nevada	
5	16 oz. Soda	$0.89	8,000	6,000	5,000	11,000	
6	32 oz. Soda	$1.59	12,000	7,500	4,000	15,000	
7	12 oz. Coffee	$1.29	7,500	8,000	5,000	11,500	
8	20 oz. Coffee	$1.59	5,400	8,500	5,500	16,000	
9	Tea	$1.29	2,500	2,000	2,300	4,000	
10	Total Dollar Values Sold						
11	16 oz. Soda	=B5*(C5+D5+E5+F5)					
12	32 oz. Soda						
13	12 oz. Coffee						
14	20 oz. Coffee						
15	Tea						
16							

7. Copy the formula in cell B11 to cells B12:B15.

8. Click cell B12. Notice that the formula multiplies the price in cell B6 by the items in row 6 for 32 oz. soda. This is correct.

9. Press ⌃Ctrl+⌂Home.

10. Save the workbook as *[your initials]*5-9 in your Lesson 5 folder.

11. Print the worksheet. Close the workbook.

Using Relative, Absolute, and Mixed References

When you copy a formula, Excel adjusts the formula relative to the row or column where the copy is located. This is known as a *relative reference* and is often exactly what you want Excel to do.

There are situations, however, when you want Excel to copy the formula exactly. A cell with an *absolute reference* does not change when a formula is copied. An absolute reference uses two dollar signs ($) in its address, one in front of the column reference and one in front of the row reference. $B$5 is an absolute reference to cell B5.

Excel can also use a *mixed reference,* in which a dollar sign is placed in front of the reference for either the row or the column. In a mixed reference, part of the cell reference is adjusted when a formula is copied, and the other part of the cell reference is not changed. $B5 is a mixed reference with an absolute reference to column B but a relative reference to row 5.

Dollar signs used in a cell address do not signify currency. They are a reserved symbol used to mark the type of cell reference.

TABLE 5-2   Cell References

ADDRESS	TYPE OF REFERENCE
B1	Relative
$B$1	Absolute
$B1	Mixed: Column letter is absolute; row number is relative.
B$1	Mixed: Row number is absolute; column letter is relative.

EXERCISE 5-10 Copy a Formula with a Relative Reference

You can place labels on two lines in a cell by pressing (Alt)+(Enter) at the point where you want the second line to start. This is known as a line break in a cell. You often also need to adjust the row height and the column width if you use line breaks.

1. Open **ShopDownTime**.
2. In cell F4, key **Cost per** and press (Alt)+(Enter).
3. Key **Down Hour** and press (Enter).
4. Adjust the column width so that the label splits only between "per" and "Down."

5. In cell F5, key **25** and format it as currency with no decimals.

6. In cell D4, key **Cost**. Its formatting matches the preceding columns.

7. Click cell D5. Key = to start the formula.

8. Click cell F5, key *, and then click cell C5. This formula uses relative references.

9. Press [Enter]. The result is $50.

10. Drag the Fill handle for cell D5 to copy the formula to cell D20. The copied formulas show a dash for zero and an error triangle. The cells that should show a cost do not do so.

11. Click the copied cells in column D and look in the formula bar. The column did not change as you copied, because you copied to the same column. But each time you went down a row in column D, the row reference increased in the formula. As a result, the copied formulas multiply by an empty cell in column F.

12. Click the Undo button . Only your copy is undone.

EXERCISE 5-11 Create a Formula with an Absolute Reference

Because absolute references are common to many calculations, Excel has a quick way of adding dollar signs to a cell reference. You press [F4] while the formula bar is open and the insertion point is positioned in the reference to cycle through options for absolute and mixed references.

1. Click cell D5 and press [F2].

REVIEW: [F2] starts Edit mode, the same as double-clicking the cell.

2. Click between F and 5 in the worksheet cell.

3. Press [F4]. Two dollar signs are inserted, one before F and one before 5.

4. Press [F4]. The dollar sign appears only with 5.

5. Press [F4] again. The dollar sign appears only with F.

6. Press [F4] again. The dollar signs are removed.

7. Press [F4] once more. The absolute reference appears again. (See Figure 5-7.)

8. Press [Enter]. Click cell D5 and look in the formula bar.

9. Use the Fill handle for cell D5 to copy the formula into cells D6:D36.

10. Click each copied cell and look in the formula bar.

11. Press [Ctrl]+[Home].

12. Save the workbook as *[your initials]*5-11 in your Lesson 5 folder.

13. Print the worksheet. Close the workbook.

FIGURE 5-7
Making a cell reference absolute

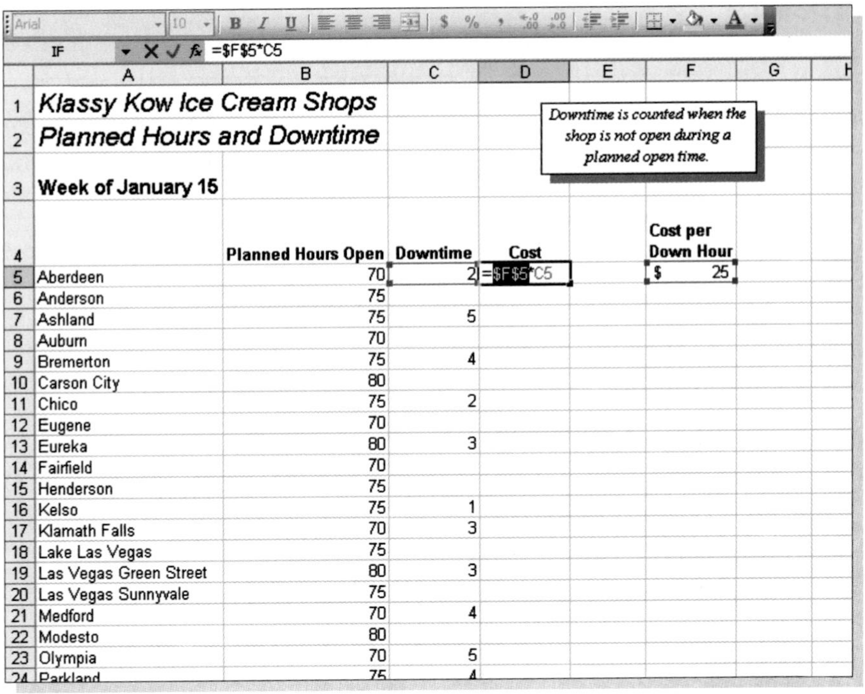
IF =$F$5*C5

	A	B	C	D	E	F	G
1	Klassy Kow Ice Cream Shops						
2	Planned Hours and Downtime						
3	Week of January 15						
4		Planned Hours Open	Downtime	Cost		Cost per Down Hour	
5	Aberdeen	70	2	=$F$5*C5		$ 25	
6	Anderson	75					
7	Ashland	75	5				
8	Auburn	70					
9	Bremerton	75	4				
10	Carson City	80					
11	Chico	75	2				
12	Eugene	70					
13	Eureka	80	3				
14	Fairfield	70					
15	Henderson	75					
16	Kelso	75	1				
17	Klamath Falls	70	3				
18	Lake Las Vegas	75					
19	Las Vegas Green Street	80	3				
20	Las Vegas Sunnyvale	75					
21	Medford	70	4				
22	Modesto	80					
23	Olympia	70	5				
24	Parkland	75	4				

EXERCISE 5-12 Use Mixed References

As a school year promotion, Klassy Kow Ice Cream Shops plan to give away multiplication tables, reduced in size and printed on cards. The same multiplication table will be posted on the company's Web site. You will create the multiplication table using mixed references.

1. Open **MultTable**.
2. Set the Zoom percent to a size that lets you see the entire worksheet.
3. Click cell B4. You want to show the result of multiplying 1 by 1 in cell B4.
4. Key = and click cell A4. This will be a mixed reference.
5. Press F4 three times to show $A4. This part of the formula will always use column A, but the row will change.
6. Press * and click cell B2.
7. Press F4 two times to show B$2. This part of the formula will always use row 2, but the column will change. (See Figure 5-8.)
8. Press Enter.
9. Use the Fill handle to copy cell B4 to cell K4.
10. Use the range Fill handle to copy cells B4:K4 down to row 13.

FIGURE 5-8
Mixed reference
formula

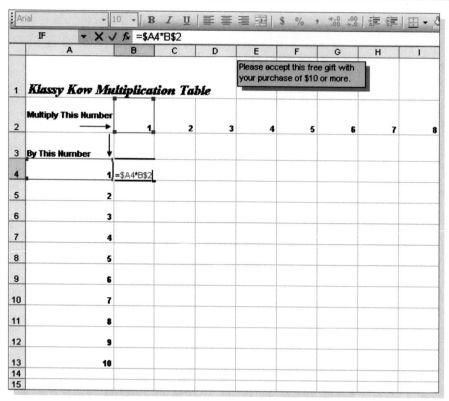

Refining Format and Print Options

This worksheet has many numbers and is too wide to print on a single page. Before printing, you can make some adjustments so that it is easy to follow and prints on one page.

EXERCISE **5-13** **Add Borders and Shading for Printing**

Printed borders and shading will make it easier to follow numbers across a wide layout.

1. If you can't see the complete label in cell A2, widen column A.
2. Select cells A2:K13 and press Ctrl+1.
3. Click the Border tab.
4. In the Border preset group, click the Top Border button.
5. Click the Middle Border and then the Bottom Border buttons. Click OK.

FIGURE 5-9
Setting top, middle, and bottom borders

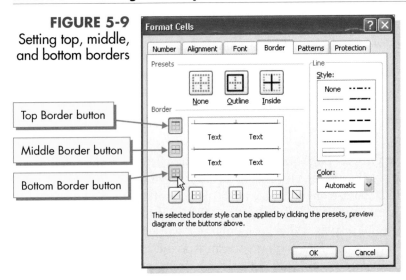

Top Border button

Middle Border button

Bottom Border button

REVIEW: Hold down the [Ctrl] key to select noncontiguous cell ranges.

6. Select cells A2:K2 and cells A3:A13.

7. Click the arrow next to the Fill Color button .

8. Choose Gray-25% in the last column, the second row from the bottom.

9. Press [Ctrl]+[Home].

EXERCISE **5-14** **Change Page Orientation**

Page orientation is a print setting that determines if the worksheet prints in landscape or portrait orientation. The default is *portrait* orientation, one that is taller than it is wide.

Many worksheets are too wide to fit in a portrait orientation. A *landscape* orientation is horizontal—the page is wider than it is tall.

1. Click the Print Preview button . The worksheet does not fit on a single page in a portrait orientation. You can see in the status bar that it requires more than one page.

2. Press [Page Down]. The part of the worksheet that does not fit appears on a second page.

TIP: Excel splits the worksheet between columns, depending on the page margins.

3. Press [Page Up] to return to page 1.

4. Click Setup. Click the Page tab.

5. Click the Landscape button in the Orientation group.

6. Click OK. The worksheet now fits on a single page with a landscape orientation.

EXERCISE **5-15** **Change Scaling and Page Margins**

In addition to changing the page orientation, Excel has a Scaling command that enables you to set a size percentage for the printed page. For example, you can set a worksheet to print at 50 percent of its size or 150 percent of its size. You might need to do this if you want to print the worksheet on a 5- by 7-inch card or if you want to enlarge it for a special display. When you enlarge a worksheet, your printer will split the pages between columns so that you can tape the parts together.

You have seen that you can change margins by dragging the margin markers. If you need to set a precise margin and have difficulty dragging a marker, you can use the Margins tab to key a specific setting.

1. Click Setup. Click the Page tab.

2. In the Scaling section, click the Adjust to button.

3. Double-click 100 and key **75**.

FIGURE 5-10
Scaling the
worksheet

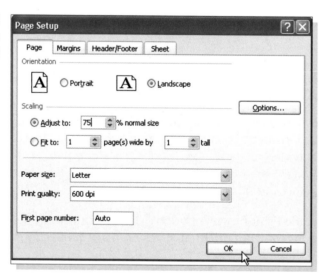

4. Click OK. The worksheet is reduced to 75 percent of its normal size. This is only a print adjustment and does not affect the font sizes specified in the worksheet.

5. Click Setup. Click the Margins tab.

6. Double-click in the Left box and key **1**.

7. Double-click in the Right box and key **1**. Click OK. Close print preview.

8. Save the workbook as *[your initials]*5-15 in your Lesson 5 folder.

9. Print the worksheet.

EXERCISE **5-16** **Copy a Worksheet and Print Formulas**

You can view the formulas within your worksheet all at once instead of checking the formula bar cell by cell. This enables you to troubleshoot problems more easily. It is also helpful to print a worksheet with the formulas visible to provide documentation for your work.

In order to keep the original version of your worksheet, you'll make a copy of it and show the formulas on the copy.

FIGURE 5-11
Copying a
worksheet

1. Rename Sheet1 as **PrintTable**.

2. Right-click the PrintTable tab and choose Move or Copy.

3. In the Move or Copy dialog box, click to place a check mark for Create a copy. Click OK. The copy is named PrintTable (2) and is inserted in front of the original.

4. Press [Ctrl]+[~]. The formulas in each cell are visible.

 NOTE: You can turn the display of formulas on and off by choosing Tools, Options. Click the View tab and turn Formulas on or off.

5. Click the column A heading.

6. Scroll right and hold down [Shift] while clicking the column K heading. All the columns are selected.

7. From the Format menu, choose Column and AutoFit Selection. Excel AutoFits each column to its longest entry.

8. Click the Print Preview button [🔍].

9. Click Setup and click the Page tab.

10. Double-click 75 in the Adjust to box and key **100**. Click OK. At its normal size, the worksheet occupies two pages, because printed formulas require more space than values.

11. Click Setup and click the Margins tab.

12. Double-click in the Left box and key **.5**. Double-click in the Right box and key **.5**.

 TIP: You can set your own scaling percentage or choose the Fit to option.

13. Click the Page tab. In the Scaling section, click the Fit to button.
14. Choose **1** page(s) wide by **1** tall.
15. Click OK. Excel does its own scaling so the worksheet fits on a single landscape page with 0.5-inch left and right margins.
16. Click Print and click OK. Press Ctrl + Home.

EXERCISE 5-17 Copy a Worksheet and Add a Background

The multiplication table for the Web uses a shaded background for the sheet rather than the borders and gray shading. A *background* is an image that appears on the screen and on the Web. It fills or spans the entire worksheet. It does not print.

1. Right-click the PrintTable tab and choose Move or Copy.
2. In the Move or Copy dialog box, click to place a check mark for Create a copy. Click OK. The copy is named PrintTable (3).
3. Rename PrintTable (3) as **Background**.
4. From the Format menu, choose Sheet and then Background. The Sheet Background dialog box opens.
5. Navigate to the folder with the **KKBack** file. Click to select the file.

FIGURE 5-12
Using a sheet background

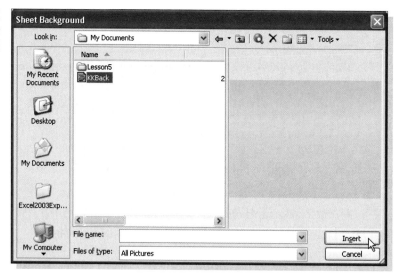

6. Click Insert. The background is a blend of colors and fills the worksheet.
7. Select cells A2:K2 and cells A3:A13.
8. Click the arrow with the Fill Color button and choose No Fill. You don't need a fill color with the background.
9. Press Ctrl + Home.

10. Click the Print Preview button . Backgrounds do not print; they are visible when the sheet is posted to the Web site.

11. Save the workbook as *[your initials]*5-17 in your Lesson 5 folder.

12. Close the workbook.

USING ONLINE HELP

You learned about simple formulas in this lesson. Use the Type a question for help box to obtain additional information about using and building formulas.

Use Help to view additional information about formulas:

1. Click in the Type a Question for help box and key **create formula**. Press Enter.

2. Click the topic Create a formula in the Search Results dialog box.

3. Click Show All in the top-right corner. Scroll and read the information in the Help window.

4. Close the Help window when you have finished reading about formulas. Close the Search Results dialog box.

LESSON 5 Summary

➤ Use a template to create workbooks that use the same labels and other basic information on a routine basis.

➤ Templates can include such elements as labels, values, formatting, formulas, and pictures.

➤ You can edit a formula in the formula bar and within the cell in Edit mode.

➤ The Percent Style converts a decimal value to its percent equivalent.

➤ In calculating formulas, Excel follows mathematical order of precedence.

➤ You can establish a different order of precedence in a formula by keying parentheses around the calculations that you want performed first.

➤ Excel has relative, absolute, and mixed references. These references determine what happens when a formula is copied.

➤ A portrait orientation prints a vertical page. A landscape page prints a horizontal page.

➤ The Scaling section of the Page tab enables you to print the worksheet in a reduced or enlarged size. You can also choose to have Excel fit the worksheet on a page.

➤ To set a precise margin, use the Margins tab in the Page Setup dialog box.

➤ You can print a worksheet with formulas displayed for documentation or help in locating problems.

➤ You can add an image as a sheet background for display on a Web page.

LESSON 5 Command Summary

FEATURE	BUTTON	MENU	KEYBOARD
Absolute/mixed reference			F4
Background		Format, Sheet, Background	
Display/hide formulas		Tools, Options	Ctrl+~
Edit mode			F2
Fit to page		File, Page Setup	
Increase Decimal		Format, Cells	Ctrl+F1
New, from template		File, New	Ctrl+N
Page margins		File, Page Setup	
Page orientation		File, Page Setup	
Percent Style		Format, Cells	Ctrl+F1
Scaling		File, Page Setup	

Concepts Review

TRUE/FALSE QUESTIONS

Each of the following statements is either true or false. Indicate your choice by circling T or F.

T F   **1.** A template opens as a new worksheet with the template name and a letter.

T F   **2.** You must use the plus symbol on the numeric keypad in a formula.

T F   **3.** The multiplication symbol in a formula is /.

T F   **4.** To multiply by a percent, you must key the decimal equivalent of the percent.

T F   **5.** You can control the order of precedence in a formula with parentheses.

T F   **6.** Division is calculated before addition in a formula without parentheses.

T F   **7.** Column widths adjust automatically when you display formulas.

T F   **8.** An absolute reference does not adjust when the formula is copied to another cell.

SHORT ANSWER QUESTIONS

Write the correct answer in the space provided.

1. What is the keyboard shortcut to display or hide formulas?

_____

2. Which page orientation is taller than it is wide?

_____

3. How would the cell reference **$F$3** be described?

_____

4. What are the four arithmetic symbols that can be used in a formula?

_____

5. What type of operation is being performed in the formula = A4*B4?

_____

6. What command option allows you to print a worksheet on a smaller piece of paper?

_____

7. What term describes a model workbook used as the basis for other workbooks?

_____

8. How can you start Edit mode to edit a formula?

_____

CRITICAL THINKING

Answer these questions on a separate page. There are no right or wrong answers. Support your answers with examples from your own experience, if possible.

1. Why is it helpful to set the Zoom percentage while working? Is this different from scaling the worksheet?

2. Why is it necessary to have an absolute cell reference in some formulas? Why can't all formulas use relative references?

Skills Review

EXERCISE 5-18

Use a template to create a new workbook. Build addition and subtraction formulas.

1. Create a workbook from a template by following these steps:
   a. Choose File, New.
   b. Click On my computer in the Templates section.
   c. Choose ChkBk and click OK.
2. In cell A4, key today's date in mm/dd/yy format.
3. Key tomorrow's date in cell A5 in the same format.
4. Press F12 and save the workbook as *[your initials]*5-18 in your Lesson 5 folder.
5. Build addition and subtraction formulas by following these steps:
   a. Click cell F5. Key = to start a formula.
   b. Click cell F4 and key – for subtraction.

    c. Click cell D5 and key **+** for addition.

    d. Click cell E5. Press (Enter) and ignore any error triangles.

 TIP: The formula subtracts amounts in column D and adds amounts in column E.

6. Copy the formula in cell F5 to cells F6:F15.

 NOTE: Key dates in this style: **mm/dd/yy**

7. Key the following information, starting in cell A6.

FIGURE 5-13

	Date	Check #	Payee	Credit Amount	Deposit
6	[2 days from today]	1002	Helpful Hand Computers	1250	
7	[3 days from today]				2500
8	[4 days from today]	1003	Greenberg and Whitefield	575	
9	[5 days from today]	1004	[your school name]	435	
10	[6 days from today]				1200

8. Widen column A to show all dates.

9. Select and hide rows 10 through 15.

 10. Click the Print Preview button . Add a custom footer with your name at the left and the filename at the right.

11. Click <u>M</u>argins in Print Preview. Drag the left and right margin markers each to about .40 to fit the worksheet on a single printed page.

12. Print the worksheet. Press (Ctrl)+(Home).

13. Save and close the workbook.

EXERCISE 5-19

Build multiplication and division formulas. Set the order of precedence.

1. Open **TasteTest**. Save the workbook as *[your initials]*5-19 in your Lesson 5 folder.

2. Build a multiplication formula by following these steps:

 NOTE: This formula is incorrect because of order of precedence. You will correct it later.

    a. Click cell F4 and key =. Click cell D4. This is a taste tester's regular hourly pay rate.

    b. Key +. Click cell E4. The tester receives a holiday rate increase, added to the regular pay rate.

    c. Key *. Click cell C4. The hourly rate is multiplied by the number of hours worked to determine the pay.

 NOTE: The total pay shown is not correct.

    d. Press (Enter).

3. Copy the formula in cell F4 to cells F5:F8.

4. Build a division formula by following these steps:

    a. Click cell H4 and key =. Click cell F4. The total pay is divided by the number of items tested.

    b. Key /. Click cell G4. Press (Enter).

    c. Copy the formula to cells H5:H8.

5. Set the order of precedence by following these steps:

    a. Click cell F4. This formula is incorrect, because it first multiplies cells E4 by C4 and then adds cell D4.

 REVIEW: Multiplication is calculated before addition.

    b. Press (F2). Click between = and D. Key (.

    c. Click before *, key), and press (Enter).

    d. Recopy the formula in cell F4 to cells F5:F8. Column H is recalculated.

 6. Select cells D4:F8 and H4:H8. Click the Currency Style button [$].

 7. Select cells A3:H3 and click the Bold button [B]. Press (Ctrl)+(1). Click the Alignment tab and turn on Wrap text. Click OK. Click the Center button [≡].

8. AutoFit each column except column A. Make column A 13.57 (100 pixels) wide. Press (Ctrl)+(Home).

9. Add a custom footer with your name at the left, the filename in the center, and the date at the right. Print the worksheet.

10. Save and close the workbook.

EXERCISE 5-20

Build formulas. Use an absolute reference.

1. Open **ClaimsCost**. Save it as *[your initials]*5-20 in your Lesson 5 folder.
2. In cell A21, key **Total Number of Claims** and make it bold. Make row 21 22.50 (30 pixels) tall.
3. Build formulas by following these steps:
   a. Click cell B21.
   b. Key = to start the formula.
   c. Click cell B7 and click + to build an addition formula.
   d. Click B10 and click + to continue.
   e. Build the formula by adding each cell in column B with a value to the formula.
   f. Press Enter.
4. Create similar formulas in cells C21 and D21. Center-align the results of the three formulas.
5. In cell A22, key **Total Processing Cost** and make it bold. Make row 22 the same height as row 21.
6. In cell C4, key **Processing Cost** and make it bold.
7. In cell D4, key **15.45** and format it as Currency with two decimals.
8. Use an absolute reference in a formula by following these steps:
   a. Click cell B22.
   b. Key = to start the formula.
   c. Click cell B21 and key * for a multiplication formula.
   d. Click D4 and press F4 to make it absolute. Press Enter.
9. Use the Fill handle to copy the formula to cells C22:D22.
10. Format cells B22:D22 as bold Currency with 2 decimal points.
11. Format all values as 10-point Arial. Press Ctrl+Home.
12. Add a custom footer with your name at the left, the tab name and the filename in the center, and the date at the right. Print the worksheet.
13. Save and close the workbook.

EXERCISE 5-21

Use relative, absolute, and mixed references. Change the page orientation. Print formulas.

1. Create a new workbook and save it as *[your initials]*5-21 in your Lesson 5 folder.
2. In cell A1, key **Klassy Kow Ice Cream Shops** and format it as 16-point Arial.

3. In cell A2, key **Henderson Shop** and format it as 14-point Arial.

4. Key **Friday** in cell B3 and make it bold. Use the Fill handle to extend the days to Sunday in cell D3. Center the labels in row 3.

5. Key the remaining labels and values to build the worksheet. Make all the labels in the column headings bold and center-aligned.

FIGURE 5-14

		Friday	Saturday	Sunday	Size Total	Cone Cost	Ice Cream Cost
4	One scoop	100	150	125			
5	Two scoops	155	175	135	Key these labels		
6	Three scoops	70	85	55			
7	Day Total						

6. Turn on <u>W</u>rap text for cells E3:G3. Format column A as 12.14 (90 pixels) wide.

7. Use relative references by following these steps:

Σ ▾

   a. Click cell B7 and click the AutoSum button **Σ ▾**. Press Enter.
   b. Copy this formula to cells C7:D7.
   c. Click cell E4 and click the AutoSum button **Σ ▾**. Press Enter.
   d. Copy this formula to cells E5:E7.

8. Key the following data in cells A10:B13 to show the costs.

FIGURE 5-15

	A	B
10	Cone cost	0.35
11	One scoop	0.8
12	Two scoops	1.1
13	Three scoops	1.6

9. Use absolute references by following these steps:

   a. Click cell F4 and key = to start a formula.
   b. Click cell E4 and key * to multiply the total number of cones sold.
   c. Click cell B10 to enter the cost per cone.
   d. Press F4 to change to an absolute reference. Press Enter.
   e. Copy this formula to cells F5:F7.

10. Use mixed references by following these steps:

   a. Click cell G4 and key = to start.
   b. Click cell E4 and key * to multiply.
   c. Click cell B11 for the cost of a one-scoop cone.
   d. Press F4 to change to an absolute reference. Press F4 again to make the row absolute. Press F4 again to make the column absolute. Press Enter.
   e. Copy this formula to cells G5:G6.

11. Format cells B4:D7 to show commas with no decimals. Format cells E4:G4, E7:F7, and B10:B13 for currency with two decimals. Format cells E5:G6 for commas with two decimals. Press Ctrl+Home.

12. Change the page orientation by following these steps:

   a. Click the Print Preview button and click Setup.
   b. Click the Page tab and choose Landscape.

13. Add your standard footer and print the worksheet. Close Print Preview.

14. Print formulas by following these steps:

   a. Right-click the Sheet1 tab and choose Move or Copy.
   b. Place a check mark for Create a copy and click OK.
   c. Rename the copied sheet as **Formulas**.
   d. Press Ctrl+~.
   e. Click the column B heading. Scroll the worksheet, hold down Shift, and click the column G heading.

    NOTE: To AutoFit a range of columns, double-click the right border of the last or rightmost column.

   f. Double-click the border between the column headings for columns G and H. The title in column A is not completely visible; but that's OK.
   g. Print the formulas worksheet.

15. Add a background to a worksheet by following these steps:

   a. Right-click the Sheet1 tab and choose Move or Copy.
   b. Place a check mark for Create a copy and click OK.
   c. Rename the copied sheet as **Background**.
   d. Choose Format, Sheet and then Background.
   e. Navigate to the folder with the **KKBack** file. Click to select the file.
   f. Click Insert.

16. Press Ctrl+Home. Save and close the workbook.

Lesson Applications

EXERCISE 5-22

Create a workbook from a template. Build addition and subtraction formulas.

1. Use the **KlassyKow** template as the basis for a workbook. Save the new workbook as *[your initials]*5-22.

 TIP: Look for recently used templates in the New Workbook task pane.

2. Edit the label in cell C3 to show the current month.

3. Edit cells A7, A12, A17, and A22 to show the date of each Friday in the current month. If the current month has a fifth Friday, do not include it.

4. In cells B10:D10, key the following actual expenses:
   1300   1000   895

5. Add actual expenses for the weeks as follows:

FIGURE 5-16

Second week	1600	900	750
Third week	1000	1300	850
Fourth week	1200	2000	500

6. In cell B11, use a formula to subtract the actual expense from the budgeted amount. Copy the formula to cells C11:D11.

7. Select cells B11:D11 and click the Copy button .

8. Click cell B16 and click the Paste button [image]. Paste again in cells B21 and B26. Press Esc when you finish.

 NOTE: Negative numbers are shown in parentheses in this workbook. A negative number means the sales rep spent more money than budgeted.

9. In cell B28, add the budget amounts for Kim Tomasaki. Copy the formula for the other salespeople.

10. In cell B29, add the actual amounts for Kim Tomasaki. Copy the formula for the other salespeople.

11. In cell B30, subtract the total actual expense from the total budgeted amount. Copy the formula.

12. Select cells E28:E30 and click the AutoSum button . Widen the column to show the data.

13. Add your usual footer.

> **NOTE:** Unless your instructor tells you otherwise, include your name, the tab name, the filename, and the date in your footer.

14. Print the worksheet. Save and close the workbook.

EXERCISE 5-23

Use a mixed reference. Add borders. Change the page orientation. Adjust the scaling percentage.

1. Open **DrinkSize** and save it as *[your initials]*5-23 in your Lesson 5 folder.

2. Select cells C4:F4. Copy/paste these cells to cells C10:F10.

3. In cell C11, multiply the item count for California by the appropriate price from column B. The cell reference from column B should be a mixed reference.

4. Copy the formula through column F and then through row 15. Check the reference for several formulas to determine its accuracy.

5. Format the values in cells C11:F15 as Currency with two decimals.

6. Select cells A3:F3 and press Ctrl+1. Center these cells across the selection.

7. Select all the cells with data and add an outside border. Then add a double bottom border to cells A9:F9.

> **NOTE:** Hidden columns/rows are used in calculations.

8. Hide column B.

9. Change the page orientation to landscape. Set the scaling to print the worksheet at 150 percent of normal size. Set the left margin at 2.00 inches.

10. Add your usual footer and print the worksheet.

11. Make a copy of the worksheet and name the tab **Formulas**.

12. Display the formulas and fit the columns as needed. Scale the worksheet to 100 percent. Print the formula worksheet.

13. Save and close the workbook.

EXERCISE 5-24

Apply borders and shading. Change print options.

1. Open **ICOrder** and save it as *[your initials]*5-24 in your Lesson 5 folder.

2. Center the two main titles across columns A:C.

3. Apply 25% gray shading to the main title cells and to cells A13:C13.

4. Selects cells A4:B11 and apply a single vertical border on the right and in the middle.

5. Select cells A1:C14. Copy and paste the cells to cell A20 so that you have a duplicate of the order form.

6. Paste the same selection in cells E1 and again in E20.

7. Check the column widths of the first copy and make the copies in columns E:G the same. You should have four copies of the order form on your worksheet.

8. Change the page orientation to landscape.

9. Scale the worksheet to 110% and set the top and bottom margins at .5 inches.

10. Add your usual footer. Print the worksheet.

11. Save and close the workbook.

EXERCISE 5-25 *Challenge Yourself*

Use parentheses and order of precedence. Print formulas.

1. Open **ICOrder**. Save it as *[your initials]***5-25** in your Lesson 5 folder.

2. For three different items, key a value of your choice indicating how many of the items were purchased on this order. Use values less than 10.

3. In cell C14, determine the amount due. The formula should multiply the quantity by the price for each item. Then multiply that total by 1 + the tax rate. (You can use the tax rate that would apply in your state, or you can use a 4.5% tax rate.)

 TIP: A 4.5% tax rate makes the final cost 104.5% of the pre-tax total.

4. Add your usual footer and print the worksheet. Save the workbook.

5. Make a copy of the worksheet, name it **Formulas**, and display the formulas. Size the columns and make other adjustments if needed to print the formula worksheet on one landscape page.

6. Save and close the workbook.

On Your Own

In these exercises you work on your own, as you would in a real-life work environment. Use the skills you've learned to accomplish the task—and be creative.

EXERCISE 5-26

Open **MultTable** and edit it into a workbook that is a division table. Apply borders and shading to make the worksheet easy to read. Print it in landscape orientation on one page. Add your usual footer. Save the workbook as *[your initials]*5-26 in your Lesson 5 folder. Print the worksheet. Make a copy of the sheet with formulas and print it. Close the workbook.

EXERCISE 5-27

Create a new workbook and save it as *[your initials]*5-27 in your Lesson 5 folder. In cell A1, key **Local Restaurants**. Enter three column titles to list the names, phone numbers, and cuisine ("Asian," "French," etc.). Key the names of five restaurants and add phone numbers and cuisine. Add a column at the right for **Average Cost per Meal**. Key a value for each restaurant and format the cells as currency with two decimals. Two rows below your last entry in column A, key **Tip Percentage**. Determine an acceptable tip percentage in your city and key it in column B on this row. Add another column to your data for **Meal with Tip**. In this column, multiply the cost by the percentage (it's an absolute reference). Apply formatting, borders, and shading so that your worksheet is consistent in its appearance. Print the worksheet, save the workbook, and close it.

EXERCISE 5-28

Develop a worksheet based on one of your interests or hobbies that contains some type of value(s). Use formulas that add, subtract, multiply, and divide the values in meaningful ways. Then use absolute and mixed references and change the order of precedence by using parentheses in formulas. Make sure that all the formulas are labeled appropriately. Make a formula worksheet. Add your usual footer. Save the worksheet as *[your initials]*5-28 in your Lesson 5 folder. Print both sheets and close the workbook.

Working with Math & Trig, Statistical, and Date & Time Functions

After completing this lesson, you will be able to:

1. **Use math & trig functions.**
2. **Use statistical functions.**
3. **Use date & time functions.**

 Estimated Time: 1½ hours

Excel has many categories of functions that perform common mathematical, statistical, financial, and other calculations. A *function* is a built-in formula.

Many functions do things automatically that would be difficult or time-consuming for you to do manually. For example, in a list of accounts with each customer's amount due, Excel can quickly calculate a total, find the largest amount due, or calculate an average amount due.

Using Math and Trig Functions

Excel functions are divided into categories. One of the large categories is Math & Trig. This category includes basic calculations such as SUM and INT, as well as many more sophisticated functions.

All functions have a *syntax,* which defines the necessary parts of the function and the order of those parts. Most functions follow a similar syntax, which in-cludes an equal sign and the name of the function, followed by parentheses. Inside the parentheses, you place arguments.

An *argument* is what the function needs to complete its calculation, usually one or more values or cell ranges. A few functions do not have arguments, but most have at least one argument. If a function has more than one argument, the arguments are sepaated by commas. A function's arguments can consist of:

- Cell references (individual cells or ranges)
- Constants (a number keyed in the formula)
- Another function (known as a nested function)
- Range names

FIGURE 6-1
Syntax for the
SUM function

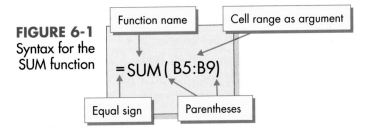

EXERCISE   6-1   **Use SUM and the Formula Bar**

SUM is a mathematical function in the Math & Trig category. It is a practical way to add long columns or rows of values. The SUM function ignores cells with:

- Text
- Error values such as #NAME?

 NOTE: Excel inserts the SUM function when you use the AutoSum button Σ ▾.

TABLE 6-1   **Examples of the SUM Function**

FUNCTION(ARGUMENT/S)	CELL DATA	RESULT
=SUM(A1:A3)	A1=10, A2=20, A3=30	60
=SUM(50,60)	None	110
=SUM(A1,250)	A1=25	275
=SUM(A1,B2,C1:C2)	A1=10, B2=20, C1=10, C2=30	70
=SUM(A1, B2)	A1=25, B2="Ice Cream"	25
=SUM (A1, B2)	A1=25, B2=#NAME?	25

1. Open **DownTime**.
2. Click cell B10.
3. Key **=sum(** to start the SUM function. An Argument ScreenTip opens to show you the syntax for the function.

FIGURE 6-2
SUM function and
Argument ScreenTip

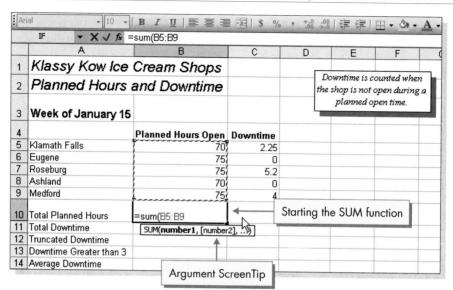

4. Click cell B5 and drag to select cells B5:B9. The function will sum the range B5:B9.

5. Press (Enter). The result is 365.

6. Click cell B10 and look in the formula bar. For the SUM function, Excel adds the closing parenthesis for you. This formula is the same as keying =b5+b6+b7+b8+b9.

EXERCISE   **6-2**   **Use Insert Function**

Although you can key functions in a cell, you can also use the Insert Function dialog box to choose the function. When you do, Excel opens a *Function Arguments dialog box* to help you complete the function. This is helpful, because each argument is described in the dialog box and you learn how to build formulas properly.

1. Click cell B11. You want to place the sum of the values from column C into cell B11.

2. Click the Insert Function button . The Insert Function dialog box opens.

3. Click the arrow next to the Or select a _category list. Choose Math & Trig.

> **TIP:** Functions are listed in alphabetical order.

4. In the Select a functio_n list, scroll to find SUM.

5. Click SUM to see its syntax and a description in the dialog box.

FIGURE 6-3
Insert Function
dialog box

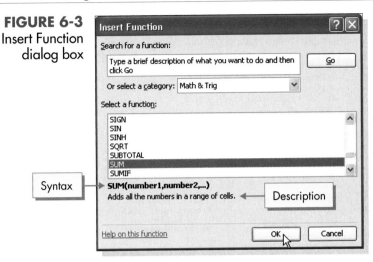

Syntax

Description

6. Click OK. The Function Arguments dialog box opens. In the Number1 box, Excel assumes that you want to sum the range just above cell B11.

7. Click and drag the dialog box down and to the right until you can see columns B and C (see Figure 6-4).

FIGURE 6-4
Function Arguments
dialog box

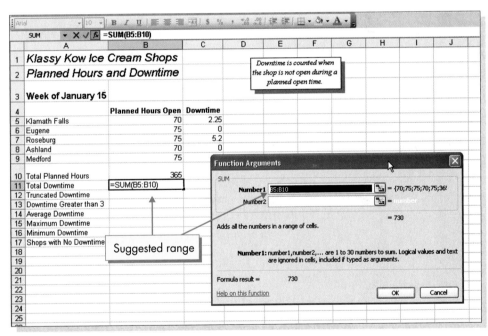

Suggested range

8. Click cell C5. A marquee appears around the cell, and its address is entered in the Number1 box in the Function Arguments dialog box.

 NOTE: If you click in the wrong cell or number box, reposition the pointer and click again in the correct location.

9. Click in the Number2 box and click cell C6. A marquee appears around the cell and the cell's address is shown. Notice that the formula appears in both the formula bar and the cell. When cells are not listed in a range, they are separated by commas in the SUM function.

10. Click in the Number3 box and click cell C7.

11. Click in the Number4 box and click cell C8.

12. Click in the Number5 box and click cell C9.

FIGURE 6-5
Function Arguments
dialog box with
cells entered
separately

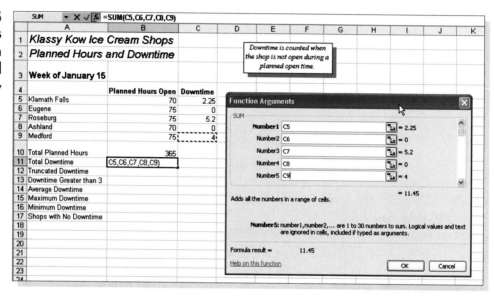

13. Press (Enter). The dialog box closes; the result (11.45) is displayed in the cell.

EXERCISE   6-3   Use TRUNC

The TRUNC function removes the decimal part of a number. You can specify if you want to keep a certain number of decimal positions, too.

1. Click cell B12. You are going to truncate the results in cell B11 so that they do not show a decimal.

2. Click the Insert Function button .

3. In the Search for a function box, key **trunc** and then press (Enter). The TRUNC function appears in the list.

NOTE: You can search for any function in any category.

4. Click OK. The Function Arguments dialog box opens. The insertion point is in the Number box.

5. Click cell B11. Its address appears in the Number box.

6. Click in the Num_digits box. Key **1** to truncate the value to show only one decimal position.

FIGURE 6-6
TRUNC function in
the Function
Arguments
dialog box

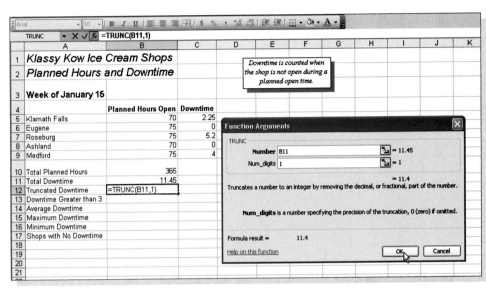

7. Click OK. The truncated value of cell B11 is 11.4.

EXERCISE **6-4** **Use SUMIF**

The SUMIF function adds cells only if they meet a condition that you set. In this case, you will determine the total number of down hours for those shops with downtime greater than three hours. The SUMIF function has two arguments, Range and Criteria. The range is the group of cells to be added. The criteria are the conditions that must be met for the cell to be included in the addition.

1. Click cell B13. Click the Insert Function button [fx].

2. Click the Or select a category arrow. Choose Math & Trig.

3. In the Select a function list, scroll to find SUMIF.

4. Click OK. The Function Arguments dialog box opens with the insertion point in the Range entry box.

5. Click cell C5 and drag to select the range C5:C9. As you drag, the Function Arguments dialog box collapses so that you can see your work better.

6. Release the mouse button. The dialog box expands, and the range you selected is entered in the Range box.

7. Click in the Criteria box. Key **>3** to set a rule that the value in the range C5:C9 must be greater than 3 to be included in the sum.

FIGURE 6-7
SUMIF function in
the Function
Arguments
dialog box

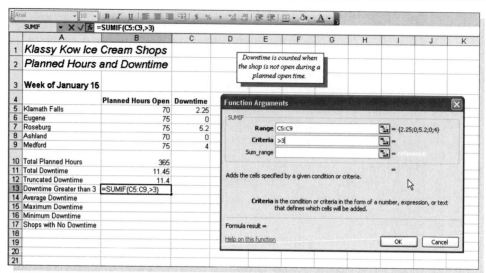

8. Click OK. The result is 9.2 because only cells C7 and C9 are included.

Using Statistical Functions

An even larger category of Excel functions is the Statistical group. Some of them are useful even if you are not a statistician.

EXERCISE **6-5** **Use the AVERAGE Function**

The AVERAGE function calculates the arithmetic mean of a range of cells. The *arithmetic mean* adds the values in the cells and then divides by the number of values. The AVERAGE function ignores:

- Text
- Blank or empty cells (but not zeros)
- Error values such as #NAME?
- Logical values

 NOTE: A logical value is "True," "False," "Yes," or "No."

1. Click cell B14. You want to place the average of the values from column C into cell B14.

2. Click the Insert Function button 𝑓𝑥.

TABLE 6-2   **Examples of the AVERAGE Function**

FUNCTION(ARGUMENT/S)	CELL DATA	RESULT
=AVERAGE(A1:A3)	A1=10, A2=20, A3=30	20
=AVERAGE(50,60)	None	55
=AVERAGE(A1,250)	A1=25	137.5
=AVERAGE(A1,B2,C1:C2)	A1=10, B2=20, C1=10, C2=30	17.5
=AVERAGE(A1, B2)	A1=25, B2="Ice Cream"	25
=AVERAGE(A1, B2)	A1=25, B2=#NAME?	25
=AVERAGE(A1:A3)	A1=20, A2=0, A3=40	20
=AVERAGE(A1:A3)	A1=20, A2=Empty, A3=40	30

3. Choose Statistical in the Or select a category list.

4. In the Select a function list, locate AVERAGE.

5. Click AVERAGE to see its syntax and description. Click OK.

6. Drag the dialog box until you can see column C. The Number1 box shows the range directly above cell B12.

7. Click cell C5 and drag to select cells C5:C9. As you drag, the Function Arguments dialog box collapses.

8. Release the mouse button. The dialog box expands, and the range you selected is entered in the Number1 box.

9. Click OK. The result is formatted as a General number.

10. Press Ctrl+1 and click the Number tab.

11. Choose Number in the Category list. Click the Down button to set 0 decimals.

12. Click OK. The value is rounded down to the next whole number.

TIP: When you round a decimal to a whole number, any decimal value that is 0.5 or greater is rounded up to the next whole number. For example, 3.6 is rounded up to 4.

EXERCISE   6-6   Use the MIN and MAX Functions

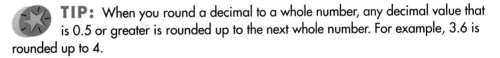

The MIN and MAX functions are statistical functions that show the minimum (smallest) value and the maximum (largest) value in a range. The MIN and MAX functions ignore:

● Text

● Blank or empty cells (but not zeros)

- Error values such as #NAME?
- Logical values

TABLE 6-3 Examples of the MIN and MAX Functions

FUNCTION(ARGUMENT/S)	CELL DATA	RESULT
=MAX(A1:A3)	A1=10, A2=20, A3=30	30
=MAX(50,60)	None	60
=MIN(A1,250)	A1=25	25
=MIN(A1,B2,C1:C2)	A1=10, B2=20, C1=10, C2=30	10
=MAX(A1, B2)	A1=25, B2="Ice Cream"	25
=MAX(A1, B2)	A1=25, B2=#NAME?	25
=MIN(A1:A3)	A1=20, A2=0, A3=40	0
=MIN(A1:A3)	A1=20, A2=Empty, A3=40	20

1. Click cell B15. You want to place the largest value from column C into cell B15.
2. Click the Insert Function button ⨍.
3. Choose Statistical in the Or select a category list.
4. In the Select a function list, double-click MAX. The dialog box opens and the Number1 box automatically shows the address of the cells directly above.
5. Arrange the Function Arguments dialog box so that you can see column C.
6. Click cell C5 and drag to select cells C5:C9. The dialog box collapses.
7. Release the mouse button. The range is shown as Number1.
8. Click OK.
9. Click cell B16 and key =min(to start the MIN function. An Argument ScreenTip appears to help you complete the function. (See Figure 6-8.)
10. Drag to select cells C5:C9 and press (Enter).
11. Click OK.

FIGURE 6-8
Argument ScreenTip

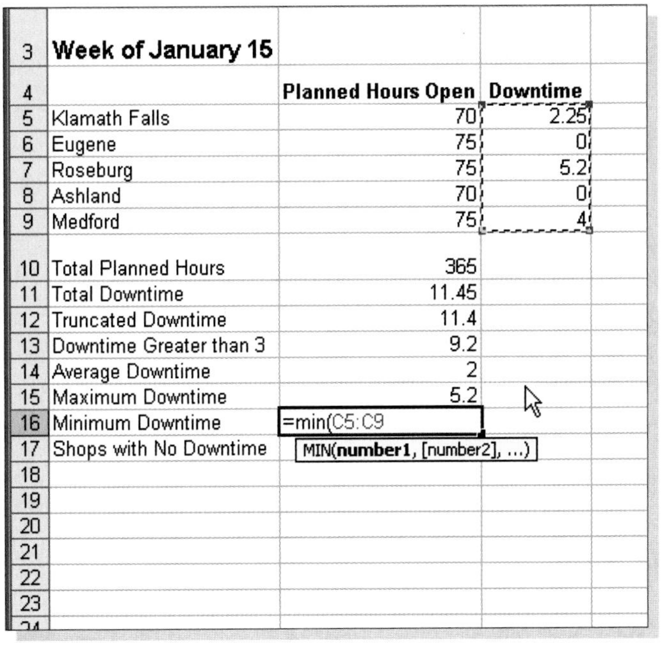

3	Week of January 15		
4		Planned Hours Open	Downtime
5	Klamath Falls	70	2.25
6	Eugene	75	0
7	Roseburg	75	5.2
8	Ashland	70	0
9	Medford	75	4
10	Total Planned Hours	365	
11	Total Downtime	11.45	
12	Truncated Downtime	11.4	
13	Downtime Greater than 3	9.2	
14	Average Downtime	2	
15	Maximum Downtime	5.2	
16	Minimum Downtime	=min(C5:C9	
17	Shops with No Downtime	MIN(**number1**, [number2], ...)	
18			
19			
20			
21			
22			
23			
24			

EXERCISE   **6-7**   Use the COUNT Function

The COUNT function tallies the number of values in a range. The COUNT function ignores:

- Text
- Blank or empty cells (but not zeros)
- Error values such as #NAME?
- Logical values

TABLE 6-4   **Examples of the COUNT Function**

FUNCTION(ARGUMENT/S)	CELL DATA	RESULT
=COUNT(A1:A3)	A1=Empty, A2=20, A3=30	2
=COUNT(A1:A3)	A1=30, A2=Empty, A3=#NAME?	1
=COUNT(A1:A3)	A1=25, A2="Ice Cream," A3=3	2
=COUNT(13, 21, 111)	None	3
=COUNT(A1, B2, C1:C2)	A1=25, B2=0, C1="Hello," C2=4	3

In order to see how the COUNT function works, copy the Downtime column so that it is duplicated in column D. You will use both columns.

1. Click cell C4 and drag to select cells C4:C9.

2. Hold down Ctrl and point at the right border of the selected range.

3. Drag the range to cells D4:D9 and release the mouse button. Then release the Ctrl key.

4. Delete the contents of cells D6 and D8. The cells should be blank.

5. Double-click cell A17. Edit mode starts.

6. Double-click No and press Delete. Delete the extra space and press Enter. The label now indicates shops with downtime.

7. Click cell B17 and click the Insert Function button _fx_.

8. Choose Statistical. In the Select a function list, double-click COUNT.

9. Select cells C5:C9. The range appears in the Value1 box.

10. Click OK. The cells with zero (0) are included in the count.

11. Click cell B17 and click the Insert Function button _fx_. The dialog box shows your current function with the Value1 range highlighted.

12. Select cells D5:D9. Click OK. Blank cells are not included in the count.

EXERCISE **6-8**   **Use the COUNTA Function**

The COUNTA function tallies values as well as labels in a range. The COUNTA function ignores:

- Blank or empty cells (but not zeros)
- Error values such as #NAME?
- Logical values

TABLE 6-5   **Examples of the COUNTA Function**

FUNCTION(ARGUMENT/S)	CELL DATA	RESULT
=COUNTA(A1:A3)	A1=Empty, A2=20, A3=30	2
=COUNTA(A1:A3)	A1=30, A2=Empty, A3=#NAME?	1
=COUNTA(A1:A3)	A1=25, A2="Ice Cream," A3=3	3
=COUNTA(13, 21, 111)	None	3
=COUNTA(A1, B2, C1:C2)	A1=25, B2=0, C1="Hello," C2=4	4

> **NOTE:** The Count option in AutoCalculate shows the same results as the COUNTA function. AutoCalculate's Count Nums option shows the same results as the COUNT function.

1. Key **Number of Oregon Shops** in cell A18.

2. Click cell B18 and key **=count(** to start the function.

3. Click cell A5 in the worksheet and drag to select cells A5:A9. Your selected range will replace value1 in the ScreenTip.

FIGURE 6-9
Keying the COUNT
function

	A	B	C
1	*Klassy Kow Ice Cream Shops*		
2	*Planned Hours and Downtime*		
3	**Week of January 15**		
4		**Planned Hours Open**	**Downtime**
5	Klamath Falls	70	2.25
6	Eugene	75	0
7	Roseburg	75	5.2
8	Ashland	70	0
9	Medford	75	4
10	Total Planned Hours	365	
11	Total Downtime	11.45	
12	Truncated Downtime	11.4	
13	Downtime Greater than 3	9.2	
14	Average Downtime	2	
15	Maximum Downtime	5.2	
16	Minimum Downtime	0	
17	Shops with Downtime	3	
18	Number of Oregon Shops	=count(A5:A9	
19		COUNT(**value1**, [value2], ...)	
20			
21			
22			
23			
24			

4. Press (Enter). The result is 0, because the Count function ignores text.

5. Double-click cell B18.

6. Position the insertion point and key **a** after COUNT.

7. Press (Enter). The new function COUNTA includes labels; there are five Oregon shops.

8. Click cell B18 and look in the formula bar.

9. Save the workbook as *[your initials]*6-8 in a folder for Lesson 6.

Using Date and Time Functions

Excel's Date & Time functions can be used to display the current date and time, determine ages, and calculate hours worked, days passed, and future dates.

When you work with dates and times, you need to understand how Excel uses a *serial number* system. A serial number is a date shown as a value. Excel's date system sets January 1, 1900, as 1 and January 2, 1900, as 2; it then counts the days from that point all the way to December 31, 9999.

EXERCISE **Use the TODAY( ) Function**

The TODAY( ) function displays the current date, using the computer's internal clock. This function has no arguments, and Excel formats the results in a standard date style. The TODAY( ) function is described as *volatile,* which means that Excel recalculates the results each time the workbook is opened.

1. With *[your initials]*6-8 open, click cell A20.
2. Key **=today()** and press (Enter). The current date is shown in the cell in the default date format.

 NOTE: Excel capitalizes function names after you complete the cell.

3. Click cell A20 and look at the formula bar. The function is shown in the formula bar, and the result is in the cell.
4. Press (Ctrl)+(1) to open the Format Cells dialog box.
5. In the Number tab, choose General.
6. Click OK. The serial number that represents today's date is shown.

 7. Click the Undo button. The format change is reversed.

EXERCISE **6-10** **Key and Format Dates**

You can key dates in a variety of ways. As you do, Excel assigns the closest matching date format to the date you key, so the format on screen may not match what you key. You can, however, use one of many built-in date formats or create your own format.

TABLE 6-6 | **Sample Keyed Dates and Initial Screen Display**

KEYED CHARACTERS	SCREEN DISPLAY
1-1-05	1/1/2005
1/1/05	1/1/2005
1-jan-05	1-Jan-05
january 1, 2005	1-Jan-05
jan 1, 2005	1-Jan-05

1. With *[your initials]*6-8 open, press Shift+F11 to insert a new worksheet.

2. Rename the sheet **Dates**. Place this sheet to the right of the Oregon sheet.

3. In cell A1, key **01/01/05** and press Enter. The date is formatted without leading zeros and shows the year with four digits.

4. In cell A2, key **1-jan-05** and press Enter. Excel recognizes the date and formats it in its default style.

 TIP: You generally do not need to capitalize months; Excel will do so automatically because months (and days) are included in its custom lists.

5. In cell A3, key **january 1, 2005** and press Enter.

6. In cell A4, key **1-1-05** and press Enter. Excel recognizes each date you key and formats it.

7. Click cell A1 and drag to select cells A1:A4. Press Ctrl+1.

8. Click the Number tab and choose Date in the Category list.

9. Choose March 14, 2001 in the Type list.

10. Click OK. All the dates are formatted in the new style.

11. Click cell A1 and drag to select cells A1:A4. Press Delete to clear the contents of these cells.

EXERCISE 6-11 **Use Fill Across Worksheets**

In addition to the Copy and Paste commands, Excel has another way for you to copy data from one worksheet to another, Fill Across Worksheets. To use this command, you first select the worksheet with the data and the one(s) where the data should be copied.

1. Click the Oregon worksheet tab. It is the active sheet.

2. Hold down the Ctrl key and click the Dates worksheet tab. Both worksheet tabs are shaded or active. The title bar shows [Group].

3. On the Oregon sheet, select cells A1:A9. These are the cells that will be copied to the Dates sheet.

4. From the Edit menu, choose Fill. Its submenu opens. (See Figure 6-10.)

5. Choose Across Worksheets. The Fill Across Worksheets dialog box has options to copy everything, only the data, or only the formatting.

6. Choose All and click OK.

7. Click the Dates worksheet tab. The data and most of the formatting has been copied.

8. Make column A 21.57 (156 pixels) wide.

9. Click cell A2 and key **Date and Initial Problem Time**. Press Enter.

FIGURE 6-10
Using Fill Across
Worksheets

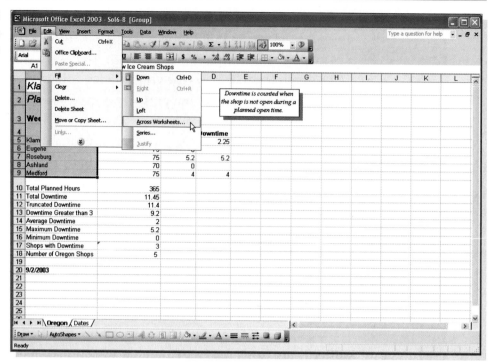

EXERCISE **6-12** **Create a Custom Date Format**

To create your own date format, you key formatting codes in the Custom category. You can see formatting codes and samples in the Format Cells dialog box.

1. Click cell B4 and key **1/15/05**. Press Enter.

2. Click cell B4 and press Ctrl+1.

3. Click the Number tab and choose Date in the Category list.

4. Scroll through the Type list. There is no preset format to show the date, the month spelled out, and a two-digit year (1 May 05).

5. Click Custom in the Category list. The Type list shows the codes for a variety of formats, not just dates. You can choose one as a starting point to build your own format.

6. Scroll the Type list to find d-mmm.

7. Click the code to select it. The Sample shows the date with that format.

8. Click in the Type box above the Type list.

9. Delete the hyphen and press Spacebar.

10. Edit the code to show dd mmmm y. Two **dd**'s show the date with a leading zero. Four **mmmm**'s spell out the month. A single **y** shows a two-digit year.

11. Look at the Sample.

FIGURE 6-11
Creating a custom
date format

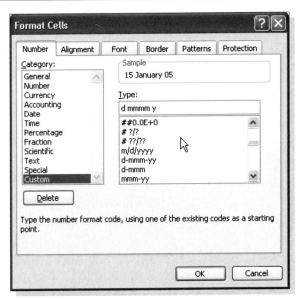

12. Click OK. The date is reformatted.
13. Use the Fill handle to extend the date in row 4 to January 19 in cell F4.
14. Format the dates as bold. AutoFit each column to show the dates.

EXERCISE **6-13** **Key and Format Times**

When you key a time in a format that Excel recognizes, it formats it with a default style.

1. Click cell B5 and key **11 am**.
2. Press Enter. The time is shown assuming no minutes and no seconds. AM is capitalized, too.
3. Click cell B5 and look at the formula bar.
4. Click cell B6 and key **4:30** and press Enter.
5. Click cell B6 and look at the time in the formula bar. If you do not key **am** or **pm**, Excel assumes the morning.
6. In cell B6 key **4:30 pm** and press Enter. Excel may format the time using a 24-hour clock.
7. In cell B7 key **13:30** and press Enter. Excel shows the time using the 24-hour clock.
8. In cell B8 key **2:45 pm**, and in cell B9 key **14:30**.
9. Click cell B5 and drag to select cells B5:B9.
10. Press Ctrl+1. Click the Number tab and choose Time in the Category list.
11. Scroll the Type list. Then choose 1:30 PM and click OK.

EXERCISE   **6-14**   Use the NOW( ) Function

The NOW( ) function is similar to the TODAY( ) function. It uses the computer's clock to show the current date and time.

1. Click cell A11. Key **=now(** and press Enter. Excel supplies the closing parenthesis. The default format may not include the time.
2. Click cell A11 and press Ctrl+1.
3. Click the Number tab and choose Time in the Category list.
4. Scroll through the Type list. Then choose 3/14/01 1:30 PM and click OK. The function now shows the current date and time.

EXERCISE   **6-15**   Create a Custom Time Format

1. Click cell A11 and press Ctrl+1.
2. Click Custom in the Category list.
3. Scroll the Type list to find m/d/yyyy h:mm.
4. Click the code to select it. The Sample shows the date and time with that format.
5. Click in the Type box before the first m.
6. Edit the code to show mmm d, yyyy--h:mm AM/PM. Be sure to insert the spaces, the comma, and the hyphens. Check the Sample box to verify your format as you build it.

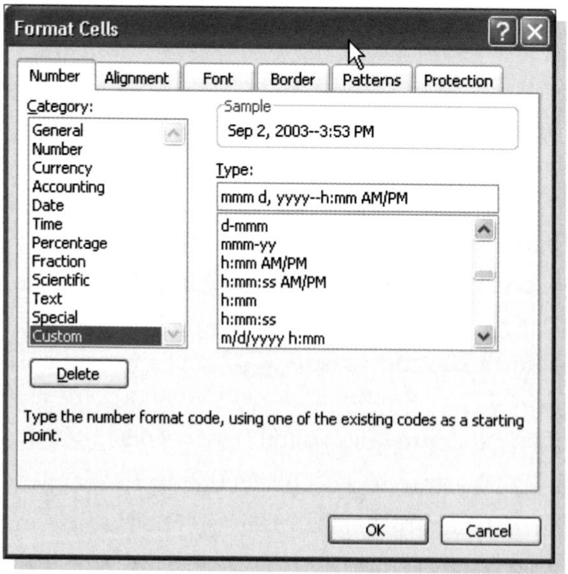

FIGURE 6-12
Creating a custom
time format

7. Click OK. The time is reformatted.

8. Press F12 and save the workbook as *[your initials]*6-15 in your Lesson 6 folder.

 NOTE: For a custom footer, include your name, the tab and filename, and the date. Include other information if your instructor asks you to do so.

9. Add your usual footer to both worksheets and print each one.

10. Save and close the workbook.

USING ONLINE HELP

You learned about creating custom date and time formats in this lesson. Use the Type a question for help box to obtain additional information about formatting codes.

Use Help to view additional information about format codes:

1. Click in the Type a question for help box and key **format codes**. Press Enter.

2. Click the topic Number format codes in the Search Results dialog box.

3. Click Dates and times. Scroll and read the information.

4. Close the Help window when you have finished. Close the Search Results dialog box.

LESSON Summary

➤ Excel has several categories of date, time, mathematical, and statistical functions. You can key them in the cell or use the Insert Function button *fx*.

➤ Functions have a syntax that must be followed. For most functions, this includes an equal sign, the name of the function, and parentheses. Inside the parentheses, you show the function's arguments.

➤ The SUM function adds the cells or values indicated in its argument.

➤ The TRUNC function removes the decimal part of a number.

➤ The SUMIF function adds cells or values only if they meet the criteria specified in the argument.

➤ The AVERAGE function calculates the arithmetic mean.

➤ The MIN function displays the smallest value in a range. The MAX function displays the largest value in a range.

➤ The COUNT function counts the number of values in a range. The COUNTA function does the same thing as the COUNT function but includes labels.

➤ The TODAY and NOW functions show the current date and time. Both functions can be formatted using preset or custom formats.

➤ You can copy data from one worksheet to another using the Fill Across Worksheets command.

LESSON 6 Command Summary

FEATURE	BUTTON	MENU	KEYBOARD
Custom format		Format, Cells	Ctrl + 1
Fill across worksheets		Edit, Fill, Across Worksheets	
Insert Function	fx	Insert, Function	

Concepts Review

TRUE/FALSE QUESTIONS

Each of the following statements is either true or false. Indicate your choice by circling T or F.

T F   **1.** To complete a function, you must include its arguments.

T F   **2.** The syntax of a function defines its category.

T F   **3.** The SUM function calculates a text value as 1.

T F   **4.** The first character for all functions is a left parenthesis.

T F   **5.** The TODAY function does not have arguments.

T F   **6.** Custom formats include **?** and ***** to show days and months.

T F   **7.** Most statistical functions ignore text in their calculations.

T F   **8.** You can copy data from one worksheet to another with the Fill handle.

SHORT ANSWER QUESTIONS

Write the correct answer in the space provided.

1. What is the keyboard shortcut to open the Format Cells dialog box?

_____

2. How can you select more than one worksheet tab?

_____

3. Name the function that adds cell values only if they meet your criteria.

_____

4. What function displays the arithmetic mean of a range of cells?

_____

5. What does Excel do if a function is volatile?

_____

6. What term is used to describe the information between parentheses in a function?

_____

7. What button displays a list of function categories and names?

_____

8. What function would display the highest sales amount in a column?

_____

CRITICAL THINKING

Answer these questions on a separate page. There are no right or wrong answers. Support your answers with examples from your own experience, if possible.

1. What are some of the Math & Trig functions that you did not use in this lesson? How might they be helpful in school work or on the job?

2. What type of calculations do you think can be accomplished with date and time functions?

Skills Review

EXERCISE 6-16

Use Math and Trig functions.

1. Open **HolidayPay**. Save it as *[your initials]***6-16** in your Lesson 6 folder.

2. Key math and trig functions by following these steps:

   a. Click cell F11.

   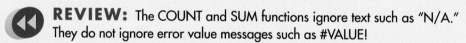 **REVIEW:** The COUNT and SUM functions ignore text such as "N/A." They do not ignore error value messages such as #VALUE!

   b. Key **=sum(** to start the function.
   c. Click cell F4 and drag to select cells F4:F10. Press Enter.
   d. In cell B11, key **=counta(** to start the function.
   e. Click cell A4 and drag to select cells A4:A10. Press Enter.

3. In cell A11, key **Number of Employees** and make it bold.

4. Make row 11 22.50 (30 pixels) high. Widen column A as needed.

5. In cell G4, key a formula to multiply the hours worked by the holiday rate. Copy the formula through row 10.

6. Format the values in column F to show two decimal places.

7. Use Insert Function to insert math and trig functions by following these steps:

   a. Click cell G11.

 b. Click the Insert Function button .

c. Click the Or select a category arrow. Choose Math & Trig.

d. In the Select a function list, scroll to find SUM. Click OK.

e. Check that the assumed range to be summed is G4:G10.

 NOTE: If the assumed range is not correct, click and drag to select the correct range.

f. Click OK. Widen column A as needed.

g. Click cell B12.

 h. Click the Insert Function button .

i. In the Search for a function box, key **countif** and press Enter. Click OK.

j. With the insertion point in the Range entry box, click cell G4 and drag to select the range G4:G10.

 NOTE: The COUNTIF function is similar to the SUMIF function.

k. Click in the Criteria box.

l. Key **>500** to count the number of employees who made more than $500.

m. Click OK.

8. In cell A12, key **Over $500** and make it bold.

9. Select cells A2:G2 and center them across the selection.

10. Add Top and Double Bottom borders to cells F11:G11.

11. Press Ctrl+Home. In the Page Setup dialog box, add your footer.

12. Print the worksheet.

13. Make a copy of the worksheet and name the tab **Formulas**.

14. Press Ctrl+~. Adjust the column widths but do not worry about the titles in the first two rows.

 NOTE: Labels that are centered across a selection are expanded when formulas are displayed.

15. Print the formula worksheet so that it fits on a single landscape page.

16. Save and close the workbook.

EXERCISE 6-17

Use Math and Trig and Statistical functions.

1. Open **Insurance**. Save it as *[your initials]*6-17 in your Lesson 6 folder.

2. Key math and trig and statistical functions by following these steps:

a. Click cell D13.

b. Key **=count(** to start the function.

c. Click cell D4 and drag to select cells D4:D11. Press Enter.

d. In cell D14, key **=sum(** to start the function.

REVIEW: For many functions, you do not need to type the ending parenthesis.

    e. Select cells D4:D11 and press Enter.

3. Use Insert Function to enter statistical functions by following these steps:

   a. In cell D15, click the Insert Function button fx.
  b. Choose Statistical and COUNTA. Click OK.
  c. Position the Function Arguments dialog box so that you can see column C.
  d. Select cells C4:C11. Click OK.

 REVIEW: COUNTA includes labels and values in its total.

   e. Click cell D16 and click the Insert Function button fx.
  f. In the Or select a category list, choose Most Recently Used and COUNTA. Click OK.

 NOTE: The Most Recently Used list shows the functions you have used during the work session.

  g. Select cells A4:A11. Click OK.

4. Format cells D13:D16 as Times New Roman.

5. Click cell A1. Apply the List 2 AutoFormat but turn off the Font, Alignment, and Width/Height changes.

6. Select cells A1:A2 and center them across the selection.

7. Add your footer, change the left margin to 1.75 inches, and print the worksheet.

8. Press Ctrl+Home. Save and close the workbook.

EXERCISE 6-18

Use Date and Time functions. Use Math and Trig functions.

1. Use the **ChkBk** template to create a new workbook. Save it as *[your initials]*6-18 in your Lesson 6 folder.

 REVIEW: Copy the template to the appropriate folder for your computer. Then choose General Templates in the New from Template section of the New Workbook task pane.

2. Key a date function by following these steps:
  a. Click cell A5.
  b. Key =**today()** and press Enter.
  c. Click cell A6 and key = to start a formula.

3. Click cell A5 to enter the cell reference in the formula.

4. Key **+5** to add five days to the date. Press Enter. The new date is five days after today.

5. Use the Fill handle to copy the formula in cell A6 through cell A12. Widen column A to show the dates. Right-align the dates.

 TIP: You can use the Fill handle for the check numbers.

6. Key the data for columns B – D as shown here.

FIGURE 6-13

	Check #	Payee	Credit Amount	Deposit	Balance
6	1002	*[your first and last name]*	1250		
7	1003	Sutter, Howe, & Jones	2500		
8	1004	Holberg Markets	575		
9	1005	*[your school name]*	435		
10	1006	Hacienda Martinez	575		
11	1007	Smithfield Stores	435		
12	1008	Grocerytown Enterprises	1200		

7. Key math and trig and statistical functions by following these steps:

 a. Click cell D14.

 b. Key **=sum(** to start the function.

 c. Click cell D5 and drag to select cells D5:D12. Press Enter.

 d. In cell B14, key **=count(** to start the function.

 e. Click cell B5 and drag to select cells B5:B12. Press Enter.

8. Select and hide columns E and F.

9. Add your footer and print the worksheet.

10. Save and close the workbook.

EXERCISE 6-19

Use Date and Time functions. Format times and dates.

1. Create a new workbook and save it as *[your initials]*6-19 in your Lesson 6 folder.

2. In cell A1, key **Klassy Kow Ice Cream Shops** and format it as 16-point Arial.

3. In cell A2, key **Olympia Shop** and format it as 14-point Arial.

4. Key **Date** in cell A3, **Open Time** in cell B3, and **Close Time** in cell C3.

5. Make these labels bold and center-align them. Make all three columns 12.14 (90 pixels) wide.

6. Use date functions by following these steps:

   a. Click cell A4.
   b. Key **=today()** and press (Enter).
   c. Click cell A5 and key **=** to start the formula.
   d. Click cell A4 and key **+1** to add one day. Press (Enter).

7. Use the Fill handle to copy the formula in cell A5 through cell A10.

8. Format dates by following these steps:

   a. Click cell A4 and drag to select cells A4:A10.
   b. Press (Ctrl)+(1).
   c. Click the Number tab and choose Date in the Category list.
   d. Choose March 14, 2001 in the Type list. Click OK.

9. Widen column A to show the dates if necessary.

10. Key the times as shown in the figure.

FIGURE 6-14

	Open Time	Close Time
4	9 am	10 pm
5	10 am	11 pm
6	10 am	12 am
7	11 am	12 am
8	11 am	9 pm
9	11 am	11 pm
10	11 am	11 pm

11. Format times by following these steps:

   a. Click cell B4 and drag to select cells B4:C10.
   b. Press (Ctrl)+(1).
   c. Click the Number tab and choose Custom in the Category list.

d. Choose h:mm in the Type list.

e. Click in the Type box.

f. Edit the code to show h AM/PM. Click OK.

12. Add your footer, change the left margin to 2.5 inches, and print the worksheet.

13. Press Ctrl + Home.

 NOTE: Dates are shown as serial numbers in a formula view. Times are shown as a fraction of a 24-hour day.

14. Make a copy of the worksheet and change the tab name to **Formulas**. Display the formulas and adjust the column widths. Print the formula worksheet to fit one landscape page.

15. Save and close the workbook.

Lesson Applications

Use Date functions. Format times and dates. Fill across a worksheet.

1. Create a new workbook using the **CSCalls** template. Save the workbook as *[your initials]***6-20**.

2. Key a formula in cell A5 that adds one day to the TODAY function in cell A3.

3. Key a formula in cell A6 that adds one day to the date in cell A5. Copy the formula in cell A6 down to row 25.

4. Select cells B5:B25 and format them to show the time using the 1:30 PM preset format.

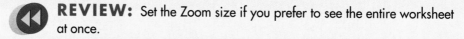 **REVIEW:** Set the Zoom size if you prefer to see the entire worksheet at once.

5. Key the times and representative names as shown. Use AutoComplete where appropriate.

FIGURE 6-15

5	9:30 am	Anderson
6	10:25 am	Olmstead
7	12:30 pm	Rogers
8	1:30 pm	Devantes
9	10:45 am	LaPluie
10	2:30 pm	Anderson
11	11:30 am	Anderson
12	8:45 am	Olmstead
13	4:30 pm	LaPluie
14	10 am	Devantes
15	8 am	Devantes

continues

FIGURE 6-15 *continued*

16	3:30 pm	Rogers
17	9:45 am	LaPluie
18	10:15 am	Olmstead
19	12 pm	Devantes
20	12:15 pm	Olmstead
21	11:15 am	LaPluie
22	11:45 am	Olmstead
23	2:25 pm	Devantes
24	9 am	Anderson
25	10:25 am	Olmstead

6. Select all the cells with data on the **Week1** worksheet.

 TIP: You can use the ⌖Shift⌗ key to select two worksheet tabs that are next to each other.

7. Hold down ⌖Ctrl⌗ and click the **Sheet2** tab. Fill all data across the worksheet(s).

8. Click **Sheet3** to deselect the first two sheets. Adjust the column width to show the date on **Sheet2**. Rename **Sheet2** as **Week2**. Delete **Sheet3**.

9. On the Week2 sheet, click cell A3. Edit the formula to add 7 days to the function.

10. Make row 4 30.00 (40 pixels) high. Make rows 5–25 18.75 (25 pixels) high.

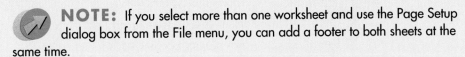 **NOTE:** If you select more than one worksheet and use the Page Setup dialog box from the File menu, you can add a footer to both sheets at the same time.

11. Click the **Week1** tab. Hold down ⌖Ctrl⌗ and click the **Week2** tab. From the File menu, choose Page Setup. Add your custom footer.

12. From the File menu, choose Print. Print the entire workbook.

13. Save and close the workbook.

EXERCISE 6-21

Use Statistical functions. Use Fill Across Worksheet to copy data.

1. Open **ShopPart** and save it as *[your initials]*6-21 in your Lesson 6 folder.

2. In cell A21 on the **California** sheet, key **Number of Shops**. Make the row 22.50 (30 pixels) high.

 3. In cell B21, click the Insert Function button . Find and choose COUNTA. Select cells B7:B20 as the Value1 argument.

4. Copy the formula to cells C21:D21. The function does not distinguish between Yes and No but just counts the labels.

5. Select cells B7:D20 and press Ctrl+H. In the Find what entry box, key **no** and press Tab. In the Replace with box, do not key anything. This will replace "No" with nothing, creating empty cells.

6. Click Find Next. Click Replace. The first occurrence of No is now an empty cell.

   ⭐ **TIP:** For multiple Find and Replace tasks, look at the first Find and Replace to make sure it is what you want. If it is, you can then click Replace All.

7. Click Replace All. Click OK and close the Find and Replace dialog box. The counts are updated.

8. Center cells B21:D21.

9. Repeat these steps on each of the other three worksheets in this workbook. Be sure to key the label for the row and match its font to the California sheet.

10. In cell C3 on the California sheet, key your first and last name. Select cell C3 and hold down Shift while clicking the Washington tab. Fill all across the worksheets. Click each worksheet tab to verify that your name is in cell C3.

11. From the File menu, choose Print. Print the entire workbook.

12. Save and close the workbook.

EXERCISE 6-22

Use Math & Trig functions.

1. Open **ORSundaes** and save it as *[your initials]*6-22 in your Lesson 6 folder.

2. Key the following values in cells C4:C13.

FIGURE 6-16

	Location	Sundaes Sold
4	Ashland	1000
5	Eugene	1500
6	Klamath Falls	2250
7	Medford	1540
8	Roseburg	1250
9	Ashland	1200
10	Eugene	1650
11	Klamath Falls	2100
12	Medford	1020
13	Roseburg	950

3. Key the following values in cells C15:C19.

FIGURE 6-17

15	Ashland	900
16	Eugene	650
17	Klamath Falls	800
18	Medford	620
19	Roseburg	550

4. In cell H6, click the Insert Function button [fx]. Choose AVERAGE and use cells C4:C8 as Number1.

5. Display the Trace Error button menu and ignore the error.

6. Compute the average sales for medium and large sundaes in cells H7 and H8. Remove all Trace Error buttons.

7. In cell H9, key **=sum(** to start the formula. Select cells C4:C8 and press Enter.

8. Edit the formula in cell H9 to multiply the sum by the price in cell A5. Use an absolute reference for the price.

 TIP: You can copy the formula in cell H9 and then edit the cell addresses for SUM as well as for the price.

9. Repeat these steps to determine revenue for medium and large sundaes.

10. In cell H13, add the three revenues to find a total.

11. Delete row 14. It is an unnecessary blank row.

12. Format the values in column C and cells H6:H8 as 12-point Times New Roman, Comma style, with no decimal places.

13. Format cells H9:H11 and H13 as 12-point Times New Roman and Currency, with two decimal places.

14. Size columns so all the data is visible.

15. Add your footer. Change the left margin to 1.25 inches. Print the sheet.

16. Make a copy of the worksheet and change the tab name to **SundaesFormulas**. Display the formulas. Make columns D, F, and G very narrow. AutoFit the other columns and disregard the labels in cells A1:A2. Print the sheet.

17. Save and close the workbook.

EXERCISE 6-23   ✚   *Challenge Yourself*

Use date arithmetic.

1. Open **SalaryAdj**. Save it as *[your initials]*6-23 in your Lesson 6 folder.

2. Insert a new column before the current column D. Key **Date Eligible** as the title for this column.

3. In cell D5, key a formula to determine the date eligible for a salary adjustment. Excel uses days in all its date arithmetic. The formula should add the appropriate number of days to the hire date to determine when the employee is eligible.

4. Format the results to match the date format in column D. Then copy the formula for the other employees. Make any other adjustments as needed.

5. Add your footer and print the worksheet.

6. Copy the worksheet and name the copy sheet **Formulas**. Display the formulas and fit the columns as necessary. Print the formulas on one portrait page.

7. Save and close the workbook.

On Your Own

In these exercises you work on your own, as you would in a real-life work environment. Use the skills you've learned to accomplish the task—and be creative.

EXERCISE 6-24

Create a new workbook and save it as *[your initials]*6-24 in your Lesson 6 folder. Key **Weekday per Date** as a main title. In column A, key yesterday's date using mm/dd/yy format. In column B on the same row, key yesterday's day of the week (Monday, Tuesday, etc.). Select both cells and use the Fill handle to extend the dates to a month from yesterday. Adjust row heights and apply borders and shading to format your worksheet. Add your footer. Print the worksheet, save the workbook, and close it.

EXERCISE 6-25

Develop a new worksheet that you can use to illustrate two of the Date & Time functions not covered in this lesson. Look at the functions in the category to determine what they do, or use the Help screens. In your worksheet, include labels that help explain what you are doing. Apply formatting, borders, and shading so that your worksheet looks professional. Save the workbook as *[your initials]*6-25 in your Lesson 6 folder. Add the footer, print the worksheet, save the workbook, and close it.

EXERCISE 6-26

Open **HolidayPay**. Delete column G. Key new labels below row 10 so that you can show these calculations: average regular rate, average rate increase, and average hours worked. Determine how to format your work or use an AutoFormat. Save the worksheet as *[your initials]*6-26 in your Lesson 6 folder. Add your footer and print the worksheet. Display the formulas and print the worksheet to fit one landscape page. Close the workbook without saving.

LESSON 7

Using Logical and Financial Functions

After completing this lesson, you will be able to:

1. Use the IF function.
2. Use AND, OR, and NOT functions.
3. Work with styles.
4. Work with page breaks.
5. Use the PMT and FV functions.
6. Use the DB function.

 Estimated Time: 1½ hours

In addition to Math & Trig, Statistical, and Date & Time functions, Excel has several other categories of functions. You will work with two different categories of functions in this lesson—Logical and Financial functions.

A *logical function* is a formula that calculates if an expression is true. There are six logical functions: IF, AND, OR, NOT, TRUE, and FALSE. Except for the IF function, a logical function shows the word "TRUE" or "FALSE" as a result.

A *financial function* performs a business calculation that involves money. These include how to figure loan payments and how to determine depreciation.

Using the IF Function

With the IF function, your worksheet has basic analysis and decision-making capabilities. When working with accounts receivable, for example, you can use a function to determine if a late fee should be assessed and the amount of the late fee.

The IF function has three arguments and follows the form "If X, then Y; otherwise Z." X, Y, and Z represent the arguments.

The syntax for the IF function is:

=IF(logical_test, value_if_true, value_if_false)

Example: =IF(C5>50,C5*2,"None")

- Logical_test is the first argument, the condition. It's a statement or expression that is either true or false. For example, the expression C5>50 is either true or false, depending on the value in cell C5.

- Value_if_true, the second argument, is what the formula shows if the condition is true. In the example, if C5 is greater than 50, the value in cell C5 is multiplied by 2. The value_if_true can be a formula, a value, text, or a cell reference.

- Value_if_false, the third argument, is what the formula shows if the condition is not true. The value_if_false can be a formula, a value, text, or a cell reference. In the example, if the value in cell C5 is not greater than 50, the result is the word "None."

EXERCISE 7-1 **Use IF to Show Text**

You can create an IF function to display text. For example, if an account is more than 30 days overdue, the cell should display "Delinquent Account." When you use the Function Arguments dialog box, Excel inserts the quotation marks around the text for you. When you key an IF function, you must key the quotation marks.

IF functions can use relational or comparison operators as well as the usual arithmetic operators.

TABLE 7-1   **Relational (Comparison) Operators**

OPERATOR	DESCRIPTION
=	Equal to
<>	Not equal to
>	Greater than
<	Less than

continues

TABLE 7-1

Relational (Comparison) Operators *continued*

OPERATOR	DESCRIPTION
>=	Greater than or equal to
<=	Less than or equal to

1. Open **BonusPay** and click cell C4.

2. Click the Insert Function button fx. In the Or select a category list, choose Logical.

3. Choose IF in the Select a function list. Click OK. The insertion point is in the Logical_test box.

 REVIEW: Move the Function Arguments dialog box so that you can see the cells you want to click.

4. Click cell B4. The address appears in the Logical_test box.

5. Key **>60000** in the Logical_test box after B4. This logical test will determine if the value in cell B4 is greater than 60000.

6. Click in the Value_if_true box.

7. Key **Yes**. If the value in cell B4 is greater than 60000, cell C4 will display the word "Yes."

8. Click in the Value_if_false box.

9. Key **No**. If the value in cell B4 is not greater than 60000, cell C4 will display the word "No."

FIGURE 7-1
Function Arguments
dialog box for IF

![Excel spreadsheet showing the Function Arguments dialog box for an IF statement. The formula bar shows =IF(B4>60000,"Yes",No). The spreadsheet shows "Klassy Kow Sales Staff" and "November Bonus Pay" with columns for Sales Representative, $ Sales, Bonus This Month?, and $ Bonus. Data includes Anderson, Michael 55,000; Carlson, Juan 45,000; Dugan, Mary 75,000; Evans, William 65,000; Jenkins, Robert 52,000; Yoto, Hashima 65,000; Adruisus, Dina 50,000; Ara, Hassan 85,000. The Function Arguments dialog shows Logical_test B4>60000 = FALSE, Value_if_true "Yes" = "Yes", Value_if_false No =. Callout: "Formula bar with IF statement"]

10. Click OK. The result of this IF formula for cell C4 is No.

11. Look at the formula in the formula bar. When you use the Function Arguments dialog box, quotation marks are inserted around text for you.

12. Click the Center button and use the Fill handle to copy the formula into cells C5:C11.

> **NOTE:** The AutoFill Options button opens after you use the Fill handle. Just ignore it.

EXERCISE | **7-2** | **Use IF to Calculate a Value**

The result of an IF formula can show a value, show a label, or compute a result. For example, Excel can determine if a salesperson fulfills the conditions to receive a bonus and calculate the bonus.

1. Click cell D4. Key =**if(** to start an IF formula. The ScreenTip displays the syntax for the function, and the argument to be keyed next is bold.

2. Click cell C4. A marquee appears around the cell, and the address appears after the left parenthesis. This starts the Logical_test.

3. Key =**"yes"** after C4. This logical test will determine if cell C4 shows "Yes." Text in a logical test is not case sensitive.

> **NOTE:** When you key text as part of the Logical_test, you must include quotation marks.

4. Key a comma after "yes" to separate the logical test from the value_if_true. Value_if_true in the ScreenTip is bold.

5. Click cell B4. A marquee appears around the cell, and the address appears after the comma.

6. Key *2.5% after B4. The formula multiplies the sales value in cell B4 by 2.5% if cell C4 shows "Yes." This is what the function will do if the test is true (C4 does show "yes").

7. Key a comma after "2.5%" to separate the value_if_true from the value_if_ false. Value_if_false in the ScreenTip is bold.

8. Key "" (two quotation marks with nothing between them). This represents no text, or nothing. If cell C4 does not show "Yes," cell D4 will show nothing. It will be blank. (See Figure 7-2 on the next page.)

9. Press Enter. Excel added the closing right parenthesis for you. Cell D4 shows nothing, because this sales rep does not receive a bonus.

10. Click cell D4 and click the Comma Style button ⟨ , ⟩.

11. Use the Fill handle to copy the formula into cells D5:D11.

FIGURE 7-2
Keying an IF
statement

	A	B	C	D	E	F	G
	IF ▾ X ✓ ƒ =if(C4="yes",B4*2.5%,"")						
1	Klassy Kow Sales Staff						
2	November Bonus Pay						
3	Sales Representative	$ Sales	Bonus This Month?	$ Bonus			
4	Anderson, Michael	55,000	No	=if(C4="yes",B4*2.5%,"")			
5	Carlson, Juan	45,000	No	IF(logical_test, [value_if_true], **[value_if_false]**)			
6	Dugan, Mary	75,000	Yes				
7	Evans, William	65,000	Yes				
8	Jenkins, Robert	52,000	No				
9	Yoto, Hashima	65,000	Yes				
10	Adruisus, Dina	50,000	No				
11	Ara, Hassan	85,000	Yes				
12							
13							

12. Click the Decrease Decimal button two times.

13. Save the workbook *[your initials]*7-2 in a folder for Lesson 7.

14. Add your footer and print the worksheet. Close the workbook.

Using AND, OR, and NOT Functions

AND, OR, and NOT are logical functions that show either "TRUE" or "FALSE" as a result. These functions ignore labels and empty cells, so you use them only with values (numbers).

EXERCISE   7-3   Use the AND Function

In an AND function, you can use multiple logical tests. All tests or expressions must be true for the result cell to show TRUE. Otherwise, it shows FALSE.

TABLE 7-2   Examples of the AND Function

EXPRESSION	RESULT IS
AND(C4>10, D4>10)	TRUE if both C4 and D4 are greater than 10; FALSE if either C4 or D4 is 10 or less.
AND(C4>10, C4<100)	TRUE if C4 is greater than 10 but less than 100; FALSE if C4 is 10 or less than 10 or 100 or greater than 100.
AND(C4>10, D4<10)	TRUE if C4 is greater than 10 and D4 is less than 10; FALSE if C4 is equal to or less than 10 or if D4 is equal to or greater than 10.
AND(C4<10, D4<100)	TRUE if C4 is less than 10 and D4 is less than 100; FALSE if C4 is equal to 10 or greater than 10 or if D4 is equal to 100 or greater.

1. Open **CustCount**.

2. Use the Fill handle for cell D3 to fill in the days of the week in cells E3:I3.

3. In cell J3, key **Over 150 on Weekend**?

4. Click cell J4.

5. Click the Insert Function button ![fx]. In the Or select a category list, choose Logical.

6. Choose AND and click OK. The insertion point is in the Logical1 box.

7. Click cell G4. The address appears in the Logical1 box.

8. Key > in the Logical1 box after G4.

9. Key **150** but don't press [Enter]. This test will determine if the value in cell G4 is greater than 150.

> **NOTE:** If you click OK or press [Enter] before completing all arguments in the Function Arguments dialog box, click the Insert Function button ![fx] button while the insertion point is still in the cell.

10. Click in the Logical2 box. Click cell H4 and key **>150**. The second condition is that the value in cell H4 is greater than 150.

11. Click in the Logical3 box. Click cell I4 and key **>150**. The third condition is that the value in cell I4 is greater than 150.

FIGURE 7-3
Function Arguments
dialog box for AND

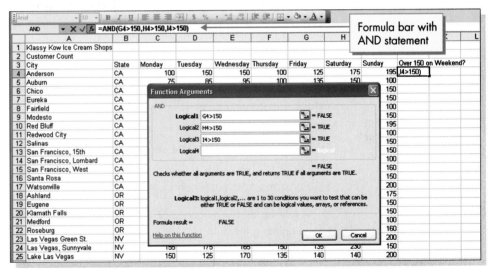

12. Click OK. The customer count must be greater than 150 each weekend day to show TRUE. Look at the formula in the formula bar.

13. Copy the formula to cells J5:J35. Only weekends in which all three days had greater than 150 customers show TRUE (Las Vegas Green Street, Reno, and Olympia). A day's count that is equal to 150 is not greater than 150.

14. Turn on Wrap text for cell J3. Format row 3 as 37.50 (50 pixels) high. AutoFit column J.

EXERCISE   **7-4**   **Use the OR Function**

In an OR function, any one of your logical tests can be true for the result cell to show TRUE. If they are all false, the result is FALSE.

TABLE 7-3   Examples of the OR Function

EXPRESSION	RESULT IS
OR(C4>10, D4>10)	TRUE if either C4 or D4 are greater than 10; FALSE only if both C4 and D4 are less than or equal to 10.
OR(C4>10, D4<100)	TRUE if C4 is greater than 10 or if D4 is less than 100; FALSE only if C4 is equal to or less than 10 and if D4 is equal to or greater than 100.
OR(C4>10, D4<10)	TRUE if either C4 is greater than 10 or if D4 is less than 10; FALSE only if C4 is equal to or greater than 10 and if D4 is equal to or less than 10.

1. Display the drag-and-drop pointer for cell J3.

    REVIEW: Point at any edge of the cell to display the drag-and-drop pointer.

2. Hold down Ctrl. Drag a copy of the label to cell K3. AutoFit column K.

3. In cell K4, key **=or(** to start the function.

4. Click cell G4. A marquee appears around the cell, and the address appears in the formula.

5. Key > after G4. Key **150** after >. This logical test will determine if the value in cell G4 is greater than 150.

6. Key a comma after 150.

7. Click cell H4. Key **>150**. The second condition will test if the value in cell H4 is greater than 150.

8. Key a comma and click cell I4. Key **>150** as the third logical test.

    REVIEW: You can click the Enter button ☑ in the formula bar to complete a formula.

FIGURE 7-4
Keying an OR
function

	B	C	D	E	F	G	H	I	J			N
1												
2												
3	State	Monday	Tuesday	Wednesday	Thursday	Friday	Saturday	Sunday	Over 150 on Weekend?	Over 150 on Weekend?		
4	CA	100	150	150	100	125	175	195	FALSE	=or(G4>150,H4>150,I4>150		
5	CA	75	85	95	100	135	150	100	FALSE	OR(logical1, [logical2], [logical3], [logical4], ...)		
6	CA	175	185	200	225	135	175	150	FALSE			
7	CA	100	150	125	100	125	135	150	FALSE			
8	CA	75	85	80	100	135	150	100	FALSE			
9	CA	175	135	200	175	135	175	150	FALSE			
10	CA	100	125	150	135	125	140	195	FALSE			

Formula bar: =or(G4>150,H4>150,I4>150

Formula bar with OR statement

9. Press Enter. If the customer count is greater than 150 people on any one of the weekend days, the result is TRUE.

10. Use the Fill handle to copy the formula into cells K5:K35.

EXERCISE   7-5   Use the NOT Function

In the NOT function, the reverse or opposite of your condition must be true for the result cell to show TRUE. The NOT function has one argument.

TABLE 7-4   Examples of the NOT Function

EXPRESSION	RESULT IS
NOT(C4>10)	TRUE if C4 is 10 or less than 10; FALSE if C4 is 11 or greater.
NOT(C4=10)	TRUE if C4 contains any value other than 10; FALSE if C4 is 10.

1. Click cell L3. Key **Sunday>150?**

2. Click cell L4. Key **=not(** and click cell I4.

3. Key **<150**. The formula tests if the value in cell I4 is less than 150. If the value is 150 or a value greater than 150, cell L4 will show TRUE.

FIGURE 7-5
Keying a NOT
function

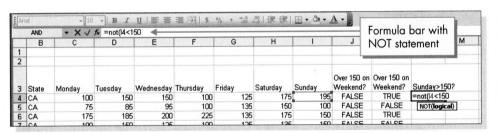

4. Press Enter.

5. Copy the formula to L35. Look at the results for counts of 150 or more on Sunday.

Working with Excel Styles

A *style* is a set of formatting specifications for labels or values. You have already used some of Excel's default styles when you clicked the Currency Style button $, the Comma Style button •, or the Percent Style button %. Excel has six predefined styles: Comma, Comma [0], Currency, Currency [0], Normal, and Percent. The default style for new data keyed in a new workbook is Normal.

EXERCISE **7-6** **Apply a Style**

1. Select cells C36:I36 and click the AutoSum button Σ ▾.

2. While the cells are selected, choose Style from the Format menu. The Style dialog box shows that the Normal style is applied to these values. The settings for the Normal style are shown in the Style includes section.

FIGURE 7-6
Style dialog box

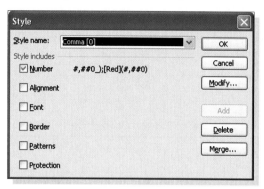

3. Click the arrow next to the Style name list. Six preset styles are listed.

4. Choose Comma [0]. This is the comma style with no decimal places.

5. Click OK. Notice that these cells are not right-aligned with other values in the columns. You will fix that in the next exercise.

EXERCISE **7-7** **Clear Cell Formats and Reapply a Style**

You can remove a style as well as your own formatting from a cell or a range of cells. The cell or range then returns to the default Normal style.

1. From the Edit menu, choose Clear and then Formats while cells C36:I36 are selected. The cells are returned to the Normal style.

2. Click cell C4 and press F8 to start Extend Selection mode.

3. Press → six times to select up to column I.

4. Hold down Ctrl and press ↓. This shortcut selects to the last row of data.

5. From the Format menu, choose Style.

6. Click the arrow next to the Style name list. Choose Comma [0].

7. Click OK. The style is applied, and all values are aligned.

8. Press Ctrl + Home.

Working with Page Breaks

A *page break* is a code that tells the printer to start a new page. When a worksheet is too wide or too tall to fit on the paper at your printer, Excel inserts an automatic page break. This page break appears as a dashed line on the screen. You can accept Excel's location for page breaks, or you can move the break to a new location.

EXERCISE 7-8   Preview and Change Page Breaks

1. Click the Print Preview button 🔍. You can see that the worksheet is too wide to print in a portrait orientation.

2. Press (Page Down). The part of the worksheet that does not fit on the first page is shown on page 2.

   NOTE: In Print Preview, (Page Down) moves to the next page if your screen is showing a reduced view. If you don't see the second page, click the Zoom button to zoom out.

3. Click Page Break Preview. A message box explains how you can adjust page breaks.

4. Click OK. The pages are shown next to each other with a background page number. The page break is the blue dashed line.

FIGURE 7-7
Page Break Preview

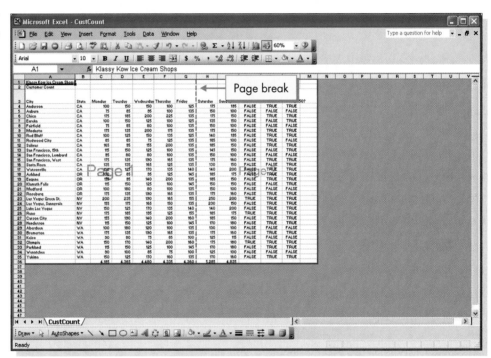

   NOTE: The background page number does not print.

5. Place the pointer on the blue dashed line to display a two-pointed arrow.

6. Click and drag the dashed blue line to the left so that it is between columns F and G.

7. Release the mouse button. The page break line is now solid blue. It turns solid blue whenever you manually set or adjust it.

8. Widen any column in which the label in row 3 is not visible.

 TIP: You can AutoFit columns while in Page Break Preview.

9. Click the Print Preview button 🔍 again. The screen shows the normal Print Preview.

10. Click Normal View to return to the worksheet. You can see dashed lines for page breaks in Normal view.

EXERCISE | **7-9** | **Insert a Page Break**

If you decide you want three columns to print per page, you can insert your own page breaks to create the look you want. You can also delete page breaks if you decide to change the page orientation and fit more columns per page. When you insert a page break, it is placed to the left of the active cell or column.

1. Click the Print Preview button 🔍.

2. Click Page Break Preview. Click OK in the message box.

3. Click cell J1. If you insert a page break here, it will be between columns I and J.

4. From the Insert menu, choose Page Break. The page break is solid blue because you inserted it manually.

FIGURE 7-8
Inserting a
page break

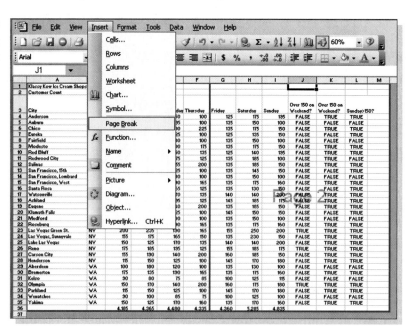

5. Click the Print Preview button ![icon].
6. Press [Page Down] to view the pages.

To make this three-page worksheet easier to follow, you can repeat the labels in column A on each printed page. Then you will see the city name on each page so that it is easy to determine which values belong with each city.

1. Click Setup in Print Preview.
2. Click the Sheet tab.
3. Click to place a check mark for Gridlines. Notice that the Print titles section is dimmed because you cannot set these titles from Print Preview.
4. Click OK. Click Normal View.
5. From the File menu, choose Page Setup.
6. Click the Sheet tab. This is the same dialog box you see from Print Preview, but the Print titles section is now available.
7. Click to place an insertion point in the Columns to repeat at left text box.
8. Click anywhere in column A. The dialog box shows $A:$A as the range for print titles.

FIGURE 7-9
Setting print titles

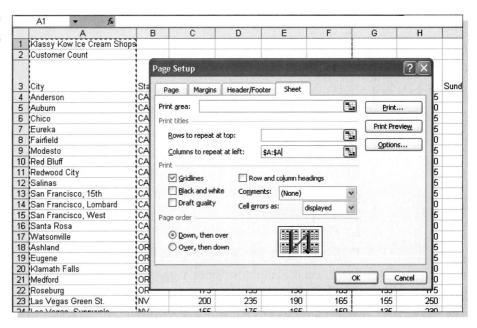

9. Click Print Preview in the dialog box.
10. Press [Page Down] and [Page Up] to view the pages.

EXERCISE 7-11 **Center a Page Horizontally**

Although you can change the left and right margins to make a page appear centered, Excel can automatically center a worksheet horizontally or vertically on the printed page.

1. Click Setup.
2. Click the Margins tab.
3. In the Center on page section, choose Horizontally.
4. Click OK. All pages are horizontally centered.

EXERCISE 7-12 **Change the Footer Font and Print Page Numbers**

The default font for data in headers and footers is 10-point Arial. You can change any section in the footer to any font and size available on your computer.

1. In Print Preview, click Setup and then the Header/Footer tab. Click Custom Footer.

 2. In the Left section, click the Font button [A].

3. Choose 8 as the Size and click OK.
4. Key *[your first and last name]*. The font is applied as you type.
5. Click in the Center section.

 6. Click the Page Number button [#]. The code is &[Page], and it is 10-point Arial.

7. Press (Spacebar) to insert a space after &[Page].
8. Key **of** and press (Spacebar).

 9. Click the Pages button [#]. The code is &[Pages]. This footer will display Page 1 of 3 on the first page.

10. Drag across &[Page] of &[Pages] to select all of it.
11. Click the Font button [A]. Choose 8 as the Size and click OK. (See Figure 7-10.)
12. Click in the Right section and click the Font button [A].
13. Choose 8 as the Size and click OK.
14. Insert the filename in the right section with the same font.
15. Close the Footer and Page Setup dialog boxes and then close Print Preview.

FIGURE 7-10
Printing page
numbers

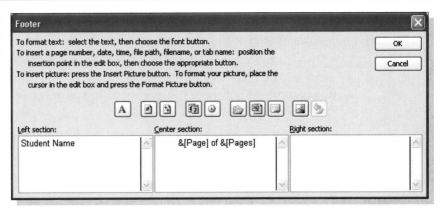

16. Save the workbook as *[your initials]*7-12 in your Lesson 7 folder.

17. Print the worksheet.

EXERCISE 7-13 Remove a Page Break

You can remove a manual page break and let Excel insert its own page breaks if they are needed.

1. Click the Print Preview button 🔍.

2. Click Page Break Preview and click OK.

3. Click cell J1. The page break is to the left of this column.

4. From the Insert menu, choose Remove Page Break.

5. From the View menu, choose Normal.

6. Close the workbook without saving.

Using the PMT and FV Functions

Financial functions analyze money transactions such as loans and savings or investment plans. Many financial functions, including the PMT and the FV functions, use the concept of an annuity. An *annuity* is a series of equal payments made at regular intervals for a specified period of time.

Many of Excel's financial functions use these arguments:

● *Rate* is the interest for the period. If you make monthly payments, you must divide the rate by 12 to find the monthly interest rate.

● *Nper* is the total number of periods during which a payment is made. It represents the total number of payments. A five-year loan with monthly payments would have an Nper of 60 (12 months a year * 5 years).

- *PV* is present value or the amount of the loan. It is the current cash value of the money transaction.

- *FV* is future value or the cash balance at the end of the time period. For a loan, the FV is 0 because you must pay back every penny. For an investment, FV is how much you will have at the end of your savings or investment time.

- *Type* specifies whether payments are made at the beginning or the end of the period.

E X E R C I S E   7-14   Use the PMT Function

The PMT (Payment) function can be used to determine monthly payments if you borrow money to buy a computer, a car, or a house.

1. Open **CU**.
2. In cell B4, key **4** to plan a four-year loan.
3. In cell B5, key **=** to use a formula to compute the number of payments.
4. Click cell B4 and key ***12**. Press (Enter). You will make a total of 48 payments (4 years * 12 months in a year).

 TIP: By using a formula in cell B5 to determine the number of payments, you only need to change the number of years to test different loan lengths.

5. In cell B6, key **20000**, the amount of money borrowed.
6. In cell B7, key **4.9%** as the interest rate.
7. Click cell B9.
8. Click the Insert Function button *fx*.
9. In the Or select a category list, choose Financial.
10. Scroll and click PMT. Click OK. The PMT Function Arguments dialog box opens. The insertion point is in the Rate box, the first argument.
11. Click cell B7, the interest rate for this loan. The cell address appears in the Rate box.
12. Key **/12** in the Rate box after B7. An annual interest rate must be divided by 12 to figure a monthly payment.
13. Click in the Nper box. This argument is the total number of payments that you calculated in cell B5.
14. Click cell B5 for the number of payments.
15. Click in the Pv box and click cell B6. The present value is the cash you receive for the loan now.

16. Click in the Fv box. The future value for a loan is what you will owe at the end of the loan, 0. You do not need to enter anything in this box.

17. Click in the Type box and key **1** for a payment at the beginning of the month.

 TIP: Most loans use Type 1 because it costs less to pay at the beginning of the month than at the end.

FIGURE 7-11
Function Arguments
dialog box for PMT

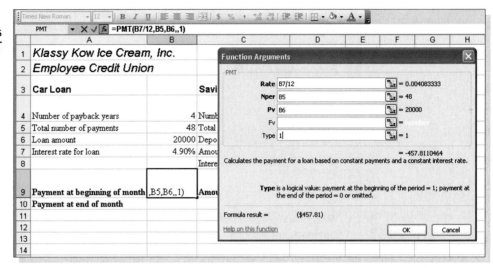

18. Click OK. The result is a negative number, because it is money that you have to pay. It is money out of your pocket.

EXERCISE 7-15 Key a PMT Function

Key a PMT function from scratch in this exercise to determine the payment if made at the end of the month.

1. Click cell B10.

2. Key **=pmt(** to start the function. The ScreenTip reminds you that the first argument is the Rate.

3. Click cell B7, the first argument in the PMT function.

4. Key **/12** to divide the rate by 12.

5. Key a comma to separate the arguments. The second argument, nper, is bold in the ScreenTip.

6. Click cell B5 for the number of payments.

7. Key another comma. The ScreenTip reminds you that the next argument is the present value or the amount of the loan.

8. Click cell B6. The square brackets with [fv] and [type] in the ScreenTip mean that these two arguments are optional in this function.

9. Press Enter. If you do not key a future value, Excel assumes it is 0. If you do not key a type, it is assumed to be a 0 type. Notice that payment at the end of the month is slightly more than at the beginning of the month.

FIGURE 7-12
Keying a PMT
function

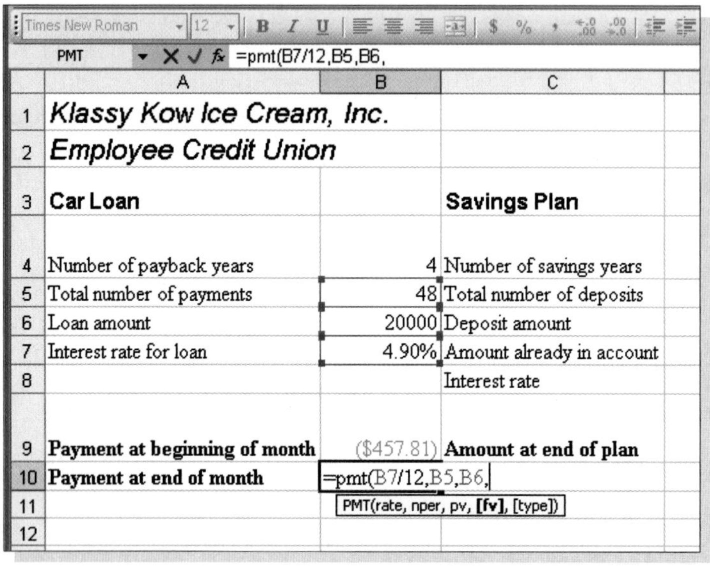

10. Click cell B4. Key **5** and press Enter for a five-year loan. Both functions are recalculated as well as the total number of payments.

11. In cell B7, key **3.9%** and press Enter. Payments with a lower interest rate are lower.

12. Click cell B6 and press F2 to edit the value.

13. Press Home to position the insertion point and key – to make this a negative number.

14. Press Enter. The payments now appear as positive numbers.

EXERCISE 7-16 **Use the FV Function**

The FV (Future Value) function can be used to determine such things as how much you will have in your savings account at some point in the future if you make regular deposits. You can include any money already in the account when you start your savings program.

1. Click cell D4 and key **5** to plan a five-year savings plan.

2. In cell D5, key = for a formula to determine the number of deposits.

3. Click cell D4 and key *12. Press Enter. You would make 60 total deposits if you save monthly for five years.

4. In cell D6, key 50 as the amount saved each month.

5. In cell D7, key 1000 as the amount of money already in the account.

6. In cell D8, key 5.25% as the interest rate.

 REVIEW: If you do not key the % sign, you must key the decimal equivalent of the value.

7. In cell D9, click the Insert Function button 𝑓𝑥.

8. Choose Financial and FV. Click OK. The insertion point is in the Rate box for the first argument.

9. Click cell D8 for the Rate. Key /12 in the Rate box after D8 to divide the rate by 12.

10. Click in the Nper box and then click cell D5.

 NOTE: The Function Arguments dialog box shows the syntax and a description of each argument when you click its box.

11. Click in the Pmt box and click cell D6. The payment is how much you plan to deposit into your savings account each month.

12. Click in the Pv box and click cell D7. The present value is what you have in the account to start.

13. Click in the Type box and key 1 for a deposit at the beginning of the month.

 TIP: In a savings plan, Type 1 pays more interest.

FIGURE 7-13
Function Arguments
dialog box for FV

Function Arguments		✕
FV		
Rate	D8/12	= 0.004375
Nper	D5	= 60
Pmt	D6	= 50
Pv	D7	= 1000
Type	1	= 1

= -4736.486919

Returns the future value of an investment based on periodic, constant payments and a constant interest rate.

Type is a value representing the timing of payment: payment at the beginning of the period = 1; payment at the end of the period = 0 or omitted.

Formula result =   -4736.486919

Help on this function   OK   Cancel

14. Click OK. The result is shown as a negative number, because the FV function assumes the bank's or lender's point of view. This is money that they would have to pay to you.

EXERCISE **7-17** **Format Negative Numbers**

Many business reports show negative numbers in red. Excel's Number and Currency formats can show negative numbers in red or black, with or without parentheses, with a leading minus sign, or simply in parentheses. The Accounting style shows negative numbers in parentheses.

 TIP: If you print to a black-ink printer, there is no need to show negative numbers in red.

1. Select cells B6, B9:B10, D6:D7, and D9.
2. Press Ctrl+1.
3. Click the Number tab and choose Currency.
4. In the Negative numbers list, choose the non-red ($1,234.10). Click OK.
5. Select cells B6 and D9. Click the Bold button B.
6. Press Ctrl+Home. Add your footer.
7. Save the workbook as *[your initials]*7-17 in your Lesson 7 folder.
8. Print the worksheet.
9. Make a copy of the worksheet and name it **CreditUnionFormulas**.
10. Press Ctrl+~ to display the formulas. Size the columns and print the worksheet fit to one landscape page.
11. Save and close the workbook.

Using Depreciation Functions

If you have taken or plan to take an accounting course, you will learn about depreciation. Depreciation represents the decline in value of an asset. Your car is a good example. Although you pay a certain amount for the car, it is not worth that much in three years because it has been used. For a business, depreciation can be used as an expense to offset income taxes. There are widely accepted methods of determining depreciation, and Excel has several functions to calculate the amounts.

Excel's depreciation functions use these basic arguments:

- *Cost* is the original price or cost of the item.
- *Salvage* is the value of the item after it has been depreciated. It is what the item is worth at the end of its life.
- *Life* is the number of periods over which the item will be depreciated. This is usually expressed in years for expensive assets.

- *Period* is the time for which depreciation is calculated. It uses the same units as Life. If an asset has a ten-year life, you would usually figure depreciation for a single year (the period).

EXERCISE 7-18 Use the DB Function

The DB (Declining Balance) function calculates depreciation at a fixed rate and considers that the value is declining each year. You calculate depreciation for each year separately.

1. Open **Depreciation**.
2. Select cells A8:A9. Use the Fill handle for the range and extend the labels down column A to "10th Year."
3. In cell B8, click the Insert Function button fx.
4. Choose Financial and DB. Click OK. The insertion point is in the Cost box for the first argument.
5. Click cell B4 for the Cost.
6. Click in the Salvage box and then click cell B5. This is the value of the tanks after ten years.
7. Click in the Life box and click cell B6. The life is how long the tanks are expected to last.
8. Click in the Period box and key **1** since you are calculating depreciation for the first year.
9. Click in the Month box. The label "Month" is not bold, which means this argument is optional. This allows you to start depreciating an asset in the middle of a year. Leave it empty.

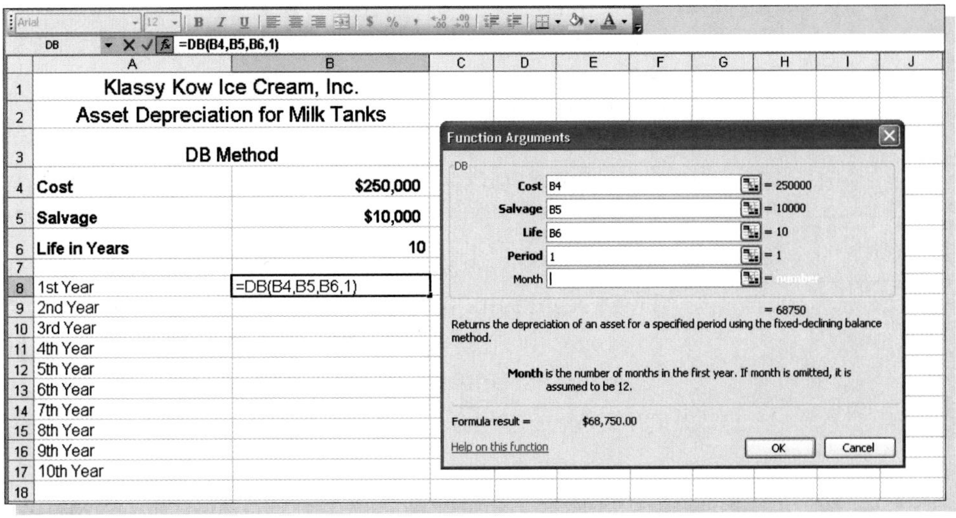

FIGURE 7-14
Function Arguments
dialog box for DB

10. Click OK. The depreciation for the first year is $68,750.

11. Click cell B9 and key the DB formula for the second year.

12. Key **=db(** to start the function. The ScreenTip reminds you that the first argument is the cost.

13. Click cell B4, the first argument in the DB function.

14. Key a comma to separate the arguments. The second argument salvage is bold in the ScreenTip.

15. Click cell B5 for the salvage value.

16. Key another comma. The ScreenTip reminds you that the next argument is the life of the asset.

17. Click cell B6 and key a comma. You must key the period argument after the comma.

FIGURE 7-15
Keying a DB function

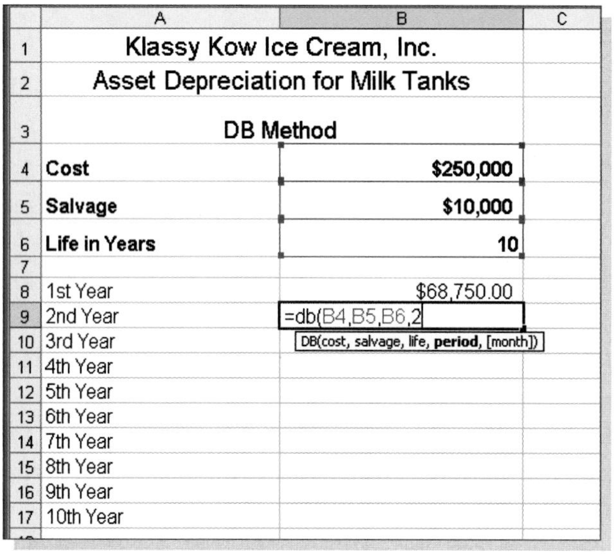

	A	B	C
1	Klassy Kow Ice Cream, Inc.		
2	Asset Depreciation for Milk Tanks		
3	DB Method		
4	Cost	$250,000	
5	Salvage	$10,000	
6	Life in Years	10	
7			
8	1st Year	$68,750.00	
9	2nd Year	=db(B4,B5,B6,2	
10	3rd Year	DB(cost, salvage, life, **period**, [month])	
11	4th Year		
12	5th Year		
13	6th Year		
14	7th Year		
15	8th Year		
16	9th Year		
17	10th Year		

18. Key **2** for the second year. The square brackets with [month] in the ScreenTip mean that this argument is optional.

19. Press (Enter). The depreciation for the second year is less because the asset was worth less at the beginning of the second year.

EXERCISE **7-19** **Edit the DB Function**

You can copy and edit the function to determine the other years. You will, however, need to change the period argument in each copied function.

1. Click cell B9 and copy the function down to row 17 with the Fill handle. These results are wrong.

2. Click cell B9 and click the Undo button. Press (F2) to edit cell B9. The references to cells B4, B5, and B6 should be absolute.

3. Click between the B and the 4 and press (F4). The reference is absolute.

4. Click between the B and the 5 and press (F4). Do the same for B6 and press (Enter).

5. Click cell B9 and copy the function again with the Fill handle to row 17. All values are duplicates of the value in cell B9.

6. Click cell B10. This is the formula for the third year. The last argument in the function should be 3 to calculate the third-year depreciation.

7. Press F2 and edit the function to **=DB($B$4,$B$5,$B$6,3)**.

8. Edit each function to show the appropriate year as the argument.

9. Press Ctrl+Home. Add your footer and save the workbook as *[your initials]***7-19** in your Lesson 7 folder.

10. Print the worksheet.

11. Make a copy of the worksheet and name it **Sheet1Formulas**. Press Ctrl+~. Print the worksheet fit to one portrait page.

12. Save and close the workbook.

USING ONLINE HELP

There are many financial functions that calculate common business arithmetic, including the many methods for determining depreciation.

Use Help to view additional information about depreciation:

1. From the Help menu, choose Microsoft Excel Help.

2. Key **depreciation** in the Search box and press Enter.

3. Click the VDB Worksheet function topic in the Search Results dialog box. Click Show All in the upper-right corner and read the Help window.

4. Click each function in the Search Results dialog box and read its Help window.

5. Close the Help window. Close the Search Results dialog box.

LESSON Summary

➤ The IF function enables you to create formulas that test whether a condition is true. If it is true, you specify what should be shown or done. You also set what appears or is done if the condition is false.

➤ The IF function can show text in its result, it can calculate a value, or it can show a cell reference.

➤ AND, OR, and NOT are logical functions that show either TRUE or FALSE as a result.

➤ Logical functions use relational or comparison operators.

➤ A style is a set of formatting specifications for labels and values.

➤ You can remove all formatting from a cell and return to the default Normal style.

➤ Page breaks determine where a new page starts. Excel inserts page breaks based on the paper size and the margins.

➤ You can insert and delete your own page breaks.

➤ Page Break Preview shows the page breaks as solid or dashed blue lines.

➤ If a worksheet requires more than one page, you can repeat column or row headings from page to page to make it easier to read the worksheet.

➤ The Margins tab in the Page Setup dialog box includes options to center a page horizontally or vertically.

➤ The Font button in the Custom Header/Footer dialog box opens the Font dialog box for regular font changes.

➤ You can print each page number as well as the total number of pages in a worksheet as a header or a footer.

➤ Financial functions include PMT and FV and other common business calculations such as depreciation.

➤ The PMT function calculates a regular payment for a loan, using an interest rate.

➤ The FV function calculates how much an amount will be worth in the future at a given interest rate.

➤ The DB function calculates how much of its value an asset loses each year during its life.

➤ Negative numbers can be shown in red, within parentheses, or with a leading minus (–) sign.

LESSON 7   Command Summary

FEATURE	BUTTON	MENU	KEYBOARD
Apply style		Format, Style	
Center page	🔍	File, Page Setup	
Delete page break		Insert, Remove Page Break	
Insert page break		Insert, Page Break	
Page break preview	🔍	View, Page Break Preview	
Print titles		File, Page Setup	

Concepts Review

TRUE/FALSE QUESTIONS

Each of the following statements is either true or false. Indicate your choice by circling T or F.

T (F)   **1.** An IF function has four arguments.

T (F)   **2.** You must key quotation marks around text that you key in a Function Arguments dialog box.

T (F)   **3.** The AND and OR functions usually show the same results.

(T) F   **4.** Excel has a preset style for each Number category in the Format Cells dialog box.

(T) F   **5.** Arguments in a function are separated by commas.

(T) F   **6.** Most of Excel's styles have a button on the Standard toolbar.

T (F)   **7.** The PMT function determines how much your money will grow over a period of time.

(T) F   **8.** The Print Titles option can repeat rows or columns on each page of a worksheet.

SHORT ANSWER QUESTIONS

Write the correct answer in the space provided.

1. What dialog box helps you complete built-in functions?

Function arguments

2. Which argument in a financial function refers to the total number of periods (also the total number of payments or deposits)?

Nper

3. Which logical function shows the opposite of the condition?

NOT

4. What Excel feature describes a set of formatting specifications?

Styles

5. What menu and menu option do you use to manually place a page break?

Insert, Page Break

6. How can you distinguish between an automatic page break and one that you placed?

Automatic page break lines are dashed, manual

7. Which financial function would help you determine how much money will be in your account at the end of a year if you make regular deposits?

FV function

8. What is the purpose of the Type argument in financial functions?

It specifies whether payments are made at the beginning or end of a period.

CRITICAL THINKING

Answer these questions on a separate page. There are no right or wrong answers. Support your answers with examples from your own experience, if possible.

1. Why are there separate logical operators for greater than (>) and greater than or equal to (>=)?

2. What other financial functions do you recognize from the Insert Function dialog box? Explain how some that you recognize work in a business.

Skills Review

EXERCISE 7-20

Use the IF function.

1. Open **CustBirth** and save it as *[your initials]*7-20 in your Lesson 7 folder.

2. Right-click the column D heading and insert a new column.

3. In cell D3, key **Born after 1995?**

4. In cell A20, key **12/31/95**. This is the last date in 1995, and you will refer to this cell in the IF function.

 NOTE: You cannot key a date as the logical test in an IF function, but you can refer to a cell with a date.

5. Use the IF function by following these steps:

   a. Click cell D4 and click the Insert Function button [fx].
   b. Choose Logical and IF. Click OK.
   c. Click cell C4 and key >.

d. Click cell A20 and press to make the reference absolute. The logical test determines if the date in cell C4 is greater than the date in cell A20 (that is, it is after that date).

REVIEW: Use an absolute reference when the cell address should not change as the formula is copied.

e. Click in the Value_if_true box. Key **Yes** to show "Yes" when the date is after 12/31/95.

TIP: You can press <kbd>Tab</kbd> to move to the next argument box.

f. Click in the Value_if_false box. Key **No** and click OK.

 6. Click the Center button ▤. Copy the formula to cells D5:D15.

TIP: Set the font and alignment before copying the formula.

7. Right-click the row 20 heading and hide the row. Add the missing border.

8. Add your footer and print the worksheet.

9. Make a copy of the worksheet and name it **CustBirthdaysFormulas.** Display the formulas and print the worksheet fit to one landscape page.

10. Save and close the workbook.

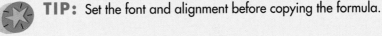

EXERCISE 7-21

Use AND, OR, and NOT functions.

1. Open the New Workbook task pane. Click On my computer in the Templates section. Choose **KlassyBirth** and click OK.

NOTE: Ask your instructor for help if you cannot find the template.

2. Save the workbook as *[your initials]***7-21** in your Lesson 7 folder.

3. Key the data shown in Figure 7-16 on the next page, starting in cell A4.

NOTE: The AND function only works for values or formulas, so you must replace M and F with numbers.

4. Select cells D4:D11. Using the option to Match entire cell contents, replace all occurrences of F with **1**. Replace all occurrences of M with **2**.

5. In cell E3, key **Female Over 5?** Copy the format from cell D3 and widen the column to show the label.

6. In cell F3, key **Age 6-8?** Copy the format from cell E3 and widen the column to show the label.

FIGURE 7-16

Name	Shop	Age	Male/Female
[Your first and last name]	Wenatchee	[your age]	[your gender]
Carole Greenfield	Olympia	10	F
Michael Westberg	Yakima	5	M
Hashima Yeng	Kelso	6	M
Krystal Chavez	Bremerton	8	F
Pedro Juarez	Yakima	7	M
David Hutchinson	Wenatchee	5	M
Melinda Brown	Kelso	6	F

7. Use an AND function by following these steps:

    a. Click cell E4 and click the Insert Function button [fx].
    b. Choose Logical and AND. Click OK.
    c. Click cell C4 and key >5 in the Logical1 box.
    d. Click in the Logical2 box. Click cell D4 and key =1. Click OK.
    e. Copy the formula in cell E4 to cells E5:E11.

8. Key an OR function by following these steps:

    a. Click cell F4 and key =or(to start the formula.
    b. Click cell C4 and key =6.
    c. Key a comma to separate the arguments.
    d. Click cell C4 again and key =7.
    e. Key another comma and then click cell C4 again. Key =8 and press (Enter).
    f. Copy the formula in cell F4 to cells F5:F11.

9. In cell G3, key **Male?** Copy the format from cell F3.

10. Use a NOT function by following these steps:

    a. In cell G4, key =not(to start the formula.

 TIP: You could use an IF function instead of NOT and test if cell D4=2.

    b. Click cell D4 and key =1. Press (Enter).
    c. Copy the formula in cell G4 to cells G5:G11.

11. Add your footer. Print the worksheet fit to one landscape page.

12. Make a copy of the sheet and name it **CustBirthdaysFormulas**. Display the formulas and print the sheet fit to one landscape page.

13. Save and close the workbook.

EXERCISE 7-22

Clear cell formats and apply styles. Work with page breaks. Set print titles.

1. Open **PerfRating**. Save the workbook as *[your initials]*7-22 in your Lesson 7 folder.

2. Clear cell formats by following these steps:
   a. Press F8 and then press Ctrl+End to select the worksheet cells.
   b. From the Edit menu, choose Clear and Formats.

3. Apply a style by following these steps:
   a. From the Format menu, choose Style.
   b. Click the arrow next to the Style name list.
   c. Choose Normal and click OK.
   d. Select cells C4:C16 and from the Format menu, choose Style.
   e. Choose Comma [0] from the Style name list and click OK.
   f. Select cells E18:E20 and from the Format menu, choose Style.
   g. Choose Percent from the Style name list and click OK.

4. Work with page breaks by following these steps:

   a. Click the Print Preview button .
   b. Click Page Break Preview. Click OK in the message box.

   REVIEW: Page breaks that you place appear as solid lines.

   c. Rest the mouse pointer on the blue dashed line to display a two-pointed arrow.
   d. Drag the dashed-line page break so that it is between columns C and D.

5. Set print titles by following these steps:
   a. From the File menu, choose Page Setup. Click the Sheet tab.
   b. In the Print titles section, click in the Rows to repeat at top box.
   c. Select cells A1:A2. Excel inserts an absolute reference for rows 1:2.
   d. Click in the Columns to repeat at left box.
   e. Click anywhere in column A and click OK.
   f. Click the Print Preview button . Notice that the labels from column A are not completely visible on the second page.

   NOTE: Print titles are cut off on all but page 1 unless you AutoFit the column to the label.

   g. Click Normal View. AutoFit column A to fit the labels in rows 1:2.

6. Add your footer, but change the font to 8 points for each section.

7. Save, print, and close the workbook.

EXERCISE 7-23

Use PMT and FV functions. Use a depreciation function.

1. Create a new workbook and save it as *[your initials]*7-23 in your Lesson 7 folder.

2. Select cells A1:A2 and make them 16-point Arial. In cell A1, key **Klassy Kow Employees Credit Union**. In cell A2, key **Auto Loan Comparison**.

3. In cells A3:A6, key the following labels:
   Loan Amount
   Rate
   Years for Loan
   Total # of Payments

4. Widen column A to fit the longest item (not the main title). Format row 3 as 27.00 (36 pixels) high.

5. Select cells A3:A6 and copy them to cells D3:D6. Make column D the same width as column A.

6. In cells B3:B5, key data for a $15,000 loan at 5.9% for 3 years. In cell B6, key = and click cell B5. Key ***12** and press [Enter].

7. In cells E3:E5, key data for a $15,000 loan at 6.5% for 4 years. Copy the formula in cell B6 to cell E6.

8. Use the PMT function by following these steps:

   a. In cell B7, click the Insert Function button [fx]. Choose Financial and PMT. Click OK.

   b. Click cell B4 and key **/12** in the Rate box.

   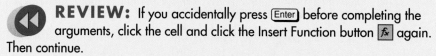

   REVIEW: If you accidentally press [Enter] before completing the arguments, click the cell and click the Insert Function button [fx] again. Then continue.

   c. Click in the Nper box and then click cell B6.
   d. Click in the Pv box and then click cell B3.
   e. Click in the Type box and key **1**. Click OK.
   f. Copy the formula in cell B7 to cell E7.

9. Select cells A1:A2 and click the Copy button [icon]. Go to Sheet2 and press [Enter].

10. Edit the label in cell A2 to say **Savings Comparison**.

11. In cells A3:A6, key the following labels:
Savings Amount
Rate
Years for Savings
Total # of Deposits

12. Widen column A to fit the longest item (not the main title). Format row 3 as 27.00 (36 pixels) high.

13. Copy cells A3:A6 to cells D3:D6. Make column D the same width as column A.

14. In cells B3:B5, key data for saving $50 a month at 6.25% for 3 years. In cell B6, key a formula to determine the number of deposits.

15. In cells E3:E5, key data for saving $100 a month at 6.5% for 4 years. Copy the formula in cell B6 to cell E6.

16. Use the FV function by following these steps:

   TIP: Check the Most Recently Used list for functions you have been using.

> *a.* In cell B7, click the Insert Function button ⎡fx⎤. Choose Financial and FV. Click OK.
> *b.* Click cell B4 and key **/12** in the Rate box.
> *c.* Click in the Nper box and then click cell B6. Click in the Pmt box and then click cell B3.
> *d.* Click in the Type box and key **1**. Click OK.
> *e.* Copy the formula in cell B7 to cell E7. Widen any columns that are not wide enough to fit the data.

17. Rename Sheet1 **AutoLoans**. Rename Sheet2 **SavingsPlans**. Rename Sheet3 **Depreciation**.

18. On the **Depreciation** sheet, select cells A1:A2 and make them 16-point Arial. In cell A1, key **Klassy Kow Ice Cream, Inc.** In cell A2, key **Asset Depreciation for Storage Tanks**.

19. Make cell A3 14-point Arial and key **DDB Method**.

20. Make both columns A and B 27.86 (200 pixels) wide.

21. Select cells A4:B6 and make them 12-point Arial bold. Key the following labels and values:
Cost $300000
Salvage $15000
Life in Years   8

22. In cell A8, key **1st Year** and in cell A9, key **2nd Year**. Select these two cells and use the Fill handle to fill down column A to **8th Year**.

23. Use a depreciation function by following these steps:

> *a.* In cell B8, click the Insert Function button ⎡fx⎤.
> *b.* Choose Financial and DDB. Click OK. The insertion point is in the Cost box for the first argument.

NOTE: The DDB depreciation function is double-declining balance.

    c. Click cell B4 for the Cost.

    d. Click in the Salvage box and then click cell B5.

    e. Click in the Life box and click cell B6.

    f. Click in the Period box and key **1** for the first year.

    g. Leave the Factor box empty. Click OK.

    h. Edit the formula in cell B8 to use absolute references for each cell reference.

    i. Make the results 12-point bold. Copy the formula down to row 15.

    j. Edit each copied formula to show the appropriate period for the year.

24. Hold down (Shift) and click the **AutoLoans** tab. Choose File and Page Setup to add a footer to all three sheets at once. Key your first and last name in the left section. In the center section, include the worksheet tab name and the filename. Add the date at the right. Close the Page Setup dialog box.

25. Print the entire workbook.

26. Save and close the workbook.

Lesson Applications

EXERCISE 7-24

Use the IF function.

1. Use the **KlassyBirth** template to create a workbook. Save it as *[your initials]*7-24 in your Lesson 7 folder.

 TIP: Look for recently used templates in the New Workbook task pane.

2. Change the label in cell C3 to show **Favorite Flavor**.
3. In cells A4:D9, key the following information:

FIGURE 7-17

	Name	Shop	Favorite Flavor	Male/Female
4	Marian Most	Las Vegas, Green	Chocolate	F
5	Tommy Dunne	Lake Las Vegas	Bubble Gum Goo	M
6	Luella Orr	Carson City	Chocolate	F
7	Patrick Adams	Reno	Vanilla	M
8	Asata Akai	Henderson	Strawberry	F
9	Efren Aldo	Las Vegas, Sunnyvale	Chocolate	M

4. Widen column B to fit the longest item. Left-align the flavors in column C.
5. Key **Chocolate?** as the label in cell E3. Copy the format from one of the other labels and adjust the column width to fit the label.
6. Use the IF function in cell E4 with C4="chocolate" as the Logical_test. Show **Yes** if the customer's favorite flavor is chocolate. Show **Other** if chocolate is not the favorite. Copy the formula for the rest of the column, and center the results.
7. Change the page orientation to landscape and center the sheet horizontally. Add your footer and print the worksheet.
8. Make a copy of the worksheet and name it **CustBirthdaysFormulas**. Press Ctrl+~. Adjust the width of each column manually to fit its longest entry.

You may need to click away from row 1 so that you can see the column headings.

 NOTE: If the Picture toolbar pops up, click its Close button ☒. Don't worry about sizing the picture.

9. Print the formulas to fit on one landscape page. Save and close the workbook.

EXERCISE 7-25

Work with page breaks.

The financial staff keeps track of the retirement accounts managed by Klassy Kow for its employees. The worksheet needs to be printed with each year on a separate page. Each year shows five funds and a total. There are a few more formatting changes, and you need to identify errors.

1. Open **RetireAcct** and save it as *[your initials]*7-25 in your Lesson 7 folder.

 TIP: Set the Zoom percentage to 75% to see more on the screen.

2. AutoFit each column that is not wide enough.

3. Select cells A7:A8 and A12:A16. Press Ctrl+1. Set a horizontal left indent of 1. Set a left indent of 2 for cells A9:A10.

4. Select cells B3:G3 and center the range across the selection. Repeat these steps for years 2003 and 2002.

5. Change the page orientation to landscape.

6. In Page Break Preview, drag the first page break to be between columns G and H, if it is not already there. The second page break should be between columns M and N. This will place each year's data on a separate page.

 7. Click the Print Preview button and view all three pages.

NOTE: If Excel inserts an automatic page break as you switch views, just drag the new dashed line on top of your solid line.

8. Close print preview. From the File menu, choose Page Setup. Repeat rows 1:2 and column A:A as print titles.

9. Add a footer with your name at the left. In the center section, show the filename and the tab name on one line. Press Enter and on the second line in the center section, show &Page of &Pages. Include the date in the right section.

10. Check column widths again and print the worksheet.

11. Make a copy of the worksheet and name it **ChangesinAssetsFormulas**.

12. From the Options dialog box (Tools menu), verify that formulas referring to empty cells will be flagged.

13. Hide column A and display the formulas. In cell A20, key the address of the first cell with an error triangle. In cell B20, key the type of error. Continue in these two columns, noting the cell address and the error type.

14. Select the cells with the error information and use the File menu to print only this selection.

15. Save and close the workbook.

EXERCISE 7-26

Use AND and OR functions.

1. Open **SerAwards**. Save it as *[your initials]*7-26 in your Lesson 7 folder.

2. In cell E4, use an AND function to show TRUE if the employee has greater than 2 years of service and a performance rating equal to 4. Copy the formula to rows E5:E16.

3. In cell F4, use an OR function to show TRUE if the employee has greater than 4 years of service or a performance rating equal to 4. Copy the formula to cells F5:F16.

4. Set the page to be horizontally centered. Add your footer using a 9-point font for all sections, and print the worksheet.

5. Make a formula sheet and print it fit to one landscape page.

6. Save and close the workbook.

EXERCISE 7-27   *Challenge Yourself*

Use the PMT function to calculate mortgage payments at different interest rates.

Klassy Kow Ice Cream, Inc., is in the process of choosing a construction loan to finance expansion at the headquarters building. They have compiled information from four lenders. You are now ready to build a worksheet to analyze the results. The loan will be for ten years, with payments made at the beginning of each month. The company wants to borrow $500,000.

1. Create a new workbook and save it as *[your initials]*7-27 in your folder for Lesson 7.

2. Key **Construction Loan Comparison** in cell A1 and choose a large font size. In cell A2, key **As of mm/dd/yy** (use today's date). Make this cell 2 points smaller than the font size you used in cell A1.

3. Key the following in cells B3:C4:
Loan Amount	-$500000
Years to Repay	15
Number of Payments	

TIP: If you key a dollar sign with a value, the value is formatted as Currency.

4. Widen column B to show the label in cell B5, and format row 3 as 22.50 (30 pixels) high.

5. Key a formula in cell C5 to determine the total number of payments.

6. Select cells A3:D6 and apply Outside Borders.

7. Key the information shown in Figure 7-18, starting in cell B9.

FIGURE 7-18

	B	C	D	E
9	Lender Name	Rate	Monthly Payment	Total Cost
10	Freedom Financial	11%		
11	Southwest Lenders	10.75%		
12	East-West Bank	11.25%		
13	State Investment Trust	10.65%		

8. Make the labels in row 9 bold and centered. Turn on Wrap text for cells D9:E9.

9. Use the PMT function in cell D10 to determine the monthly payment for the first lender. Because you will copy the formula for the other lenders, use absolute references where appropriate. Copy the formula.

 NOTE: If you make the loan amount a negative number, the payment amounts will be positive values.

10. In cell E10, key a formula to multiply the monthly payment by the total number of payments. Use an absolute reference where appropriate so that you can copy this formula, too. Copy the formula.

11. Make any formatting changes so that your worksheet is attractive and easy to read.

12. Add your footer and print the worksheet.

13. Make a formula sheet and print it fit to one portrait page.

14. Save and close the workbook.

On Your Own

In these exercises you work on your own, as you would in a real-life work environment. Use the skills you've learned to accomplish the task—and be creative.

EXERCISE 7-28
As a banker who expects a 6% return on money you lend, you can determine how much to lend a customer who can afford to pay $200 a month for five years. Create a new workbook that illustrates this idea as if you were the banker. Use Help to learn about the PV function. Then use PV in the new workbook to determine what you can lend this customer. Add a footer. Save the workbook as *[your initials]*7-28 in your Lesson 7 folder. Print the worksheet, save the workbook, and close it.

EXERCISE 7-29
Use Excel's Help system to learn more about styles. Then create a new workbook and key two labels and two values. Create two different styles for the labels, each using different fonts, colors, and perhaps borders or shading. Create two different styles for values that are different from what you have already seen in Excel's styles. Apply these styles to your data. Add your footer. Save the workbook as *[your initials]*7-29 in your Lesson 7 folder. Print the worksheet, save the workbook, and close it.

EXERCISE 7-30
Open **AcctRec** and save it as *[your initials]*7-30 in your Lesson 7 folder. Select and copy cells A2:E16 to cell A17. Paste again in cells A32 and A47. Add a custom footer that shows your name at the left and the page number in the center. Look at the worksheet in regular Print Preview and then in Page Break Preview. (Note that Excel prints the pages down and then across on a worksheet like this.) On the Sheet tab of the Page Setup dialog box, change the page order and print the worksheet with this new setting. Save and close the workbook.

Rounding and Nesting Functions

After completing this lesson, you will be able to:

1. **Use the INT function.**
2. **Use the ROUND function.**
3. **Use date and time arithmetic.**
4. **Create nested functions.**
5. **Create a hyperlink.**

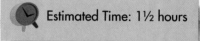 Estimated Time: 1½ hours

In this lesson, you learn about the INT and ROUND functions, which can be used with your own formulas or Excel functions. You continue to work with Date and Time functions to perform date or time arithmetic. You also learn how to nest one function inside another to solve complex problems. Finally, you learn how to create hyperlinks in an Excel worksheet.

Using the INT Function

Excel stores the full number of decimals that are keyed or calculated in a cell, even if the cell is formatted to show fewer decimal places. For example, if you key 1.2345 but format the cell for two decimal places, Excel displays 1.23 in the cell. In a calculation, however, Excel uses the full value, 1.2345, which you see in the formula bar.

If you want Excel to use the value shown in the cell (not the one in the formula bar), you can use the INT or ROUND functions.

INT stands for "Integer." An *integer* is a whole number, a number with no decimal or fractional parts. The INT function (in the Math & Trig category) shows only the nondecimal portion of a number. To do this, it truncates or cuts off all digits after the decimal point. The INT function has one argument, the value or cell to be adjusted.

TABLE 8-1   Examples of the INT Function

EXPRESSION	CELL DATA	RESULT
INT(C4)	C4=9.7	9
INT(9.792)	None	9
INT(A1)	A1=-9.7	-9

EXERCISE   **8-1**   **Use INT with a Value**

1. Create a new workbook.

 TIP: Key a font size that is not in the list.

2. In cell A1, key **Integer and Round Training**. In cell A2, key **Human Resources Department**. Select both cells and make them 17-point Arial.

3. In cell A3, key **Integer Samples**. Format it as 10-point bold Arial. Format row 3 as 27.00 (36 pixels) high.

4. Key the following values in cells A4:A8:
   1.2
   3.4
   5.6
   7.8
   9.0

 NOTE: The General number format shows only significant digits after the decimal point, so 0 after the decimal point is not displayed.

5. In cell B4, key **=int(** and click cell A4.

 REVIEW: You will see an Argument ScreenTip for the INT function.

6. Press (Enter). The integer value of 1.2 is 1.

7. Copy the formula in cell B4 to cells B5:B8.

8. Select cells A9:B9.

9. Click the AutoSum button . The integer values are used in column B and the result is 25. The decimal values in column A add up to 27.

EXERCISE 8-2 Compare Formula Results Using INT

1. In cell A10, press Ctrl+B to start bold.

2. Key **Multiplication Samples** and press Enter. Make row 10 27.00 (36 pixels) high.

3. In cell A11, key **10.2** and press Enter.

4. Key **5.8** in cell A12 and press Enter.

5. Key = in cell A13 and click cell A11.

6. Key * and click cell A12. Press Enter. This is a simple multiplication formula.

7. Select cells A11:A13 and drag and drop a copy to cells B11:B13.

 REVIEW: Hold down the Ctrl key to copy with drag and drop.

8. Click cell B13 and press F2.

9. Position the pointer after the equal sign. Key **int(** and press Enter. The result is formatted as an integer, and the result is 59.

FIGURE 8-1
Changing a formula
to an integer result

	A	B	C	D	E	F	G
1	Integer and Round Training						
2	Human Resources Department						
3	Integer Samples						
4	1.2	1					
5	3.4	3					
6	5.6	5					
7	7.8	7					
8	9	9					
9	27	25					
10	Multiplication Samples						
11	10.2	10.2					
12	5.8	5.8					
13	59.16	=int(B11*B12					
14		INT(number)					
15							

10. In cell C11, key **=int(** and click cell B11. Press Enter.

11. In cell C12, key **=int(** and click cell B12. Press Enter. Both cells show integer values now.

12. Key = in cell C13. Click cell C11, key *, and then click cell C12. Press Enter. This result (50) is different because it uses the integer values, not the full decimal values.

13. Click cell B13 and display the Trace Error button shortcut menu. The formula is inconsistent, because it is different from those in cells A13 and C13. It includes INT in the formula.

14. Choose Ignore Error.

Using the ROUND Function

The ROUND function "rounds" a value to a specified digit to the left or right of the decimal point. *Rounding* a number means that it is made larger or smaller, a greater or lesser value. The ROUND function uses two arguments: the value to be rounded and the number of digits used for rounding. If the second argument is zero or a negative number, the rounding occurs to the left of the decimal point.

TABLE 8-2 **Examples of the ROUND Function**

EXPRESSION	CELL DATA	RESULT
ROUND(C4, 1)	C4=9.736	9.7
ROUND(C4, 2)	C4=9.736	9.74
ROUND(C4, 0)	C4=9.736	10
ROUND(C4, -1)	C4=9.736	10
ROUND(C4, -2)	C4=9.736	0

 TIP: Rounding is often used in financial calculations to round to the nearest dollar.

EXERCISE **8-3** **Use Insert Function for ROUND**

1. Select cells A3:C13 and drag and drop a copy to cells E3:G13.
2. Edit cell E3 to show **Round Samples**. Delete the contents of cells F4:F8.
3. In cell F4, click the Insert Function button 🔲.
4. In the Or select a category list, choose Math & Trig.
5. In the Select a function list, choose ROUND. Click OK.
6. In the Number box, click cell E4.
7. In the Num_digits box, key **0**. The value in cell E4 will be rounded to show no decimal positions. (See Figure 8-2 on the next page.)
8. Click OK. The value 1.2 is rounded to 1. It rounds down because the value after the decimal point is less than 5.
9. Display the Fill handle for cell F4 and copy the formula down to cell F8.

FIGURE 8-2
Using ROUND in
the dialog box

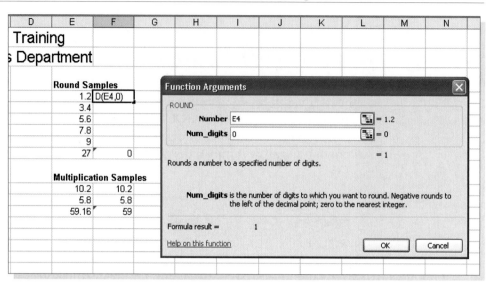

10. Edit cells E4:E8 to show the following values. As you do, notice how the values in column F are rounded up or down.

1.3
3.5
5.4
7.7
9.2

EXERCISE | **8-4** | **Key a ROUND Formula**

1. Click cell E13. Note that the result is 59.16.
2. Press Delete.
3. Key **=round(** and click cell E11. Key * and click cell E12.
4. Key a comma. The ScreenTip shows that num_digits is the next argument to be entered.
5. Key **1** and press Enter. This rounds the result to one decimal position. (See Figure 8-3 on the next page.)
6. Click cell G11 and press Delete.
7. Key **=round(** and click cell F11.
8. Key a comma, key **0**, and press Enter. Notice the result in cell G13.

 REVIEW: Ignore error triangles as you work through these exercises.

9. Click cell G12 and press Delete.

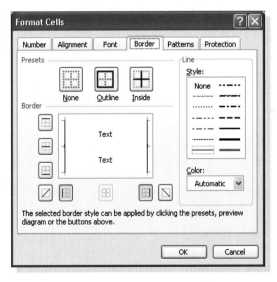

FIGURE 8-3
Keying a ROUND
formula

10. Key **=round(** and click cell F12. Key a comma, key **0**, and press [Enter]. Notice the result in cell G13.

11. Select cells D4:D13 and press [Ctrl]+[1].

FIGURE 8-4
Adding side
borders

12. Click the Border tab. In the Border preview area, click the left and right side borders. Click OK.

13. Make column D 3.00 (20 pixels) wide.

14. Select cells A1:G2 and press [Ctrl]+[1]. Click the Alignment tab and center the cells across the selection. Click OK.

15. On the Margins tab in the Page Setup dialog box, set the worksheet to be horizontally centered.

Using Date and Time Arithmetic

Because of its serial number system, Excel's Date & Time functions can calculate ages, hours worked, or days passed. The serial number system treats dates as values. January 1, 1900, is 1; January 2, 1900, is 2; and so on.

TIP: Macintosh systems start counting at January 1, 1904.

EXERCISE 8-5 **Determine Ages**

To determine a person's age, subtract the person's birthday from today. The result is a serial number that can be converted to the person's age.

1. Select cell A2 and press Ctrl+C to copy it to the Clipboard.
2. Click the Sheet2 tab and press Enter. The label is copied with the Center Across Selection alignment.
3. Click the Align Left button ▤. Now you can see the label.
4. Make rows 1 and 2 30.00 (45 pixels) high.
5. In cell A2, key **Determining a Person's Age** and make it 17-point Arial.
6. Make row 3 37.50 (50 pixels) high.
7. In cell A3, key **Name**. Key **Birth Date** in cell B3. Key **Age** in cell C3.
8. Drag across the column headings for columns A, B, and C. Then make them 17.14 (125 pixels) wide.
9. In cell A4, key your first name and last name.
10. In cell B4, key your birthday in the **mm/dd/yy** format.
11. Click cell A15, key **=today()**, and press Enter.
12. In cell C4, key = to start the formula.
13. Click cell A15. The first part of the formula is today's date.
14. Press F4 and make it an absolute reference.

 REVIEW: An absolute reference does not change when the formula is copied.

15. Key a minus sign and click cell B4 to subtract your birthday from today's date.
16. Press Enter. Your age is formatted as a date. Widen the column to see the result.
17. Click cell C4 and press Ctrl+1.
18. Click the Number tab. Choose Number with 2 decimal places and click OK. This is your age in days.
19. Press F2. Press Home and → to position the insertion point after the equal sign.
20. Key a left parenthesis (after the equal sign.

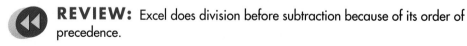 **REVIEW:** Excel does division before subtraction because of its order of precedence.

21. Press End and key a right parenthesis) after B4.

FIGURE 8-5
Converting the age
formula to years

	A	B	C
1	Human Resources Department		
2	Determining a Person's Age		
3	Name	Birth Date	Age
4	Student Name	1/1/1980	=($A$15-B4)/365.25
5			
6			
7			
8			
9			
10			
11			
12			
13			
14			
15	9/5/2003		
16			

22. Key **/365.25** to divide by the number of days in a year. Press Enter.

 NOTE: Dividing by 365.25 includes a leap year once every four years.

23. Copy the formula in cell C4 to row 5. The results are not correct until you enter a birth date.

24. In row 5, key another person's name and birth date.

25. Make the labels in row 3 bold. Right-align the labels in cells B3 and C3.

26. Set the worksheet to be horizontally centered.

EXERCISE **8-6** **Determine Time Worked**

Figuring time worked or time passed is similar to figuring your age. You subtract the beginning time from the ending time.

1. Select cell A1 and press Ctrl+C to copy it to the Clipboard.

2. Click the Sheet3 tab and press Enter.

3. Format rows 1 and 2 as 33.75 (45 pixels) high.

4. Format cell A2 as 17-point Arial and key **Determining Hours Worked**.

5. Key these labels in row 3 and make them bold.

Name	**Time In**	**Time Out**	**Hours Worked**

6. Make row 3 22.50 (30 pixels) high.

7. In cell A4 key your first and last name. Widen columns as needed.

8. In cell B4, key **8:30 am** and press →. Excel capitalizes the AM/PM reference.

9. In cell C4, key **4:30 pm**. Excel shows times as you key them, using a 12-hour AM/PM clock.

10. In cell D4, key = and click cell C4. This is the ending time.

11. Key a minus sign (–) and click cell B4, the starting time.

12. Press Enter. The result is formatted as time, because the two cells in the formula are time.

EXERCISE 8-7 **Format Time Results**

Excel shows time as a fraction of a 24-hour day. To convert to hours, you multiply the results by 24.

1. Click cell C4 and press Ctrl+1. Click the Number tab.
2. Choose Number with 2 decimal places. Click OK.
3. Press F2 and press Home.
4. Press → and key a left parenthesis (after the equal sign.

 REVIEW: Excel does multiplication before subtraction unless you insert parentheses.

5. Press End and key a right parenthesis).
6. Key *24 to multiply by the number of hours in a day. Press Enter.
7. Set the worksheet to be horizontally centered.

EXERCISE 8-8 **Group Sheets and Add a Footer**

You have already learned how to select more than one worksheet tab at a time. When you do so, the worksheets are grouped. If you use the File menu and the Page Setup command when worksheets are grouped, you can add the same footer to all sheets in the group.

1. Rename the worksheet tabs as follows:
   Sheet1 **Integer**
   Sheet2 **Age**
   Sheet3 **Time**
2. Save the workbook as *[your initials]*8-8 in a folder for Lesson 8.
3. While the Time sheet is active, hold down Shift and click the Integer tab. The three worksheets are selected, and the title bar shows [Group]. (See Figure 8-6 on the next page.)
4. Choose File and then Page Setup.
5. Click the Header/Footer tab. Add your name in the left section, the worksheet tab name in the center, and the date in the right section. Click OK.
6. Click Print Preview in the Page Setup dialog box. This is the first page of 3.
7. Press Page Down to see the other worksheets. Press Page Up to return to previous pages.
8. Click Close to close print preview.

FIGURE 8-6
Grouped
worksheets

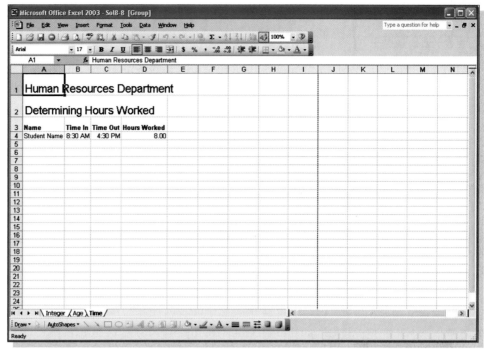

9. Click the Print button 🖨 while the worksheets are still grouped. All three sheets print with the same footer.

EXERCISE 8-9 Hide and Unhide a Worksheet

You have already learned how to hide columns and rows in a worksheet. You can also hide a worksheet so that you do not see its tab while the workbook is open. This allows you to hide sheets that include sensitive information that should not be easily visible.

1. Right-click any worksheet tab and choose Ungroup Sheets. The three sheets are no longer grouped.
2. Click the Age sheet so that it is active.
3. From the Format menu, choose Sheet and then Hide. The Age sheet no longer appears in the workbook.
4. Save and close the workbook. If you save and close a workbook with hidden sheets, the workbook will reopen just like that.
5. Open *[your initials]*8-8 in your Lesson 8 folder. There is no Age sheet visible.
6. From the Format menu, choose Sheet and then Unhide. The Unhide dialog box shows which sheets are hidden.
7. Click Age in the list and click OK. The Age sheet is visible.
8. Save and close the workbook.

Creating Nested Functions

A *nested* function is a function inside another function. The logical test or argument for the main function is another function. The IF function is a function that is often used in nested functions. The ROUND function is another function in which other functions can be nested.

E X E R C I S E **8-10** **Nest SUM and ROUND**

---

1. Open **CookieCrunch**.
2. Click cell C4 and then click cell D4. This worksheet uses a formula to compute a 5 percent sales increase from one day to the next.

 NOTE: A 5 percent increase multiplies the previous day's sales by 105 percent.

3. Click cell H9. Click the Insert Function button ⨍.
4. In the Search for a function box, key **round** and press Enter. Click OK.
5. Move the Function Arguments dialog box to see column headings and column H.
6. In the Number box, you need to show the sum of Sunday's sales. This will be the SUM function nested in the ROUND function.
7. While the insertion point is in the Number box, click the arrow next to the Function Name box.

 NOTE: If SUM is not in the Function Name list, click More Functions and find SUM in the Math & Trig or Most Recently Used category.

8. Choose SUM and click OK. The Function Arguments dialog box now shows the SUM function, but it is nested in the ROUND function in the formula bar. The SUM function is bold in the formula bar, and the suggested range for the argument is highlighted and is correct (H4:H8). (See Figure 8-7 on the next page.)
9. Click anywhere in the word ROUND in the formula bar. The Function Arguments dialog box shows SUM(H4:H8) as the Number argument for the ROUND function.
10. Click in the Num_digits box and key **2**. Click OK.
11. Display the Fill handle for cell H9.
12. Drag the handle left to copy the formula to cells G9:B9.

FIGURE 8-7
Nesting SUM in a
ROUND function

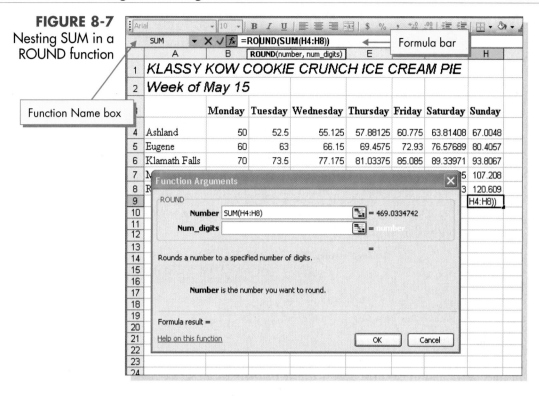

EXERCISE 8-11   Create a Nested IF Function

A nested IF function tests for more than one logical test. In your worksheet, you will first check to see if the daily total is greater than 400, and then you'll test if it is greater than 375.

1. Select cells B4:H9. Press Ctrl + 1. Use the Number format with 0 decimal places.

2. Click cell B10 and click the Insert Function button 𝑓𝑥. In the Logical category, choose IF and click OK.

3. In the Logical_test box, click cell B9. Key **>400** after B9 in the box. This tests if the value in cell B9 is greater than 400.

4. Click in the Value_if_true box. Key **Over 400**. If the value in cell B9 is greater than 400, the text "Over 400" will be shown.

5. Click in the Value_if_false box. If the value is not over 400, you will check if it is over 375. This is another IF function.

6. While the insertion point is in the Value_if_false box, click the arrow next to the Function Name box and choose IF. The Function Arguments dialog box updates to show another IF statement. You can see both in the formula bar. The second IF function is bold in the formula bar to show that it is the one you are now building.

7. In the Logical_test box, click cell B9. Key **>375** after B9. Now you are determining if the value in cell B9 is greater than 375.

8. Click in the Value_if_true box. Key **Over 375** as the result text.

9. Click in the Value_if_false box. Key **Under Quota** and click OK.

FIGURE 8-8
Nesting IF functions

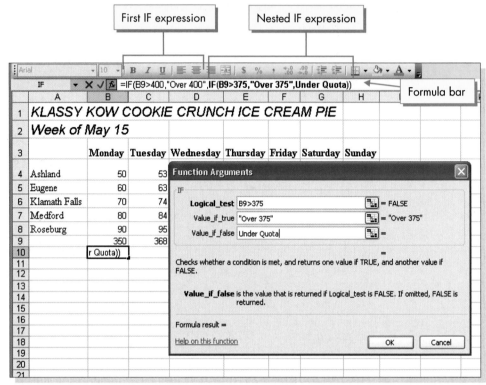

10. Copy the formula to cells C10:H10 and widen columns.

11. Right-align cells C10:H10.

Creating a Hyperlink

A *hyperlink* is a clickable object or text that, when clicked, displays another file, opens another program, shows a Web page, or displays an e-mail address. A hyperlink is a shortcut to files on your computer, your network, or the World Wide Web. As you insert hyperlinks in your work, Excel keeps a list of the addresses and shows them in the Insert Hyperlink dialog box. You can key a new entry or choose an existing name from the list.

A text hyperlink is shown in color and underlined. There are several ways to add a hyperlink to your worksheet:

- Click the Insert Hyperlink button 🔗 on the Standard toolbar.
- Choose Hyperlink from the Insert menu.
- Right-click the cell and choose Hyperlink from the shortcut menu.
- Press Ctrl+K.

EXERCISE **8-12** **Create a Hyperlink**

1. Click cell G12.
2. Click the Insert Hyperlink button 🔗. The Insert Hyperlink dialog box opens.
3. Click the E-mail address button in the Link to bar. Key **distance learning@mcgraw-hill.com** in the E-mail address text box. Excel adds mailto: for your e-mail address.
4. Drag to select the address in the Text to display box.
5. Key **Click here to return to sender**. Click OK. Hyperlink text appears in color and underlined.

FIGURE 8-9
Insert Hyperlink
dialog box

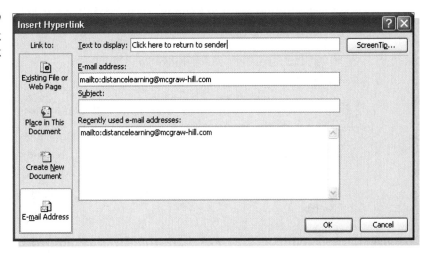

6. Position the mouse pointer on cell G12 to see the ScreenTip. (See Figure 8-10 on the next page.)

✦ **TIP:** To edit or delete a hyperlink, right-click the cell and choose Edit Hyperlink or Remove Hyperlink.

7. Press Ctrl+Home. Save the workbook as *[your initials]*8-12 in your folder.

FIGURE 8-10
Hyperlink and
ScreenTip

	C	D	E	F	G	H	I	J
	OOKIE CRUNCH ICE CREAM PIE							
	Tuesday	Wednesday	Thursday	Friday	Saturday	Sunday		
	53	55	58	61	64	67		
	63	66	69	73	77	80		
	74	77	81	85	89	94		
	84	88	93	97	102	107		
	95	99	104	109	115	121		
	368	386	405	425	447	469		
	Under Quota	Over 375	Over 400	Over 400	Over 400	Over 400		
					Click here to return to sender			
					mailto:distancelearning@mcgraw-hill.com - Click once to follow. Click and hold to select this cell.			

EXERCISE   8-13   Save a Workbook in a Different Format

If you send a workbook to someone who uses a different version of Excel or a different electronic spreadsheet program, you can save the file in an appropriate format for them. Two popular formats are WK4 (Lotus worksheet) and CSV (comma-separated values).

1. Press F12. The Save As dialog box opens.
2. Click the Save as type arrow.

 NOTE: 1-2-3 is an electronic spreadsheet program. Excel can open a 1-2-3 Lotus workbook.

3. Choose WK4(1-2-3) for a Lotus format. The filename is the same, but the workbook will have the **wk4** filename extension.
4. Click Save. A message box alerts you about possible problems in converting the file.
5. Click Yes.

FIGURE 8-11
Message box about
converting file

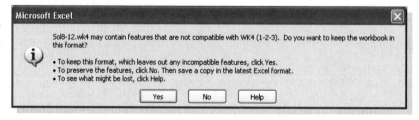

6. Close the workbook without saving.

USING ONLINE HELP

Although you might often print your worksheets for immediate use, many times it is necessary to electronically send the workbook to someone else for further editing or additions. Excel is a *mail-enabled* program, which means you can e-mail a workbook to someone without leaving Excel.

Use Help to learn about Excel's e-mail capabilities:

1. Click in the Type a question for help box and key **email**. Press (Enter).
2. Click the topic Sending a workbook or worksheet in e-mail.
3. Click Show All in the upper-right corner. Read the information.
4. Close the Help window when you are finished reading about e-mail. Close the Search Results dialog box.

LESSON Summary

➤ Use the INT function to display a value without any decimal positions. It shows only the part of the value to the left of the decimal.

➤ The ROUND function adjusts a value up or down, depending on how many digits you use for rounding. It can round to the left or right of the decimal point.

➤ Excel uses a serial number system for dates and times. This enables it to make date and time calculations.

➤ In most date and time calculations, you need to convert the results to the proper format. For example, in determining a person's age, Excel initially shows the result in days. Time results are initially shown in fractions of a 24-hour day.

➤ You can hide a worksheet so that its tab is not visible.

➤ A nested function is a function within a function.

➤ Hyperlinks enable you to jump to other files, e-mail addresses, or Web sites.

➤ Workbooks can be saved in a variety of file formats for exchanging data with others.

LESSON 8 Command Summary			
FEATURE	**BUTTON**	**MENU**	**KEYBOARD**
Hide sheet		Format, Sheet, Hide	
Insert hyperlink	🔗	Insert, Hyperlink	(Ctrl)+(K)
Unhide sheet		Format, Sheet, Unhide	

Concepts Review

TRUE/FALSE QUESTIONS

Each of the following statements is either true or false. Indicate your choice by circling T or F.

T **(F)**   **1.** The INT and ROUND functions use the same arguments.

(T) F   **2.** An integer is a whole number, a nondecimal number.

(T) F   **3.** Excel uses a serial number system for dates.

T **(F)**   **4.** A nested function is placed in the cell below the first formula.

(T) F   **5.** You can hide a worksheet in a workbook.

T **(F)**   **6.** A hyperlink is a flashing cell with a formula.

(T) F   **7.** You can determine if sheets are grouped from the title bar.

T **(F)**   **8.** To convert a fraction of a day to hours, multiply by 365.25.

SHORT ANSWER QUESTIONS

Write the correct answer in the space provided.

1. What is the term used to describe a function inside a function?

Nested function

2. How would you group Sheet1 and Sheet2 in a workbook?

Holding down shift and clicking on other worksheet tabs.

3. What is the keyboard shortcut for displaying the Save As dialog box?

_F12_

4. What does a hyperlink do?

displays another file, opens another program, shows a webpage, or displays an e-mail address

5. Which function inserts the current date?

=today()

6. What does the INT function do?

It shows the nondecimal partion of a number

7. How would Excel display this value =ROUND(1.567,2)?

_1.57_

8. Name two functions that are often used in nested formulas.

IF, ROUND

CRITICAL THINKING

Answer these questions on a separate page. There are no right or wrong answers. Support your answers with examples from your own experience, if possible.

1. How would you determine the number of days until Christmas?

2. Which function do you think has more value in business use: INT or ROUND? Why?

Skills Review

EXERCISE 8-14

Use the INT and ROUND functions.

1. Open **Miles&Disc** and save it in your Lesson 8 folder as *[your initials]*8-14.

2. On the DeliveryMiles sheet, format cell A1 as 18-point Arial.

3. Delete row 2.

 REVIEW: Right-click a row heading and choose Delete.

4. Make the labels in row 2 bold and click the Center button ≣. Widen column C to fit the label in row 3.

5. Format rows 2 and 3 as 22.50 (30 pixels) high.

6. Use the INT function by following these steps:

   a. Key **=int(** in cell C3.
   b. Click cell B3 and press Enter.
   c. Copy the formula in cell C3 to cell C4:C7.

7. Add a custom header to your worksheet but change the font to 9-point in each section. Key your name at the left, add the filename and the tab name in the center, and add the date at the right.

8. Print the worksheet.

9. On the Discounts sheet, click cell C6.

10. Key = and click cell B6. Key * and click cell C5. Press F4 to make it an absolute reference. Press Enter.

 NOTE: The formula multiplies the cost per unit by a quantity of 575 units.

11. Copy the formula in cell C6 to cells C7:C14.

12. Use the ROUND function by following these steps:

    a. Click cell D6 and click the Insert Function button fx.
    b. Choose Math & Trig and ROUND. Click OK.
    c. Click cell C6 for the Number box. Click in the Num_digits box and key **2**. Click OK.
    d. Copy the formula in cell D6 to cells D7:D14.

13. Edit the label in cell D5 to show **Round to the Nearest Penny**.

14. Select cells A4:B4 and drag them to cells A5:B5. Then delete rows 3 and 4. Format row 4 as 22.50 (30 pixels) high.

 REVIEW: Include your name at the left, the filename and the tab name in the center, and the date at the right for a footer.

15. Add a footer to the worksheet and print it.

16. Save and close the workbook.

EXERCISE 8-15

Use date and time arithmetic.

1. Open **PTWorkers** and save it as *[your initials]***8-15** in your Lesson 8 folder.

2. On the Status sheet, key **=today( )** in cell E1. Edit cell A5 to show your first and last name.

3. Use date arithmetic by following these steps:

 NOTE: Subtract the hire date from today to determine how long an employee has worked at the shop.

    a. Click cell C4 and key = to start the formula.
    b. Click cell E1 and press F4.
    c. Key – and click cell B4. Press Enter.
    d. Select cell C4 and press Ctrl+1. Choose Number as the Category and use 2 decimal places. Click OK.
    e. Copy the formula in cell C4 to cells C5:C8.
    f. Click cell D4, key =(and click cell E1. Press F4.

 REVIEW: The subtraction is enclosed in parentheses, so it is calculated first.

> *g.* Key – and click cell B4.
>
> *h.* Key **)/365.25** and press [Enter].
>
> *i.* Format cell D4 as Number with 2 decimal places.
>
> *j.* Copy the formula in cell D4 to cells D5:D8. Format cells D4:D8 as 12-point Times New Roman.
>
> *k.* Print the worksheet.

4. On the PartTimeHours sheet, replace Tom Santana's name with your first and last name.

5. Use time arithmetic by following these steps:

 NOTE: You will subtract the start time from the finish time to determine hours worked.

> *a.* Click cell D5, key **=(** and click cell C5.
>
> *b.* Key **–** and click cell B5.
>
> *c.* Key **)*24** and press [Enter].
>
> *d.* Copy the formula in cell D5 to cells D6:D15.

6. From the Tools menu, choose Options. Click the View tab. Turn off Zero values. Click OK.

 TIP: You can set a worksheet to show or hide zeros.

7. Print the worksheet. Save and close the workbook.

EXERCISE 8-16

Create nested functions by using Insert Function. Key a nested function.

1. Open **CASupplies**. Save it in your Lesson 8 folder as *[your initials]*8-16.

2. Use Insert Function to create a nested function by following these steps:

> *a.* Click cell B18. Click the Insert Function button [*fx*].
>
> *b.* Choose Statistical and AVERAGE. Click OK.
>
> *c.* Click the arrow next to Function Name and choose AVERAGE again. The suggested range is B4:B17 for Number1.
>
> *d.* Click in the Number2 box and select cells C4:C17.
>
> *e.* Click in the Number3 box and select cells D4:D17.
>
> *f.* In the formula bar, click anywhere in the first occurrence of AVERAGE. Click OK.

3. Key a nested function by following these steps:

> *a.* Click cell B19. Key **=average(average(** to start the nested function.
>
> *b.* Select cells E4:E17 and key a comma to separate the arguments.
>
> *c.* Select cells F4:F17 and key **)** to close the second AVERAGE function.
>
> *d.* Key **)** to close the first AVERAGE function. Press [Enter].

   e. Click cell B20. Key **=average(average(** and select cells G4:G17.

   f. Key a comma and select cells H4:H17.

   g. Key a comma and select cells I4:I17.

   h. Key **))**, one parenthesis for the first AVERAGE function and one for the second function. Press Enter.

4. Format cells A1:A2 as 18-point Arial. Apply the Comma Style with 0 decimal places to all values. Right-align the labels in row 3, but leave them rotated.

5. Add a footer and print the worksheet, fit to one landscape page.

6. Make a formula copy of the worksheet and print it fit to one landscape page.

7. Save and close the workbook.

EXERCISE 8-17

Insert a hyperlink.

1. Open **CACount** and save it as *[your initials]*8-17 in your Lesson 8 folder.

2. From the Format menu, choose Sheet and then Unhide. Click CustCount (2) in the list and click OK. Repeat these steps to unhide CustCount (3).

3. While CustCount (3) is active, hold down Shift and click the CustCount tab name to group the sheets.

4. While the sheets are grouped, right-click the column B heading and hide it.

5. Right-click any worksheet tab and choose Ungroup Sheets.

6. Insert a hyperlink by following these steps:

   a. On the CustCount sheet, right-click cell G1 and choose Hyperlink.

   b. Click in the Text to display box and key **Show Supplies Sheet**.

   c. Click the Existing File or Web Page in the Link to list at the left of the dialog box.

   d. Find **CASupplies**, click the filename, and click OK.

7. Add a footer and print the worksheet, fit to a portrait page.

8. Save and close the workbook.

Lesson Applications

EXERCISE 8-18

Use date arithmetic. Create a nested function.

1. Open **PastDue** and save it as *[your initials]*8-18.

2. Select cells C4:C13. Replace all occurrences of "2000" with the current year. If, after replacing, you have some dates in the future, change those cells to last year.

 TIP: You can limit a Find and Replace task to selected cells.

3. In cell D4, key a formula to compute the due date 30 days after the invoice date. Copy the formula.

4. In cell E4, use a formula to subtract cell D4 from today. Format the result with no decimal places. Copy the formula. Some customers might be very late, and some might show a negative number of days, meaning bills are not yet due.

5. Format negative numbers in Column E to show in red without parentheses or a minus sign. You may not have negative numbers at this point, but apply the format anyway.

6. In cell F4, create an IF formula. The first logical test is that cell E4 be greater than 120 days. If this is so, the Value_if_true is **Over 120**. As the Value_if_false, nest another IF function. The logical test for the second IF function is that cell E4 be greater than 60. The Value_if_true for this IF statement is **Over 60**. The Value_if_false entry for the second IF statement is **Acceptable**. Copy the formula and right-align the results.

7. Add your footer and print the worksheet.

8. Make a copy of the sheet and display the formulas. Fit the column widths without regard for the main titles. Print the formula sheet fit to one landscape page.

9. Save and close the workbook.

EXERCISE 8-19

Use time arithmetic.

1. Create a new workbook and save it as *[your initials]*8-19.

2. Format cells A1:A2 as 18-point Arial. In cell A1, key **Klassy Kow Parkland Shop**. Key **Part-Time Hours** in cell A2.

3. In cell B3:D3, key the following labels. Make them bold, turn on Wrap text, and center them.

Starting Time   **Ending Time**   **Hours Worked**

4. In cell A4, key **Monday** and make it bold.

5. Key the data shown in Figure 8-12. Widen column A to fit the longest worker name.

 NOTE: When the time is on the hour, you do not need to key the colon or the zeros. Excel inserts them and capitalizes AM and PM.

FIGURE 8-12

		Starting Time	Ending Time	
5	Keiko Yang	11 am	8:30 pm	
6	Eugene Sanchez	12 pm	10 pm	
7	Millie Hanes	9:30 am	4 pm	
8	Michael Bianciotto	10 am	5:30 pm	
9	Aneta Monroe	2 pm	10 pm	

6. In cell D5, key a formula to determine hours worked. Format the result as a Number with 2 decimal places. Copy the formula.

 REVIEW: Convert a fraction of a day to hours by multiplying by 24.

7. Make sure that all data is visible. Format rows 3 and 4 as 30.00 (40 pixels) high.

8. Add your footer and print the worksheet.

9. Save and close the workbook.

EXERCISE 8-20

Create a nested function.

In this worksheet, you create a nested IF function. The IF statement shows the name of the state with the maximum value for each product.

1. Open **JulyDrinks**. Save it as *[your initials]*8-20.

 2. In cell G5, click the Insert Function button ⨍ₓ. Choose Logical and then IF. Click cell B5 to start the first the Logical_test.

3. Key = after B5 and then click the arrow next to Function Name. Click More Functions, choose Statistical, MAX and then click OK. The MAX function is now nested in the IF function.

4. Select cells B5:E5 as Number1 for the MAX function.

 NOTE: You cannot include the Totals column as you check for the highest sales.

5. Click anywhere in the word IF in the formula bar. Click the Value_if_true box and key **California**. Your function currently states that "California" will be shown in cell G5 if the value in cell B5 is the maximum value in the range B5:E5.

6. Click the Value_if_false box. Now you need to do the same thing for cell C5 to determine if Washington had the highest sales.

7. Click the arrow next to Function Name and choose IF. Click cell C5 for the Logical_test. Key = after C5 and then click the arrow next to Function Name. Choose MAX and select cells B5:E5 as Number1.

8. Click anywhere in the second occurrence of IF in the formula bar. Click the Value_if_true box and key **Washington**. This part of the function says that "Washington" will be shown in cell G5 if the value in cell C5 is the maximum value in the range B5:E5.

9. Click the Value_if_false box. Click the arrow next to Function Name and choose IF. Click cell D5 for the Logical_test. Key = after D5 and then click the arrow next to Function Name. Choose MAX and select cells B5:E5.

10. Click anywhere in the third occurrence of IF in the formula bar. Click the Value_if_true box and key **Oregon**. You have now checked three states. If none of them are the maximum value, then Nevada has the highest sales.

11. Click the Value_if_false box. Key **Nevada**. Click OK.

12. Center the results and copy the formula to row 9.

13. Add a Top and Double Bottom border to cells B10:F10.

14. Set the page to be horizontally centered. Add your footer and print the worksheet.

 REVIEW: Page centering options are on the Margins tab. Because you copy the sheet for the formulas, you must turn off centering on that sheet.

15. Copy the worksheet and display the formulas. Fit the columns according to the data, not the main titles. Print this sheet fit to one landscape page, but not horizontally centered.

16. Save and close the workbook.

EXERCISE 8-21 *Challenge Yourself*

Use date arithmetic and the INT function.

The human resources department is responsible for maintaining records that list an employee's birthday, age, and other related data. You have been asked to create a worksheet with new employees (hired within the last two months).

1. Create a new workbook and save it as *[your initials]*8-21.

2. Key **Klassy Kow New Employees** in cell A1. Key **Birthday and Age** in cell A2. Choose a font and size for both cells.

3. Key these labels in cells A3:C3 and make them bold:

   Name   **Birthday**   **Age**

4. In cells A4:A10, key the first and last names of six new employees. Use classmates' or family members' names, or create new names.

5. Key birthdays in column B for each of your employees. Format the birthdays in a date format that you like.

    TIP: Key birthdays in **mm/dd/yy** format for speed, and format them later.

6. Key a formula that determines the person's age and show the result as an integer.

    TIP: Nest the formula to determine an age in the INT function.

7. Adjust the height of rows 3 and 4 to show more white space. Make other adjustments to format your worksheet in a professional manner.

8. Add your footer and print the worksheet.

9. Copy the worksheet and make a formula printout.

10. Save and close the workbook.

On Your Own

In these exercises you work on your own, as you would in a real-life work environment. Use the skills you've learned to accomplish the task—and be creative.

EXERCISE 8-22

In a new workbook, key your name and the names of three family members in a column. In the next column, key birthdays for each person. In the third column, calculate the number of days until the person's next birthday. Apply an AutoFormat or use your own format choices to make the worksheet attractive. Add a footer. Save the workbook as *[your initials]*8-22 in your Lesson 8 folder. Print the worksheet, save the workbook, and close it.

EXERCISE 8-23

Use Excel's Help system to explore hyperlinks. In a new workbook, key each type of hyperlink that is available in the Insert Hyperlink dialog box. Test each link to see if it works. Save the workbook as *[your initials]*8-23 in your Lesson 8 folder. Print the worksheet, save the workbook, and close it.

EXERCISE 8-24

Create a new workbook with a list of ten persons' first names in column A. In column B, key each person's height in inches, using heights between 60 and 75 inches. In column C, use an IF formula to show "Tall" if the person is 72 inches or more, "Average" if the person is between 64 and 71 inches, and "Short" if the person is less than 63 inches tall. Add a main title and column headings. Format the worksheet with an AutoFormat or your own formatting. Add a footer. Save the workbook as *[your initials]*8-24 in your Lesson 8 folder. Print the worksheet and close the workbook.

Unit 2 Applications

UNIT APPLICATION 2-1

Use an absolute reference. Use the ABS and MIN functions. Apply a border.

Klassy Kow Ice Cream has a contest in which customers guess how many gumballs are in a large jar. You need to keep track of customers and their guesses to determine who has won. The correct count for this month's contest is shown in cell B4.

1. Open **Gumballs**. Save the workbook as *[your initials]*u2-1 in a new folder for Unit 2.

2. In cell C5, key **Difference**. In cell D5, key **Lowest Difference**. Copy the format from cell D5 to the other labels in row 5.

3. In cell C6, click the Insert Function button 𝑓𝑥. From the Math & Trig category, choose **ABS**. In the Number1 entry box, click cell B4 and make it absolute. Then subtract cell B6. Copy the formula.

> **NOTE:** The ABS function shows the absolute value without a minus sign for a negative number. Some of the guesses are greater than the real number, and these results would be negative numbers.

4. In cell D6, use the MIN function to determine which difference in column C is the smallest.

5. Format all values as 12-point Times New Roman with commas and no decimal places.

6. Select the cells in columns A, B, and C for the winner and apply a double top and double bottom border.

7. Add your footer. Print the worksheet.

8. Save and close the workbook.

UNIT APPLICATION 2-2

Use order of precedence and an absolute reference. Determine an age. Nest AND and IF functions.

On the customer birthday list, you need to indicate whether a customer is between 1 and 4 years old, between 5 and 10 years old, or over 10. The formula uses AND functions nested in IF functions.

1. Open **CustAge** and save the workbook as *[your initials]*u2-2 in your Unit 2 folder.

2. In cell E1, key **=today( )**. In cell E3, key **Category** and copy the format from one of the other labels in this row.

3. Use a formula in cell D4 to determine the customer's age. Format the results as a number with two decimals. Copy the formula.

REVIEW: The IF function is in the Logical category.

4. Click cell E4 and click the Insert Function button . Choose IF.

5. In the Logical_test box, click the arrow next to the Function Name box and choose AND. If AND is not in the list, click More Functions and locate it.

6. In the Logical1 box, click cell D4 and key **>=5**. Click the Logical2 box, click cell D4, and key **<=10**. This AND function tests if a customer is between 5 and 10 years old.

7. Click in the word IF in the formula bar. You are now returned to the IF Function Arguments dialog box with the nested AND function as the Logical_test.

8. In the Value_if_true box, key **Between 5 and 10**. If the results of the AND function are true, this statement will be shown.

9. In the Value_if_false box, click the arrow next to the Function Name box and choose IF. If the customer is not between 5 and 10 years old, you will test for another age range.

10. In the Logical_test box, click the arrow next to the Function Name box and choose AND.

11. In the Logical1 box, click cell D4 and key **>1**. In the Logical2 box, click cell D4 and key **<5**. This tests if the customer is between 1 and 4 years old.

12. Click in the second occurrence of IF in the formula bar. In the Value_if_true box, key **Between 1 and 4**.

13. In the Value_if_false box, key **Over 10**. Click OK.

14. Format the results in column E to match the font and size of the other labels in the row. Then copy the formula.

NOTE: You can use the Increase Indent button 📇 or the Format Cells dialog box to set an indent.

15. Select cells E4:D14 and set a horizontal left indent of 1. Make sure all data is visible.

16. Apply a single-line bottom border to cells A3:E3. Widen column E so the border is as long as the longest item. Format row 4 as 22.50 (30 pixels) high.

17. Change the birthday for Maureen Weinberg to one that will make her between 1 and 4 years old.

18. Add your footer and print the worksheet.

19. Copy the worksheet and name the copy **CustBirthdaysFormulas**. Display the formulas. Fit all the columns to the data and print the formula sheet fit to one landscape page.

TIP: Position the pointer in cell A1 before you save a workbook.

20. Save and close the workbook.

UNIT APPLICATION 2-3

Use mixed references.

Klassy Kow Ice Cream shops buy supplies from the main office in San Francisco. Each shop receives a discount based on the quantity ordered. You need to determine the total cost based on the quantity and the discount.

1. Open **SupplyDisc**. Rename Sheet1 as **Discounts**. Delete Sheet2 and Sheet3. Save the workbook as *[your initials]***u2-3** in your Unit 2 folder.

2. In cell C6, key a formula to determine the price if 500 cups are ordered. First multiply the quantity by the price; both of these are mixed references. Continue to build this formula to multiply the result of your first calculation by 1 minus the discount in row 3. The discount is a mixed reference.

3. Copy the formula to the remaining rows in column C and determine if your formula is correct. Once the formula is correct in column C, you should be able to select cells C6:C14 and copy the formulas to the other columns.

4. Select cells C4:F4 and center the label across the selection.

5. Apply the List 1 AutoFormat without the Number, Font, and Alignment settings. Make column A narrower and make columns C through F wider. Columns C through F should all be the same width.

6. Format all values as Currency with 2 decimals.

7. Add your footer and print the worksheet.

8. Copy the worksheet and name the copy **DiscountsFormulas**. Display the formulas. Fit all the columns to the data and print the formula sheet fit to one landscape page.

9. Save and close the workbook.

UNIT APPLICATION 2-4   *Using the Internet*

Search online travel sites to determine travel times for five trips. For each trip, choose a departure city and a destination city. (For a challenging option, develop your data so that one trip is by train, one is by bus, and the others are by air.)

 NOTE: If your trips are between time zones, convert all times to your current time zone before calculating the travel time.

Prepare a worksheet that lists the departure and arrival cities and times, and travel time. (Include type of transportation if you included train or bus options.) Use a formula to determine the actual time in transit, regardless of time zone changes.

Add an appropriate title and your standard footer. Show the current date in a worksheet cell. Apply an AutoFormat. Save your workbook as *[your initials]***u2-4** and print the worksheet. Close the workbook.

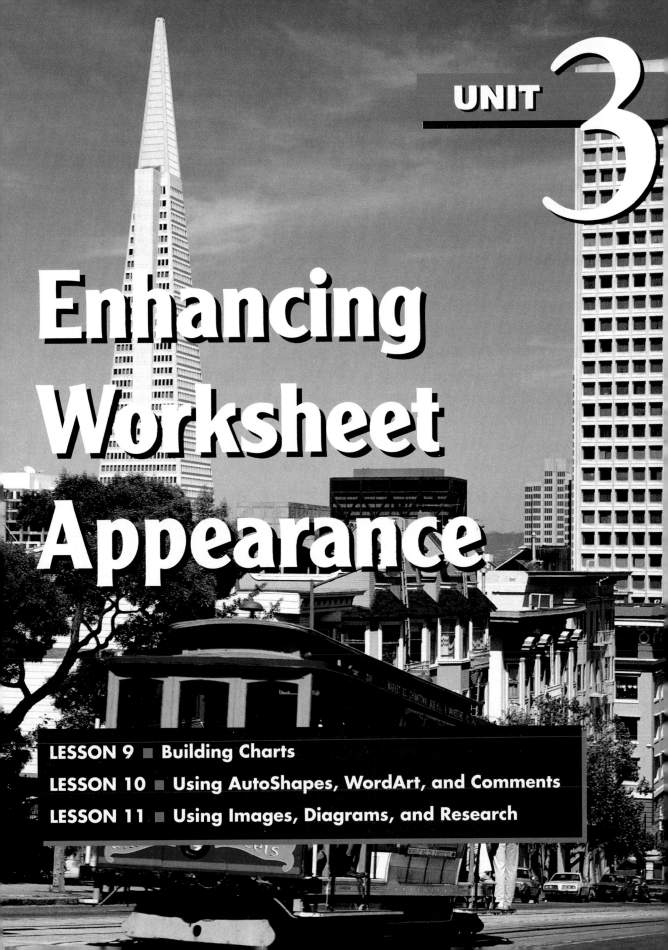

Enhancing Worksheet Appearance

Building Charts

OBJECTIVES

MICROSOFT OFFICE SPECIALIST ACTIVITIES

In this lesson:
XL03S-2-5
XL03E-2-4

See Appendix.

After completing this lesson, you will be able to:

1. **Preview and print charts.**
2. **Edit chart objects.**
3. **Create charts.**
4. **Edit chart data.**
5. **Use images and patterns for a data series.**
6. **Create combination charts.**

 Estimated Time: 2 hours

A *chart* is a visual display of information in a worksheet. Charts can help you make comparisons, identify patterns, and recognize trends.

You can create a chart on its own sheet or within a worksheet. In either case, a chart is linked to worksheet data that is used to create that chart. Because they are linked, a chart is updated when you edit worksheet data.

Previewing and Printing a Chart

An *embedded chart* is a chart that appears on the same sheet as the data. It is a graphic object and can be selected, sized, moved, and edited. An *object* is a separate element or part of a worksheet or chart.

EXERCISE 9-1 Preview a Chart

When you select a chart, the Data menu is replaced by the Chart menu. Depending on how your computer is set, the Chart toolbar might also open.

1. Open **SeptChart**.

2. Change the Zoom size to 75% so that you can see more of the worksheet and the chart at the same time.

3. Click the Print Preview button . This chart shows the value from column F for each city. The chart is positioned below the worksheet data.

   NOTE: If you're using a black-and-white printer, Print Preview shows the chart in shades of gray.

4. Close the preview.

5. Click in the white chart background area to select the chart. It is surrounded by small black rectangles, known as *selection handles*. The data that is plotted on the chart is outlined in the worksheet. The Name box shows that the Chart Area is the active object.

FIGURE 9-1
Chart selected in the worksheet

Name box

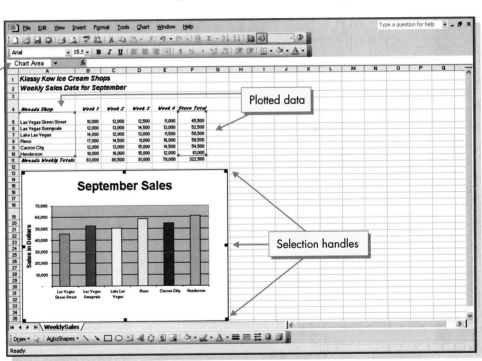

6. Click the Print Preview button . Only the chart is shown, because it is selected.

NOTE: If the Chart toolbar is open, close it for this exercise.

7. Close the preview.

EXERCISE **9-2** **Print a Chart**

1. Click cell D1 to deselect the chart. The selection handles are removed from the chart.
2. Click the Print Preview button . Excel displays the worksheet and its chart.
3. Click <u>S</u>etup and add your standard footer.
4. Click Prin<u>t</u> and click OK. The worksheet and chart print on a single page.
5. Click in the white background chart area to select the chart. The selection handles are visible.
6. Click the Print button. The chart prints by itself in landscape orientation. When you print a selected object, the footer is not included, because the footer is a page setting.

Editing Chart Objects

A chart is made up of objects or elements. You can format each object by using many of the same format settings that you use for a worksheet. Here are descriptions of Excel chart objects:

- The *chart area* is the background for the chart. It can be filled with a color or pattern.
- The *category axis* is created from the row or column headings in the data. A category describes what is shown in the chart.
- The *category title* is an optional title for the chart's categories.
- The *value axis* shows the values on the chart. Excel creates a range of values (the *scale*) based on the data.
- The *plot area* is the rectangular area bounded by the category and value axes.
- The *chart title* is an optional title or name for the chart.
- A *data series* is a collection of related values from the worksheet. These values are in the same column or row and translate into the columns, lines, pie slices, and so on.
- A *data point* is a single value or piece of data from the data series.
- A *data marker* is the object that represents individual values. The marker can be a bar, a column, a symbol, an image, or some other symbol.

- A *legend* is an object that explains the symbols, patterns, or colors used to differentiate the series in the chart.
- A *gridline* is a horizontal or vertical line that extends across the plot area to make it easier to read and follow the values.
- A *tick mark* is a small line or marker on the category (*x*) and value (*y*) axes to help in reading the values.

FIGURE 9-2
Excel chart objects

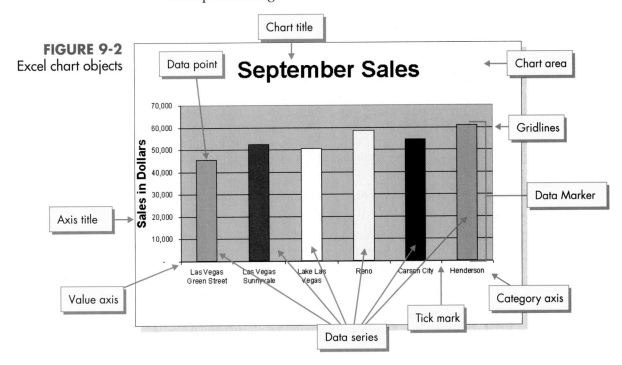

All chart objects show a ScreenTip when you position the mouse pointer on the object. To edit a chart object, select it by pointing and clicking. When an object is selected, it shows selection handles and its name appears in the Name box.

EXERCISE 9-3 **Format the Chart Title**

1. Position the mouse pointer on the chart title "September Sales." A ScreenTip appears showing that it is the Chart Title.
2. Click the chart title. It is selected and shows selection handles with an outline border. Its name appears in the Name box.
3. Click to the left of the **S** in "September." The text insertion point is in position, and the border and selection handles are removed.
4. Key **Nevada** and press the (Spacebar). The word is inserted.
5. With the I-beam pointer, drag across the entire chart title to select it.

6. Point anywhere in the selected text and right-click. A shortcut menu opens.

7. Choose Format Chart Title. The Format Chart Title dialog box has Font and Properties tabs.

8. On the Font tab, choose Bold Italic and click OK. The title is reformatted.

9. Click the white background area of the chart to deselect the title.

EXERCISE **9-4** **Format the Data Series**

The series of values shown in this chart are the values in column F. Each value is represented by the height of its column. The values are plotted against the *y*-axis in this chart, the column of numbers at the left. The category for this chart is the city name, shown along the bottom axis (the *x*-axis).

1. Scroll the window to see the city names along the chart's category axis (the x-axis).

2. Rest the mouse pointer on the Reno column to see its ScreenTip. It is one data point from the series.

3. Right-click the Reno column. The entire data series is selected, and each column has a single selection handle in its middle. The Name box shows Series1, because this is the first (and only) series in this chart.

4. Choose Format Data Series.

5. Click the Data Labels tab. A *data label* is an optional title shown for each value. It is the value from column F in this case.

6. Click to place a check mark for Value in the Label Contains group.

FIGURE 9-3
Format Data Series
dialog box

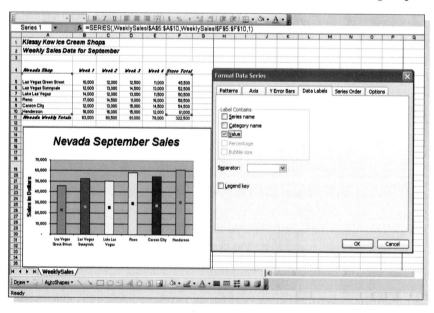

7. Click OK. The value of each data point appears above its column.

8. Rest the mouse pointer on one of the data labels to see the ScreenTip.

9. Right-click any of the labels and choose Format Data Labels. The Format Data Labels dialog box includes tabs for the patterns (colors), font, number, and alignment.

10. Click the Font tab and choose 9 points as the Size. Click OK. The data labels look better in a smaller font.

EXERCISE **Change the Data Series Colors**

1. Right-click any column and choose Format Data Series.

2. Click the Options tab.

3. Click to remove the check mark for Vary colors by point. Click OK. All the columns are now the same color.

4. Right-click a column again and choose Format Data Series.

5. Click the Patterns tab. The Area group includes solid colors for the columns.

6. Click any color swatch in the Area group. Click OK. All the columns are changed to the new color.

7. Right-click a column and choose Format Data Series. Click the Options tab.

8. Click to place a check mark in the Vary colors by point box. Click OK. The colors are not varied, though you just turned on that setting.

 TIP: The Automatic option must be turned on for colors to be varied.

9. Right-click a column again and choose Format Data Series.

10. Click the Patterns tab again. Click the Automatic button in the Area group. Click OK.

EXERCISE **9-6** **Format the Category Axes**

1. Position the mouse pointer on a city name to see its ScreenTip. The Category Axis is the x-axis in this chart. It represents the city names.

2. Right-click any city name and choose Format Axis.

3. On the Font tab, choose Bold.

4. Click the Patterns tab. Notice that the Major tick mark type is Outside (outside the bottom border of the chart). Move the dialog box so that you can see a tick mark clearly.

5. Choose Cross for Major tick mark type. Click OK. The tick mark now crosses the bottom border.

EXERCISE 9-7 **Format the Value Axes**

The Chart toolbar includes buttons for many of the same commands that are shown in the shortcut menus. To display or hide the Chart toolbar, right-click any other toolbar and click Chart. You can also display the Chart toolbar by choosing Toolbars and Chart from the View menu.

You can change the shape of the toolbar by dragging an edge to make it taller or wider. You can also position the toolbar by dragging it by its title bar.

TABLE 9-1 Chart Toolbar

BUTTON		DESCRIPTION
Chart Title ▾	Chart Objects	Lists all the objects in the chart and allows you to choose one for editing.
	Format Object (varies)	Opens the format dialog box for the selected object.
	Chart Type	Lists the chart types available.
	Legend	Displays or hides a legend.
	Data Table	Displays or hides a table showing the data series.
	By Row	Plots a data series by rows.
	By Column	Plots a data series by column.
	Angle Clockwise	Rotates text downward.
	Angle Counterclockwise	Rotates text upward.

1. Display the Chart toolbar.

2. Click one of the values along the y-axis, the sales in dollars. You can see selection handles at the top and bottom of the vertical axis that show it is selected. The Chart Objects box on the toolbar shows Value Axis; so does the Name box.

3. Click the Format Axis button ⊞ on the Chart toolbar. The Format Axis dialog box opens.

TIP: The Format button 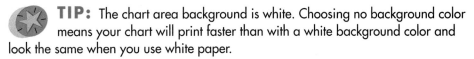 on the Chart toolbar shows the name of the selected object. The name changes depending on what is selected.

4. Click the Number tab. Choose Currency with 0 decimals and $ as the Symbol.

5. Click the Font tab and key **7** as the size. Click OK.

6. Click the title "Sales in Dollars" along the left edge of the chart. Its name, Value Axis Title, appears in the Chart Objects box, and it shows selection handles.

7. Click the Format Axis Title button 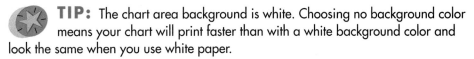 on the Chart toolbar.

8. On the Font tab, choose 10-point italic. Click OK.

9. Click the arrow next to the Chart Objects button on the toolbar. The list includes all the objects in the chart.

10. Click Plot Area. The plot area is the background grid for the columns. It is selected, and the data is outlined in the worksheet.

11. Click the Format Plot Area button 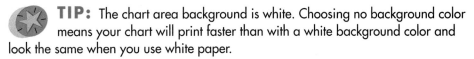 on the Chart toolbar.

12. In the Area section, click the None button. Click OK. The grid color is removed.

13. Click the arrow next to the Chart Objects button on the toolbar. Choose Chart Area. The chart's background is selected.

14. Click the Format Chart Area button 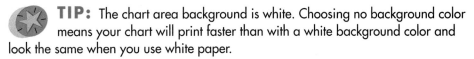 on the Chart toolbar.

15. On the Patterns tab, click the None button in the Area section. Click OK. The chart background is removed.

TIP: The chart area background is white. Choosing no background color means your chart will print faster than with a white background color and look the same when you use white paper.

16. Click a cell in the worksheet. Press Ctrl+Home.

17. Save the workbook as *[your initials]*9-7 in a new folder for Lesson 9.

18. Print and close the workbook.

Creating Charts

Before you build you own chart, you must answer two questions. First, what data should you use to create the chart? Second, what type of chart is best for your data? With practice and experience, you can develop a good sense of how to identify data and choose chart types.

You can create basic chart types such as column charts, bar charts, pie charts, and line charts. You can also create specialized charts such as doughnut and radar charts. Table 9-2 describes the chart types available.

TABLE 9-2 Chart Types in Excel

TYPE		DEFINITION
	Column	A column chart is the most popular chart type. Column charts show how values change over a period of time or make comparisons among items. They can be prepared with 3-D effects or stacked columns. Categories are on the horizontal axis (x), and values are on the vertical axis (y).
	Bar	Bar charts illustrate comparisons among items or show individual figures at a specific time. Bar charts can use 3-D effects and stacked bars. Categories are on the vertical axis (y). Values are on the horizontal axis (x).
	Line	Line charts show trends in data over a period of time. They emphasize the rate of change. 3-D effects are available. Lines can be stacked and can show markers, a symbol that indicates a single value.
	Pie	Pie charts show one data series and compare the sizes of each part of a whole. Pie charts should have less than six data points to be easy to interpret. A pie chart can use 3-D effects and can show exploded slices.
	XY (Scatter)	XY (Scatter) charts are used to show relationships between two values, such as comparing additional advertising to increased sales. Scatter charts do not have a category; both axes show numbers/values.
	Area	Area charts look like colored-in line charts. They show the rate of change and emphasize the magnitude of the change. 3-D effects are available.
	Doughnut	Doughnut charts compare the sizes of parts. A doughnut chart has a hole in the middle. A doughnut chart shows the relative proportion of the whole. A doughnut chart can show more than one data series, with each concentric ring representing a series.
	Radar	Radar charts show the frequency of data relative to a center point and to other data points. There is a separate axis for each category, and each axis extends from the center. Lines connect the values in a series.
	Surface	Surface charts illustrate optimum combinations of two sets of data. They show two or more series on a surface. Surface charts can use 3-D effects.
	Bubble	Bubble charts compare sets of three values. They are like XY scatter charts with the third value displayed as the size of the bubble. Bubble charts can be 3-D.
	Stock	Stock charts are often called "high-low-close charts." They use three series of data in high, low, close order. They can also use volume as a fourth series.
	Cylinder	Cylinder charts use a cylindrical shape to show more effect for 3-D column and bar charts.
	Cone	Cone charts use a conical shape for dramatic effect in 3-D column and bar charts.
	Pyramid	Pyramid charts use a pyramid shape for dramatic effect in 3-D column and bar charts.

EXERCISE **9-8** **Create and Edit an Automatic Chart**

After you select values and labels for a chart, press (F11) to create an automatic column chart. It is inserted on its own sheet, and you can edit it like any chart.

To create an automatic chart, select the range of data to be plotted. This range should include category information and values.

1. Open **MayChart**. There is no chart yet.

2. Select cells A3:B7. This range includes the state category and the values.

3. Press (F11). A column chart is created on its own sheet.

4. Click the chart title and click the Format Chart Title button 🖼 on the Chart toolbar.

5. Click the Font tab. Format the title as 18-point bold and click OK.

6. Click in the title to place an insertion point. Edit the title to **Number of Kowabungas Sold**.

7. Click any column and then click the Format Data Series button 🖼 on the Chart toolbar.

8. Click the Options tab. Click to place a check mark for Vary colors by point. Click OK.

9. While all columns are selected, click the "Oregon" column. It is selected alone.

10. Click the Format Data Point button 🖼 on the toolbar.

11. Click the Patterns tab and choose a different color in the Area group. Click OK. Only the selected column is changed.

FIGURE 9-4
Changing an
individual column

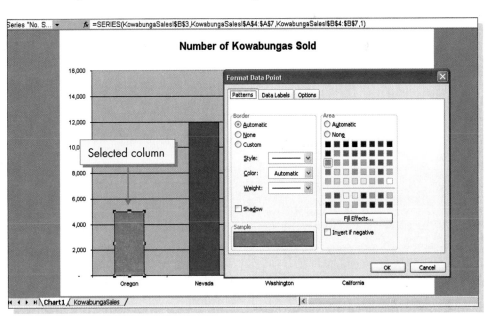

EXERCISE 9-9 Create an Embedded Chart

An embedded chart appears on the same sheet as the data. You create it by using the Chart Wizard. A *wizard* is a series of dialog boxes that leads you step-by-step through the process of creating an object or using a complex feature. You can start the Chart Wizard by:

- Clicking the Chart Wizard button 🗠 on the Standard toolbar.
- Choosing Chart from the Insert menu.

1. Click the **KowabungaSales** tab. Cells A3:B7 are still selected.

2. Click the Chart Wizard button 🗠. The first Chart Wizard dialog box lists the types of charts available.

 TIP: When you have time, experiment with Custom Types to see other chart types.

3. On the Standard Types tab, choose Pie in the Chart type list. Several sub-types for pie charts are shown on the right, with the first one selected. A description appears below the list.

FIGURE 9-5
Creating a pie chart
by using the wizard

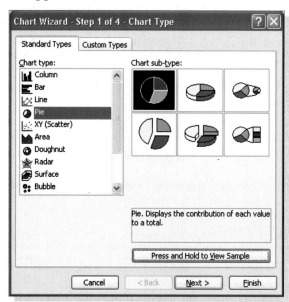

4. Click Press and Hold to View Sample and hold down the mouse button. A sample of your pie chart is shown. Release the mouse button.

5. Click Next. The second dialog box shows the Data range that you selected, A3:B7. The range is shown with absolute references and the worksheet tab name. Excel assumes that the series is in a column, because the values are in column B.

6. Click the Rows button. The sample changes to show what your chart looks like if the series is in rows. This pie chart does not make sense.

 TIP: If you are not sure if your data is in rows or columns, click each button to see which chart seems more logical.

7. Click the Columns button.

8. Click the Series tab. There is one series or one set of values in this chart. Because the series is in a column, Excel has named the series by using the label from column B.

9. Click Next. The third Chart Wizard dialog box has three tabs of Chart Options for a pie chart.

10. On the Titles tab, drag across the current Chart title to select it.

11. Key **Comparison of State Sales** in the Chart title box. After a few seconds, the new title appears in the preview area.

12. Click the Legend tab. You can choose where to place the legend.

13. Choose Bottom. The legend is below the chart.

14. Click the Data Labels tab. For a pie chart, you can show names, labels, or percents.

15. Click to place a check mark for Percentage in the Label Contains area. The percent of the pie that each slice represents is shown.

FIGURE 9-6
Embedding the
chart in the
worksheet

16. Click Next. The Chart Location dialog box shows that the chart will be placed as an object in the worksheet.

17. Click Finish. The chart is on the worksheet with its data.

EXERCISE **9-10** **Move and Size a Chart**

1. Point at the white background chart area. Drag the chart so that its top-left corner aligns at cell D1.

 NOTE: Move the Chart toolbar so that you can see your work area.

2. Point at the bottom-right selection handle. A two-pointed sizing pointer appears.

 NOTE: Change the Zoom size so that you can see column K and row 19.

3. Click and drag the bottom-right selection handle to cell K19. As you drag, the chart is made larger.

4. Click in column B to deselect the chart.

EXERCISE **9-11** **Format a Legend and Pie Slices**

1. Right-click the legend and choose Format Legend.

2. Click the Font tab. Change the font size to 9 points and click OK.

3. Right-click the pie and choose Format Data Series.

4. Click the Data Labels tab.

5. Click to remove the check mark for Percentage. Click OK. The pie is larger because there's more room without the data labels (percents).

6. While the pie is selected, left-click the California slice. Only that slice is selected.

7. Right-click the California slice and choose Format Data Point.

FIGURE 9-7
Pie chart with a
single slice selected

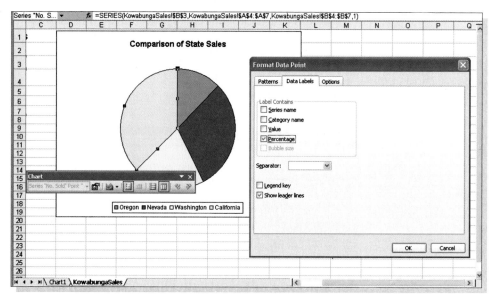

8. Click the Data Labels tab and Percentage. Click OK. The data point percentage is shown for the California slice.

9. Click any cell in the worksheet.

10. Click the Print Preview button. The chart and worksheet are shown. You will rearrange the chart later so that it is not cut off.

11. Close print preview.

EXERCISE **9-12** **Create a Chart Sheet**

A chart sheet shows a chart by itself on a separate sheet. It is still linked to the data in the worksheet.

1. Select cells A3:B7 and click the Chart Wizard button .
2. On the Standard Types tab, choose Bar in the Chart type list.
3. In the Chart sub-type group, choose Clustered bar with a 3-D visual effect, the first sub-type in the second row.
4. Click Press and Hold to View Sample and hold down the mouse button.
5. Release the mouse button.
6. Click Next. The Data range is cells A3:B7, the states and values. In this bar chart, the category is along the left side of the chart. The values are along the bottom of the chart.
7. Click Next. A bar chart has six tabs of Chart Options.
8. On the Titles tab, key **Comparison of Weekly Sales** in the Chart title box.

> ⤢ **NOTE:** You might notice a slight delay before titles appear in the preview area.

FIGURE 9-8
Chart options for a
bar chart

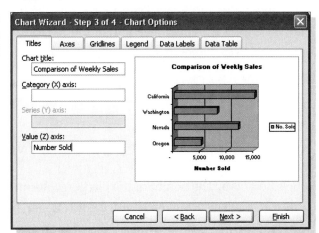

9. Click in the Value (Z) axis box. Key **Number Sold**.
10. Click the Axes tab. The chart shows the categories and the values on the chart. Both show a check mark.

EXERCISE **9-13** **Add Gridlines and a Data Table**

1. Click the Gridlines tab. Only major gridlines are shown along the value axis.
2. Click to place a check mark for Minor gridlines in the Value (Z) axis group.
3. Click the Legend tab. The legend is shown on the chart.
4. Click to remove the check mark for Show legend.
5. Click the Data Labels tab. It is not necessary to show any labels on this chart.

6. Click the Data Table tab. A data table shows the values and categories below the chart.

7. Click to place a check mark for Show data table.

8. Click Next. You can place a chart in the worksheet or in a separate sheet.

9. Choose As new sheet. Key **BarChart** in the box.

10. Click Finish. The bar chart is on a new sheet named BarChart.

Editing Chart Data

After you create a chart, you might need to change values in the worksheet. Because the chart is linked to the data, changes that you make in the worksheet are shown in the chart.

You might also discover that you need to add another category or data series to your chart. Both are easy to accomplish.

EXERCISE 9-14 Change Chart Data

1. Click the KowabungaSales tab. Notice the pie-slice size for Oregon and its corresponding value in the worksheet.

2. Click the BarChart tab. Note the length of the bar for Oregon.

3. Click the Chart1 tab. Note the height of the Oregon column.

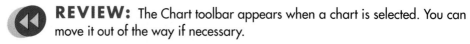 **REVIEW:** The Chart toolbar appears when a chart is selected. You can move it out of the way if necessary.

4. Click the KowabungaSales tab.

5. Click cell B4, key **10000**, and press Enter. Notice the larger pie slice for Oregon.

6. Click the Chart1 tab. The height of the Oregon column is increased.

7. Click the BarChart tab. Note the length of the Oregon bar.

EXERCISE 9-15 Add a Data Point

If you add another state and its total to the worksheet, you add a data point. If you insert the new data point within the chart's data range, it appears automatically in all charts linked to the data. If you add new data below or above the chart's original source data range, you need to reset the data range for each chart.

1. On the KowabungaSales sheet, key **Idaho** in cell A8.

2. Key **5000** in cell B8. This new data point is not within the existing data range for the charts.

3. Click the white background area for the pie chart. The data range is highlighted in the worksheet.

4. Position the pointer on the bottom-right handle for cell B7. A two-pointed sizing arrow appears.

5. Drag the sizing arrow to include the Idaho information in the data range. The chart is updated when you release the mouse button.

FIGURE 9-9
Adding a
data point

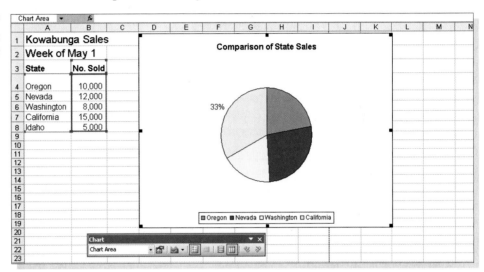

6. Click the Chart1 tab.

7. Right-click the white chart background. Choose Source Data. The Source Data dialog box opens on top of the KowabungaSales tab with the current data range selected.

8. In the Data range entry box, edit the address to show **$B$8** instead of $B$7. Click OK. The column chart is updated to include Idaho. (See Figure 9-10 on the next page.)

9. Click the BarChart tab. Right-click the white chart background.

10. Choose Source Data. The current data range is selected in the worksheet.

 REVIEW: The dialog box collapses as you drag. It expands when you release the mouse button.

11. Click cell A3 and drag to select cells A3:B8. Click OK. There is now an Idaho bar.

12. Right-click the row 8 heading on the KowabungaSales sheet.

13. Choose Insert. One blank row is inserted.

14. Key **Arizona** in cell A8 and **25000** in cell B8. This data point is within the existing data range for the charts.

FIGURE 9-10
Source Data
dialog box

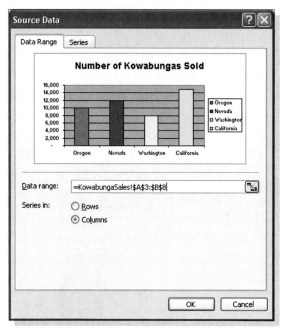

15. Click each sheet tab to see the Arizona data.

EXERCISE 9-16 **Add a Data Series**

If you add another column of values to the worksheet, listing a second product, you add another series.

 NOTE: A pie chart has only one series.

1. On the KowabungaSales sheet, key the following values in cells C4:C9:
6000
12000
4500
15000
30000
25000

2. In cell B3, key **Kowabunga**. In cell C3, key **KowOwow**.

3. Match the format in cell C3 to cell B3 and widen the columns. Format the values in column C to match the other values in the worksheet.

4. Click the white background for the pie chart. Drag the chart to the right so that its left edge aligns at the left side of column E.

5. Click the Chart1 tab. Right-click the white chart background and choose Source Data.

6. Click cell A3 and drag to select cells A3:C9. Click OK. The column chart now shows two columns for each state, one for each product. Oregon has a different color scheme because you changed it earlier.

FIGURE 9-11
Adding a
data series

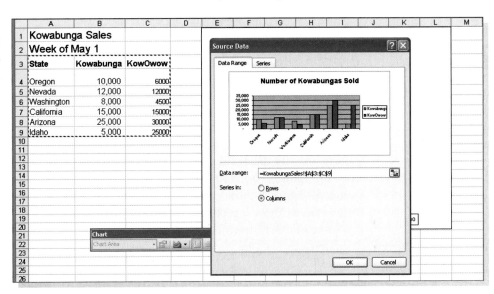

REVIEW: Look at the legend or display the ScreenTip to determine which column represents "Kowabunga."

7. Right-click any column for Kowabunga products. Choose Format Data Series.

8. Click the Patterns tab and choose a different color in the Area group. Click OK.

9. Point at the chart title and click to select it.

10. Click within the text to display a text insertion point.

11. Edit the title to **Number of Kowabungas and KowOwows Sold**.

12. Click the white background.

EXERCISE 9-17 **Delete a Data Point and a Data Series**

1. Click the KowabungaSales tab.

2. Select the headings for rows 8 and 9. Right-click either heading and delete the rows. The pie chart is updated.

3. Click the BarChart tab. Click the Chart1 tab. The Arizona and Idaho data is removed from all charts.

4. Click the KowabungaSales tab.

NOTE: You can delete any chart object or the entire chart by selecting it and pressing Delete.

5. Select cells C3:C7 and press Delete. This deletes the KowOwow series on the column chart.

6. Click the Chart1 tab. The second column is gone, but the legend still shows a marker for the data series.

7. Right-click the white chart background and choose Source Data.

8. In the Data range box, edit the last cell reference to show **b7**. Click OK.

9. Click the legend and press Delete.

Using Images and Patterns for a Data Series

Charts initially use solid colors in the columns, bars, pie slices, and other objects. You can change from a solid color to a pattern or an image. Patterns can be used to better distinguish bars, columns, or slices, on a black-and-white printer. Images allow you to show a picture to represent the data.

You can insert an image in a worksheet by:

- Clicking the Insert Picture from File button on the Drawing toolbar.
- From the Insert menu, choosing Picture and then From File.

The Drawing toolbar usually appears at the bottom of the window. You can display the Drawing toolbar by:

- Right-clicking any toolbar and choosing Drawing.
- From the View menu, choosing Toolbars and then Drawing.

EXERCISE 9-18 Use an Image for a Data Series

If you want to use an image in a bar or column chart, it looks best if you use a two-dimensional chart rather than 3-D.

1. Click the BarChart tab. Click the chart background to display the Chart toolbar (or click View, Toolbars, Chart).

2. Click the arrow next to the Chart Type button on the Chart toolbar. A palette with several chart types opens.

3. Choose Bar Chart (first icon, second row) to change the chart to a two-dimensional chart.

4. Click any bar in the chart. All the bars show selection handles.

5. Click the Insert Picture From File button on the Drawing toolbar. (If the Drawing toolbar is not open, click View, Toolbars, Drawing.) The Insert Picture dialog box opens.

6. Navigate to the folder with **Kowabunga** to find the image.

 NOTE: Ask your instructor for help if you cannot find the image.

FIGURE 9-12
Inserting a picture

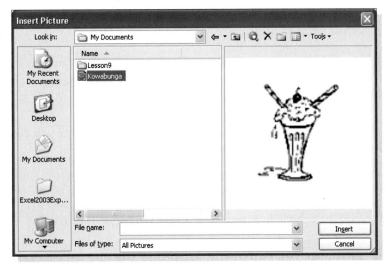

7. Choose **Kowabunga** and click Insert. The picture is inserted in the bars and stretched to fit the length of the bar.

EXERCISE **9-19** **Format the Image**

FIGURE 9-13
Changing
the picture
format setting

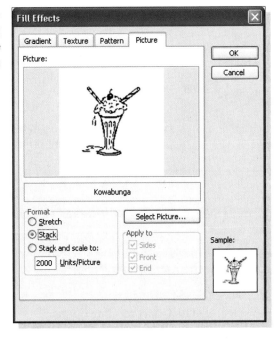

1. Right-click any bar and choose Format Data Series.

2. Click the Patterns tab.

3. Click Fill Effects in the Area group. The Fill Effects dialog box opens. You can apply gradients (blended colors), textures, patterns, and picture settings.

4. Click the Picture tab. The default for most images is a Stretch format.

5. In the Format group, choose Stack and click OK.

6. Click OK again. The image tiles (stacks) inside the length of the bar.

EXERCISE 9-20 **Use a Gradient for a Data Series**

A *gradient* is a blend of colors. In Excel, you can build color blends that use one or two colors, or you can choose from preset gradients. A gradient can give a special effect to bars, columns, or pie slices in a chart.

1. Click the Chart1 tab.
2. Right-click any column and choose Format Data Series.
3. Click the Patterns tab and Fill Effects.

 TIP: A one-color gradient uses the color that you choose and blends to dark (black) or light (white).

4. Click the Gradient tab.
5. In the Colors group, choose Two colors.
6. Click the arrow for Color 1 and choose a dark color.

FIGURE 9-14
Using a gradient
for fill

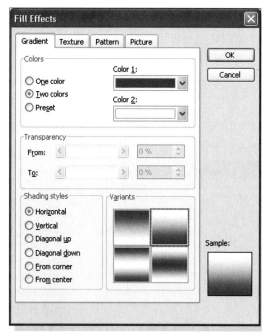

7. Click the arrow for Color 2 and choose a light color.
8. In the Shading styles box, choose Horizontal.

 NOTE: The Variants area controls how the two colors blend, top to bottom or left to right.

9. In the Variants box, choose the top-right variant. Click OK.
10. Click OK again. All the columns show the gradient.

 NOTE: If you're using a black-and-white printer, the gradient prints as shades of gray.

EXERCISE 9-21 **Use a Texture and a Pattern for a Data Series**

A *texture* is a background that appears as a grainy, nonsmooth surface. A *pattern* is a cross-hatched, dotted, dashed, or similar pattern.

1. Click the KowabungaSales tab.
2. Click the pie to select it. The Chart toolbar opens.

NOTE: If the Chart toolbar does not open, right-click any open toolbar and choose Chart to open it.

3. Click the California slice to select only it.

4. Click the Format Data Point button ⬚ on the Chart toolbar.

5. Click the Patterns tab. Click Fill Effects.

6. Click the Texture tab. Notice that some textures look similar to marble, wood, and canvas.

7. Click any texture tile. Its description appears below the group.

8. Choose White marble. Click OK and then click OK again.

9. Click to select only the Nevada slice. Click the Format Data Point button ⬚ on the Chart toolbar.

10. Click the Patterns tab. Click Fill Effects.

11. Click the Pattern tab. The patterns in the first two columns are described as percentages. They are dotted blends of the Foreground and Background colors. The other patterns have descriptive names.

12. Click several different pattern tiles and read their descriptions.

13. Click the arrow for the Foreground color. Choose Black (first tile).

14. Click the arrow for the Background color. Choose White (last column, fifth row).

FIGURE 9-15
Using a pattern as a
fill effect

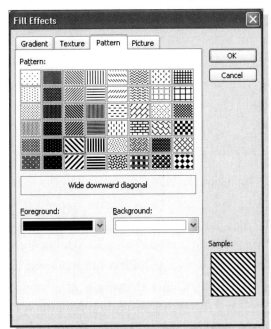

15. Choose one of the patterns, not a dotted percentage. Click OK.

16. Click OK again. Click a cell in the worksheet.

17. Drag the chart so that its top-left corner aligns at cell A9.

18. Save your workbook as *[your initials]*9-21 in a Lesson 9 folder.

19. Click the Chart1 tab name. Hold down (Shift) and click the KowabungaSales tab name. The sheets are grouped.

20. From the File menu, choose Page Setup. Add your footer to the landscape pages.

21. Show the portrait page and add the same footer.

22. Print the workbook.

Creating a Combination Chart

A *combination chart* is a single chart that uses more than one chart type or different number scales. A combination chart usually has at least two series or sets of values. Some combination charts use the same chart type for each series, but a secondary number scale. A *secondary scale* is a set of axis values that is different from the first (primary) set.

E X E R C I S E 9-22 **Create a Chart with Two Chart Types**

1. Key the data in Figure 9-16 to add another series for the number of KowOwows sold and two series for the dollar value sold of both products.

FIGURE 9-16

	A	B	C	D	E
3	State	Kowabunga	KowOwow	$Kowabunga	$KowOwow
4	Oregon	5000	12000	=b4*2.39	=c4*2.19
5	Nevada	12000	15000		
6	Washington	8000	10000		
7	California	15000	25000		

 NOTE: The formula multiplies the price by the number sold.

2. Copy the formulas into rows 5 through 7. Format the results as 12-point Arial and Currency with no decimals and a dollar sign.
3. Match the label formats and AutoFit columns D and E.
4. Click the Chart1 tab. Right-click the white background for the chart.
5. Choose Source Data. The chart currently plots cells A3:B7.
6. Click cell A3 and drag to select cells A3:C7. Click OK. Now the chart plots two sales values.

 7. Click the Legend button ▤ on the Chart toolbar. A legend is placed on the sheet.

FIGURE 9-17
Changing the
chart type for
a data series

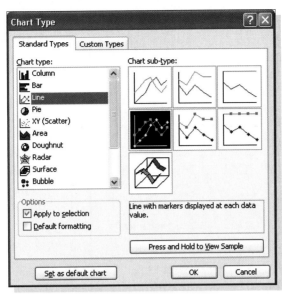

8. Right-click any Kowabunga bar and choose Chart Type. These are the same chart types you see in the Chart Wizard.

9. Choose Line in the Standard Types tab.

10. Choose Line with markers displayed at each data value. Click OK. The Kowabunga series is now a line chart.

11. Print the chart sheet.

EXERCISE **9-23** **Build a Chart with Two Series**

You can show the dollar sales and the number of items sold on the same chart. These values will be two different series on the chart.

1. Click the KowabungaSales tab.

 REVIEW: Use Ctrl to select noncontiguous ranges. Ranges for a chart need not be contiguous.

2. Select cells A3:A7, C3:C7, and E3:E7. This includes the number of items sold and the dollar values for KowOwows.

3. Click the Chart Wizard button ▦. Choose a Column chart type and a Clustered Column sub-type.

4. Click Next. The series or values are in columns, but the dollar values are disproportionately larger than the number sold.

5. Click the Series tab. There are two series, one for the product and one for the dollars. For the name of each series, Excel uses the label at the top of the column.

6. In the Series list, choose KowOwow.

7. In the Name box, drag across the reference to select it.

8. Key **Number Sold**.

9. In the Series list, choose $KowOwow. In the Name box, drag across the reference and key **Dollar Sales**. (See Figure 9-18 on the next page.)

10. Click Next. The Chart Options include six tabs.

FIGURE 9-18
Changing a
series name

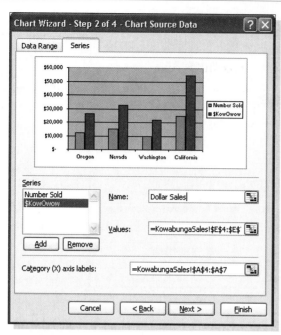

11. On the Titles tab, key
Units and Dollars as
the Chart title.

12. Click Next.

13. Choose As new sheet
and name the sheet
ComboChart.

14. Click Finish. Both series
use the same value axis,
so the dollar column is
disproportionately taller.

EXERCISE   **9-24**   **Add a Secondary Axis**

Because the values are very different, you should use two axes on the chart, one to
show the number of items and one to show the dollar amounts. This makes it easier to understand the values in the chart. To use a secondary axis, use different
chart types for each data series.

1. Right-click a Dollar Sales bar and choose Chart Type.

2. Choose Line in the Standard Types tab.

3. Choose Line with markers displayed at each data value. Click OK.

4. Right-click a Number Sold bar and choose Format Data Series.

5. Click the Axis tab.

6. Click the radio button for Secondary axis. The selected series will be plotted
on a separate value axis. Click OK.

7. Right-click the Dollar Sales line. Choose Format Data Series.

8. Click the Patterns tab. In the Line group, click the arrow next to Color: and
choose Black.

9. In the Marker group, click the arrow next to Style. A list of shapes for the line
markers is shown.

10. Choose a style.

11. Click the arrow for the Foreground color. Choose Black.

12. Click the arrow for the Background color. Choose Black.

13. Click the up spinner button for Si<u>z</u>e to reach 10 pts.
14. Click OK. Click the white chart background to see the changes.
15. Add your footer to this sheet.
16. Save the workbook as *[your initials]*9-24 in your Lesson 9 folder.
17. Print the chart sheet and then close the workbook.

USING ONLINE HELP

In addition to charts, you can build diagrams and organization charts in a worksheet. Unlike charts, however, diagrams are not based on worksheet data. In this unit, you will use Office on Microsoft.com to view the most current help information.

Use Help to learn about diagrams:

1. Establish an Internet connection and start Internet Explorer. Minimize the window.
2. In a blank workbook, choose Help and Microsoft Excel Help. Click Table of Contents. You may see a prompt Downloading from Microsoft.com as the latest help files are accessed.
3. Click the topic Working with Data. Related subtopics are listed.
4. Click Charts and Graphics. Click Drawings, Pictures, and Diagrams. Click Diagrams and Organization Charts.
5. Click About diagrams. Click Show All in the upper-right corner. Read the information.
6. Close the Help window. Close the Help task pane.
7. Close Internet Explorer and end your Internet connection if appropriate.

LESSON 9 Summary

➤ Charts can be embedded within a worksheet. They can also be placed in a separate sheet.
➤ A chart is linked to the data that it is plotting. If the data is edited, the chart reflects the changes.
➤ A chart includes many individual objects that can be edited.
➤ Right-click a chart object to see its shortcut menu.
➤ Charts show data series, which are the chart's values. A pie chart can have only one series, but other types of charts can show multiple data series.

➤ You can make many chart changes directly from the Chart toolbar.

➤ If you select data and press F11, Excel creates an automatic column chart.

➤ The Chart Wizard is a series of dialog boxes in which you choose options for creating a chart.

➤ Excel's standard types of business charts include bar, column, line, and pie charts.

➤ Move a chart by selecting it and dragging it. Size a chart by dragging one of its selection handles.

➤ After a chart is created, you can add a data point or an entire series to it.

➤ Although charts typically use solid color for columns, slices, and bars, you can use images, patterns, textures, or gradients to add visual appeal to your charts.

➤ A combination chart typically has at least two series and uses different chart types for each series.

➤ Some combination charts use a single chart type but a secondary axis because the series values are disproportionate.

LESSON 9   Command Summary

FEATURE	BUTTON	MENU	KEYBOARD
Axis, format	🖼	Chart, Chart Options	
Chart, create	📊	Insert, Chart	F11
Chart title, format	🖼	Chart, Chart Options	
Data labels, format	🖼	Chart, Chart Options	
Data series, format	🖼	Chart, Chart Options	
Legend, format	🖼	Chart, Chart Options	

Concepts Review

TRUE/FALSE QUESTIONS

Each of the following statements is either true or false. Indicate your choice by circling T or F.

T **F**   **1.** A chart sheet includes the related worksheet data.

T F   **2.** A selected object displays selection handles.

T F   **3.** You can change the color of all or individual bars or columns in a chart.

T **F**   **4.** Excel determines the best type of chart for your data in the Chart Wizard.

T F   **5.** A data series can be in rows or columns.

T F   **6.** If you insert another item in a range used in a chart, you add a data point.

T **F**   **7.** Each slice in a pie chart represents a data series.

T F   **8.** You can use a crisscrossed pattern to fill a bar or column.

SHORT ANSWER QUESTIONS

Write the correct answer in the space provided.

1. What name describes a chart that appears on the worksheet with the data?

Embedded chart

2. What Chart toolbar button do you use to change a bar chart to a column chart?

Chart type

3. What is the keyboard shortcut to create an automatic chart?

_F11_

4. What name is used for the small black rectangles that appear around an active chart object?

Selection handles

5. What term describes a blend of colors for filling a bar or column?

Gradient

6. What can you use when two data series have drastically different values?

You can use two axes on the chart

7. What happens if you delete a data series used in a column chart from the worksheet?

The entire chart is deleted

8. What are the other common names for the x- and y-axes used in most charts?

The category axis and the value axis

CRITICAL THINKING

Answer these questions on a separate page. There are no right or wrong answers. Support your answers with examples from your own experience, if possible.

1. Discuss and determine what data and related charts might be developed for your school.

2. What are some advantages of using charts over printed data? What are some pitfalls of charts?

Skills Review

EXERCISE 9-25

Preview and print a chart.

1. Open **DecChart** and save it in your Lesson 9 folder as *[your initials]*9-25.

2. Preview a chart by following these steps:

   a. Click the Print Preview button . The chart is below the worksheet. Close the preview.

   ◀◀ REVIEW: When the chart is selected, the ranges are outlined in the worksheet.

   b. Click the white chart background. The chart is selected.
   c. Click the Print Preview button . Only the chart is previewed. Close the preview.

3. Print a chart by following these steps:

   a. Click the Print button . The chart prints by itself.
   b. Click cell A1. The chart is deselected.
   c. Add your footer to the worksheet.
   d. Click the Print button . The worksheet and chart print on the same page.

4. Save and close the workbook.

EXERCISE 9-26

Edit chart titles. Format axes.

1. Open **NovChart** and save it as *[your initials]*9-26 in your Lesson 9 folder.

2. Format chart and axis titles by following these steps:

   a. Click the chart title to select it.

   b. Double-click **November** and key **December**.

 REVIEW: In editing mode, a double-click selects a word.

   c. Right-click **Sales in Dollars** along the *y*-axis.

   d. Choose Format Axis Title.

   e. Click the Font tab and use 10-point bold. Click OK.

3. Format the axis by following these steps:

   a. Right-click any value on the *y*-axis.

   b. Choose Format Axis.

 NOTE: The value axis is vertical in this column chart. The category axis (the state names) is horizontal.

   c. Click the Number tab.

   d. Choose Currency with the dollar sign as the Symbol and 0 decimal places. Click OK.

   e. Right-click any state name and choose Format Axis.

   f. Click the Font tab and choose 9 points. Click OK.

 REVIEW: Drag across row headings to select multiple rows.

4. Delete row 3. Next delete rows 8 and 9.

5. Add a footer and print the worksheet with the chart.

6. Save and close the workbook.

EXERCISE 9-27

Create charts. Edit chart data. Edit chart objects. Add a data point.

1. Create a new workbook and save it as *[your initials]*9-27 in your Lesson 9 folder.

2. In cell A1, key **Sales of Waffle Cones**. Make it 18-point Times New Roman.

3. In cell A2, key **May 1** and press (Enter). Use the Fill handle in cell A2 and fill in dates to reach May 15 in cell A16.

4. Key the following values in column B:

FIGURE 9-19

01-May	1000
02-May	1200
03-May	1000
04-May	1500
05-May	1400
06-May	1000
07-May	1200
08-May	1000
09-May	1500
10-May	1400
11-May	1400
12-May	1500
13-May	1200
14-May	1000
15-May	800

5. Create a chart by following these steps:

   a. Select cells A2:B16 and click the Chart Wizard button .

   b. Choose Line in the Standard Types tab.

   c. Choose Line with markers displayed at each data value.

   d. Click Next. Verify that the data range is in columns.

   e. Click Next. Click the Titles tab.

   f. In the Chart title box, key **Waffle Cone Sales**. In the Category (X) axis box, key **May 1 through May 15**.

   g. Click the Axes tab. Click to remove the check mark for Category (X) axis in the Primary axis group.

> **NOTE:** Turning off the category x-axis turns off the display of the dates along the primary axis (the horizontal axis).

   h. Click the Legend tab. Click to remove the check mark for Show legend.

   i. Click Next. Choose As object in and use Sheet1. Click Finish.

REVIEW: Point anywhere in the chart's background to drag a chart. Use a corner handle to size a chart.

  j. Move the chart so that its top-left corner is at cell E1.

  k. Size the chart so that its bottom-right corner is at cell L21.

 6. Edit chart data by following these steps:

  a. Edit cell B5 to show **600**.

  b. Edit cell B12 to show **800**.

 7. Edit chart objects by following these steps:

  a. Right-click the line and choose Format Data Series.

  b. Click the Patterns tab. In the Line group, choose a thicker (heavier) Weight for the line.

  c. In the Marker group, click the Style arrow and choose a rectangle shape.

  d. Click to place a check mark for Shadow. Click OK.

 TIP: Click away from the chart to see your changes.

 8. Add a data point by following these steps:

  a. Key **May 16** in cell A17 and **2000** in cell B17.

  b. Select the chart.

  c. Place the mouse pointer on the bottom-right handle of the data range and drag the two-pointed sizing pointer to include the new data.

 9. Click the x-axis title in the chart and change it to **May 1 through May 16**.

 10. Click cell A1. Add your footer. Print the sheet in landscape orientation.

 11. Save and close the workbook.

EXERCISE 9-28

Create a combination chart. Use a gradient for a data series. Format a data series.

 1. Open **ConeSales** and save it as *[your initials]*9-28 in your Lesson 9 folder.

 2. Create a combination chart by following these steps:

 NOTE: Some chart types cannot be combined. Excel displays a message if you choose charts that cannot be combined.

   a. Select cells A2:C17 and click the Chart Wizard button .

  b. Choose Line in the Standard Types tab.

  c. Choose Line with markers displayed at each data value.

  d. Click Next. Verify that the data range is in columns.

  e. Click Next. Click the Titles tab. In the Chart title box, key **Waffle and Sugar Cone Sales**.

  f. In the Category (X) axis box, key **May 1 through May 15**.

g. Click the Axes tab. Click to remove the check mark for Category (X) axis in the Primary axis group.

h. Click the Gridlines tab. Click to place a check mark for Minor gridlines for the Value (Y) axis.

i. Click Next. Choose As new sheet and key **SalesComparison** as the sheet name.

j. Click Finish.

k. Right-click the waffle cone line and choose Chart Type.

l. Choose Area in the Chart type list.

 REVIEW: Click the Press and Hold to View Sample button to test your chart combination.

m. Choose the first sub-type, Area. Displays the trend of values over time or categories. Click OK.

3. Use a gradient for a series by following these steps:

a. Right-click in the area for the waffle cone series. Choose Format Data Series.

b. Click the Patterns tab. Click Fill Effects.

 TIP: Preset gradients are preselected color blends.

c. Click the Gradient tab. In the Colors section, click Preset.

d. Click the arrow for the Preset colors box and choose Fog.

e. In the Shading styles group, choose Horizontal.

f. In the Variants section, choose the bottom-right sample. Click OK.

g. Click OK again.

4. Format data series by following these steps:

a. Right-click the sugar cone line and choose Format Data Series.

b. Click the Color arrow in the Line group.

c. Choose Black.

d. In the Marker group, choose Black as the Foreground and Background colors. Click OK.

5. Click the white chart background area.

6. Add a footer to the chart sheet.

7. Go to Sheet1 and choose Format, Sheet, and Hide. The sheet with the data for the chart is hidden but the data is still used in the chart.

8. Print the chart and close the workbook.

Lesson Applications

EXERCISE 9-29

Create a scatter chart. Edit chart objects. Preview and print a chart.

A scatter chart is commonly known as an XY scatter chart or a "scattergram." This type of chart does not have a category axis. Both axes show values instead. In this chart, you show the relationship between a price decrease and increased sales.

1. Open **Scatter** and save it as *[your initials]***9-29** in your Lesson 9 folder.

2. Format cell A1 as 18-point Times New Roman. Delete row 2.

3. Format cells A2:B2 as 12-point Times New Roman bold. Format row 2 as 22.50 (30 pixels) high. Format column A as 16.43 (120 pixels) wide. AutoFit column B.

4. Select cells A2:B8 and create an XY (Scatter chart), using data points connected by smoothed lines. Create the chart as an object in the worksheet.

5. Place the chart below the worksheet data and size it to reach cell G30.

6. Right-click a value on each axis and use a 9-point font. On the vertical axis (Y), format the numbers to show commas with no decimal places.

7. Delete the legend.

8. Edit the chart title to **Percentage Price Decrease and Increased Sales**.

9. Select the Chart Area and click the arrow next to the Fill Color button . Choose No Fill.

> **REVIEW:** The Fill Color button shows the most recently selected color.

10. Click the Plot Area and click the Fill Color button . It should be No Fill like the chart area.

> **NOTE:** A chart with no background fill color prints more quickly.

11. Add a footer. Print the worksheet and chart.

12. Save and close the workbook.

EXERCISE 9-30

Create a stock chart. Edit chart data. Preview and print a chart.

A stock chart plots daily stock price information. In a stock chart, you list the prices in this order from left to right: high price, low price, closing price. There are five sub-types for this chart, with some that include the volume of stocks sold.

1. Create a new workbook and save it as *[your initials]*9-30 in your Lesson 9 folder.

2. Format cell A1 as 16-point Arial and key **Klassy Kow Stock Investments**.

3. In cell B2, key **High**. In cell C2, key **Low**. In cell D2, key **Close**. Make these labels bold, and format the row as 26.25 (35 pixels) high.

4. In cell A3, key **Greenbriar Dairy Services**. This is the company whose stock prices will be shown in the chart. Format column A as 21.43 (155 pixels) wide.

5. In cell A4, key **April 1**. Use the Fill handle to fill down to April 10. Delete rows 9 and 10. You will show stock prices for eight days in April.

 NOTE: When preparing a stock chart, you should eliminate weekend and other nontrading days.

6. Key the values shown in Figure 9-20.

FIGURE 9-20

	High	Low	Close
April 1	28.25	22.125	24
April 2	27	21.5	24.5
April 3	26.75	20	26.75
April 4	30	27.5	29.75
April 5	28	24.25	27.15
April 8	32.75	30	32.75
April 9	35	27.5	32.125
April 10	38	34.25	34.35

 NOTE: If you key a fraction, Excel converts it to a decimal. You can display a fraction by choosing Fraction in the Format Cells dialog box.

7. Select cells A4:D11 and create a stock chart, using the first sub-type. In the Series tab in the wizard, name Series1 **High**. Name Series2 **Low** and Series3 **Close**.

8. Key **Greenbriar Dairy Services** as the main chart title. On the Axes tab, turn off the labels along the bottom of the chart. On the Gridlines tab, show minor gridlines for the value axis.

9. Do not show a legend but show the data table. Place the chart in a separate sheet. Click Finish.

NOTE: The chart shows markers that you might not see until you format them differently.

10. Right-click one of the lines. Choose Format High-Low Lines. Choose a heavy (thick) weight for the line.

 TIP: The marker size is shown in points, like a font.

11. Right-click the top of any line and choose Format Data Series. Use a circle for the marker and make its Size 10 pts. Choose the same color for the foreground and background, but use a color different from the line color. This formats the high price on the line.

 NOTE: Excel sets the number scale according to the values used in the chart.

12. Right-click the bottom of any line and choose Format Data Series. Use a pyramid shape for the marker and make its Size 10 pts. Choose the same color for the foreground and background, but use a color different from the line color and the high marker. This formats the low price on the line.

 NOTE: The Close value might be the same as either the high or low value. The markers then cover one another and you'll see the close marker.

13. Change the Zoom size to 200%. Scroll the chart to see a line, and right-click the marker between the high and low prices on any line. The marker is tiny and difficult to see. (If you think you may have formatted the wrong marker in Step 11 or 12, make your adjustments now.) Choose Format Data Series. Use a rectangle shape for the marker and make its Size 10 pts. Choose the same color for the foreground and background, but use a color different from the line color, the high marker, and the low marker.

14. Change the Zoom size to 75%.

15. Right-click a value along the vertical axis and choose Format Axis. Click the Scale tab. Make the minimum number 15. Click OK.

16. Add a footer and print the chart.

17. Save and close the workbook.

EXERCISE 9-31

Create an exploded pie chart. Edit chart objects.

The custom charts are variations of the standard chart types. When you print to a black-and-white printer, you can choose an option to create a black-and-white chart. An exploded pie chart shows one of the slices detached from the rest of the pie to emphasize the slice.

1. Open **ExPie** and save it as *[your initials]*9-31 in your Lesson 9 folder.

    REVIEW: Because a pie chart has only one series, it does not have category titles.

2. Create a pie chart, using the Custom Types to choose a B&W Pie Chart.

3. Key **Shake Flavor Comparison** as the chart title. Show only the category names and no legend. Place the chart in a separate sheet named **PieChart**.

4. Format the chart title to be 24 points.

    TIP: You can change the font for a chart object from the Font and Size buttons on the Formatting toolbar.

5. Select the pie. Then click the Butterscotch slice.

6. Point at the slice and drag it up and away from the other slices, not dragging it too far.

7. Select the Vanilla slice and format it to show solid white.

8. Add a footer and print the chart.

9. Save and close the workbook.

EXERCISE 9-32 *Challenge Yourself*

The Klassy Kow Credit Union maintains savings records for employees who contribute regularly to their accounts. You want to prepare a bubble chart to show employees that it is best to start saving as soon as possible. A bubble chart is similar to an XY scatter chart, but it can show an additional series.

1. Open **BubbleChart** and save it as *[your initials]*9-32 in your Lesson 9 folder.

2. In cell D5, use the FV function to determine the value of an account with the interest rate in cell B3 and the other information as shown. The original amount is the PV, the amount in the account when the savings program starts. Assume that payments are made at the beginning of the month. Copy the formula.

    REVIEW: Divide the interest rate by 12 for monthly payments. Multiply the number of years by 12 to determine the Nper. Use absolute references.

3. Select cells A4:A9, B4:B9, and D4:D9 and create a bubble chart. In the Series tab, make sure column A is the x-axis, column B is the y-axis, and column D shows the Sizes.

4. As a main chart title, key **Growth of Your Deposits**. Place the chart in a separate sheet named **Bubbles**.

5. Format the bubbles to show different colors for each one.

6. Rename Sheet1 as **Savings**. Delete Sheet2 and Sheet3. Group the sheets and click the Print Preview button . Add a footer to each sheet while they are grouped. Print both sheets.

NOTE: Worksheets and chart sheets can be grouped. However, the footer must be added separately to the chart sheet and to the worksheet.

7. Save and close the workbook.

On Your Own

In these exercises you work on your own, as you would in a real-life work environment. Use the skills you've learned to accomplish the task—and be creative.

EXERCISE 9-33
In a new workbook, key your city, state, and ZIP code in cell A1. In cells A3:A12, key the month and date for the past ten days. Use the local newspaper or an Internet site to determine the high temperature for each of those days and key the values in column B. Create a line chart that plots the daily temperature. Decide on a main title and whether or not you need axis titles, gridlines, a legend, or a data table. Embed the chart in the worksheet. Format the line chart and its markers in an attractive manner. Position the chart appropriately in relation to the worksheet data. Add a second title in cell A2 and format both titles with a larger font. Add a footer and print the worksheet and chart. Save the workbook as *[your initials]* **9-33** in your Lesson 9 folder and close it.

EXERCISE 9-34
Build an embedded pie chart to show your weekly expenses. Use at least four categories or types of expenses. Add a main title and decide whether to show labels or percentages on the chart. Save the workbook as *[your initials]***9-34** in your Lesson 9 folder. Add a footer if necessary. Print the worksheet with the chart, save the workbook, and close it.

EXERCISE 9-35
Create a worksheet that lists the first names of six acquaintances in one column and their heights in inches in the next column. Create a column chart that shows the names on the category axis and the heights on the value axis. Add an appropriate title and vary the colors of the data points. Place the chart in a separate sheet. Make other formatting changes so that your chart is easy to interpret. Hide the worksheet. Save the workbook as *[your initials]***9-35** in your folder for Lesson 9. Add a footer and print the chart. Save and close the workbook.

Using AutoShapes, WordArt, and Comments

After completing this lesson, you will be able to:

1. Add callouts to a worksheet.
2. Change an object's font, color, size, and position.
3. Use the adjustment handle.
4. Edit an AutoShape.
5. Insert WordArt.
6. Insert comments.

 Estimated Time: 1¾ hours

In addition to charts, Excel has other features to increase the visual appeal of your worksheets. These are design objects that can be sized, moved, and formatted. Design objects include text boxes, lines (with or without arrows), and callouts.

Design objects are placed on a draw layer. The *draw layer* is an invisible layer that is separate from the worksheet data.

 REVIEW: An *object* is a separate element (part) of a worksheet.

Adding Callouts to a Worksheet

An *AutoShape* is a common, recognized figure, shape, or outline. AutoShapes, as well as other drawing objects, are located on the Drawing toolbar. AutoShapes include common callout shapes. A *callout* is descriptive text enclosed in a shape. Callouts typically include a line or arrow that points to data or an object on the worksheet.

TABLE 10-1   Drawing Toolbar

BUTTON		FUNCTION
Draw ▾	Draw	Displays a list of commands for adjusting drawing objects.
▲	Select Objects	Activates a pointer for selecting objects.
AutoShapes ▾	AutoShapes	Displays a list of preset objects.
╲	Line	Draws a vertical, horizontal, or diagonal line.
↘	Arrow	Draws a line with an arrow.
▢	Rectangle	Draws a rectangle or square. Hold down Shift to make a square.
○	Oval	Draws an oval (an ellipse) or circle. Hold down Shift to make a circle.
▣	Text Box	Draws a rectangle to hold text.
◢	Insert WordArt	Inserts an image from the WordArt Gallery.
⚙	Insert Diagram or Organization Chart	Inserts a blank organization chart, a radial diagram, a pyramid diagram, or other business diagrams.
▨	Insert Clip Art	Inserts clip art from the Clip Organizer or from the Web.
▨	Insert Picture from File	Inserts an image from disk.
◇ ▾	Fill Color	Sets the background color for an object.
◢ ▾	Line Color	Sets the color of a line or the outline of an object.
A ▾	Font Color	Changes the color of text in an object.
≡	Line Style	Displays a list of line thicknesses (weights) and styles (single, double, and so on).

continues

TABLE 10-1   Drawing Toolbar *continued*

BUTTON		FUNCTION
▦	Dash Style	Displays a list of dash styles.
⇄	Arrow Style	Displays a list of arrow sizes, shapes, and positions.
▣	Shadow Style	Displays a list of shadow styles and positions for drawing objects.
▤	3-D Style	Displays a list of 3-dimensional effects for drawing objects.

EXERCISE **10-1**   **Add a Callout to a Worksheet**

Callouts and most other AutoShapes have the following features:

- *Selection handles*, small white circles surrounding the shape's bounding box.
- An *adjustment handle*, a yellow diamond used to change the appearance and design of the shape. Each shape has its own type of adjustments.
- A *rotation handle*, a green circle that acts as a wand to rotate an object.
- A *bounding box*, a rectangular outline around an object.

1. Create a new workbook from the **K&KSales** template.

    REVIEW: Click On my computer in the Templates group on the New Workbook task pane.

2. Add the following data to columns B and C in the worksheet. Green error triangles will be removed as you key values.

FIGURE 10-1

State	Kowabunga	KowOwow	
Oregon	2575	2000	
Nevada	3550	3000	
Washington	5600	4500	
California	6500	6700	

3. Display the Drawing toolbar by right-clicking any visible toolbar and choosing Drawing. The Drawing toolbar usually appears at the bottom of the screen.

4. Click AutoShapes on the Drawing toolbar. Choose Callouts.

 TIP: Each callout AutoShape has a ScreenTip with its name.

5. Choose Rounded Rectangular Callout, first row, second shape. The pointer changes to a thin cross.

FIGURE 10-2
Choosing a callout

3	State	Kowabunga	KowOwow	$ Kowabunga	$KowOwow		
4	Oregon	2,575	2,000	$ 6,154	$ 4,380		
5	Nevada	3,550	3,000	$ 8,485	$ 6,570		
6	Washington	5,600	4,500	$ 13,384	$ 9,855		
7	California	6,500	6,700	$ 15,535	$ 14,673		
8							
9							
10							
11							
12							
13							
14							
15							
16							
17							
18		Lines ▶					
19		Connectors ▶					
20		Basic Shapes ▶					
21							
22		Block Arrows ▶					
23		Flowchart ▶					
24		Stars and Banners ▶					
25							
26		Callouts ▶					

Draw ▼   AutoShapes ▼   Rounded Rectangular Callout

Ready

6. Click and drag to draw a rectangular shape starting at cell F1 and extending to column G and almost reaching row 3. The shape appears with a text insertion point in the callout, round white selection handles, and diagonal lines outlining the shape.

7. Click the arrow for the Font Size box and choose 9 points.

8. Key **KowOwow prices were decreased early in the year**.

FIGURE 10-3
New callout on the worksheet

	A	B	C	D	E	F	G	H
1	Kowabunga and KowOwow Sales							
2	Week of							
3	State	Kowabunga	KowOwow	$ Kowabunga	$KowOwow			
4	Oregon	2,575	2,000	$ 6,154	$ 4,380			
5	Nevada	3,550	3,000	$ 8,485	$ 6,570			
6	Washington	5,600	4,500	$ 13,384	$ 9,855			
7	California	6,500	6,700	$ 15,535	$ 14,673			
8								
9								

Selection handles → *KowOwow prices were decreased early in the year.*

Diagonal lines outlining shape

9. Click cell F7. The AutoShape is deselected.

10. Using the four-pointed arrow, click the outline of the callout. It is selected and shows a dotted pattern as its bounding box. The dotted pattern boundary means the entire callout is active and can be edited. You can now see the adjustment handle (yellow diamond).

FIGURE 10-4
Selected callout

	A	B	C	D	E	F	G	H
1	Kowabunga and KowOwow Sales							
2	Week of							
3	State	Kowabunga	KowOwow	$ Kowabunga	$KowOwow			
4	Oregon	2,575	2,000	$ 6,154	$ 4,380			
5	Nevada	3,550	3,000	$ 8,485	$ 6,570			
6	Washington	5,600	4,500	$ 13,384	$ 9,855			
7	California	6,500	6,700	$ 15,535	$ 14,673			
8								
9								

Dotted pattern → *KowOwow prices were decreased early in the year.*

Adjustment handle

11. Click inside the callout. The text insertion point appears, and the dotted lines become diagonal lines. The diagonal lines boundary means you can work with the text inside the box.

12. Click cell F7. The shape is deselected.

EXERCISE 10-2 **Add a Text Box to a Chart Sheet**

A text box is similar to a callout but does not have connector lines or arrows. You can use a text box to display titles, comments, or notes.

1. From the Format menu, choose Sheet and Unhide.

2. Choose the ComboChart sheet and click OK. A chart related to the data is displayed.

3. Click the Text Box button on the Drawing toolbar. The pointer changes to an upside-down lowercase "T."

4. Place the intersection of the lines in the "T" pointer on the gridline for 7,000, vertically aligned with the Oregon bar. Click and drag to draw a rectangular shape that extends to the 6,000 gridline and the Nevada bar. The shape appears with the diagonal lines bounding box and a text insertion point.

 NOTE: If you draw a shape that you do not like, click to select it (it will show the dotted pattern outline), and press (Delete). Then try again.

5. Key **California shops report on Friday; others report on Monday**.

6. Click somewhere in the chart. The text box is deselected. When you draw a text box on a chart, it does not have a border.

7. Using the four-pointed arrow, click where the border of the text box would be. When the text box is selected, it shows a dotted pattern outline.

8. Click inside the text box. When you click inside the box, it is ready for text editing and shows diagonal lines.

 NOTE: When an AutoShape, text box, or other drawing object is selected, its name appears in the Name box.

9. Click the white chart background.

E X E R C I S E   10-3   Add a Text Box and a Line to a Worksheet

1. Click the K&KSales tab to return to the data.

 2. Click the Arrow button ↘ on the Drawing toolbar. The pointer changes to a thin cross.

3. Point to the right and slightly below the "a" in "California" in cell A7.

4. Hold down (Shift) and drag down and to the right to point at cell B10. Release the mouse button and then release (Shift). The arrow appears where you finish drawing. The line has two round selection handles.

 TIP: Holding down (Shift) while drawing a line keeps it straight.

5. Click cell A7. The line is deselected.

6. Using the four-pointed arrow, click the line. It is selected again.

 7. Click the Arrow Style button ⇄ on the Drawing toolbar. A palette of lines and arrows opens.

8. Choose Arrow Style 7 for a line with arrows at both ends.

 9. Click the Line Style button ≡. A palette of weights or thickness settings opens.

10. Choose 1½ point. The line is slightly thicker.

11. Click the Text Box button on the Drawing toolbar. The pointer changes to the upside-down lowercase "T."

12. Draw a box that starts at cell B10 and extends to cell C11. Release the mouse button.

13. Key **California shops did co-op advertising with coupons.** Click an empty cell. A text box on a worksheet has a border.

Change the Font, Color, Size, and Position of Objects

Many drawing objects have a fill color, an outline or border color, a line thickness or weight, and a font style and size. You can also change the size and position of drawing objects and add special effects, such as shadows.

EXERCISE 10-4 Change the Font in Drawing Objects

1. With the four-pointed arrow, click the outline of the rounded rectangle callout shape. The shape displays the dotted pattern outline. This means edits will affect all text in the shape or the shape itself.

 TIP: If you cannot click to select an object, click the Select Objects button on the Drawing toolbar.

2. Choose 10-point Times New Roman as the font. All the text in the callout changes.

FIGURE 10-5
Entire callout
selected, changing
the font for all
the text

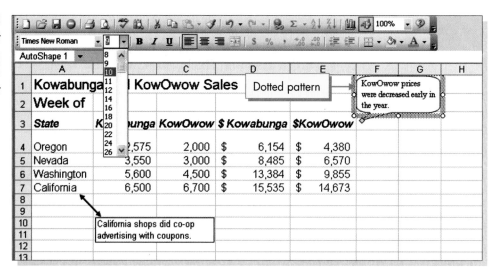

3. Click inside the rounded rectangle callout to display a text insertion point. The outline displays diagonal lines with the selection handles, meaning that your edits will affect only selected text.

4. Double-click "KowOwow" to select the word.

FIGURE 10-6
Changing font
of selected text in
a callout

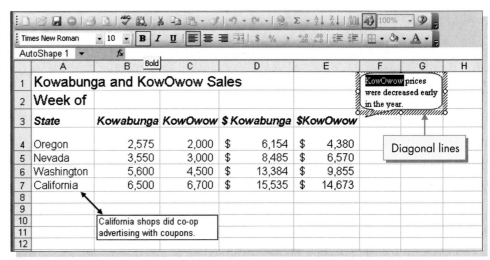

5. Click the Bold button **B**. Only the selected text is changed.

6. Click an empty cell.

EXERCISE 10-5 Change the Colors of Drawing Objects

1. With the four-pointed arrow, click the double-arrowed line.

 2. Click the Line Color button ✐▾ on the Drawing toolbar. The color on the button is applied to the line.

TIP: The Line Color button ✐▾ shows the last selected color. The palette swatches have ScreenTips with the color name.

3. Click the arrow next to the Line Color button ✐▾. A color palette shows available colors.

4. Choose Green in the second row, fourth column. The new color is applied to the line.

5. Using the four-pointed arrow, click the text box. The dotted pattern outline appears, indicating that the shape is selected.

6. Click the Line Color button ✐▾. The color on the button (Green) is applied to the outline of the text box.

 7. Click the Fill Color button ◇▾. The color on the button is applied to the background of the text box.

8. Click the arrow next to the Fill Color button . The color palette opens.

9. Choose Light Green in the last row, fourth swatch.

10. Click the ComboChart tab. This text box has no color for its border.

11. With the four-pointed arrow, click where the text box border would be located.

12. Click the arrow next to the Line Color button ✐▾.

13. Choose Black (first swatch, first row). The text box has a solid border.

 14. Click the Dash Style button ▦ on the Drawing toolbar. A palette of dash options opens.

15. Choose Long Dash (six in the list). The text box has a dashed border.

16. Click the white chart background.

EXERCISE **10-6** **Size and Move Drawing Objects**

1. Click the K&KSales tab.

2. Using the four-pointed arrow, click the text box to show the dotted pattern border.

3. Place the pointer on the bottom-middle selection handle to display a two-pointed arrow. This is a sizing pointer.

4. Drag down to reach the bottom of row 12. The text box is taller.

5. Place the pointer on the middle-right selection handle to display a two-pointed arrow.

6. Drag left to reach the middle of column C. The text box is narrower and the text rewraps.

    TIP: When an object is selected with the dotted pattern outline, you can nudge it by pressing any arrow key.

7. Place the mouse pointer on the outline of the text box. The four-pointed arrow appears again.

8. Drag the object left or right so that the arrow points to the middle of the top edge of the text box.

 9. Click the arrow next to the Font Color button �A▾ and choose White. White text is difficult to see on a light background.

   NOTE: You can use the Font Color button ▲▾ or the Fill Color button ⬧▾ on the Drawing or Formatting toolbar.

10. Click the arrow next to the Fill Color button ⬧▾ and choose Black. Now you can see the text.

11. Click the arrow next to the Line Color button and choose No Line. The border is not necessary with black fill.

12. With the four-pointed arrow, click to select the line with two arrow ends.

13. Click the arrow next to the Line Color button and choose Black. The line and text box colors match.

14. Click an empty cell.

Using the Adjustment Handle

Most drawing objects have one or more adjustment handles, shown as a yellow diamond. The adjustment handle allows you to change the appearance of the object. For example, you can change the rounded rectangle callout to point to a different location. What an adjustment handle does depends on the object.

Some shapes do not have adjustment handles. If they don't, they can only be resized with one of the sizing pointers.

In addition to the adjustment handle, most objects have a rotation handle. This allows you to move the object so that it angles differently from the original.

EXERCISE **10-7** **Reshape a Drawing Object**

1. With the four-pointed arrow, click the rounded rectangle callout. It has one adjustment handle.

2. Point at the adjustment handle. The pointer changes to a solid white arrowhead.

3. Click the adjustment handle and drag it down to row 6. The connector part of the callout adjusts.

> **TIP:** If an object appears to be anchored to its adjustment handle, deselect the object. Then select it by clicking the bounding box.

4. Double-click the adjustment handle. It returns to its default location and size for the shape.

5. With the four-pointed arrow, click the text box. It does not have an adjustment handle.

6. With the four-pointed arrow, click the line. It does not have an adjustment handle either.

7. Click an empty cell.

EXERCISE   10-8   **Rotate a Drawing Object**

The rotation handle enables you to rotate an object in any direction. It is a small green circle.

1. Click A<u>u</u>toShapes on the Drawing toolbar. Choose Block <u>A</u>rrows.
2. Choose Curved Down Arrow, fourth row, fourth column. The pointer changes to a thin cross.
3. Click and drag from cell C8 to about cell E12. The shape appears with round white selection handles, a green rotation handle, and three adjustment handles.

FIGURE 10-7
Ready to rotate

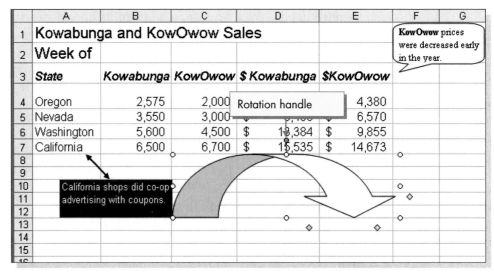

4. Place the mouse pointer over the green rotation handle. A circulating arrow surrounds the handle.
5. Drag straight down to about row 13. This actually rotates the shape 180 degrees or upside down.
6. Place the mouse pointer over the green rotation handle again.
7. Drag in any direction, moving the mouse in a small arc.
8. Click the Undo button . Try this again so that you get an idea for how the rotation handle moves the shape.

   TIP: Click the Undo button to practice rotating objects until you are comfortable with the results.

9. Finish with the arrow pointing at cell C7.

Editing an AutoShape

Once an AutoShape is on the sheet, you can change it to another shape, add text, or make a variety of other format changes. Most edits can be accomplished from the Drawing toolbar.

EXERCISE   **10-9**   **Change an AutoShape**

1. Select the text box. It shows the dotted pattern with the selection handles.
2. Choose Draw on the Drawing toolbar. A menu of additional commands appears.
3. Choose Change AutoShape. A list of shape categories opens.
4. Choose Basic Shapes. A palette of common shapes displays.
5. Choose Change Shape to Bevel (fourth row, third column). This shape has one adjustment handle. You cannot see the bevel well with black fill.

FIGURE 10-8
Changing the
AutoShape

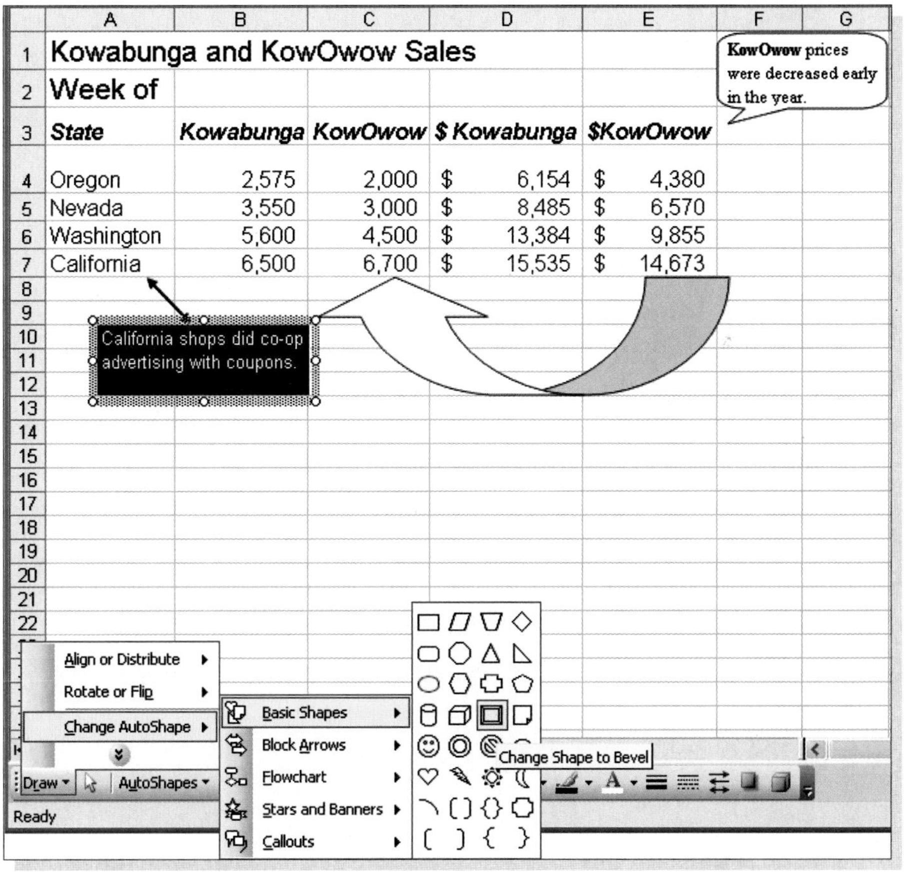

6. Click the arrow with the Fill Color button 🖌▾. Choose Gray-25% from the palette. The shape may be a bit small now for the text.

7. Place the mouse pointer on the middle bottom selection handle and drag down to row 14.

8. Click the arrow with the Font Color button A▾. Choose Black from the palette.

9. Click the Bold button B and then click the Center button ≡. Many object changes can also be made from the Formatting toolbar.

10. Click the adjustment handle and drag it to the left. You remove the bevel this way.

11. Double-click the adjustment handle to return to the original bevel shape.

12. Click the adjustment handle and drag it to the right. This is a different bevel change.

13. Double-click the adjustment handle. Click an empty cell.

E X E R C I S E   **10-10**   **Add Text to an AutoShape**

You can add text to any shape. You draw the shape, select it, and then key the text. Some shapes are not well suited to text, so give some thought to what you might use to display text.

1. Click the ComboChart tab.

2. Click AutoShapes and choose More AutoShapes. The Clip Art task pane opens with images that can be used as shapes.

3. Scroll to find Documents.

4. Click the image in the task pane. It is placed on the chart sheet at a default size and position. This shape does not have an adjustment handle. (See Figure 10-9.)

5. Click the shape and drag the shape to the middle of the chart above the Nevada and Washington columns.

6. Click the arrow next to the Fill Color button 🖌▾. Choose White.

7. Key **This report is completed each week at corporate headquarters.**

8. Click the shape's edge with the four-pointed arrow to display the dotted pattern. Change the font to 9-point Arial.

9. Click the white chart background.

10. Close the Clip Art task pane.

FIGURE 10-9
Using more
AutoShapes

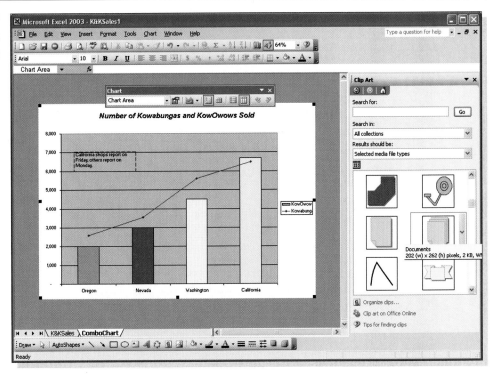

EXERCISE 10-11 Use the Format AutoShape Dialog Box

Although you can make one change at a time to objects using the Drawing or For-matting toolbars, you can use the Format AutoShape dialog box to make several changes at once.

You can open the Format AutoShape dialog box by:

- Right-clicking the shape outline and choosing Format AutoShape from the shortcut menu.
- Selecting the shape so that it displays the dotted pattern and pressing [Ctrl]+[1].
- Selecting the shape so that it displays the dotted pattern and choosing AutoShape from the Format menu.

1. Click the K&KSales tab.
2. Right-click the outline of the rounded rectangle callout and choose Format AutoShape. The Format AutoShape dialog box includes several tabs for making changes to the shape.
3. Click the Colors and Lines tab.
4. In the Fill group, click the arrow for Color.
5. Choose Gray-25% in the fourth row, last swatch. (See Figure 10-10 on next page.)

FIGURE 10-10
Format AutoShape
dialog box

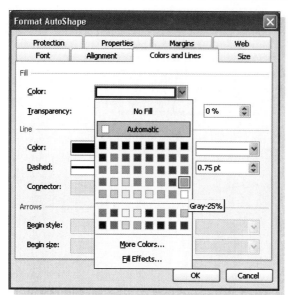

6. Click OK. The fill color of the callout is changed.

EXERCISE 10-12 Add a 3-D Effect

A *3-D effect* applies a three-dimensional look to an object so that it appears to have a depth, as well as a height and width.

1. Click the ComboChart tab.

2. Click to select the text box so that it shows the dotted pattern outline.

3. Press Ctrl+1 to open the Format Text Box dialog box.

4. Click the Colors and Lines tab.

5. In the Fill group, click the arrow for Color. Choose White.

6. In the Line group, click the arrow for Dashed. Choose Solid.

7. Click OK. The 3-D effect will be more discernible now.

8. Click the 3-D Style button on the Drawing toolbar. A palette of three-dimensional designs opens. (See Figure 10-11.)

9. Click 3-D Style 1, the first button in the first row. The text box is a three-dimensional shape with highlights and shadows. The colors are adjusted, too.

10. Click the white chart background.

FIGURE 10-11
3-D options

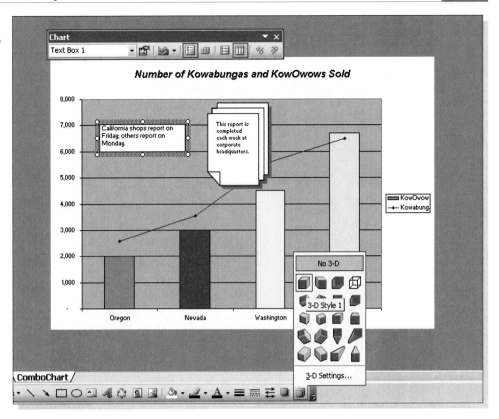

EXERCISE 10-13 Align Drawing Objects

When you use more than one drawing element on your worksheet, you can arrange the objects so that they align at the top edges, the left edges, the right edges, and so on. To align objects, you must select more than one object. With only one object selected, the Align and Distribute commands are not available. The alignment of objects uses each object's bounding box and its selection handles.

1. Click the edge of the 3-D text box to select it.
2. Hold down Ctrl and click an edge of the Documents AutoShape. Both objects are selected.

 NOTE: The Name box is empty when more than one object is selected.

3. Click Draw on the Drawing toolbar.
4. Choose Align or Distribute. Alignment options appear in the submenu. The horizontal alignment choices are first, followed by the vertical alignment options. Distribute options are dimmed, because only two objects are selected.

5. Choose Align Top. The two shapes are aligned on their top bounding box edges relative to the object that was highest on the screen.

FIGURE 10-12
Aligning objects

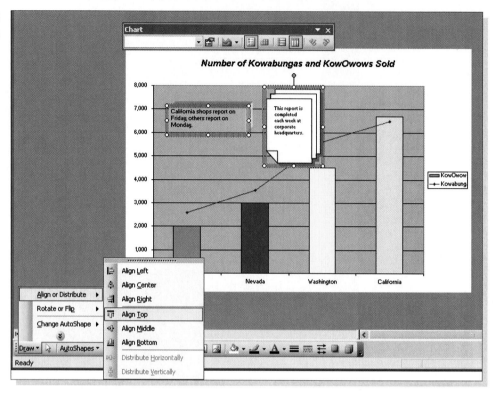

6. Click the white chart background. The objects themselves may not appear to be aligned because it is their bounding boxes that are aligned.

7. Click the edge of the 3-D text box to select it. Hold down Ctrl and click the Documents AutoShape.

8. Click Draw on the Drawing toolbar. Choose Align or Distribute.

9. Choose Align Middle. The two shapes are aligned vertically in the middle.

10. Click the gray page background. Nothing is selected.

EXERCISE 10-14 **Distribute Drawing Objects**

The Distribute command spaces objects evenly across the area occupied by the objects. You must select at least three objects for the Distribute command to be available.

1. Click the K&KSales tab.

2. Using the four-pointed arrow, drag the beveled text box so that its bottom-left corner covers cell A19.

3. Drag the curved arrow so that its bottom-right selection handle is at cell G19.

4. Drag the line with two arrow ends so that it touches the middle-right edge of the beveled text box.

 NOTE: You can hold down (Shift) or (Ctrl) to select multiple objects.

5. Hold down (Shift) and click the curved arrow. Two objects are selected.

6. Hold down (Shift) and click the beveled text box. Three objects are selected.

FIGURE 10-13
Distributing objects

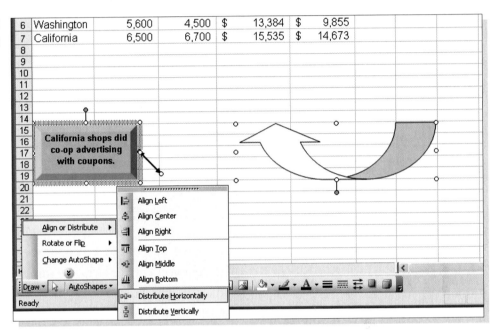

7. Click Draw. Choose Align or Distribute and then Distribute Horizontally. The three objects are spaced evenly between the left edge of the beveled text box and the right edge of the curved arrow.

8. Click an empty cell.

Inserting WordArt

WordArt is an application that is included with Microsoft Office and works in all the Office applications. A WordArt image is text that is shaped and colored. A image from the WordArt Gallery is an object with selection handles, an adjustment handle, and a rotation handle.

You can insert WordArt by:

● Clicking the Insert WordArt button ◢ on the Drawing toolbar.

● From the Insert menu, choosing Picture and WordArt.

EXERCISE 10-15 Insert WordArt on a Worksheet

1. Click cell B25.
2. Click the Insert WordArt button 🔲 on the Drawing toolbar. The WordArt Gallery displays 30 variations.
3. Click the style in the bottom row, second from the right.

FIGURE 10-14
WordArt Gallery

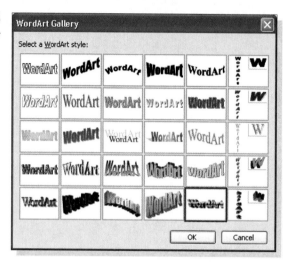

4. Click OK. The Edit WordArt Text dialog box opens with default sample text.
5. Key **Klassy Kow**. The text you key replaces the sample text.
6. Click the arrow for the Size and choose 24.
7. Click OK. The WordArt image appears on the worksheet in a default location, and the WordArt toolbar opens. (See Figure 10-15.)

 NOTE: You can place WordArt on a chart sheet, too.

8. With the four-pointed arrow, drag the WordArt object so that its top-left handle is in the middle of cell B9.
9. Place the mouse pointer on the bottom-right handle to display a two-arrow sizing pointer. Hold down (Shift) and drag the handle down and to the right to make the image slightly larger.

 NOTE: If you hold down the (Shift) key while sizing an object, it is sized horizontally and vertically at the same time.

10. Click cell A1.
11. Save your workbook as *[your initials]***10-15** in your Lesson 10 folder.
12. Group the worksheets and click the Print Preview button 🔲.

FIGURE 10-15
WordArt image
and toolbar

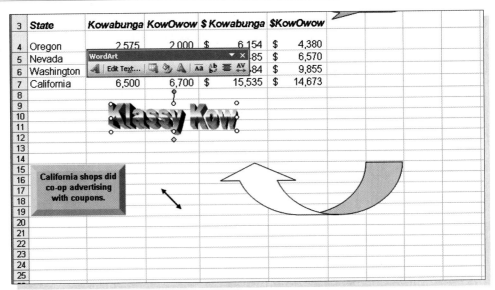

3	State	Kowabunga	KowOwow	$ Kowabunga	$KowOwow			
4	Oregon	2,575	2,000	$ 6,154	$ 4,380			
5	Nevada			85	$ 6,570			
6	Washington			84	$ 9,855			
7	California	6,500	6,700	$ 15,535	$ 14,673			
8								
9								
10								

NOTE: When sheets are grouped, you can add a header/footer to each page separately from Print Preview.

13. Add your standard footer to both sheets. Then print both worksheets.

Inserting Comments

In addition to using AutoShapes and WordArt, you can annotate a cell with a comment. A *comment* is pop-up explanatory text attached to a cell. In a comment you can inform others what you did or what they should do in the sheet.

Cells with comments initially show a small red triangle in the upper-right corner. The comment appears in a text box when you move the pointer over the cell with the comment.

EXERCISE **10-16** **Insert and Display a Comment**

1. On the K&KSales sheet, right-click cell A2.

2. Choose Insert Comment. The comment text box opens and displays the user name for your computer, followed by a colon.

3. Key **Edit this cell to enter the appropriate date**. (See Figure 10-16 on the next page.)

4. Click cell A4 to close the comment text box. If it does not disappear, choose View and then Comments.

TIP: You can click any cell to close and hide the comment.

FIGURE 10-16
Inserting a comment

	A	B	C	D	E	F	G
1	Kowabunga ~~and KowOwow~~ Sales					KowOwow prices	
2	Week of	User Name: Edit this cell to enter the appropriate date.				were decreased early in the year.	
3	*State*		wow	*$ Kowabunga*	*$KowOwow*		
4	Oregon	2,575	2,000	$ 6,154	$ 4,380		
5	Nevada	3,550	3,000	$ 8,485	$ 6,570		
6	Washington	5,600	4,500	$ 13,384	$ 9,855		
7	California	6,500	6,700	$ 15,535	$ 14,673		
8							
9							
10							
11		Klassy Kow					
12							
13							
14							
15							
16	California shops did co-op advertising with coupons.						
17							
18							
19							
20							
21							
22							
23							
24							
25							

5. Move the mouse pointer over cell A2 to display the comment.

 NOTE: Check with your instructor if the comment is not visible on your computer.

6. Click the Print Preview button ▣. Comments do not print as a default. Close the preview.

EXERCISE 10-17 Edit, Print, and Delete a Comment

1. Right-click cell A2 and choose Edit Comment.

2. Edit the text to read **Edit this cell each week. . .**

3. Click any cell to finish and hide the comment.

4. Move the pointer over cell A2 to see the edited comment.

5. Right-click cell A2 and choose Show/Hide Comments. The comment stays visible.

6. Click the Print Preview button ▣. Comments do not print even when they show onscreen.

7. Close the preview.

8. Choose File, Page Setup. Click the Sheet tab.

9. In the Print group, click the Comments arrow. You must use this setting to print comments.

10. Choose As displayed on sheet. Click OK.

 NOTE: You can print comments as they appear on the sheet or at the end of the data on a separate sheet.

11. Click the Print button 🖨. The comment prints as it appears on the worksheet.

12. Right-click cell A2 and choose Delete Comment.

13. Close the workbook without saving.

USING ONLINE HELP

Excel has another type of comment, known as *discussion comments*. These are annotations you can attach to a worksheet for viewing across the Web.

Use Help to learn about discussion comments:

1. Establish an Internet connection and start Internet Explorer. Minimize the window.

2. In a blank workbook, choose Help and Microsoft Excel Help.

3. Key **discussion** in the Search box and press Enter. A prompt may tell you that the Microsoft Office site is being searched.

4. Scroll and click the topic About Web Discussions in the Search Results dialog box.

5. Click Show All in the upper-right corner. Read the information.

6. Close the Help window. Close the Search Results dialog box.

7. Close Internet Explorer and end your Internet connection.

LESSON Summary

➤ An AutoShape is a common shape or form. A callout is used to attach a text description to a cell or other object.

➤ AutoShapes and callouts are placed on the draw layer, an invisible layer separate from the worksheet data.

➤ You can change the font within an AutoShape or change its size, shape, rotation angle, and colors.

➤ Many AutoShapes have a fill color, as well as an outline or border color. Text within an AutoShape has a color, too.

➤ To show text in a shape other than a rectangle, start with a text box and change its shape.

➤ Lines, with or without arrows, are objects that can be placed on the draw layer.

➤ AutoShapes can be formatted with 3-D effects and shadows. They can also be aligned and distributed for a balanced appearance on the sheet.

➤ You can use WordArt to create a design object that is shaped text. The WordArt Gallery includes 30 WordArt styles.

➤ Comments display when the mouse pointer touches a cell with the comment. Comments can be used as annotations, notes, or explanations for data on a worksheet.

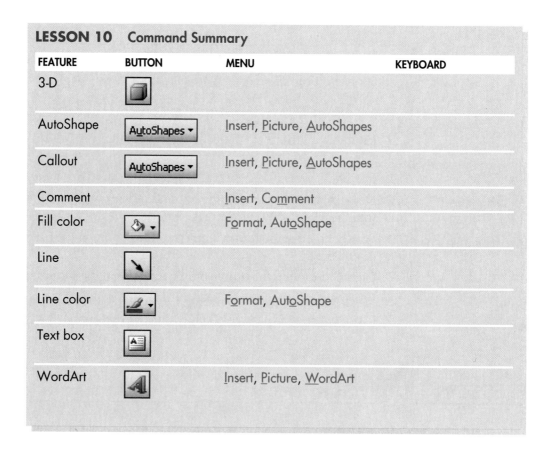

LESSON 10 Command Summary

FEATURE	BUTTON	MENU	KEYBOARD
3-D			
AutoShape	AutoShapes ▾	Insert, Picture, AutoShapes	
Callout	AutoShapes ▾	Insert, Picture, AutoShapes	
Comment		Insert, Comment	
Fill color		Format, AutoShape	
Line			
Line color		Format, AutoShape	
Text box			
WordArt		Insert, Picture, WordArt	

Concepts Review

TRUE/FALSE QUESTIONS

Each of the following statements is either true or false. Indicate your choice by circling T or F.

T   F   **1.** Drawing objects are placed on a draw layer.

T   F   **2.** Callouts can use various shapes to display text.

T   F   **3.** You can change the font and fill color of a drawing object from the Drawing toolbar.

T   F   **4.** AutoShapes cannot be changed, but they can be deleted and redrawn.

T   F   **5.** WordArt is an Excel application.

T   F   **6.** The adjustment handle is a small green circle.

T   F   **7.** When aligning objects, you can choose the option to group them.

T   F   **8.** A cell with a comment displays a small red triangle.

SHORT ANSWER QUESTIONS

Write the correct answer in the space provided.

1. What is the small green circle that appears when a drawing object is selected?

_____

2. What does the pointer look like when you move a drawing object?

_____

3. What does the pointer look like if you want to size a drawing object?

_____

4. What name describes an annotation that appears only when the mouse pointer passes over the cell?

_____

5. What command spaces objects evenly across the area?

_____

6. What type of AutoShape usually includes a connector line?

_____

7. How can you determine if a cell has a comment without moving the pointer around the sheet?

_____

8. What is the difference between the dotted pattern bounding box and the diagonal lines bounding box?

_____

CRITICAL THINKING

Answer these questions on a separate page. There are no right or wrong answers. Support your answers with examples from your own experience, if possible.

1. What are the differences between comments and callouts? Why and when would you use each?

2. Discuss uses for WordArt in a workbook.

Skills Review

EXERCISE 10-18

Add callouts to a worksheet. Change the color of an object. Use the adjustment handle.

1. Create a new workbook from the **K&KSales** template.

2. Save the workbook as *[your initials]***10-18** in your Lesson 10 folder.

3. Key the values shown in Figure 10-17 on the worksheet:

FIGURE 10-17

State	Kowabunga	KowOwow
Oregon	5000	5700
Nevada	8000	9300
Washington	7570	8050
California	10000	11500

4. Add a callout to a worksheet by following these steps:

    a. Click AutoShapes and choose Callouts.

    b. Choose Cloud Callout.

    c. Click and drag to draw a rectangle shape starting at cell B9 and extending to cell C13.

    d. Key **Kowabunga and KowOwow are popular novelty products.**

    e. Place the pointer on the bottom-middle handle to display a sizing pointer.

    f. Drag the pointer down to the bottom of row 14.

5. Change the fill color by following these steps:

    a. Click anywhere in the text in the callout.

     b. Click the Center button ▤.

    c. Use the four-pointed arrow to click the callout bounding box and display the dotted pattern outline.

     d. Click the arrow next to the Fill Color button ▥ ▾.

    e. Choose Light Turquoise in the bottom row (fifth swatch).

6. Use the adjustment handle by following these steps:

    a. Click the adjustment handle (the yellow diamond) on the callout.

    b. Drag the handle up and through column A, toward the bottom of the label "California" in cell A7.

7. Edit cell A2 to show the date for Tuesday of the current week. Widen columns so that you can see all of the text.

8. Select cells A1:E2 and center them across the selection.

9. Add your standard footer and print the worksheet horizontally centered.

10. Save and close the workbook.

EXERCISE 10-19

Add, copy, and edit an AutoShape. Use the adjustment handle.

1. Open **Contest** and save it as *[your initials]***10-19** in your Lesson 10 folder.

2. Add an AutoShape by following these steps:

    a. Click AutoShapes and choose Basic Shapes.

    b. Choose Smiley Face.

    c. Click and drag to draw a shape starting at cell D7 and extending to cell D12.

3. Select cells D5:D6. Copy and paste these two cells in cells D14:D15.

4. Edit the label in cell D14 to show **Biggest Difference**.

5. Edit the formula in cell D15 to use MAX instead of MIN.

6. Copy an AutoShape by following these steps:

    a. Click the Smiley Face AutoShape to display its selection handles.

      b. Point at the border of the shape and hold down the Ctrl key. Drag a copy of the shape to cells D16.

      c. Release the mouse and the Ctrl key.

7. Edit an AutoShape by following these steps:

      a. Click the second Smiley Face AutoShape to select it.

      b. Click the arrow with the Fill Color button on the Drawing toolbar.

      c. Click Gray-25% in the palette.

8. Use the adjustment handle by following these steps:

      a. Click the second Smiley Face AutoShape to select it.

      b. Click the yellow diamond handle and drag it slightly up to make the smiley face into a sad face.

9. Click cell A6 and key your first and last name.

10. Center the sheet horizontally on the page and print it.

11. Save and close the workbook.

EXERCISE 10-20

Insert WordArt. Format WordArt.

1. Open **CASales** and save it as *[your initials]***10-20** in your Lesson 10 folder.

2. Delete the contents of cells A1:A2. Insert a row at row 3.

3. Insert WordArt by following these steps:

      a. Click the Insert WordArt button .

      b. Click the first style in the second row. Click OK.

      c. Key **Klassy Kow Ice Cream** and press Enter.

       NOTE: WordArt text wraps on the worksheet only where you press Enter.

      d. Key **Weekly Sales Data**.

      e. Change the Size to 24 points. Click OK.

      f. Using the four-pointed arrow, drag the WordArt image so that its top-left selection handle is at cell A1.

4. Format WordArt by following these steps:

      a. Click the Format WordArt button on the WordArt toolbar.

       NOTE: Display the WordArt toolbar by right-clicking any toolbar and choosing WordArt.

      b. Click the Colors and Lines tab.

      c. In the Fill group, click the arrow for Color.

      d. Choose Gray-25%, the last swatch in the fourth row. Click OK.

      e. Click the WordArt Alignment button on the WordArt toolbar.

      f. Choose Left Align.

5. Click cell F1. Add your standard footer and print the worksheet.

6. Save and close the workbook.

EXERCISE 10-21

Insert comments. Print comments.

1. Create a new workbook from the **ExpRpt** template.

2. Save the workbook as *[your initials]***10-21** in your Lesson 10 folder.

3. Add your usual footer to the Expenses sheet.

4. Insert comments by following these steps:

   a. Right-click cell C3 and choose Insert Comment.
   b. Key **Edit cell C3 to show the current month.**
   c. Click cell A7. From the Insert menu, choose Comment.
   d. Key **Edit cell A7 to show the date of the first Monday in the month.**
   e. Right-click cell A12 and choose Insert Comment.
   f. Key **Edit cell A12 to show the date of the second Monday in the month.**
   g. Right-click cell A17 and add this comment: **Edit cell A17 to show the date of the third Monday in the month.**
   h. Right-click cell A22 and add this comment: **Edit cell A22 to show the date of the fourth Monday in the month.**

5. Print comments on the worksheet by following these steps:

   a. From the View menu, choose Comments. All comments are shown and the Reviewing toolbar opens.
   b. From the File menu, choose Page Setup. Click the Sheet tab.
   c. Click the arrow for Comments in the Print group.
   d. Choose As displayed on sheet.
   e. Click Print in the dialog box and then click OK.

6. From the View menu, choose Comments. All comments are hidden.

    NOTE: Hide the Reviewing toolbar by right-clicking any toolbar and choosing Reviewing.

7. Print comments on a separate sheet by following these steps:

   a. From the File menu, choose Page Setup. Click the Sheet tab.
   b. Click the arrow for Comments in the Print group.
   c. Choose At end of sheet.
   d. Click Print in the dialog box and then click OK.

8. Close and save the workbook.

Lesson Applications

Add a comment in an AutoShape. Format the AutoShape.

The default comment box is a rectangle shape. You can replace the rectangle with a callout shape from AutoShapes.

1. Create a new workbook, using the **K&KSales** template. Save the workbook as *[your initials]*10-22 in your Lesson 10 folder.

2. Key the values shown in Figure 10-18 in the appropriate cells.

FIGURE 10-18

State	Kowabunga	KowOwow	
Oregon	15000	16500	
Nevada	18000	19200	
Washington	17570	18050	
California	19000	19500	

3. Add a comment in cell C7. Delete the user name and colon and key this text (do not use bold type): **California's best sales this year!** Right-click the cell and show the comment.

4. Use the four-pointed arrow to select the comment. Then click Draw and choose Change AutoShape. Use the cloud callout. Size the callout so you can see the text. Position the callout below and to the right of cell C7. Use the adjustment handle to make the connector clouds angle toward the cell.

5. Choose a size and color for the text and the fill. Center the text horizontally.

6. Choose File, Page Setup to print the worksheet with the comment as displayed.

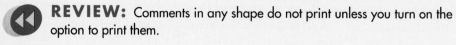 **REVIEW:** Comments in any shape do not print unless you turn on the option to print them.

7. Add your standard footer and print the sheet.

8. Save and close the workbook.

EXERCISE 10-23

Add and format callouts.

The Stars and Banners category has shapes that can highlight a cell in eye-catching ways.

1. Open **CASales** and save it as *[your initials]***10-23** in your Lesson 10 folder.

2. Select rows 6 through 18 and format them as 25.50 (34 pixels) high.

3. Use Explosion 1 from the Stars and Banners AutoShapes and draw a shape around cell F16. While the shape is selected, right-click it and choose Format AutoShape. Use no fill.

    NOTE: No fill means you can see the cell contents through the shape.

4. From the Basic Shapes category, draw a lightning bolt in cells D1 through F3. While the bolt is selected, choose Draw, and then choose Rotate or Flip. Flip the object horizontally so that it points toward the data.

5. Apply a light yellow or orange color as fill.

    6. Select the bolt and click the 3-D button . Choose 3-D Style 7 in the second row.

7. Add your standard footer and print the worksheet.

8. Save and close the workbook.

EXERCISE 10-24

Link a cell to an AutoShape.

Although you can type text in many AutoShapes, you can also link an AutoShape to a cell. Then the cell's contents are displayed in the AutoShape.

1. Open **Contest**. Save the workbook as *[your initials]***10-24** in your Lesson 10 folder.

2. From the Stars and Banners category in the AutoShapes, draw a Curved Up Ribbon from cell D9 to E13.

3. While the shape is selected, click in the formula bar. Key **=d6** and press Enter. The value from cell D6 appears in the shape.

4. Right-click the AutoShape to format it. Use 19-point bold for the font. Center the text horizontally and vertically.

   REVIEW: Use the Alignment tab to set centering options.

5. Move the AutoShape so that it does not cover any of column C.

6. Format cells D5:D6 to use white as the font color.

7. Edit cell B8 to show **25300**. This becomes the lowest difference and the new winner.

8. Add your standard footer and print the worksheet horizontally centered.

9. Save and close the workbook.

EXERCISE 10-25 *Challenge Yourself*

You can link a cell on one worksheet to an AutoShape on another sheet in the same workbook. In this way you can create a separate display about your data.

1. Open **CASales** and save it as *[your initials]***10-25** in your Lesson 10 folder.

2. Insert a new sheet and name it **BestWeek**.

 REVIEW: Press ⇧Shift+F11 to insert a new worksheet.

3. On the new sheet, insert WordArt using the style from the fourth row, second column. It should display **Best California Sales!** and use the default font size.

4. Drag the object so that its bottom edge rests on row 5 and so that the object starts in column A.

5. Draw a 16-point star (Stars and Banners AutoShapes) that covers approximately cells B8:F22.

 6. Click the Shadow Style button 🔲. Choose Shadow Style 6 in the second row.

7. After the shadow is applied, click the Shadow Style button 🔲 again. Click Shadow Settings. The Shadow toolbar opens. Change the shadow color to darker gray or black. Close the Shadow toolbar.

8. On the WeeklySales sheet, key **Best Week** in cell A20. Match its format to cell A19.

9. In cell B20, use the MAX function with the range B5:E18.

10. On the BestWeek sheet, click the star. In the formula bar, key = to start a formula. Next click the WeeklySales tab and click cell B20. Press Enter. The formula in the shape refers to a cell on the WeeklySales tab.

11. Right-click the star shape and format it with a larger font. Experiment with centering options.

12. Add your standard footer. Center the sheet horizontally and vertically. Print the sheet.

13. Save and close the workbook.

On Your Own

In these exercises you work on your own, as you would in a real-life work environment. Use the skills you've learned to accomplish the task—and be creative.

EXERCISE 10-26

Create a workbook using the **K&KSales** template. Fill in amounts for each of the products. Unhide each of the chart sheets. Add appropriate WordArt as a title to each chart sheet. Save the workbook as *[your initials]*10-26 in your Lesson 10 folder. Add your standard footer to both chart sheets and print each one. Save and close the workbook.

EXERCISE 10-27

Open **CASales**. Review the formulas used in the total row and column. Draw a wide text box below the worksheet data and explain the formulas and how they can be built. Write your text as if you are giving instructions to someone who might use this sheet in the future. Format the text box with a shadow. Save the workbook as *[your initials]*10-27 in your Lesson 10 folder. Print the worksheet and close the workbook.

EXERCISE 10-28

In a new workbook, draw five text boxes and key your name in each. Then change each text box to a different AutoShape. Adjust each AutoShape's handles to reshape the object. Try changing fill and line colors. Save your worksheet as *[your initials]*10-28 in your Lesson 10 folder. Add your standard footer and print the sheet. Save and close the workbook.

Using Images, Diagrams, and Research

OBJECTIVES

MICROSOFT OFFICE
SPECIALIST
ACTIVITIES

In this lesson:
XLO3S-1-3
XLO3S-1-4
XLO3S-2-5
XLO3S-3-4
XLO3S-5-5
XLO3S-5-10
XLO3E-2-3
XLO3E-2-4

See Appendix.

After completing this lesson, you will be able to:

1. **Insert a picture.**
2. **Use a background picture.**
3. **Add an image to a header or footer.**
4. **Save a workbook as a Web page.**
5. **Create an organization chart.**
6. **Build a diagram.**
7. **Use the Research task pane.**

 Estimated Time: 1 hour

There are many design objects available to enhance worksheet data. You can insert images from disk, from the Clip Organizer, or from Web galleries. You can build organization charts as well as other common business diagrams.

The Research tool is available so that you can insert information from other sources into your worksheet, too. You can find information on your own computer, a network, or the Web.

Inserting a Picture

Like shapes and WordArt, images add visual appeal to your work. You can insert clip art from the Clip Organizer. You can use your own images from various sources. When you insert an image, Excel treats it as an object, like WordArt or an

AutoShape. You can edit the size, position, and other properties, depending on what type of image it is.

 TIP: For best effect, don't use too many images on a sheet. One or two related images or objects should work.

EXERCISE 11-1 Insert a Picture from a File

To insert a picture from a file, the picture must be in a graphics format that Excel can use. The **KowOwow** file used in this exercise is a *TIF* file (Tagged Image Format), a popular graphics format for printing images.

You can insert a picture from a file by:

- Clicking the Insert Picture From File button on the Drawing toolbar.
- From the <u>I</u>nsert menu, choosing <u>P</u>icture and <u>F</u>rom File.

 NOTE: Display the Drawing toolbar by right-clicking any toolbar and choosing Drawing.

1. Open **KowSales**.

2. Click the Insert Picture From File button on the Drawing toolbar. The Insert Picture dialog box opens.

3. Navigate to the folder with the **KowOwow** file and click the filename to select it.

4. Click the arrow next to the Views button and choose Pre<u>v</u>iew. A preview of the image is on the right.

FIGURE 11-1
Inserting a picture from a file

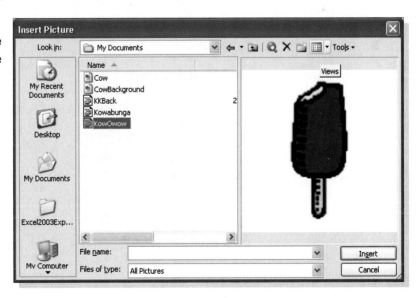

5. Double-click **KowOwow**. The image is inserted at a default size in a default position on the worksheet. Images are placed on the drawing layer, like other objects. If the Picture toolbar has opened, close it.

EXERCISE **11-2** **Check Properties and Scale the Picture**

Depending on the type of picture, the Format Picture dialog box shows various options. An important feature is the option to scale the image. *Scaling* means that you can resize the picture by a percentage, larger or smaller.

1. Click the white background for the picture. Drag the image below the worksheet data.

2. Double-click the white background. The Format Picture dialog box opens.

 TIP: You can double-click the background or right-click an object and choose from the shortcut menu to format a picture.

3. Click the Properties tab. The settings on this tab depend on the picture format and whether it is used on a worksheet or a chart sheet.

4. If it's not already selected, select Move but don't size with cells. This will allow you to size the picture separately.

5. If it's not already selected, place a check mark for Print object. You can turn this setting off if you want to print the sheet without the picture.

6. Click the Size tab. The Scale group shows how the image is sized, based on its original size.

7. In the Scale group, double-click the value in the Height box, key **50**, and press Tab. The Width is adjusted automatically because Lock aspect ratio is selected.

FIGURE 11-2
Format Picture
dialog box

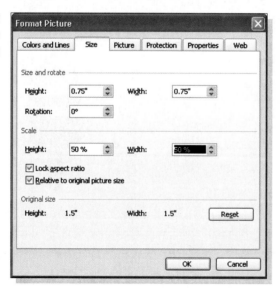

NOTE: The aspect ratio keeps an image proportional as you resize it.

8. Click OK. The image is half its original size.

9. Make column C 24.29 (175 pixels) wide. Then make row 3 56.25 (75 pixels) high.

10. Point at the image and drag it to the right of the label in cell C3. It appears that the white background could be a problem.

11. Click the Print Preview button . Since the gridlines do not print and the paper is white, the background does not show.

12. Close the preview. Click an empty cell.

EXERCISE 11-3 Insert a Clip Art Image

The Clip Organizer organizes images from Microsoft and other sources that are on your hard disk. These images are installed on your computer or network drive and have been cataloged so that they appear in the Insert Clip Art task pane.

1. Click the Insert Clip Art button on the Drawing toolbar. The Clip Art task pane opens.

2. In the Search for box, key **money**. This searches for images on your computer that have the word "money" in the title or the description.

3. Click Go. Clip art images that illustrate money are shown in the task pane. Your images may not be the same as those shown in this text.

FIGURE 11-3
Searching for an image in the Clip Art task pane

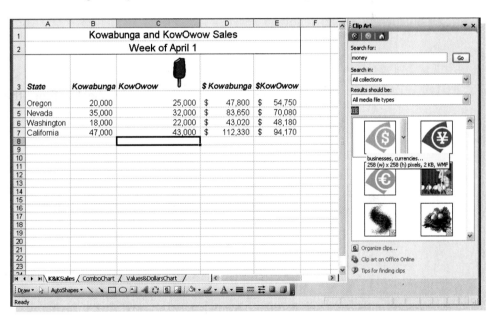

4. Double-click the first image (or any available picture). It is inserted on the worksheet.

EXERCISE **11-4** **Crop an Image**

Cropping an image allows you to remove part of the picture, working from any of the edges. It takes some guesswork and practice to learn how to crop an image so that it shows what you want to see.

1. Right-click the image background and choose Format Picture.
2. Click the Picture tab.
3. In the Crop from group, key **1** for the Left crop amount.

 NOTE: You need not key the inch mark ("). It is assumed.

4. Key **.5** for the Top crop amount.
5. Key **.35** for the Right amount. Key **.5** for the Bottom amount.

FIGURE 11-4
Crop settings
for an image

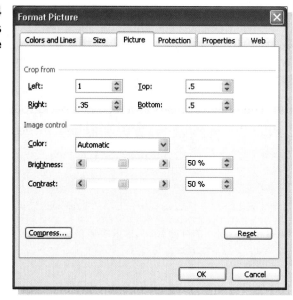

6. Click OK. The image is rectangular in shape but still too large.
7. Press [Ctrl]+[1] to open the Format Picture dialog box.
8. Click the Size tab. In the Scale group, double-click the value in the Height box, key **80**, and press [Tab]. The Width is adjusted automatically.
9. Click OK.
10. Make column E 24.29 (175 pixels) wide.
11. Point at the image and drag it to the right of the label in cell E3.

12. Click an empty cell. Close the Clip Art task pane.
13. Save the workbook as *[your initials]***11-4** in a new folder for Lesson 11.
14. Add your standard footer and print the sheet horizontally centered on the page.

Using a Background Picture

You can choose any graphics file as a background for a worksheet. A background image is *tiled*, or repeated across the worksheet. A background is for screen display and does not print. If you use a background image, you should check that it does not make your data difficult to read.

EXERCISE 11-5 **Insert a Tiled Image**

1. Click the ComboChart tab.
2. Right-click the gray plot area and choose Format Plot Area.
3. In the Area group, choose None and click OK. The plot area is now transparent.
4. Click the white sheet background.
5. From the Format menu, choose Sheet and then Background. The Sheet Background dialog box opens.

6. Click the arrow next to the Views button and choose Preview.
7. Navigate to find the **Kowabunga** image. Click the filename to select it.
8. Click Insert. The image appears as a repeated background picture.

9. Click the Print Preview button ⬚. Background images do not print.
10. Close the preview.

Adding an Image to a Header or Footer

You can also insert images in headers and footers. A company logo or symbol is an example of an image that might be used in a header or footer.

EXERCISE 11-6 **Insert and Format an Image in a Footer**

1. Click the Values&DollarsChart tab.

2. Click the Print Preview button ⬚.
3. Click Setup. Click the Header/Footer tab.
4. Choose Custom Footer.
5. Key your name in the left section.
6. Click in the Right section box.

7. Click the Insert Picture button . The Insert Picture dialog box opens.

8. Navigate to the folder with **Kowabunga** and click to highlight the filename.

9. Click Insert. You do not see the image in the Header/Footer dialog box. The code is &[Picture].

FIGURE 11-5
Inserting a picture
in a footer

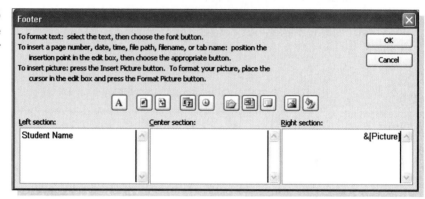

10. Click OK to close the Header/Footer dialog box. The image is a bit large for the footer.

11. Click OK again to close the Page Setup dialog box. You can see the image in Print Preview, and it is too big.

12. Click Setup. Click the Header/Footer tab. Choose Custom Footer.

13. Click in the Right section box.

14. Click the Format Picture button. The Format Picture dialog box has two tabs when in a footer.

15. Click the Size tab. In the Scale group, double-click the value in the Height box, key **30**, and press Tab.

16. Click OK to return to print preview.

17. Save the workbook as *[your initials]***11-6** in your Lesson 11 folder.

18. Print the sheet.

Saving a Web Page

You can save an Excel workbook as an HTML file so that it can be viewed on the World Wide Web, using most browsers. An *HTML* file uses *Hypertext Markup Language,* a widely used and recognized format for Web pages. Web pages are saved with an **.html** extension.

EXERCISE **11-7** Save a Workbook as a Web Page

You can save the entire workbook or an individual worksheet as a Web page. When you save the entire workbook, the Web page shows the worksheet tabs.

1. Click the K&KSales tab and click cell A1.

2. From the File menu, choose Save as Web Page.

 NOTE: Do not use Single File Web Page to save a Web page unless you are familiar with HTML and can edit it on your own.

3. Click the arrow for Save as type and choose Web Page.

4. Set the Save in folder to your Lesson 11 folder.

5. In the Save area, choose Entire Workbook.

6. Click Change Title. This will be the title that appears in the title bar of the browser.

7. Key **Kowabunga and KowOwow Sales** and click OK.

FIGURE 11-6
Saving a Web page

8. Name the Web page *[your initials]*11-7. Click Save.

EXERCISE **11-8** Use Web Page Preview

You can use Web Page Preview before or after you save a file to see what your Web page will look like in your browser. When you choose Web Page Preview, the browser on your computer is launched and the browser displays the file.

1. From the File menu, choose Web Page Preview. The browser on your computer starts and shows your file.

2. Maximize the browser window. Look for the title of the Web page in your browser's title bar.

3. Click the worksheet tabs to see the charts. You will see the tiled image on the ComboChart sheet.

4. Click the Close button ☒ to close the browser.

5. Close the workbook.

> **NOTE:** You must have a workbook open to use Web Page Preview. However, the open workbook does not need to be the file you want to preview.

6. Click the New button 🗋. A blank workbook opens.

7. From the File menu, choose Web Page Preview. The blank workbook opens in the browser.

8. From the File menu, choose Open.

9. Click the Browse button.

10. Find *[your initials]***11-7** and click to select it.

11. Click Open and then click OK.

12. Close the browser and then the blank workbook.

EXERCISE **Delete a Tiled Image**

---

1. Open *[your initials]***11-6**. You do not need to keep the background image on the ComboChart sheet.

2. Click the ComboChart tab.

3. From the Format menu, choose Sheet.

4. Choose Delete Background. The background is removed.

5. Save the workbook as *[your initials]***11-9** in your Lesson 11 folder.

6. Close the workbook.

Creating an Organization Chart

An *organization chart* is an object that shows relationships, usually among workers in a company. Organization charts generally show hierarchical associations between people. This means there is someone at the top (the superior) with assistants, subordinates, or coworkers. Organization charts, unlike worksheet charts, are not linked to data in the worksheet.

You can insert an organization chart file by:

- Clicking the Insert Diagram or Organization Chart button ☼ on the Drawing toolbar.
- From the Insert menu, choosing Picture and Organization Chart.

EXERCISE 11-10 Create and Scale an Organization Chart

1. Create a new workbook.
2. Click the Insert Diagram or Organization Chart button ☼ on the Drawing toolbar. The Diagram Gallery dialog box shows six types of diagrams that can be built. As you click each one, a description appears in the dialog box.
3. Click the Organization Chart icon in the Diagram Gallery dialog box and click OK. An organization chart with four shapes opens with the Organization Chart toolbar.

FIGURE 11-7
New organization
chart

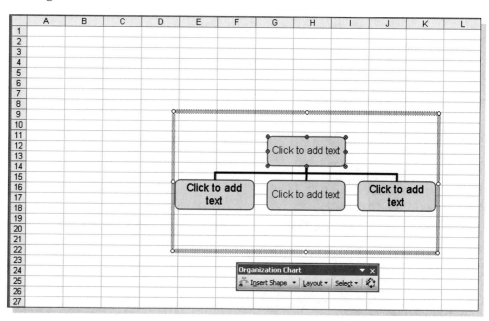

4. Right-click the bounding box border and choose Format Organization Chart. The Format Organization Chart dialog box has seven tabs with properties that can be edited.
5. Click the Size tab. The Scale group shows that the chart is at 100% of its original size.
6. In the Scale group, double-click the value in the Height box, key **200**, and press (Tab). This will double the size of the chart. Make sure Lock aspect ratio shows a check mark.

7. Click OK. The chart object is resized.

8. Point at the border to display the four-pointed arrow. Drag the chart object so that its top-left selection handle is in cell A1.

EXERCISE 11-11 Add Shapes to an Organization Chart

The shapes in an organization chart can be one of four types. The *superior shape* is the top shape, the highest in the hierarchy. There is one superior shape. The *assistant shape* generally represents a helper to the superior. It is attached to the line that connects the superior shape to the rest of the chart. The other two shapes are *subordinate* and *coworker,* both employees of the superior shape.

1. Click the border of the superior shape, the top rounded rectangle. It shows selection handles. A code to identify it appears in the Name box.

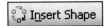

2. Click the arrow with the Insert Shape button on the Organization Chart toolbar. Choose Assistant. A shape is added below the superior shape but above the subordinates.

> **TIP:** If you insert a shape in the wrong location, right-click it and choose Delete.

3. Click the border of the leftmost subordinate shape. Handles appear and its code appears in the Name box.

FIGURE 11-8
Adding shapes

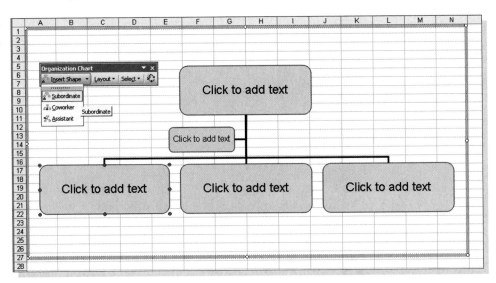

4. Click the arrow with the Insert Shape button [Insert Shape]. Choose Subordinate. A shape is added below the subordinate, indicating another subordinate.

EXERCISE 11-12 **Add Text to the Shapes**

The quickest way to add text to a shape is to click inside it to place the text insertion point and type. You can change the font, alignment, and color as you would for any text in a worksheet.

1. Click inside the superior shape. The text insertion point appears.
2. Key **Conrad Steele** and press (Enter). You can add multiple lines inside a shape.
3. Key **President and CEO** on the second line.
4. Click inside the assistant shape.
5. Key **[your first and last name]**. If your name is long, it may split into two lines. Press (Enter).
6. Key **Executive Assistant** on the second line. You may not see everything you keyed at this point.
7. Click inside the leftmost subordinate shape, key **Juan Sante** and press (Enter).
8. Key **Vice-President for Finance** as his title.

 NOTE: Type the text for the boxes and adjust the sizing when the text is finalized.

9. Click inside the middle subordinate shape, key **Keiko Sumara** and press (Enter).
10. Key **Sales and Marketing** as her second line.
11. Click inside the rightmost subordinate shape, key **Robin McDonald**, and press (Enter).
12. Key **Human Resources**.
13. Click inside the bottom subordinate shape and key **[your instructor's first and last name]**. It may split into two lines like your name.
14. Click the dotted pattern border for the chart.
15. Click the arrow with the Layout button |Layout ▾| on the Organization Chart toolbar.
16. Click to turn off AutoLayout. When AutoLayout is off, you can size each object in the chart individually.

EXERCISE 11-13 **Format an Organization Chart**

You can change properties of a chart as you would change those for an AutoShape or a worksheet cell. In addition to basic format changes, organization charts have AutoFormats. These AutoFormats are part of a gallery of styles for charts and diagrams.

1. Click the border of the superior shape. Click the Bold button **B**. The text is bold.

2. Click the border of the assistant shape. Hold down (Shift) and click the border of each of the other four shapes. Five shapes are selected.

FIGURE 11-9
Selecting multiple shapes

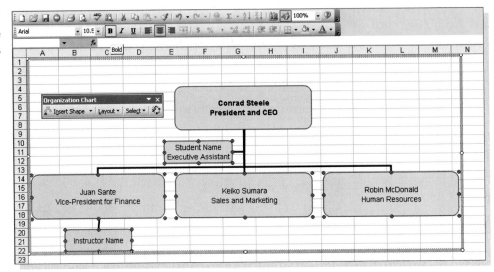

3. Click the Bold button **B**. All the shapes are bold.

4. Hold down (Shift) and click the superior shape to add it to the selection.

5. Set the font size to 14-point Arial.

6. Click the AutoFormat button on the Organization Chart toolbar. The Organization Chart Style Gallery lists styles for this type of chart.

7. Click Fire in the list. The preview area displays the colors used in this style.

FIGURE 11-10
Style Gallery for charts and diagrams

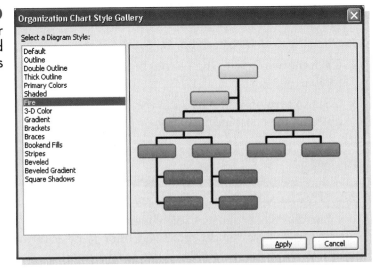

8. Click Beveled Gradient and click OK. The chart is reformatted in a different style. With this style, you need a smaller font.

9. Click to select one text box. Hold down (Shift) and click to add each text box to the selection.

10. Set the font to 10 point.

11. Position the chart with its top-left selection handle in cell A1.

12. Print the organization chart fit to one landscape page and horizontally centered.

Building a Diagram

A *diagram* is an object that illustrates a concept. Excel can build several styles of business diagrams, including Cycle, Target, Radial, Venn, and Pyramid. Diagrams are not linked to worksheet data.

TABLE 11-1   Diagram Types

DIAGRAM TYPE		PURPOSE
	Cycle	Shows a process that has a continuous cycle.
	Target	Shows steps toward a goal.
	Radial	Shows the relationships of parts to a core part or element.
	Venn	Shows areas of overlap between and among parts.
	Pyramid	Shows foundation-based relationships.

EXERCISE 11-14 Create a Cycle Diagram

1. Click the Sheet2 tab.

2. Click the Insert Diagram or Organization Chart button 🔿 on the Drawing toolbar.

3. Click the Cycle Diagram icon in the Diagram Gallery dialog box and click OK. A cycle diagram with three shapes and three labels opens with the Diagram toolbar.

4. Click the top-left text label. An insertion point appears in a bounding box.

5. Key **Promotion** and click the top-right label.

6. Key **Sales** and click the bottom label.

7. Key **Feedback** and click one of the arc shapes.

FIGURE 11-11
Cycle diagram

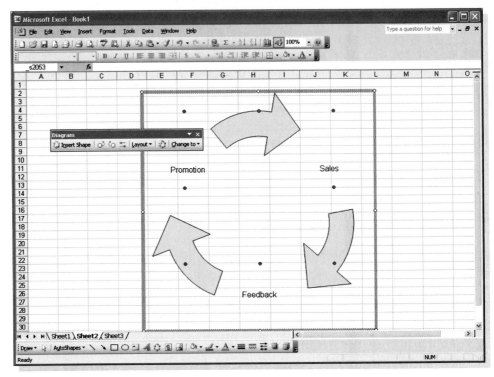

EXERCISE 11-15 Format a Cycle Diagram

1. Click the border of the diagram.

2. Click the AutoFormat button 🔯 on the Diagram toolbar. The Diagram Style Gallery lists styles for a cycle diagram.

3. Click 3-D Color in the list and click OK.

4. Click one of the text areas. It shows diagonal lines for text editing.

5. Click the diagonal lines border. Only selection handles are shown.

6. Hold down Shift and click each of the other two labels. All three are selected.

7. Change the font to 16-point Arial.

8. Click the border of the diagram. Click the arrow with the Layout button Layout ▾. Choose Expand Diagram.

9. Drag the diagram so that the top-left selection handle is in cell A1.

10. Save the workbook as *[your initials]*11-15 in your Lesson 11 folder.

11. Add a footer to this sheet and print it.

Using the Research Task Pane

The Research task pane helps you find and insert data from an outside source into your worksheets. You can use information from your in-house network or from the Web. Excel has a Research Library that includes a multilanguage thesaurus and dictionary, a translation utility, and an Internet encyclopedia. A *thesaurus* is a reference that lists words that mean the same thing as the word you select.

You can open the Research task pane by:

- Clicking the Research button 📖 on the Standard toolbar.
- Clicking a word while holding down the (Alt) key.
- From the View menu, choosing Task Pane, and then clicking the Other Task Panes arrow.

E X E R C I S E **11-16** **Find Synonyms**

A *synonym* is a word that means the same thing as another word. You will revise the diagram to use different words. In order to look up a word using the Research options, you need to rekey the word in a worksheet cell. Your text is currently objects in a diagram, and the Research feature ignores them.

1. Right-click the Sheet2 tab and choose Move or Copy.
2. Click to place a check mark for Create a copy. Click OK.
3. Rename the copied sheet **Revised**.
4. In cell L1, key **sales** and press (Enter). Key **promotion** in cell L2 and **feedback** in cell L3.
5. Hold down the (Alt) key and click cell L1. The Research task pane opens with some preliminary results for the word "sales." It has checked All Reference Books that are installed on your computer. Each resource has an expand or collapse button (+ or –) to indicate whether its list is hidden or shown.
6. Collapse each of the resource items to start.
7. Click the Expand button ➕ for Thesaurus: English (US). It expands to show similar words. There is only one related word, **sale**.
8. Click the Collapse button ➖ for Thesaurus: English (US).

NOTE: If you have different reference books and resources on your computer, expand/collapse each one and check its findings.

9. Click the Expand button ➕ for Thesaurus: French (France). There are many possibilities here.

FIGURE 11-12
Using the Research
task pane

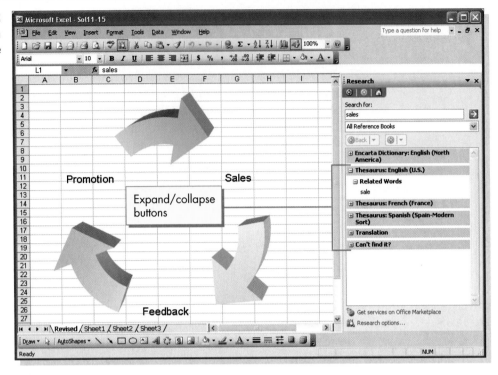

10. Click the Collapse button ☐ for Thesaurus: French (France).
11. Click the Expand button ☐ for Thesaurus: Spanish (Spain-Modern Sort). You need to know Spanish to recognize if these words are possible substitutions.
12. Click the Collapse button ☐ for Thesaurus: Spanish (Spain-Modern Sort).

 NOTE: Close the Research task pane if you cannot see a cell that you need to click.

13. Hold down the [Alt] key and click cell L2. The task pane updates to show related words for "promotion."
14. Click the Expand button ☐ for Thesaurus: English (US). You will replace the word "promotion" in cell L2 with "advertising."
15. Place the mouse pointer on advertising in the advertising (n.) category. (See Figure 11-13.)
16. Click the drop-down arrow and choose Insert. The replacement is made in cell L2.
17. Hold down the [Alt] key and click cell L3.
18. Place the mouse pointer on response in the criticism (n.) category.
19. Click the drop-down arrow and choose Insert.
20. Close the Research task pane.
21. Double-click Promotion in the cycle diagram and key **Advertising** as its replacement.

FIGURE 11-13
Choosing a word
from the thesaurus

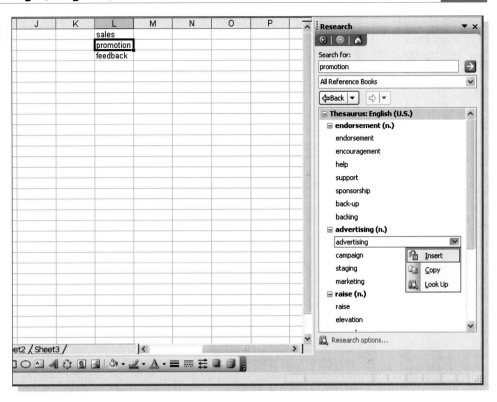

22. Double-click Feedback in the diagram and key **Response**.
23. Click an empty cell and print the sheet.

EXERCISE 11-17 Translate Words

As part of the Research task pane, Excel can help you translate words into French or Spanish. Although this is a handy feature, you will find that you must be familiar with the language you choose so that you can use the correct gender, tense, or grammar.

1. Right-click the Revised tab and choose Move or Copy. Click to place a check mark for Create a copy. Click OK.
2. Rename the copied sheet **French**.
3. Hold down the Alt key and click cell L1.
4. Click the Expand button ⊞ for Translation.
5. In the To box, choose French (France). (See Figure 11-14 on the next page.)
6. Click the Expand button ⊞ for Bilingual dictionary if it is not expanded. The translation for "sales" is "vente."

FIGURE 11-14
Using translation in
the Research
task pane

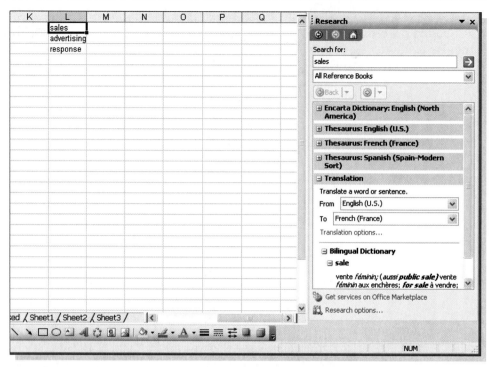

7. Double-click Sales in the diagram and key **Ventes** adding the "s" to make it plural.

8. Hold down the Alt key and click cell L2. The Translation group should be expanded, since you just used it. You have to review the possible translations and determine which one is the best.

9. Double-click Advertising in the diagram and key **Campagne**.

10. Hold down the Alt key and click cell L3.

11. Double-click Response in the diagram and key **Reponse**.

EXERCISE 11-18 **Use a Special Symbol**

You should add the accent to the first "e" in "Réponse" so that it is shown correctly according to the French language. Accented characters are special symbols and can be easily inserted.

1. Drag to select the first "e" in "Reponse."

2. From the Insert menu, choose Symbol.

3. Click the Symbols tab. Set the Font to Arial if it is not already there.

 NOTE: When inserting a symbol for an accented character, use the same font as the rest of the text.

FIGURE 11-15
Inserting a symbol

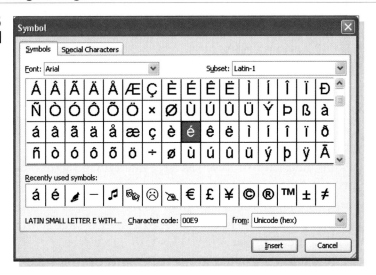

4. Scroll to find **é**, the accented lowercase "e."

5. Click the character to select it and click Insert. The accented é replaces the original character.

6. Click Close. Click an empty cell on the worksheet.

7. Save the workbook as *[your initials]***11-18** in your Lesson 11 folder.

 TIP: When you copy a worksheet, the footer is copied with it.

8. Print the French sheet.

9. Close the workbook. Close the Research task pane.

USING ONLINE HELP

Excel can accept many types of images. You can use Help to learn about many of the formats available for use in a workbook.

Use Help to learn about image formats:

1. Establish an Internet connection and start Internet Explorer. Minimize the window.

2. In a blank workbook, choose Help and Microsoft Excel Help.

3. Key **images** in the Search box and press Enter.

4. Scroll to find the topic Graphic file types Excel can use and click it.

5. Click Show All in the upper-right corner. Read the information.

6. Close the Help window and the Search Results dialog box.

7. Close Internet Explorer and end your Internet connection.

LESSON 11 Summary

➤ You can place images on a sheet or a chart. Images can be taken from a disk or the Clip Organizer.

➤ Images have properties that depend on how the image was originally created. You can edit many of these properties.

➤ A background picture appears as a repeated image across the worksheet. It does not print.

➤ You can use images in headers and footers.

➤ A workbook or worksheet can be saved as a Web page so that it can be viewed with an Internet browser.

➤ You can create organization charts with various levels to illustrate relationships among workers.

➤ Excel can build several common business diagrams including Cycle, Target, Radial, Venn, and Pyramid.

➤ Charts and diagrams have their own AutoFormats.

➤ Charts and diagrams are not linked to worksheet data.

➤ You can use the Research task pane to find words that mean the same thing in the same or a different language.

LESSON 11   Command Summary

FEATURE	BUTTON	MENU	KEYBOARD
Background picture		Format, Sheet, Background	
Clip art	🖼	Insert, Picture, Clip Art	
Diagram	🖼	Insert, Diagram	
Header/footer image	🖼	File, Page Setup	
Picture/image	🖼	Insert, Picture, From File	
Organization chart	🖼	Insert, Picture, Organization Chart	
Research	🖼	View, Task Pane	Alt + Click
Symbol		Insert, Symbol	
Web page		File, Save as Web Page	

Concepts Review

TRUE/FALSE QUESTIONS

Each of the following statements is either true or false. Indicate your choice by circling T or F.

T F   **1.** A scaled image has been resized proportionally.

T **F**   **2.** To remove part of a picture from the image onscreen, you must rotate it.

T **F**   **3.** A thesaurus translates words into another language.

T F   **4.** You can edit a worksheet while viewing it as a Web page with a browser.

T F   **5.** The text boxes in an organization chart are called *shapes*.

T F   **6.** The Clip Organizer includes images from a variety of subjects and categories.

T F   **7.** A background image appears behind the worksheet data.

T **F**   **8.** In the Research task pane, you can find and use images from the Clip Organizer.

SHORT ANSWER QUESTIONS

Write the correct answer in the space provided.

1. Name two types of diagrams that you can build in Excel.

   Cycle, Target,

2. How can you display this character á?

   Select the letter "a", choose symbol from insert, click the
   symbols tab, scroll to "á", and double-click it.

3. What type of reference includes words that mean the same thing?

   Thesaurus

4. What two buttons on the Drawing toolbar allow you to insert pictures in a worksheet?

5. What term describes an image that repeats across the page?

   Tiling

6. How do you insert an image in a header?

Print preview, setup, header/footer tab, custom header,

7. What can you do so others can see your worksheet on the Internet?

You can save it as an HTML file

8. How can you restyle a diagram with different colors or shadows?

CRITICAL THINKING

Answer these questions on a separate page. There are no right or wrong answers. Support your answers with examples from your own experience, if possible.

1. The Research task pane allows you to add other reference sources to the ones that come with Excel. What types of references might be helpful to business workers? What references might help students?

2. What kinds of images might be appropriate for a header or footer?

Skills Review

EXERCISE 11-19

Insert a picture. Format and scale a picture. Copy and flip a picture.

1. Create a new workbook from the **ExpRpt** template.

2. Save the workbook as *[your initials]*11-19 in your Lesson 11 folder.

3. Insert a picture by following these steps:

  a. Click cell A1.

  b. Click the Insert Picture from File button on the Drawing toolbar.

  c. Find and select the **Cow** file. Click Insert.

> **NOTE:** The **Cow** file is a GIF image file, a popular format used for Web display. The image format determines what type of format changes you can make in Excel.

  d. With the four-pointed arrow, click and drag the image slightly down and to the right so you can see all the handles.

4. Format a picture by following these steps:

  a. Right-click the image and choose Format Picture.

b. Click the Colors and Lines tab.

c. In the Fill group, choose Orange (second row, second swatch) for the Color.

d. In the Line group, choose Orange (second row, second swatch) for the Color. Click OK. The color is applied only to the outline of the bounding box. You cannot change the fill color of this type of image in Excel.

 NOTE: To change the image colors of a GIF file, you need to use a graphics editing program.

5. Scale a picture by following these steps:

   a. Right-click the image and choose Format Picture.

   b. Click the Size tab.

   c. In the Scale group, double-click the value in the Height box, key **50**, and press `Tab`. The Width is adjusted. Click OK.

6. Position the image so that its center is aligned on the border between columns A and B in rows 1 and 2.

7. Point at the image and hold down the `Ctrl` key. Drag a copy of the picture to be just below the original in rows 3:5.

8. Flip a picture by following these steps:

   a. While the copied image is selected, click Draw on the Drawing toolbar.

   b. Choose Rotate or Flip and then choose Flip Horizontal.

   c. Choose Rotate or Flip again and choose Flip Vertical.

9. Hold down `Ctrl` and click the original image so that both pictures are selected.

10. Click Draw on the Drawing toolbar and choose Align or Distribute. Choose Align Left.

11. Click cell A1. Add your standard footer and print the worksheet.

12. Save and close the workbook.

EXERCISE 11-20

Use a background picture. Save a workbook as a Web page. Delete a background picture. Add an image to a header/footer.

1. Open **ICOrder** and save it as *[your initials]***11-20** in your Lesson 11 folder.

2. Add a background image by following these steps:

   a. From the Format menu, choose Sheet and then Background.

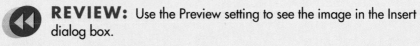 **REVIEW:** Use the Preview setting to see the image in the Insert dialog box.

   b. Navigate to the folder with **KKBack** and click to select the filename. Click Insert.

3. Save a workbook as a Web page by following these steps:

   a. From the File menu, choose Save as Web Page.

   b. Set the Save in folder to your Lesson 11 folder.

   c. Choose Selection: Sheet in the Save area. This will automatically save your file as a Single File Web Page.

   d. Click Change Title. Key **Online Order Form** and click OK.

 NOTE: You can use the same filename for the workbook and the Web file because they use different filename extensions.

   e. In the File name box, key *[your initials]***11-20**. Click Save.

4. Preview a Web page by following these steps:

   a. From the File menu, choose Web Page Preview.

   b. Maximize the browser window.

   c. Close the browser.

5. Delete a background image by following these steps:

   a. From the Format menu, choose Sheet.

   b. Choose Delete Background. The background is removed.

6. Add an image to a footer by following these steps:

   a. Click the Print Preview button .

   b. Click Setup. Click the Header/Footer tab.

   c. Choose Custom Footer. Click the Center section.

   d. Click the Insert Picture button .

   e. Navigate to the appropriate folder to find **KowOwow** to select it. Click Insert.

   f. Key your name in the Right section. Click OK.

   g. Click OK. Close the preview.

7. Press Ctrl + Home.

8. Print the worksheet. Save and close the workbook.

EXERCISE 11-21

Create an organization chart. Add a shape. Add text. Format an organization chart.

1. Open **Personnel** and save the workbook as *[your initials]***11-21** in your Lesson 11 folder.

2. Rename the Sheet2 tab as **OrgChart**.

3. Create an organization chart by following these steps:

   a. Click the Insert Diagram or Organization Chart button.

   b. Click the Organization Chart icon and click OK.

   c. Right-click the border and choose Format Organization Chart.

   d. Click the Size tab. In the Scale group, double-click the value in the Height box, key **150**, and press Tab.

4. Add a shape to an organization chart by following these steps:

   a. Click the border of the leftmost subordinate shape.

   b. Click the arrow with the Insert Shape button . Choose Coworker.

5. Add text to a shape in an organization chart by following these steps:

   a. Click inside the superior shape.

   b. Key **Heinrich Kraus** and press (Enter). Key **President-Elect**.

   c. Click inside the leftmost subordinate shape, key **Glenn Ladewig**.

   d. Click inside the second subordinate shape, key **Nassar Eassa**.

   e. Click inside the third subordinate shape, key **Ted Artagnan**.

   f. Click inside the fourth subordinate shape, key **Maria Calcivechia**.

6. Format an organization chart by following these steps:

   a. Click the chart border.

   b. Click the AutoFormat button 🗘 on the Organization Chart toolbar.

   c. Click Shaded in the list and click Apply.

   d. Click the arrow with the Layout button Layout ▾. Choose Fit Organization Chart to Contents.

7. Move the organization chart so that its top-left handle is at cell A4.

8. In cell A1, key **Owners Association**. In cell A2, key the current month and year. Format the date to show the month spelled out and four digits for the year with no date.

9. Use 16-point Arial for cells A1:A2.

10. Select cells A1 to J2 and center these labels across this range.

11. Add your usual footer to the sheet.

12. Print the worksheet landscape and horizontally centered.

13. Save and close the workbook.

EXERCISE 11-22

Build a diagram. Edit a diagram. Use the Research tool.

1. Open **Personnel** and save the workbook as *[your initials]*11-22 in your Lesson 11 folder.

2. Rename the Sheet2 tab as **Venn**.

3. Build a Venn diagram by following these steps:

   a. Click the Insert Diagram or Organization Chart button 🗘.

   b. Click the Venn Diagram icon and click OK.

4. Edit a Venn diagram by following these steps:

   a. Click the Insert Shape button .

   TIP: There are no choices for what type of shape to insert in a Venn diagram.

    b. Click the top text label and key **Finance**.

    c. Click the left label and key **Marketing**.

    d. Click the bottom label and key **Owners**.

    e. Click the right label and key **Human Resources**.

     f. Click the arrow with the Layout button Layout ▾. Choose Fit Diagram to Contents.

    g. Click the diagram's border. Click the arrow with the Layout button Layout ▾. Choose Expand Diagram. Repeat this step until all the labels can be seen.

5. Move the diagram so that its top-left handle is at cell A4.

6. Use the Research task pane by following these steps:

    a. Right-click the Venn tab and choose Move or Copy.

    b. Click to place a check mark for Create a copy. Click OK.

    c. Rename the copied sheet **NewLabels**.

    d. In cell L1, key **finance** and press Enter. Key **marketing** in cell L2, **human resources** in cell L3, and **owners** in cell L4.

    e. Hold down the Alt key and click cell L1. Verify that All Reference Books are used.

    f. Click the Expand button ➕ for Thesaurus: English (US).

    TIP: You can collapse references that you are not using.

    g. Place the mouse pointer on funding in the money (n.) category.

    h. Click the drop-down arrow and choose Insert.

    i. Hold down the Alt key and click cell L2.

    j. Place the mouse pointer on promotion in the advertising (n.) category. Click the drop-down arrow and choose Insert.

    k. Hold down the Alt key and click cell L3.

    l. Place the mouse pointer on workforce in the workers (n.) category. Click the drop-down arrow and choose Insert.

    m. Hold down the Alt key and click cell L4. There are no good substitutions.

    n. Close the Research task pane.

7. Double-click Marketing in the diagram and key **Promotion**.

8. Double-click Finance in the diagram and key **Funding**. Replace Human Resources with **Workforce**.

9. In cell A1, key **Possible Name Changes**. Use 16-point Arial.

10. Add your usual footer to the sheet.

11. Print the worksheet horizontally centered on one page.

12. Save and close the workbook.

Lesson Applications

EXERCISE 11-23

Insert a background image. Save a file as a Web page.

Using WordArt and a background image, you have been asked to create a simple promotional Web page.

1. Create a new workbook and save it as *[your initials]*11-23 in your Lesson 11 folder.

2. Format the sheet to use **CowBackground** as a background image.

3. Create a WordArt image using the fifth style in the second row. Make it 48 points and key **Klassy Kow Ice Cream** on a single line. Place this image so that the rotation handle is at row 1 and the top-left handle is near cell A2.

4. Create a second WordArt image using the second style in the second row. Make it 36 points, key **Sundaes,** and press Enter. On the second line, key **Shakes** and press Enter. Key **Cones** and press Enter. On the fourth line, key **And more. . ..** Place this image so that it appears a couple of rows below and centered in relation to your first WordArt image.

5. Create a third WordArt image using the fourth style in the fourth row. Make it 36 points and key **Come See Us Soon!** Place this image below and centered in relation to your second WordArt image.

6. Add your standard footer, save the workbook, and print the sheet. The background does not print.

 NOTE: Use Web page as the file type, not Single File Web page.

7. Save the workbook as a Web page with the same name. Change the title to **Klassy Kow Ice Cream.** Preview your Web page in your browser.

8. Close the browser. Close the workbook without saving.

EXERCISE 11-24

Use the Research task pane.

Klassy Kow Ice Cream, Inc., wants to prepare a supermarket order sheet that shows the flavor names in Spanish. Use the Research task pane and other resources to change the names of the flavors.

1. Open **SpanishOrderSheet** and save it as *[your initials]***11-24** in your Lesson 11 folder.

2. Hold down (Alt) and click **Vanilla** in cell A7. Expand the Translation group and change the To choice to Spanish (Spain-Modern Sort). Key the Spanish spelling in cell A7.

 TIP: To insert a symbol, select the character in the formula bar.

3. Repeat these steps to find a Spanish translation for each of the flavors. Use symbols if needed.

 NOTE: Adjectives usually follow the noun, so "French Vanilla" would be "Vainilla Francés."

4. Add your standard footer and print the worksheet.

5. Save and close the workbook. Close the Research task pane.

EXERCISE 11-25

Create and format an organization chart.

Although organization charts usually show relationships among people, you can also show relationships between events, activities, or ideas.

1. Create a new workbook and save it as *[your initials]***11-25** in your Lesson 11 folder.

2. Create an organization chart.

3. Click the leftmost subordinate shape and add three subordinate shapes.

 NOTE: Click the shape to which the subordinate should be added. Then click the Insert Shape button to insert the first shape in the list.

 4. While the leftmost subordinate shape is selected, click the arrow with the Layout button [Layout ▾]. Choose Right Hanging.

5. Repeat steps 3 and 4 for each of the other subordinate shapes.

6. Select the chart and use the corner selection handles to make the chart larger. Size and position it so that the top-left handle is at cell A1 and the bottom-right handle is about at cell M25.

7. Key **Sales** in the superior shape.

8. In the leftmost subordinate shape on the second row, key **Campaigns**. In the middle shape, key **Locations**. In the rightmost shape, key **Products**. Nothing will fit as you key the labels.

9. In the three shapes for Campaigns, key these labels:
   Timing
   Nature
   Purpose

10. In the three shapes for Locations, key these labels:
    Geography
    Demographics
    Cost

11. In the three shapes for Products, key these labels:
    Cost
    Testing
    Success Rate

12. Click the chart border when finished keying the labels. Fit the chart to the contents. Reposition the chart so that it starts in cell A1.

13. Add your standard footer and print the worksheet so that it fits on one portrait page.

14. Save and close the workbook.

EXERCISE 11-26 *Challenge Yourself*

You can paste a "picture" of cells to another sheet in the same workbook. A cell picture can be pasted and linked on the same worksheet so that when the cells are edited, the picture updates.

1. Open **CASales** and save it as *[your initials]***11-26** in your Lesson 11 folder.

2. Select cells F4:F18 and copy the range.

  REVIEW: You can click the Copy button or right-click and choose Copy from the shortcut menu.

3. Go to the chart. Hold down (Shift) and open the Edit menu. Choose Paste Picture. The picture of the cells is an object with selection handles.

 NOTE: You must hold down (Shift) to see the Paste Picture command.

4. Drag the picture object to the white chart background at the right, with the top of the object aligned with the "San Francisco, West" bar.

5. Format the picture object to have a black line color and light gray fill.

6. Add your standard footer and print the chart sheet.

7. Save and close the workbook.

On Your Own

In these exercises you work on your own, as you would in a real-life work environment. Use the skills you've learned to accomplish the task—and be creative.

EXERCISE 11-27

Search the Web to find sites from which you can download images. Download an image and save it in your Lesson 11 folder. In a new workbook, insert the image. Then size and format it. In cells away from the image, key an explanation of where you found the image and how you formatted it. Use two rows for your explanations. Add your standard footer and print the sheet. Save the workbook as *[your initials]*11-27 in your Lesson 11 folder and close it.

EXERCISE 11-28

Create a new workbook and save it as *[your initials]*11-28 in your Lesson 11 folder. Create an organization chart that illustrates the descendants in your family with a great-grandfather or grandfather as the superior shape. Add or delete shapes as necessary. Format the chart according to your tastes. Print the chart. Save and close the workbook.

EXERCISE 11-29

In a new workbook, explore possibilities for using the Target or the Radial diagram to illustrate a business idea. Create the diagram, add the text, and format the diagram. Save your worksheet as *[your initials]*11-29 in your Lesson 11 folder. Add your standard footer and print the sheet. Save and close the workbook.

Unit 3 Applications

UNIT APPLICATION 3-1

Create a combination chart. Format chart objects.

Klassy Kow Ice Cream sells cases of ice cream to supermarkets. The cases come in sizes of 6 gallons, 12 gallons, 18 gallons, and 24 gallons. You need to build a combination chart that plots the cost per case to Klassy Kow and the selling price to the supermarket.

 NOTE: The *cost* is what Klassy Kow incurs to make and ship the ice cream case. The *markup* is an additional amount added to the cost. The *selling price* equals the cost + the markup.

1. Open **ICCases** and save it in a new folder for Unit 3 as *[your initials]***u3-1**.

2. In cell C6, key a formula to multiply the cost in cell B6 by the number of half-gallons specified in column A. Key a similar formula to calculate the cost of each case. Copy the format from cell B6 to the results in column C.

 NOTE: The formula to determine the markup should use parentheses to control what is done first and an absolute reference.

3. In cell D6, key a formula to multiply the case cost by 1 plus the markup for the month. Copy the formula to cell D9 and then copy the format from a value in column C.

4. Select cells A6:A9, C6:C9, and D6:D9 and create a clustered column chart. In the wizard on the Series tab, name Series1 **Cost**. Name Series2 **Selling Price**. As the chart title, key **October Markup**. Place the chart on a separate sheet.

5. Format the chart title as 24 points. Right-click any Selling Price column and change its chart type to a line with markers at each data value.

6. Format the line and its markers so that the chart is easy to read. Change the colors to colors that print well on your printer.

7. Position the legend on the bottom and show the data table.

8. Add your usual footer and print the chart.

9. Save and close the workbook.

UNIT APPLICATION 3-2

Insert WordArt. Add a comment in an AutoShape. Format the AutoShape.

Klassy Kow Ice Cream Shops keep track of sales promotions and incentives to determine which are the best sales generators. You need to create a workbook that shows recent promotions and the increase in sales.

1. Create a new workbook and save it as *[your initials]***u3-2** in your Unit 3 folder. Delete Sheet2 and Sheet3. Rename Sheet1 **Promotions**.

    TIP: Group the sheets and delete them at once.

2. Key **Promotions** in cell B1. Key **Percent Increase** in cell C1. Make both cells bold.

3. Key the information in Figure U3-1 in cells B2:C5. Adjust the column widths.

FIGURE U3-1

	B	C
1	Promotions	Percent Increase
2	Guess gumballs	12%
3	Tip calculator	8%
4	10% Off	15%
5	Multiplication table	8%

4. Click the Insert WordArt button . In the far-right column, choose a vertical style and click OK. Set the font to 20 points. Key **Klassy Kow Ice Cream**. Click OK. Move the object to column A.

5. Insert a comment in cell C2. Delete the user name and key the following (do not use bold type):
   These are company-wide averages. Individual shops experience various increases based on location, weather, and other factors.

    REVIEW: Show a comment from the View menu so that it stays on screen.

6. Show the comment and select it. Change the shape to a rounded rectangular callout. Size the callout to show the text and position it so that you can drag the adjustment handle to point at cell C2.

   REVIEW: Use File, Page Setup to print comments.

7. While the comment is shown on the worksheet, print the sheet with your standard footer.

 NOTE: If it appears that you cannot click to select a cell after working with a drawing object, click the Select Objects button 🔲 in the Drawing toolbar.

8. Save and close the workbook.

UNIT APPLICATION 3-3

Create a target diagram. Add drawing objects.

1. Create a new workbook and save it as *[your initials]*u3-3 in your Unit 3 folder. Delete Sheet2 and Sheet3. Rename Sheet1 **Target**.

2. Create a target diagram. Change the top label to **20% Sales Increase**. Change the middle label to **15% Sales Increase** and the bottom label to **10% Sales Increase**.

3. Format the diagram to use Square Shadows. Drag the diagram so that the top-left handle is at cell A1.

4. Draw a text box and key **Local promotion on radio and in newspapers**. Format this text box to have no line and no fill. Size it to show the text on two lines. Position the text box with its top-left handle at cell E21.

5. Draw an arrow that points from the outer ring to the text box. Choose a length that corresponds to how far the text box is from the outer ring.

6. Copy and paste the text box. Move the copy to the lower-left part of the circle near cell A24. Change the text to **State-wide coupon campaign and free decal with purchase**. Draw an arrow that points from the middle ring to this text box.

7. Create one more text box for the inner ring. Position it at the top-left edge of the target. The text is **Regional TV ads with free gift with purchase**. Draw the arrow.

8. Preview the diagram and make changes so that your sheet is easy to understand and well designed.

9. Add your footer and print the sheet.

10. Save and close the workbook.

UNIT APPLICATION 3-4 *Using the Internet*

Search online office supply and computer equipment Web sites to build a price list for six items in an office. You might include objects such as a desk, a chair, a bookcase, file cabinet(s), a computer, a monitor, or a printer. For each item, list the name and a price on the worksheet.

Build a custom pie chart that shows the proportion each item represents of the entire cost of all six items. Use a main title for the chart that includes your name. You might need a legend, depending on your other design choices. Place the chart on a separate sheet. Save the workbook as *[your initials]*u3-4 in your Unit 3 folder. Add your footer and print the chart sheet. Save and close the workbook.

Improving Uses of Worksheet Data

Working with Multiple Worksheets

OBJECTIVES

MICROSOFT OFFICE
SPECIALIST
ACTIVITIES
In this lesson:
XLO3S-1-1
XLO3S-2-3
XLO3S-2-4
XLO3S-5-2
XLO3S-5-4
XLO3S-5-8

See Appendix.

After completing this lesson, you will be able to:

1. **Copy and group worksheets.**
2. **Create a 3-D reference.**
3. **Use functions and formulas in a 3-D reference.**
4. **Print multiple worksheets.**

 Estimated Time: 1½ hours

An Excel workbook can have up to 255 worksheets. This enables you to place data on different sheets for ease in building and reviewing information. Through grouped worksheets and 3-D references, you can gather information from multiple sheets to calculate grand totals, differences, averages, and more.

Copying and Grouping Worksheets

Suppose you use Excel to track monthly sales for several stores. It would be a good practice to keep each month's data on a separate worksheet. The sheets are basically the same except for the month and the values. You can copy the first sheet and edit it to prepare the second sheet. You can group the sheets and change the formatting for all of them.

EXERCISE 12-1 **Copy and Rename Worksheets**

You have already made copies of worksheets to prepare formula printouts. When you use the Move or Copy dialog box, all formatting is copied with the data.

1. Open **JanKow0**.

2. Right-click the January tab. The shortcut menu opens.

3. Choose Move or Copy. The Move or Copy dialog box opens. The To book list includes the names of open workbooks as well as a new book. The Before sheet list allows you to move or copy the sheet before the current sheet or place it last in the tabs.

 NOTE: If you do not turn on Create a copy, the worksheet is moved.

4. Select (move to end) in the Before sheet list.

5. Click to place a check mark in the Create a copy check box.

FIGURE 12-1
Copying
a worksheet
to the end

6. Click OK. A new worksheet named January (2) is inserted after the January sheet. It is an exact duplicate of the January sheet.

7. Rename January (2) tab as **February**.

8. Change "January" to **February** in cell A2.

9. Right-click the February tab. Choose Move or Copy.

10. Choose (move to end) in the Before sheet list.

11. Click to place a check mark in the Create a copy box.

12. Click OK. A new worksheet named February (2) is inserted after the February sheet.

13. Rename the February (2) tab **March**.

 REVIEW: You can double-click or right-click a sheet tab to rename it.

14. Change "February" to **March** in cell A2.

EXERCISE 12-2 **Group Worksheets and Delete Data**

When worksheets are grouped, editing and formatting commands affect all sheets in the group. This is an easy way to make changes to several worksheets at once, as long as the worksheets are identical.

1. While the March worksheet is active, hold down ⌷Ctrl⌷ and click the February tab. Both worksheets are selected or active.

 NOTE: The word [Group] appears in the title bar.

2. Click cell B4 and drag to select cells B4:C8.

FIGURE 12-2
Grouped
worksheets

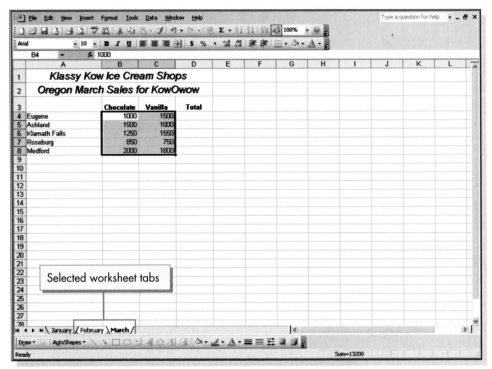

3. Press ⌷Delete⌷. The values are cleared from both sheets.

4. Click the January tab. The other two worksheets are ungrouped.

 TIP: You can ungroup sheets by clicking a sheet that is not in the group or by right-clicking a sheet in the group and choosing Ungroup Sheets.

5. Click the February tab to see that the cells are cleared. Click the March tab.

EXERCISE **12-3** **Group Worksheets and Insert Data**

1. While the March worksheet is active, hold down ⌷Shift⌷ and click the January tab. All three worksheets are active.

2. Click cell A3 and key **Shop** to add the label to all three sheets.

3. Right-click any sheet tab and choose Ungroup Sheets.

4. Click the February tab and key the values in Figure 12-3 to complete the worksheet.

FIGURE 12-3

Shop	Chocolate	Vanilla
Eugene	1200	1025
Ashland	1500	1600
Klamath Falls	975	1035
Roseburg	1050	1200
Medford	1800	1560

5. Click the March tab and key the values in Figure 12-4.

FIGURE 12-4

Shop	Chocolate	Vanilla
Eugene	1300	1225
Ashland	1675	1650
Klamath Falls	1975	935
Roseburg	1450	1175
Medford	1645	1800

EXERCISE **12-4** **Format Values and Insert a Function**

1. While the March worksheet is active, hold down (Shift) and click the January tab.

2. Click cell B4 and drag to select cells B4:D8.

3. Click the Comma Style button .

4. Click the Decrease Decimal button ⊡ two times.

5. Select cells D4:D8 and click the AutoSum button ⊡.

6. Right-click any sheet tab and choose Ungroup Sheets.

7. Check each sheet for its formatting and SUM function.

EXERCISE 12-5 **Insert and Move a Worksheet**

1. Click the January tab and press Ctrl + Home.
2. Press Shift + F11. A blank worksheet is inserted in front of (to the left of) the January sheet.

 REVIEW: You can also insert a sheet by choosing Insert, Worksheet or by right-clicking a worksheet tab and choosing Insert.

3. Press Shift + F11 again. Another worksheet is inserted.

 NOTE: New sheet numbers start at the next available number.

4. Right-click the Sheet2 tab and choose Delete.
5. Rename Sheet1 as **FirstQuarter**.
6. Right-click the FirstQuarter tab and choose Move or Copy.
7. Choose (move to end) and click OK. This moves the sheet without making a copy.

 REVIEW: You can also drag a worksheet tab to reposition it.

EXERCISE 12-6 **Fill Data to a Worksheet**

1. Click the March tab and select cells A1:D3.
2. Hold down Ctrl and click the FirstQuarter tab. The two sheets are grouped.
3. From the Edit menu, choose Fill. From the submenu, choose Across Worksheets.
4. Choose All and click OK. The labels are copied, but the column widths and row heights are not.
5. Right-click the FirstQuarter tab and choose Ungroup Sheets.
6. Format column A as 21.57 (156 pixels) wide.

 TIP: Drag across the column headings to select multiple columns and adjust the width.

7. Format columns B, C, and D each as 10.00 (75 pixels) wide.
8. Format row 3 as 22.50 (30 pixels) high.
9. Change the label in cell B2 to **First Quarter Sales for KowOwow**.

EXERCISE 12-7   **Copy Multiple Worksheets**

1. While the FirstQuarter tab is active, hold down (Shift) and click the January tab. All four worksheets are grouped.
2. Right-click any sheet in the group and choose Move or Copy.
3. Choose (move to end).
4. Click to place a check mark for Create a copy.
5. Click OK. Four new worksheets are inserted, one copy of each grouped sheet.

EXERCISE 12-8   **Scroll Multiple Worksheets**

Now that you have eight worksheets in your workbook, you cannot see all the worksheet tabs at once. The worksheet tab scrolling buttons are at the left edges of the tab names. These buttons allow you to scroll tabs.

The tab scrolling buttons share space with the horizontal scroll bar and are separated from it by the tab split box. You can drag the tab split box to change the number of visible tabs or the size of the horizontal scroll bar.

1. Position the mouse pointer on the tab split box. The pointer is a two-pointed arrow.
2. Click and drag the pointer to the right until you see all the tabs.

 NOTE: Depending on your screen size, you might not be able to drag the tab split bar far enough to see all the tabs.

FIGURE 12-5
Dragging the tab split box

	A	B	C	D
1	Klassy Kow Ice Cream Shops			
2	Oregon January Sales for KowOwow			
3	Shop	Chocolate	Vanilla	Total
4	Eugene	1,000	1,500	2,500
5	Ashland	1,500	1,000	2,500
6	Klamath Falls	1,250	1,550	2,800
7	Roseburg	850	750	1,600
8	Medford	2,000	1,800	3,800

Tab split box

Tab scrolling buttons

⏮ ◀ ▶ ⏭ \ January ╱ February ╱ March ╱ FirstQuarter ╲ January (2) ╱ February (2) ╱ March (2) ╱ FirstQuarter (2) ╱

Draw ▾ | AutoShapes ▾ \ \ □ ○ ▭ ◄ ۞ ▨ ▨ | ◇ ▾ ✎ ▾ A ▾ ≡ ≡ ⛶ ◻ ▣

Ready

3. Rename the copied sheets as follows (in the order shown):
   April
   May
   June
   SecondQuarter

4. Position the mouse pointer on the tab split box.

5. Click and drag the pointer to the left so that you see the worksheet tabs up to FirstQuarter.

6. Click each tab scrolling button to see how it moves through the tab names.

7. Right-click any of the tab scrolling buttons. A shortcut menu with a list of the tab names opens.

8. Choose April. The sheet is visible and active.

9. Double-click cell A2 and change the month to **April**.

10. Click the far-right tab scrolling button. The tab names at the end are visible.

11. Change cell A2 on the May sheet to show **May** as the month. Change the month on the June sheet to **June**.

12. On the SecondQuarter sheet, edit the label in cell A2 to show **Second Quarter Sales for KowOwow**.

13. Position the mouse pointer on the tab split box. Click and drag the pointer so that you can see the March sheet through the SecondQuarter sheet.

14. Click the March tab. Hold down ⎈Ctrl and click the FirstQuarter sheet. Hold down ⎈Ctrl and click the SecondQuarter sheet. Three sheets are grouped with the March sheet visible.

15. Select the labels in the range A4:A8.

16. From the Edit menu, choose Fill. From the submenu, choose Across Worksheets.

17. Choose Contents and click OK. The labels are copied.

18. Right-click the March tab and choose Ungroup Sheets.

Creating a 3-D Reference

If a formula refers to cells in another worksheet, the formula is described as a *3-D reference*. The formula is a dynamic link between worksheets. If the value in the referenced cell is edited, the formula recalculates the result.

A 3-D reference is valuable when you want to calculate a total based on data on several sheets. In your workbook, for example, you can use a 3-D reference to determine first quarter sales by adding each shop's January, February, and March values.

EXERCISE **12-9** Create a 3-D Reference

You can create a 3-D reference by pointing to the cells in the appropriate worksheet. Excel inserts the worksheet tab name followed by an exclamation point with the cell address.

1. Click the far-left tab scrolling button. Then click the FirstQuarter tab.
2. Click cell B4 and key = to start a formula.
3. Click the January tab and click cell B4. The formula bar shows =January!B4, and a marquee appears around the cell.
4. Key + to add the next reference.
5. Click the February tab and click cell B4. The worksheet tab names are followed by an exclamation point.
6. Key + to continue.
7. Click the March tab and click cell B4.

FIGURE 12-6
Creating a
3-D formula

	A	B	C	D	E	F
	IF ▾ X ✓ ƒx	=January!B4+February!B4+March!B4				
1	*Klassy Kow Ice Cream Shops*					
2	*Oregon March Sales for KowOwow*					
3	Shop	Chocolate	Vanilla	Total		
4	Eugene	1,300	1,225	2,525		
5	Ashland	1,675	1,650	3,325		
6	Klamath Falls	1,975	935	2,910		
7	Roseburg	1,450	1,175	2,625		
8	Medford	1,645	1,800	3,445		
9						
10						
11						

8. Press Enter. The formula is completed, and the result is shown on the FirstQuarter sheet.
9. Click cell B4 and look at the formula bar.
10. Display the Fill handle and copy the formula to cells B5:B8.

 TIP: Ignore the AutoFill Options button.

11. While the filled range is selected, display the Fill handle again and copy the formula to column C.
12. Click cell C4. The reference is adjusted to show the correct cell address and the worksheet tab name.
13. Select cells D4:D8 and click the AutoSum button Σ ▾.

EXERCISE 12-10 Use Paste Special

If you have created a format with several attributes on one worksheet, you can copy only the format by using the Format Painter. You can use the Format Painter from the Paste Special dialog box when you work across multiple sheets.

1. Click the March tab and click cell B4. This value is formatted with commas and no decimal positions.

2. Click the Copy button.

3. Click the FirstQuarter tab.

4. Click cell B4 and drag to select cells B4:D8.

5. From the Edit menu, choose Paste Special. The Paste Special dialog box opens. You can copy everything, only the values, only the formats, or other choices depending on your data.

FIGURE 12-7
Paste Special
dialog box

6. Click the button for Formats.

7. Click OK. The values are formatted.

EXERCISE 12-11 Edit Underlying Data

If you change the value in a cell used in a 3-D reference, the formula is automatically recalculated. Before you begin, notice that the First Quarter total for "Eugene" in cell D4 is 7,250.

1. Click the January tab.

2. Click cell B4 and key **0**.

3. Click the FirstQuarter tab. The result is recalculated.

4. Click the January tab and click cell B4.

5. Key **2000** and click the FirstQuarter tab.

EXERCISE 12-12 **Enter Data in Grouped Worksheets**

You can enter the same data in grouped sheets by keying it once. As you complete this exercise, the sheets for April, May, and June will have the same values.

1. Click the far-right tab scrolling button and click the April tab.

2. Hold down (Shift) and click the June tab. Three sheets are grouped.

3. Select cells B4:C8.

4. Key the following values and press (Enter) after each. These values appear in column B:

   1000
   2000
   1000
   2000
   1000

5. Continue to key the next set of values in column C, pressing (Enter) after each:

   2000
   1000
   2000
   1000
   2000

6. Click the SecondQuarter tab. The sheets are ungrouped.

7. Click cell B4 and key = to start a formula.

8. Click the April tab and click cell B4. Key + to add the next reference.

9. Click the May tab and click cell B4. Key + to continue.

10. Click the June tab, click cell B4, and press (Enter).

11. Copy the formula to cells B5:B8 and then to column C.

12. Select cells D4:D8 and click the AutoSum button Σ ▾.

13. Select cells B4:D8 and format them as Comma Style, with no decimal places.

Using Functions and Formulas in a 3-D Reference

In addition to simple addition, subtraction, multiplication, and division, you can use functions in a 3-D reference. Although you can key a 3-D formula, you are less likely to make an error by pointing at the references. In addition, when you point, Excel includes the worksheet tab name and the exclamation point so that you don't have to key them.

EXERCISE 12-13 Use AVERAGE in a 3-D Reference

1. With the SecondQuarter tab active, press (Shift)+(F11).
2. Move the new sheet after the SecondQuarter sheet and name it **AverageSales**.
3. Click the SecondQuarter tab and click cell A1.
4. Press (Ctrl)+(C), click the AverageSales tab, and press (Enter). The Center Across Selection format is copied and makes the label partially visible.
5. Press (Ctrl)+(1). On the Alignment tab, change the Horizontal text alignment to General. Close the dialog box.
6. Key **Average Monthly Sales** in cell A2. Format the font and size to match cell A1.
7. Copy cells A3:A8 on the SecondQuarter sheet to cell A3 on the AverageSales sheet.
8. Copy cells B3:C3 on the SecondQuarter sheet to cells B3:C3 on the AverageSales sheet.
9. Format columns A:C as 13.57 (100 pixels) wide. Format row 3 as 22.50 (30 pixels) high.
10. Click and drag the tab split box to the right so that you can see all the worksheet tab names (or as many as possible). Then scroll the names to show the January tab.
11. Click cell B4 on the AverageSales sheet and key **=average(** to start the function.
12. Click the January tab and click cell B4. Its address is inserted in the formula.
13. Key a comma to separate the arguments in the function.
14. Click the February tab and click cell B4.
15. Key a comma and click the March tab.
16. Click cell B4, key a comma, and click the April tab.
17. Click cell B4, key a comma, and click the May tab.
18. Click cell B4, key a comma, and click the June tab. (See Figure 12-8 on the next page.)
19. Click cell B4 and press (Enter).
20. Click cell B4 and view the formula in the formula bar.
21. Press (F2) and key **round(** after the = sign in the formula.
22. Press (End) and key **,0)** to round the average with no decimal places. Press (Enter).
23. Copy the formula to cells B5:B8 and then to cells C5:C8.
24. Format the values to show commas with no decimal positions.

FIGURE 12-8
Using AVERAGE in
a 3-D reference

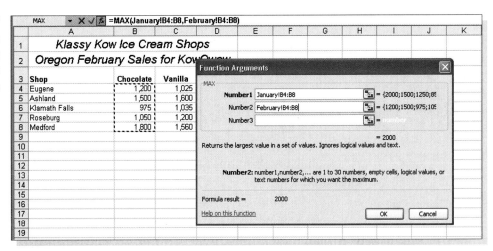

EXERCISE **12-14** **Use MAX and Paste Functions in a 3-D Reference**

1. On the AverageSales tab, copy cell A2 to cell A10. Copy cells B3:C3 to cell A11.

2. Format row 11 as 22.50 (30 pixels) high. Edit cell A10 to show **Maximum Monthly Sales**.

3. Click cell A12 and click the Insert Function button .

4. Choose MAX and click OK. Move the Function Arguments dialog box so that you can see the cells you need to click.

   REVIEW: MAX is in the Statistical category.

5. Click the January tab. Click cell B4 and drag to select cells B4:B8.

6. Click in the Number2 box in the Function Arguments dialog box.

7. Click the February tab. Click cell B4 and drag to select cells B4:B8.

FIGURE 12-9
Using the Function
Arguments dialog
box for a 3-D
reference

8. Click in the Number3 box and click the March tab.

9. Click cell B4 and drag to select cells B4:B8.

10. Click in the Number4 box and click the April tab.

11. Select cells B4:B8, click in the Number5 box, and click the May tab.

 TIP: Scroll the number boxes in the Function Arguments dialog box if they do not automatically appear.

12. Select cells B4:B8, click in the Number6 box, and click the June tab.

13. Select cells B4:B8 and click OK.

14. Copy the formula to cell B12.

15. Click the May tab. Click cell C4 and key **12000**.

16. Click the AverageSales tab and note the new maximum for "Vanilla." The "Vanilla" average for "Eugene" changes, too.

17. Format these cells to match the other values.

EXERCISE **12-15** **Use Multiplication in a 3-D Reference**

---

1. Right-click the SecondQuarter tab and choose Move or Copy.

2. Create a copy of the sheet at the end of the tabs. Name the copied worksheet **ProjectedSales**.

3. Edit cell A2 to show **Third Quarter Projected Sales**.

4. Select and delete cells B4:C8.

5. Click cell B4 and key = to start the formula.

6. Click the SecondQuarter tab and click cell B4.

7. Key *110% and press Enter.

 NOTE: The formula multiplies second quarter sales by 110 percent to determine projected sales that are 10 percent higher.

8. Copy the formula in cell B4 to cells B5:B8 and then to column C.

Printing Multiple Worksheets

When sheets are grouped, you can view them one after another in Print Preview. If you click the Print button while viewing multiple sheets, they print one after the other.

From the Page Setup dialog in Print Preview, you can add a footer or header but must prepare each sheet separately. It's quicker to add the same footer to grouped sheets using Page Setup from the File menu because you only need to create it once.

EXERCISE **12-16** **View Grouped Worksheets**

1. Save the workbook as *[your initials]***12-16** in a folder for Lesson 12.
2. Hold down Ctrl and click the FirstQuarter tab. It is selected with the ProjectedSales tab.
3. Hold down Ctrl and click the SecondQuarter tab. Three worksheets are selected or grouped.
4. Hold down Ctrl and click the AverageSales tab. Four worksheets are selected or grouped.

5. Click the Print Preview button . These four sheets are shown in the preview.
6. Press Page Down or Page Up to view the pages.
7. Close print preview. The sheets are still grouped.

EXERCISE **12-17** **Add a Footer to Grouped Worksheets**

1. From the File menu, choose Page Setup.

2. Create a custom footer with your name in the left section. In the center, include the filename and the tab name. In the right section, click the Page Number button. Click OK.
3. Click Print Preview in the Page Setup dialog box. The first page has the footer.
4. Press Page Down to display page 2. Each page has the same footer.
5. Click Print and click OK to print the grouped sheets.

NOTE: If you save a workbook while sheets are grouped and reopen it, the workbook opens with grouped sheets.

6. Save the workbook using the same name.

EXERCISE **12-18** **Print Formulas for Grouped Worksheets**

1. Press Ctrl+~. The formulas are displayed on each of the grouped worksheets.
2. Right-click a sheet in the group and ungroup them.
3. Group the FirstQuarter and the SecondQuarter sheets. These sheets are the same, so you can format them for printing together.

4. AutoFit each of the columns while the formulas are displayed.

5. Click the Print Preview button .

6. Click Setup. Change the first sheet to landscape orientation, fit to one page. Close the Page Setup dialog box.

7. Press Page Down and click Setup again. Change to landscape orientation, and choose the option to fit the worksheet on one page.

8. Print both sheets.

9. Close the workbook without saving.

USING ONLINE HELP

References in a formula to different worksheets are a common business task. Use Help to learn more about this type of formula.

Use Help to learn about 3-D references:

1. Establish an Internet connection and start Internet Explorer. Minimize the window.

2. In a new workbook, choose Help and Microsoft Excel Help.

3. Key **3-d reference** in the Search box and press Enter.

4. Click the topic Refer to the same cell or range on multiple sheets.

5. Click Show All in the upper-right corner. Read the information.

6. Close the Help window when you are finished reading about 3-D references. Close the Search Results dialog box.

7. Close Internet Explorer and end your Internet connection if appropriate.

LESSON Summary

➤ You can copy an entire worksheet and choose where to place it in the workbook. All data and formats are copied when you use the Move or Copy dialog box.

➤ You can move worksheet tabs to rearrange them by dragging or with the Move or Copy dialog box.

➤ Group worksheets by clicking the first tab and holding down Ctrl or Shift while clicking the other worksheet tabs.

➤ Group worksheets to print several sheets with one command, to format them in the same way, or to delete or key data on all of them at the same time.

➤ The tab scrolling buttons allow you to move through worksheet tabs when you cannot see all of them at once. The buttons share space with the horizontal scroll bar.

➤ You can use the Fill Across Worksheets command to copy data and formats from one worksheet to another. Column widths and row heights are not copied.

➤ A 3-D reference is a formula that refers to cells or values in a different worksheet. A 3-D reference can use simple formulas or functions.

➤ Grouped worksheets are shown in print preview one after the other. In print preview mode, you add a footer to each sheet separately.

➤ To add the same footer to multiple sheets, group them and use File and Page Setup.

LESSON 12   Command Summary

FEATURE	BUTTON	MENU	KEYBOARD
Copy formats		Edit, Paste Special	
Copy sheet		Edit, Move or Copy Sheet	
Fill data		Edit, Fill, Across Worksheets	
Formulas		Tools, Options	Ctrl + ~

Concepts Review

TRUE/FALSE QUESTIONS

Each of the following statements is either true or false. Indicate your choice by circling T or F.

T F **1.** Grouped worksheets can be formatted all at once.

T F **2.** Grouped worksheets are permanent.

T F **3.** The Edit, Paste Special command can be used to copy formats from one worksheet to another.

T F **4.** You can create the same footer once for multiple sheets from Print Preview.

T F **5.** A 3-D reference is a formula that refers to another worksheet.

T F **6.** If you cannot see all worksheet tabs, use the horizontal scroll bar to move them into view.

T F **7.** When you edit a cell used in a 3-D reference, you need to update the formula to include the new data.

T F **8.** If sheets are grouped, you can display formulas for all of them at once.

SHORT ANSWER QUESTIONS

Write the correct answer in the space provided.

1. What is the difference between using Shift and Ctrl to group worksheets?

_____

_____

2. What keyboard shortcut inserts a blank worksheet?

_____

3. Describe how a 3-D reference appears in the formula bar.

_____

4. How would you copy a sheet so that all data and formats are copied?

_____

5. Name the buttons that allow you to move worksheet tabs into view.

_____

6. How can you determine if worksheets are grouped?

_____

7. What menu command enables you to paste formats, formulas, or links?

_____

8. How do you ungroup sheets?

_____

CRITICAL THINKING

Answer these questions on a separate page. There are no right or wrong answers. Support your answers with examples from your own experience, if possible.

1. In your school or the company where you work, how could you use 3-D references? Give examples of worksheets that might be used in such a reference.

2. Using your school or the company where you work, give an example of a workbook that might use multiple sheets. What would be the main purpose of the workbook and how would multiple sheets be used?

Skills Review

EXERCISE 12-19

Copy worksheets. Group and format worksheets.

1. Open **AdvExp** and save it as *[your initials]***12-19** in your Lesson 12 folder.

2. Add your standard footer and use landscape orientation.

3. Copy worksheets by following these steps:

   a. Right-click the July tab and choose Move or Copy.
   b. Choose (move to end).
   c. Click to place a check mark for Create a copy. Click OK.
   d. Double-click the July (2) tab and key **August**. Press Enter.
   e. Right-click the August tab and choose Move or Copy.
   f. Choose (move to end) and click to place a check mark for Create a copy. Click OK.
   g. Double-click the August (2) tab and key **September**. Press Enter.

NOTE: The worksheets should be July, August, September in that order.

4. Group and format worksheets by following these steps:

a. Click the July tab.

b. Hold down (Shift) and click the September tab.

c. Select cells D4:D7 and click the AutoSum button Σ▼.

d. Select and format the values to show commas and no decimals.

e. Select cells B4:D4. Format them to show currency with no decimal places.

f. Right-click any tab. Choose Ungroup Sheets.

5. Edit cell A2 on the monthly sheets to show the correct month.

6. Group the sheets again and print them.

7. Save and close the workbook.

EXERCISE 12-20

Copy worksheets. Group sheets and delete data. Create a 3-D reference.

1. Open **Charity** and save it as *[your initials]*12-20 in your folder.

2. Add your standard footer.

TIP: If you add the footer to the original sheet, it is copied to the new sheets.

3. Copy worksheets by following these steps:

a. Right-click the 2003 tab and choose Move or Copy.

b. Choose (move to end).

c. Click to place a check mark for Create a copy. Click OK.

d. Double-click the 2003 (2) tab and key **2004**. Press (Enter).

e. Repeat these steps to make two more copies, naming the new sheets **2005** and **ToDate**.

4. Group worksheets and delete data by following these steps:

a. While the ToDate tab is selected, hold down (Shift) and click the 2004 tab.

b. Select cells B3:B7 and press (Delete).

5. Right-click one of the tabs in the group and ungroup the sheets.

6. On the 2004 tab, edit the title to show the correct year. Then key these values in cells **B3:B7**:

2000
1500
3200
1800
3500

7. On the 2005 tab, edit the title to show the correct year. Key these values in cells **B3:B7**:

   2200

   1600

   2800

   2300

   3000

8. Create a 3-D reference by following these steps:

   a. Click the ToDate tab and click cell B3.

   b. Key = to start a formula.

   c. Click the 2003 tab and click cell B3. Key + to add.

   d. Click the 2004 tab and click cell B3.

   e. Key + to add, click the 2005 tab, and click cell B3. Press (Enter).

9. Copy the formula to cells B4:B7. Change the label in cell A2 to **To Date Charitable Contributions**.

10. Print the ToDate sheet.

11. Make a copy of the ToDate sheet and place it at the end of the tab names.

12. Display the formulas. Widen each column to show the data. Print the formulas, fit to one portrait page.

13. Save and close the workbook.

EXERCISE 12-21

Use functions in a 3-D reference. Create 3-D references by using formulas.

1. Open **EstAdv** and save it as *[your initials]*12-21.

2. Use functions in a 3-D reference by following these steps:

   a. Click the FirstQtr tab and click cell B4.

   b. Click the Insert Function button . Find and choose AVERAGE.

   REVIEW: AVERAGE is in the Statistical category.

   c. Click the July tab and click cell B4.

   d. Click in the Number2 box. Click the August tab and click cell B4.

   e. Click in the Number3 box. Click the September tab and click cell B4. Click OK.

3. Copy the formula to cells B5:B7 and then to cells C4:C7. Format cells B4:D7 as currency with no decimals.

4. Add your standard footer and print the FirstQtr worksheet.

5. Make a copy of the FirstQtr worksheet and name it FirstQtrFormulas.

6. Press Ctrl+~ to display the formulas. Widen each column to show the data. Print the formulas, fit to one landscape page.

7. Create a 3-D reference using a formula by following these steps:

   a. Click the Estimated tab and cell B4.

   b. Key = and click the FirstQtr tab.

   c. Click cell B4. Key *115% and press Enter.

    NOTE: Multiplying a value by 115 percent calculates a new value that represents a 15 percent increase.

   d. Copy the formula to cells B5:B7 and then to cells C4:C7. Format cells B4:D7 as currency with no decimals.

8. Add your standard footer and print the Estimated worksheet.

9. Make a copy of the Estimated worksheet and name it EstimatedFormulas.

10. Display the formulas. Widen each column to show the data. Print the formulas, fit to one landscape page.

11. Save and close the workbook.

EXERCISE 12-22

Group worksheets. Print multiple worksheets.

1. Open **ProductList**. Save it as *[your initials]*12-22. This workbook has four worksheets, each listing products for a single category.

2. Group worksheets by following these steps:

   a. Click the Beverages tab.

   b. Hold down Shift and click the NoveltyItems tab.

3. Print multiple worksheets by following these steps:

   a. Click the Beverages tab.

   b. Hold down Shift and click the NoveltyItems tab.

   c. From the File menu, choose Page Setup.

    d. Create a custom footer with your name in the left section. In the center, include the filename and the tab name. In the right section, click the Page Number button.

   e. Click Print Preview in the Page Setup dialog box. Press Page Down to view the sheets.

   f. Click Print and click OK to print all sheets.

4. Save and close the workbook.

Lesson Applications

EXERCISE 12-23

Copy data. Create a 3-D reference.

In addition to statistical and mathematical functions and formulas, you can use most other categories of functions in a 3-D reference. The IF statement you create in this workbook tests whether employees have worked for five or more years.

1. Open **Personnel** and save it in your Lesson 12 folder as *[your initials]*12-23.

2. Change the year in cells D3 and D13 to the current year.

3. Rename Sheet2 **Vested**. In cell A1, key **Vested Employees** and make it 16-point Arial.

4. In cell A2, key **As of** and apply the same font as cell A1. Right-align this label.

5. Key **=now( )** in cell B2 and use the same font again. Left-align the date and format it to show the month spelled out, the date, a comma, and four digits for the year.

 REVIEW: You can move between worksheets by pressing Ctrl + Page Up and Ctrl + Page Down.

6. Copy cells A2:B15 on Sheet1 to cell A3 on the Vested sheet.

7. Widen columns as needed. Center the labels in row 3. Format rows 3 and 4 as 18.75 (25 pixels) high.

8. In cell C3, key **Vested?** Format it like the other labels in row 3.

9. Click cell C4. Use an IF function. In the Logical_test box, click cell B2 (the current date) and press F4 to make it an absolute reference.

10. Key – to subtract the hire date from today.

 NOTE: Date arithmetic uses serial numbers; five years is equal to 1825 days.

11. Click the Sheet1 tab and click cell D3 for the first hire date. Key **>1825** after D3 in the entry box. The logical test asks if today minus the hire date is greater than 1,825 days or more than five years.

12. In the Value_if_true box, key **Yes**. In the Value_if_false box, key **No**. Click OK.

13. Center the results and copy the formula for the other employees.

 REVIEW: Use the Margins tab in the Page Setup dialog box to center the worksheet.

14. Add your standard footer and print the worksheet horizontally centered.

15. Make a copy of the Vested sheet and name it **VestedFormulas**. Display the formulas and print the sheet fit to a portrait page.

16. Save and close the workbook.

EXERCISE 12-24

Copy worksheets. Create a 3-D reference. Group and ungroup worksheets.

1. Create a new workbook and save it as *[your initials]***12-24**.

2. Key **Klassy Kow Ice Cream Shops** in cell A1. Make it 18-point Times New Roman. Key **Ice Cream Sandwich Sales** in cell A2 and use the same font.

3. Key **Week 1** in cell B3 and make it 10-point Arial bold. Use the Fill handle to fill in to Week 4 in cell E3. Center these labels and make each column 6 pixels wider than its current size.

4. Key the following labels in cells A4:A7:
Vanilla
Chocolate
Strawberry
Chocolate Chip

5. Widen column A as needed. Format row 4 as 18.75 (25 pixels) tall. Rename Sheet1 **March**.

6. Key the data in Figure 12-10 to complete the worksheet.

FIGURE 12-10

	Week 1	Week 2	Week 3	Week 4
Vanilla	15000	14500	12500	15000
Chocolate	10000	12000	10500	12500
Strawberry	8000	7500	9000	8500
Chocolate Chip	15000	20000	16000	14000

7. Make two copies of the March sheet so that you have sheets for April and May. Rename the sheets accordingly. Group Sheet2 and Sheet3 and delete them.

8. On the April sheet, delete the values. Key a formula in cell B4 to multiply the March value by 110 percent to determine the April value. Copy the formula to the other value cells.

9. On the May sheet, delete the values and key a formula to multiply the April value by 115 percent. Copy the formula.

10. Group the worksheets. Format the values to show commas and no decimals. Ungroup the sheets.

 NOTE: You cannot draw AutoShapes or insert images when worksheets are grouped.

11. Click the March tab. From the Basic Shapes category, draw a Sun in cells E1:E2. While the sun is selected, fill it with an appropriate color.

12. Select the sun object and click the 3-D Style button . Choose 3-D Style 1.

13. Click the 3-D Style button . Choose 3-D Settings. Click the Depth button on the toolbar. Choose Custom and make the new depth half the value of its default setting. Close the 3-D Settings toolbar.

14. Select the sun object and click the Copy button 📋. Click the April tab and click the Paste button 📋. Drag the sun into position on the April tab.

15. Click the May tab and paste and position the sun.

16. Group the sheets, and key your name in cell A12. Print the sheets.

17. Ungroup the worksheets. Save and close the workbook.

EXERCISE 12-25

Group and ungroup worksheets. Copy data to another workbook.

When you copy data from one workbook to another, you should check any 3-D references. They might not be the same in different workbooks.

1. Create a new workbook and save it as *[your initials]***12-25**.

2. Rename Sheet1 **October**, Sheet2 **November**, and Sheet3 **December**. Group all three sheets.

3. Open **SandwichSales**. Your new workbook is still open.

4. Click cell B10. The cell has a formula that refers to cell B5 on this worksheet.

5. Click cell B15. This formula refers to cell B10 on this worksheet.

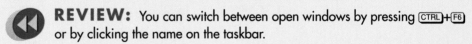 **REVIEW:** You can switch between open windows by pressing CTRL+F6 or by clicking the name on the taskbar.

6. Copy cells A1:A2 from **SandwichSales** to cell A1 in *[your initials]***12-25**.

7. Key your first and last name in cell A15 in *[your initials]***12-25**. Ungroup the sheets.

8. Copy cells A3:E8 in **SandwichSales** to cell A3 in the October sheet of *[your initials]***12-25**.

9. Copy cells A9:E13 in **SandwichSales** to cell A3 in the November sheet. The copied cells cause a #REF error message to display, because the formula reference is now wrong.

10. Delete the cells with #REF messages. Key a formula in cell B4 that multiplies the October values in your workbook 108%. Copy the formula to cells B5:E7.

11. Copy cells A14:E18 from **SandwichSales** to the December sheet. Delete the cells with errors and key and copy a formula that multiplies the November values by 108%.

12. Group the November and December sheets. Insert a row at row 4. Key **Week 1** in cell B4. Center it and make it bold. Use the Fill handle to show up to Week 4 in row 4. Adjust the column widths on the grouped sheets.

13. Group all sheets and add your standard footer using File, Page Setup. Print the sheets.

14. Make copies of the November and December sheets. Rename each to include **Formulas** in the tab name. Display the formulas and print these two sheets, each fit to a landscape page.

15. Save and close your workbook.

16. Close **SandwichSales** without saving.

EXERCISE 12-26 *Challenge Yourself*

Copy worksheets.

If data is all on one worksheet in a workbook, you can easily create new sheets and copy the data to other sheets. Then when you hide the unnecessary data on each sheet, the formulas are still correct.

1. Open **SandwichSales** and save it as *[your initials]***12-26** in your Lesson 12 folder.

2. Center the sheet horizontally on the page and add your standard footer.

3. Make two copies of the sheet and name the copies **November** and **December**. Arrange the sheets in proper month order.

4. On the November sheet, hide rows 3–8 and rows 14–18. The hidden cells are still referenced in the formulas in the remaining cells.

5. On the December sheet, hide the rows that should be hidden. Do the same on the October sheet.

6. Group the sheets and print them.

7. Save and close the workbook.

On Your Own

In these exercises you work on your own, as you would in a real-life work environment. Use the skills you've learned to accomplish the task—and be creative.

EXERCISE 12-27

In a new workbook, key the first and last names of students in your class or co-workers in your company in separate columns. Include a label for each column. Add a footer to the sheet and then make a copy of it. On the second sheet, add columns to show each person's height and weight (you can estimate this data). Make another copy of the first sheet and add two columns to show the person's city and state. Name each sheet with an appropriate name. Save the workbook as *[your initials]*12-27 in your Lesson 12 folder. Group the sheets and print them. Save and close the workbook.

EXERCISE 12-28

Open **Personnel**. On Sheet2, create a 3-D reference for the label in cell A1 to display the same label as the one on Sheet1. Copy the reference to rows 2:15 and then to columns B:G to create a "duplicate" of Sheet1 on Sheet2. Save the workbook as *[your initials]*12-28 in your Lesson 12 folder. Display the formulas on Sheet2 and widen the columns to show the complete reference. Add your standard footer and print the formula worksheet fit to a landscape page. Save and close the workbook.

EXERCISE 12-29

Create a new workbook that will use two sheets. Develop an idea, labels, and values for the first sheet. You can use a business problem, personal finance, school grades, or other things of interest to you. On the second sheet, develop additional data that can use values from the first sheet in 3-D references. Create the 3-D references using functions or simple formulas. Format both sheets attractively. Save your workbook as *[your initials]*12-29 in your Lesson 12 folder. Add your standard footer and print both sheets. Make formula sheets and print them. Save and close the workbook.

Working with Lists

OBJECTIVES

MICROSOFT OFFICE SPECIALIST ACTIVITIES
In this lesson:
XLO3S-2-1
XLO3S-2-4
XLO3S-5-6
XLO3S-5-7
XLO3S-5-10
See Appendix.

After completing this lesson, you will be able to:

1. **Copy data to a different workbook.**
2. **Sort and name a list.**
3. **Filter a list.**
4. **Use wildcards in a filter.**
5. **Use COUNTA in a 3-D reference.**
6. **Set print areas and print selections.**
7. **Create a custom view.**

 Estimated Time: 1 hour

I n this lesson, you will begin to learn about lists. A *list* is a table of information with a row of headers (titles) followed by rows of data. Excel has several list commands that enable you to work with data much like a database. For example, you can sort a list to arrange the rows in different orders, or you can filter a list to display only certain rows.

Copying Data to a Different Workbook

In addition to copying data within a workbook, you can copy or move data from one workbook to another. You can create a new workbook from existing workbooks, eliminating the need to rekey labels and values. When you work with multiple workbooks, you can arrange them so that you can see all of them on the screen at once in different layouts.

EXERCISE **13-1** **Copy Data by Using Tiled Windows**

The **Departments** workbook has four worksheets, each listing employees in a particular department. You can create a new workbook that lists all employees on one sheet by copying data from each of the sheets.

The **Departments** workbook was saved with the sheets grouped.

1. Open **Departments**. The sheets are grouped.

2. Click the New button 🗋. A new workbook opens. It is maximized and on top of the **Departments** workbook.

> **TIP:** When two workbooks are open, you can use the Compare Side by Side command from the Window menu to horizontally tile the windows.

3. From the Window menu, choose Arrange. The Arrange dialog box opens.

4. Choose Horizontal and click OK. Both workbooks are displayed in tiled windows that are the same size. The active workbook has a darker title bar and shows shaded row and column headings for the active cell.

FIGURE 13-1
Tiled windows

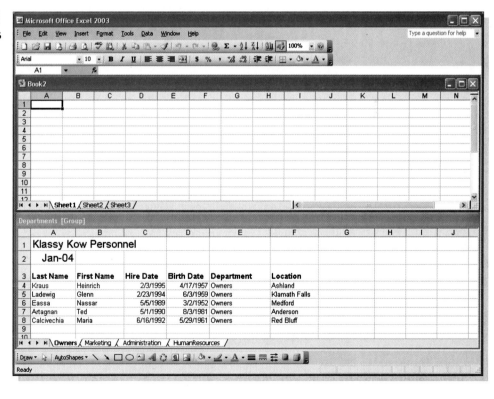

TIP: The workbook that is active when you tile the windows horizontally appears in the top half of the screen.

5. Right-click any tab in the **Departments** workbook and ungroup the sheets.

6. Click the Owners tab and click cell A1.

7. Press [F8] to start Extend Selection mode. Use [→] to extend the selection to column F.

REVIEW: EXT appears in the status bar when Extend Selection mode is on.

8. Use [↓] to extend the selection to row 8.

9. Click the Copy button .

10. Click cell A1 in the blank workbook and press [Enter]. Data and cell formatting are copied, but row heights and column widths are not.

NOTE: You can format the new workbook after copying all the data.

EXERCISE **13-2** **Copy Data by Using Maximized Windows**

You can copy data from one workbook to another even if both windows are maximized. You switch between workbooks by using the taskbar.

1. Maximize the new workbook.

2. Click Departments on the taskbar.

3. Click the Marketing tab. Click cell A4 and drag to select cells A4:F8.

4. Press [Ctrl]+[C].

REVIEW: New workbooks are named Book1, Book2, and so on during a work session.

5. Click Book1 on the taskbar, click cell A9, and press [Enter]. The second set of names is added to the list.

6. Press [Ctrl]+[F6] to return to the Departments workbook. Click the Administration tab.

7. Click cell A4 and drag to select cells A4:F7. Press [Ctrl]+[C].

8. Press [Ctrl]+[F6], click cell A14, and press [Enter]. Another set of names is added to the list.

TIP: You can click the workbook name on the taskbar or press [Ctrl]+[F6] to move between open workbooks.

9. Switch to the Departments workbook and click the HumanResources tab. Select cells A4:F6 and copy them to cell A18 in Book1.

10. Switch to the Departments workbook and close it.

11. In your workbook, format column A as 13.57 (100 pixels) wide. AutoFit each of the other columns.

Sorting and Naming a List

The workbook you just created by copying data is a list. Excel's list commands include sorting, which allows you to arrange the rows in order by the data in one of the columns.

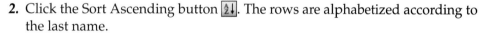

EXERCISE 13-3 **Sort a List**

An *ascending sort* sorts rows in A-to-Z order or lowest value to highest value. A *descending sort* sorts rows in Z-to-A order or highest value to lowest. If you select a range of cells on the screen and sort them, the sort uses the first column of the range.

1. Select cells A4:F20. You should not include titles when selecting data to be sorted.

 2. Click the Sort Ascending button . The rows are alphabetized according to the last name.

 3. Click the Sort Descending button . The rows are alphabetized in reverse, from Z to A.

 4. Click the down arrow next to the Undo button . Undo the last two actions. The rows are returned to the original order.

 REVIEW: Undo keeps a history of your edits.

5. Click cell F4 to deselect the range.

6. With cell F4 selected, click the Sort Ascending button . The rows are alphabetized according to the data in column F, but the titles are included in the sort because you did not first select the data. You learn one way to avoid this in the next exercise.

7. Click the Undo button .

EXERCISE **13-4** **Name a List as a Range**

Excel has requirements for using List commands effectively. One requirement is that you must name the list as a range. A named range is a descriptive label for a selection of cells. Rather than referring to the range as cells A4:F20, you can call it "Employees," for example.

 REVIEW: A range is a rectangular group of cells.

If you name the range of cells in a list, you do not need to select the cells before sorting. You just need to click anywhere in the column that you want to sort. Naming the range also gives you the ability to sort easily by other columns. When you name a list as a range, you need to include the title or label row with the rows of information.

Excel recognizes the range name "Database" automatically as a list. Using this range name makes many of Excel's List commands easier and faster. "Database" is a special, reserved word in Excel.

1. Select cells A3:F20. Remember that titles are included when you name a list range.

2. Click the Name box. Key **Database** and press Enter. This names the selected cells "Database."

FIGURE 13-2
Naming a range
for a list

Name box

	A	B	C	D	E	F	G
1	Klassy Kow Personnel						
2	Jan-04						
3	Last Name	First Name	Hire Date	Birth Date	Department	Location	
4	Kraus	Heinrich	2/3/1995	4/17/1957	Owners	Ashland	
5	Ladewig	Glenn	2/23/1994	6/3/1959	Owners	Klamath Falls	
6	Eassa	Nassar	5/5/1989	3/2/1952	Owners	Medford	
7	Artagnan	Ted	5/1/1990	8/3/1981	Owners	Anderson	
8	Calcivechia	Maria	6/16/1992	5/29/1961	Owners	Red Bluff	
9	Stewart	Kathleen	5/2/1997	9/7/1975	Marketing	San Francisco	
10	Sumara	Keiko	11/21/1999	2/20/1962	Marketing	San Francisco	
11	Nguyen	Luni	6/7/2000	5/23/1978	Marketing	San Francisco	
12	Grabowski	Harry	3/1/2001	5/5/1975	Marketing	San Francisco	
13	Adams	Angelina	6/6/2000	8/3/1982	Marketing	Klamath Falls	
14	Sante	Juan	3/18/1996	5/8/1960	Finance	San Francisco	
15	Steele	Conrad	1/1/2004	12/24/1984	President	San Francisco	
16	Steinbeck	Sarah	2/15/1999	1/28/1955	Finance	San Francisco	
17	Alvarez	Juan	7/8/1999	3/17/1975	Finance	San Francisco	
18	McDonald	Robin	7/6/1996	7/23/1965	Human Resources	San Francisco	
19	Alverez	Toni	4/15/1999	3/30/1975	Human Resources	San Francisco	
20	Gillard	Michelle	9/1/2000	2/15/1976	Human Resources	San Francisco	
21							
22							

3. Click cell A4 to deselect the cells.

4. Click the Sort Ascending button 📊. The rows are arranged in alphabetical order by last name.

5. Click any department name in column E and click the Sort Descending button 📊. The data is arranged by department in reverse alphabetical order.

6. Undo the last two sort actions to return the rows to the original order.

7. Click cell A4 to deselect the range.

Filtering a List

A *filter* is a criterion or a specification for data in your list. A filter hides rows that do not meet your criteria. Filters enable you to keep a large list but display only required information. For example, an employee list includes all the workers in a company. To print a report of employees in a certain department, you can filter the list to show only those workers.

When you filter a list, you display records that meet some requirement that you choose. You can print your list while it is filtered so that you see only the records that match your requirements.

EXERCISE **13-5** **Filter a List with AutoFilter**

The AutoFilter command adds drop-down arrows next to the row headings so that you can choose from a list of labels or values in the list. What you choose in the list is used to display the rows matching your choice.

1. From the Data menu, choose Filter and then AutoFilter. An AutoFilter arrow appears in each of the labels in row 3.

2. Click the Department AutoFilter arrow and choose Human Resources. Only the rows that match are displayed. The other rows are hidden. The row headings for the visible rows are blue to remind you that the list is filtered.

FIGURE 13-3
Creating an
AutoFilter

The AutoFilter arrow for Department is blue, too.

3. Click the Department AutoFilter arrow and choose (All). All the rows are shown.

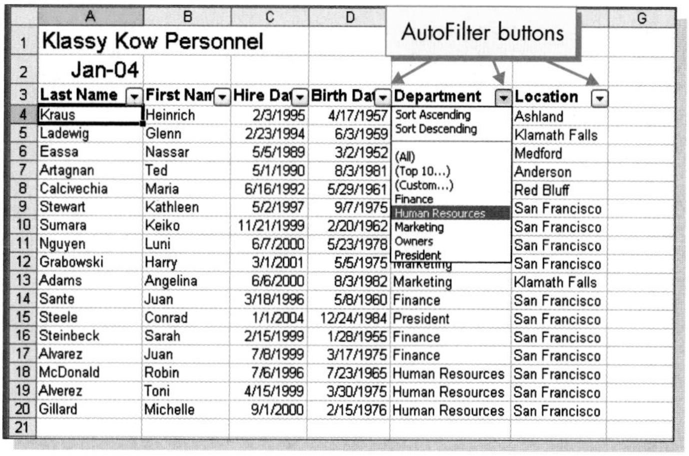

4. Click the Location AutoFilter arrow and choose Klamath Falls. Only the employees located in that city are listed.

5. Click the Location AutoFilter arrow and choose San Francisco. The list changes to show only the San Francisco employees.

6. Click the Department AutoFilter arrow and choose Marketing. This adds another requirement to the list, which now shows employees in the Marketing department in San Francisco.

 NOTE: A filter does not rearrange or sort the rows.

7. Choose (All) from the Department list. Choose (All) from the Location list.

EXERCISE | **13-6** | **Create a Custom AutoFilter by Using Or**

A simple AutoFilter chooses one item from the list. A Custom AutoFilter gives you the ability to filter by more than one item and to use operators such as "greater than."

1. Click the Department AutoFilter arrow and choose (Custom. . .). The dialog box shows the name of the column.

2. In the first entry box, choose equals. This means the department will be equal to your next choice.

3. Click the down arrow for the entry box to the right and choose Finance. The department should be "Finance."

4. Click the Or button. This adds another option to the filter.

5. Click the down arrow for the first box below the And/Or buttons. Choose equals.

6. Click the down arrow for the entry box to the right and choose Marketing. This filter requires that the department be either "Finance" or "Marketing."

FIGURE 13-4
Creating a Custom
AutoFilter with Or

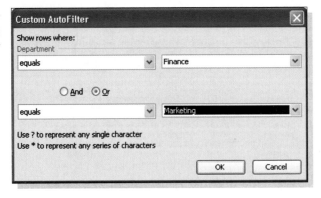

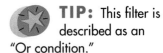 **TIP:** This filter is described as an "Or condition."

7. Click OK. The employees are either in the Finance or the Marketing department.

8. Choose Data, Filter, Show All. All the rows are shown.

EXERCISE 13-7 Create a Custom AutoFilter by Using And

1. Click the Hire Date AutoFilter arrow and choose (Custom. . .).
2. In the first entry box, choose is greater than.
3. Click in the entry box to the right and key **1/1/90**. The first filter is that the date be greater than January 1, 1990, which means a date later than that date.

    NOTE: You can key a value in an entry box. You do not need to choose from the list.

4. Click the And button.
5. Click the down arrow for the first box below the And/Or buttons.
6. Choose is less than.
7. Click in the entry box to the right and key **12/31/95**. The second filter requires that the hire date be less than December 31, 1995 (that is, it must be before that date).
8. Click OK. These employees were hired between 1990 and 1995.
9. Choose Data, Filter, Show All.

Using Wildcards in a Filter

A *wildcard* is a keyboard character (* or ?) used in filters to represent characters that you do not know. For example, if you know that an employee's name ends in "ish" but you don't remember the first part of the name, you could use a wildcard to find all employees whose names end with "ish" by keying "*ish" in the entry box to be matched. You can key the wildcard characters or use Excel's operators. Excel has operators in its list that enable you to build wildcard filters by using words.

EXERCISE 13-8 Use Wildcards in a Custom AutoFilter

1. Click the Last Name AutoFilter arrow and choose (Custom. . .).
2. In the first entry box, choose equals.
3. Click in the entry box to the right and key **s***. This entry finds last names that begin with "S." The asterisk means that any number of characters can come after the "S." (See Figure 13-5 on the next page.)
4. Click OK. The employees whose names begin with "S" are listed.
5. Click the Last Name AutoFilter arrow and choose (Custom. . .). Excel replaces the asterisk with a filter from its list.
6. In the first entry box, choose equals.

FIGURE 13-5
Keying a wildcard

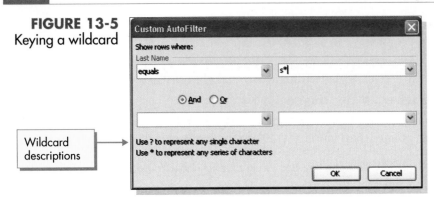

Wildcard descriptions

7. Click in the entry box to the right and key ***ar*** to find employees whose names have "ar" anywhere in them.

8. Click OK. The last names are filtered.

9. Click the Last Name AutoFilter arrow and choose (Custom. . .). Using the wildcard in this case is the same as using the "contains" filter.

10. Click Cancel. Click the Last Name arrow and choose (All).

EXERCISE **13-9** **Filter Dates and Text**

In many cases, it is easy to use Excel's own wildcard words. Some wildcards work with text and some with values.

1. Click the Birth Date AutoFilter arrow and choose (Custom. . .).

2. In the first entry box, choose ends with.

3. Click in the entry box to the right and key **1975** to find employees born in 1975.

4. Click OK. No records are filtered because "ends with" is a text filter and does not work with dates.

5. Click the Birth Date AutoFilter arrow and choose (Custom. . .). In the first entry box, choose is greater than. In the entry box to the right, key **12/31/74** to mark the last day in 1974.

6. Click the And button.

 TIP: Excel recognizes the year in two- or four-digit formats.

7. In the box below the And/Or buttons, choose is less than.

8. In the entry box to the right, key **1/1/76**. Click OK. These are employees who were born in 1975.

9. Choose Data, Filter, Show All.

10. Click the First Name AutoFilter arrow and choose (Custom. . .).

11. In the first entry box, choose ends with. Click in the entry box to the right and key **n** to find employees whose names end in "n."

 TIP: Using "ends with" is the same as keying *n.

12. Click OK. The filter works with a label.

13. Choose Data, Filter, Show All.

14. Choose Data, Filter, AutoFilter. The AutoFilter buttons are removed.

Using COUNTA in a 3-D Reference

The COUNTA function counts cells that have values or labels. You can use it to count the number of employees per department.

EXERCISE 13-10 Create a 3-D Reference with COUNTA

1. Select cells A1:A2. Copy them to cell A1 on Sheet2. Widen column A to show the date.

2. On Sheet2, key **Department** in cell A3. Key **# of Employees** in cell B3.

3. Format the labels in row 3 as bold and make the row 22.50 (30 pixels) high.

4. Key the following department names in cells A4:A7:
   Marketing
   Finance
   Human Resources
   Owners

5. Select cells A4:A7 and click the Sort Ascending button ⬇️. A Sort Warning message box tells you that you might not have selected all the data.

   ⏪ **REVIEW:** Because there is no range name, you must select the cells to be sorted.

6. Choose Continue with the current selection. Click Sort. The department names are in alphabetical order.

FIGURE 13-6
Sort Warning
message box

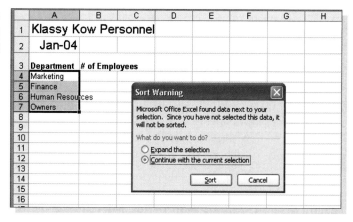

7. Format column A as 15.71 (115 pixels) wide.

8. In Sheet1, click any department name and sort in ascending order. This list has a range name, so you don't need to select any cells.

9. Click cell B4 in Sheet2 and click the Insert Function button fx.

10. Choose COUNTA in the Statistical category and then click OK.

11. Click Sheet1. Move the Function Arguments dialog box so that you can see the department.

12. Select cells E4:E6. The reference appears in the Value1 box. This will count the number of people in the Finance department.

FIGURE 13-7
Using COUNTA in
a 3-D reference

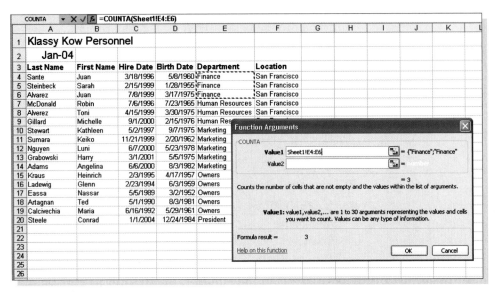

13. Click OK. There are three employees in the Finance department.

14. Repeat these steps or key the formula for each of the departments listed in Sheet2.

15. Save the workbook as *[your initials]*13-10 in a folder for Lesson 13.

16. Add your standard footer to the sheet and print the sheet.

Setting Print Areas and Print Selections

When you give a Print command, Excel prints the entire worksheet because that is the default print area. A *print area* is the range of cells to be printed. If you want to print only a portion of the worksheet, you can select the cells and define them as the print area. When you set your own print area, it is saved with the workbook.

You can also select cells on the worksheet and print them by using the Selection choice in the Print what area of the Print dialog box. When you use this method, the selection is not saved with the workbook.

EXERCISE 13-11 Set and Clear a Print Area

1. On the Sheet1 tab, add your standard footer.
2. Click the Name box arrow and choose Database. The list range is selected.
3. From the File menu, choose Print Area, and then Set Print Area. The range is outlined by a dashed outline.
4. Click cell G1 to see the outline better.

5. Click the Print Preview button. As you can see, only the print area will be printed.
6. Print the area and close the preview.
7. From the File menu, choose Print Area and then Clear Print Area. The print selection is removed.

EXERCISE 13-12 Print a Selection

1. Click the Name box arrow and choose Database.
2. From the File menu, choose Print.
3. Click the button for Selection in the Print what group.
4. Click Preview. This is the same range as you printed previously.
5. Close the preview without printing.
6. Click cell G1. The print range is deselected.

EXERCISE 13-13 Print Noncontiguous Selections

If you select ranges that are not next to each other, Excel prints each one on a separate page. Although you cannot change this feature, you can copy and paste a live link for each range to another area of the worksheet. Then you can print multiple ranges on a single page.

A *live link* is a simple formula that refers to a cell such as =A4. If you change the original data, the link is updated.

1. Select cells A4:F6 to select the employees in the Finance department.
2. Hold down Ctrl and select cells A10:F14 to include employees in the Marketing department. (See Figure 13-8 on the next page.)
3. From the File menu, choose Print. Click the button for Selection in the Print what group.
4. Click Preview. Each selection will be printed on its own page.

FIGURE 13-8
Selecting two
ranges for printing

	A	B	C	D	E	F	G
1	Klassy Kow Personnel						
2	Jan-04						
3	**Last Name**	**First Name**	**Hire Date**	**Birth Date**	**Department**	**Location**	
4	Sante	Juan	3/18/1996	5/8/1960	Finance	San Francisco	
5	Steinbeck	Sarah	2/15/1999	1/28/1955	Finance	San Francisco	
6	Alvarez	Juan	7/8/1999	3/17/1975	Finance	San Francisco	
7	McDonald	Robin	7/6/1996	7/23/1965	Human Resources	San Francisco	
8	Alverez	Toni	4/15/1999	3/30/1975	Human Resources	San Francisco	
9	Gillard	Michelle	9/1/2000	2/15/1976	Human Resources	San Francisco	
10	Stewart	Kathleen	5/2/1997	9/7/1975	Marketing	San Francisco	
11	Sumara	Keiko	11/21/1999	2/20/1962	Marketing	San Francisco	
12	Nguyen	Luni	6/7/2000	5/23/1978	Marketing	San Francisco	
13	Grabowski	Harry	3/1/2001	5/5/1975	Marketing	San Francisco	
14	Adams	Angelina	6/6/2000	8/3/1982	Marketing	Klamath Falls	
15	Kraus	Heinrich	2/3/1995	4/17/1957	Owners	Ashland	
16	Ladewig	Glenn	2/23/1994	6/3/1959	Owners	Klamath Falls	
17	Eassa	Nassar	5/5/1989	3/2/1952	Owners	Medford	
18	Artagnan	Ted	5/1/1990	8/3/1981	Owners	Anderson	
19	Calcivechia	Maria	6/16/1992	5/29/1961	Owners	Red Bluff	
20	Steele	Conrad	1/1/2004	12/24/1984	President	San Francisco	
21							

5. Press **Page Down** and **Page Up** to view the print selections.

6. Close the preview without printing.

7. Select cells A4:F6 and click the Copy button 🗐.

8. Go to cell H4.

9. From the <u>E</u>dit menu, choose Paste <u>S</u>pecial.

10. Click Paste <u>L</u>ink. The range is copied to cell H4 and linked to the original range.

11. Press **Esc** to remove the marquee.

12. Select cells A10:F14 and click the Copy button 🗐.

13. Go to cell H7.

14. From the <u>E</u>dit menu, choose Paste <u>S</u>pecial. Click Paste <u>L</u>ink.

15. Press **Esc** to remove the marquee.

16. Widen columns to accommodate the longest text in columns H:M.

17. Select cells H4:M11. From the <u>F</u>ile menu, choose <u>P</u>rint.

18. Click the button for Selectio<u>n</u> in the Print what group.

19. Click Previe<u>w</u>. You can print the two ranges on one page now.

20. Print the ranges.

Creating Custom Views

A *view* is a set of display and print settings for a workbook. It includes column widths, gridlines, window size and position, the active sheet, and more. You can use a view to keep certain arrangements of your data so that you do not need to keep making the same changes. For example, you can save one view of your worksheet with a particular sheet on top and no gridlines. Then you can save another view with gridlines and a different sheet active.

EXERCISE 13-14 Create Custom Views

1. Press Ctrl + Home.
2. From the View menu, choose Custom Views. The Custom Views dialog box shows that there are currently no views for your workbook.
3. Click Add. The Add View dialog box opens.
4. Key **Normal** as the name for this view.
5. Make sure there is a check mark for Print settings and Hidden rows, columns and filter settings.

FIGURE 13-9
Adding a
custom view

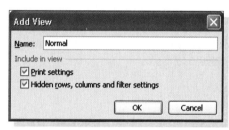

6. Click OK.
7. Select and delete cells H4:M11.
8. From the Tools menu, choose Options.
9. On the View tab, click to remove the check mark for Gridlines. Click OK.

10. Right-click the column D heading and hide the column. Press Ctrl + Home.
11. Go to Sheet2.
12. From the View menu, choose Custom Views.
13. Click Add and key **Revised** as the name for this view.
14. Make sure there is a check mark for Print settings and Hidden rows, columns and filter settings. Click OK.

 NOTE: Custom views are saved with the workbook.

15. Save the workbook as *[your initials]***13-14** and close it.

EXERCISE 13-15 Display Views

1. Open *[your initials]***13-14** from your Lesson 13 folder. It opens in the most recently used view with Sheet2 active.
2. Click the Sheet1 tab. This view does not show gridlines or column D.
3. From the View menu, choose Custom Views.

4. Click Normal and click Show. This is your original worksheet.

 TIP: You cannot create a custom view while worksheets are grouped.

EXERCISE **13-16** **Save a List as a Text File**

In addition to saving a workbook as a Web page, you can also save a worksheet as a text file. A *text file* is a file format that includes text only with no formatting. It does include spacing characters such as tabs and line returns. It is a format that is easily interchangeable with most software programs, including word processing and database software.

1. From the File menu, choose Save As. The Save As dialog box opens.

2. Navigate to your Lesson 13 folder.

 NOTE: If your computer does not show filename extensions, you will see only Text in the Save as type list.

3. Click the arrow for Save as type. Scroll to find Text (Tab delimited). You can use the same filename because a text file has an extension different from a workbook.

FIGURE 13-10
Saving a worksheet
as a text file

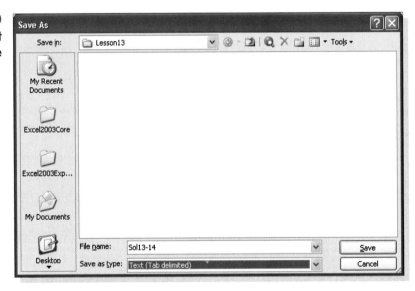

4. Click Save. A message box informs you that you can only save the active sheet, not the entire workbook.

5. Click OK. Another message box informs you that the text file may not include all the formatting.

6. Click Yes. The workbook is saved as a text file.

 TIP: To open the text file in Word or another word processor, check the Files of type choices in the Open dialog box and choose Text.

7. Close the workbook without saving.

USING ONLINE HELP

Filters are like queries in a database. They allow you to display only those rows that meet your conditions.

Use Help to learn about filters:

1. Establish an Internet connection and start Internet Explorer. Minimize the window.

2. In a new workbook, choose Help and Microsoft Excel Help.

3. Key **filters** in the Search box and press Enter.

4. Click the topic About filtering in the Search Results dialog box. Click Show All. Read the information.

5. Click the topic Wildcard characters in the Search Results dialog box. Click Show All. Read the information.

6. Close the Help window. Close the Search Results dialog box.

7. Close Internet Explorer and end your Internet connection if appropriate.

LESSON 13 Summary

➤ You can copy data from one workbook to another by opening both workbooks. Tile the windows, if desired, or use maximized windows.

➤ A list is a table of data with a row of labels as titles, followed by any number of rows of data.

➤ Sort an unnamed list by selecting the rows to be sorted, not including titles or totals. Then specify the type of sort (ascending or descending).

➤ You can select a range of cells and name it by keying the name in the Name box.

➤ If you name a list, you can sort it by clicking any column and using the Sort Ascending button and Sort Descending button.

➤ A filter allows you to display certain rows from a list. You can use AutoFilters by selecting from a list.

➤ Create a custom filter to use more than one requirement or to use wildcard features.

➤ You can use wildcard characters in a filter.

➤ The print area is the range of cells to be printed. You can set a print area that is different from the entire worksheet. A print area can be saved for future use.

➤ A print selection is not saved for future use. If you choose more than one selection, each one prints on a separate page.

➤ To print multiple selections on one page, paste a link to each range on an unused part of the worksheet and print that selection.

➤ A custom view is a set of display and print choices for a worksheet. You can save several views with the workbook.

LESSON 13 Command Summary

FEATURE	BUTTON	MENU	KEYBOARD
Arrange windows		Window, Arrange	
AutoFilter		Data, Filter, AutoFilter	
Custom view		View, Custom Views	
Paste Link		Edit, Paste Special	
Print area, clear		File, Print Area, Clear Print Area	
Print area, set		File, Print Area, Set Print Area	
Sort, ascending	A/Z↓	Data, Sort	
Sort, descending	Z/A↓	Data, Sort	

Concepts Review

TRUE/FALSE QUESTIONS

Each of the following statements is either true or false. Indicate your choice by circling T or F.

T F　　***1.*** You can arrange two workbooks to be side-by-side vertically or horizontally.

T F　　***2.*** A range of cells can be given a name using the formula bar.

T F　　***3.*** A filter is a wildcard character.

T F　　***4.*** You can copy data only when the windows are tiled, not maximized.

T F　　***5.*** A simple AutoFilter uses the column titles and an item from the column.

T F　　***6.*** An ascending sort arranges rows in alphabetical order.

T F　　***7.*** If you want to use more than one condition and an operator such as "greater than," use a Custom AutoFilter.

T F　　***8.*** A print area can be set to include selections that are not next to each other.

SHORT ANSWER QUESTIONS

Write the correct answer in the space provided.

1. What name describes workbook settings such as sort orders and column widths that have been saved for repeated displaying as needed?

_____

2. How could you name cells B3:D5 as Sales?

_____

3. Name two file formats other than xls that can be used to save a workbook.

_____

4. What does a filter do?

_____

5. What type of sort would arrange rows so that the largest number is first?

_____

6. What command allows you to paste a link to cells on a different sheet?

_____

7. What is the default print area for a worksheet?

_____

8. Describe one way to print only cells A5:D10.

_____

CRITICAL THINKING

Answer these questions on a separate page. There are no right or wrong answers. Support your answers with examples from your own experience, if possible.

1. In your school or the company where you work, what kinds of uses can you think of for sorting and filtering data?

2. What do you think is the difference between using AND and using OR in a custom filter?

Skills Review

EXERCISE 13-17

Copy data to a different workbook.

1. Create a new workbook and save it as *[your initials]***13-17** in your Lesson 13 folder.

2. Open **ProductList**.

3. Copy data to a new workbook by following these steps:

   a. From the Window menu, choose Arrange.
   b. Choose Vertical and click OK.
   c. Select cells A1:C13 on the Beverages sheet.
   d. Click the Copy button 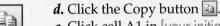.
   e. Click cell A1 in [your initials]13-17 and press Enter.
   f. Click the Cakes&Pies tab. Select cells A4:C10.
   g. Click the Copy button and click cell A14 in [your initials]13-17. Press Enter.

      h. Click the IceCream tab. Copy cells A4:C19 to cell A21 in [your initials]13-17.

      i. From the NoveltyItems tab, copy the appropriate cells to the bottom of the list in [your initials]13-17.

4. Close ProductList and the Clipboard task pane, if it is open.

5. Maximize your workbook. Widen the columns to show the data.

6. Name the worksheet tab **Products**. Add your standard footer and print the sheet.

7. Save and close the workbook.

EXERCISE 13-18

Name and sort a list. Filter a list with AutoFilter. Use wildcards in a filter.

1. Open **Products** and save it as *[your initials]*13-18.

2. Name and sort a list by following these steps:

      a. Select cells A3:C3 and press F8.

      REVIEW: F8 starts Extend Selection mode.

      b. Press Ctrl + ↓ to select to the bottom of the list.

      c. Click the Name box and key **Database**. Press Enter.

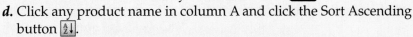   *d.* Click any product name in column A and click the Sort Ascending button ⬇.

3. Add your standard footer and print the worksheet.

4. Filter a list with AutoFilter by following these steps:

      a. Click anywhere in the list.

      b. From the Data menu, choose Filter and then AutoFilter.

      c. Click the Price AutoFilter arrow and choose $1.89.

      d. Print the filtered worksheet.

      e. Click the Price arrow and choose (Custom. . .).

      f. In the first entry box, choose is greater than. In the entry box to the right, key **2**. Click OK.

      g. Print the filtered worksheet.

      h. Click the Price AutoFilter arrow and choose (All).

5. Use wildcards in a filter by following these steps:

      a. Click anywhere in the list.

      b. Click the Product AutoFilter arrow and choose (Custom. . .).

      c. In the first entry box, choose equals. In the entry box to the right, key **c***. Click OK. Products that start with "c" are listed.

      d. Print the filtered worksheet.

      e. Click the Product AutoFilter arrow and choose (All).

      f. Click the Size AutoFilter arrow and choose (Custom. . .).

 g. In the first entry box, choose equals. In the entry box to the right, key ***inch***. Click OK. Products that have "inch" somewhere in the size are listed.

 h. Print the filtered worksheet.

 i. Click the Size AutoFilter arrow and choose (All).

6. From the Data menu, choose Filter and AutoFilter.

7. Save and close the workbook.

EXERCISE 13-19

Use COUNTA in a 3-D reference. Create a custom view. Set and clear a print area.

1. Open **ProductList** and save it as *[your initials]***13-19**.

2. Press Shift+F11 and rename the new sheet **ProductCount**. Move the sheet so that it is the last one (the far right) in the workbook.

3. Key **Klassy Kow Product Count** in cell A1 on the ProductCount sheet. Make it 14-point Arial.

4. In cell A2, key today's date. Format the date with the same font as the label in cell A1. Format the date to show the month spelled out, the date, a comma, and four digits for the year.

5. Use COUNTA in a 3-D reference by following these steps:

 a. In cell A3, click the Insert Function button .

 b. Choose COUNTA from the Statistical category.

 c. Click the Beverages tab and select cells A4:A13 for the Value1 box.

 d. Click in the Value2 box and select cells A4:A10 on the Cakes&Pies tab.

> ✸ **TIP:** Use F8 and arrow keys to select ranges that are not easy to select by dragging.

 e. Click in the Value3 box and select cells A4:A19 on the IceCream tab. Use cells A4:A6 on the NoveltyItems tab for Value4. Click OK.

6. Format the results with the same font and size as cells A1:A2.

7. Add your standard footer and print the worksheet.

8. Make a copy of the sheet and name it **ProductCountFormulas**. Display the formulas and print the sheet fit to one landscape page.

9. Save and close the workbook.

EXERCISE 13-20

Create a custom view. Show a view. Set and clear a print area.

1. Open **RetireAcct** and save it as *[your initials]***13-20**.

2. Add your standard footer and set landscape orientation.

3. Create custom views by following these steps:

  a. From the View menu, choose Custom Views.
  b. Click Add and key **Normal** as the name. Click OK.
  c. Hide columns H:S so that only information for 2004 is visible.
  d. Adjust the column widths and print the worksheet.
  e. From the View menu, choose Custom Views.
  f. Click Add and key **2004** as the name. Click OK.
  g. Show columns H:S and hide columns B:G and N:S. Only data for 2003 is visible.
  h. From the View menu, choose Custom Views. Click Add and key **2003** as the name. Click OK.
  i. Adjust column widths and print the worksheet.
  j. Show all the columns. Hide the columns and create a custom view for 2002. Print the worksheet.

4. Show a custom view by following these steps:

  a. From the View menu, choose Custom Views.
  b. Select **Normal** and click Show.

5. Set a print area by following these steps:

  a. Select cells H3:M18.
  b. From the File menu, choose Print Area and then Set Print Area.
  c. Click the Print Preview button [image].
  d. Print the worksheet.

6. Clear a print area by following these steps:

  a. From the File menu, choose Print Area and then Clear Print Area.
  b. Click cell A1.

7. Save and close the workbook.

Lesson Applications

Name and sort a list. Filter a list.

1. Open **CountCust** and save it as *[your initials]***13-21** in your Lesson 13 folder.
2. Select cells A3:I35 and name the range **Database**.
3. Add your standard footer. Change to landscape orientation and set the left and right margin to 0.5 inches.
4. Sort the list alphabetically by city. Print the worksheet.
5. Undo the sort.
6. Use an AutoFilter to show those rows in which the Saturday count is greater than 150. Print the sheet.
7. Show all the rows.
8. Save and close your workbook.

Create a filter. Create and display custom views.

You can save filtered results in a custom view for display at any time. If you add records in the Normal view, the added records appear in the custom view the next time you show it.

1. Open **Personnel** and save it as *[your initials]***13-22** in your folder.
2. Select the column labels (row 2) and the data rows, and name the range **Database**.
3. Add your standard footer and change the page orientation to landscape.
4. Create a custom view named **Normal**.
5. Create an AutoFilter to show the employees in the Marketing department. While the records are filtered, create a custom view named **Marketing**.

 TIP: You can copy the label from the row immediately above by pressing
Ctrl + '.

6. While the records are filtered, add yourself as an employee of the Marketing department in your home city. Print the filtered worksheet.
7. Show the Normal view to make sure you are listed in that view.
8. Save and close the workbook.

EXERCISE 13-23

Create filters using OR. Copy data to a different workbook. Use COUNTA.

1. Create a new workbook and save it as *[your initials]*13-23.
2. Open **CountCust**. Arrange the windows so that they are vertically tiled.

 REVIEW: Name the range of cells that make up the list to use an AutoFilter.

3. In CountCust, create an AutoFilter that shows shops in Oregon and shops in Washington.

 NOTE: Use the OR option in a custom AutoFilter when you want to show both states.

4. While the rows are filtered, select all cells in columns A and B. Copy these cells to cell A1 in *[your initials]*13-23.
5. Close CountCust without saving and maximize your workbook window. Adjust the column widths as necessary.
6. Insert a row at row 9. In cell A9 key **# of Shops** and make it bold. Make the row 22.50 (30 pixels) high.
7. Use COUNTA in cell B9 to show how many shops are in Oregon. Make the results bold.
8. Show the same information in row 17 for Washington.
9. Add your standard footer. Print the worksheet.
10. Save and close the workbook.

EXERCISE 13-24   *Challenge Yourself*

Print noncontiguous selections.

You can paste a link to cells on a different sheet to print ranges that are not next to each other on one page.

1. Open **RetireAcct** and save it as *[your initials]*13-24.

 NOTE: When there is nothing on a worksheet, use File, Page Setup to add a footer.

2. Insert a new worksheet and name it **Totals**. Add your standard footer.
3. Select cells A1:A18 on the ChangesInAssets sheet and click the Copy button ⬜.
4. Go to cell A1 on the Totals sheet.
5. From the Edit menu, choose Paste Special. Click Paste Link.

6. Widen column A to show the longest item. Delete the contents of cells A3:A5.

7. Select cells G5:G18 on the ChangesInAssets sheet. Click the Copy button [image].

8. Go to cell B5 on the Totals sheet. From the Edit menu, choose Paste Special. Click Paste Link. Widen the column to show the values.

9. Repeat these steps to paste a link to cells M5:M18 in column C and a link to cells S5:S18 in column D. Widen the columns as needed.

10. Edit the labels in row 5 to show **2004, 2003,** and **2002** in place of the word "Total." Key an apostrophe (') before the year to indicate that the value should be treated as a label. Make these labels bold and right-aligned.

11. Add your standard footer and print the sheet.

12. Make a copy of the Totals sheet and name it **TotalsFormulas**. Display the formulas and print the sheet fit to one portrait page.

13. Save and close the workbook.

On Your Own

In these exercises you work on your own, as you would in a real-life work environment. Use the skills you've learned to accomplish the task—and be creative.

EXERCISE 13-25

In a new workbook, use three columns to key the first and last names of students in your class or coworkers in your company and each person's favorite food. Make some of the foods the same so that you can use AutoComplete. Include a label for each column. Name the range **Database**. Sort the rows alphabetically by last name. Save the workbook as *[your initials]*13-25 in your Lesson 13 folder. Add your standard footer and print the worksheet. Sort the rows in descending order by food type and print the worksheet. Save and close the workbook.

EXERCISE 13-26

Open **CountCust**. Hide the columns to create a custom view that shows only Monday data. Save your workbook as *[your initials]*13-26 in your Lesson 13 folder. Add your standard footer and print the worksheet in this view. Create six additional views to show each day separately. Print each view. Save and close the workbook.

EXERCISE 13-27

Use the Office Assistant to look up "lists." Print the guidelines for reference. In a new workbook, create a list of 12 company names, retail stores, or restaurants in your city. In separate columns, list a phone number, the year they started in business, and an average hourly wage for someone who works at this establishment. Format the list attractively and name the range according to the guidelines. Add your standard footer and print the worksheet. Sort the rows by year started in business, with the oldest establishment listed first. Print the worksheet in this sort order. Sort the rows by average hourly wage in ascending order. Print the worksheet again. Close the workbook without saving.

Using Worksheet Templates

After completing this lesson, you will be able to:

1. **Use an Excel workbook template.**
2. **Edit an Excel template.**
3. **Use the Template Gallery.**
4. **Redesign a Gallery template.**
5. **Add worksheet protection.**

 Estimated Time: 1 hour

A template is a model workbook. You use it as the basis for a new workbook. A template helps you eliminate repetitive work. Suppose you create a sales report each week with summary calculations by state and accompanying charts. If you create a template for the worksheet with all the basic data, you simply need to start a new workbook based on the template, fill in the week's sales figures, and print.

Using an Excel Workbook Template

In addition to the default workbook template, Excel has a few sample custom templates. A *custom template* is a workbook template that may include values, formulas, labels, images, and more.

 NOTE: When you create a new blank workbook, you are using the default workbook template with three blank worksheets.

When you create a workbook based on a template, it has the same name as the template, followed by a number.

EXERCISE   14-1   Create a Workbook Based on an Excel Template

If another task pane is open, you can open the New Workbook task pane by clicking the Other Task Panes arrow and choosing from the list. You can also open the New Workbook task pane from the File menu by choosing New.

1. Click the Other Task Panes arrow in the task pane. Choose New Workbook from the list.

2. Click On my computer in the Templates section. The Templates dialog box has two tabs: General and Spreadsheet Solutions.

> **NOTE:** Spreadsheet Solutions are templates that were created by a company that sells and develops templates for Excel users.

3. Click the Spreadsheet Solutions tab. There are five sample workbook templates.

4. Double-click ExpenseStatement. A new workbook opens with the template name followed by a number. It is a copy of the template.

5. Click the Print Preview button 🔍. This worksheet uses a variety of design principles. The gridlines are off, an unused cell has black shading, and borders are used in unique ways.

FIGURE 14-1
Worksheet based on ExpenseStatement template

								Statement No.	

Expense Statement

Employee

Name	Emp #	Pay Period
SSN	Position	From
Department	Manager	To

Date	Account	Description	Lodging	Transport	Fuel	Meals	Phone	Entertainment	Other	TOTAL

	Sub Total
Approved	Notes	Advances
	TOTAL

Office Use Only   *Insert Fine Print Here*

6. Close the preview.

EXERCISE **14-2** **Fill In Data in the Worksheet**

This template opens with the insertion point in cell E12, the cell where the employee's name is keyed.

1. Key *[your first and last name]*. Press Tab.

2. Key 12345 as your employee number.

3. Press Tab. A prompt pops up to tell you what date to use.

 NOTE: The keyboard shortcut to enter the current date is Ctrl+;.

4. Press Ctrl+; and press Tab. Scroll the window to see the left side of the worksheet if necessary.

5. Key **888-44-8888** as the social security number.

6. Click cell D17 for the first date entry. Press Ctrl+;.

7. Press Tab and key **111** as the Account.

8. Press Tab and key **Travel to school** as the Description.

9. Key **10** for Fuel and **5** for Phone in cells I17 and K17.

10. Press Tab. The total is calculated.

11. Scroll to the bottom of the worksheet. Click the fine-print cell and read the message.

12. Press Esc to remove the message and click cell E12.

EXERCISE **14-3** **Save and Hide the Workbook**

A template opens as a copy of the original. To save the version with your data, you must save the workbook as usual. A *hidden workbook* is open but not visible.

1. Press F12. The Save As dialog box opens.

2. Save the workbook as *[your initials]***14-3** in a folder for Lesson 14.

3. Preview and print the worksheet.

4. From the Window menu, choose Hide. The workbook is open but hidden from view. You will unhide it later.

Editing an Excel Template

You can open an Excel template and save it as a new template using a different name. This allows you to use the existing template as the basis for creating your own template.

Templates are easiest to use when they appear in the General Templates group of the New Workbook task pane. You can store templates anywhere, but only certain folders are listed in this task pane.

EXERCISE **14-4** **Open a Template**

You need to know where a template is stored so that you can open it as a regular workbook. When you open a template, the original opens, not a copy.

1. Click the Open button .

   > ✦ **TIP:** To find where your templates are stored, choose Search from the Start menu, choose All files and folders, and key ***.xlt** as All or part of the file name. Look for ExpenseStatement and note the folder. Ask your instructor for additional help.

2. Navigate to the folder where **ExpenseStatement** (and the other Spreadsheet Solution templates) is stored.

3. Double-click **ExpenseStatement**. The original template file is opened.

EXERCISE **14-5** **Edit an Excel Template**

Most templates have some type of *cell protection.* Cell protection locks the contents of cells so that you cannot edit them. Since you now want to edit this template, you need to turn off the Protection feature.

1. From the Tools menu, choose Protection and then Unprotect Sheet. This turns off the protection setting so that you can now edit the template.

2. Click cell D6 and format it as 18-point Arial.

3. Key **Klassy Kow Ice Cream, Inc.**

   > ✏ **NOTE:** The green error triangles mark formulas that refer to empty cells. Ignore them for now.

4. Press (F5), key **n17**, and press (Enter). This cell has an IF function that sums the range G17:M17. If the result is greater than 0, the sum is shown. Otherwise, the cell is left blank.

5. Right-click the column I heading and delete the column.

6. Change **Department** to **Store** in cell D14.

EXERCISE 14-6 Edit the Template Properties

A *property* is a setting or attribute, and all workbooks have properties. A useful property for templates is the preview image. A *preview image* is a replica or picture of the workbook displayed in the Open and Templates dialog boxes when the file is selected.

1. From the File menu, choose Properties. The Properties dialog box has five tabs.

2. Click the Summary tab. Because your template is a copy of the original, the author and company is Microsoft Corporation.

3. Change the author entry to *[your first and last name]*.

4. Change the company to *[your school or company name]*.

 NOTE: You can toggle a check mark on/off by pressing the (Spacebar).

5. Click to place a check mark for Save preview picture. Click OK.

FIGURE 14-2
Editing workbook properties

ExpenseStatement Properties	☒

General | **Summary** | Statistics | Contents | Custom

Title:

Subject:

Author: Student Name

Manager:

Company: School or Company Name|

Category:

Keywords:

Comments:

Hyperlink base:

Template:

☑ Save preview picture

[OK]   [Cancel]

EXERCISE 14-7   Save a New Template

In order to preserve the original template, you should save this revised version using a different name. It is good practice to save your own templates in the General templates folder, not the Spreadsheet Solutions folder. On most computers, the folder for your templates is C:\Documents and Settings\UserName\Application Data\Microsoft\Templates.

1. Press F12 to open the Save As dialog box.
2. Note the Save in folder. This is the folder where the Spreadsheet Solutions templates are stored.
3. Navigate to the folder for your templates.
4. Key *[your initials]*14-7 as the new File name. Excel will add the **xlt** extension to identify this as a template.
5. Note the Save as type. It should be Template, since you started with a template.
6. Click Save.
7. Close the template and open the New Workbook task pane.
8. Click On my computer in the Templates section. Click General. **Templates that you create are displayed in this tab.**

 NOTE: You may need to move your template to a folder that displays in the Templates dialog box. Check with your instructor.

9. Click once to select your template and see its preview image.
10. Click OK. A copy of the template opens as a new workbook. The filename includes a number after the template name.

 NOTE: The number after your template filename is probably "1."

11. Print the sheet.

EXERCISE 14-8   Unhide a Workbook and Compare Side by Side

You can now unhide the first workbook that you created from the original template. Then you can compare it to the edited one.

1. From the Window menu, choose Unhide. The workbooks that are hidden appear in the list.
2. Click to select *[your initials]*14-3 and click OK. Both workbooks are open.

3. From the Window menu, choose Compare Side by Side with [your initials] 14-71. The workbooks are tiled horizontally, and the Compare Side by Side toolbar opens.

FIGURE 14-3
Using Compare
Side by Side

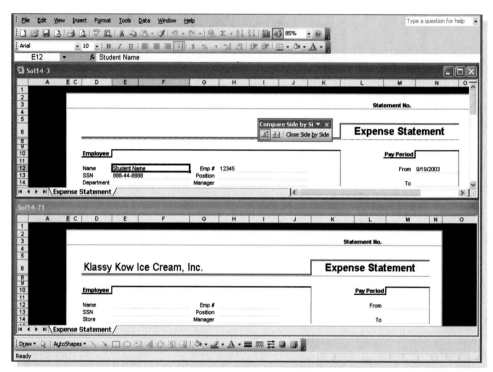

4. Click the Synchronous Scrolling button so that it shows an outline. It may show the outline as you start. This means the feature is active. Synchronous scrolling means that the windows will move in tandem.

5. Press the down arrow until you see both windows scroll vertically.

6. Click Close Side by Side on the toolbar. Both workbooks are open and maximized.

EXERCISE **14-9** **Close Multiple Files**

You can close several workbooks at once by using the Close All command. This command appears in the File menu when you hold down the [Shift] key as you click File.

 NOTE: The Close All command is available in most Windows applications.

1. Hold down the [Shift] key.

FIGURE 14-4
Closing multiple files

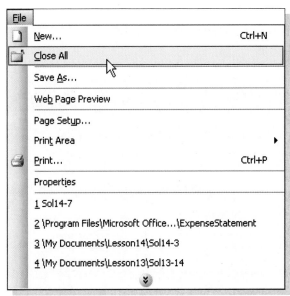

2. Click File on the menu bar. Release the Shift key.

3. Choose Close All. If any of the workbooks has been changed since its last save, the usual prompt appears.

4. Close the workbooks without saving.

EXERCISE 14-10 Delete a Template

You should delete your template from the classroom computer.

1. Open the New Workbook task pane.
2. Click On my computer in the Templates section. Click General.
3. Right-click your template icon and choose Delete.
4. Choose Yes. Click Cancel.

Using the Template Gallery

Microsoft.com maintains a *Template Gallery* that is a collection of templates for Word, Excel, PowerPoint, and Access. You can preview templates, find ones that you like, edit them in Excel, and save them to your computer. Then you can add your own design elements or ideas.

EXERCISE 14-11 Preview and Open a Gallery Template

The gallery lists categories of templates to help you find one that fits your purpose. You must be online and using Internet Explorer to use the Template Gallery.

1. Establish an Internet connection and start Internet Explorer.
2. Key **http://officeupdate.microsoft.com/templategallery/** in the Address box and press Enter.

NOTE: Excel can be running when you establish your Internet connection.

3. Key **vehicle service record** in the Search box and press $\boxed{\text{Enter}}$.

FIGURE 14-5
The Microsoft
Template Gallery

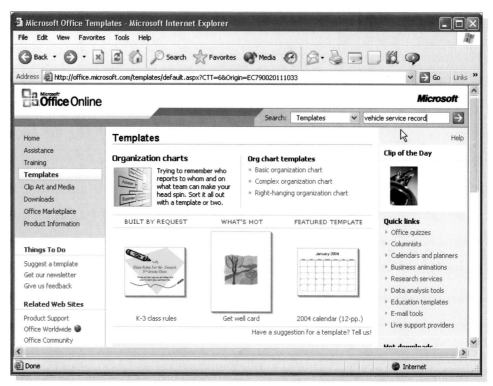

4. Scroll the list and view the names. Check the icons that identify Word, Access, Excel, or PowerPoint.

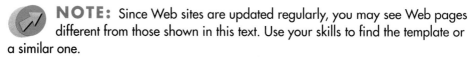 **NOTE:** Since Web sites are updated regularly, you may see Web pages different from those shown in this text. Use your skills to find the template or a similar one.

5. Find and click Vehicle Service Record. The template is previewed to show its purpose and appearance. (See Figure 14-6 on the next page.)

6. Click Download Now. The template opens as a workbook in Excel. There may also be a message box about additional resources related to this template.

7. Click No. The title bar shows the template name followed by a number. The template does include sample data.

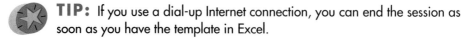 **TIP:** If you use a dial-up Internet connection, you can end the session as soon as you have the template in Excel.

8. End your Internet connection if appropriate.

FIGURE 14-6
Template previewed
in the Gallery

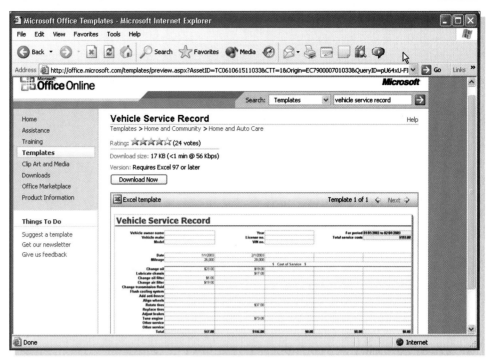

Redesigning a Gallery Template

When you download a template from the Template Gallery, you have a regular workbook that you can edit. You can then save this workbook as a template so that you have your own template.

EXERCISE 14-12 Add a Custom Footer to a Template

You can create a custom footer in a template, so that the footer is part of any new workbook based on that template.

1. Click the Print Preview button 🔍.
2. Click Setup. Click the Header/Footer tab.
3. Click Custom Footer.
4. In the Left section box, key *[your first and last name]*.
5. In the Center section box, add the filename and the tab name.
6. In the Right section box, click the Date button 📅. Click OK.
7. Close the Page Setup dialog box.
8. Close print preview.

EXERCISE **14-13** **Edit Data and Change Colors**

1. Click cell A1 and press F2. Press Home.

 REVIEW: The Home key positions the insertion point at the left edge of the cell.

2. Key **Klassy Kow** and press Spacebar before the existing text. Press Enter.
3. Click cell F3. This cell has a nested formula. It converts and formats the earliest and latest dates in the range B8:F8.
4. Click cell F4. This cell has a SUM function.
5. Click cell B25. The cells in this row have SUM functions.
6. Select cells B8:C9 and press Delete. You will fill in data here.
7. Select cells B11:C22 and press Delete.
8. Select the cells that have light yellow shading.
9. Click the arrow with the Fill Color button 🖌▾.
10. Choose Pale Blue in the last row.

EXERCISE **14-14** **Add Labels and a Formula**

1. Click cell A27 and key **Total This Record**. Since there are several rows that precede this row with bold and right alignment, those settings are applied to your label.
2. Click cell B27 and key **=sum(** to start a formula.
3. Click cell B25 and drag to select the range B25:F25. Press Enter. The result will show zero.
4. Format the result as bold.
5. Click cell B3 and key **Klassy Kow Ice Cream, Inc.**

EXERCISE **14-15** **Add a Comment**

On this worksheet that you are building from the Template Gallery original, you can set comments to show onscreen. Since comments do not print, this is a logical setting for templates, because you can use comments to provide help to those using the template.

 REVIEW: Comments are toggled on/off from the View menu.

1. Right-click cell E27 and choose Insert Comment.

2. Delete the user name and key the following:
   Complete the vehicle information and submit this record to Accounting by the 30th of the month.

3. Click an edge of the comment and size it so that the text fits on two lines.

4. Position the comment so that it is centered below columns E and F near rows 27:28.

FIGURE 14-7
Adding a comment

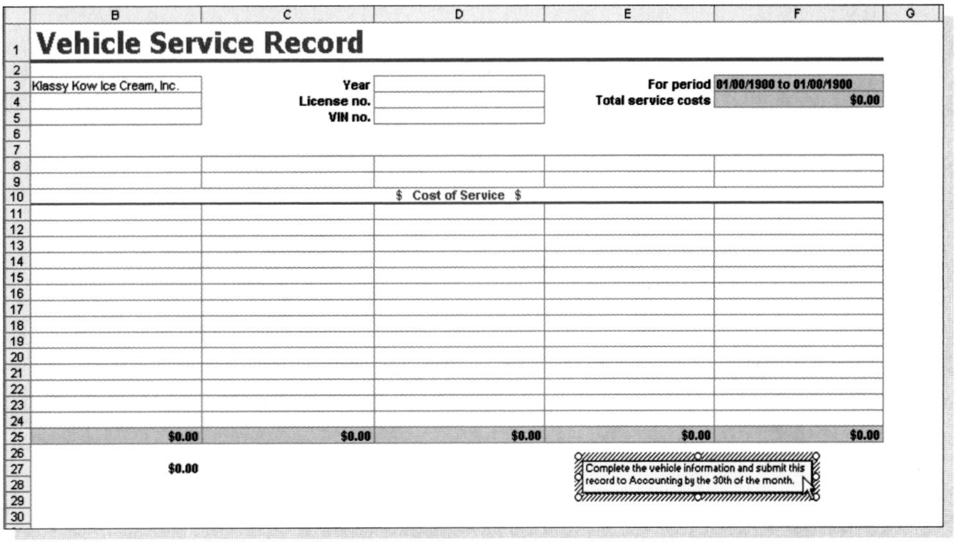

5. Click an empty cell. Press Ctrl + Home.

6. Choose View and Comments if your comment is not visible.

7. Click the Print Preview button. The comment will not print.

Adding Worksheet Protection

After all your work to create a template, you can make sure that others do not accidentally delete formulas, change colors, edit data, or make other errors. You can protect or prohibit cells from being changed. You can lock drawing objects and images so that they cannot be selected or changed. The Locked property in the Format Cells dialog box and the Protect Sheet command in the Tools menu work together to allow you to do this.

EXERCISE **14-16** **Change the Locked Property**

Cells and objects, like workbooks, have properties. One of those properties is whether or not the cell or object is *locked*. When a cell is locked, it cannot be changed if the worksheet is protected.

By default, all cells on a worksheet are locked. However, the Locked property has no effect until the worksheet is protected. The Protection setting is not active until you turn it on.

1. Right-click the comment and choose Format Comment.

2. Click the Protection tab. The Locked property has a check mark. When the worksheet protection is activated, you will not be able to edit the comment.

3. Read the message about the Protection command.

4. Click OK.

5. Select the range B4:B5. Hold down Ctrl and select cells D3:D5. Hold down Ctrl and select cells B8:F24. These cells should not be locked, because this is where you will key information about each vehicle.

6. Right-click one of the selected cells and choose Format Cells.

7. Click the Protection tab.

8. Remove the check mark for Locked.

FIGURE 14-8
Changing the
Locked property

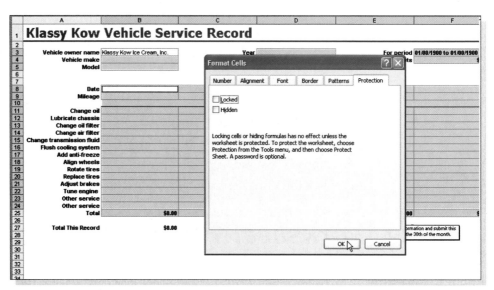

9. Click OK.

EXERCISE 14-17 Protect the Worksheet

When you protect a worksheet, the Locked property takes effect. If Worksheet Protection is on, locked cells and objects cannot be changed.

 NOTE: You can assign an optional password when setting worksheet protection.

1. Press Ctrl + Home.

2. From the Tools menu, choose Protection and then Protect Sheet. You can choose what users can do when this sheet is protected.

3. Make sure there are check marks for Select locked cells and Select unlocked cells. This means that a user can click to select any cell.

4. Place a check mark for Format rows. This means that they will also be able to format a row. Click OK.

FIGURE 14-9
Protect Sheet
dialog box

5. Click cell F3 and press Delete. You cannot delete the contents, because this cell is locked and protected.

6. Click OK in the message box.

7. Try to select the comment. You cannot do so for the same reason.

8. Click cell B8 and key today's date. Press Tab. This cell was unlocked, so your entry is allowed.

9. Delete the contents of cell B8.

10. Press Ctrl + Home.

REVIEW: Position the insertion point where you would like it to be when a new workbook is opened.

EXERCISE 14-18 Save a Template

This workbook has not yet been saved, since it was created from a Template Gallery template. Use the Save As command to change the Save as type to template.

1. From the File menu, choose Properties.

2. Click the Summary tab.

3. Change the author to *[your first and last name]*.

4. Change the company to *[your school or company name]*.

5. Make sure there is a check mark for Save preview picture. Click OK.

6. Press F12.

7. In the File name box, key *[your initials]*14-18.

8. Click the Save as type arrow.

9. Choose Template. The Save in folder changes to the template location for your computer. Note the name and location of this folder.

10. Click Save. (See Figure 14-10 on the next page.)

11. Close the template.

FIGURE 14-10
Saving a workbook
as a template

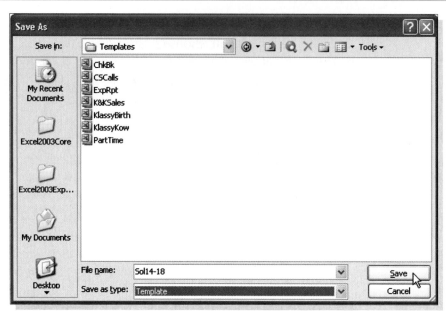

EXERCISE 14-19 Create a Workbook from a Template

1. Open the New Workbook task pane.
2. Click On my computer in the Templates section.
3. Click the General tab.
4. Double-click *[your initials]*14-18. A new workbook opens with the template name followed by a number.
5. Complete the data as shown here using the current year for the dates.
6. Preview and print the worksheet.
7. Save the workbook as *[your initials]*14-19 in your Lesson 14 folder.
8. Close the workbook.
9. Open the New Workbook task pane.
10. Click On my computer in the Templates section. Click General.
11. Right-click your template and choose Delete.
12. Choose Yes. Click Cancel.

FIGURE 14-11

Vehicle owner name	Klassy Kow Ice Cream, Inc.	Year	2004	For period 07/01/2004 to 08/31/2004
Vehicle make	Buick	License no.	KK001	Total service costs
Model	Regal	VIN no.	123B456YY02	

Date	7/1/xx	8/15/xx			
Mileage	15,500	16,750			
		$ Cost of Service $			
Change oil	27.93				
Lubricate chassis					
Change oil filter	7.5				
Change air filter					
Change transmission fluid					
Flush cooling system					
Add anti-freeze					
Align wheels		55			
Rotate tires		23			
Replace tires					
Adjust brakes					
Tune engine					
Other service					
Other service					
Total	$0.00	$0.00	$0.00	$0.00	$0.00

USING ONLINE HELP

Workbooks have file properties such as the preview image. Properties can help you identify a file.

Use Help to learn about file properties:

1. Establish an Internet connection and start Internet Explorer. Minimize the window.
2. In a new workbook, choose Help and Microsoft Excel Help.
3. Key **properties** in the Search box and press Enter.
4. Click the topic About file properties in the Search Results dialog box. Click Show All. Read the information.
5. Click the topic Create custom file properties in the Search Results dialog box. Click Show All. Read the information.
6. Close the Help window. Close the Search Results dialog box.
7. Close Internet Explorer and end your Internet connection if appropriate.

LESSON Summary

➤ Excel includes several custom workbook templates that can be opened, edited, and resaved. A custom workbook template can have single or multiple worksheets.

➤ When you create a new workbook from a template, the new workbook is named with the template name and a number. Use the Save As command to save the workbook with an appropriate filename.

➤ You can open a template to edit it. You can resave it with the same name if you prefer.

➤ You can hide an open workbook so that it is not visible.

➤ Microsoft's Template Gallery is a Web site with professionally designed templates for each product in the Office suite including Excel.

➤ The Close All command is available if you hold down the Shift key while clicking File in the menu bar.

➤ A property is a workbook setting or attribute. Properties allow you to add identifying information about the file.

➤ The Save preview picture property creates a preview of the worksheet in the Open and Templates dialog box.

➤ The Locked property is a cell setting that controls whether or not the cell or object can be edited. This property works with the Protection setting.

➤ The Protection setting can be applied to a worksheet or to a workbook. When you use worksheet protection, the user cannot edit or change cells or objects unless they have been unlocked.

LESSON 14 Command Summary

FEATURE	BUTTON	MENU	KEYBOARD
Compare side by side		Window, Compare Side by Side	
Hide workbook		Window, Hide	
Lock or unlock cell		Format, Cells	Ctrl+1
Properties, set		File, Properties	
Protect worksheet		Tools, Protection, Protect Sheet	
Template, use		File, New	
Template, open		File, Open	Ctrl+O
Unhide workbook		Window, Unhide	
Unprotect worksheet		Tools, Protection, Unprotect Sheet	

Concepts Review

TRUE/FALSE QUESTIONS

Each of the following statements is either true or false. Indicate your choice by circling T or F.

T   F   **1.** Templates can include values, labels, comments, and images.

T   F   **2.** You can use, but not edit, Excel's custom workbook templates.

T   F   **3.** A protected worksheet may have cells that cannot be edited.

T   F   **4.** Click the Open button 📖 to edit a template.

T   F   **5.** You can edit workbook properties from the File menu.

T   F   **6.** The name of a hidden workbook does not appear in the Open dialog box.

T   F   **7.** All templates appear on the General tab of the Templates dialog box.

T   F   **8.** Comments have the Locked property like cells.

SHORT ANSWER QUESTIONS

Write the correct answer in the space provided.

1. What is the first option you would click in the New Workbook task pane to use a template in a folder on your computer?

_____

2. What can you do if you must edit a workbook that is protected?

_____

3. What is a preview image?

_____

4. How can you activate the Close All command?

_____

5. What property works with worksheet protection?

_____

6. What part of Microsoft's Web site has a variety of templates available for download?

_____

7. How do you create a new template from an existing one?

_____

8. How can you display a workbook that is hidden?

_____

CRITICAL THINKING

Answer these questions on a separate page. There are no right or wrong answers. Support your answers with examples from your own experience, if possible.

1. In your school or the company where you work, what types of documents might be good candidates for templates?

2. Why might you want to hide a workbook?

Skills Review

EXERCISE 14-20

Use an Excel template. Change template properties.

1. Use an Excel template by following these steps:

a. In the New Workbook task pane, click On my computer.
b. Click the Spreadsheet Solutions tab. Double-click Balance Sheet.

2. Save the workbook as *[your initials]*14-20 in your Lesson 14 folder.

3. In cell C9, key **Klassy Kow Receivables and Payables,** *[your last name]*. Press Tab.

 NOTE: This template can be used as a checkbook register. It includes a line chart on the Balance over time sheet.

4. In cell H9, key **10000**. Press Tab. Click cell C14.

5. Key the following, using the current year for all dates.

FIGURE 14-12

Date	Item Description	Received	Payment
1/1/??	Grandview Markets	450	
2/3/??	Klamath Falls Dairy		2375
4/4/??	Office House		235
5/5/??	Santorini Groceries	1750	

6. Print the worksheet.

7. Save and close the workbook.

EXERCISE 14-21

Open and edit an Excel template. Change template properties. Delete a template.

1. Open an Excel template by following these steps:

    a. Click the Open button . Navigate to the folder that contains the Spreadsheet Solutions templates.

     NOTE: On many computers, the Spreadsheet Solutions folder is C:\ Program Files\Microsoft Office\Templates\1033.

    b. Double-click Balance Sheet.

    c. Press F12. Name the new template *[your initials]***14-21**.

    d. Click the arrow with Save in and navigate to the folder for general templates. Click Save.

     REVIEW: On many computers, the general templates folder is C:\ Document and Settings\UserName\Application Data\Microsoft\Templates.

2. Edit an Excel template by following these steps:

    a. From the Tools menu, choose Protection and Unprotect Sheet.

    b. Make cell C9 14-point bold.

     NOTE: Press Alt+Enter within a cell to insert a line break.

    c. In cell C9, key **Klassy Kow Receivables and Payables** and press Alt+Enter.

    d. Key *[your first and last name]*.

    e. Select cells I14:I25. Choose a different light fill color.

f. Click the Print Preview button . Click Setup.

      g. On the Margins tab, turn off vertical centering and set a 1.5-inch top margin.

      h. Close the preview.

3. Change template properties by following these steps:

      a. From the File menu, choose Properties. Click the Summary tab.

      b. Change the author entry to *[your first and last name]*.

      c. Change the company to *[your school or company name]*.

      d. Place a check mark for Save preview picture. Click OK.

      e. Click the Save button .

      f. Print the template and close it.

4. Delete a template by following these steps:

      a. In the New Workbook task pane, click On my computer.

      b. Click the General tab.

      c. Right-click *[your initials]***14-21** and choose Delete.

      d. Choose Yes and click Cancel.

EXERCISE 14-22

Use the Template Gallery. Redesign a Gallery template. Edit properties. Delete a template.

1. Use the Template Gallery by following these steps:

      a. Establish an Internet connection while Excel is running.

      b. Key **http://officeupdate.microsoft.com/templategallery/** in the Address box and press Enter.

      c. Key **packing slip** in the Search box and press Enter.

> **NOTE:** Check the icons with the template to make sure it is for Excel. Remember that Web pages are changed regularly.

      d. Find and click Packing slip to select it.

      e. Click Download Now. Click No in the message box about additional resources if it appears.

      f. End your Internet connection if appropriate.

2. Redesign a Gallery template by following these steps:

      a. Add your usual footer to the workbook. Set the sheet to be horizontally centered.

      b. Click cell A1 and key **Klassy Kow Ice Cream, Inc.**

      c. Delete the contents of cell A2.

      d. In cell A4, key **5613 South Thomson Road**.

      e. In cell A5, key **Klamath Falls, OR 97601**.

      f. In cell A6, key **1-800-555-0023**.

      g. Delete the contents of cells B8:B10 and cells D8:D10.

h. Delete column C. The label in cell E1 moves to cell D1 and becomes partially visible.

i. Click cell D1 and drag the label to cell E1.

j. Delete the contents of cells C13:C17.

3. Edit properties by following these steps:

a. From the File menu, choose Properties. Click the Summary tab.

b. Change the author entry to *[your first and last name]*.

c. Change the company to *[your school or company name]*.

d. Place a check mark for Save preview picture. Click OK.

4. Press F12 and save the workbook as a template named *[your initials]*14-22 in the General templates folder. Close the template.

5. Create a new workbook based on your template and fill in the data shown here.

Order Date:	=now()
Order Number:	KK70403
Purchase Order:	P70403

6. In cells B13:B16, key the following address information:
Diamond Groceries
432 Mountain View Avenue
Medford, OR 97501
1-800-222-5555

7. Delete the contents of cell B17.

8. Key the following product information.

FIGURE 14-13

Product	Description	Order Quantity	Ship Quantity
KK103	24-gallon pack, French Vanilla	3	3
KK234	6-gallon pack, Raspberry Swirl	3	3

9. Save the workbook as *[your initials]*14-22 in your Lesson 14 folder.

10. Print and close the workbook.

11. Delete a template by following these steps:

a. In the New Workbook task pane, click On my computer.

b. Click the General tab.

c. Right-click *[your initials]*14-22 and choose Delete.

d. Choose Yes and click Cancel.

EXERCISE 14-23

Open and edit a template. Add worksheet protection. Delete a template.

 NOTE: Copy the **ExpRpt** template to the General templates folder before starting this exercise.

1. Open a template by following these steps:

   a. Click the Open button 📂. Navigate to the General templates folder.
   b. Double-click ExpRpt.
   c. Press F12. Name the new template *[your initials]*14-23.
   d. Change to a 75% Zoom size.

2. Add worksheet protection by following these steps:

   a. Click to select cell D3.
   b. Hold down Ctrl and select cells B10:D10.
   c. Hold down Ctrl and select cells B15:D15.
   d. Hold down Ctrl and select cells B20:D20. Repeat for cells B25:D25. These cells should not be locked.
   e. Press Ctrl+1.
   f. Click the Protection tab. Remove the check mark for Locked.
   g. Click the Patterns tab. Choose light gray shading for the cells. Click OK.
   h. Press Ctrl+Home. From the Tools menu, choose Protection and Protect Sheet. Click OK.

3. Add your standard footer to the sheet. Print the worksheet.

4. Save and close the template.

5. Delete a template by following these steps:

   a. In the New Workbook task pane, click On my computer. Click the General tab.
   b. Right-click *[your initials]*14-23 and choose Delete.
   c. Choose Yes and click Cancel.

Lesson Applications

Open and edit a template. Edit workbook properties. Add a comment to a template. Protect a worksheet.

1. Open the **ExpRpt** template to be edited.

2. Save the template with a preview image and your name as author in a new template named *[your initials]***14-24** in the General templates folder for your computer.

3. Add a comment in cell C3 that tells the user to press F2 to edit the cell and key the current month.

 REVIEW: You can paste multiple times.

4. Key a formula in cell B11 to subtract the actual expense from the budget amount. Copy the formula through column D. Then copy cells B11:D11 to the same columns in rows 16, 21, and 26.

5. Create formulas in cells B28:B30 and copy them through column D.

6. Select the Actual Expense cells for each salesperson and unlock them. Unlock cell C3 also.

7. Insert, size, and position the COW image so that it displays across cells A1:B5.

8. Add a footer with **Klassy Kow Ice Cream Shops** in the Left section. Show your name in the middle and the date at the right.

9. Delete Sheets 2 and 3.

10. Protect the worksheet.

11. Save the template and print a copy.

12. Remove the protection and delete the image.

13. Press Ctrl+~. AutoFit the columns and print the formulas fit to one landscape page. Print the comment as displayed on the sheet.

14. Close the template without resaving it.

15. Delete *[your initials]***14-24** from your General templates folder.

Use the Template Gallery. Edit a Gallery template. Add worksheet protection.

The Template Gallery includes a template that uses the Depreciation functions that you learned earlier. When you get a template from the Gallery, worksheet protection may be removed. If you want to create your own template, you should set it again.

1. Establish an Internet connection and go to the Template Gallery.

2. Look for a category such as Finance and Accounting. Find and preview the Asset depreciation schedule and download it.

3. End your Internet connection if appropriate.

4. Edit cell B3 to use **=now( )** and format it to show the month spelled out, the date, a comma, and four digits for the year.

     NOTE: The Trace Error message tells you that the function is unprotected.

5. Add your standard footer.

6. Check the Locked property for cells D6:D8. These are the only cells that should be unlocked on this template.

7. Press Ctrl + Home. Save this workbook as a template named *[your initials]***14-25** in the General templates folder. Close the template.

8. Create a workbook from your template for an asset that initially cost $10,000 and that has a salvage value of $1,000 and a useful life of ten years. Save this workbook as *[your initials]***14-25** in your Lesson 14 folder.

9. Print the worksheet.

     REVIEW: Right-click the worksheet tab and choose Move or Copy to copy a sheet with all its formatting and data.

10. Make a copy of the worksheet. Change the data on the copied sheet to determine depreciation for an asset that cost $76,000 and will have a useful life of eight years. It is expected to be worth $15,000. Print the worksheet.

11. Save and close the workbook.

Use an Excel template.

1. Create a new workbook from the Loan Amortization template in the Spreadsheet Solutions folder.

2. Save the workbook as *[your initials]***14-26** in your Lesson 14 folder.

3. Fill in data for a mortgage loan of $200,000 for 30 years at 5.375%. The loan will start on the first day of the next month. Assume that there will be no extra payments.

     NOTE: Press Esc to remove a comment from view.

4. Add a footer with your name at the left and the filename in the center. In the right section, click the Page Number button . Then press Spacebar and key **of** and press Spacebar. Then click the Total Pages button .

5. Preview the worksheet before printing. Adjust the top and bottom margins as needed.

6. Print the worksheet.

7. Save and close the workbook.

EXERCISE 14-27 *Challenge Yourself*

Edit an Excel template.

1. Create a new workbook from the Timecard template in the Spreadsheet Solutions folder.

2. Save the workbook as a template named *[your initials]***14-27** in the General templates folder.

3. Remove worksheet protection. Change to a 75% view. Insert a new blank worksheet.

4. Select cells D3:Q17 and copy them to cell A1 on the blank sheet. Adjust column widths as necessary.

5. Change the page orientation to landscape and set the page to fit on one page.

6. Copy cells J18:Q38 to cell B16 on the new sheet. Preview the sheet to determine what you should fix.

7. In cell A1, key **Klassy Kow Ice Cream, Inc.** and make it 18-point Arial bold italic.

8. Add a footer with the filename at the left and your name at the right.

9. Print the worksheet.

10. Save and close the template.

11. Delete the template from the General templates folder.

On Your Own

In these exercises you work on your own, as you would in a real-life work environment. Use the skills you've learned to accomplish the task—and be creative.

EXERCISE 14-28

Create a workbook from the Sales Invoice template in the Spreadsheet Solutions folder. Add a company name, a customer name, and products to complete the invoice using a business concept of interest to you. Save the workbook as *[your initials]***14-28** in your Lesson 14 folder. Add a footer, print the worksheet, and close the workbook.

EXERCISE 14-29

Create a workbook that you can use to track your monthly living expenses. Design the workbook as a model by keying labels and formulas, but do not key specific values. Develop at least ten categories of expenses. Use labels as main titles for the worksheet. One label should be the cell in which you key the month; add a comment here to remind yourself about that. Format the sheet attractively or use an AutoFormat. Unlock the cells in which you will key values and protect the worksheet. Add the standard footer. Save the workbook as a template named *[your initials]*14-29 in the General templates folder. Create a new workbook from your template and key expenses for the current month. Print the worksheet and close it without saving. Delete the template file from your computer.

EXERCISE 14-30

Use the Internet to find information about Excel templates available for purchase from other sources. Create a workbook to list the vendor's name, web site, and the type of template. Include purchase prices. Add a standard footer. Save the workbook as *[your initials]*14-30 in your Lesson 14 folder. Print the worksheet and close it.

Unit 4 Applications

UNIT APPLICATION 4-1

Move data to another worksheet. Use a 3-D reference with a nested IF function.

Employees receive a salary increase based on their performance ratings. Your first task is to move the ratings and increase percentages to a separate sheet. Then you must create a nested IF function to determine each employee's increase and new salary.

1. Open **SalaryInc** and save it as *[your initials]*u4-1 in your Unit 4 folder.

2. Insert a new worksheet and name it **Increases**. Place it after the SalaryProjections sheet.

3. On the SalaryProjections sheet, select cells D17:E20. Cut and paste these cells to cell A1 on the Increases sheet. Return to the SalaryProjections sheet.

> **REVIEW:** The IF function is in the Logical category. The Function Name arrow is the same as the Name box arrow.

4. Click cell E4 and click the Insert Function button. Choose IF. In the Logical_test box, click cell D4. Key **=2** for the first rating possibility. In the Value_if_true box, click cell C4 and key * to multiply. Click the Increases tab and cell B2. Press F4 to make the reference absolute.

> **NOTE:** If the employee's rating is 2, his/her salary is multiplied by 4 percent. If the rating is not 2, you run another IF function to determine if the rating is 3.

5. In the Value_if_false box, click the Function Name down arrow and find/ choose IF. In the Logical_test box, click cell D4 and key **=3** for the next rating. In the Value_if_true box, click cell C4 and key *. Click the Increases tab and cell B3. Press F4.

> **NOTE:** If the employee's rating is neither 2 or 3, his/her salary is multiplied by 6 percent.

6. In the Value_if_false box, click cell C4 and key *. Click the Increases tab and cell B4. Press F4. Click OK.

7. Copy the formula through cell E16.

8. In cell F4, key a formula to add the increase to the current salary. Copy the formula through cell F16. Format the values in column E to be the same as those in column F.

NOTE: GIF means Graphics Interchange Format, a good format for many Web images.

9. Add a footer with the **COW.gif** file at the left. Place the filename and the tab name in the Center section and your name in the Right section. Format the filename, the tab name, and your name as 10 points.

10. Press Ctrl+Home. Print the worksheet.

11. Make a copy of the worksheet and name it **SalaryProjectionsFormulas**. Display the formulas and AutoFit the columns. Set the worksheet to show column A on each printed sheet. Print the formula sheet.

12. Save and close the workbook.

UNIT APPLICATION 4-2

Name a list. Sort rows. Filter a list.

The Human Resources department keeps a list that tracks vacation days taken by employees. The list is built in chronological order so that the data is sorted by date by default.

1. Open **VacDays** and save it as *[your initials]***u4-2** in your Unit 4 folder.

2. Select the cells that should be used to create a list and name it **Database**. Sort the rows by last name.

3. Create a custom autofilter to show those employees who took vacation days during the first six months of 2003.

 NOTE: For a range of dates, use "is greater than" and "is less than" with the appropriate dates.

4. Add your footer and print the filtered list.

5. Edit the filter to show employees who took vacation days in the second six months of 2003. Print the filtered list.

6. Show all the records and remove the filter. Then sort ascending by date.

7. Make two copies of the sheet and name the copies **2004** and **2005**. Edit the label in cell A2 to show the appropriate year.

8. On the respective sheets, replace the year with either **2004** or **2005** in the Date column.

9. Group the sheets and print them.

10. Save and close the workbook.

UNIT APPLICATION 4-3

Open and redesign a template. Add worksheet protection.

The Customer Service Department has a template that is used every day to log calls. You have been asked to redesign it to include more information.

 NOTE: Copy the CSCalls template file from the CD to the General templates folder on your computer.

1. Create a new workbook based on the **CSCalls** template. Save the workbook in the General templates folder as *[your initials]*u4-3.

2. Change the alignment for the date to left.

 TIP: You need to use a constant in your formula for the number of gallons.

3. Key **Request** in cell D4 and format it to match the other labels. Fix the borders for the label row and center-align the labels.

4. Change to landscape orientation. Make all the columns wider, with the Request column being the widest.

5. Add horizontal borders as needed for the new column. Add vertical borders that start at row 5 between the Date/Time, Time/Representative, and Representative/Request columns.

6. Unlock the cells in which you would key new data. Protect the worksheet. Position the insertion point where it should be when a new workbook is created from this template.

7. Change the top and bottom margins to 0.5 inch. Add your standard footer and print the worksheet.

8. Save and close the workbook.

9. Delete the template from the General templates folder.

UNIT APPLICATION 4-4 *Using the Internet*

Review the templates in the Microsoft Template Gallery to find one that you can use for personal interest or on the job. Edit the template and reformat it so that it looks different from the original. Add a label or formula to the template that can make it more useful to you. Add a footer and print the template.

After you redesign the template, save it in the General templates folder. Create a workbook based on this template and key your own data. Save the workbook as *[your initials]*u4-4 in your Unit 4 folder. Print the workbook. Close the workbook without saving.

Increasing Productivity

Working with Ranges and Lookup & Reference Functions

OBJECTIVES

MICROSOFT OFFICE SPECIALIST ACTIVITIES

In this lesson:
XL03E-1-9
XL03E-1-11
XL03E-1-14

See Appendix.

After completing this lesson, you will be able to:

1. **Use named ranges for navigation.**
2. **Use named ranges in formulas.**
3. **Use a named constant.**
4. **Modify range names.**
5. **Print range names.**
6. **Use lookup functions.**
7. **Use reference functions.**

 Estimated Time: 1½ hours

Y ou have already learned that you can give a descriptive name to a list. In addition to lists, you can assign a range name to any group of cells. Range names can be used in formulas and to move around the workbook. There are several reasons for using range names.

- Range names are easier to remember than cell addresses.
- You are less likely to make an error keying a range name than keying a cell address.
- You can use range names for navigation.
- Range names make formulas easier to understand.

Range names are helpful in many functions, such as those in the Lookup & Reference category. This group of functions obtains data or displays information from the current worksheet or other workbooks.

Using Named Ranges for Navigation

Excel has a few requirements for naming ranges. Here are the basic rules for you to follow:

- Begin range names with a letter.
- Keep range names fewer than 255 characters.
- Do not use range names that resemble cell addresses, such as "A5."
- Do not use single-letter range names, such as "n."
- Do not use spaces in a range name; use uppercase letters, an underscore, or a period to separate words in a name (FirstQuarter, First_Quarter, or First.Quarter).
- Do not use special characters such as hyphens (-) or symbols ($, %, &, #) in a range name.

Excel has some reserved range names that you should not use. These special names are Print_Area, Print_Titles, Consolidate_Area, and Sheet_Title. If you name a range on your worksheet with one of these names, you override Excel's use of the names.

 TIP: Use short, recognizable range names.

TABLE 15-1   Examples of Acceptable and Unacceptable Range Names

ACCEPTABLE NAMES	UNACCEPTABLE NAMES
Week1	Week 1
Week_1	Week-1
Week.1	Week:1
WeekNo1	Week#1
Wk1	W1 or W

EXERCISE   15-1   Use Ranges for Navigation

You can use the Name Box or the Go To command to quickly move around a worksheet.

1. Open the file **JuneExp**.
2. Click the down arrow next to the Name Box. The range names in the workbook are listed.

FIGURE 15-1
Range names in
the workbook

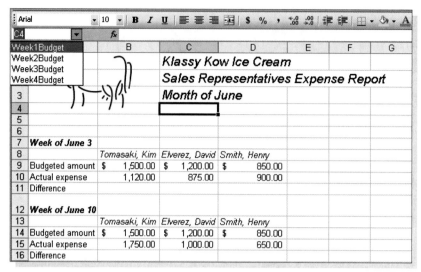

3. Choose Week1Budget. The range is highlighted on the worksheet.

 REVIEW: Another keyboard shortcut for the Go To command is F5.

4. Press Ctrl+G. The Go To dialog box shows range names and recently used cell addresses.

5. Choose Week2Budget. Click OK. The new range is highlighted.

Using Named Ranges in Formulas

When you use a range name instead of a cell address range in a formula, the formula is often easier to understand at first glance. For example, a formula such as

=sum(FirstQtrSales)

conveys a meaning more quickly than the formula

=sum (B12:F12).

EXERCISE **15-2** **Use Ranges in a Formula**

1. Select cell B28. Key **=sum(** to start the SUM function.

2. Press F3. The Paste Name dialog box lists the range names in the workbook.

 NOTE: You can key range names instead of using the Paste Name dialog box.

3. Under Paste name, choose Week1Budget.

FIGURE 15-2
Pasting range
names in a formula

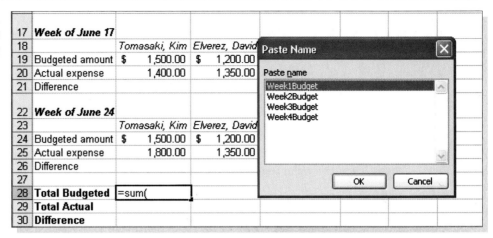

4. Click OK. The named range is added to the formula. Next, you'll add more named ranges to the formula, separating them with commas.

5. Key a comma followed by a space (,) and press F3. Choose Week2Budget and click OK.

6. Key a comma followed by a space (,) and press F3. Double-click Week3Budget.

7. Key a comma followed by a space (,) and press F3. Double-click Week4Budget.

8. Press Enter to complete the formula.

9. Select cell B28 and look at the formula in the formula bar.

EXERCISE **15-3** **Create Named Ranges by Using the Name Box**

The easiest way to create a range name is the Name Box. Just select the range of cells on the worksheet and key the name in the Name Box.

1. Select the range B10:D10. Click the Name Box (not the down arrow next to the box).

2. Key **ActualWk1** and press Enter.

3. Select the range B15:D15. Click the Name Box, key **ActualWk2**, and press Enter.

4. Name the range B20:D20 **ActualWk3** and the range B25:D25 **ActualWk4**.

5. Click the down arrow next to the Name Box and choose one of your new ranges.

6. Press F5 and choose a different range from the Go To dialog box.

7. Select cell B29. Key **=sum(** and press F3. Choose ActualWk1 and click OK.

8. Key a comma followed by a space (,) and press F3. Double-click ActualWk2.

9. Add the other two names for actual expenses to the formula. Press Enter when finished.

Range names are assigned and used in the entire workbook, not just the worksheet where you create the name. If you use a name on one worksheet, you should not use the same name on a different sheet in the same workbook.

> ⚝ **TIP:** You can create worksheet-specific range names by preceding the range name with the sheet name and an exclamation point. This enables you to use the same name more than once in a workbook.

1. Click the YTD sheet tab to display the YTD worksheet. Select cell A2.

2. From the Insert menu, choose Name and then choose Define. The Define Name dialog box shows the selected range, a suggested name, and the existing names.

3. Key **YTD** in the Names in workbook text box and click OK.

FIGURE 15-3
Naming a range in
the dialog box

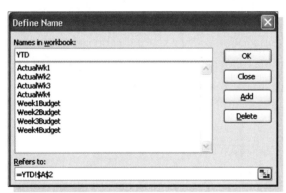

4. Click the down arrow next to the Name Box and choose Week1Budget. The pointer returns to the Expenses sheet, because that is where the range is located.

5. Press F5, key **ytd**, and press Enter. The pointer is now in the YTD worksheet. (See Figure 15-4.)

Depending on how a worksheet is arranged, you can assign range names automatically. If columns and rows have labels and the data is consistent, you can quickly name several ranges with one command.

1. Make sure the YTD worksheet is displayed and select the range A3:D9.

2. Choose Insert, Name from the menu and then choose Create. The Create Names dialog box shows how it will create range names based on what you have selected. (See Figure 15-4.)

3. Click OK. Range names have been created for each of the months and each of the salespersons.

4. Click the down arrow next to the Name Box. Choose January.

FIGURE 15-4
Creating
range names
automatically

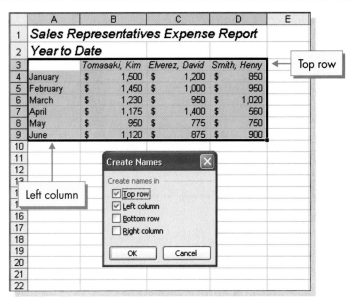

	A	B	C	D	E
1	*Sales Representatives Expense Report*				
2	*Year to Date*				
3		Tomasaki, Kim	Elverez, David	Smith, Henry	
4	January	$ 1,500	$ 1,200	$ 850	
5	February	$ 1,450	$ 1,000	$ 950	
6	March	$ 1,230	$ 950	$ 1,020	
7	April	$ 1,175	$ 1,400	$ 560	
8	May	$ 950	$ 775	$ 750	
9	June	$ 1,120	$ 875	$ 900	

Top row

Left column

Create Names

Create names in
☑ Top row
☑ Left column
☐ Bottom row
☐ Right column

[OK]   [Cancel]

NOTE: Range names are sorted alphabetically in the Name Box list.

5. Click the down arrow next to the Name Box and choose any salesperson's name.

Using a Named Constant

A *constant* is a value used in a formula that does not change. For example, if you multiply all prices by 110% to determine increased prices, 110% is a constant. Constants can be named. You can use these named constants in your formulas instead of the actual values. This makes it easier to understand the purpose of the constant in the formula.

EXERCISE   15-6   Create a Constant Range Name

You use the Define Name dialog box to name a constant. The value does not need to appear anywhere in the workbook for you to name it.

1. Press Ctrl + F3. This is the keyboard shortcut to open the Define Name dialog box.
2. In the Names in workbook text box, key **Increase**.
3. In the Refers to text box, delete any existing data and key **=500**. (See Figure 15-5 on the next page.)
4. Click OK.

FIGURE 15-5
Naming a constant

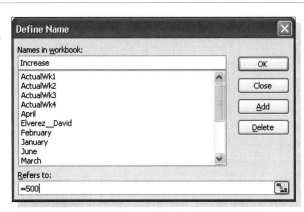

5. Click the down arrow next to the Name Box. Look for the Increase range name; it's not shown. Named constants do not appear in this list, because they are not worksheet cell addresses.

6. Choose YTD from the drop-down list.

EXERCISE 15-7 Use a Constant in a Formula

You can see the usefulness of constants in a formula. They help you quickly understand the calculation.

1. Copy the range A3:D9 to cells A11:D17. Delete the values in the range B12:D17.

2. Click cell B12. Key **=b4+increase** and press (Enter). The constant value (500) is added to the value in cell B4.

3. Copy the formula in B12 to the range B13:B17.

4. Copy the formulas in the range B12:B17 to the range C12:D17. All the formulas use the constant range name.

Modifying Range Names

Range names can be deleted, redefined, or renamed. You can delete a range name if it is no longer needed in a workbook. However, it is important not to delete any range name that is used in a formula. A formula with a deleted range name displays an error message.

You might want to redefine a range name so that it refers to different cells in the worksheet. Sometimes you might want to simply rename a range. Excel does not have a one-step command to change a range name. You need to create the new name and then delete the old one.

EXERCISE 15-8 Delete a Range Name

When you delete a named range that is used in a formula, the formula displays an error in the cell.

1. Click the Expenses tab and press (Ctrl)+(F3). The Define Name dialog box opens.

2. Select ActualWk1 in the list of range names.

3. Click Delete. The name is removed from the list.

4. Click OK.

5. Select cell B29. The formula refers to the range name that you just deleted. Now the cell shows #NAME?, which indicates that a name in the formula is not recognized. Leave the error for now.

FIGURE 15-6
Error after deleting
a range name

22	**Week of June 24**				
23		Tomasaki, Kim	Elverez, David	Smith, Henry	
24	Budgeted amount	$ 1,500.00	$ 1,200.00	$ 850.00	
25	Actual expense	1,800.00	1,350.00	600.00	
26	Difference				
27					
28	**Total Budgeted**	$ 14,200.00			
29	**Total Actua** ◇	#NAME?			
30	**Difference**				

E X E R C I S E **15-9** **Change a Range Name**

To change a range name, you first define the new range name with the same address and then delete the old name.

1. Click the down arrow next to the Name Box and choose January. The range refers to the first set of values in the YTD sheet.

2. Press Ctrl+F3. The Define Name dialog box opens.

3. Choose January in the list of names.

4. In the Names in workbook text box, edit the name to **Jan**.

5. Click Add. Now the ranges Jan and January both refer to the same cells.

6. Choose January in the list. Click Delete.

7. Click OK. This range is not used in any formulas, so no error messages appear.

E X E R C I S E **15-10** **Redefine a Range**

When you redefine a range name, you change the cells to which it refers. This might be necessary if you have made changes to your worksheet.

1. Press Ctrl+F3. Choose February in the list.

2. Place the insertion point in the Refers to text box. A marquee surrounds the current cell range for the name in the worksheet.

3. Select the address in the Refers to box to highlight it, including the = sign.

4. In the worksheet, select the range B13:D13. This changes the range in the text box so that it refers to the second set of values for February.

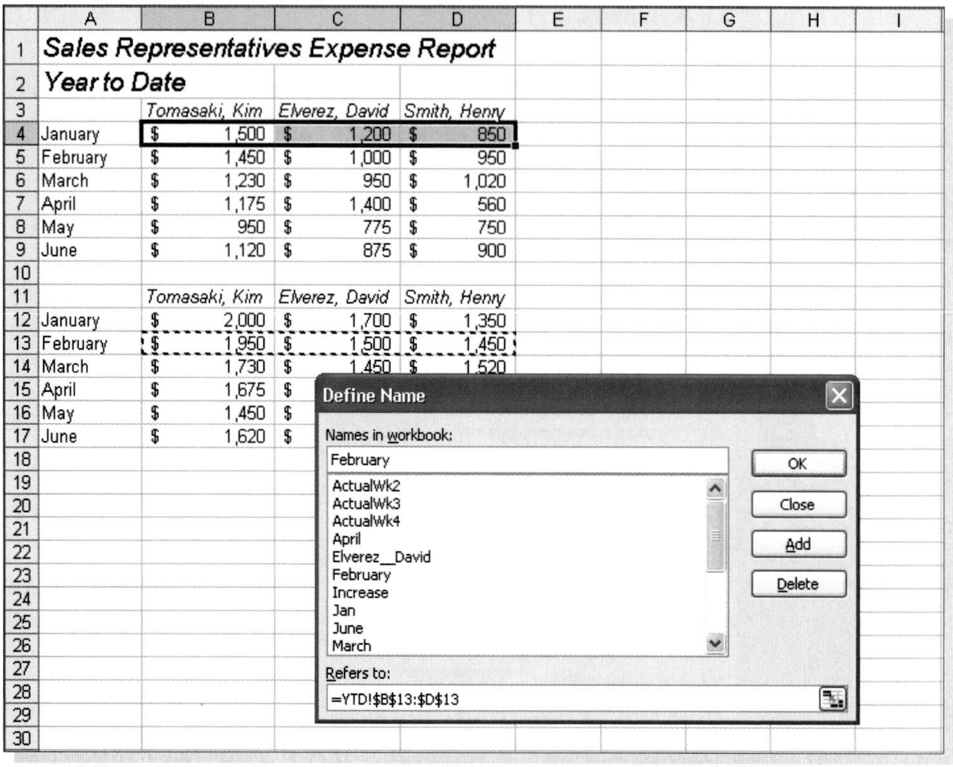

FIGURE 15-7
Redefining a
range name

	A	B	C	D	E	F	G	H	I
1	*Sales Representatives Expense Report*								
2	*Year to Date*								
3		Tomasaki, Kim	Elverez, David	Smith, Henry					
4	January	$ 1,500	$ 1,200	$ 850					
5	February	$ 1,450	$ 1,000	$ 950					
6	March	$ 1,230	$ 950	$ 1,020					
7	April	$ 1,175	$ 1,400	$ 560					
8	May	$ 950	$ 775	$ 750					
9	June	$ 1,120	$ 875	$ 900					
10									
11		Tomasaki, Kim	Elverez, David	Smith, Henry					
12	January	$ 2,000	$ 1,700	$ 1,350					
13	February	$ 1,950	$ 1,500	$ 1,450					
14	March	$ 1,730	$ 1,450	$ 1,520					
15	April	$ 1,675	$						
16	May	$ 1,450	$						
17	June	$ 1,620	$						

Define Name ☒

Names in workbook:

February

ActualWk2
ActualWk3
ActualWk4
April
Elverez__David
February
Increase
Jan
June
March

OK
Close
Add
Delete

Refers to:
=YTD!$B$13:$D$13

5. Click OK. The February range is redefined.

6. Click the Name Box arrow and choose February. The redefined range is highlighted.

Printing Range Names

The Paste List command in the Paste Name dialog box creates a table of the workbook's range names. You can create this list on a separate worksheet and print it as documentation for your workbook.

EXERCISE **15-11** **Create a Range Name Table**

You can insert the current date as a value by pressing Ctrl + ;. Note that this is a fixed date that is not updated by the computer's internal clock.

1. Rename Sheet3 as **Documentation**.

2. In cell A1, key **Monthly Expense Report**.

3. In cell A2, key *[your first and last name]*.

4. In cell A3, press Ctrl+; and press Enter. The date is inserted in one of Excel's standard date formats.

5. Make the range A1:A3 bold.

6. In cell B4, key **Name**. In cell C4, key **Range**. Make these labels bold.

7. Select cell B5 and press F3. The Paste Name dialog box opens.

8. Click Paste List. The range names and references are pasted in two columns starting in cell B5.

9. Widen the columns to show the data.

FIGURE 15-8
A pasted range
name list

	A	B	C	D
1	Monthly Expense Report			
2	Student Name			
3	1/1/2005			
4		Name	Range	
5		ActualWk2	=Expenses!$B$15:$D$15	
6		ActualWk3	=Expenses!$B$20:$D$20	
7		ActualWk4	=Expenses!$B$25:$D$25	
8		April	=YTD!$B$7:$D$7	
9		Elverez__David	=YTD!$C$4:$C$9	
10		February	=YTD!$B$13:$D$13	
11		Increase	=500	
12		Jan	=YTD!$B$4:$D$4	
13		June	=YTD!$B$9:$D$9	
14		March	=YTD!$B$6:$D$6	
15		May	=YTD!$B$8:$D$8	
16		Smith__Henry	=YTD!$D$4:$D$9	
17		Tomasaki__Kim	=YTD!$B$4:$B$9	
18		Week1Budget	=Expenses!$B$9:$D$9	
19		Week2Budget	=Expenses!$B$14:$D$14	
20		Week3Budget	=Expenses!$B$19:$D$19	
21		Week4Budget	=Expenses!$B$24:$D$24	
22		YTD	=YTD!$A$2	
23				

10. Click anywhere in the worksheet to deselect the range.

EXERCISE **15-12** **Suppress Errors When Printing**

The Expenses worksheet has an error message from your range name deletion. You can suppress the printing of errors. This lets you review the worksheet without your attention being drawn to errors that will be corrected later.

1. Press Shift and click the Expenses sheet tab. The three worksheets are grouped.

2. Click the Print Preview button on the Standard toolbar. You can see the error message on the Expenses worksheet. Close print preview.

3. Choose File, Page Setup from the menu. Click the Sheet tab.

4. In the Print group, click the down arrow next to the Cell errors as text box and choose <blank>. This tells Excel to not show errors.

5. Click the Header/Footer tab and then click Custom Footer. The Footer dialog box opens.

6. In the Left section, key your name. In the Center section, click the Filename button and press Spacebar.

7. Click the Tab Name button and press Tab.

8. In the Right section, click the Date button 🗓.

9. Close the Footer dialog box and the Page Setup dialog box.

10. Save the workbook as *[your initials]*15-12 in a new folder for Lesson 15.

⏪ **REVIEW:** If you save a workbook while the sheets are grouped, it will open with the sheets grouped.

11. Print the entire workbook and then close the workbook.

Using Lookup Functions

Lookup functions display information from a table by scanning the table's columns or rows to look up, or find, data. The lookup table is often on a separate sheet. There are two lookup functions, VLOOKUP and HLOOKUP. Think of them as vertical lookup and horizontal lookup. The VLOOKUP function scans the table's columns to find data that match a value. The HLOOKUP function works the same way but scans the table's rows to find the data.

EXERCISE **15-13** **Use VLOOKUP**

The workbook for this exercise has three worksheets. The first worksheet lists account names, the second worksheet lists discount percentages allowed by account name, and the third worksheet shows payment methods based on the discounts.

The vertical lookup table is located on the Discounts worksheet. The lookup value is in column A, which is the first column of the table. The function uses this column to find the correct discount, which is column B of the table. The rows in a vertical lookup table must be sorted by column A for the function to work properly.

It is a good practice to name the lookup table as a range so that you can refer to it easily in the VLOOKUP function.

1. Open the file **AcctPay**.

2. Click the Discounts sheet tab. This sheet contains the lookup table that will be used by the VLOOKUP function. The table lists the discount that Klassy Kow receives from each vendor.

3. On the Discounts worksheet, select the range A2:B10.

4. Click the Name Box. Key **TDisc** and press (Enter). You'll use this range name to refer to the table when you create the VLOOKUP function.

 TIP: Precede range names for lookup tables with a "T" so you can easily recognize that they are lookup tables.

 5. Click cell A2. Click the Sort Ascending button 🔼 on the Standard toolbar. The first column of the lookup table must be sorted in ascending order.

6. Click the Accounts tab and select cell C4. You'll enter the VLOOKUP function to look up a discount rate for the company name in column B.

 7. Click the Insert Function button 🔣. The Insert Function dialog box opens.

8. Choose the Lookup & Reference category. Choose VLOOKUP and click OK. The Function Arguments dialog box opens.

9. Make sure the insertion point is located in the Lookup_value text box. The Lookup_value is the label or value that the function will search for in the TDisc table.

10. Click cell B4 in the worksheet. Excel will look for this company name in column A of the lookup table.

11. Click in the Table_array text box. The Table_array is the range name or address of the table that shows the discounts.

12. Press (F3). The Paste Name dialog box opens. Double-click TDisc, the range name for your lookup table.

13. Click in the Col_index_num box. The Col_index_num identifies which column in the TDisc lookup table contains the discounts.

14. Key **2**. Column B is the second column. In Lookup functions, you cannot key the column letter but must identify it by counting columns from the left.

15. Leave the Range_lookup text box empty. This tells Excel to look for approximate matches to your lookup value, the company name. This is an optional argument for Lookup functions. (See Figure 15-9 on the next page.)

NOTE: Use the Range_lookup text box if you want Excel to find exact matches to the lookup value in your lookup table. The argument for this text box is either TRUE or FALSE. If it is TRUE or omitted, Excel finds an approximate match. If it is FALSE, Excel looks for an exact match. If none is found, the error value #N/A is displayed.

16. Click OK. The discount for the company, Greenfield Supermarkets, is .05 (the decimal equivalent of 5%).

17. Click the Discounts tab. Verify that Greenfield Supermarkets gives a 5% discount.

18. On the Accounts sheet, copy the formula to the range C5:C15. #N/A appears in the blank rows in cells C13:C15.

FIGURE 15-9
Using VLOOKUP

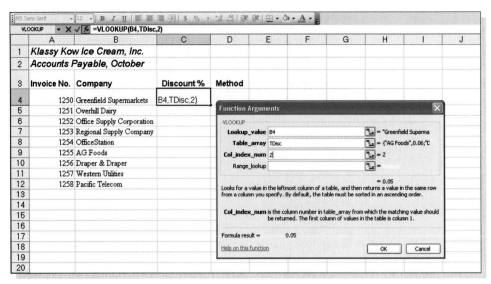

19. Format the results as percent with two decimals and 12-point Times New Roman.

20. In cell A13, key **1259**.

21. In cell B13, key **ov** and press ⟨Enter⟩ to accept the AutoComplete suggestion. The formula looks up the company name in the TDisc table and displays the appropriate discount.

EXERCISE 15-14 Use HLOOKUP

Depending on the discount, Klassy Kow pays by check, credit card, or electronic funds transfer. You will use HLOOKUP to determine the payment method. The HLOOKUP function is similar to VLOOKUP, but the lookup table is arranged in rows. You should name the table as a range.

1. Click the PayMethod sheet tab. This is a horizontal lookup table.

2. Select the range A2:E3. Click the Name Box, key **TPay**, and press ⟨Enter⟩.

3. On the Accounts sheet, select cell D4. You'll use the HLOOKUP function in this cell to look up the discount rate in the TPay table and display the payment method.

4. Click the Insert Function button 𝑓ₓ. In the Lookup & Reference category, choose HLOOKUP and click OK.

5. Make sure the insertion point is located in the Lookup_value text box. The Lookup_value is the label or value to be checked.

6. Click C4. Excel will look up the discount shown in cell C4.

7. Click in the Table_array box. This is the lookup table with the payment methods.

8. Key **TPay**.

9. Click in the Row_index_num text box. The Row_index_num identifies which row in the TPay lookup table contains the payment method.

10. Key 2. The payment methods are in row 2 of the lookup table.

11. Leave the Range_lookup text box empty so that Excel will look for approximate matches. When no exact match to the lookup value is found, Excel displays the largest value that is less than the lookup value.

12. Click OK. A 5% discount is paid by credit.

13. Copy the formula to the range D5:D15.

14. Format the results as 12-point Times New Roman and adjust the column width as necessary.

> **NOTE:** Invoice #1252 has a 4.5% discount, but that value is not in the lookup table. Because the Range_lookup text box was left empty, Excel uses the largest value in the lookup table (4%, Write check) that is less than 4.5%.

15. In the Discounts worksheet, change the Greenfield discount to **3%**.

16. Return to the Accounts worksheet. The HLOOKUP function now shows #N/A for that company, because there is no value in the lookup table that is less than 3%. If the lookup value (cell C4) is less than the smallest value in the first row of TPay, the function shows #N/A.

EXERCISE 15-15 Create and Remove a Circular Reference

A *circular reference* is a cell address in a formula that refers to the formula's location. Formulas with circular references display an error message. Create an IF function that shows "Less than 5%" or "Greater than 5%" in column C.

1. Click the Discounts sheet tab and select cell C2.

2. Click the Insert Function button ⨍. Choose the Logical category, choose IF, and then click OK.

3. Click cell C2 to set the Logical_test argument. Notice that this is the same cell in which you are entering the function. This will be a circular reference.

4. Key <=5% after C2 to check if the discount is less than or equal to 5%.

5. Click in the Value_if_true text box and key **Less than 5%**.

6. Click in the Value_if_false text box and key **Greater than 5%**.

7. Click OK. The circular reference message box alerts you that there is a problem.

FIGURE 15-10
Message box about
a circular reference

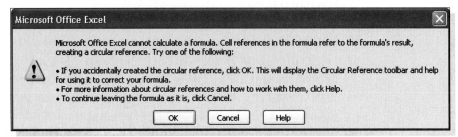

8. Click OK in the message box. Excel opens a Help screen.

9. Read the information and close the Help screen. The Circular Reference toolbar is open, and the status bar shows the location of the error.

FIGURE 15-11
Circular reference
in the worksheet

	A	B	C	D	E	F
	C2 ▼ fx =IF(C2<=5%,"Less than 5%","Greater than 5%")					
1	**Lookup Table for Discounts**					
2	AG Foods	6.00%	0			
3	Draper & Draper	5.75%				
4	Greenfield Supermarkets	3.00%	Circular Reference ▼ ×			
5	Office Supply Corporation	4.50%	$C$2 ▼			
6	OfficeStation	7.00%				
7	Overhill Dairy	7.00%				
8	Pacific Telecom	6.25%				
9	Regional Supply Company	8.00%				
10	Western Utilities	5.50%				
11						
12						
13						
14						
15						
16						
17						
18						
19						
20						
21						
22						
23						
24						

Accounts \ **Discounts** / PayMethod /

Draw ▼ AutoShapes ▼ \ \ □ ○ 🔲 🔺 ⬡ 🔳 🔳 🔳 ▼ 🖉 ▼ A ▼ ≡ ≡ ⇄ ◻ ◻

Ready   Circular: C2

10. Click the formula bar to edit the reference. Change the reference from C2 to **b2**.

11. Press (Enter). The toolbar closes, and the result is displayed.

12. Format cell C2 as 12-point Times New Roman.

13. Copy the formula to cells C3:C10.

EXERCISE   **15-16** **Increase the Indent**

You've already learned how to use the Format Cells dialog box to indent values or labels from the left edge of the cell. You can also use the Increase Indent button 🔳 on the Formatting toolbar to add a 1-space left indent to the cell.

1. Select the range C2:C10.

2. Click the Increase Indent button 🔳 on the Formatting toolbar. The labels are indented 1 space from the left edge of the cell.

3. Adjust the width of column C to accommodate the data.

Using Reference Functions

Reference functions obtain and display information from various sources, including the active workbook and other workbooks. They do this by matching values, counting rows or columns, showing cell addresses, and more.

EXERCISE   **15-17** **Create a HYPERLINK Function**

The HYPERLINK function creates a shortcut to a document on your computer, a location on the Internet, or a location on your local network. To complete the arguments for this function, you must know the complete path to the document or location that you want to use, including filename extensions.

In this exercise, you'll use the HYPERLINK function to create a shortcut to the file you saved at the end of Exercise 15-12.

1. Select cell F1 on the Accounts sheet.

2. Click the Insert Function button 𝑓ₓ.

3. Find and choose HYPERLINK in the Lookup & Reference category, and then click OK.

4. In the Link_location text box, key *[your initials]***15-12.xls**, preceding the filename with the complete drive and path.

NOTE: If your Lesson 15 folder is on the C drive, your path might be C:\lesson15\[your initials]15-12.xls. Ask your instructor for assistance if you are unsure of the drive and path of your file.

5. In the Friendly_name box, key **Expense Workbook**. This is the link name that will appear in cell F1.

FIGURE 15-12
Using HYPERLINK

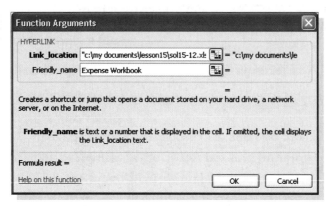

6. Click OK. A hyperlink is inserted in the cell and shows the friendly name.

7. Click cell F1. The June Expense Report workbook that you saved in Exercise 15-12 is opened and active. The Web toolbar also opens.

 NOTE: If an error message says the file cannot be opened, right-click the cell and click the Insert Function button 🔎. Check and edit the pathname.

8. Close the June Expense Report workbook without saving.

9. Right-click any toolbar and choose Web to hide the Web toolbar.

EXERCISE **15-18** Use the ROWS and INDEX Functions

The ROWS function is a reference function that displays the number of rows in a range or in an array. An *array* is a collection of cells that is used as a group. An array might be a single range of cells, but it can also be a group of ranges. You could use the ROWS function to count the number of invoices or the number of employees in a workbook.

The INDEX function displays the value or label of the cell at the intersection of a particular row and column. You could use this function to display a name or value from another worksheet in the same workbook.

1. On the Discounts worksheet, select cell A13.

2. Click the Insert Function button 🔎. Find and choose ROWS in the Lookup & Reference category, and then click OK. There is one argument, Array.

3. Press F3 to display the Paste Name dialog box. Choose TDisc and click OK to enter the range name in the Array text box.

4. Click OK. The formula shows that there are nine rows in the table.

5. On the Accounts sheet, select cell A17 and key **Discounts greater than 7%**.

6. Select cell A18. Click the Insert Function button .

7. Find and choose INDEX in the Lookup & Reference category and click OK. The Select Arguments dialog box opens. There are two ways to use the INDEX function; each has a different argument list.

8. Choose reference, row_num, column_num, area_num in the Arguments text box. Click OK.

FIGURE 15-13
Choosing
arguments for
INDEX

9. In the Reference text box, key **tpay**. This is your horizontal lookup table.

10. In the Row_num text box, key **2** to display data from the second row of the TPay table.

11. In the Column_num text box, key **4** to display data from the fourth column of the TPay table. Leave Area_num blank.

12. Click OK. The formula returns the payment method in column D in the second row of the TPay table range.

> **NOTE:** There is a COLUMNS function that performs a similar task with columns.

EXERCISE 15-19 Use TRANSPOSE in an Array Formula

The TRANSPOSE function displays row data in a column or vice versa. It is a quick way to change the orientation of a horizontal table to vertical.

Array formulas are similar to regular formulas but perform multiple calculations on one or more sets of values, returning either a single result or multiple results. Array formulas calculate entire ranges at once.

To create an array formula, press Ctrl + Shift + Enter after the arguments are completed. An array formula appears with curly braces {} in the formula bar.

1. Click the PayMethod sheet tab. The TPay range has five columns and two rows. In a vertical layout, this requires two columns and five rows.

2. Select the range A5:B9. This the same number of cells as the TPay range.

3. Click the Insert Function button .

4. Find and choose TRANSPOSE in the Lookup & Reference category, and then click OK.

5. In the Array text box, key **tpay**.

6. Press Ctrl + Shift + Enter. The rows are converted to column format. Format the values in column A as percents with no decimals.

7. Click any cell in the range to see the array formula in curly braces in the formula bar.

8. Group the worksheets. Use File and Page Setup to add your usual footer to the sheets but change the font size in each section to 10-point. Set landscape orientation.

9. Save the workbook as *[your initials]***15-19** in your Lesson 15 folder. Print the grouped sheets.

 REVIEW: Right-click one of the sheets in the group and choose Move or Copy to create copies for formula display.

10. Make a copy of the grouped sheets. You will see message boxes about the range names already existing in the worksheets. Click Yes to preserve the names.

FIGURE 15-14
Message box
about duplicate
range names

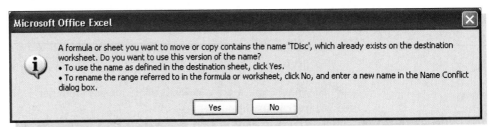

11. Ungroup the sheets. On each of the copies, display the formulas and use AutoFit for the columns. Print each sheet so that it fits to one page.

12. Choose File and Properties. As the Title, key **Lookup and Reference Functions**.

13. Key your name as the author and your school or company name as the company.

14. Save and close the workbook.

USING ONLINE HELP

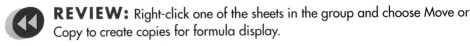

You can create named ranges that span more than one sheet. For example, a workbook with four quarters of financial results each on separate worksheets might have a range named "GrossRevenues" on each sheet.

Use Help to learn how to name ranges in more than one worksheet.

1. With Internet Explorer and Excel running, find topics about naming ranges. Look for a subtopic about naming ranges in more than one sheet.

2. Read the information. Close the windows.

3. Close Internet Explorer and end your Internet connection.

LESSON 15 Summary

➤ Range names must begin with a letter, cannot use spaces or special characters, and should be short and descriptive.

➤ Use range names rather than cell addresses for navigation and in formulas. In a formula, key the range name or display a list of available names and choose the name.

➤ A constant is a value that does not change. You can name a constant with a range name and use that name in a formula rather than keying the value.

➤ Range names can be deleted, changed, or redefined. Ctrl+F3 displays the Define Name dialog box.

➤ You can paste a table of range names and references on the worksheet.

➤ Insert the current date as a value by pressing Ctrl+;.

➤ You can suppress the printing of errors by using the Page Setup dialog box.

➤ A circular reference is a cell address in a formula that refers to itself. Excel displays circular references as errors.

➤ Lookup functions display data from a table by scanning the table's columns or rows to look up or find that data. There are two lookup functions, VLOOKUP and HLOOKUP.

➤ Use the Increase Indent button 🔢 on the Formatting toolbar to add a 1-space left indent to a cell.

➤ The HYPERLINK function creates a shortcut to another document or Web page.

➤ An array is a collection of cells used as a group. Use the ROWS function to display the number of rows in an array. Use the INDEX function to display a cell's value at the intersection of a particular row and column.

➤ Use the TRANSPOSE function to display row data in columns or vice versa.

➤ Array formulas perform multiple calculations on one or more sets of values. Press Ctrl+Shift+Enter to create an array formula.

LESSON 15 Command Summary

FEATURE	BUTTON	MENU	KEYBOARD
Name Range		Insert, Name, Define	Ctrl+F3
Go to Range		Edit, Go To	F5 or Ctrl+G
Today's date			Ctrl+;
Paste Names		Insert, Name, Paste	F3

Concepts Review

TRUE/FALSE QUESTIONS

Each of the following statements is either true or false. Indicate your choice by circling T or F.

T F   **1.** A range name can use some special characters, including * and ?.

T F   **2.** Range names can be keyed or pasted in formulas.

T F   **3.** A constant is a value that does not change.

T F   **4.** The Paste List command creates a new worksheet for the range names.

T F   **5.** You can print a worksheet with or without formula errors such as #NAME? or #N/A.

T F   **6.** When you delete a range name, Excel substitutes cell addresses in formulas.

T F   **7.** Lookup functions are categorized with the Database functions.

T F   **8.** A circular reference repeats a formula across the range.

SHORT ANSWER QUESTIONS

Write the correct answer in the space provided.

1. What is the box next to the formula bar that you use to go to a named range?

_____

2. What keyboard shortcut displays the Paste Name dialog box?

_____

3. Which function creates a shortcut to an Internet address or another document on your computer?

_____

4. Which range name is acceptable: 1stQtr, FirstQtr, Qtr 1?

_____

5. What term describes a value that does not change in formulas?

_____

6. What term describes a formula that refers to its own location?

_____

7. Which lookup function scans a table by columns?

_____

8. What function lets you display row data in columns?

_____

CRITICAL THINKING

Answer these questions on a separate page. There are no right or wrong answers. Support your answers with examples from your own experience, if possible.

1. Think of a worksheet application you might create for your school or the company where you work. What types of information might be constants? How would these constants be used in formulas?

2. In your school or the company where you work, what lookup tables might be created? How would these lookup tables be used in a workbook?

Skills Review

EXERCISE 15-20

Create named ranges. Use range names for navigation. Use ranges in a formula.

1. Open the file **Products**.

2. Create a named range by following these steps:

    a. Select cell A3 and press `F8`. Press `→` two times. Press `Ctrl` and `↓`.
    b. Click the Name Box and key **Database**. Press `Enter`.

3. Click anywhere in column A within the named range.

4. Click the Sort Ascending button on the Standard toolbar.

5. Select the ranges A15:C15 and A19:C20.

6. Click the Name Box and key **Novelties**. Press `Enter`.

    NOTE: Named ranges need not be contiguous.

7. Select the range C4:C39, click the Name Box, and name the range **Prices**.

8. Use range names for navigation by following these steps:
   a. Press Ctrl+Home.
   b. Click the Name Box arrow and choose Database.
   c. Click the Name Box arrow and choose Novelties.
   d. Press Ctrl+Home.

9. Use a named range in a formula by following these steps:

   a. Select cell F3 and click the Insert Function button fx. Choose AVERAGE in the Statistical category.
   b. With the insertion point in the Number1 text box, press F3 and choose Prices. Click OK.
   c. Select cell F4. Key **=max(prices** and press Enter.
   d. Find the minimum price in cell F5.

10. Format the formula results as currency with two decimals.

11. Add the standard footer with your name, the filename, and the date.

12. Save the workbook as *[your initials]***15-20** in your Lesson 15 folder. Print the sheet.

13. Make a copy of the sheet. Hide columns B and D. Display the formulas and AutoFit the visible columns. Print the formula sheet.

14. Save and close the workbook.

EXERCISE 15-21

Name constants. Modify range names. Use names in a formula. Print range names.

1. Open the file **PriceIncreases**.

2. Name constants by following these steps:

   NOTE: Clicking an empty cell that has an empty cell above it opens the Define Name dialog box with a blank Names in workbook text box.

   a. Select cell D2 and press Ctrl+F3.
   b. In the Names in workbook text box, key **Increase1**.
   c. Place the insertion point in the Refers to text box, delete the existing information, and key **=110%**.
   d. Click Add. (The Define Name dialog box remains open.)

   NOTE: If you accidentally click OK, open the Define Name box again.

   e. In the Names in workbook text box, edit the name to **Increase2**.
   f. In the Refers to text box, edit the value to **=115%**. Click Add.
   g. Add the range name **Increase3** to refer to =120%. Close the Define Name dialog box.

3. Modify range names by following these steps:

    a. Press Ctrl + F3.

    b. Select Database in the list and click Delete.

    c. Choose Shakes in the list. Its reference is shown.

    d. Edit the existing text in the Names in workbook text box to **ShakesMalts**. Click Add.

    NOTE: The Shakes and ShakesMalts ranges are duplicates until you delete one.

    e. Choose Shakes in the list. Click Delete. Click OK.

4. Use range names in a formula by following these steps:

    a. Select cell D4, key **=c4***, and press F3.

    b. Choose Increase1 and click OK. Press Enter.

    c. Select cell E4, key **=c4*increase2**, and press Enter.

    d. Select cell F4, and key a formula to multiply cell C4 by the named range Increase3.

5. Format these results as 12-point Times New Roman.

6. Copy the formulas to the remainder of the products.

7. Add a footer with your name at the left and the filename and tab name in the center. In the Right section click the Page Number button ▣. Press Spacebar and key **of** and press Spacebar. Click the Total Pages button ▣. Set the worksheet orientation to landscape.

8. Save the workbook as *[your initials]***15-21** in your Lesson 15 folder.

9. Use File and Page Setup to set rows 1:3 to repeat on each printed page. Print the worksheet.

10. Insert a new worksheet, position it after the Products sheet, and name it **Documentation**.

11. In cell A1, key **Product List**. In cell A2, key *[your first and last name]*. In cell A3, press Ctrl + ; to insert today's date. Make the labels bold.

12. In cell B4, key **Name**. In cell C4, key **Range**. Make these labels bold.

13. Print range names by following these steps:

    a. Select cell B5 and press F3.

    b. Click Paste List. Widen the columns to show the data.

    c. Print the sheet.

14. Save and close the workbook.

EXERCISE 15-22

Use lookup functions. Print range names.

1. Open the file **TastersPay**.

2. Rename Sheet2 **BonusAmt**. Rename Sheet3 **Group**.

3. In the BonusAmt worksheet, select cell A1 and key **Rate**. In cell B1, key **Bonus**. Make the labels bold.

4. Starting in cell A2, key the information shown in Figure 15-15.

FIGURE 15-15

	A	B
2	18	300
3	15	225
4	16.75	250
5	13.75	150

5. Use VLOOKUP by following these steps:

   a. Select the range A2:B5 and click the Sort Ascending button .
   b. With the range still selected, click the Name Box and key **TBonus**. Press (Enter).
   c. Select cell D4 on the Tasters worksheet. Click the Insert Function button 𝑓ₓ, choose VLOOKUP from the Lookup & Reference category, and click OK.
   d. With the insertion point in the Lookup_value text box, select cell C4 in the worksheet. The function will look for this pay rate in the table to determine the bonus.
   e. Click in the Table_array text box. Press (F3) and double-click TBonus.
   f. In the Col_index_num text box, key **2** and click OK.

6. Copy the formula to the range D5:D13. Format the results as currency with two decimal places.

7. Use HLOOKUP by following these steps:

   a. Select cell A1 in the Group worksheet and key **Group Assignment**. Make it bold.
   b. Key the information shown in Figure 15-16, starting in cell A2.

FIGURE 15-16

	A	B	C	D
2	$13.00	$15.00	$16.75	$18.00
3	Group D	Group C	Group B	Group A

c. Select the range A2:D3, click the Name Box, and key **TAssign**. Press Enter.

   d. Select cell E4 on the Tasters worksheet. Click the Insert Function button fx. Choose HLOOKUP from the Lookup & Reference category and click OK.

   e. Place the insertion point in the Lookup_value text box and select cell C4 in the worksheet.

   f. Place the insertion point in the Table_array text box. Press F3 and double-click TAssign.

   g. In the Row_index_num text box, key **2** and click OK.

  8. Copy the formula to the range E5:E13. With the range E4:E13 selected, click the Increase Indent button on the Formatting toolbar.

  9. Print range names by following these steps:

   a. Select cell A15.

   b. Press F3 and choose Paste List.

 10. Add your usual footer.

 11. Save the workbook as *[your initials]***15-22** in your Lesson 15 folder. Print the Tasters worksheet.

 12. Make a copy of the Tasters worksheet and display the formulas. AutoFit the columns. Print the worksheet in landscape orientation, fit to one page.

 13. Close and save the workbook.

EXERCISE 15-23

Use a reference function.

  1. Create a new workbook. Right-click any toolbar and choose Drawing to turn on the Drawing toolbar.

  2. Click the Insert WordArt button on the Drawing toolbar. Choose the fourth style in the fourth row and click OK. Key **Klassy Kow Ice Cream**. Press Enter and key **Product List and Prices**. Click OK.

  3. Use a reference function by following these steps:

   a. Select cell A1 and click the Insert Function button fx. Choose HYPERLINK from the Lookup & Reference category, and click OK.

   b. In the Link_location text box, key **Products.xls**, preceding the filename with the complete drive and path.

> **NOTE:** Ask your instructor for assistance if you are unsure of the drive and path of the file.

   c. In the Friendly_name text box, key **Click here to see list**. Click OK.

  4. Change the font size of cell A1 to 16-point and test the hyperlink. If you see a message warning you about hyperlinks from unknown sources, click Yes. Close the **Products** workbook.

5. Add your footer. Position the WordArt object so that the worksheet will print on one portrait page.

6. Save the workbook as *[your initials]***15-23** in your Lesson 15 folder and print the worksheet.

7. Save the worksheet as a Web page with the title **Product and Price List**. Do not use Single Web page as the Save as type.

8. Preview the page in your browser. Close the browser. Close the workbook. Hide the Web toolbar.

Lesson Applications

Name ranges. Suppress error messages. Use lookup functions.

Klassy Kow keeps a list of customer accounts and their invoices. When a customer number is entered, Excel looks up the customer's name so that it need not be keyed. You need to create the lookup formula and complete the worksheet.

1. Open the file **CustAccts**.

2. In cell A2 in the Accounts worksheet, key **=now( )** and press Enter. Format the date with a Custom format to show the date as three characters for the month, two digits for the date, no comma, and four digits for the year. Widen the column if necessary.

3. Select the range A4:F15 and format it as 12-point Times New Roman.

4. Key a formula in cell F4 to add the late fee and the amount. Copy the formula to the range F5:F15.

5. In the CustTable worksheet, select the customer lookup table and name the range **TCust**.

6. Select cell B6 in the Accounts worksheet and insert a VLOOKUP function that will display the company name based on the customer number in column A. Since the data is incomplete, the result is an error message. Copy the formula to the range B7:B15.

7. Key the information shown in Figure 15-17, starting in cell A6. Press Tab for the company name and key the current date by pressing Ctrl+; as indicated. Format as necessary.

FIGURE 15-17

Customer No.	Company Name	Invoice Date	Amount	Late Fee
1018		Ctrl+;	$500	$25
1020		Ctrl+;	$1000	$55
1019		Ctrl+;	$1500	$75
1014		Ctrl+;	$2500	$85

8. Set a print area to exclude the rows with #N/A. Increase the indent four times for the customer numbers.

9. Add your footer. Save the workbook as *[your initials]*15-24 in your Lesson 15 folder. Print the Accounts sheet.

10. Make a copy of the Accounts sheet and display the formulas. Fit the columns and print the sheet fit to one landscape page.

11. Close and save the workbook.

EXERCISE 15-25

Name a range. Use a range in a formula. Print range names.

The COUNTIF function counts cells in a range if they match your specifications. You can determine how many products are priced under certain levels by using COUNTIF and a range name.

1. Open the file **PriceGroups**.

2. Select the product, size, and price rows, including the column labels. Name the range **Database**. Select cells C4:C39 and name it **Prices**.

3. Select cell F4 and use the Insert Function button to insert COUNTIF from the Statistical category. Specify the Range as **Prices**. Specify the Criteria as **<1** to count prices that are less than $1. Format the result as 12-point Times New Roman.

4. Copy the formula to the range F5:F7. Edit each formula so that the price criteria are correct. For example, use **<5** to find prices less than $5.

5. Select cell E9 and key **Number of Products**. Format it as bold italic.

6. Use COUNT in cell F9 to count the total number of products; use **Prices** for Value1. Format the result to match the values in column F.

7. Paste a list of range names starting in cell A41.

8. Add your footer. Fit the worksheet to one page in portrait orientation.

9. Save the workbook as *[your initials]*15-25 in your Lesson 15 folder and print the worksheet.

10. Copy the sheet and show the formulas. Print the formula sheet in landscape orientation, fit to one page.

11. Edit the file properties to show your name as the author and an appropriate title for this workbook.

12. Close and save the workbook.

EXERCISE 15-26

Name a range. Use VLOOKUP.

A lookup table can have more than one column. This exercise has a lookup table that shows a description and a category for each account number.

1. Open the file **Journal**.
2. In the Table worksheet, name the lookup table **TAccounts**. Notice that there are two columns that can be searched, columns B and C (2 and 3).

 TIP: Do not include the column labels when naming a lookup table range.

3. In the Journal worksheet, select cell B4 and use a VLOOKUP formula that looks up the account number and shows the related description. Select cell C4 and use another VLOOKUP formula that looks up the same account number but shows the related category.
4. Copy both formulas down to row 15.
5. Key the information shown in Figure 15-18, starting in cell A7.

FIGURE 15-18

Account #	Description	Category	Amount
101			5000
202			1200
101			8000
103			12000
202			4300
303			1000

6. Insert the picture file **KowOwow.tif** so that its top-left edge starts in cell E1.
7. Set a print area to exclude the rows that display #N/A but do include the image. Increase the indent three times for the account numbers.
8. Save the workbook as *[your initials]*15-26 in your Lesson 15 folder.
9. Add your footer and print the worksheet.
10. Make a copy of the sheet and create a formula printout. Delete the image and print the formulas landscape and fit to one page.
11. Save and close the workbook.

EXERCISE 15-27 *Challenge Yourself*

Use a reference function.

Array formulas are popular in programming. They are similar to regular formulas but are entered by pressing Ctrl+Shift+Enter. As you learned in this lesson, the TRANSPOSE function is entered as an array formula.

1. Create a new workbook.
2. Key the information shown in Figure 15-19 in the range A1:B9.

FIGURE 15-19

	A	B
1	Sugar Cones	100
2	Waffle Cones	200
3	Sundaes	275
4	Shakes	150
5	Malts	200
6	Sodas	125
7	Kowabungas	250
8	KowOwows	175
9	Sandwiches	105

3. Name the range A1:B3 **IceCream**. Name the range A4:B6 **Beverages**. Name the range A7:B9 **Novelties**.
4. On Sheet2, key **Sunday Sales, Klamath Falls** in cell A1. Format it as 18-point Times New Roman.

 TIP: Select the cells for the transposed range. Then start the TRANSPOSE function. Press Ctrl+Shift+Enter to close the Functions Arguments dialog box.

5. Transpose the Beverages range to A2:C3 on Sheet2. Transpose the Novelties range to D2:F3. Transpose the IceCream range to G2:I3.
6. Format row 2 as bold and make it 36 pixels high. Adjust column widths appropriately.

7. Add your footer. Set the worksheet to print in landscape orientation. Rename Sheet2 as **Transposed**.

8. Save the workbook as *[your initials]***15-27** in your Lesson 15 folder and print the Transposed sheet.

9. Create a formula sheet and fit the columns to show the data. Set row 1 to print on each page. Print your formula sheet.

10. Save and close the workbook.

On Your Own

In these exercises you work on your own, as you would in a real-life work environment. Use the skills you've learned to accomplish the task—and be creative.

EXERCISE 15-28
In a new workbook, AutoFill 12 months in column A starting with January. In columns B:F, key labels to describe five expense categories for your personal finances. Insert a row for a main title. Create range names that will allow you to total each expense for the year and to total all expenses each month. Add labels where these totals will be located. Add formulas using the range names. Add your footer. Save the workbook as *[your initials]***15-28** in your Lesson 15 folder. Make a copy of the worksheet to show the formulas. Print the formula sheet fit to one page. Save and close the workbook.

EXERCISE 15-29
Use Excel Help to determine the difference between the ROW and ROWS functions. Create a new workbook that demonstrates the difference, showing your formulas. Use an AutoShape or a callout to describe the function and/or the difference. Add a standard footer. Save the workbook as *[your initials]***15-29** in your Lesson 15 folder and print the worksheet. Save and close the workbook.

EXERCISE 15-30
Open the file **JuneExp** and name the ranges B9:D9, B14:D14, B19:D19, and B24:D24 as **Budgeted**. Name the ranges B10:D10, B15:D15, B20:D20, and B25:D25 as **Actual**. Rename Sheet3 as **Documentation**. In cell A1, key **Information about the Expenses Sheet**. In cell A2, key **Prepared by** *[your first and last name]*. In the range A3:C3, key **Name**, **Range**, and **Areas**. Paste a list of range names in cell A4. Look up the AREAS function and use it in the Areas column to identify how many areas are in each range. Add your footer and save the workbook as *[your initials]***15-30** in your Lesson 15 folder. Create a formula printout of the worksheet.

Creating Worksheet and Workbook Templates

After completing this lesson, you will be able to:

1. **Create a default workbook.**
2. **Create a default worksheet.**
3. **Create a user template.**
4. **Set data validation and conditional formatting.**
5. **Protect a template.**
6. **Create a templates folder.**
7. **Create a workbook template.**
8. **Use workbook protection.**

 Estimated Time: 1½ hours

Although you can use and edit Excel templates, you can create your own template from scratch. A template starts as a regular workbook but is saved in a specially identified folder as a template.

Creating a Default Workbook

When you create a new workbook, it has a default font and a default number of worksheets. It shows gridlines and displays values in a General number format. New workbooks are based on built-in default settings.

You can change these settings so that new workbooks use your design preferences. To do this, you create a template named **Book.xlt** and save it in the XLStart folder. The XLStart folder is a folder that Excel checks each time it starts. The XLStart folder is empty by default. If you save **Book.xlt** in this folder, however, Excel uses it as a template for new workbooks instead of its built-in settings.

E X E R C I S E   **16-1**   **Create a New Default Workbook**

To create a default workbook, start with a new workbook.

1. Open a new workbook. Delete Sheet2 and Sheet3.

2. Click the Select All button to the left of and above the column A and row 1 headings. This selects all cells on the worksheet.

3. Change the font to 12-point Times New Roman. Click cell A1.

 NOTE: When there is nothing on a sheet, you cannot use Print Preview to add the footer. Use the File menu and Page Setup.

4. Create a footer that includes your name, the filename and tab name, and the date.

5. From the File menu, choose Properties.

6. Add your name as the author. Delete all other information.

7. Place a check mark for Save preview picture.

8. Click OK. Your new default workbook is going to include one sheet with the settings you just made.

9. Click the Save button .

10. Change the Save as type to Template. The default folder for templates is shown.

 NOTE: The XLStart folder is usually in C:\Program Files\Microsoft Office\ Office11 or C:\Documents and Settings\UserName\Application Data\ Microsoft\Excel. Check with your instructor.

11. Navigate to the XLStart folder and open it. The Save in folder should be XLStart.

12. Edit the File name to **Book**. (See Figure 16-1 on the next page.)

 REVIEW: If your computer shows filename extensions, the template name will be **Book.xlt**.

13. Click Save.

14. Close the workbook and exit Excel.

FIGURE 16-1
Saving Book.xlt in
the XLStart folder

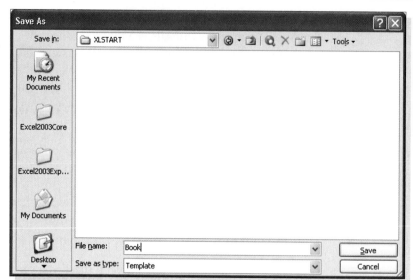

EXERCISE 16-2 Create a New Workbook

If there is a template named **Book.xlt** in the XLStart folder, it is used for new work-books rather than Excel's built-in settings.

1. Start Excel with a new workbook.
2. Note the number of sheets and the default font.
3. Check the file properties.
4. Use File and Page Setup to check the footer.
5. Press (Shift)+(F11) to insert a new sheet.
6. Check the font on Sheet2. It does not use 12-point Times New Roman.
7. Use File and Page Setup to check the footer. Your footer is only on Sheet1.
8. Check the file properties again. These settings pertain to the workbook. Close the dialog box.

Creating a Default Worksheet

The **Book.xlt** file does not include settings for new sheets inserted in a workbook. Excel uses its built-in settings unless you create a file named **Sheet.xlt** and place it in the XLStart folder.

The **Sheet** file should have one worksheet with the font, formatting, and other information that you want on new sheets inserted in a workbook.

EXERCISE **16-3** Size and Crop an Image

If you place an image on the worksheet, it will appear on all new worksheets. It will not appear on the first sheet, however, which is part of your default workbook.

When you size an image on screen using the handles, the Name box shows the scaling percentage as you drag.

1. Delete Sheet2.
2. Click the Insert Picture From File button .
3. In the Look in text box, navigate to the folder with the **Cow.gif** image.
4. Double-click Cow. The image is inserted at a default size.
5. Click the image to select it. A selected object shows eight round white selection handles at the edges.

 NOTE: The Picture toolbar may open when you select the image.

6. Right-click any toolbar and choose Picture to display the Picture toolbar.
7. Drag the toolbar and the image so that both are in the middle of the screen.
8. Place the mouse pointer on the bottom-right handle to display a two-pointed arrow. This is a sizing pointer.
9. Drag down and to the right to make the image about 200 percent of its current size. Watch the Name box for the percentage.

FIGURE 16-2
Sizing an image
on screen

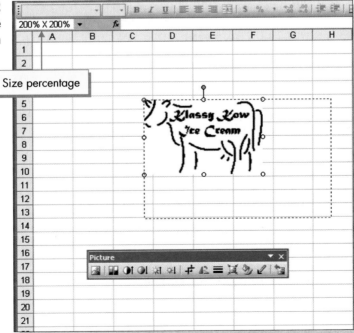

10. Click the Crop button on the Picture toolbar. The handles change shape.

11. Place the mouse pointer on the bottom-right handle. It changes to a corner shape. You will crop everything but the head.

12. Drag up and to the left to crop out the body and leave only the head. Release the mouse button.

FIGURE 16-3
Cropping an image

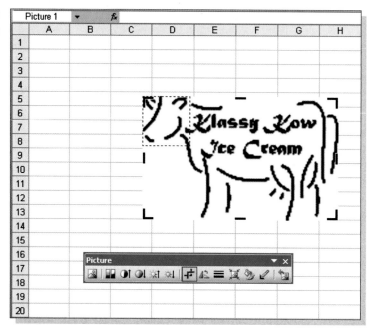

13. Reposition the image so that the top-left corner is at cell A1.

14. Click cell C1. Close the Picture toolbar.

EXERCISE **16-4** **Save a Default Worksheet Template**

This worksheet has the font and footer settings from your Book template. Those settings will be included on new worksheets now, too.

1. Press F12 to open the Save As dialog box.

2. Change the Save as type to Template. Your Templates folder is shown.

3. Navigate to the XLStart folder and open it.

4. Edit the File name to **Sheet**. You may or may not see filename extensions. (See Figure 16-4.)

5. Click Save.

6. Close the workbook and exit Excel.

 NOTE: Exit and restart Excel so that the XLStart folder is read again.

FIGURE 16-4
Saving Sheet.xlt in
the XLStart folder

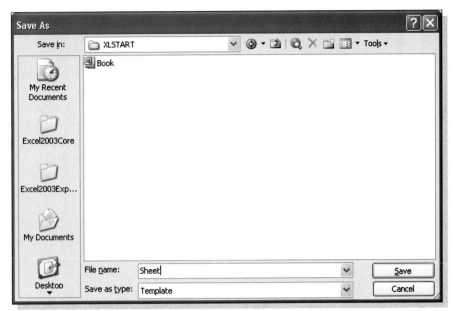

Creating a User Template

A *user template* is one that you create and use for your day-to-day tasks. Templates often include labels, formatting, range names, and formulas. Most templates include everything except the data that changes each time the template is used.

EXERCISE **16-5** **Format and Enter Labels for a Template**

1. Start Excel and a new workbook.
2. Note the number of sheets and the default font. Check the file properties. This workbook is based on Book in the XLStart folder.
3. Press Shift+F11. The new worksheet includes the same settings and the image.
4. On Sheet2, format the range C1:C2 as 18 point.
5. Key **Klassy Kow Ice Cream Shops** in cell C1. In cell C2, key **Advertising Expenses for** and press Spacebar.
6. In cell C4, key **Week 1**. Make it bold and centered.
7. Use the Fill handle to fill to Week 4 in cell F4.
8. Key **Store Total** in cell G4 and match its format to the other labels.
9. Select columns C:G and make the column width 12.14 (90 pixels).
10. Format cell A5 as bold and key **Shop Location**.

EXERCISE **16-6** **Hide Zeros in a Template**

You can hide zero values so that a formula with nothing to calculate shows an empty cell.

1. Select cell G6. This cell will show a sum of the four weeks.

2. Click the AutoSum button ⟨Σ ▾⟩. Because there are no values above or to the left of the cell, AutoSum does not suggest a range.

3. Select the range C6:F6.

4. Press ⟨Enter⟩. A zero may be displayed.

5. Copy the formula through row 20. All the formula cells display zero values if that is how your computer is set.

6. From the Tools menu, choose Options. The Options dialog box opens.

7. Click the View tab.

8. In the Window options group, remove the check mark for Zero values.

9. Click OK. Zero values are hidden. This setting affects the entire worksheet.

 NOTE: If your Error Checking options are set to note formulas referring to empty cells, you will see Trace Error buttons for column G.

10. Select cell G6 to deselect the range.

FIGURE 16-5
Template labels and formatting

	A	B	C	D	E	F	G	H
1			Klassy Kow Ice Cream Shops					
2			Advertising Expenses for					
3								
4			Week 1	Week 2	Week 3	Week 4	Store Total	
5	Shop Location							
6						◇		
7								
8								
9								
10								
11								
12								
13								
14								
15								
16								
17								
18								
19								
20								
21								
22								

Setting Data Validation and Conditional Formatting

Data validation is a process by which Excel checks the value or label in a cell to make sure it matches conditions that have been set. For example, you can set data validation for a range of cells so that values are between 5 and 15. If you key **16,** you will see an error message.

When you set data validation, you can include a message that explains what should be done to correct the error. You can also decide whether to allow the error but give a warning.

Conditional formatting is a cell format applied only when the cell or range meets specified conditions. For example, you might set conditional formatting for values over 1000 to be shown in a different color.

E X E R C I S E   **16-7**   **Create Data Validation Settings**

1. Select the range C6:F20. These are cells in which advertising amounts will be keyed.

2. From the Data menu, choose Validation. The Data Validation dialog box opens.

3. Click the Settings tab. Click the down arrow with the Allow text box.

4. Choose Whole number. This criterion specifies that only whole numbers can be keyed. You will not be able to key a decimal or fraction. Additional options for specifying the range of values appear.

5. Click the down arrow next to the Data text box. These operators allow you to specify a range for keyed values.

6. Choose greater than from the drop-down menu.

7. In the Minimum box, key **25.** This criterion sets a minimum expense of 25 that can be keyed in the range of cells. (See Figure 16-6 on the next page.)

FIGURE 16-6
Data validation
settings

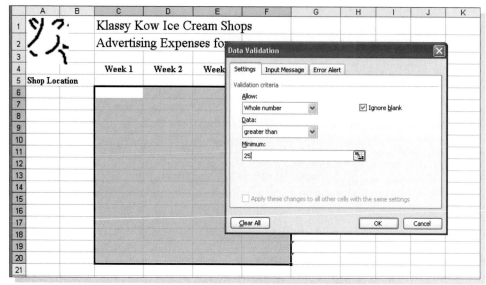

EXERCISE | **16-8** | **Set Error Messages for Data Validation**

Excel displays an error message if an entry violates your settings. You can determine what the message says.

1. Click the Error Alert tab.
2. Click the down arrow next to the Style text box. The menu shows three error alerts for message boxes.
3. Choose Warning. This Style displays an exclamation point in a yellow triangle. It will show a message but allow the entry to be made.
4. In the Title text box, key **Minimum Advertising Required** and press Tab to move to the next text box.
5. In the Error message text box, key **Each shop must spend a minimum of $25 per week on local advertising.** (See Figure 16-7.)
6. Click OK. The data validation settings and the error alert are applied to the range C6:F20.

FIGURE 16-7
Data validation
error alert

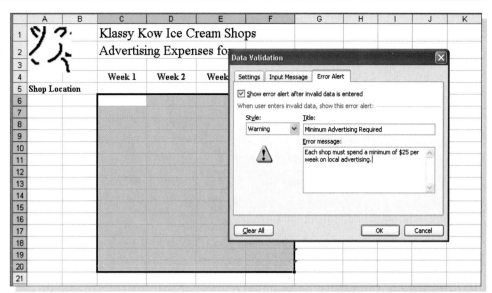

EXERCISE **16-9** **Create an Input Message for Data Validation**

You can have Excel display an input message as soon as the pointer enters the cell. It guides the user's input before any entry is made.

1. Select the range C6:F6. You will show an input message only in the first row of amounts.
2. From the Data menu, choose Validation.
3. Click the Input Message tab.
4. In the Title text box, key **Minimum Amount**.
5. In the Input message text box, key **Each week, each shop must spend a minimum of $25 on local advertising.**
6. Click OK. The input message is displayed because the range is selected.
7. Click cell C6. Your input message appears.
8. Key **35** and press Tab. This entry meets the data validation setting, because it is greater than 25.
9. Key **20** and press Tab. You have violated the data validation setting, but your error alert choices will allow you to continue.
10. Click Yes. The value is entered into the cell.
11. Press Ctrl + Home.

 TIP: You can override a data validation setting by copying data and pasting it in the cell with data validation.

E X E R C I S E 16-10 Use Go To Special

You can verify which cells have data validation with the Go To Special command. Note that you can see the actual data validation settings only by opening the Data Validation dialog box.

1. Select cell C6. This cell has data validation, the error alert, and the input message.
2. Press Ctrl+G. The Go To dialog box opens.
3. Click Special. The Go To Special dialog box opens.
4. Select Data validation.
5. Select Same. All cells with the same validation settings as cell C6 will be highlighted.
6. Click OK. The range C6:F6 is selected.
7. Select cell C7. This cell has data validation and the error alert, but no input message.
8. Press Ctrl+G. Click Special. Select Data validation and Same.
9. Click OK. The range C7:F20 is selected.

E X E R C I S E 16-11 Add Conditional Formatting

Conditional formatting can include font, color, size, and style. Because your data validation warning will allow an entry larger than 25, you can apply conditional formatting to highlight cells that violate your data validation settings.

1. Select the range C6:F20.
2. From the Format menu, choose Conditional Formatting. The Conditional Formatting dialog box opens.
3. In the Condition 1 text box, choose Cell Value Is.
4. Click the down arrow next to between and choose less than.
5. Place the insertion point in the rightmost text box and key **25**. Your condition states that if the cell value is less than 25, conditional formatting will be applied. Next, you'll define the formatting to be applied when the condition has been met.
6. Click Format. The Format Cells dialog box opens.
7. Click the Font tab. Click the down arrow next to the Color list box and choose red, the first color in the third row of the palette.
8. Click OK. The preview shows your conditional formatting. (See Figure 16-8.)

FIGURE 16-8
Setting conditional
formats

9. Click OK. Conditional formatting is now applied to the selected range.

10. Click any cell to deselect the range. The value in cell C7 is shown in red because it is less than 25.

11. Delete the contents of the range C6:F6.

EXERCISE 16-12 **Add a Comment and Formatting**

1. Right-click cell C2. Choose Insert Comment.

2. Delete the user name and key **Press F2 to edit this cell. Key the month and press Enter.**

3. Select the range C6:G20.

 REVIEW: Use the Format Cells dialog box to apply formats when there are no visible values to check.

4. Format the range as Accounting with a dollar sign and no decimals.

Protecting a Template

After all your work to create the template, you can ensure that others using it do not accidentally delete formulas, move pictures, or make changes. You can lock cells so that they cannot be edited. You can lock images so that they cannot be selected.

EXERCISE 16-13 **Set the Locked Property**

When a cell or image is locked, it cannot be changed if the worksheet is protected. The Locked property and the Protection command work together.

1. Right-click the picture and choose Format Picture.

2. Click the Protection tab. Notice that Locked has a check mark. When worksheet protection is activated, you will not be able to edit the image.

3. Read the information in the dialog box about protection.

4. Click OK.

5. Select the range A6:F20.

6. Press (Ctrl) and click cell C2. All of these cells should not be locked, because you will key shop names, amounts, and the date.

7. Right-click one of the selected cells and choose Format Cells.

8. Click the Protection tab. Remove the check mark for Locked.

FIGURE 16-9
Changing the
Locked property

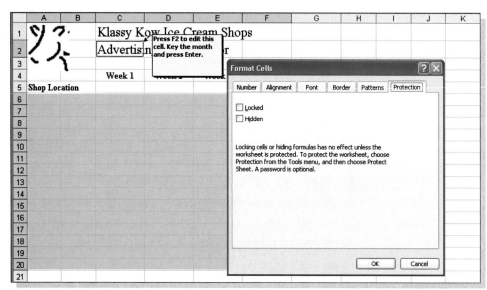

9. Click OK.

EXERCISE **16-14** **Activate Protection with a Password**

When setting worksheet protection, you can assign a password. Then you must key the password before you can change the Protection setting.

1. Press (Ctrl)+(Home). In a template, comments may display at all times.

2. From the View menu, choose Comments. The red triangle indicator is visible and the comment is hidden.

3. From the Tools menu, choose Protection and then Protect Sheet. The Protect Sheet dialog box opens.

4. Make sure Select locked cells and Select unlocked cells are selected. This allows the user to select any cell on the sheet.

5. Select Format rows. This allows the user to change row heights.

6. In the Password to unprotect sheet text box, key **123**. Passwords are optional.

FIGURE 16-10
Protect Sheet
dialog box

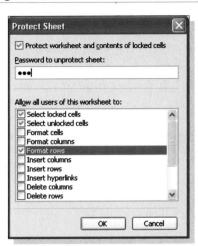

7. Click OK. The Confirm Password dialog box opens. You must re-key your password to make sure you keyed it correctly the first time.

8. Key **123** to confirm your password. Click OK.

9. Click cell G6 and press (Delete). You cannot delete the formula, because this cell is locked and protected.

10. Click OK.

11. Try to select the picture. The image is protected and locked.

12. Select cell C6 and key **100**. Press (Tab). This cell is unlocked, so your entry is allowed.

13. Delete the contents of cell C6.

14. Click cell A6.

15. Rename Sheet2 **AdvExpense**.

 TIP: Position the insertion point where you would like it to be when a new workbook is opened.

Creating a Templates Folder

Templates are listed in the Templates dialog box on either the General tab or the Spreadsheet Solutions tab. Usually, the General tab shows templates that are in C:\Documents and Settings\[User]\Application Data\Microsoft\Templates. *User* is the user name for your computer. If you create a new folder within this folder, it appears in the Templates dialog box as a third tab.

 NOTE: The folder for Spreadsheet Solutions templates is usually C:\Program Files\Microsoft Office\Templates\1033.

EXERCISE **16-15** **Create a Templates Folder**

1. Press (F12).

2. Change the Save as type setting to Template. The default Templates folder is opened.

 3. Click the Create New Folder button . You will create a folder within the Templates folder.

4. Key **MyTemplates** and click OK. The new folder is opened.

5. In the File name box, key *[your initials]***16-15**.

6. Click Save. The workbook is saved as a template.

7. Close the workbook.

8. Open the New Workbook task pane. Click On my computer. Your new folder appears as a tab.

FIGURE 16-11
New tab in
Templates
dialog box

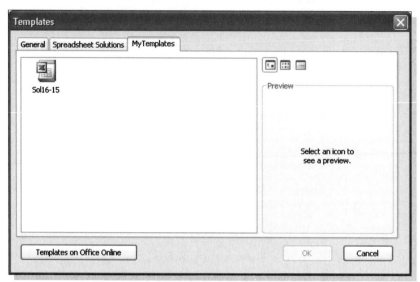

9. Click the MyTemplates tab.

10. Double-click the file *[your initials]***16-15**. A copy of the template opens named with the template filename followed by a number.

EXERCISE 16-16 Create a Workbook from a Template

1. Select cell C2 and edit its contents according to the instructions in the comment.

 NOTE: Values greater than 25 are acceptable, but values 25 or less than 25 are noted. Accept the error.

2. Key the information in Figure 16-12 in the range A6:F10.

3. Save the workbook as *[your initials]***16-16** in a new folder for Lesson 16.

4. Print the worksheet and close the workbook.

FIGURE 16-12

Shop	Week 1	Week 2	Week 3	Week 4
Ashland	27	32	35	28
Eugene	25	20	24	32
Klamath Falls	45	55	50	34
Medford	50	35	37	48

EXERCISE 16-17 Remove Protection and the Password

If you've applied protection and a password to the template, you need to remove the protection and password before you can make changes.

1. Click the Open button 📂.
2. Open the folder where the templates are stored and then your new templates folder.
3. Select the file *[your initials]*16-15 and click Open. This is the original template file, not a copy.
4. From the Tools menu, choose Protection and Unprotect Sheet. The Unprotect Sheet dialog box opens, prompting you to key the password for the file.
5. In the Password text box, key **123**. Click OK. Protection for this workbook is turned off.
6. Select the image. It is no longer locked because protection is off.
7. Delete the formula in cell G6. It is no longer protected.
8. Close the template without resaving.
9. Choose File, New from the menu to open the New Workbook task pane. Click On my computer. Click the MyTemplates tab. Delete the file *[your initials]*16-15.xlt and then click Cancel.

NOTE: Make sure you complete the last step of this exercise. Template files remain on the computer until they are deleted.

Creating a Workbook Template

A workbook template has multiple predesigned worksheets. You create and save a workbook template the same way you create an individual worksheet template.

EXERCISE 16-18 Create a Workbook Template

In this exercise, you'll create a workbook template with four worksheets—one for each of the four states in which Klassy Kow has stores.

1. Create a new workbook and insert four worksheets. Delete Sheet1.

2. Rename the worksheets with these names: **California**, **Oregon**, **Nevada**, and **Washington**.

3. Group all four worksheets.

4. Format cells C1:C2 as 16-point Arial.

5. Key **Klassy Kow Ice Cream Shops** in cell C1.

6. In cell C2, key **Monthly Sales for** and press (Spacebar). You will fill in the state later.

7. In cell C4, key **Week 1**. Make it bold and centered.

8. Use the Fill handle to fill to Week 4 in cell F4.

9. Key **Store Total** in cell G4 and make it bold and centered.

10. Set the width for columns C:G to 12.14 (90 pixels) and column A to 20.71 (150 pixels). Delete column B. Set the height for row 5 to 22.50 (30 pixels).

11. Key **Shop** in cell A5 and make it bold.

12. Ungroup the worksheets.

13. In the California worksheet, edit the label in cell B2 to show **Monthly Sales for California**.

14. Repeat the previous step for each of the other worksheets.

15. Group the worksheets.

16. From the File menu, choose Page Setup. Click the Page tab and choose Landscape.

17. Click the Header/Footer tab. The footer is part of the default worksheet. Close the dialog box.

18. Ungroup the worksheets. Click the California tab.

Using Workbook Protection

You can apply both worksheet and workbook protection to a workbook. Workbook protection can prevent the workbook window from being sized and moved. You can also prevent adding, deleting, renaming, moving, or hiding worksheets.

EXERCISE **Set Properties and Add Protection**

1. Click cell A6.
2. From the File menu, choose Properties. Click the Summary tab.
3. Change the title to **Monthly Sales**. Your name should be the author, because you set that in your default workbook.
4. Change the company to *[your school or company name]*.
5. Verify that there is a check mark for Save preview picture and click OK.

 TIP: You cannot change the properties if the workbook is protected.

6. From the Tools menu, choose Protection, Protect Workbook. The Protect Workbook dialog box opens. The Structure option refers to deleting, moving, hiding, inserting, or renaming worksheets. The Windows option applies to resizing, moving, or closing windows.
7. Select both Structure and Windows. Do not use a password.

FIGURE 16-13
Protect Workbook
dialog box

8. Click OK.
9. Click the Save button 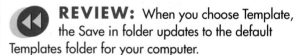. The Save As dialog box opens. In the File name text box, key *[your initials]***16-19**.
10. For Save as type, choose Template.

REVIEW: When you choose Template, the Save in folder updates to the default Templates folder for your computer.

11. Double-click the MyTemplates folder and click Save.
12. Print the entire workbook.
13. From the File menu, choose Close.

  NOTE: There is no Close Window button ☒ for a protected workbook.

EXERCISE **16-20** **Test a Workbook Template**

1. Open the New Workbook task pane. Click On my computer. Click the MyTemplates tab.
2. Select the file *[your initials]***16-19** and click OK.
3. Press Shift+F11. Nothing happens.

4. Choose Insert from the menu. Worksheet is unavailable. You cannot insert or delete worksheets in a protected workbook.

5. Try to maximize the window. There are no sizing buttons. Workbook protection prevents you from maximizing the window.

6. From the File menu, choose Close.

EXERCISE 16-21 **Delete a Folder and Files**

You should delete the personal templates folder that you created as well as the default workbook and worksheet files in the XLStart folder. When there are no files in the XLStart folder, Excel uses its built-in settings.

 REVIEW: The Templates folder is usually C:\Document and Settings\ User\Application Data\Microsoft\Templates.

1. Click the Open button. Navigate to the Templates folder for your computer.

2. Click to highlight the MyTemplates folder.

 3. Click the Delete button X. Click Yes. The folders and its contents are deleted.

FIGURE 16-14
Deleting a templates folder and contents

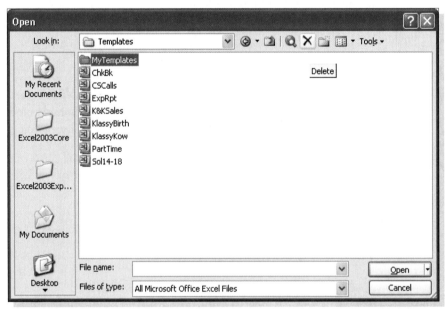

4. Navigate to the XLStart folder. Double-click the folder name to open it.

REVIEW: The XLStart folder is usually in C:\Program Files\Microsoft Office\Office11 or C:\Documents and Settings\UserName\Application Data\Microsoft\Excel. Check with your instructor.

5. Click Book to highlight it. Hold down Ctrl and click Sheet.

6. Click the Delete button ✖. Click Yes. The files are deleted.

FIGURE 16-15
Deleting files in the
XLStart folder

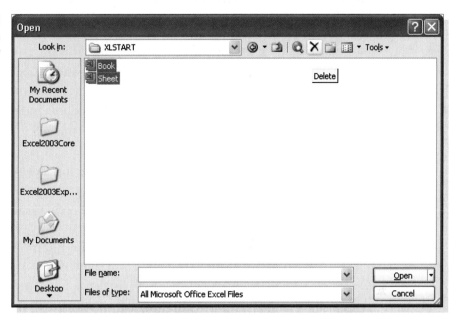

7. Click Cancel to close the Open dialog box.

8. Exit Excel to reset the defaults.

 NOTE: Always leave Excel in its default settings for the next class or student to use.

USING ONLINE HELP

Data validation offers many options for checking data entry.

Use Help to learn more about data validation.

1. With Internet Explorer and Excel running, find topics about data validation. Look for a topic detailing how to designate cell validation.

2. Read the information. Close the windows.

3. Close Internet Explorer and end your Internet connection.

LESSON 16 Summary

➤ Workbooks are based on built-in default settings. You can create a template named **Book.xlt** and save it in the XLStart folder to use your own default settings.

➤ New worksheets use built-in settings. You can create a template named **Sheet.xlt** and save it in the XLStart folder to use your own settings for new worksheets.

➤ You can size objects on screen by dragging a selection handle.

➤ Click the Crop tool 🖅 on the Picture toolbar and drag a handle to hide part of an object.

➤ When you create your own template, begin by keying labels and values and formatting them.

➤ You can suppress the display of zeros when there are no values for a formula to calculate.

➤ Data validation checks your cell entries against conditions that you specify. You can set data validation to display an error message when an incorrect entry is made in a cell.

➤ The Go To command includes a feature that enables you to select cells with data validation.

➤ Conditional formatting is a cell format applied only when cell contents meet specific conditions. Conditional formatting can include font, color, size, and style.

➤ The Locked property controls whether a cell or object can be edited when the worksheet is protected.

➤ A workbook template has multiple, predesigned worksheets.

➤ Protection can be applied to a worksheet or to a workbook.

➤ Workbook protection prevents the user from resizing or moving the windows and from adding, deleting, or changing the worksheets.

➤ You can assign a password to a protected worksheet.

➤ If you create a folder in the default Templates folder, it appears as a separate tab in the Templates dialog box.

LESSON 16   Command Summary

FEATURE	BUTTON	MENU	KEYBOARD
Template, use		<u>F</u>ile, <u>N</u>ew	
Template, open		<u>F</u>ile, <u>O</u>pen	Ctrl+O
Properties, set		<u>F</u>ile, Proper<u>t</u>ies	
Crop image		F<u>o</u>rmat, P<u>i</u>cture	
Hide zeros		<u>T</u>ools, <u>O</u>ptions	
Validate data entry		<u>D</u>ata, Va<u>l</u>idation	
Conditional formatting		F<u>o</u>rmat, Con<u>d</u>itional Formatting	
Go To Special		<u>E</u>dit, <u>G</u>o To	Ctrl+G
Protect worksheet		<u>T</u>ools, <u>P</u>rotection, <u>P</u>rotect Sheet	
Protect workbook		<u>T</u>ools, <u>P</u>rotection, Protect <u>W</u>orkbook	
Lock or unlock picture		F<u>o</u>rmat, P<u>i</u>cture	Ctrl+1
Lock or unlock cell		F<u>o</u>rmat, C<u>e</u>lls	Ctrl+1
Unprotect worksheet		<u>T</u>ools, <u>P</u>rotection, Unprotect Sheet	
Unprotect workbook		<u>T</u>ools, <u>P</u>rotection, Unprotect <u>W</u>orkbook	

Concepts Review

Each of the following statements is either true or false. Indicate your choice by circling T or F.

T   F   **1.** Templates can include one or multiple worksheets.

T   F   **2.** You cannot change Excel's default workbook settings.

T   F   **3.** The XLStart folder includes all templates on your computer.

T   F   **4.** Zeros must be shown as a digit or a hyphen.

T   F   **5.** Data validation checks formula results and displays an error when the result is incorrect.

T   F   **6.** Passwords can be assigned with worksheet protection.

T   F   **7.** Worksheet and workbook protection use the same settings.

T   F   **8.** You must store all templates in the default Templates folder.

Write the correct answer in the space provided.

1. What file can you create to hold your own default workbook settings?

_____

2. What folder holds your personalized default workbook and worksheet files?

_____

3. What button on the Picture toolbar allows you to mask or hide part of a picture?

_____

4. What command would you use to display values over 500 in bold?

_____

5. How can you hide zero values on a worksheet?

_____

6. What command would you use to ensure that no value less than 100 is keyed in a range?

_____

7. How can you create your own folder for templates?

_____

_____

8. Name two ways to enhance a template's usefulness.

_____

_____

CRITICAL THINKING

Answer these questions on a separate page. There are no right or wrong answers. Support your answers with examples from your own experience, if possible.

1. What are the advantages of using workbook protection?
2. How can data validation contribute to your productivity?

Skills Review

EXERCISE 16-22

Create a default workbook. Create a default worksheet.

1. Create a default workbook by following these steps:
    a. Open a new workbook. Delete Sheet2 and Sheet3.
    b. Click the Select All button .
    c. Change the font to 11-point Times New Roman. Click cell A1.
    d. Create a header that includes your name at the left and the filename and tab name at the right. Leave the center section blank.
    e. From the File menu, choose Properties. Add your name as the author. Delete all other information.
    f. Place a check mark for Save preview picture. Click OK.
    g. Click the Save button . Change the Save as type to Template.

    REVIEW: Look for the XLStart folder at C:\Program Files\Microsoft Office\XLStart.

    h. Navigate to the XLStart folder and open it.
    i. Edit the File name to **Book**. Click Save.
    j. Close the workbook.

2. Create a default worksheet by following these steps:

   a. Open a new workbook.

   b. Check that the font is 11-point Times New Roman. If it is not, exit Excel and restart.

   c. Check for the header.

   d. Insert the **Cow.gif** file and position it so that its top-left handle is about at cell A20.

   e. Click the Save button . Change the Save as type to Template.

   f. Navigate to the XLStart folder and open it.

   g. Edit the File name to **Sheet**. Click Save.

   h. Close the workbook. Exit Excel.

REVIEW: You may need to exit and restart Excel for your default workbook and worksheet to take effect.

3. Create a new workbook by following these steps:

   a. Start Excel with a new workbook. It uses one sheet with a new font setting.

   b. Key **Klassy Kow Ice Cream, Inc.** in cell A1.

   c. Insert a new worksheet. It includes the image.

   d. Key **Klassy Kow Ice Cream, Inc.** in cell A1 on the new sheet. It includes the font and header from your default sheet.

   e. Print both sheets. Close the workbook.

4. Delete default templates by following these steps:

TIP: You can delete files from the XLStart folder from any Explorer or My Computer window.

   a. Click the Open button .

   b. Navigate to the XLStart folder and open it.

   c. Click Book. Hold down Ctrl and click Sheet.

   d. Click the Delete button . Click Yes.

   e. Click Cancel to close the Open dialog box.

NOTE: Make sure you complete this exercise to delete the Sheet and Book template files.

EXERCISE 16-23

Create a user template. Add data validation settings with error messages. Apply conditional formatting.

1. Create a new workbook. Delete Sheet2 and Sheet3. Rename Sheet1 **PartTimeHours**.

2. Format cells A1:A2 as 16-point Arial and key **Klassy Kow Ice Cream Shops** in cell A1. Key **Part-Time Hours** in cell A2.

3. Make the range B3:D3 bold and key the following labels in the range:
Start Time   End Time   Hours

4. Set the width for columns B:D to 10.71 (80 pixels). Set the width for column A to 27.86 (200 pixels). Set the height for rows 3 and 4 to 22.50 (30 pixels).

5. Key **Monday** in cell A4 and make it bold.

6. Create data validation settings by following these steps:

   a. Select cells B5:C20.
   b. From the Data menu, choose Validation. Click the Settings tab.
   c. Click the down arrow next to the Allow text box and choose Time.
   d. In the Data text box, make sure between is selected.
   e. In the Start time text box, key **10 AM**.
   f. In the End time text box, key **11 PM**.

7. Set error messages by following these steps:

   a. Click the Error Alert tab.
   b. In the Style box, choose Information.
   c. In the Title box, key **Standard Hours**.
   d. In the Error message text box, key **Standard available part-time hours are between 10 a.m. and 11 p.m.**
   e. Click OK.

8. Apply conditional formatting by following these steps:

   a. Select cells D5:D20.
   b. From the Format menu, choose Conditional Formatting.
   c. Make sure Cell Value Is appears in the Condition 1 text box.
   d. Click the down arrow next to the second text box and choose greater than.
   e. In the third text box, key **8**.

 TIP: You can use multiple conditional formats by clicking Add.

   f. Click Format.
   g. Make sure the Font tab is displayed. Set the Font style as Bold Italic. Click OK twice.

9. Select cell A5. Add the usual footer.

10. Save the worksheet as a template by following these steps:

   a. Click the Save button .
   b. In the File name box, key **[your initials]16-23**.
   c. Click the down arrow next to the Save as type text box and choose Template.

   REVIEW: Excel switches to the Templates folder for your computer when you choose Template as the file type.

   d. Click Save.
   e. Print and then close the template.

11. Use a template by following these steps:

   a. Choose File, New from the menu and click On my computer.
   b. Click the General tab and double-click *[your initials]*16-23.
   c. Starting in cell A5, key the information shown in Figure 16-16.

FIGURE 16-16

Monday	Start Time	End Time	Hours
[your name]	10:30 am	4:30 pm	6
Keiko Yang	11 am	8:30 pm	9.5

   d. Press F12 and save the workbook as *[your initials]*16-23 in your Lesson 16 folder.
   e. Print the worksheet and close the workbook.

12. Choose File, New and click On my computer. Click the General tab. Right-click *[your initials]*16-23 and choose Delete. Choose Yes and click Cancel.

 NOTE: Make sure you complete the last step of this exercise. Template files remain on the computer until they are deleted.

EXERCISE 16-24

Protect a template. Create a templates folder.

 NOTE: Copy the PartTime template file from the CD to the Templates folder for your computer.

1. Open the template file **PartTime.xlt** in the Templates folder for your computer.

2. Insert a comment at cell D5 with the text shown here.

FIGURE 16-17

Hours are computed by subtracting the Start Time from the End Time. The result is divided by 24 to convert to hours. The result is formatted as Number.

3. Size the comment box to show all the text.

 REVIEW: Format a picture in a header/footer from the Header/Footer dialog box.

4. Add a footer with your name at the left, the filename and the tab name in the center, and the **Cow.gif** file at the right. Scale the picture to 35%.

5. Protect a worksheet by following these steps:

    a. Select cells A5:C20 and press Ctrl+1.
    b. Click the Protection tab.
    c. Remove the check mark for the Locked option. Click OK.
    d. Click cell A5.
    e. From the Tools menu, choose Protection, Protect Sheet.
    f. Make sure the options Select locked cells and Select unlocked cells are selected.
    g. Click OK.

6. Create a templates folder by following these steps:

    a. Press F12.
    b. Change Save as type to Template.
    c. Click the Create New Folder button [icon].
    d. Key **MyTemplates** and click OK.
    e. In the File name box, key *[your initials]*16-24. Click Save.
    f. Close the workbook.

7. Open the New Workbook task pane. Click On my computer. Click the MyTemplates tab.

8. Double-click the file *[your initials]*16-24.

9. In the new workbook, set the comment to print on a separate sheet. (*Hint:* Choose File, Page Setup, click the Sheet tab, click the down arrow next to the Comments text box.)

10. Display the formulas. Print the workbook fit to a landscape page.

11. Close the workbook without saving.

12. Click the Open button [icon]. Navigate to the Templates folder and delete the MyTemplates folder and its contents.

> **NOTE:** Make sure you complete the last step of this exercise. Always leave Excel in its default settings for the next class or student to use.

EXERCISE 16-25

Create a workbook template. Protect a workbook.

1. Open the file **ORKowO**. Center the worksheet horizontally.

2. Make two copies of the January sheet. Name the new sheets **February** and **March** and position the sheets in month-to-month order.

3. Edit cell A2 on the February and March worksheets to show the correct month.

4. Group the worksheets to add the standard footer. Ungroup the sheets.

5. In the file properties, set the Author to your name and the Company to your school or company name. Place a check mark for Save preview picture. Click OK.

6. Protect a workbook by following these steps:

   a. From the Tools menu, choose Protection, Protect Workbook.
   b. Make sure the Structure option is selected. Do not select Windows or use a password. Click OK.

7. Save a workbook template by following these steps:

   a. Press F12.
   b. In the File name text box, key *[your initials]*16-25.
   c. Click the down arrow next to the Save as type text box and choose Template.
   d. Make sure the Save in location is the regular Templates folder. Click Save.

8. Print the entire workbook template and then close the workbook.

9. Choose File, New and click On my computer. Click the General tab. Right-click the file *[your initials]*16-25 and choose Delete. Choose Yes and click Cancel.

> **NOTE:** Make sure you complete the last step of this exercise. Template files remain on the computer until they are deleted. Always leave Excel in its default settings for the next class or student to use.

Lesson Applications

EXERCISE 16-26

Create a worksheet template. Add data validation. Create a workbook from a template.

Klassy Kow uses a check register for deposits and payments to customers. Using an existing worksheet, create a template for the register. The worksheet has a nested function (OR inside IF). The data validation in this template will use a drop-down list of customer names.

1. Open the file **CheckReg**.
2. Select cells A14:F14. Use the Fill handle to extend the register to row 25.
3. Select cells A3:F3 and apply a Gray-25% fill color. This marks the balance so that no entry is made in this row.
4. Rename Sheet1 **Register**. Rename Sheet2 **Payees**. Delete Sheet3.
5. On the Payees worksheet, select the names and sort them alphabetically. Then name the range **Payees**.
6. Select cells C4:C25 on the Register sheet for data validation. In the Allow text box, choose List. In the Source text box, press F3 and choose Payees.
7. Review the IF formula in cell F4. Note that cell F3 holds a beginning balance and does not use the formula. Copy the formula through row 25.
8. Add your standard footer to the Register sheet. Set the worksheet to fit to one portrait page.
9. Save the workbook as a template named *[your initials]***16-26** in the Templates folder. Print the worksheet and close it.
10. Create a new workbook based on your template.
11. Key the information shown in Figure 16-18, starting in cell A4. Choose the payee from the list.

FIGURE 16-18

Date	Check #	Payee	Credit Amount	Deposit
Ctrl + :	1234	Glencoe Dairy Products	1000	
Ctrl + :	1235	eZone Services, Ltd.	2000	
Ctrl + :				300

12. Adjust the columns so that all data is visible.
13. Save the workbook as *[your initials]***16-26** in your Lesson 16 folder.

14. Print the worksheet to fit to one portrait page and close it.

15. Choose File, New and click On my computer. From the General tab, right-click and delete *[your initials]*16-26. Close the Templates dialog box.

 NOTE: Make sure you complete the last step of this exercise. Template files remain on the computer until they are deleted.

EXERCISE 16-27

Add data validation. Apply conditional formatting. Protect a worksheet.

1. Open the template file **KlassyBirth.xlt**.

2. Set the worksheet to landscape orientation, horizontally centered.

 TIP: Use different handles to crop an image as desired.

3. Crop the image to show only the text and as little as possible of the cow. After cropping, make the image larger. Reposition the image to align on the right with the last column.

4. Set data validation for cells C4:C20 to allow a whole number between 2 and 12. Set an error message that will allow the entry.

5. Apply conditional formatting to the same range to show any value outside the range in bold italic. Add Condition 2 to do this.

6. Add a footer with **Klassy Kow Ice Cream Shops** in the Left section. Key your name in the middle and add the filename in the right.

7. Unlock cells in which you will key data. Protect the worksheet without a password.

8. Save the template as a new template named *[your initials]*16-27 in the Templates folder. Close the template.

9. Create a workbook based on the template with the data shown here.

FIGURE 16-19

Name	Shop	Age	Male/Female
Barry Hartman	Salinas	3	Male
Lisa Haywood	Klamath Falls	13	Female
Anna Pawlowitz	Medford	2	Female
John Daniels	Klamath Falls	4	Male
Sally Booth	Reno	1	Female

10. Save the workbook as *[your initials]*16-27 in your Lesson 16 folder. Print the sheet and close the workbook.

11. Choose File, New and click On my computer. Click the General tab and delete *[your initials]*16-27.

 REVIEW: Template files remain on the computer until they are deleted.

EXERCISE 16-28

Create a workbook template. Edit properties. Protect worksheets.

Klassy Kow keeps track of sales by quarter. You can create a workbook template with a worksheet for each quarter. You can enter the formulas and formatting and key appropriate labels.

1. Create a new workbook. Set the properties to show a preview image and your name as author.

2. Use four worksheets, naming them as follows: **1stQtr**, **2ndQtr**, **3rdQtr**, **4thQtr**.

3. Group the worksheets and format the range A1:A2 for 18-point Times New Roman. Key **Klassy Kow Dollar Sales** in cell A1. In cell A2, key **State Totals**.

4. In the range A4:A7, key these states: **California**, **Oregon**, **Nevada**, **Washington**. Widen the column to show the longest label.

5. Format the range B3:E3 as bold and centered.

6. In cell E3, key **Total**. In cell E4, create a formula to sum the range B4:D4. Copy the formula to the range E5:E7. Hide the zeros.

7. Select and unlock the cells in the range B4:D7.

8. Ungroup the worksheets. On each worksheet, key the months for the quarter in the range B3:D3. For example, the 1stQtr worksheet should show **January**, **February**, and **March** in the range B3:D3. Adjust column widths as needed.

9. Group the worksheets and add your standard footer. Ungroup the worksheets.

 TIP: You cannot protect grouped worksheets.

10. Protect each worksheet without a password.

11. Save the workbook as a template named *[your initials]*16-28 in the Templates folder for your computer. Print the entire workbook and close the template.

12. Choose File, New and click On my computer. From the General tab, delete *[your initials]*16-28.

NOTE: Make sure you complete the last step of this exercise. Template files remain on the computer until they are deleted. Always leave Excel in its default settings for the next class or student.

EXERCISE 16-29 *Challenge Yourself*

Create a workbook from a template. Use a formula for data validation.

Klassy Kow's management would like the expense report for their sales representatives to note when actual expenses are more than 150 percent of budgeted expenses. You can accomplish this with a formula as data validation. A formula used as data validation must calculate a logical value, which means the result must be True or False.

1. Create a new workbook from the **ExpRpt** template.

2. Select cell B10. Choose Data, Validation from the menu and click the Settings tab. Click the down arrow next to the Allow text box and choose Custom. In the Formula box, key **=b10** to start the formula. Your formula should determine that the value in cell B10 is less than or equal to 150% of the value in cell B9. Key those operators and cell references after **b10**.

3. Add an error alert message titled **Over Allowance**. Key your own message to note that the expenses exceed 150% of budget.

4. Key various values in cell B10 to test your validation setting. Delete your test values after you are confident your formula is correct.

5. With cell B10 selected, click the Copy button . Select the range C10:D10 and use Paste Special to paste the validation. (Press Esc after the Paste Special command to cancel the marquee.)

6. Copy the range B10:D10. Use Paste Special to paste the validation in the remaining rows with Actual expense cells. Don't cancel the marquee until you've pasted all the rows.

7. Rename Sheet2 **Documentation**. Key your name in cell A1. In cell A2, key **Using a Formula for Data Validation**.

8. On the Expenses worksheet, select any cell with the data validation setting. Open the Data Validation dialog box and select and copy the formula to the clipboard. Close the dialog box.

9. On the Documentation worksheet, paste the formula in cell A3 and display the formulas. The references are relative.

10. In cell A4, key **The data validation formula is used in cells B10:D10, B15:D15, B20:D20, and B25:D25.**

11. AutoFit column A.

12. Select rows 1 through 4 on the Documentation worksheet and set the height to 22.50 (30 pixels).

13. Add the standard footer to the Documentation worksheet.

14. Save the workbook as *[your initials]***16-29** in your Lesson 16 folder.

15. Print the Documentation sheet and close the workbook.

On Your Own

In these exercises you work on your own, as you would in a real-life work environment. Use the skills you've learned to accomplish the task—and be creative.

EXERCISE 16-30

Create a template you might find useful at work or at school for a task, activity, or topic of interest to you. Use formulas, data validation, and conditional formatting where appropriate. Unlock cells and protect the worksheet. Add a standard footer. Save the workbook as a template named *[your initials]***16-30** in your computer's Templates folder. Print the template. Delete the template from the computer.

EXERCISE 16-31

Create a new workbook that uses conditional formatting with two conditions. For example, you might show a value/label in one of two different colors/styles depending on what the value/label is. Develop a worksheet using something of interest to you at work, school, or home. In a comment in an appropriate cell, explain how the conditional formatting works. Key sample data to test and display the conditional formatting. Add a standard footer and save the workbook as *[your initials]***16-31** in your Lesson 16 folder. Print the workbook with the comment displayed at the end of the sheet. Save and close the workbook.

EXERCISE 16-32

Explore the types of data validation settings in the dialog box and in Help. Then create a new workbook to illustrate two uses of data validation settings. Use a documentation worksheet that explains your validation settings. Add the standard footer to both worksheets and save your workbook as *[your initials]***16-32** in your Lesson 16 folder. Print the workbook and close it.

Working with Macros

OBJECTIVES

After completing this lesson, you will be able to:

1. **Run a macro from the menu.**
2. **Edit a macro.**
3. **Record a new macro.**
4. **Assign a macro to a button.**
5. **Create a custom toolbar.**
6. **Customize an Excel toolbar.**
7. **Create a macros workbook.**

 Estimated Time: 1½ hours

A *macro* is a sequence of commands and/or keystrokes that automate a task. A macro can perform data entry, formatting, menu command execution, and dialog box selections. For example, you can create a macro that keys your company name in a specific font and size. Then you run the macro whenever you need to enter the company name in the worksheet. Macros help you work more quickly and with fewer mistakes.

Excel macros are recorded in Visual Basic for Applications programming language (VBA), but you don't need to know that language to create and use macros.

Running a Macro from the Menu

When you run a macro, each step in the macro is carried out. Macros are stored in workbooks, and the workbook with a macro must be open for the macro to be run. Macros are "run" or executed from the Tools menu.

E X E R C I S E   **17-1** **Set Macro Security**

Macros have become easy places for hackers to store viruses. Because of this possibility, Excel has a Macro Security feature that allows you to choose whether to open and use macros from others.

Macro security can be set to one of three levels: High, Medium, or Low. High security means that you can run only those macros that have been digitally signed and are from trusted sources. A *digital signature* is an electronically encrypted authentication stamp on a macro or document. It confirms that the macro or document originated from the signer and has not been altered.

With Medium security, you can choose whether to run macros. With a Low security setting, you are not protected from potentially unsafe macros, and you receive no warning if you open workbooks containing macros. Low security is not recommended unless you are running virus-scanning software or are sure all documents and macros you receive are safe.

 NOTE: Digital signatures are usually created by a network or project administrator.

1. From the Tools menu, choose Macro and then Security. The Security dialog box opens.
2. Click the Security Level tab. Read each option and its description.
3. Select Medium.
4. Click the Trusted Publishers tab. If you use High security, your list of acceptable sources is listed here.
5. Click OK.

E X E R C I S E   **17-2** **Run a Macro**

When you open a workbook with a macro, a message box alerts you that macros might contain viruses. You choose to enable or disable the macros with the Medium security setting. You must enable macros in order for them to be used.

1. Open **ORSales**. This workbook contains macros, and the message box about macros opens.

FIGURE 17-1
Macro alert
message

2. Click Enable Macros. The workbook opens.

3. From the Tools menu, choose Macro and then Macros. The Macro dialog box opens. This workbook has one macro named CompanyName. It is selected and its name is entered in the Macro name text box.

FIGURE 17-2
Macro dialog box

4. Click Run. The dialog box closes, and the macro inserts and formats two labels.

EXERCISE **17-3** **View a Macro in the Visual Basic Editor**

You can use the *Visual Basic Editor* to view, edit, or create a macro. The Visual Basic Editor is made up of several windows. The code that makes up the macro is displayed in the *Code window. Code* is written in the Visual Basic language. Some lines in the Code window are preceded by an apostrophe and shown in green. These are comments and explanations.

You open the Visual Basic Editor from the Tools menu. The macro in this exercise is a *subroutine macro,* which is a command sequence that can be run from the worksheet or run from another macro. Subroutine macros start with the word *Sub* followed by the macro name. Subroutine macros end with *End Sub*.

1. From the Tools menu, choose Macro and Visual Basic Editor. The Visual Basic Editor starts. The Code window is the larger window on the right. The smaller windows on the left are the Project Explorer and the Properties window. Look in the Project Explorer window for the Modules folder. Macros are stored as modules in the workbook. This macro is in Module1.

   NOTE: If you do not see the Project Explorer window, choose View, Project Explorer from the Visual Basic Editor menu. If the Properties window is not displayed, choose View, Properties Window. If you do not see the macro code, choose View, Code.

FIGURE 17-3
Visual Basic Editor

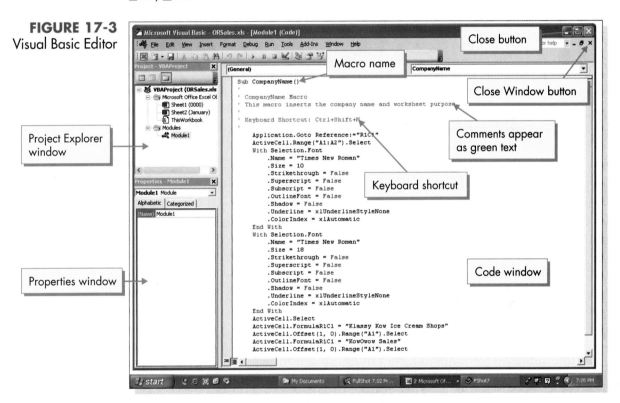

2. Look for the macro code in the Code window. The macro begins with Sub followed by the macro name, CompanyName. The next lines are green and begin with an apostrophe. These are comment lines that describe the macro, show the shortcut, and insert blank lines for ease in reading the code.

3. Look for the comment indicating the keyboard shortcut.

4. Scroll to the bottom of the macro. Look for EndSub. This marks the end of the macro.

5. Click the Close button in the Visual Basic title bar. The Visual Basic Editor closes, and Excel reappears.

  NOTE: The Close Window button closes the CompanyName macro but leaves the Visual Basic Editor open.

Editing a Macro

You edit a macro in the Visual Basic Editor. Even if you have no knowledge of Visual Basic programming, you will probably be able to determine how to make text and formatting edits to macros.

For example, the code ".Name=Times New Roman" formats a cell to use that font. To change the font to Arial, you simply type "Arial" in place of "Times New Roman" in that line in the macro. When editing a macro, you must be careful not to change spaces and punctuation, because such changes could have unexpected results.

EXERCISE `17-4` **Edit a Macro**

While you are editing code in the Visual Basic Editor, a line might display in red. This signifies an error in the code. If you cannot determine what the error is, press `Ctrl`+`Z` to undo and try again.

1. Press `Alt`+`F11`, the keyboard shortcut to open the Visual Basic Editor.

2. In the Code window, locate the line .Size=18. This line sets the font size for the text.

 TIP: The first .Size=10 in the macro shows the default font size.

3. Change 18 to **24**. The next time you run this macro, the labels will use a larger font size.

4. Locate the line that includes the text "Klassy Kow Ice Cream Shops" near the end of the macro.

5. Position the insertion point after the word Shops, inside the quotation marks.

NOTE: Text that should be displayed when the macro is run is enclosed in quotation marks.

6. Key **Inc.** inside the quotation marks. The label will include "Inc." as part of the name the next time the macro is run.

7. Locate the line that includes "KowOwow Sales."

8. Delete KowOwow and key **Kowabunga**. The label will display "Kowabunga Sales" the next time the macro is run.

FIGURE 17-4
Editing a macro

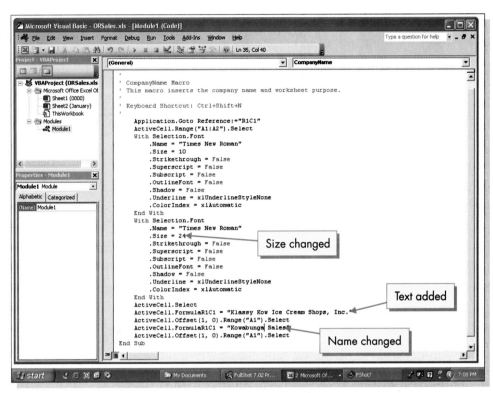

EXERCISE **17-5** **Print a Macro**

1. Scroll to the top of the Code window. Position the insertion point to the right of the first apostrophe under Sub CompanyName().

2. Press [Spacebar] and key *[your name]*. Press ↓. Your name is shown in green, indicating that it has been added as a comment.

3. Choose File from the menu, and then choose Print. The Print – VBAProject dialog box opens.

4. In the Range group, choose Current Module if it is not already selected. Macros are stored in modules.

5. In the Print What group, choose Code if it is not already selected. (See Figure 17-5 on the next page.)

6. Click OK. The macro is printed.

7. Click the Close button ⊠ on the Visual Basic title bar.

FIGURE 17-5
Printing a macro

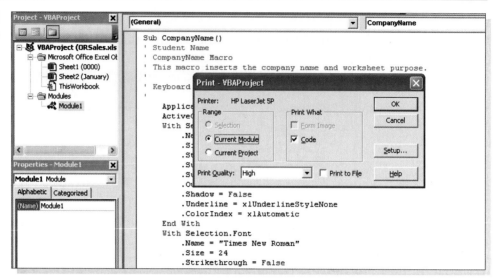

 NOTE: Changes to your macro code are saved in the Visual Basic Editor. However, you must save the workbook containing the macro to permanently save the changes.

EXERCISE | **17-6** | **Run a Macro with a Shortcut**

If a macro is recorded with a keyboard shortcut, you can use keystrokes to run the macro. This is faster than running a macro from the Tools menu. To test your edited macro, you should reset the worksheet to the way it was when you first opened it.

1. Select the range A1:A2.
2. From the Edit menu, choose Clear and then All. This deletes the contents and the formatting.
3. Select cell B4. This is the location of the insertion point when you opened the workbook.

 NOTE: This macro includes a command to go to cell A1.

4. Press Ctrl+Shift+N. The macro inserts the labels in the new font size with "Inc." added as well as "Kowabunga."
5. Select the range A1:A2.
6. From the Edit menu, choose Clear and then All.
7. Select cell B4. The worksheet is reset once again.

Recording a New Macro

You create a macro by "recording" it. When you record a macro, Excel stores information about each step and command as you go through the task. Macros are stored in workbooks. As long as the workbook with a macro is open, you can use that macro in any open workbook.

Follow these guidelines to help you decide where to store a macro:

- Special-purpose macros that will be used with only one workbook should be stored in that workbook. Templates might have special-purpose macros.

- General-purpose macros used on a regular basis can be stored in a workbook that contains only macros. Anytime this workbook is open, any other open workbook can use its macros.

- General-purpose macros that should be available at all times can be stored in the Personal Macro Workbook. Excel creates a Personal Macro Workbook, named **Personal.xls**, in the XLStart folder if you choose this option while creating a macro. The Personal Macro Workbook opens as a hidden workbook each time you start Excel.

 NOTE: Explore Help topics about the Personal Macro Workbook if you have your own computer at work or home.

EXERCISE 17-7 Name a Macro

Macro names must begin with a letter and cannot contain spaces or special characters. If you use a keyboard shortcut, you should enter an uppercase letter in the Record Macro dialog box so that you do not override existing Windows or Excel shortcuts. For example, if you enter "s" in the Record Macro dialog box as the shortcut key, you override the Save command shortcut Ctrl+S.

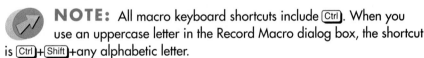 **NOTE:** All macro keyboard shortcuts include Ctrl. When you use an uppercase letter in the Record Macro dialog box, the shortcut is Ctrl+Shift+any alphabetic letter.

1. From the Tools menu, choose Macro and then Record New Macro. The Record Macro dialog box opens.

2. In the Macro name box, key **CompanyInfo**.

3. Position the insertion point in the Shortcut key box. Press Shift and key **k**. The complete shortcut is shown.

4. Make sure that Store macro in shows This Workbook.

5. In the <u>D</u>escription text box, delete any existing information and key **Displays company name and date**.

 NOTE: The Record Macro dialog box shows the default user name/ID in the <u>D</u>escription text box.

FIGURE 17-6
Record Macro
dialog box

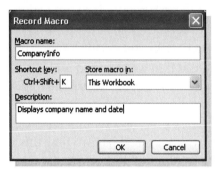

6. Click OK. The Stop Recording toolbar opens and Recording appears at the left of the status bar. You're now ready to begin recording your macro.

 NOTE: If you do not see the Stop Recording toolbar, right-click any toolbar and choose Stop Recording to display it.

FIGURE 17-7
Stop Recording
toolbar

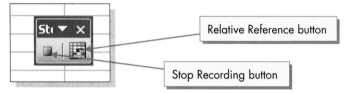

Relative Reference button

Stop Recording button

EXERCISE **17-8** **Record a Macro with Absolute References**

You click the Stop Recording button ■ when you finish recording your macro. The Relative Reference button ▦ allows you to choose between relative and absolute cell references as you record macros.

When Relative Reference is active, the macro carries out its actions relative to the current cell or range. It does not record specific cell addresses but records positioning commands. If Relative Reference is not active when you record a macro, cell addresses are recorded as part of the macro. Pointer movement is not recorded.

1. Check that the Relative Reference button is not active. (The button appears outlined when it is on.) If it is on, click it to use absolute references.
2. Press ⬆ three times to position the insertion point in cell B1. This cell address is recorded in the macro.
3. Press ⬅ once to position the insertion point in cell A1. The cell address A1 is recorded.
4. Format the cell for 18-point Times New Roman. The font setting is recorded in the macro.
5. Key **Klassy Kow Ice Cream Shops** and press Enter. The insertion point is in cell A2.
6. Format the cell for 14-point Times New Roman.

7. Press `Ctrl`+`;` and press `Enter`. The insertion point is in cell A3.

8. Click the Stop Recording button . Your macro is complete, the toolbar closes, and Recording is no longer displayed in the status bar.

> **NOTE:** Do not click the Close button ✕ on the toolbar. This closes the toolbar but does not stop recording.

9. Select the range A1:A2. From the Edit menu, choose Clear and All. The worksheet is reset and ready for you to test your macro.

10. Select cell A10 and press `Ctrl`+`Shift`+`K` to run your macro. The macro carries out its actions in cells A1:A2, because the cell addresses were absolute.

EXERCISE 17-9 Review Macro Code

1. From the Tools menu, choose Macro and Macros. The workbook now contains two macros. Your macro, CompanyInfo, is selected.

2. Click Edit. The Visual Basic Editor starts.

3. Locate the line Range("A1").Select near the beginning of the code. Because you used absolute references, Excel did not record your pressing ⬆ and ⬅. Instead, it recorded the exact cell address, cell A1.

4. Locate the line Range("A2").Select in the middle of the code. Locate the third absolute reference at the end of the macro, indicating where the insertion point finishes.

5. Click the Close button ✕ on the Visual Basic Editor title bar.

EXERCISE 17-10 Delete a Macro

1. Select the range A1:A2. From the Edit menu, choose Clear and All.

2. Press `Alt`+`F8`. This is the keyboard shortcut to open the Macro dialog box.

3. Click to select CompanyInfo and click Delete.

4. Choose Yes to delete your macro.

5. Select cell B4. This is where the insertion point was located when you first opened the workbook.

EXERCISE 17-11 Record a Macro with Relative References

For many macros, a relative reference is best. You can change the reference type as often as necessary while recording a macro.

1. From the Tools menu, choose Macro and Record New Macro.

2. In the Macro name text box, key **CompanyInfo**.

3. Position the insertion point in the Shortcut key box. Press (Shift) and key **k**.

4. Make sure the Store macro in option is This Workbook.

5. Delete the existing information in the Description box and key **Displays company name and date**.

6. Click OK. The Record Macro dialog box closes, and the Stop Recording toolbar opens. The status bar shows that you are recording.

 7. Click the Relative Reference button 🔲 on the Stop Recording toolbar. An outline surrounds the button when Relative Reference is active.

8. Press (↑) three times. Press (←). These pointer movement commands are recorded in the macro.

9. Format the cell as 18-point Times New Roman.

10. Key **Klassy Kow Ice Cream Shops** and press (Enter).

11. Format cell A2 as 14-point Times New Roman and press (Ctrl)+(;). Press (Enter).

12. Click the Stop Recording button 🔲. The status bar indicates that you are no longer recording a macro.

13. Select the range A1:A2. From the Edit menu, choose Clear and then All.

14. Select cell C12 and press (Ctrl)+(Shift)+(K) to run the macro. The macro performs its tasks relative to the position of the insertion point when you start the macro. The labels are inserted three rows up from cell C12 and to the left one column.

15. Clear all from the range B9:B10 and select cell C12.

EXERCISE 17-12   Add a Comment Line

1. Press (Alt)+(F11) to start the Visual Basic Editor.

2. In the Project window, scroll to display the Modules folder if it is not already displayed. Expand the Modules folder if it is not open. The workbook has two macros, so there are two modules.

NOTE: Although these two macros are in separate modules, a module can contain more than one macro. Macros within the same module are separated by a horizontal line.

3. If the Code window does not show the CompanyInfo macro, double-click Module2 in the Project window.

4. In the Code window, locate the line ActiveCell.Offset(-3, -1).Range("A1").Select. When you use relative references, Excel records positioning commands.

This code is a command to go up three rows (–3) and to the left one column (–1) ending in cell A1 when you recorded this macro.

5. Scroll to the top of the Code window. Position the insertion point to the right of the first apostrophe under Sub CompanyInfo().

6. Press (Spacebar) and key *[your name]*. Press (↓). Your name is shown in green, indicating that it has been added as a comment.

7. From the File menu, choose Print. In the Range group, make sure Current Module is selected. In the Print what group, make sure Code is selected. Click OK. The macro is printed.

8. Click the Close button ☒ on the Visual Basic Editor title bar to close the editor and return to Excel.

9. Save the file as *[your initials]*17-12 in a new folder for Lesson 17.

Assigning a Macro to a Button

You can assign a macro to a *button* so that the macro runs when you click the button. A button is a *control,* an object that lets the user direct tasks or activities. You can use controls to run macros, display information, make choices, or perform a specific action.

 TIP: Templates are good locations for button-activated macros.

EXERCISE 17-13 Display, Size, and Hide Toolbars

You use the Button tool on the Forms toolbar to create buttons. Toolbars can float on the window or be anchored. When a toolbar is floating, you can size it and move it on the screen. An anchored toolbar appears at the top, bottom, left, or right of the window.

1. Right-click anywhere in the Standard or Formatting toolbar. A list of available toolbars opens. Those showing check marks are currently displayed.

2. Choose Forms. The Forms toolbar opens as a floating toolbar.

3. Drag the toolbar by its title bar to the middle of the screen.

4. Position the pointer on the left or right edge of the toolbar to display a two-pointed arrow.

5. Click and drag to make the toolbar four columns wide. Position the pointer over the rightmost image on the top row. The ScreenTip indicates that this is the Button tool ◢.

FIGURE 17-8
Forms toolbar

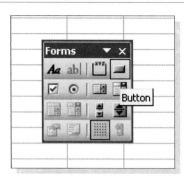

6. Double-click the toolbar's title bar. The Forms toolbar is anchored with other toolbars at the top of the screen.

7. Right-click the Forms toolbar and choose Forms from the list of toolbars. The toolbar is hidden.

8. Right-click anywhere in the Standard or Formatting toolbars.

9. Choose Forms again. It is anchored at the top of the screen with the other toolbars.

10. Position the pointer on the dashed vertical line at the left of the Forms toolbar to display a four-pointed arrow.

11. Drag the toolbar down into the worksheet.

EXERCISE 17-14 Draw a Command Button

Buttons are objects. When you edit a button, it displays the diagonal lines or the dotted pattern around its edges. The diagonal lines mean you can edit the text. The dotted pattern allows you to edit other properties for the button.

1. Click the Button tool on the Forms toolbar. The pointer turns into a thin crosshair.

2. Click at the top-left corner of cell G3 and drag to the bottom-right corner of cell H4.

3. Release the mouse button. The Assign Macro dialog box opens with the names of macros in your workbook. (See Figure 17-9.)

4. Select CompanyName and click OK. The button shows default text, "Button 1."

5. Right-click the border of the button and choose Format Control. The Format Control dialog box opens.

6. On the Font tab, choose 10-point Arial bold. Click OK. The button text changes to bold.

7. Click inside the button to display a text insertion point.

NOTE: You can right-click the button and choose Edit Text from the shortcut menu to display a text insertion point.

8. Delete the default text and key **Display Name**.

9. Select cell C12. The button is deselected.

FIGURE 17-9
Assign Macro
dialog box

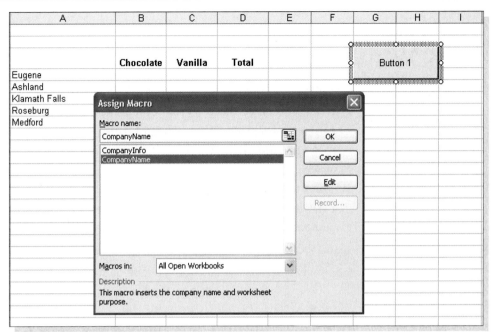

EXERCISE **17-15** **Run a Macro from a Command Button**

You must right-click a button to select it and change its properties because left-clicking a button runs the macro. In addition to setting a button's properties, you can also change its formatting.

1. Click the button control. The macro runs and places the labels in the range A1:A2. The CompanyName macro uses absolute references, so you can run the macro from any cell location.

2. Click the Print Preview button . Notice that button controls do not print.
3. Close the preview.
4. Right-click the button. Choose Format Control. Click the Properties tab.
5. Select Print object and click OK.
6. Preview the worksheet. Close the preview.
7. Print the worksheet.
8. Right-click the button. The button is selected, and the shortcut menu is open.
9. Left-click the edge of the button. The shortcut menu closes, but the button is still selected.
10. Press Delete. The button is removed, but the macro is still stored in the workbook.
11. Close the Forms toolbar. Clear all from the range A1:A2.

Creating a Custom Toolbar

You can create your own toolbar and add menu items to it. You can add any Excel command to your toolbar, and you can place macros on it.

When you place macros on a toolbar, keep these features in mind:

- Macros on toolbars are available whenever the toolbar is visible and as long as the macro workbook is accessible on the computer.
- A macro on a toolbar includes an identifier to locate the workbook with the macro.
- If you move or rename the macro workbook, you must reassign the macro to the button to reestablish the identifier.

 NOTE: Begin Exercise 17-16 when you can complete through Exercise 17-19. You will be adding a toolbar that will be deleted in Exercise 17-19.

EXERCISE **17-16** **Create a Toolbar and a Menu Item**

1. From the Tools menu, choose Customize. The Customize dialog box opens.
2. Click the Toolbars tab if it is not already displayed. The list shows names of standard Excel toolbars.
3. Click New. The New Toolbar dialog box opens.
4. In the Toolbar name text box, key **Macros**. Click OK. The Customize dialog box remains open and the toolbar name is added to the list. The new toolbar appears in the worksheet.
5. Drag the Customize dialog box so that you can see both the dialog box and the toolbar. The toolbar is not wide enough to show its name.
6. Click the Commands tab. The categories of Excel commands are listed on the left. The command names and buttons are on the right.
7. In the Categories list, locate and select Macros. The right side of the dialog box shows two options under Commands.
8. In the Commands list, select Custom Menu Item.
9. Click and drag Custom Menu Item to the open area of your Macros toolbar below the title bar.
10. Release the mouse button when you see an I-beam insertion point. The text appears as a menu item on the toolbar and the toolbar expands.

FIGURE 17-10
Creating a custom
toolbar

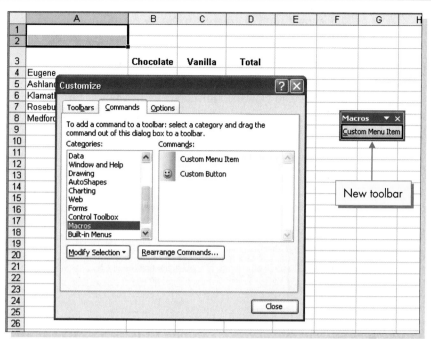

EXERCISE 17-17 Assign a Macro to a Menu Item

After you've created a toolbar and added a command to it, you must assign the macro to the command.

1. Click Modify Selection in the Customize dialog box. The list of command options opens.
2. Choose Assign Macro. The Assign Macro dialog box opens and lists macros in your workbook.
3. Select CompanyName and click OK. The macro is assigned to your toolbar command. The Customize dialog box is still open.

EXERCISE 17-18 Change the Menu Name

You can change the command name on your toolbar to a name that describes the command's function.

1. Click Modify Selection in the Customize dialog box.
2. Select Name near the top of the menu. The text box adjacent to Name contains the text of the menu command. The ampersand character (&)

marks which character in the name will be underlined for use as a keyboard shortcut. In the default text, the first letter in the command receives the underline because the ampersand precedes the "C."

3. Place the insertion point in the text box adjacent to Name.

4. Delete the existing information and key **&Display Info**.

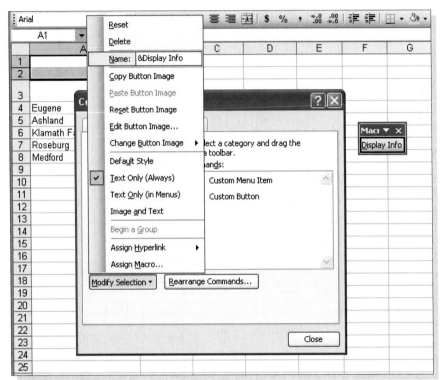

FIGURE 17-11
Changing the
menu name

5. Press (Enter). The menu name on the toolbar is changed. The first letter is underlined because the ampersand preceded the letter "D."

6. Click Close to close the Customize dialog box.

7. Click Display Info on the Macros toolbar. The command runs the CompanyName macro.

EXERCISE **17-19** **Delete a Toolbar**

1. Right-click the Macros toolbar and choose Customize. The Customize dialog box opens.

2. Click the Toolbars tab. A check mark indicates whether a toolbar is displayed.

3. Scroll to find Macros in the list and click once to select it. A selected toolbar is highlighted in blue.

4. Click Delete. A message box asks if you are sure you want to delete the toolbar.

5. Click OK. Click Close. The Macros toolbar is deleted, but your macros are still stored in *[your initials]***17-12**.

 NOTE: Make sure you complete this exercise. Custom toolbars remain on the computer until they are deleted.

Customizing an Excel Toolbar

You can add a macro button to an existing Excel toolbar as an alternative to creating a separate macro toolbar. When you add a macro button to an Excel toolbar, the steps are the same as when you create your own toolbar.

EXERCISE **17-20** **Add a Button to the Standard Toolbar**

1. From the Tools menu, choose Customize. Click the Commands tab.

2. In the Categories list, choose Macros.

3. In the Commands list, select Custom Button.

 4. Click and drag Custom Button to the right of the AutoSum button on the Standard toolbar. Release the mouse button. The button image is a smiley face. (See Figure 17-12 on the next page.)

5. Click Modify Selection in the Customize dialog box.

6. Choose Assign Macro. Select CompanyName and click OK. The button has been assigned the CompanyName macro.

7. Click Modify Selection again to display the shortcut menu.

8. Choose Name and delete the existing information in the text box.

9. Key **&Company** and press Enter.

10. Click Modify Selection and choose Change Button Image. A palette of button images is displayed.

11. Click any image for your button.

12. Click Modify Selection again. Choose Image and Text. This will show the name as well as the image.

13. Click Close.

14. Insert a new worksheet.

15. Click the new button you just added on the Standard toolbar. The macro inserts the company information.

FIGURE 17-12
Adding a button to
the Standard
toolbar

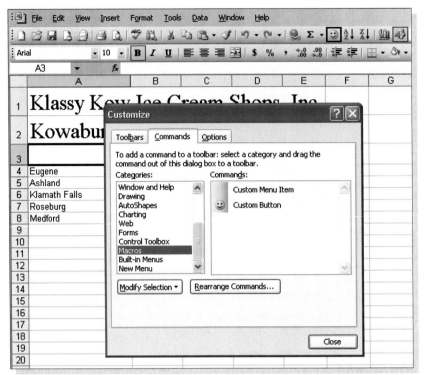

EXERCISE `17-21` **Delete a Button from the Standard Toolbar**

1. Press and hold [Alt] and drag your button off the toolbar, down into the worksheet. The button is removed.
2. Close the workbook without saving.

  NOTE: Make sure you complete this exercise. Buttons you add to Excel toolbars remain until they are deleted.

Creating a Macros Workbook

If you have macros that you use on a regular basis, you can create a workbook that includes only these macros. Then you can open this macro workbook every time you use Excel, and the macros are available.

EXERCISE `17-22` **Record a Macro with AutoFill**

You'll create one macro to fill in Weeks 1 through 4 on a worksheet.

1. Open a new workbook.

2. From the Tools menu, choose Macro and Record New Macro.

3. In the Macro name text box, key **Weeks**.

4. In the Shortcut key box, press (Shift) and key **w**.

5. Make sure the Store macro in text box shows This Workbook.

6. In the Description text box, replace the existing text with **Displays Weeks 1-4**. Click OK. The Stop Recording toolbar opens, and the status bar indicates that you are now recording a macro.

7. Make sure that the Relative Reference button 🖻 is not selected.

8. Press (Ctrl)+(G), key **b3**, and press (Enter). The macro records these keystrokes to position the insertion point in cell B3.

9. Select the range B3:E3 and make them bold and centered. The macro will select cells B3:E3 and make them bold and centered.

10. Key **Week 1** in cell B3. Use the Fill handle to fill in the weeks up to Week 4.

11. Click the Stop Recording button 🔳. The status bar indicates that you are no longer recording.

12. Clear all from the range B3:E3.

EXERCISE 17-23 Create a Second Macro

Create another macro in the same workbook to display the company name.

1. From the Tools menu, choose Macro and Record New Macro.

2. In the Macro name text box, key **KKInc**.

3. In the Shortcut key box, press (Shift) and key **k**.

4. Make sure the Store macro in text box shows This Workbook.

5. In the Description text box, key **Displays company name**. Click OK.

6. Make sure that the Relative Reference button 🖻 is not selected.

7. Select the range A1:A2 and set 18-point Times New Roman.

8. Key **Klassy Kow Ice Cream, Inc.** in cell A1 and press (Enter).

9. Key **Monthly Sales for** and press (Spacebar). Press (Enter).

10. Click the Stop Recording button 🔳.

11. Clear all from the range A1:A2.

EXERCISE 17-24 Save and Hide the Workbook

Your workbook appears to be blank but does include two macros. You can hide the workbook but still use its macros.

1. Save the workbook as *[your initials]***17-24** in your Lesson 17 folder.

2. Choose Hide from the Window menu. The macros workbook is open but hidden.

3. Create a new workbook.

4. In cell A1, press Ctrl+Shift+K to run the company name macro.

5. Press Ctrl+Shift+W to run the Weeks macro.

6. Close the new workbook without saving. Your macros workbook is still open and hidden.

7. Choose Unhide from the Window menu. Choose *[your initials]***17-24** and click OK.

8. Press Alt+F11. Expand the Modules folder if necessary. Then double-click Module1 to see the code.

9. From the File menu, choose Print. In the Range group, choose Current Module. In the Print what group, make sure Code is selected. Click OK.

10. Click the Close button ⊠ on the Visual Basic Editor title bar.

11. Save and close the workbook.

USING ONLINE HELP

As security becomes more important, you should understand how digital signatures are used. In most cases, you need to purchase a commercial certificate or get authentication from the IT department where you work.

Use Help to learn more about digital signatures.

1. With Internet Explorer and Excel running, find topics about digital signatures.

2. Read the information and print some of the windows if you think you can use them.

3. Close the windows and Internet Explorer. End your Internet connection.

LESSON Summary

➤ A macro is a sequence of commands and keystrokes that automate tasks. Macros are converted to Visual Basic for Applications (VBA) as you record them.

➤ Use the Visual Basic Editor to review and edit macro code.

➤ Macro security can be set to High, Medium, or Low. With Medium security, you can choose whether to enable or disable macros when opening the workbook.

➤ You must enable macros to run them.

➤ You can run a macro from the Tools menu, with a keyboard shortcut, or from a button or menu item.

➤ Subroutine macros can be run from the worksheet or from another macro. They start with the word "Sub" followed by the macro name. Subroutine macros end with "End Sub."

➤ Press Alt+F11 to open the Visual Basic Editor.

➤ You print macro code from the Visual Basic Editor.

➤ Macros are stored in workbooks. Delete a macro if you no longer need it.

➤ Macro names must begin with a letter and cannot use spaces or special characters. Keyboard shortcuts should include Shift so that you do not override Excel's own shortcuts.

➤ You can record macros with relative or absolute cell references.

➤ Use the Button tool on the Forms toolbar to create button controls. You can assign a macro to a button.

➤ You can create a new toolbar and place your macros on it.

➤ You can add a macro button to an existing Excel toolbar as an alternative to creating a separate macro toolbar.

LESSON 17 Command Summary

FEATURE	BUTTON	MENU	KEYBOARD
Run macro		Tools, Macro, Macros	Alt+F8
Edit macro		Tools, Macro, Visual Basic Editor	Alt+F11
Macro security		Tools, Macro, Security	
Create macro		Tools, Macro, Record New Macro	
Delete macro		Tools, Macro, Macros	Alt+F8
Display and hide toolbar		View, Toolbars	
Create and remove toolbar		Tools, Customize	
Add and delete button		Tools, Customize	

Concepts Review

TRUE/FALSE QUESTIONS

Each of the following statements is either true or false. Indicate your choice by circling T or F.

T F **1.** Macros are stored in workbooks.

T F **2.** Macros are recorded and converted to Visual Basic for Applications.

T F **3.** An acceptable name for a macro is **&MyName**.

T F **4.** To run a macro, choose Tools, Execute and then Macro.

T F **5.** Existing macros can be edited on the worksheet.

T F **6.** You must set the security level for each macro you write.

T F **7.** You can add new toolbars but cannot change Excel toolbars.

T F **8.** You must know Visual Basic to record a macro.

SHORT ANSWER QUESTIONS

Write the correct answer in the space provided.

1. What button should you click when you have finished creating your macro?

_____

2. What does the acronym "VBA" stand for?

_____

3. How can you determine if a line in a macro is explanatory and not part of the code?

_____

4. How do you remove a button from a toolbar?

_____

5. What dialog box allows you to make changes to toolbars and menus?

_____

6. What two types of cell references can Excel use in macros?

_____

7. What is the keyboard shortcut to open the Visual Basic Editor?

_____

8. What would happen if you used Ctrl+P as a shortcut to run a macro?

_____

CRITICAL THINKING

Answer these questions on a separate page. There are no right or wrong answers. Support your answers with examples from your own experience, if possible.

1. What advantages might there be to studying Visual Basic as a programming language?

2. As a student, what types of macros might be helpful to you in completing your class work?

Skills Review

EXERCISE 17-25

Run a macro. Edit and print a macro.

1. Open the file **AprilExp**. Click Enable Macros.

2. Run a macro by following these steps:
  a. Select cell B8.
  b. From the Tools menu, choose Macro and then Macros.
  c. Select Salesmen and click Run.

3. Select the range B8:D8. From the Edit menu, choose Clear and then All.

4. Edit a macro by following these steps:
  a. Press Alt+F11.
  b. Expand the Modules folder in the Project Explorer window. Then double-click Module1. Note the keyboard shortcut for the Salesmen macro subroutine.

 NOTE: If you do not see the Project Explorer window, choose Project Explorer from the View menu.

  c. In the Code window, locate the line that includes the text "Your name here."

d. Delete your name here and key your name. Be sure to leave the quotation marks.

e. Locate the line "Your Instructor" and key your instructor's name between the quotation marks.

f. Locate the line "Your Friend" and key the name of a friend between the quotation marks.

g. Scroll to the top of the Code window. Position the insertion point just after the first apostrophe under Sub Salesmen().

> **NOTE:** This module has two macros.

h. Press ⌨Spacebar once and key *[your name]*.

5. Print a macro by following these steps:

a. From the File menu, choose Print.

b. In the Range group, choose Current Module.

c. In the Print what group, make sure Code is selected. Click OK.

d. Click the Close button ☒ on the Visual Basic Editor title bar.

6. Run a macro by following these steps:

a. Select cell B8. Press ⌨Ctrl+⌨Shift+⌨S. Widen the columns to show each name.

b. Run the macro in cells B13, B18, and B23.

7. Add the standard footer. Save the workbook as *[your initials]***17-25** in your Lesson 17 folder.

8. Print the sheet and close the workbook.

EXERCISE 17-26

Name and record a macro. Run a macro. Print a macro.

1. Open the file **SalinasHoliday**.

2. Select cell A7. You will record and run a macro from this cell.

> **REVIEW:** This worksheet has a formula in column D that multiplies the hours worked by a constant named Rate. You can see what the rate is in the Define Name dialog box.

3. Name a macro by following these steps:

a. From the Tools menu, choose Macro and Record New Macro.

b. In the Macro name text box, key **ApplyRowShading**.

c. In the Shortcut key box, hold ⌨Shift and key **s**.

d. Make sure that the Store macro in option is This Workbook.

e. Delete text in the Description box and key **Applies shading to the current row**.

f. Click OK.

4. Record a macro with relative references by following these steps:

  a. Click the Relative Reference button 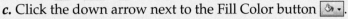 on the Stop Recording toolbar to activate it.

  b. Press Ctrl+Shift+→ to select all cells with data in the row.

  c. Click the down arrow next to the Fill Color button 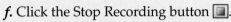.

  d. Choose Gray-25%, the rightmost color in the fourth row.

  e. Press Home and then ↓ two times to position the insertion point in cell A9.

  f. Click the Stop Recording button ◼.

5. Run a macro by following these steps:

  a. Press Ctrl+Shift+S to apply the shading to the cells in row 9.

  b. Run the macro in the odd-numbered rows with data.

6. Add a standard footer. Save the workbook as *[your initials]*17-26 in your Lesson 17 folder. Print the worksheet.

7. Display and print macro code by following these steps:

  a. Press Alt+F11. If the ApplyRowShading macro does not appear in the Code window, expand the Modules folder in the Project window, and then double-click Module1.

  b. Position the insertion point after the first apostrophe under Sub ApplyRowShading(). Press Spacebar and key *[your name]*.

  c. Choose File, Print from the menu. In the Range group, choose Current Module. In the Print what group, choose Code. Click OK.

8. Close the Visual Basic Editor. Save and close the workbook.

EXERCISE 17-27

Assign a macro to a button. Run a macro. Create a custom toolbar.

1. Open **AprilExp**. Click Enable Macros.

2. Draw a button by following these steps:

  a. Right-click any toolbar and choose Forms.

  b. Click the Button tool ▣ on the Forms toolbar.

  c. Click and drag to draw a button that covers the range F4:F5.

  d. Select BudgetAmounts in the Assign Macro dialog box and click OK.

  e. Click inside the button to display a text insertion pointer. Delete the existing text and key **Insert Budget $**.

  f. Right-click an edge of the button and choose Format Control.

  > **NOTE:** If you see only a Font tab in the Format Control dialog box, close the dialog box and select the button again to show the dotted pattern outline.

  g. On the Font tab, choose 9-point bold.

  h. Click the Properties tab and select Print object.

i. Click the Size tab. In the Size and rotate group, set the Height to **.4**. Click OK.

3. Run a macro from a button by following these steps:

   a. Select cell B9.

   b. Click the button.

   c. Run the macro in cells B14, B19, and B24.

4. Add a standard footer. Save the workbook as *[your initials]***17-27** in your Lesson 17 folder.

5. Print the worksheet and close the Forms toolbar.

6. Right-click the button and choose Cut.

7. Select the values in rows 9, 14, 19, and 24 and delete them.

8. Create a custom toolbar by following these steps:

   a. From the Tools menu, choose Customize. Click the Toolbars tab.

   b. Click New. In the Toolbar name text box, key **Macros**. Click OK.

   c. Arrange the screen so that you can see the dialog box and the toolbar.

   d. Click the Commands tab. In the Categories list, locate and select Macros.

   e. From the Commands list, click and drag Custom Menu Item to the open area of your toolbar below the title bar.

   f. Click Modify Selection in the Customize dialog box. Choose Assign Macro.

   g. Select BudgetAmounts and click OK.

   h. Click Modify Selection again. Select Name. In the Name text box, delete existing information and key **&Budget$** and press Enter.

   i. From the Commands list, drag Custom Button to the right of your menu item in the toolbar.

   j. Click Modify Selection. Choose Assign Macro. Select Salesmen and click OK.

   k. Click Modify Selection again. Select Name. In the Name text box, key **&Salesmen** and press Enter.

   l. Click Modify Selection again. Select Image and Text.

   m. Click Close to close the Customize dialog box.

 TIP: Steps 9–10 create a screen capture. These steps work in most Windows programs.

9. Drag the toolbar to start in cell C4. Press Print Screen. A picture of the worksheet is copied to the Clipboard.

 10. Insert a new worksheet and click the Paste button 📋▾. The image is pasted.

11. Right-click the image and size it to be 50% of its current size. Position its top-left corner at cell A1. Add a footer and print this sheet.

12. Close and save the workbook.

13. Delete a toolbar by following these steps:

   a. Right-click the Macros toolbar and choose Customize.

   b. Click the Toolbars tab. In the Toolbars list, select Macros.

   c. Click Delete. Click OK. Close the dialog box.

EXERCISE 17-28

Record a macro. Create a macros workbook. Customize an Excel toolbar. Print macros.

1. Create a new workbook.

2. Record a macro by following these steps:

   a. Choose Tools and Macro. Then choose Record New Macro. In the Macro name box, key **InsertKowabunga**.

   b. In the Shortcut key box, press (Shift) and key **b**. Verify that the Store macro in option is This Workbook. In the Description text box, key **Insert Kowabunga image**. Click OK.

   c. Turn on Relative Reference if it is not already active.

   d. With the macro recording, click the Insert Picture From File button [image]. (If the Drawing toolbar is not open, choose Insert, Picture, From File.) Open the folder with the image file **Kowabunga**. Double-click it to insert it.

   e. Right-click the image and choose Format Picture. Click the Size tab. In the Scale group, set Height to 50%. Click OK.

   f. Click the Stop Recording button [image].

   g. Select and delete the image.

3. Record a macro by following these steps:

   a. Choose Tools, Macro, and Record New Macro. Name this macro **KKInc**.

   b. In the Shortcut key box, press (Shift) and key **k**. Verify that the Store macro in option is This Workbook. In the Description box, key **Show name**. Click OK.

   c. With a relative reference, key **Klassy Kow Ice Cream, Inc.** in an empty cell. Press (Enter). Key **Monthly Sales** and press (Enter).

   d. Click the Stop Recording button [image].

   e. Clear all from the two cells.

4. Save a macros workbook by following these steps:

   a. Save the workbook as *[your initials]***17-28** in your Lesson 17 folder.

   b. Choose Hide from the Window menu.

   c. Create a new workbook.

   d. In cell A1, press (Ctrl)+(Shift)+(K).

   e. Press (Ctrl)+(Shift)+(B).

   f. Close the new workbook without saving. Your macros workbook is still open.

   g. Choose Unhide from the Window menu. Select your workbook and click OK.

5. Customize an Excel toolbar by following these steps:

   a. From the Tools menu, choose Customize.

   b. Click the Commands tab. In the Categories list, select Macros.

   c. From the Commands list, drag the Custom Button to any location on the Formatting toolbar.

  d. Click <u>M</u>odify Selection. **Choose** Assign <u>M</u>acro. **Select** InsertKowabunga and click OK.

  e. Click <u>M</u>odify Selection **and choose** Change <u>B</u>utton Image.

  f. Select any image. Click Close.

6. Go to Sheet2. Click the new toolbar button.

7. Delete a button by following these steps:

  a. Hold down Alt and drag the button off the toolbar and into the worksheet.

8. Print macros by following these steps:

  a. Press Alt+F11. Expand the Modules folder and then double-click Module1 in the Projects window if you do not see the InsertKowabunga macro code.

  b. Position the insertion point just after the first apostrophe under Sub InsertKowabunga(). Press Spacebar and key *[your name]*.

  c. Choose <u>F</u>ile, <u>P</u>rint. In the Range group, choose Current <u>M</u>odule. In the Print what group, make sure <u>C</u>ode is selected. Click OK.

  d. Close the Visual Basic Editor.

9. Close and save the workbook.

 NOTE: Make sure you complete step 7 of this exercise. Custom buttons remain on the computer until they are deleted.

Lesson Applications

EXERCISE 17-29

Record a macro to open a workbook. Assign a macro to a button. Test the macro. Print a macro.

Klassy Kow Ice Cream wants to design an order form template that includes a button to open a price list workbook.

1. Create a new workbook.

2. Format cells A1:A2 as 16-point Arial. Key **Klassy Kow Ice Cream** in cell A1 and **Online Order** in cell A2.

3. In the range A3:C3, key the following labels, starting in cell A3:
   Product   Quantity   Price

4. Make the labels in row 3 bold and centered. Set the width for all three columns to 20.71 (150 pixels). Set the height for row 3 to 26.25 (35 pixels).

5. Delete Sheet2 and Sheet3 and rename Sheet1 **OrderForm**.

6. Record a macro named **OpenPrices**. Do not use a shortcut. Store it in This Workbook. For the Description, key **Opens the price list**.

 TIP: A macro does not need a keyboard shortcut if you plan to run it from a button.

7. When the macro begins recording, open the file **ProductList**. Then stop recording.

8. Close the file **ProductList**.

9. Draw a button that covers the range C1:C2. Assign the OpenPrices macro to it. Edit the text on the button to show **Price List** and format it as bold.

10. Add the standard footer.

11. Save the file as a template named *[your initials]***17-29** in the Templates folder for your computer.

 REVIEW: The usual default folder location for Excel templates is C:\Documents and Settings*[User]*\Application Data\Microsoft\Templates.

12. Print the template and then close it. Close the Forms toolbar.

13. Create a new workbook based on your template, enabling the macros.

14. Test the button.

15. Click the Cakes&Pies tab in the **ProductList** workbook, select the range A9:C9, and copy and paste it to cell A4 in your workbook. Copy and paste one product from the NoveltyItems sheet in the **ProductList** workbook to cell A5 in your workbook. Close **ProductList** when you are finished copying and pasting.

16. Delete the sizes that were copied to column B and key a quantity for each item.

17. Format the button control so that it will print.

18. Save the workbook as *[your initials]*17-29 in your Lesson 17 folder. Print the worksheet.

19. Print the macro with your name as a comment after the macro name.

20. Close the Visual Basic Editor and your workbook.

21. Choose File, New and click On my computer. From the General tab, delete the template file *[your initials]*17-29.

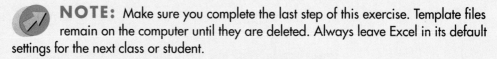 **NOTE:** Make sure you complete the last step of this exercise. Template files remain on the computer until they are deleted. Always leave Excel in its default settings for the next class or student.

EXERCISE 17-30

Record a macro to copy and position a worksheet. Run a macro.

Klassy Kow Ice Cream has a worksheet file for California soda sales that they would like to use for the other states. The workbook needs a macro that automates creating copies of the worksheet.

1. Open the file **CASodas**.

2. Record a new macro named **CopySheet**. For a shortcut, use Ctrl + Shift + C. The description is **Copies worksheet**. Use a relative reference when recording the macro.

3. When recording begins, right-click the worksheet tab and choose Move or Copy. In the Before sheet list, select (move to end). Select Create a copy and click OK. Stop recording.

4. Run the macro for a total of four worksheets. Rename the copied worksheets **Oregon**, **Nevada**, and **Washington**.

5. Group the Oregon, Nevada, and Washington worksheets and delete the contents of the range B4:D12.

 **REVIEW:** Use File and Page Setup to add the same footer to grouped sheets.

6. Add the California worksheet to the group. Select cell B4. Add the standard footer. Ungroup the worksheets.

7. Print the macro with your name as a comment after the macro name.

8. Save the workbook as *[your initials]*17-30 in your Lesson 17 folder.

9. Print the entire workbook and then close it.

EXERCISE 17-31

Edit a macro. Create a custom toolbar. Delete a toolbar.

In its blank phone order form, Klassy Kow has found that the macros have errors. You need to run the macros to find the errors and edit them. Then you need to build a toolbar with custom menu items for the macros.

1. Open **OrderForm** and enable the macros.

2. Determine what macros are in this workbook. Run them in logical order. Edit each macro to correct its errors.

3. Clear the contents and formats from the worksheet.

4. Create a new toolbar with a custom menu item for each of these macros. Edit the menu text to show an appropriate name for each macro.

5. Test the menu items on your toolbar.

6. Print the macros with your name as a comment.

7. Delete the toolbar.

8. Add the standard footer. Save the workbook as *[your initials]***17-31** in your Lesson 17 folder.

9. Print the worksheet and close the workbook.

 NOTE: Make sure you complete step 7 of this exercise. Custom toolbars remain on the computer until they are removed.

EXERCISE 17-32   *Challenge Yourself*

Record, test, edit, and print a macro.

When you write a macro, Excel records the results of commands. It also places in the macro current settings from the workbook. For example, if you write a macro while the workbook is set for portrait orientation, that setting is included in the macro code.

You can write a macro to place your name in a footer for a portrait worksheet. If the workbook with this macro is open, you can apply the footer to any other worksheet with one keystroke.

 TIP: On your own computer at work or home, store a footer macro in the Personal Macro Workbook so that it is always available.

1. Create a new workbook.

 REVIEW: Use File and Page Setup to create a footer on a blank worksheet.

2. Record a macro that inserts your standard footer. Choose a shortcut and description. Remember that this macro is for portrait orientation.

3. Delete the footer that was created as you recorded the macro.

4. Run your macro. If it does not work, delete it and try again.

 TIP: Type sample text in a cell so that you can use Print Preview to see if your macro worked.

5. Print the macro with your name as a comment.

6. Save the workbook as *[your initials]***17-32** in your Lesson 17 folder.

7. Close the workbook.

On Your Own

In these exercises you work on your own, as you would in a real-life work environment. Use the skills you've learned to accomplish the task—and be creative.

EXERCISE 17-33
In a new workbook, create a macro that you would find helpful in your school work or at your job. Key a description for the macro to describe what it will do. Add your name as a comment in the macro. Save the workbook as *[your initials]***17-33** in your Lesson 17 folder. Test your macro. Print your macro when it is complete and close the workbook.

EXERCISE 17-34
Use the Internet to find information about macros that are available from expert users or from Microsoft or its partners. Create a new workbook to describe what macros you found, where they can be purchased, what they do, and how much they cost. Add a standard footer. Save the workbook as *[your initials]***17-34** in your Lesson 17 folder, print the worksheet, and close the workbook.

EXERCISE 17-35
Create a new workbook. Create a new toolbar; use your name as the title and include five of Excel's commands that are not on the Standard or Formatting toolbar and that you would like to have available. Explore the options in the Customize dialog box to learn what you can do with this toolbar. After the toolbar is created, practice floating and anchoring it on your worksheet. Then float it near the middle of the screen. Press Print Screen to copy the screen image to the Clipboard. Insert a new sheet and press Ctrl+V to paste an image of the worksheet. Scale the picture to 50%. Add a standard footer and set the worksheet to print in landscape orientation. Save the workbook as *[your initials]***17-35** in your Lesson 17 folder. Print the worksheet and close the workbook. Delete the toolbar.

Unit 5 Applications

UNIT APPLICATION 5-1

Create a workbook template. Name ranges and constants. Include a chart in a template. Use a template.

Klassy Kow performs an analysis of its health insurance claims each year. They count the claims by month, build a chart, and estimate the number of claims for the next year. You have been asked to create a template with basic information so that it can be used each year.

1. Open the file **StateClaims**.

2. Use the Fill handle to fill the months across row 3 from Jan to Dec.

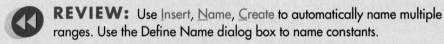 **REVIEW:** Use Insert, Name, Create to automatically name multiple ranges. Use the Define Name dialog box to name constants.

3. Select the range A3:M7 and use the top row and left column to automatically name the ranges.

4. Create a constant named **Increase1** and set it equal to **104%**. Create another constant named **Increase2** and set it equal to **106%**.

 NOTE: Use cell addresses in the SUM formula. You cannot copy the formula if you use range names.

5. Key a SUM formula for the first month in row 8. Copy the formula for the remaining months. Key a label in cell A8 for this row.

6. Use a formula in cell N4 to total the state. When Excel inserts the range name in a formula, you cannot copy the formula. So use a SUM formula for each state's total in column N.

7. Key **State Total** in cell N3 and adjust the column width.

8. Use a formula in cell N8 for the grand total. Hide the zeros. Format the range B4:N8 as Comma with no decimals.

9. Rename Sheet1 **Actual**. Rename Sheet2 **Estimated**. Delete Sheet3.

10. Copy the labels in cells A1 and A4:A7 from the Actual worksheet to the Estimated worksheet in the same locations. On the Estimated worksheet, in cell A2, key **Estimated State Total Next Year**. Copy the format from cell A1 to cell A2.

11. On the Estimated worksheet, key **4%** and **6%** in cells B3 and C3. Format these labels as bold and centered.

12. On the Estimated worksheet in cell B4, enter a 3-D formula to multiply California's total on the Actual sheet by the appropriate constant. Copy the formula through row 7. Enter a similar formula in cell C4. Copy this formula through row 7. Hide the zeros. Format the range B4:C7 as Comma with no decimals.

13. On the Actual worksheet, select the range B3:M3 and the range B8:M8. Create a line chart with markers at each value as a new sheet. In the wizard, name Series1 **Number of Claims**. Title the chart **Current Monthly Claims**. Place the chart between the other two worksheets. Delete the legend.

 NOTE: Chart sheets require that the footer be created separately.

14. Group the Actual and Estimated sheets and add your standard footer. Ungroup the worksheets and set the Actual worksheet to print on one page in landscape orientation. Add the same footer to the chart sheet.

15. Save the workbook as a template named *[your initials]***u5-1** in the Templates folder for your computer. Close the template.

16. Create a new workbook based on the template and key the information shown in Figure U5-1.

FIGURE U5-1

	Jan	Feb	Mar	Apr	May	Jun	
California	40	42	35	25	15	32	
Oregon	30	25	15	22	27	23	
Nevada	42	27	35	28	32	29	
Washington	18	21	7	21	19	21	
	Jul	Aug	Sep	Oct	Nov	Dec	
California	30	42	45	28	18	38	
Oregon	20	28	19	32	24	17	
Nevada	32	32	23	28	38	34	
Washington	16	27	17	23	29	16	

17. Save the workbook as *[your initials]***u5-1** in a new folder for Unit 5.

18. Print the entire workbook and close the workbook.

19. Delete the template from your Templates folder.

REVIEW: Template files remain on the computer until they are deleted. Always leave Excel in its default settings for the next class or student.

UNIT APPLICATION 5-2

Create a worksheet template. Add an image and a footer to a template. Protect a worksheet.

A balance sheet is a financial statement that shows a company's assets, its liabilities, and its owners' (or shareholders') equity. Klassy Kow Ice Cream, Inc. prepares a monthly balance sheet and needs a template to automate the process.

1. Open the file **BalanceSheet**.
2. Widen column A to accommodate the widest label in the column. Delete rows 4 and 5. Set the height of the new row 4 to 26.25 (35 pixels). Delete row 17 and then set its row height to 26.25 (35 pixels).
3. Use AutoSum in cell C10 to add the range C6:C9. Format cell C10 with a single top border.
4. Enter a formula in cell C14 to subtract cell C13 from C12. Format cell C14 with a single top border.
5. In cell C16, enter a formula that adds cells C10, C14, and C15. Format the formula cell with a single top and double bottom border.
6. Sum the current liabilities in cell C22. Use a single top border. Sum cells C23 and C24 in cell C25. Use a single top border.
7. In cell C27, add cells C22, C25, and C26. Format this cell with a single top and double bottom border.
8. Insert a comment in cell A2 that tells the user to edit the cell to show the current month.
9. Insert the image file **Cow.gif** and place it to appear at the top-right margin of the sheet. Make sure the worksheet fits on a portrait page.

 REVIEW: You must show a comment in order for it to print.

10. Add your standard footer. Set the comment to print on the sheet.
11. Unlock cell A2 and the cells in column C that will have values. Protect the template to allow selection of cells and formatting of columns without a password.
12. Save the workbook as a template named *[your initials]***u5-2** in your Unit 5 folder. Print the template.

 NOTE: Because you are not using the template to create a new workbook, you can save this template in your Unit 5 folder.

13. Make a copy of the worksheet and remove the protection. Display the formulas. Delete the comment and the image. Adjust column widths. Print the formulas fit to one portrait page.

14. Save and close the template.

UNIT APPLICATION 5-3

Record a macro to copy a worksheet and delete a range.

Klassy Kow contributes to its employees' retirement funds. Each year the amounts are totaled by state. Write macros that will make it easy to create each year's worksheet. These include a macro to copy the worksheet and delete the existing values.

1. Open the file **401K**.

2. Record a macro in this workbook named **CopySheet** with the shortcut Ctrl+Shift+C. Use an appropriate description. When recording begins, make sure the Relative Reference button is off. Copy the worksheet by using the tab shortcut menu so that the sheet for the new year precedes the current year sheet.

3. On the copied sheet, select and delete the contribution amounts but not the total formulas. Click cell B5. Stop recording.

4. Delete the copied sheet that you created while writing the macro.

5. Run the macro. Rename the new sheet **2005**. Edit the label in cell A3 accordingly.

6. Key a 3-D reference in cell B5 to multiply the value from the previous year by 107.5%. Copy the formula down the column to row 16 and then copy the formulas in column B through column E.

7. Add your standard footer to the copied sheet. Edit the properties to show a title, your name, and **Klassy Kow Ice Cream, Inc.** as the company. Use a preview image.

8. Save the workbook as *[your initials]***u5-3** in your Unit 5 folder. Print the copied sheet.

9. Print the macro with your name entered as a comment.

10. Save and close the workbook.

UNIT APPLICATION 5-4 *Using the Internet*

Create a template. Insert an image. Use VLOOKUP and HYPERLINK. Apply conditional formatting.

Explore consumer retail sites on the Internet to find a site that sells products of interest to you. Look for sites that show pictures of the products. Make a list of five products, descriptions, and prices from one site.

Create a template order form for the site. On the sheet, enter the company name and a logo or image. Use an image or logo from the Web site if possible. In a cell near the top of the order form, use the HYPERLINK function with appropriate text to link to the Web site.

 TIP: Right-click an image on a Web site and save it to your hard drive.

Use five columns in the body of the sales invoice: Product ID, Description, Unit Price, Quantity, and Extension. Create a formula in the Extension column to multiply the price by the quantity. These cells must be unlocked. Set conditional formatting in the Quantity column for any quantities over 6.

On a lookup sheet, create a lookup table that includes the Product ID, Description, and Unit Price. Remember that the lookup table must be sorted alphabetically by the first column. Then use the VLOOKUP function on the order sheet to display the description and the price after the Product ID is keyed.

Protect the worksheet and add the standard footer. Save it as a template named *[your initials]***u5-4** in your Templates folder. Print the template and close it. Create a new workbook from the template, keying sample data. Save the workbook as *[your initials]***u5-4** in your Unit 5 folder. Print the workbook and close it. Delete the template from the Templates folder.

Using Analysis, Linking, and Workgroup Features

18

Using Auditing Tools

OBJECTIVES

After completing this lesson, you will be able to:

1. **Evaluate a formula.**
2. **Trace precedents and dependents.**
3. **Select errors with Go To Special.**
4. **Correct errors.**
5. **Use the Watch window.**
6. **Troubleshoot errors.**

MICROSOFT OFFICE SPECIALIST ACTIVITIES

In this lesson:
XL03E-1-11
XL03E-1-12
XL03E-1-13
XL03E-3-2

See Appendix.

 Estimated Time: 1 hour

Errors can creep into a worksheet in many ways. For example, you could accidentally refer to an empty cell in a formula. You might delete a range name used in a formula. *Auditing* is the practice of examining cells and formulas for accuracy, similar to proofreading an essay. It is good business practice to audit your work before printing or e-mailing.

Excel contains many tools and features that help you audit your worksheets. Many errors show a message in the cell and are easy to spot. For almost all errors, you can get help from the Formula Auditing toolbar.

 NOTE: "Auditing" applies to many types of financial records and documents.

Evaluating a Formula

Excel performs background error checking each time you open a workbook and while you are working. It looks for patterns, expected ranges, consistencies, and other issues. Cells with a potential problem display the tiny green triangle in the upper-left corner. Some formula errors also display an error value message in the cell. Table 18-1 describes the error value messages.

The Error Checking tab in the Options dialog box lists the types of errors for which Excel can look. These include formulas that refer to empty cells, inconsistent formulas, and formulas that display an error value message.

 NOTE: You can turn background error checking on/off by choosing Tools, Options and clicking the Error Checking tab.

TABLE 18-1

Excel Error Value Messages

ERROR VALUE IN CELL	DESCRIPTION
#DIV/0	The formula (or macro) divides by zero. This message might also appear when the formula divides by an empty cell.
#N/A	The formula uses a value that is not available.
#NAME?	The formula uses unrecognized text, such as a range name that does not exist.
#NULL!	The formula refers to an intersection of cell ranges that do not intersect.
#NUM!	The formula uses an invalid numeric value, such as a negative number when a positive number is needed.
#REF!	The formula refers to a cell reference that is not valid.
#VALUE!	The formula uses the wrong type of argument or operand.

EXERCISE **18-1** **Evaluate a Formula**

If a cell displays an error value message, you can review the formula, step-by-step, to determine where the mistake is located. When you evaluate a formula, Excel shows each part of the formula and its results. This can help you see where the problem is or where it starts.

 NOTE: Check that your macro security setting is Medium. Choose Tools, Macro, and Security.

1. Open **ConsolidatedPies**. The medium security setting alerts you when a workbook has a macro.

2. Click Enable Macros. You cannot use macros unless they are enabled.

3. If you do not see green triangles to mark errors, press ⬇ to reach cell A30 and then press ⬆ to return to cell A1. This refreshes or rewrites the screen.

4. Select cell B19. Position the pointer on the Trace Error button ◈. The ScreenTip indicates that the problem is the wrong data type.

FIGURE 18-1
ScreenTip about
the error

		Q1	Q2	Q3	Q4	Total
5	Unit Sales					
6	Flavors	Q1	Q2	Q3	Q4	Total
7						
8	Vanilla	10,000	14,500	15,000	15,000	54,500
9	Chocolate	12,000	13,000	16,000	18,000	59,000
10	Strawberry	9,500	14,750	12,500	10,500	47,250
11	Chocolate Chip	13,500	14,500	16,000	17,000	61,000
12	Turtle	12,000	11,500	18,000	15,000	56,500
13	Total	57,000	68,250	77,500	75,500	278,250
14						
15	Dollar Sales					
16	Flavors	Q1	Q2	Q3	Q4	Total
17						
18	Vanilla	$129,500.00	$187,775.00	$194,250.00	$511,525.00	$511,525.00
19	Chocolate ◈ ▾	#VALUE!	#VALUE!	#VALUE!	#VALUE!	#VALUE!
20	Strawberry	#NAME?	#NAME?	#NAME?	#NAME?	#NAME?
21	Chocolate Chi	A value used in the formula is of the wrong data type.			-	-
22	Turtle	203,400.00	194,925.00	305,100.00	703,425.00	703,425.00
23	Total	#VALUE!	#VALUE!	#VALUE!	#VALUE!	#VALUE!
24						
25		Pie Prices		Avg Unit Sales		
26	Vanilla	$ 12.95		#DIV/0!		
27	Chocolate	-				
28	Strawberry	$ 13.50				
29	Chocolate Chip	$ 14.95				
30	Turtle	$ 16.95				
31						

Trace Error button

5. Click the down arrow with the Trace Error button ◈. The first menu item is an explanation of the error. The other choices are error-checking options for this type of error. Show Calculation Steps is an option for errors that display an error value message.

6. Choose Show Calculation Steps. The Evaluate Formula dialog box opens and shows the cell reference and its initial evaluation. The formula in cell B19 multiplies 12000 by a hyphen (-). The hyphen is in quotation marks, which means it is text. (See Figure 18-2.)

7. Click Evaluate. When this formula is calculated, Excel shows the error value message #VALUE!.

8. Click Restart. The formula is shown with its cell references this time, B9*$B27. The underline with B9 indicates that it will be the first part of the formula checked.

9. Click Step In. The first step in the formula calculates that cell B9 = 12000. That's correct.

FIGURE 18-2
Evaluate Formula
dialog box

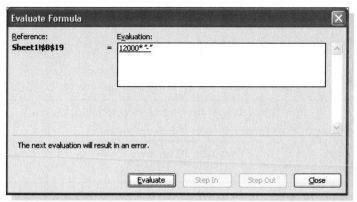

10. Click Step Out. The next element (cell B27) is underlined and ready to be checked.

11. Click Step In. Cell B27 does not have a value; it has a hyphen that Excel has identified as a constant. This is the source of the error.

12. Click Step Out and then click Close. The Evaluate Formula dialog box does not correct the formula. It checks each part to help you determine what is wrong.

13. Select cell C19 and position the pointer over the Trace Error button. Click the down arrow with the button.

14. Choose Help on this error. A related Help window opens.

15. Click the topic Entering text when the formula requires a number or a logical value, such as TRUE or FALSE.

16. Read the explanation and close the Help window. You will correct the error later.

Tracing Precedents and Dependents

In addition to evaluating a formula in steps, you can use other auditing tools for fixing errors. Some of these tools trace the relationships between a formula and its related cells by displaying arrows on the screen. The Formula Auditing toolbar has tools to show the flow of a formula and how one formula relates to another. (See Table 18-2 on the next page.)

EXERCISE **18-2** **Trace Precedents**

One way to correct errors in formulas is to trace a formula's precedent cells. A *precedent* is a cell that "precedes" and contributes to the formula's results. It provides

TABLE 18-2 Formula Auditing Toolbar Buttons

NAME	BUTTON	DESCRIPTION
Error Checking		Starts an error-checking routine that opens a dialog box about each error with options for correcting the error.
Trace Precedents		Traces the source of a formula's result.
Remove Precedent Arrows		Removes the arrows shown by Trace Precedents.
Trace Dependents		Traces the cells dependent on a cell's contents or results.
Remove Dependent Arrows		Removes the arrows shown by Trace Dependents.
Remove All Arrows		Removes all precedent, dependent, and trace error arrows.
Trace Error		Locates all cells that contribute to an error in a cell.
New Comment		Inserts a comment into a cell.
Circle Invalid Data		Displays circles around cells with data that does not meet data validation settings.
Clear Validation Circles		Removes circles displayed by Circle Invalid Data.
Show Watch Window		Displays or hides the Watch window for viewing a formula's results.
Evaluate Formula		Shows each part of the formula with its results in steps.

data for the formula. A precedent cell that contains an error will generate an error in the formula.

1. Right-click any toolbar and choose Formula Auditing. The Formula Auditing toolbar opens.

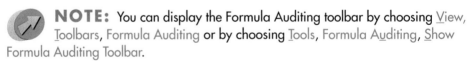

NOTE: You can display the Formula Auditing toolbar by choosing View, Toolbars, Formula Auditing or by choosing Tools, Formula Auditing, Show Formula Auditing Toolbar.

2. Select cell B19.

3. Click the Trace Precedents button . Blue dots and lines connect the formula to the cells providing the data (cells B9 and B27). Something is

wrong in one or both of those cells. Although the lines pass through several cells, the cells with the dots are the precedents.

TIP: For a complicated worksheet, you can click the Trace Precedents button a second time to trace precedents of the precedent cells.

FIGURE 18-3
Precedents traced in
the worksheet

		Q1	Q2	Q3	Q4	Total
5	**Unit Sales**					
6	**Flavors**	**Q1**	**Q2**	**Q3**	**Q4**	**Total**
7						
8	Vanilla	10,000	14,500	15,000	15,000	54,500
9	Chocolate	12,000	13,000	16,000	18,000	59,000
10	Strawberry	9,500	14,750	12,500	10,500	47,250
11	Chocolate Chip	13,500	14,500	16,000	17,000	61,000
12	Turtle	12,000	11,500	18,000	15,000	56,500
13	**Total**	**57,000**	**68,250**	**77,500**	**75,500**	**278,250**
14						
15	**Dollar Sales**		Formula Auditing		▼ ×	
16	**Flavors**					Total
17						
18	Vanilla	$129,500.00	$187,775.00	$194,250.00	$511,525.00	$511,525.00
19	Chocolate	#VALUE!	#VALUE!	#VALUE!	#VALUE!	#VALUE!
20	Strawberry	#NAME?	#NAME?	#NAME?	#NAME?	#NAME?
21	Chocolate Chip	-	-	-	-	-
22	Turtle	203,400.00	194,925.00	305,100.00	703,425.00	703,425.00
23	**Total**	**#VALUE!**	**#VALUE!**	**#VALUE!**	**#VALUE!**	**#VALUE!**
24						
25		**Pie Prices**		**Avg Unit Sales**		
26	Vanilla	$ 12.95		#DIV/0!		
27	Chocolate	-				
28	Strawberry	$ 13.50				
29	Chocolate Chip	$ 14.95				
30	Turtle	$ 16.95				
31						

 4. Click the Remove Precedent Arrows button . The arrows are removed.

NOTE: The Trace Precedents and Dependents buttons show plus (+) signs. The buttons to remove arrows show minus (−) signs.

5. Click the Trace Error button 🔘 on the Formula Auditing toolbar. The same precedents are shown.

 6. Click the Remove All Arrows button 🔘. The arrows are removed.

EXERCISE **18-3** **Trace Dependents**

A *dependent* is a cell that "depends" or relies on another cell. You can use this feature to see what formulas are affected by a specific cell.

 1. Click the Trace Dependents button 🔘. Red arrows point to cells that depend on the value in cell B19 (cells E19 and B23).

2. Click the Remove Dependent Arrows button ⬕.

3. Select cell F19.

4. Click the Trace Error button ⬕ on the Formula Auditing toolbar. This cell has precedent (blue) and dependent (red) arrows. The precedent dots (blue) show that something in either cell B9 or B27 contributes to the error in cell B19. The dependent dots (red) show that cells B19 and E19 depend on either B9 or B27. All of this affects cell F19.

5. Click the Remove All Arrows button ⬕.

Selecting Errors with Go To Special

You can use the Go To Special dialog box to select cells with errors, cells that are blank, cells with constants, and other data types. Some of these options can help you find various types of problems in your worksheet. Table 18-3 summarizes the options available in the Go To Special dialog box.

TABLE 18-3 Go To Special Selections

OPTION	DESCRIPTION
Comments	Selects all cells that contain comments.
Constants	Selects all cells with values that do not change.
Formulas	Selects all cells with formulas. You can choose to find cells that result in numbers, text, logicals (Yes or No, True or False), or error values.
Blanks	Selects all cells that are empty.
Current region	Selects all cells up to the first blank cell.
Current array	Selects all cells in the array.
Objects	Selects all objects, such as AutoShapes and images.
Row differences	Selects all cells in the current row with contents different from the active cell.
Column differences	Selects all cells in the current column with contents different from the active cell.
Precedents	Selects all cells that support the active cell.
Dependents	Selects all cells that depend on the active cell.
Last cell	Selects the last cell with data on the worksheet.
Visible cells only	Selects only cells that can be seen and excludes hidden cells and cells in hidden rows or columns.
Conditional formats	Selects all cells that have a conditional format applied.
Data validation	Selects cells that have data validation settings applied.

EXERCISE **Select Cells with Formulas**

1. Press Ctrl+Home.
2. Press Ctrl+G. The Go To dialog box opens.

   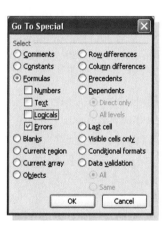 **REVIEW:** You can press F5 to display the Go To dialog box or choose Edit, Go To.

3. Click Special. The Go To Special dialog box opens.
4. Select Formulas. This option will highlight all cells with formulas. The results of those formulas can be values, text, logical TRUE or FALSE entries, or error value messages.
5. Make sure each of these is selected: Numbers, Text, Logicals, and Errors.
6. Click OK. All cells with formulas are selected.
7. Press Ctrl+Home. Press Ctrl+G. Click Special.
8. Select Formulas. Deselect Numbers, Text, and Logicals. Leave a check mark for Errors.

FIGURE 18-4
Selecting cells with errors

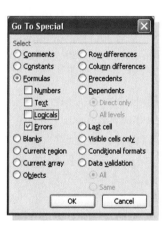

9. Click OK. All cells with error value messages are selected.
10. Press Ctrl+Home. Press Ctrl+G. Click Special.
11. Choose Blanks. Click OK. Empty cells are highlighted.
12. Press Ctrl+Home.

Correcting Errors

Although Excel has numerous tools for finding errors in your worksheet, it can't correct them for you. You must manually correct errors. You can use tools such as the Evaluate Formula button 🔍 to assist you in tracking down the source of an error. With practice, you can learn to use these tools to quickly correct problems in your worksheet.

EXERCISE **18-5** **Check and Correct Identified Errors**

1. Select cell B27. Unlike the other pies, the Chocolate pie has no price.

2. Look at the formula bar. The cell is not empty, because it has a hyphen. A simple typing error like this can affect much of the worksheet.

3. Key **12.95** and press Enter. Several errors in row 19 are corrected, because they depended on cell B27.

4. Select cell B20.

5. Click the Trace Error button ⬇ on the Formula Auditing toolbar. This error traces to cell B10.

6. Click the Remove All Arrows button ⬚.

7. Click the Evaluate Formula button ⬚ on the Formula Auditing toolbar. The Evaluate Formula dialog box opens. The formula in cell B20 multiplies cell B10 by Strawberry. The contents of cell B10 will be evaluated first.

> **NOTE:** The Evaluate Formula button ⬚ on the Formula Auditing toolbar and Show Calculation Steps in the shortcut menu both display the Evaluate Formula dialog box.

8. Click Evaluate. The value for cell B10 is 9500. This seems acceptable. Strawberry is underlined for evaluation next.

9. Click Evaluate. Excel shows the #NAME? error.

10. Click Evaluate. The formula tries to compute but returns #NAME?. Strawberry is a range name used in this formula, but the name is invalid.

11. Click Close.

12. Click the down arrow next to the Name box. The ranges are listed, but there is no range name for Strawberry.

13. Press Esc.

14. Press Ctrl+F3. The Define Name dialog box opens. The name Strawberry is shown in the Names in workbook text box, because Excel accepts the label in the adjacent cell A20. The Refers to entry is wrong.

> **REVIEW:** You can open the Define Name dialog box by choosing Insert, Name, Define or by pressing Ctrl+F3. Existing range names appear in the list box.

15. Place the insertion point in the Refers to text box.

16. Delete the entry and select cell B28, the price of the Strawberry pie.

17. Click Add. Click Close. Errors in rows 20 and 23 are corrected.

18. Widen the columns to show all the data.

Using the Watch Window

The *Watch window* is a separate window that displays a formula and its results. You can add cell references with formulas to the window and watch what happens as you edit precedent or dependent cells on the worksheet. This is helpful for large worksheets or 3-D references in which you cannot see dependent, precedent, and formula cells all at once.

 NOTE: Do not begin this exercise unless you can complete Exercise 18-9. You will be changing default settings in Exercise 18-6, and you restore them in Exercise 18-9.

EXERCISE **18-6** **Use the Watch Window**

You can use the Watch window to observe cells with errors as you add data to the dependent cells.

1. Choose Tools and Options. Click the Error Checking tab.

2. Verify that there is a check mark for Formulas referring to empty cells and click OK. Cells in row 21 and column F show green triangles, indicating problems with the formulas. If you do not see triangles, move the insertion point around the worksheet to refresh the screen.

 3. Click the Show Watch Window button in the Formula Auditing toolbar. The Watch window opens. Currently, no cell is being watched. Drag the Watch window so that you can see row 23.

4. Click Add Watch in the Watch window. The Add Watch dialog box opens so that you can select cells to be watched.

5. Select the range B23:F23 in the worksheet. (See Figure 18-5 on the next page.)

6. Click Add. Information about each cell and its formula is listed in the window.

7. Move the Watch window so that you can see row 21.

 NOTE: If the Watch window snaps or anchors to the top or bottom of the screen, float it by clicking its title bar and dragging the window.

8. Select cell B21. Position the pointer on the Trace Error button and click its drop-down arrow. The first item in the menu indicates that the formula refers to empty cells.

FIGURE 18-5
Preparing the
Watch window

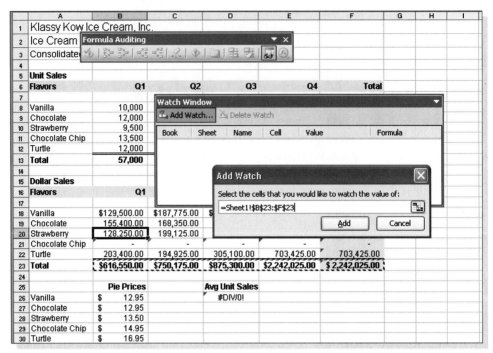

9. Press Esc to hide the menu. Look at the formula in the formula bar. It refers to cell C29, but the price is in cell B29.

10. Press F2 and look at cell B21. Color coding can help you follow an error to determine what is wrong. Cell C29 is outlined in green and shown in green in the formula. Cell B11 and its reference are shown in blue.

11. In the cell, edit $C29 to **$B29**.

12. Press Enter. The Watch window shows the new result for cell B23, as does the worksheet. (See Figure 18-6.)

13. Copy the formula in cell B21 to the range C21:E21. Widen columns to show the data.

EXERCISE **18-7** **Delete a Watch and Close the Window**

You can delete a formula from the Watch window when you no longer need to monitor it.

1. Click the row for cell B23 in the Watch window.

2. Click Delete Watch. The reference is removed.

3. Click the row for cell C23 in the Watch window.

FIGURE 18-6
Changing a formula

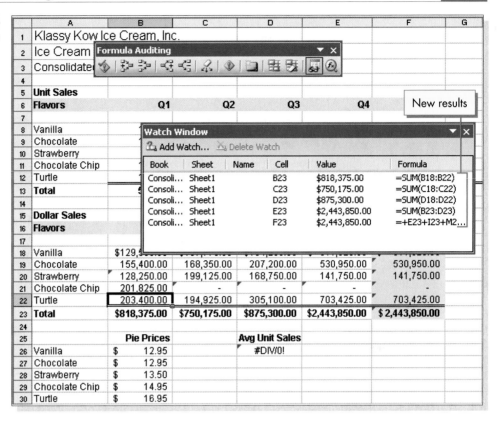

4. Press and hold (Shift) and click the row for cell F23. All the rows in the Watch window are selected.

5. Press (Delete). All the cell references are removed.

6. Click the Show Watch Window button 🖾 on the Formula Auditing toolbar. The window is hidden.

Troubleshooting Errors

Not all errors are apparent or found by Excel. For example, two columns of data might contain exactly the same values for different time periods. Excel would not see this as an error, but you'd probably be suspicious of such data if you spotted it and would almost certainly examine it.

Excel also might flag some cells with errors when, in fact, the formulas are correct. You'll want to examine all cells that Excel marks with the green triangles. Sometimes you can tell Excel to ignore the errors.

EXERCISE 18-8 **Ignore Errors**

The worksheet still contains cells that Excel marked with errors. You can remove the green triangles if you decide the problem can be ignored.

1. Select cell B20. It displays a green triangle and shows a Trace Error button 🔽.

2. Position the pointer on the button and click its arrow. The first item on the menu is Inconsistent Formula. The second menu item suggests Copy Formula from Above. That's a hint about what is wrong.

3. Select cell B19. This formula does not use a range name, but the formula in cell B20 does. Excel notes this as being inconsistent.

4. Select cell B20 again. Click the down arrow next to the Trace Error button 🔽.

5. Choose Ignore Error. The green triangle is removed.

6. Select the range C20:E20.

7. Click the down arrow next to the Trace Error button 🔽 and choose Ignore Error. The green triangles are removed from cells in the selected range.

EXERCISE 18-9 **Look for Other Errors**

You've set Excel to show errors in formulas that refer to empty cells. The default setting is for this option to be turned off. When the default setting is in place, some of the formulas in your worksheet would not show errors. You'd have to spot these errors yourself.

1. Compare the values in the range E18:E22 and F18:F22. The values are the same in both columns, but they should not be the same. The column F values should show a total of all four quarters.

2. Select cell F18. Position the pointer on the Trace Error button 🔽 and click the down arrow. The first shortcut menu item indicates that the formula refers to empty cells.

3. Click the Trace Error button 🔽 on the Formula Auditing toolbar. An information box opens. You can use this button only for errors that display an error value message such as #NAME?. Click OK.

4. Click the Trace Precedents button 📑 on the Formula Auditing toolbar. The formula in cell F18 refers to cells to the right that have no data. (See Figure 18-7.)

5. Click the Remove Precedent Arrows button 📑.

FIGURE 18-7
Formula referring to
empty cells

	Q2	Q3	Q4	Total			
16	Q2	Q3	Q4	Total			
17							
18	$187,775.00	$ 194,250.00	$ 611,52◇0	$ 611,525.00			
19	168,350.00	207,200.00	530,950.00	530,950.00			
20	199,125.00	168,750.00	141,750.00	141,750.00			
21	216,775.00	239,200.00	254,150.00	254,150.00			
22	194,925.00	305,100.00	703,425.00	703,425.00			
23	$966,950.00	$ 1,114,500.00	$2,899,825.00	$ 2,899,825.00			
24							
25		Avg Unit Sales					
26		#DIV/0!					
27							

6. Select cell E18. The value for this cell is substantially larger than the three previous quarters. Look at the formula in the formula bar. The formula shows a sum of the three previous columns, but it should multiply the unit sales by the price (E8*B26). Look at the remaining cells in the range E19:E22. Several have unnoticed errors.

7. Select and delete the contents of the range E18:E22.

8. In cell E18, key = and then select cell E8 to start the formula.

9. Key * and select cell B26. The range name for cell B26 appears in the formula. Press ⌈Enter⌋.

10. In cell E19, key = and select cell E9. Key ***chocolate** and press ⌈Enter⌋.

11. In cell E20, key = and select cell E10. Key ***strawberry** and press ⌈Enter⌋.

12. Complete the formulas for the range E21:E22.

13. Delete the contents of the range F18:F23.

14. While the cells are selected, click the AutoSum button . New totals are entered into the selected range.

15. Select cell E23. Notice that its total is substantially larger than corresponding quarters. This is an error that Excel has not noted. The formula should sum cells E18:E22, not the values in row 23.

16. Delete the contents of cell E23 and click the AutoSum button Σ ▾. Press ⌈Enter⌋.

17. Choose Tools and Options. Click the Error Checking tab. Remove the check mark for Formulas referring to empty cells and click OK.

 NOTE: Make sure you complete the last step of this exercise. By default, Excel does not show formulas that refer to empty cells as errors.

EXERCISE 18-10 Correct Division by Zero

There is one more cell in the worksheet with an error. It displays the error message value #DIV/0 to indicate that the formula is dividing by zero.

1. Select cell D26. Position the pointer on its Trace Error button 🔷 to see the ScreenTip for the error.

2. Press F2. The sum of B13:E13 should be divided by the number of quarters. This is a constant value.

3. Delete the zero and key **4**. Press Enter.

4. Format cell D26 to show no decimals. Remember that Excel rounds the value when you choose no decimals.

5. Add your standard footer.

EXERCISE 18-11 Create a Digital Certificate

This worksheet includes a macro to insert the company name. When a workbook has macro or other Visual Basic features, you can add your own digital certificate to the file. When you add your own digital certificate, it is valid for only the machine where you create it. If authenticity is important for documents that you send or receive, you should work with a commercial source for digital certificates.

1. Click the Start button on the taskbar. Choose All Programs.

 NOTE: Your workstation may show Microsoft Office Tools in the All Programs menu.

2. Choose Microsoft Office and then Microsoft Office Tools.

3. Choose Digital Certificate for VBA Projects. The Create Digital Certificate dialog box opens.

4. Read the information about certificates.

5. Key *[your first initial and last name]* in this format, ASmith.

FIGURE 18-8
Creating a digital
certificate

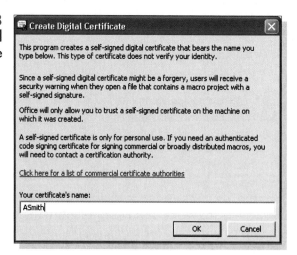

6. Click OK. The message box shows that the certificate has been created.

7. Click OK.

8. Save the workbook as *[your initials]*18-11 in a new folder for Lesson 18.

9. Close the Formula Auditing toolbar. Print the worksheet and close the workbook.

USING ONLINE HELP

Background error checking and the Formula Auditing toolbar both are helpful for checking your work. Use Microsoft Excel Help to learn more about auditing worksheet formulas.

Use Help to learn about auditing worksheets.

1. With Internet Explorer and Excel running, look for topics about correcting formulas. Look for subtopics such as Find and correct errors in formulas and Trace the relationships between formulas and cells.

2. Read the information. Close the windows.

3. Close Internet Explorer and end your Internet connection.

LESSON 18 Summary

➤ Auditing is the practice of examining cells and formulas for accuracy. Excel provides several tools to help you audit your worksheet for accuracy.

➤ Excel performs background error checking. Errors are noted with a tiny green triangle. Some cells display an error value message.

➤ When a cell displays an error value message, you can review each element in the formula step-by-step.

➤ The Formula Auditing toolbar includes most tools for tracing and evaluating formula errors.

➤ A precedent contributes or provides data to a formula's result.

➤ A dependent is a cell that relies on another cell for its value.

➤ You can use the Go To Special dialog box to select cells with errors, blanks, and other types of data.

➤ Although Excel can help you locate errors, you must manually correct them. You can use the Evaluate Formula button to analyze problem formulas.

➤ The Watch window displays formula cells and related information in a separate window.

➤ Delete a formula from the Watch window when you no longer need to monitor it, or close the Watch window.

➤ You can have Excel show formulas that refer to empty cells as errors.

➤ The error message value #DIV/0 indicates division by zero.

LESSON 18   Command Summary

FEATURE	BUTTON	MENU	KEYBOARD
Evaluate Formula		Tools, Formula Auditing, Evaluate Formula	
Digital Certificate		Start, Microsoft Office, Microsoft Office Tools, Digital Certificate for VBA Projects	
Trace Precedents		Tools, Formula Auditing, Trace Precedents	
Trace Dependents		Tools, Formula Auditing, Trace Dependents	
Trace Error		Tools, Formula Auditing, Trace Error	
Remove Precedent Arrows		Tools, Formula Auditing, Remove All Arrows	
Remove Dependent Arrows		Tools, Formula Auditing, Remove All Arrows	
Remove All Arrows		Tools, Formula Auditing, Remove All Arrows	
Show Watch Window		Tools, Formula Auditing, Show Watch Window	

Concepts Review

TRUE/FALSE QUESTIONS

Each of the following statements is either true or false. Indicate your choice by circling T or F.

T   F   **1.** Excel finds and corrects most formula errors.

T   F   **2.** Precedent arrows point to cells used in the formula.

T   F   **3.** You can press Ctrl+G to find specific types of cells.

T   F   **4.** Any digital certificate can authenticate your identity.

T   F   **5.** The Evaluate Formula dialog box shows each argument in a formula and its reference.

T   F   **6.** The Watch window displays the current time, date, and number of edits.

T   F   **7.** The Formula Auditing toolbar includes a button to display the Watch window.

T   F   **8.** #NAME? is an error value message.

SHORT ANSWER QUESTIONS

Write the correct answer in the space provided.

1. If a cell provides data for a formula, what is that cell called?

_____

2. What toolbar is used for checking the accuracy of formulas and cell relationships?

_____

3. A cell that relies on other cells for data is called what?

_____

4. How can you monitor a formula if the worksheet is large and you cannot see the formula cell?

_____

5. What does the error value #DIV/0 mean?

_____

6. Name two categories of cells that can be selected by using the Go To Special dialog box.

   _____

7. What is the term for examining a worksheet's cells and formulas for accuracy?

   _____

8. What can be assigned to a document to electronically verify its authenticity?

   _____

CRITICAL THINKING

Answer these questions on a separate page. There are no right or wrong answers. Support your answers with examples from your own experience, if possible.

1. How do you think the online book industry might use digital certificates?
2. The Go To Special dialog box is helpful when auditing a workbook. Think of instances when you might use selection options in this dialog box that you did not try in this lesson.

Skills Review

EXERCISE 18-12

Evaluate a formula. Trace precedents and dependents.

1. Open the file **UnitAndDollarSales** and enable macros. This workbook has a circular reference, so a message box opens.
2. Click OK in the message box. A Help window about circular references and the Circular Reference toolbar open.
3. Close the Help window. Close the Circular Reference toolbar.
4. Evaluate a formula by following these steps:
   a. Right-click any toolbar and choose Formula Auditing.
   b. Select cell D21.

   c. Click the Evaluate Formula button on the Formula Auditing toolbar. The formula multiplies cell D11 by ChocolateChip.
   d. Click Step In. The first step evaluates cell D11 as 16,000.
   e. Click Step Out. ChocolateChip is underlined.
   f. Click Evaluate. The error message #NAME? marks the error.

g. Click Close.

5. Save the workbook as *[your initials]*18-12 in your Lesson 18 folder.

6. Trace precedents and dependents by following these steps:

a. Select cell F9. This is the circular reference.
b. Click the Trace Precedents button .
c. Select cell D21. Click the Trace Dependents button ⬚.
d. Click the Circle Invalid Data button ⬚ on the Formula Auditing toolbar. Scroll the window if necessary to see the circled cells.

> **NOTE:** The Circle Invalid Data button ⬚ identifies cells in which the contents do not match what is set in the Data Validation dialog box.

7. Add a standard footer. On the Sheet tab, make sure Cell errors as shows displayed.

8. Print the worksheet.

> **NOTE:** Invalid data circles do not print. All arrows and circles are removed when you save the file.

9. Save and close the workbook. Close the Formula Auditing toolbar.

EXERCISE 18-13

Use Go To Special and correct errors.

1. Open **UnitAndDollarSales** and enable macros. The circular reference is noted.

2. Click OK. If the Help window opens, close it.

> **NOTE:** The Help window may not open the second time you open a workbook with a circular reference during a class session.

3. Close the Circular Reference toolbar if it is open.

4. Use the Go To Special dialog box to select cells by following these steps:

a. Press Ctrl+G. Click Special. Select Formulas.
b. Remove the check marks for Numbers, Text, and Logicals.
c. Click OK. Only cells with error value messages are selected.

5. Correct errors by following these steps:

a. Select cell D21. The formula shows ChocolateChip as the range name, but the range name is spelled Chocolate_Chip.
b. Press F2. Delete ChocolateChip in the cell.
c. Press F3 and double-click Chocolate_Chip. Press Enter.

d. Select cell A26. Click the data validation list arrow. Choose Vanilla from the list.

e. Select cell A27. Click the data validation list arrow. Choose Chocolate.

f. Select cell B20. Position the pointer over the Trace Error button and click the down arrow.

g. Choose Ignore Error.

h. Select cell C20. Repeat the previous steps to ignore the error.

i. Select cell F9, the cell with the circular reference.

j. Press Delete.

k. Click the AutoSum button Σ ▾. Verify that the range is B9:E9. Press Enter.

REVIEW: Open the Macros dialog box to determine macro names. To see a macro shortcut, open the Visual Basic Editor.

6. Select cell A1 and run the macro.

7. Add a standard footer.

8. Save the workbook as *[your initials]*18-13 in your Lesson 18 folder.

9. Print the worksheet and close the workbook.

EXERCISE 18-14

Use the Watch window. Delete a watch. Create a digital certificate.

1. Open the file **SalinasSales** and enable macros. Display the Formula Auditing toolbar.

2. Use the Watch window by following these steps:

a. Click the Show Watch Window button on the Formula Auditing toolbar.

b. Select cells B13:E13 and click Add Watch in the Watch window.

c. Click Add.

NOTE: The formulas in row 13 refer to cells in the Prices worksheet.

d. Click the Prices sheet tab.

e. Change the prices as shown in Figure 18-9 and watch the changes in the formulas in the Watch window.

f. Return to the 4thQtr worksheet.

3. Delete a watch by following these steps:

a. Click the first watch row in the Watch window.

b. Press and hold Shift and click the last row in the Watch window.

c. Press Delete.

d. Click the Close button ✗ on the Watch window.

4. Run the macro in rows 3 and 13.

FIGURE 18-9

Product	Price
Cakes	10.59
Pies	11.99
Kowabunga	2.29
KowOwow	2.19
Sodas	2.35
Sundaes	2.25
Cones	1.29
Malts	1.69
Shakes	1.89

5. Create a digital certificate by following these steps:

   a. Click the Start button on the taskbar. Choose All Programs.
   b. Choose Microsoft Office and then Microsoft Office Tools.
   c. Choose Digital Certificate for VBA Projects.
   d. Key [your first initial and last name]. Click OK.

6. Add a standard footer. Center the page horizontally.

7. Save the workbook as [your initials]18-14 in your Lesson 18 folder.

8. Print the sheet. Close the Formula Auditing toolbar and the workbook.

EXERCISE 18-15

Troubleshoot errors. Evaluate a formula. Correct errors.

1. Open the file **2QtrReport**.

2. Troubleshoot errors by following these steps:

   a. Select cell B9. Click the down arrow with the Trace Error button ⬛.
   b. Choose Help on this error. Read and then close the Help window.
   c. Click the down arrow next to the Trace Error button ⬛ again.
   d. Choose Edit in Formula Bar.
   e. Correct the spelling of the function name (AVERAGE) and press Enter.

3. Evaluate a formula by following these steps:

a. Select cell B12.

b. Display the Formula Auditing toolbar if it is hidden.

c. Click the Evaluate Formula button 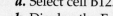 on the Formula Auditing toolbar. Cell B4 will be evaluated first.

d. Click Step In. Cell B4 = 10000.

e. Click Step Out. Cell B18 is next for evaluation.

f. Click Step In. Cell B18 = Prices. This is the label in cell B18, not a range name.

g. Click Step Out. Click Close.

4. Correct errors by following these steps:

a. Press F2. Edit the cell reference to show **$B$19**. Press Enter.

b. Copy the formula to the range B13:B15.

c. Select cell C12 and display the error's ScreenTip. Read the reason for the error.

d. Press Delete.

e. Key = and select cell C4. Key * and select cell B20. Press F4 and press Enter. The formula multiplies the number of waffle cones sold by the price.

f. Copy the formula to the range C13:C15.

g. Select cell D12 and review its formula. Press F2 and edit the formula to show the correct cell. Copy the formula to the range D13:D15.

 NOTE: Because Excel is always checking for errors in the background, more errors might be noted as you work.

h. Check the formulas in cells E12 and F12. Correct the errors and copy the formulas through row 15.

5. Format the values in rows 12 through 15 to show dollar signs with two decimal positions.

6. Add a standard footer. Save the workbook as *[your initials]*18-15 in your Lesson 18 folder.

7. Print the worksheet and close the workbook. Close the Formula Auditing toolbar.

Lesson Applications

Trace precedents and dependents. Locate and fix errors.

One of the sales workbooks has several errors. You must find and correct these errors before a consolidated worksheet can be prepared.

1. Open the file **2QtrSales**.
2. In the California worksheet, trace the precedents of cell D8. Correct the error and remove the arrows.
3. In the Oregon worksheet, trace the dependents of cell C5. Correct the error and remove the arrows.

 TIP: Use the Data Validation list to correct errors.

4. In the Nevada worksheet, circle invalid data. Check another worksheet for the correct products, correct the Nevada worksheet errors, and remove the circles. (*Hint:* Select the cells with errors and use the Data Validation drop-down list to correct the errors.)
5. Correct the error in cell D8.
6. In the Washington worksheet, determine what is wrong and correct the errors.
7. Group the worksheets and add a standard footer from the Page Setup dialog box.
8. Save the workbook as *[your initials]*18-16 in your Lesson 18 folder.
9. Print the entire workbook and close the workbook. Close the Formula Auditing toolbar.

Troubleshoot and correct errors.

Klassy Kow Ice Cream makes sales projections based on a year's sales and an estimated percentage increase. Before you can complete projections for the next two years, you need to correct errors in the formulas.

1. Open the file **2YrProjected**.
2. Starting in cell C4, key the following values in the range C4:C7.

    14,000,000   10,000,000   13,500,000   10,500,000

     NOTE: The #DIV/0 error is corrected when you key values in column C.

3. Cut cells in the range A10:A14 and insert them at cell F3, shifting the cells to the right.

4. Determine what is wrong in cell D4. Edit the formula and copy it through row 7. (*Hint:* A percentage increase divides the difference by the previous year's total.)

5. In column E, multiply this year's sales by 1 plus the percentages in column D. Then multiply this result by 108%. Remember the order of precedence for arithmetic operators. The 108% is an additional sales goal for the year. Copy the formula through row 7.

6. Format the values in column F to be the same as those in column D.

7. The column G values should use the percentages in column F to project sales. There is no additional sales goal.

8. Format dollar amounts with dollar signs and no decimals. Widen columns as needed.

9. Add a standard footer.

10. Save the workbook as *[your initials]*18-17 in your Lesson 18 folder and print the worksheet.

11. Make a copy of the sheet and display the formulas. Adjust column widths, and print the worksheet in landscape orientation fit to one page.

12. Save and close the workbook.

EXERCISE 18-18

Troubleshoot errors and correct errors. Use Go To Special.

There are several errors on the Oregon sales worksheet for sundaes. One includes a format error that Excel does not detect. In addition, you have been asked to print the comments on the worksheet.

1. Open the file **SundaeSalesOR**.

2. Evaluate the formulas in cells H1 and H6 and correct them.

3. Determine what is wrong in cell H9 by checking similar formulas in cells H10 and H11. Correct the error.

4. Find the error in cell H13 and correct it. Format the cell appropriately.

5. Press Ctrl+G and use Special to select only the cells with comments. While the cells are selected, choose View and then Comments. Close the Reviewing toolbar if it opens.

 NOTE: The Reviewing toolbar is useful when working with comments.

6. Add the standard footer. Set the comments to print as they appear on the sheet.

7. Save the workbook as *[your initials]*18-18 in your Lesson 18 folder and print the worksheet.

8. Make a copy of the sheet and display the formulas. Do not print comments with the formulas. Set the formula sheet to print on one page in landscape orientation. Adjust column widths, hide columns that do not have data, and print the worksheet.

9. Save and close the workbook.

EXERCISE 18-19 *Challenge Yourself*

Troubleshoot errors in a template.

The Balance template needs to be audited. Because it is a template, it does not contain any values. You can still trace most errors and see error value messages.

1. Open the template file **Balance** in the Templates folder.

2. Examine all cells with formulas; they show a hyphen or an error value message. Use whatever tools seem appropriate to determine what is wrong and correct the errors.

3. Select all cells with formulas and lock them. Protect the worksheet without a password.

4. Set the file properties to show an appropriate title, your name, and the correct company name. Include a preview image.

5. Add the standard footer. Save the workbook as a template named *[your initials]*18-19 in the Templates folder.

6. Create a new workbook based on your template.

7. Key the values in Figure 18-10 in the appropriate cells to test your template.

8. Save the workbook as *[your initials]*18-19 in your Lesson 18 folder and print the worksheet.

9. Go to the Formulas sheet. Delete the image and add your footer. Print the formula sheet.

10. Save and close the workbook.

11. Choose File, New and click On my computer in the New Workbook task pane. Click the General tab. Delete *[your initials]*18-19.

 NOTE: Make sure you complete the last step of this exercise. Template files remain on the computer until they are removed.

FIGURE 18-10

Current assets		
Cash and securities	1500	
Accounts receivable	1750	
Inventories	550	
Other	235	
Total current assets		
Fixed assets		
Property, plant, and equipment	2500	
Less depreciation	250	
Net fixed assets		
Other assets	100	
Total assets		
Liabilities and Owner's Equity		
Current liabilities		
Debt due for repayment	1250	
Accounts payable	1000	
Other current liabilities	335	
Total current liabilities		
Long-term debt	1000	
Other long-term liabilities		
Total long-term liabilities		
Owners' Equity	2800	
Total liabilities and owners' equity		

On Your Own

In these exercises you work on your own, as you would in a real-life work environment. Use the skills you've learned to accomplish the task—and be creative.

EXERCISE 18-20
Create a new workbook with labels, values, and formulas that tracks something of interest to you. Create deliberate errors in your formulas. Add a standard footer. Save the workbook as *[your initials]*18-20 in your Lesson 18 folder and print it with the errors. Trade workbooks with a classmate and locate and correct each other's errors. Change the footer to include your name with your classmate's name. Save your corrected version of your classmate's workbook as *[your initials]*18-20b in your Lesson 18 folder and print it. Close the workbook.

EXERCISE 18-21
Create a new workbook with labels, values, and formulas that you might use in your personal life. Review the error value messages in Table 18-1 and create a situation that will display each type of error. Use Excel Help to find more information about each error value message. Add a standard footer and save the workbook as *[your initials]*18-21 in your Lesson 18 folder. Print the worksheet with the error value messages displayed and close the workbook.

EXERCISE 18-22
Use the Internet to research the most common types of errors found in accounting and other financial work. Create a new workbook. In this workbook, list and describe at least five common errors and create an example to illustrate the problem. Add a standard footer and save the workbook as *[your initials]*18-22 in your Lesson 18 folder. Print the worksheet in landscape orientation and close the workbook.

Using What-If Analysis

OBJECTIVES

MICROSOFT OFFICE
SPECIALIST
ACTIVITIES
In this lesson:
XL03E-1-6
XL03E-1-7
XL03E-2-4
XL03E-3-2

See Appendix.

After completing this lesson, you will be able to:

1. **Create a scenario.**
2. **Manage scenarios.**
3. **Forecast with a trendline.**
4. **Use Goal Seek.**
5. **Use Solver.**

 Estimated Time: 1½ hours

What-if analysis is a procedure in which you test values in a worksheet to predict future results. For example, you can analyze what your company revenues would be if you charge $12 for ice cream cakes or if you raise the price to $14.

Excel has several analytical tools for forecasting values and results. You can create scenarios that let you save and review various possibilities. You can solve common and sophisticated mathematical problems by using Solver or Goal Seek. You can even add trendlines to charts.

Creating a Scenario

A *scenario* is a set of values saved with the workbook. You can save several scenarios and then view different solutions for your worksheet. Scenarios allow you to perform what-if analysis by entering new values for certain cells to see what happens.

EXERCISE 19-1 Change Security Settings

When you use high macro security, all macros are automatically disabled when you open a workbook.

1. With a blank or no workbook open, choose Tools, Macro, and Security.
2. Choose High and click OK.
3. Open the file **ConsolidatedReport**. This workbook has a macro that will be disabled because of the high security setting.

FIGURE 19-1
High macro security
message box

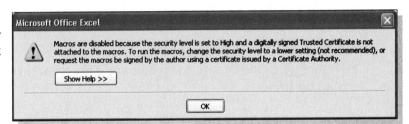

4. Click OK in the message box.
5. Press Ctrl + Shift + K. This is the shortcut for the macro. The same dialog box informs you that the macro is disabled.
6. Click OK in the message box.
7. Close the workbook.
8. With no workbook open, choose Tools, Macro, and Security.
9. Choose Medium and click OK.
10. Open **ConsolidatedReport**. Medium security offers you a choice about enabling macros.
11. Choose Enable Macros.
12. Press Ctrl + Shift + K. The company name is inserted in cell A1.

EXERCISE 19-2 Name Ranges for a Scenario

In a scenario, you normally refer to ranges of cells. These include cells that can change and cells that show results. If you name these ranges, managing scenarios is easy.

1. Select the range B22:B26.
2. Click the Name box and key **Prices**. Press Enter.
3. Name the range F14:F18 as **DollarSales**.
4. Name cell F19 as **TotalSales**.

EXERCISE　**19-3**　**Create a Scenario**

1. From the Tools menu, choose Scenarios. The Scenario Manager dialog box opens. There are now no scenarios in your workbook.
2. Click Add. The Add Scenario dialog box opens.
3. In the Scenario name text box, key **Current Prices**. Press Tab.

REVIEW: When you press Tab to move to the next text box, the existing entry is highlighted and ready to be replaced.

4. In the Changing cells box, press F3. The Paste Name dialog box opens with the named ranges.
5. Choose Prices and click OK. The Add Scenario dialog box is still open.
6. Press Tab. In the Comment text box, key **This scenario shows sales at current prices**.

FIGURE 19-2
Adding a scenario

7. Notice the Protection options. Protection settings work only if the worksheet is protected. When Prevent changes is selected, the values in a scenario are locked and cannot be edited. You can also hide a scenario if the workbook is protected.
8. Click OK. The Scenario Values dialog box shows each of the cells from the Prices range with its current value. Do not change any values.
9. Click OK. The Scenario Manager dialog box lists the scenario you just created.

EXERCISE　**19-4**　**Add Scenarios to the Worksheet**

The Scenario Manager dialog box shows the names of all the scenarios for a workbook. You will now add two more scenarios with different prices for each of the pies.

1. With the Scenario Manager dialog box open, click Add.
2. In the Scenario name text box, key **Reduced Prices**.
3. Press Tab. Excel shows the last range you used for Changing cells, the Prices range, B22:B26. A marquee appears around the range in the worksheet. Your new scenario will be for this same range of cells.

4. Press (Tab). In the Comment text box, key **This scenario shows sales at reduced prices**.

5. Click OK. The Scenario Values dialog box opens. Now you need to change each price.

6. Key each new price as shown in Figure 19-3, pressing (Tab) to move from one text box to the next. If you press (Enter) before you have completed the changes, click Edit and then click OK to return to the Scenario Values dialog box.

FIGURE 19-3

Vanilla	10.95
Chocolate	10.95
Strawberry	12.5
Chocolate_Chip	13.5
Turtle	15

FIGURE 19-4
Changing scenario values

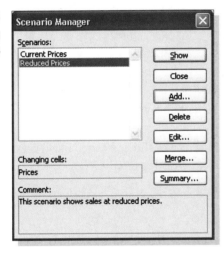

7. Click OK. The Scenario Manager shows the names of both scenarios that you created.

8. Click Add. The Add Scenario dialog box opens again.

9. In the Scenario name text box, key **Increased Prices**.

10. Press (Tab) two times. In the Comment text box, key **This scenario shows sales at higher prices**.

11. Click OK. Original prices are shown. Key each new price as shown in Figure 19-5.

FIGURE 19-5

Vanilla	13.95
Chocolate	13.95
Strawberry	14.5
Chocolate_Chip	16
Turtle	18

12. Click OK. The Scenario Manager shows all three scenario names.

13. Click Close. The CurrentPrices scenario is displayed in the worksheet.

14. Click a blank cell in the worksheet. Worksheet formulas dependent upon the scenario's changing cells are outlined in the worksheet.

Managing Scenarios

Scenarios are saved with the workbook. You can edit them, show them, or print a summary report for them. While the workbook is open, you can display each set of values and decide which might be the best.

EXERCISE **19-5** **Show Scenarios**

You can watch the changes in the relevant cells as you switch from one scenario to another.

1. From the Tools menu, choose Scenarios. The Scenario Manager dialog box opens.

2. Position the dialog box so that you can see the pie prices and the total dollar sales.

3. Select Reduced Prices in the Scenarios list.

4. Click Show. The worksheet shows reduced pie prices and the resulting total dollar sales.

5. Double-click Increased Prices in the Scenarios list. The worksheet now shows higher pie prices with new dollar results.

 NOTE: You can delete a scenario by clicking its name and clicking Delete.

6. Double-click Current Prices in the Scenarios list. The worksheet shows current prices and the dollar results.

EXERCISE **19-6** **Edit a Scenario**

There may be times when you need to change values in a scenario. You can edit an existing scenario.

1. With the Scenario Manager dialog box open, choose Increased Prices in the Scenarios list.

2. Click Edit. The Edit Scenario dialog box is the same as the Add Scenario dialog box.

3. Press Tab to place the insertion point in the Comment box. Each time you edit a scenario, Excel adds a line to the comment with the user's name and the current date.

4. Edit the comment to show **Modified by** *[your name]* **on** *[current date]*.

5. Click OK. The Scenario Values dialog box opens.

 NOTE: The values in the Scenario Values dialog box are formatted as General numbers.

6. Change the Chocolate_Chip price to **17.5**. Click OK. The Scenario Manager dialog box is open with the Current Prices scenario still displayed on the worksheet.

EXERCISE **19-7** **Print a Scenario Summary Report**

A *scenario summary report* is a formatted description for each scenario in the worksheet. It shows the cells that change and the results in an outline format on a separate worksheet.

1. With the Scenario Manager dialog box open, click Summary. The Scenario Summary dialog box opens.

2. Make sure the Report type is Scenario summary.

3. In the Result cells box, select the range F14:F19 on the worksheet.

FIGURE 19-6
Scenario Summary
dialog box

Q1	Q2	Q3	Q4	Tot
10,000	14,500	15,000	15,000	
12,000	13,000	16,000	18,000	
9,500	14,750	12,500	10,500	
13,500	14,500	16,000	17,000	
12,000	11,500	18,000	15,000	
57,000	68,250	77,500	75,500	2

Scenario Summary

Report type
◉ Scenario summary
○ Scenario PivotTable report

Result cells:
=$F$14:$F$19

OK   Cancel

	Q1	Q2	Q3	Q4	Total
$	129,500.00	$ 187,775.00	$ 194,250.00	$ 194,250.00	$ 705,775.00
	155,400.00	168,350.00	207,200.00	233,100.00	764,050.00
	128,250.00	199,125.00	168,750.00	141,750.00	637,875.00
	201,825.00	216,775.00	239,200.00	254,150.00	911,950.00
	203,400.00	194,925.00	305,100.00	254,250.00	957,675.00
$	818,375.00	$ 966,950.00	$ 1,114,500.00	$ 1,077,500.00	$ 3,977,325.00

4. Click OK. A new worksheet appears, summarizing the scenarios.

 NOTE: If you had named the cells in the range F14:F18 individually, you would see those range names instead of cell addresses in the summary report.

5. Click the plus symbol (+) to the left of row 3. The top section of the report expands to show the scenario descriptions.

6. Click the minus symbol (–) to the left of row 5. The Changing Cells section is hidden.

7. Click the plus symbol (+) to the left of row 5 to display the Changing Cells section again.

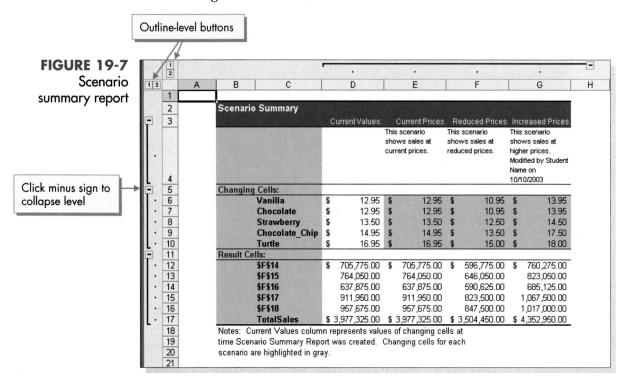

FIGURE 19-7
Scenario summary report

8. Add your standard footer. Set the worksheet to fit on a portrait page.

9. Save the workbook as *[your initials]***19-7** in a new folder for Lesson 19.

10. Print the summary worksheet.

Forecasting with a Trendline

A common way to analyze and predict business data is to forecast future results on the basis of past results. A *trendline* is a line in a chart that points out and predicts general tendencies or directions in the values. For example, you can add a line to a chart that shows how many pies might be sold next year given how many were sold this year.

EXERCISE 19-8 Create a Column Chart

A trendline can be added to a column chart. In this exercise, you'll create a column chart showing chocolate chip pie sales.

1. Click the Sheet1 tab.
2. Choose Tools and Scenarios. Select Current Prices and click Show. Click Close.
3. Select the range B9:E9, quarterly totals for the chocolate chip pie.

4. Click the Chart Wizard button ▥ on the Standard toolbar. The Chart Wizard – Step 1 of 4 dialog box opens.
5. Make sure Column is selected as the Chart type and Clustered Column is selected as the Chart sub-type.
6. Click Next. The Chart Wizard – Step 2 of 4 dialog box opens.
7. Click the Series tab and name Series1 **Chocolate Chip Pies**.
8. Click Next. In the Chart Wizard – Step 3 of 4 dialog box, edit the Chart title to **Projected Sales of Chocolate Chip Pies**.
9. Click Next. Place the chart on a separate worksheet.
10. Click Finish. The column chart is created on its own sheet.

EXERCISE 19-9 Format a Chart

1. Right-click any one of the columns. Choose Format Data Series.
2. On the Patterns tab, click the black color tile in the Area group. Click OK.
3. Right-click one of the values along the vertical axis. Choose Format Axis.
4. On the Font tab, choose 9-point bold. Click OK.
5. Left-click any value on the category axis. Choose Edit and Repeat Format Axis. The same format is applied to the selected object.

EXERCISE 19-10 Add a Trendline to a Chart

After you've created your chart, you can add a trendline to it.

1. From the Chart menu, choose Add Trendline. The Add Trendline dialog box opens. On the Type tab, there are six types of trendlines.
2. Make sure that Linear is darkened to show that it is selected. A linear trendline is a straight line. (See Figure 19-8 on the next page.)
3. Click the Options tab.

FIGURE 19-8
Adding a linear
trendline to a chart

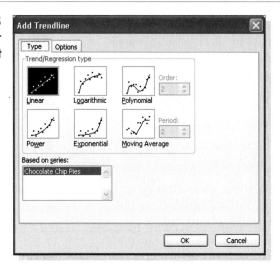

4. In the Forecast group, place the insertion point in the Forward text box.

5. Delete 0 and key **4** to project sales for the next four quarters.

FIGURE 19-9
Forecasting four
future periods

6. Click OK. Given current sales, the trendline shows that sales will gradually increase in each of the next four quarters.

EXERCISE 19-11 Format a Trendline

1. Right-click the trendline and choose Format Trendline. The Format Trendline dialog box opens.

2. On the Patterns tab, choose a heavier (thicker) line in the Weight box.

3. On the Patterns tab, choose red in the Color box.

4. Click the Options tab.

5. In the Trendline name group, select Custom.

6. Key **Next Four Quarters Projection** in the Custom text box. Click OK. The name for the trendline is added to the legend.

7. Click the Sheet1 tab.

8. In the range C9:E9, key these values.
   12000   10000   18000

9. Click the Chart1 tab and view the change. Even with some lower values, the trend is for greater sales.

10. Add the standard footer. Print the chart.

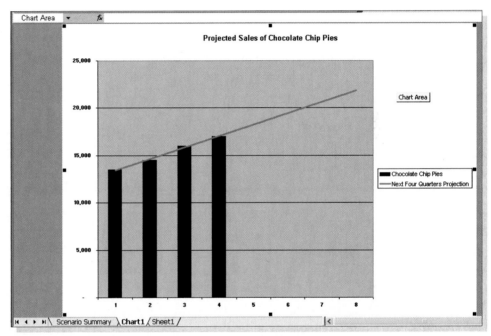

FIGURE 19-10
Trendline in a chart

Using Goal Seek

Goal Seek allows you to adjust or "backsolve" a cell value to reach a desired outcome. *Backsolving* might be considered what-if analysis in reverse. That is, you know the results of a formula and you adjust values or arguments in the formula to reach those results. For example, suppose you want to reach a particular total dollar sales for pies. You can backsolve to determine how many pies you would have to sell or what price to set.

EXERCISE 19-12 Use Goal Seek to Determine a Price

Suppose you want to sell $800,000 worth of vanilla pies. You can use Goal Seek to set the formula cell to $800,000 by changing the pie price.

1. Rename Sheet1 as **PieSales** and select cell F14.

2. From the Tools menu, choose Goal Seek. The Goal Seek dialog box opens. The Set cell text box shows the active cell. This is the cell that Excel will change.

3. In the To value text box, key **800000**. This is the result that you want the formula in cell F14 to show.

4. Position the insertion point in the By changing cell text box. This is the cell that can be changed to reach your goal of $800,000.

5. Select cell B22 in the worksheet, the current price of the pie. You will determine the price required to reach $800,000 in sales.

FIGURE 19-11
Using Goal Seek to set a price

12	**Dollar Sales**					
13	**Flavors**	**Q1**	**Q2**	**Q3**	**Q4**	**Total**
14	Vanilla	$ 129,500.00	$ 187,775.00	$ 194,250.00	$ 194,250.00	$ 705,775.00
15	Chocolate	155,400.00	168,350.00	207,200.00	233,100.00	764,050.00
16	Strawberry	128,250.00	199,125.00	168,750.00	141,750.00	637,875.00
17	Chocolate Chip	201,825.00	179,400.00	149,500.00	269,100.00	799,825.00
18	Turtle	203,400.00	194,925.			957,675.00
19	**Total**	$ 818,375.00	$ 929,575.			3,865,200.00
20						
21			**Pie Prices**			
22	Vanilla	$ 12.95				
23	Chocolate	$ 12.95				
24	Strawberry	$ 13.50				
25	Chocolate Chip	$ 14.95				
26	Turtle	$ 16.95				
27						
28						

Goal Seek

Set cell: F14
To value: 800000
By changing cell: $B$22

OK   Cancel

6. Click OK. The Goal Seek Status dialog box shows that a solution was found. It is shown in cell B22. You would have to increase the price to $15.34 to reach total sales of $800,000.

FIGURE 19-12
Goal Seek status after a solution is found

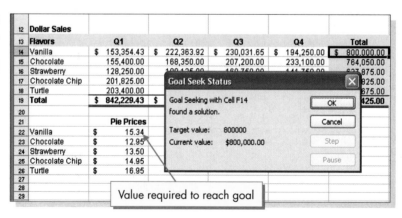

Value required to reach goal

7. Click Cancel. Nothing is changed in the worksheet.

E X E R C I S E 19-13 Use Goal Seek to Determine Units Sold

Another way to reach $800,000 is to sell more pies with the price unchanged.

1. From the Tools menu, choose Goal Seek. The Set cell entry shows the active cell.

2. In the To value text box, key **800000**.

3. Position the insertion point in the By changing cell text box. Select cell F6 in the worksheet, the current total number of vanilla pies sold. This cell has a formula.

4. Click OK. Excel displays an error message, because Goal Seek cannot adjust a cell that has a formula. It can change only a cell that has a value.

 NOTE: Goal Seek can use one adjustable cell with a value. It cannot be used for more than one cell at a time.

5. Click OK in the error message box. Click Cancel. Nothing is changed in the worksheet.

Using Solver

Solver is an Excel add-in for what-if analysis. An *add-in* is a feature or command added to the program that makes the program easier to use or supplies additional functionality. Excel has several add-ins, some of which are installed separately from the main program.

Solver backsolves the value for a cell with a formula. It is useful for more complex backsolving problems.

Solver has the following components:

● A target cell with a formula that you want to result in a particular value.

● Adjustable cells that relate directly or indirectly to the formula in the target cell and that Solver adjusts to produce the desired result.

● Limitations, or *constraints*, placed on the target cell or adjustable cells. A constraint is applied to adjustable cells, the target cell, or other cells directly or indirectly related to the target cell.

E X E R C I S E 19-14 Use Solver to Determine Units Sold

Solver uses parameters in its dialog box. A *parameter* is the data or information that Solver needs to determine a solution. It is similar to the arguments in a function.

NOTE: If Solver does not appear in the Tools menu, choose Add-Ins from the menu to install it.

1. Select cell F14. From the Tools menu, choose Solver. The Solver Parameters dialog box opens.

2. In the Set Target Cell box, verify that $F$14 is shown.

 NOTE: Set Target Cell shows the active cell address but it can be changed.

3. In the Equal To group, select Value of and key **800000** in the Value of text box. This tells Solver that you want the value in cell F14 to be 800,000.

4. Position the insertion point in the By Changing Cells text box. Position the dialog box so that you can see row 6.

5. Select the range B6:E6 in the worksheet, the current sales figures for vanilla pies. Changing these numbers controls the value in the target cell.

FIGURE 19-13
Solver Parameters
dialog box

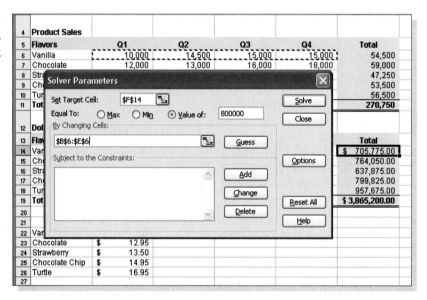

6. Click Solve. The suggested solution is in cells B6:E6. The Solver Results dialog box allows you to keep the solution or return to the original. You can also save the results as a scenario.

7. Click Save Scenario. The Save Scenario dialog box opens.

8. In the Scenario Name text box, key **Solver 1**.

9. Click OK. The Solver Results dialog box is open.

10. Select Restore Original Values.

11. Click OK. The worksheet is not changed.

EXERCISE 19-15 Add Solver Constraints

Suppose you want sales of vanilla pies in the first quarter to be 12,000 and 16,000 in the third quarter. The second and fourth quarter sales can be any values.

1. With cell F14 still selected, choose Tools and Solver. Excel remembers your most recent parameters.
2. In the Equal To group, verify that Value of is set to 800000.
3. Verify that the By Changing Cells text box shows $B$6:$E$6.
4. In the Subject to the Constraints group, click Add. The Add Constraint dialog box opens.
5. With the insertion point in the Cell Reference text box, select cell B6 in the worksheet.
6. Click the down arrow next to the middle (operator) box and choose = from the drop-down list.
7. In the Constraint text box, key **12000**. This sets a requirement that the value in cell B6 be 12,000.

FIGURE 19-14
Adding a constraint

8. Click Add. The Add Constraint dialog box is still open. You can add another constraint.
9. With the insertion point in the Cell Reference box, select cell D6 in the worksheet.
10. Click the down arrow next to the operator box and choose =.
11. In the Constraint text box, key **16000**. This requirement is that the value in cell D6 be 16,000.
12. Click OK. The Solver Parameters dialog box lists both constraints.

FIGURE 19-15
Multiple constraints

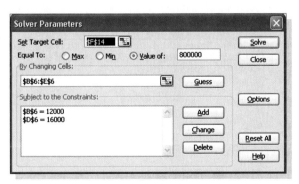

13. Click Solve. The results are shown on the worksheet.
14. Click Save Scenario. In the Scenario Name text box, key **Solver 2**. Click OK.
15. Select Restore Original Values in the Solver Results dialog box. Click OK. The worksheet returns to its original values.

EXERCISE 19-16 Edit and Print a Scenario Report

Because you saved your Solver solutions as scenarios, you can create a scenario summary report to show those two possibilities.

1. From the Tools menu, choose Scenarios. Click Summary.

 NOTE: It does not matter which scenario name is highlighted when you create a summary report.

2. In the Scenario Summary dialog box, make sure Scenario summary is selected. Move the dialog box if row 14 is obscured.

3. Specify the Result cells by selecting the range B14:F14 in the worksheet. Click OK.

4. Delete columns D through G, the Current Values, Current Prices, Reduced Prices, and Increased Prices columns.

5. Hide rows 6 through 10.

6. Add the standard footer.

7. Save the workbook as *[your initials]***19-16** in your Lesson 19 folder.

FIGURE 19-16
Edited summary report

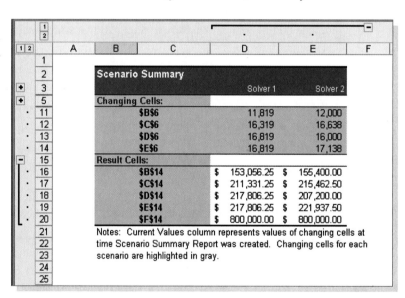

8. Print the Scenario Summary 2 worksheet.

9. Close the workbook.

USING ONLINE HELP

Solver, Goal Seek, and scenarios can be used to find solutions to fairly sophisticated business problems. Learn more about what-if analysis in general.

Ask a question about what-if analysis.

1. With Internet Explorer and Excel running, look for topics about what-if analysis. Look for subtopics about projecting values, data tables, and using Solver.

2. Read the information and close the windows.

3. Close Internet Explorer and end your Internet connection.

LESSON Summary

➤ What-if analysis tests values in a worksheet to predict future results.

➤ A scenario is a saved set of values for specific cells, saved with a name in the workbook.

➤ You can add multiple scenarios to a workbook.

➤ Scenarios can be edited, displayed, or deleted when necessary.

➤ A scenario summary report is an outline about each scenario in the worksheet. You can print a scenario summary report.

➤ Business forecasting can be accomplished with a trendline added to a chart. A trendline illustrates and predicts general tendencies of values.

➤ Goal Seek adjusts a cell value to reach a desired outcome in a formula. In backsolving, you know the results of a formula and adjust values to reach those results.

➤ Goal Seek can change only a cell that has a value.

➤ Solver is a what-if analysis tool. Its parameters are a target cell, adjustable cells, and constraints or limitations on the target or adjustable cells.

LESSON 19 Command Summary			
FEATURE	**BUTTON**	**MENU**	**KEYBOARD**
Create/edit scenario		Tools, Scenarios	
Create trendline		Chart, Add Trendline	
Goal Seek		Tools, Goal Seek	
Solver		Tools, Solver	
Repeat command		Edit, Repeat command name	Ctrl+Y

Concepts Review

TRUE/FALSE QUESTIONS

Each of the following statements is either true or false. Indicate your choice by circling T or F.

T   F   **1.** High and medium macro security settings allow you to enable or disable macros.

T   F   **2.** A scenario summary report is created on its own worksheet.

T   F   **3.** Goal Seek uses parameters to set restrictions on each cell.

T   F   **4.** A trendline highlights the most common data points in a series.

T   F   **5.** You can use named ranges or cell addresses to build a scenario.

T   F   **6.** What-if analysis allows you to use an IF statement in more than one formula.

T   F   **7.** You can run Goal Seek and save the results as a scenario.

T   F   **8.** In Solver, you can have more than one adjustable cell.

SHORT ANSWER QUESTIONS

Write the correct answer in the space provided.

1. What does Solver call a limitation or restriction on a cell?

_____

2. What term describes testing various values in a worksheet to see how the results change?

_____

3. Name the dialog box used to display a saved scenario.

_____

4. What term describes the data that Solver needs to determine a solution?

_____

5. In what menu are Goal Seek and Solver listed?

_____

6. In a scenario summary report, what do the expand and collapse buttons do?

_____

7. What term might be described as what-if analysis in reverse?

_____

8. How can you prepare a chart to show projected future sales?

_____

CRITICAL THINKING

Answer these questions on a separate page. There are no right or wrong answers. Support your answers with examples from your own experience, if possible.

1. In your current school work or job, how could you use scenarios?

2. Think of what-if analysis problems that you face as an employee or a student. How could you use the tools covered in this lesson, such as trendlines, Goal Seek, and Solver?

Skills Review

EXERCISE 19-17

Create a scenario. Add scenarios. Create a scenario summary report.

1. Set macro security to medium. Open the file **Shakes&Malts** and enable macros.

2. Run the macro stored in this workbook.

3. Select the range B3:D4. From the Insert menu, choose Name and then Create. Use the top row for range names. Click OK.

 NOTE: This worksheet already includes a named constant for the price.

4. Select cell B5 and name it **OctDollars**. Name cell C5 **NovDollars** and cell D5 **DecDollars**.

5. Create a scenario by following these steps:

a. From the Tools menu, choose Scenarios. Click Add.

b. In the Scenario name text box, key **Modest Sales**. Press Tab.

c. With the insertion point in the Changing cells text box, select the range B4:D4 in the worksheet. Press Tab.

    d. Delete the existing information in the Comment text box and key **Assumes modest sales**. Click OK.

    e. Do not change any values. Click OK.

6. Add scenarios by following these steps:

    a. Click Add. Key **Best Sales** in the Scenario name text box.

    b. Press Tab. Do not change the Changing cells.

    c. Press Tab. For the Comment, key **Assumes high sales**. Click OK.

    d. Key the following new values for each of the changing cells:

        Oct   **18000**

        Nov   **20000**

        Dec   **19000**

    e. Click OK. Click Add.

    f. Key **Worst Sales** in the Scenario name text box. Press Tab two times.

    g. For the Comment, key **Assumes low sales**. Click OK.

    h. Key the following new values for each of the changing cells:

        Oct   **9000**

        Nov   **10000**

        Dec   **9500**

    i. Click OK. Click Close.

7. Create a scenario summary report by following these steps:

    a. From the Tools menu, choose Scenarios.

    b. Click Summary. Make sure that Scenario summary is selected.

    c. In the Result cells text box, select the range B5:D5 in the worksheet. Click OK.

    d. Click the plus symbol (+) next to row 3.

8. Add the standard footer.

9. Save the workbook as *[your initials]***19-17** in your Lesson 19 folder.

10. Print the Scenario Summary worksheet and close the workbook.

EXERCISE 19-18

Edit a scenario. Show a scenario. Create a scenario summary report.

1. Set macro security to medium. Open the file **Malts&Shakes** and enable macros.

2. Run the macro. Its shortcut is Ctrl+Shift+K.

3. Edit a scenario by following these steps:

    a. From the Tools menu, choose Scenarios.

    b. Choose Modest Sales in the Scenarios list.

    c. Click Edit.

    d. Press Tab two times.

    e. For the new Comment, key **Assumes average sales**. (Key the period.)

    f. Click OK.

g. Key the following new values for each of the changing cells:

    Oct   10500

    Nov   10000

    Dec   9000

h. Click OK.

i. Choose Best Sales in the Scenarios list. Click Edit.

j. Press [Tab] two times. For the new Comment, key **Assumes high sales**. Click OK.

k. Key the following new values for each of the changing cells:

    Oct   **23000**

    Nov   **24000**

    Dec   **25000**

l. Click OK.

m. Choose Worst Sales in the Scenarios list. For the new Comment, key **Assumes low sales**. Do not change the values. Click OK.

4. Show a scenario by following these steps:

  a. Choose Best Sales and click Show.

  b. Click Close.

5. Name cell B5 **OctDollars**. Name cell E5 **Totals**.

6. Create a scenario summary report. Make sure that Scenario summary is selected, and in the Result cells text box, select the range B5:E5.

7. Click the plus symbol (+) next to row 3. Hide rows 5–8.

8. Set the width of column A to 3.57 (30 pixels).

9. Add your standard footer.

10. Save the workbook as *[your initials]***19-18** in your Lesson 19 folder.

11. Print the Scenario Summary sheet and close the workbook.

EXERCISE 19-19

Show a scenario. Forecast with a trendline. Format a trendline.

1. Open the file **Sodas**.

2. Show the Best Sales scenario.

3. Select the range B4:D5 and create a clustered column chart. On the Series tab in the Chart Wizard, name Series1 **# of Sodas**. Name Series2 **Dollars**. Key **Projected Sales of Sodas** for the chart title and place the chart on a separate worksheet.

4. Forecast with a trendline by following these steps:

  a. From the Chart menu, choose Add Trendline.

  b. On the Type tab, make sure that Linear is selected.

  c. Click the Options tab.

  d. In the Trendline name group, select Custom.

e. Key **Next Six Months** in the Custom text box.

f. In the Forecast group, position the insertion point in the Forward box. Delete 0 and key **6**.

 NOTE: Projecting six periods means six months in this chart.

g. Click OK.

5. Format a trendline by following these steps:

a. Right-click the trendline and choose Format Trendline.

b. On the Patterns tab, click the down arrow next to Weight and choose a thicker line.

c. Click OK.

6. Add the standard footer.

7. Save the workbook as *[your initials]***19-19** in your Lesson 19 folder.

8. Print the chart and close the workbook.

EXERCISE 19-20

Use Goal Seek. Use Solver. Save a scenario. Add Solver constraints. Create a scenario summary report.

1. Open the file **XmasCakes**.

2. Use Goal Seek by following these steps:

a. In the CreditUnion worksheet, select cell B9. The formula uses the PMT function to determine the monthly car payment.

b. From the Tools menu, choose Goal Seek.

c. With the insertion point in the To value text box, key **350**, the desired car payment.

 NOTE: Goal Seek sets the borrowed amount to a negative number, because the PMT function assumes the lender's (the credit union's) perspective.

d. With the insertion point in the By changing cell text box, select cell B6 in the worksheet, the amount to be borrowed.

e. Click OK to display the solution in the worksheet.

f. Click OK to keep the solution.

g. Select cell D9. The formula uses the FV function to determine what the savings account will be worth in four years.

h. From the Tools menu, choose Goal Seek. Position the insertion point in the To value text box and key **7000**, the amount you would like to have in four years.

i. Position the insertion point in the By changing cell text box and select cell D8 in the worksheet, the interest rate. Click OK. Excel tries but cannot find a solution to the problem in this way.

TIP: Goal Seek cannot always find a solution.

    j. Click Cancel.

    k. From the Tools menu, choose Goal Seek. In the To value text box, key **7000**. Position the insertion point in the By changing cell text box and select cell D6 in the worksheet, the monthly deposit.

    l. Click OK. Excel finds a solution to the problem with cell D6 as the changing cell.

    m. Click OK to keep the solution.

3. Format cell D9 so that its font matches the rest of the worksheet.

4. Add your standard footer.

5. Use Solver by following these steps:

    a. Click the DecoratingSchedule tab.

    b. Select cell D4. The formula in cells D4:D8 multiplies hours worked per week by the number of cakes decorated in an hour. This determines how many cakes a decorator can complete in a week.

    c. Select cell F4. The formula in the range F4:F8 multiplies the worker's hourly wage by hours worked.

     d. Select the range B9:F9 and click the AutoSum button Σ ▾.

    e. Select cell D9.

    f. From the Tools menu, choose Solver. Cell D9 is the target cell, because you want to make a certain number of cakes.

    g. Select Value of and key **750** in the Value of text box, the number of cakes that must be completed this week.

    h. Position the insertion point in the By Changing Cells text box and select the range B4:B8 in the worksheet. You will vary how much each person works to get the most cakes made.

    i. Click Solve.

6. Save a scenario by following these steps:

    a. Click Save Scenario.

    b. Key **Any Hours** in the Scenario Name text box. Click OK.

TIP: Key spaces between words in scenario names so that the summary report includes spaces in the names.

    c. Select Restore Original Values. Click OK.

7. Add constraints to a Solver problem by following these steps:

    a. From the Tools menu, choose Solver. Your most recent Solver parameters are remembered.

    b. Click Add in the Subject to the Constraints group.

    c. With the insertion point in the Cell Reference text box, click cell B4 in the worksheet.

    d. Click the down arrow next to the middle (operator) text box and choose =.

    e. In the Constraint text box, key **30**. This constraint means that Carl can work only 30 hours.

    f. Click Add to add another constraint.

    g. With the insertion point in the Cell Reference text box, select cell B7 in the worksheet.

    h. Choose = as the operator. In the Constraint text box, key **30**.

    i. Click OK.

    j. Click Solve.

    k. Click Save Scenario. Key **Restricted Hours** as the Scenario Name. Click OK.

    l. Select Restore Original Values. Click OK.

8. Create a scenario summary report. Make sure Scenario summary is selected and D9 is shown in the Result cells text box.

9. Add your standard footer.

10. Save the workbook as *[your initials]*19-20 in your Lesson 19 folder.

11. Print the CreditUnion and Scenario Summary sheets and close the workbook.

Lesson Applications

EXERCISE 19-21

Create scenarios. Project sales with a trendline.

Given a daily customer count, you can forecast the general direction in the number of customer visits. You can create average, better, and best scenarios and have the trendline update for each scenario.

1. Create a new workbook.
2. Delete Sheet1 and Sheet2. Name Sheet3 **CustomerCount**.
3. Format the range A1:A2 for 16-point Arial. Key **Klassy Kow Ice Cream** in cell A1. Key **Daily Customer Count** in cell A2.
4. In cell B3, key **Mon**. Using the Fill handle, add the remaining days of the week across row 3 to **Sun** in cell H3. Make these labels bold and centered. Increase the height of row 3.
5. In cell A4, key **Week 1**. Fill to **Week 4** in cell A7. Increase the height of rows 4 through 7.
6. Key the values shown in Figure 19-17, starting in cell B4. Format the values to show commas with no decimals.

FIGURE 19-17

	Mon	Tue	Wed	Thu	Fri	Sat	Sun
Week 1	9000	11000	12000	10000	15000	12325	14350
Week 2	10000	12300	13000	9000	16000	15425	12550
Week 3	19000	14500	14000	8000	10000	8325	11350
Week 4	9500	16000	15000	11000	8000	7525	15350

7. Save the current values as a scenario named **Average**. The values that will change are Saturday counts, G4:G7. Key a comment that includes your name.
8. Create a column chart for Saturday counts on a separate sheet. Name the series **# of Customers**. Key an appropriate title for the chart.
9. Add a trendline to the chart to project the next four weeks. Name the trendline **Next Four Weeks**. Add the standard footer to the chart.
10. Save the workbook as *[your initials]*19-21 in your Lesson 19 folder and print the chart.

11. In the CustomerCount worksheet, create a scenario named **Poor** with your name in the comment. The changing cells are still the Saturday values (G4:G7). Key the following new values for each of the changing cells:

$G$4   **9500**

$G$5   **8700**

$G$6   **7500**

$G$7   **7000**

12. Show the Poor Sales scenario and print the chart.

13. Save and close the workbook.

EXERCISE 19-22

Create scenarios. Use Goal Seek. Create a scenario summary report.

Klassy Kow sold $800,000 worth of KowOwows, Kowabungas, and ice cream sandwiches during the fourth quarter last year. You have been asked to determine what growth rate would result in $4,000,000 in yearly sales for these three products.

1. Open the file **GrowthRate**.

 REVIEW: Verify the current total sales (cells B13:B15) with AutoCalculate by using Sum.

2. In cell C13, build a formula to calculate first quarter next year KowOwow sales. Use the information about the Sales Forecast Formula on the worksheet.

 NOTE: The formula will have absolute and mixed references.

3. Copy the formula for each product and to the fourth quarter. Fix cell borders and column widths after copying the formula.

4. Format the values to show no decimal positions. Display dollar signs with the values in row 13.

 5. In cell G13, click the AutoSum button **Σ ▾** but adjust the range so that it does not include cell B13. Copy the formula through row 15. Show a dollar sign with the value in cell G13 and no decimals for the range G13:G15.

6. Use AutoSum in cell G16. Show a dollar sign with the result and no decimal positions. This cell will be the target cell.

7. Adjust the width of column H to be very narrow so that its borders looks like a border for column G.

8. Create a scenario named **1.5% Growth** for the worksheet with its current values. The changing cell is cell G4. Include your name in the comment.

 NOTE: The Scenario Values dialog box shows 1.5% in its decimal equivalent of 0.015. The dialog box does not show the percent sign.

9. Use Goal Seek to adjust the Quarterly Growth Rate to a percent that will result in $4,000,000 in sales (cell G16).

10. Save the Goal Seek values in a scenario named **New Growth** and include your name in the comment.

11. Create a scenario summary report.

12. Group the worksheets and set the orientation to landscape. Horizontally center the worksheets. Add the standard footer.

13. Save the workbook as *[your initials]*19-22 in your Lesson 19 folder. Print the entire workbook.

14. Make a copy of the SalesForecast worksheet and prepare a formula printout to fit on one landscape page.

15. Save and close the workbook.

EXERCISE 19-23

Use Solver. Create scenarios. Create a scenario summary report.

The Easter Rainbow Ice Cream Cake is very popular. The corporate office wants to determine the maximum number of cakes a shop can make and still be profitable. Profits start to decline after 200 cakes are made. This decline in profits is represented by the formula noted in the worksheet. The extra number of cakes shown in the worksheet is a sample.

1. Open the file **EasterCake**.

2. Select the range C4:D6 and create automatic range names by using the left column. Do the same for the ranges C8:D9, C11:D12, and C13:D13.

3. In cell D11, build a formula to calculate profit at the shop's capacity. This formula should multiply Maximum Cakes*Price*Profit Margin.

 TIP: A profit margin is the percentage or dollars earned on each cake.

4. In cell D12, build a formula to calculate profit for extra cakes made over 200. This formula is explained in the text box on the worksheet.

 NOTE: By making 50 extra cakes with the 2% multiplier, a shop makes no extra money.

5. In cell D13, build a formula that sums profits from shop capacity and from overcapacity.

6. Use Solver to determine how many extra cakes should be made to maximize total profit. The target cell is the total profit, and the changing cell is the extra cakes cell. Set the target cell to find the maximum.

7. While the Solver solution is displayed, save it as a scenario named **2% Multiplier**.

8. Restore the original values. On the worksheet, change the multiplier to **1%**. Run Solver again to see how the multiplier affects the results. Save the solution as a scenario named **1% Multiplier**.

9. Repeat the previous step using a 3% multiplier and save the solution as a scenario named **3% Multiplier**.

10. Create a scenario summary report to show cell D13 as a result cell.

11. Group the worksheets and add your footer. Ungroup the worksheets. Set the EasterCakes worksheet to print in landscape orientation.

12. Save the workbook as *[your initials]*19-23 in your Lesson 19 folder.

13. Print the entire workbook.

14. Make a copy of the EasterCakes worksheet and display formulas. Delete the text box. Make necessary adjustments. Print the worksheet to fit to one page.

15. Save and close the workbook.

EXERCISE 19-24 *Challenge Yourself*

Use Solver.

You have been asked to help determine the minimum labor cost for a holiday weekend. The weekend consists of 100 hours, and the ice cream shop has four employees. Some employees are limited in the number of hours they can work, but the total hours worked must be 100 hours.

1. Create a new workbook.

2. Key **Klassy Kow Ice Cream Shops** in cell A1. Key **Holiday Weekend** in cell A2. Format both cells with your choice of font and size.

3. In cell B3, key **# of Hours**. In cell C3, key **Hourly Rate**. In cell D3, key **Weekend Pay**. Make these labels bold and centered. Adjust column widths and increase the row height.

4. In cell A4, key **Employee 1**. Using the Fill handle, fill column A to **Employee 4** in cell A7. Adjust the column width and increase the height of the rows. In cell A8, key the label **Total** and make it bold.

5. Starting in cell C4, key the hourly rates for each employee in the range C4:C7 as follows:

   Employee 1 $9.25

   Employee 2 $10.50

   Employee 3 $9.75

   Employee 4 $8.50

6. In column D, build a formula to multiply the hourly rate by the number of hours for each employee. Copy the formula.

7. In column B, key **25** hours for each employee so that the total is 100. Use AutoSum in cells B8 and D8 to show totals for the hours and weekend pay.

8. Use Solver to find the lowest total weekend pay, changing the number of hours for each employee. Use the following constraints:

   ● Employee 1 hours <=25
   ● Employee 2 hours =30
   ● Employee 3 hours >=30
   ● Employee 4 hours <=25
   ● Cell B8 =100

9. Keep the Solver solution. Make other row height, font, or style changes to format your worksheet in a professional manner.

10. Add the standard footer with your name, the filename, and the date.

11. Save the workbook as *[your initials]*19-24 in your Lesson 19 folder.

12. Print the worksheet and close the workbook.

On Your Own

In these exercises you work on your own, as you would in a real-life work environment. Use the skills you've learned to accomplish the task—and be creative.

EXERCISE 19-25

Create a new workbook with labels, values, and formulas for a sports activity with which you are familiar. Use players or team names, scores, and other statistics related to the sport. Save your first set of values as a scenario. Add the standard footer. Create and save best and worst case scenarios for your players/teams. Show the best scenario. Create a scenario summary report and add the standard footer. Save the workbook as *[your initials]*19-25 in your Lesson 19 folder. Print the entire workbook and close the workbook.

EXERCISE 19-26

Create a new workbook with labels, values, and formulas for some daily activity or aspect of your life. For example, you might track how many miles you drive your car per day, how many times you drink a glass of water per day, or how many times you answer the telephone per day. Include a count of your activity each day from Monday through Friday. Build a column chart that represents your data. Then add a trendline to project the next five days. Add the standard footer to both worksheets. Save the workbook as *[your initials]*19-26 in your Lesson 19 folder, print the entire workbook, and close it.

EXERCISE 19-27

Use the Internet to learn about add-ins or other utilities that are not part of a typical Excel software installation. Create a new workbook. List and describe five add-ins or tools that you learned about in your search. Add a standard footer. Save the workbook as *[your initials]*19-27 in your Lesson 19 folder. Print the worksheet and close the workbook.

LESSON 20

Using Data Consolidation and Linking

OBJECTIVES

MICROSOFT OFFICE SPECIALIST
A C T I V I T I E S
In this lesson:
XL03E-4-5

See Appendix.

After completing this lesson, you will be able to:

1. **Create a static data consolidation.**
2. **Create a dynamic data consolidation.**
3. **Consolidate data by using other functions.**
4. **Link workbooks.**
5. **Examine and edit links.**
6. **Use a workspace.**

 Estimated Time: 1½ hours

Consolidation is a process in which data from multiple worksheets or work-books is combined and summarized. For example, if each ice cream shop submits weekly data in a separate workbook, the corporate office can consolidate all workbooks to create a summary workbook.

Worksheets and workbooks can be consolidated when:

- Common data appears in the same position on each worksheet. This is known as consolidating *by position.*

- Worksheets have the same row or column labels. This can be referred to as consolidating *by category.*

Linking is a process in which formulas refer to cells in another workbook. Linking is similar to using a 3-D reference within a workbook.

 REVIEW: A 3-D reference is a formula that refers to another worksheet in the same workbook.

Creating a Static Data Consolidation

A *static consolidation* summarizes values and enters a result. The resulting value does not change if a value in one of the worksheets or workbooks changes. You might use a static consolidation when you are preparing a final report and know that all supporting data is final.

The Data, Consolidate command can use one of several functions to summarize values, including SUM, AVERAGE, COUNT, and others.

EXERCISE 20-1 Copy and Prepare a Worksheet for Consolidation

This workbook includes a worksheet for each month in the fourth quarter.

1. Open the file **4QtrSandwiches**.
2. Right-click the December tab. Choose Move or Copy.
3. Choose (move to end) and select Create a copy. Click OK. The new worksheet is named December (2).
4. Rename the copied worksheet **4thQtr**.
5. Edit cell A3 to show **Fourth Quarter**.
6. On the 4thQtr worksheet, delete the contents of the range B5:E8. The new sheet is ready for consolidating data.

EXERCISE 20-2 Create a Static Consolidation

On each of these worksheets, the labels in A5:A8 and B4:E4 are the same. The related values are in the same positions on each worksheet, too. You can consolidate data by position when the values are in the same locations on each worksheet.

1. Make sure the range B5:E8 is selected on the 4thQtr worksheet.
2. From the Data menu, choose Consolidate. The Consolidate dialog box opens.
3. In the Function text box, check that Sum is the function to be used.
4. Position the insertion point in the Reference text box.
5. Click the October tab. The reference shows the name of the worksheet with an exclamation point.
6. Select the range B5:E8. The cell addresses are added to the entry box with absolute references. (The Consolidate dialog box collapses when you select a range on the worksheet.)
7. Click Add. The selected range appears under All references. You can add another reference to include in the consolidation.

8. Click the November tab. The same range is selected in the November worksheet, and the Reference text box shows the new worksheet name and cell addresses.

9. Click Add. The second reference appears under All references. You still need to add the December figures.

10. Click the December tab. The same range is selected in the December worksheet, and the Reference text box again shows the new worksheet name and cell addresses. Because everything is in the same position on these worksheets, your work in consolidating the data is minimal.

FIGURE 20-1
Using the
Consolidate
dialog box

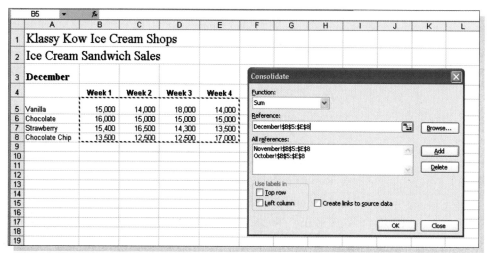

11. Click Add. The All references text box lists the three ranges that will be summed on the 4thQtr worksheet.

12. Click OK. The 4thQtr worksheet shows the sum of the values from the three monthly worksheets.

EXERCISE 20-3 Edit Underlying Data

The 4thQtr worksheet has values, not formulas. If you change a value in one of the monthly worksheets, the consolidated worksheet does not change to reflect the new figures.

1. Select cell B5 on the 4thQtr worksheet.

2. Look at the formula bar. It holds a value, not a formula.

3. Click the October tab. Select cell B5 and key **0**.

4. Click the 4thQtr tab. The value is not updated.

5. Delete the contents of the range B5:E8 in the 4thQtr worksheet.

Creating a Dynamic Data Consolidation

A *dynamic consolidation* creates a formula that refers to the other worksheets or workbooks. Because it is a formula, the results are recalculated if you make a change in the supporting worksheet or workbook.

Dynamic consolidation is appropriate when the values in the supporting worksheets might be changed after you consolidate, and you always want your workbook to reflect the most current information.

E X E R C I S E   20-4   Create a Dynamic Consolidation

Excel saves the references used in the most recent Data, Consolidate command. To edit or change the consolidation, you might not need to re-enter the references if you have not closed Excel.

When you choose the option to link to the source data in the Consolidate dialog box, Excel creates an outline with 3-D references. An *outline* is a summary worksheet that can display or hide details.

1. Select the range B5:E8 on the 4thQtr worksheet.
2. From the Data menu, choose Consolidate. The Consolidate dialog box opens. The three references to the other worksheets are still shown.
3. Place a check mark for Create links to source data. This option creates a dynamic consolidation.
4. Click OK. The worksheet shows the same results as the static consolidation, displayed in an outline. Outline symbols appear to the left of the row numbers and column letters. The numbers to the left of column A indicate how many levels of detail are in the outline. The plus and minus symbols (Expand and Collapse buttons) are used to display and hide the levels of detail. This outline has two levels of detail.

 REVIEW: You saw an outline in the scenario summary reports.

5. Click the plus (+) symbol for row 8. Excel displays details for the Vanilla data. Immediately above row 8 are the monthly values for vanilla from the other worksheets. (See Figure 20-2 on the next page.)

 NOTE: Bold formatting is copied from the labels in row 4 to the first set of values.

6. Click the minus (–) symbol for row 8. The individual values are hidden.
7. Click the plus (+) symbol for row 20. The individual monthly values for chocolate chip are displayed.

FIGURE 20-2
Displaying detail
in an outline

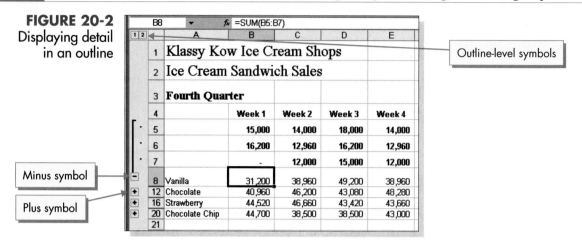

Outline-level symbols

Minus symbol

Plus symbol

8. Select cell B17. Notice in the formula bar that it is a 3-D formula.

9. Click the minus (–) symbol for row 20 to hide the details.

10. Select cell B8 and note its value.

11. Click the October tab. In cell B5, key **10000**.

12. Click the 4thQtr tab. The new result in cell B8 includes the value you just keyed.

13. Click the plus (+) symbol for row 8. The October value is in cell B7.

14. Collapse row 8.

EXERCISE **20-5** **Display Formulas in an Outline**

The level symbols are at the top of the outline column. They display 1 and 2 be-cause this outline has two levels. Level 1 shows the totals; Level 2 shows details.

1. Click the Level 2 outline symbol. The entire worksheet expands.

 REVIEW: You can display formulas by choosing Tools, Options, clicking the View tab, and selecting Formulas.

2. Press [Ctrl]+[~] to display the formulas. You can see the name of each worksheet used in a formula. (See Figure 20-3.)

 NOTE: Close the Formula Auditing toolbar if it opens.

3. Adjust column A to show the labels. AutoFit columns B:E. Change the orientation to landscape fit to one page. Add your standard footer.

 REVIEW: For footers, key your name in the left section, add the filename and tab name in the center, and add the date at the right.

Level 1 symbol   Level 2 symbol

FIGURE 20-3
Displaying formulas
in an outline

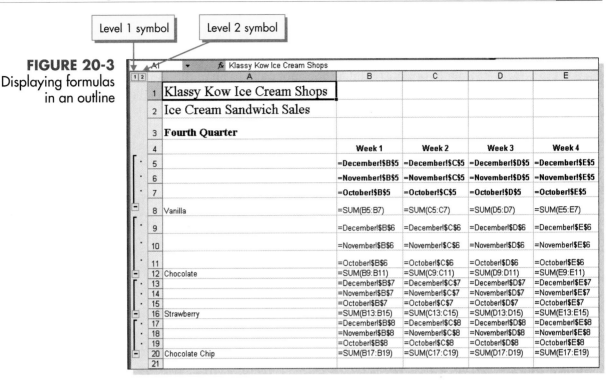

	A	B	C	D	E
1	Klassy Kow Ice Cream Shops				
2	Ice Cream Sandwich Sales				
3	**Fourth Quarter**				
4		**Week 1**	**Week 2**	**Week 3**	**Week 4**
5		=December!$B$5	=December!$C$5	=December!$D$5	=December!$E$5
6		=November!$B$5	=November!$C$5	=November!$D$5	=November!$E$5
7		=October!$B$5	=October!$C$5	=October!$D$5	=October!$E$5
8	Vanilla	=SUM(B5:B7)	=SUM(C5:C7)	=SUM(D5:D7)	=SUM(E5:E7)
9		=December!$B$6	=December!$C$6	=December!$D$6	=December!$E$6
10		=November!$B$6	=November!$C$6	=November!$D$6	=November!$E$6
11		=October!$B$6	=October!$C$6	=October!$D$6	=October!$E$6
12	Chocolate	=SUM(B9:B11)	=SUM(C9:C11)	=SUM(D9:D11)	=SUM(E9:E11)
13		=December!$B$7	=December!$C$7	=December!$D$7	=December!$E$7
14		=November!$B$7	=November!$C$7	=November!$D$7	=November!$E$7
15		=October!$B$7	=October!$C$7	=October!$D$7	=October!$E$7
16	Strawberry	=SUM(B13:B15)	=SUM(C13:C15)	=SUM(D13:D15)	=SUM(E13:E15)
17		=December!$B$8	=December!$C$8	=December!$D$8	=December!$E$8
18		=November!$B$8	=November!$C$8	=November!$D$8	=November!$E$8
19		=October!$B$8	=October!$C$8	=October!$D$8	=October!$E$8
20	Chocolate Chip	=SUM(B17:B19)	=SUM(C17:C19)	=SUM(D17:D19)	=SUM(E17:E19)
21					

4. Save the workbook as *[your initials]*20-5 in a new folder for Lesson 20 and print the worksheet.

5. Click the Level 1 symbol. The details are hidden.

6. Press Ctrl+~ to hide the formulas.

7. Save the workbook and close it.

 TIP: You can remove an outline by choosing Data, Group and Outline, and then Clear Outline.

Consolidating Data by Using Other Functions

You are not limited to using SUM for data consolidation. You can use any of several statistical functions, including AVERAGE, MIN, MAX, COUNT, and others.

In the previous exercises, you consolidated data by position. All the source data was arranged in identical order and location. You can also consolidate data by category. In this case, the supporting worksheets have the same row and column labels, but the data is organized differently.

EXERCISE **20-6** **Rearrange Data to be Consolidated**

Data to be consolidated does not have to be in the same row and column order. However, the rows and columns must have the same labels.

1. Open the file **4QtrSandwiches**.
2. Make a copy of the December sheet as the rightmost sheet. Rename the copied worksheet **Averages**. Edit cell A3 to show **Averages**.
3. In the October worksheet, right-click the column E heading and choose Cut.
4. Right-click the column B heading and choose Insert Cut Cells. The week order on this worksheet is now different from the order on the other worksheets. Select any cell to deselect the column.

 REVIEW: If you do a regular cut-and-paste, Excel replaces the existing data with the cut cells.

5. In the November worksheet, right-click the row 7 heading. Choose Cut.
6. Right-click the row 6 heading and choose Insert Cut Cells. The flavor order on this worksheet is different from the order on the other worksheets. Select any cell.

EXERCISE **20-7** **Use AVERAGE to Consolidate by Category**

When you consolidate data by category, you must include labels in the consolidation ranges. The consolidation worksheet should not show any labels as you start the consolidation.

1. In the Averages worksheet, delete the contents of the range A4:E8. Leave the range selected on the worksheet.
2. Choose Data and Consolidate. The Consolidate dialog box opens.
3. Click the down arrow next to the Function text box and choose Average.
4. Position the insertion point in the Reference text box.
5. Click the October tab and select cells A4:E8. This range includes the labels for the rows and the columns.
6. Click Add in the Consolidate dialog box. The selected range appears under All references.
7. Click the November tab. The same range is assumed.
8. Click Add. The second selected range appears under All references.
9. Click the December tab and click Add. The third selected range appears under All references.

10. In the Use labels in group, place check marks for Top row and Left column. These settings will consolidate the data according to the labels in the column and the row.

FIGURE 20-4
Consolidating
by category

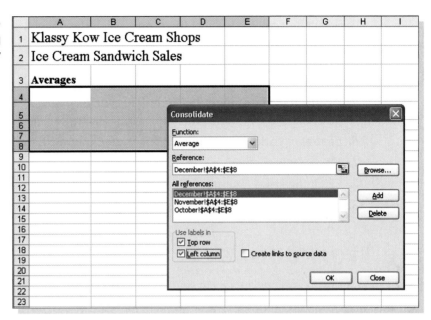

11. Click OK. The Averages worksheet shows the averages of the three supporting worksheets. The Vanilla average for Week 1 is 15,400.

EXERCISE **20-8** **Consolidate Data by Using MAX**

You can consolidate worksheets and summarize the data to show the maximum values in the supporting worksheets.

1. Select any cell in the Averages worksheet to deselect the range. Create a copy of the Averages worksheet, move it to the end, and rename it **Maximums**. Edit cell A3 in the Maximums worksheet to show **Maximums**.

2. On the new worksheet, delete the contents of the range A4:E8. Leave the range selected.

3. Choose Data and Consolidate. The Consolidate dialog box opens.

4. Click the down arrow next to the Function text box and choose Max. You'll use the same references as before. The options in the Use labels in group are also still selected.

5. Place a check mark for Create links to source data. This will create a dynamic consolidation with 3-D references.

6. Click OK. The Maximums worksheet shows the maximum values in the three supporting worksheets. The Vanilla maximum for Week 1 is 16,200. There are two outline levels, one to show the weekly numbers and one to show the maximum.

7. Select any cell to deselect the range. Click the Level 2 symbol. The outline expands to show all the references.

8. Press Ctrl+`. The formulas show worksheet references. Column B is inserted in a dynamic consolidation by category. It identifies the workbook.

9. Adjust the column widths so that all data is visible. Set the orientation to landscape to fit to one page and add the standard footer.

10. Save the workbook as *[your initials]*20-8 in your Lesson 20 folder.

11. Print the worksheet.

12. Click the Level 1 symbol. Press Ctrl+` to hide the formulas.

13. Save the workbook and close it.

Linking Workbooks

Linking combines data from several workbooks into a summary workbook. When any workbook is changed, the summary workbook will reflect those changes.

Linked workbooks depend on one another. The *dependent workbook* is the file that obtains data from other workbooks. Dependent workbooks use *external reference formulas,* which are formulas that refer to cells in another workbook. The *source workbook* is the file with data used by a dependent workbook in an external reference formula.

You can create an external reference formula in several ways. You can:

- Point to the cell(s) if the source workbook is open. This creates a link.

- Use Edit, Paste Special, and Paste Link if the source workbook is open. This is the same as pointing to the open source workbook.

- Use the Data, Consolidate command and create links. Both workbooks must be open.

- Key the formula with the workbook, worksheet, and cell references. This can be tedious and requires that you type accurately, but the source workbook need not be open.

EXERCISE **20-9** **Link Workbooks by Pointing**

When you point to an external reference, Excel fills in the correct syntax for the reference. The syntax for an external reference is:

=[WorkbookName]WorksheetName!CellAddress

NOTE: When you point to an external reference, Excel inserts an absolute reference. You can change it if you want to copy the formula.

1. Open the file **YogurtOR**. This workbook contains Oregon sales for frozen yogurt. This will be the source workbook.

2. Add your standard footer and save the workbook as *[your initials]***20-9OR** in your Lesson 20 folder. Leave the workbook open.

3. Open the file **YogurtNV**. These are Nevada sales for frozen yogurt. This will be the dependent workbook.

4. Add the standard footer and save the workbook as *[your initials]***20-9NV** in your Lesson 20 folder.

5. From the Window menu, choose Arrange.

6. Select Vertical. Click OK. When you arrange windows, the active window is tiled on the left.

7. Select cell A11 in *[your initials]***20-9NV**, the Nevada workbook. Key **Vanilla**.

8. In cell B11, key = to start a formula.

9. Click cell B5 in the Nevada workbook and key + to add.

10. Double-click cell B5 in *[your initials]***20-9OR**, the Oregon workbook. An external reference is entered with the name of the workbook and an absolute reference to the cell or range.

REVIEW: The first click in the source workbook activates the workbook. The second click selects the cell. You can double-click.

FIGURE 20-5
Creating an external reference

| DCOUNT | | =B5+[Sol20-9OR.xls]Oregon1$B$5 |

Sol20-9NV

	A	B	C	D	E	F
1	Klassy Kow Ice Cream Shops					
2	Frozen Yogurt Sales					
3	**Nevada**					
4		**Week 1**	**Week 2**	**Week 3**	**Week 4**	
5	Vanilla	16,200	12,960	16,200	12,960	
6	Chocolate	12,960	16,200	14,580	17,280	
7	Strawberry	15,120	15,660	15,120	15,660	
8	Chocolate Chip	16,200	13,500	13,500	13,500	
9						
10						
11	Vanillla	=B5+[Sol20-9OR.xls]Oregon1$B$5				
12						
13						
14						
15						
16						
17						
18						
19						
20						
21						
22						
23						
24						

Nevada

Sol20-9OR

	A	B	C	D	E
1	Klassy Kow Ice Cream Shops				
2	Frozen Yogurt Sales				
3	**Oregon**				
4		**Week 1**	**Week 2**	**Week 3**	**Week 4**
5	Vanilla	15,000	12,000	15,000	12,000
6	Chocolate	12,000	15,000	13,500	16,000
7	Strawberry	14,000	14,500	14,000	14,500
8	Chocolate Chip	15,000	12,500	12,500	12,500
9					
10					
11					
12					
13					
14					
15					
16					
17					
18					
19					
20					
21					
22					
23					
24					

Oregon

11. Press Enter. The formula in cell B5 in the Nevada workbook adds the Vanilla values from both workbooks.

12. Select cell B11 in the Nevada workbook, *[your initials]***20-9NV**.

13. Edit the formula to remove the absolute reference. Delete only the dollar signs ($).

14. Copy the formula to the range B12:B14. These are the totals for the other flavors for Week 1.

15. Select the range A6:A8 in the Nevada workbook. Copy and paste the range to cell A12 to add labels for the copied formulas.

Examining and Editing Links

While a source workbook is open, the external reference in the dependent workbook does not show a path in the filename. A *path* is an identifier preceding a filename that includes the name of the disk drive and the series of folders specifying the file location on the drive. If you close the source workbook, the dependent workbook shows the full filename and path.

When you open a workbook with linked formulas, Excel updates the values and recalculates the formulas.

EXERCISE **20-10** **Examine Links**

You can see the path of a link when you close the source workbook. Excel alerts you to the existence of links when you open a dependent workbook.

1. Close the Oregon workbook, *[your initials]***20-9OR**, the source workbook in this case.

2. Maximize the Nevada workbook, *[your initials]***20-9NV**.

3. Select cell B11 and view the formula in the formula bar. It now includes the path to identify the source workbook.

4. From the Edit menu, choose Links. The Edit Links dialog box lists information about source files for this workbook. Update is set to Automatic. (See Figure 20-6.)

5. Click Close without making any changes. Make a note of the Vanilla total in cell B11.

6. Save and close the Nevada workbook, *[your initials]***20-9NV**.

7. Open the Oregon workbook, *[your initials]***20-9OR**, the source workbook.

8. Select cell B5 and change the Vanilla value for Week 1 to **0**. Then save and close the workbook.

9. Open the Nevada workbook, *[your initials]***20-9NV**, the dependent workbook. A dialog box alerts you to the links. (See Figure 20-7.)

FIGURE 20-6
Edit Links
dialog box

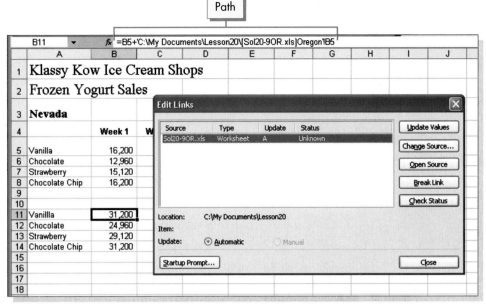

Path

FIGURE 20-7
Message to
update links

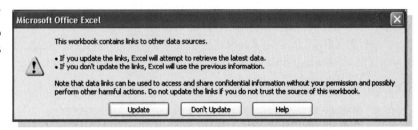

10. Click Update. The workbook shows the new Vanilla total based on the change you made in the Oregon workbook.

11. Save and close the Nevada workbook.

EXERCISE **20-11** Move a Source Workbook

If you move the source workbook to another location, Excel will not be able to find it when you open the dependent workbook.

1. Open the Oregon workbook, *[your initials]*20-9OR, the source workbook.

2. Change the Vanilla value in cell B5 to **50000**.

3. Save and close the workbook.

4. Click the Open button on the Standard toolbar.

5. Right-click *[your initials]*20-9OR, the Oregon source workbook. A shortcut menu opens.

6. Choose Cut.

7. Click the Desktop icon on the Places bar (the vertical bar on the left side of the Open dialog box).

8. Right-click in unused white space and choose Paste. This moves the workbook from your folder to the desktop. Leave the Open dialog box open.

EXERCISE 20-12 Edit Links

As you open the dependent workbook, you can edit the link to show the new location of the source workbook.

1. Click the down arrow next to the Look in text box and navigate to your Lesson 20 folder.

> **NOTE:** If you're not sure of the path for your Lesson 20 folder, ask your instructor for assistance.

2. Open the file *[your initials]***20-9NV**, the Nevada dependent workbook. The same message appears about the links.

3. Click Update. Excel displays a message that the links cannot be updated, because the workbook is not in the folder where it was when you created the link.

FIGURE 20-8
Message that links
cannot be updated

4. Click Continue. The formula is not updated to show a new total in cell B11.

5. From the Edit menu, choose Links. The Edit Links dialog box opens.

6. Click Change Source. The Change Source dialog box opens so that you can set a new location for the source workbook.

7. Click the Desktop icon on the Places bar.

8. Click *[your initials]***20-9OR** and click OK. The Edit Links dialog box shows the new location, and the formula has been updated with the new value.

> **TIP:** If someone else is working on the source workbook while you are working on the dependent workbook, you can force an update by clicking Update Values in the Edit Links dialog box.

9. Click Close. The formula shows the recalculated Vanilla total (66,200).

10. Save the file.

EXERCISE 20-13 Break Links

If you no longer need external references in a workbook, you can delete the contents of those cells. As long as you delete the contents of all cells with links, the external reference is removed. You can also keep the results in the dependent workbook but break the link to the source workbook.

1. In the Nevada workbook, *[your initials]*20-9NV, select the range with links, B11:B14.
2. From the Edit menu, choose Links. The Edit Links dialog box opens.
3. Click Break Link. Excel displays a message warning you that when you break a link, the linked formulas are converted to values.
4. Click Break Links. Click Close.
5. Click cell B11. The formula bar shows the value from the linked formula, but the formula is now removed.
6. Save and close the workbook.
7. Click the Open button 📖. Click the Desktop icon 📖 on the Places bar.
8. Right-click *[your initials]*20-9OR, the Oregon source workbook.
9. Choose Cut.
10. Click the down arrow next to the Look in text box and navigate to your Lesson 20 folder.
11. Right-click in unused white space and choose Paste. This moves the workbook from the desktop to your Lesson 20 folder.
12. Close the Open dialog box.

Using a Workspace

A *workspace* is a file that saves display information about open workbooks, including workbook names, screen positions, and window sizes. For example, if you frequently work with two workbooks and always tile them vertically, you can save this arrangement as a workspace. When you open the workspace, the workbooks are arranged the way you prefer them to be.

A workspace file does not include the actual workbook files, just a reference to them. You still need to save the workbooks separately after making changes. And if you want to send a workspace to a coworker, you must include the actual workbook files.

EXERCISE **20-14** **Create a Workspace**

You create a workspace by first arranging your workbooks as you'd like them to appear each time you open them. Then you save them as a workspace.

1. Open the file **YogurtCA**. Add your standard footer. Save the workbook as *[your initials]***20-14CA** in your Lesson 20 folder. Leave the file open.

2. Open the file **YogurtWA**. Add the footer. Save the workbook as *[your initials]***20-14WA** in your Lesson 20 folder.

3. Press ⌃Ctrl+F6 to switch to the California workbook.

 NOTE: The keyboard shortcut ⌃Ctrl+F6 switches to other open documents in most Windows applications. You can also click the document name on the taskbar.

4. Arrange the windows vertically. The California workbook is on the left, because it was active when you executed the Arrange command.

5. From the File menu, choose Save Workspace. The Save Workspace dialog box opens. The File name text box shows a default filename. The Save as type text box shows Workspaces. Workspaces use the xlw filename extension.

 **REVIEW:** Your Windows settings determine whether you see filename extensions.

6. Navigate to your Lesson 20 folder in the Save in box if it is not already shown.

7. In the File name box, key *[your initials]***20-14WS**.

FIGURE 20-9
Creating a
workspace

8. Click <u>S</u>ave. The arrangement of the two workbooks is saved as a workspace. When you open the workspace, the two workbooks will be arranged the way you've saved them.

9. Press and hold (Shift). From the <u>F</u>ile menu, choose <u>C</u>lose All. Both workbooks are closed.

 REVIEW: Close All appears in the File menu only when you press and hold (Shift).

10. Click the Open button 📂.

11. Open the file *[your initials]***20-14WS**. Both workbooks open in the same arrangement.

EXERCISE 20-15 **Consolidate Data in a Workspace**

You can use the <u>D</u>ata, <u>C</u>onsolidate command to create a static consolidation in a workspace.

1. Set each workbook to a 75% view for easier selecting.

2. In the Washington workbook, select the range A10:E14. These cells are empty. They represent the same number of cells as the range A4:E8.

3. From the <u>D</u>ata menu, choose <u>C</u>onsolidate. The Consolidate dialog box opens.

4. In the <u>F</u>unction text box, make sure that Sum is selected.

5. Position the insertion point in the <u>R</u>eference text box.

6. Select the range A4:E8 in the Washington workbook. This range includes the labels and the values.

7. Click <u>A</u>dd. The selected range is shown in the All r<u>e</u>ferences text box.

8. Select the range A4:E8 in the California workbook.

9. Click <u>A</u>dd. The second range, which includes the workbook name in square brackets, is shown under All r<u>e</u>ferences.

10. In the Use labels in group, make sure both <u>T</u>op row and <u>L</u>eft column have a check mark.

11. Place a check mark for Create links to <u>s</u>ource data.

12. Click OK. A message box indicates that Excel cannot create links in a workspace.

13. Click OK in the message box.

14. From the <u>D</u>ata menu, choose <u>C</u>onsolidate.

15. Deselect Create links to <u>s</u>ource data. (See Figure 20-10 on the next page.)

16. Click OK. Excel can create a static consolidation in a workspace. Click any cell in the Washington workbook to deselect the range.

FIGURE 20-10
Consolidating data
in a workspace

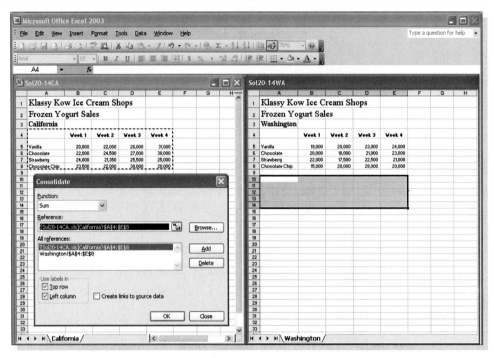

17. Save the Washington workbook, *[your initials]*20-14WA, and print the worksheet.

18. Press and hold (Shift). From the File menu, choose Close All.

 NOTE: When you use File, Close All, you are prompted to save each file individually if you have made changes to any of them.

19. Save all files if prompted.

USING ONLINE HELP

If you use data from multiple worksheets on a regular basis, there are numerous ways in which linking might be helpful. Use Microsoft Excel Help to get ideas about how you might use linking in other ways.

Use Help to learn about linking workbooks.

1. With Internet Explorer and Excel running, look for topics about linking workbooks. Look at several subtopics of interest to you.

2. Read the information and close the windows.

3. Close Internet Explorer and end your Internet connection.

LESSON Summary

➤ In data consolidation, information from several worksheets or workbooks is combined and summarized. Linking occurs when formulas in a worksheet refer to cells in another workbook.

➤ The results of a static consolidation are not updated if the supporting data changes.

➤ You can consolidate data by position when the values are in the same location on each worksheet.

➤ Dynamic consolidations create links by using 3-D cell references to the supporting worksheets. The results appear in an outline, in which you can hide or display details.

➤ In a dynamic consolidation, changes made in the supporting worksheets are reflected in the consolidated worksheet.

➤ In a consolidation by category, the supporting worksheets have the same row and column labels, but the data is organized differently.

➤ Formulas that refer to cells in another workbook are called external reference formulas. Linked workbooks are either dependent or source workbooks.

➤ When you create an external reference by pointing, Excel uses proper formula syntax for the source workbook.

➤ After workbooks have been linked, you can review and update the links. A path is the identifier preceding a filename that indicates the drive and folder location of the file.

➤ Excel alerts you to the existence of links when you open a dependent workbook.

➤ External references can be deleted from the dependent workbook. You can also break the links but keep the results in the dependent workbook.

➤ If you move a source workbook, you need to edit the link in the dependent workbook so that Excel can reestablish the link.

➤ A workspace is a file that saves display information about open workbooks, including workbook names, screen positions, window sizes, and other data.

➤ You create a workspace by first arranging your workbooks as you'd like them to appear each time you open them. Workspace files use the extension xlw.

➤ In a workspace, you can perform static data consolidation.

LESSON 20   Command Summary

FEATURE	BUTTON	MENU	KEYBOARD
Consolidate data		Data, Consolidate	
Close all files		[Shift] + File, Close All	
Edit links		Edit, Links	
Create workspace		File, Save Workspace	

Concepts Review

TRUE/FALSE QUESTIONS

Each of the following statements is either true or false. Indicate your choice by circling T or F.

T F   **1.** Static and dynamic consolidations initially show the same results.

T F   **2.** Linking refers to formulas that depend on cells in another workbook.

T F   **3.** Workspaces can be used for linking workbooks.

T F   **4.** Data to be consolidated must be in the same position on each worksheet.

T F   **5.** A dependent workbook has external reference formulas.

T F   **6.** An external reference shows the complete path if the source workbook is closed.

T F   **7.** After you establish a link in a workbook, you cannot move the source workbook from its folder.

T F   **8.** A workspace is the memory used by the dependent and source workbooks.

SHORT ANSWER QUESTIONS

Write the correct answer in the space provided.

1. What type of data consolidation updates the summary worksheet each time a source worksheet is changed?

_____

2. Name three functions that can be used for data consolidation.

_____

3. In what menu is the Consolidate command listed?

_____

4. How can you convert a linked formula to its value?

_____

5. What name describes a file that includes workbook names, positions, and sizes?

_____

6. How do you hide details in an outline?

_____

7. When you consolidate by category, what do you include when selecting the range in the supporting worksheet?

_____

8. What is the filename extension for a workspace file?

_____

CRITICAL THINKING

Answer these questions on a separate page. There are no right or wrong answers. Support your answers with examples from your own experience, if possible.

1. If you are creating a year-end report, would you use a static or dynamic consolidation? Explain your decision.
2. Why is it important to know how to edit or break links?

Skills Review

EXERCISE 20-16

Copy a worksheet for consolidation. Create a static data consolidation. Create a dynamic consolidation. Show and hide detail in an outline.

1. Open the file **WorkersComp**.
2. Copy a worksheet for consolidation by following these steps:
   a. Right-click the 4thQtr tab. Choose Move or Copy.
   b. Choose (move to end) and select Create a copy. Click OK.
3. Rename the copied sheet **Static**. In the Static worksheet, delete the contents of the range B5:D10.
4. Create a static data consolidation by following these steps:
   a. Select the range B5:D10 in the Static worksheet.
   b. From the Data menu, choose Consolidate.
   c. In the Function text box, verify that Sum is displayed.

   d. Position the insertion point in the Reference text box.

   e. Click the 1stQtr worksheet tab and select the range B5:D10.

   f. Click Add.

   g. Click the 2ndQtr worksheet tab and click Add.

   h. Repeat these steps for the 3rdQtr and 4thQtr worksheets.

   i. When all four references are shown in the All references text box, click OK.

5. In the Static worksheet, select the range E5:E10 and click the AutoSum button on the Standard toolbar.

> **NOTE:** The three consolidated columns must be summed to determine each city's yearly total.

6. Starting in cell B4, change the labels in the range B4:D4 as follows:

   1st Month   **2nd Month**   **3rd Month**

7. Key **Total** in cell E4.

8. Add your standard footer. Edit the file properties to show your name as the author and your school/company name. Add a preview picture.

9. Save the workbook as *[your initials]*20-16 in your Lesson 20 folder and print the Static worksheet.

10. Make a copy of the 4thQtr sheet, move it to the end, and name it **Dynamic**.

11. Create a dynamic consolidation by following these steps:

   a. In the Dynamic worksheet, delete the contents of the range B5:D10.

   b. From the Data menu, choose Consolidate while the range B5:D10 is selected.

   c. Click the 1stQtr worksheet tab and select the range B5:D10. Click Add.

   d. Repeat these steps for the other quarters.

   e. Place a check mark for Create links to source data. Click OK.

12. Use outline symbols by following these steps:

   a. Click the Level 2 outline symbol next to the column headings.

   b. Click the Level 1 outline symbol to hide the summary detail.

   c. Click the plus (+) symbol next to row 34 to show the Henderson detail.

13. Add your footer. Print the Dynamic worksheet.

14. Hide the Henderson detail and deselect the range.

15. Make a copy of the Dynamic sheet. Display the formulas. Click the Level 2 outline symbol. AutoFit the columns and set the orientation to landscape. Print the formula sheet.

16. Save and close the workbook.

EXERCISE 20-17

Consolidate data by using MIN. Show outline levels.

1. Open the file **4QtrSandwiches**.
2. Edit the values in the November worksheet as shown in Figure 20-11.

FIGURE 20-11

	Week 1	Week 2	Week 3	Week 4
Vanilla	17000	12000	19200	12760
Chocolate	13060	15100	14320	13350
Strawberry	15000	15560	14220	15000
Chocolate Chip	18200	13400	16400	13400

3. Copy the December sheet to the end and rename the new sheet **Minimums**. Delete the contents of the range B5:E8.
4. Use MIN to consolidate data by following these steps:

   a. From the Data menu, choose Consolidate.
   b. Click the down arrow next to the Function text box and choose Min.
   c. Position the insertion point in the Reference text box.
   d. Click the October worksheet tab and select the range B5:E8.
   e. Click Add.
   f. Repeat these steps for the November and December worksheets.
   g. Place a check mark for Create links to source data.
   h. Click OK.

5. Edit cell A3 to show **Minimum Sales**.
6. Add the standard footer. Save the workbook as *[your initials]*20-17 in your Lesson 20 folder.
7. Print the Minimums worksheet.
8. Make a copy of the Minimums sheet and move it to the end. Show the outline detail by clicking the Level 2 outline symbol.
9. Display the formulas on this copied sheet and AutoFit the columns. Set the orientation to landscape. Print the formulas sheet.
10. Save and close the workbook.

EXERCISE 20-18

Link workbooks. Edit and copy an external reference. Examine and edit links.

1. Create a new workbook.

2. Format the range A1:A2 as 18-point Times New Roman. Key **Klassy Kow Ice Cream Shops** in cell A1. Key **Frozen Yogurt Sales** in cell A2.

3. Starting in cell A3, key the following labels in the range A3:A6:
   Vanilla   Chocolate   Strawberry   Chocolate Chip

4. Set the height of rows 3 through 6 to 24.00 (32 pixels). Widen column A.

5. Insert a row at row 3 and key **Week 1** in cell B3. Make it bold and centered. Fill to **Week 4** in cell E3.

6. Link workbooks by following these steps:

   a. Click the Open button on the Standard toolbar. Navigate to the folder with the files for this lesson.

   b. Select the files **YogurtCA**, **YogurtNV**, **YogurtOR**, and **YogurtWA**.

    TIP: If the workbook names are not contiguous, select the first filename and then press and hold Ctrl while selecting each of the others.

   c. Click Open. All four workbooks are opened as well as your new workbook.

   d. From the Window menu, choose Arrange. Tile the windows vertically.

   e. Click in each window and scroll it so that you can see cell B5.

   f. Select cell B4 in your new workbook window and key = to start a formula.

   g. Double-click cell B5 in **YogurtCA** and key + to continue the formula.

   h. Double-click cell B5 in **YogurtNV** and key +.

   i. Repeat these steps to add cell B5 from **YogurtOR** and **YogurtWA** to the formula. Press Enter when finished.

    REVIEW: If you key a plus sign (+) at the end of the formula, Excel will suggest a correction.

7. Maximize your new workbook window and select cell B4.

8. Edit and copy an external reference by following these steps:

   a. With cell B4 selected, press F2.

   b. Edit the formula to remove the absolute references and make them relative.

   c. Press Enter when finished.

   NOTE: The dependent workbook does not have the row with the state name, so the totals are a row higher than they are in the source workbooks.

   d. Copy the linked formula in cell B4 for the rest of the totals. Format the values to show commas and no decimals.

9. Add the standard footer. Save the workbook as *[your initials]*20-18 in your Lesson 20 folder and print the worksheet.

10. Press and hold (Shift). From the File menu, choose Close All.

11. Examine and edit links by following these steps:

    a. Open the file *[your initials]*20-18 and click Update. Note the total for Vanilla in Week 1.
    b. From the Edit menu, choose Links.
    c. Select YogurtNV in the list and click Open Source.
    d. Change the Vanilla total for Week 1 in the YogurtNV worksheet to **0**. Close the workbook without saving.

12. Print Sheet1 in *[your initials]*20-18 with the updated total.

13. Close and save the workbook.

EXERCISE 20-19

Create a workspace. Consolidate data in a workspace.

1. Open the files **YogurtNV** and **YogurtOR**. Save the Oregon workbook as *[your initials]*20-19OR in your Lesson 20 folder. Save the Nevada workbook as *[your initials]*20-19NV in the same folder.

2. Create a workspace by following these steps:

   a. From the Window menu, choose Arrange. Tile the windows vertically.
   b. From the File menu, choose Save Workspace.
   c. Make sure the Save in location is your Lesson 20 folder.
   d. In the File name text box, key *[your initials]*20-19. Click Save.

3. Press and hold (Shift). From the File menu, choose Close All.

4. Open the workspace file *[your initials]*20-19. Set each workbook to a 75% view for easier viewing.

5. Consolidate data in a workspace by following these steps:

   a. In the Oregon workbook, select the range A10:E14.
   b. From the Data menu, choose Consolidate and set the Function to Average.
   c. Position the insertion point in the Reference text box.
   d. Select the range A4:E8 in the Nevada workbook. Click Add.
   e. Select the range A4:E8 in the Oregon workbook. Click Add.
   f. In the Use labels in group, select both Top row and Left column.
   g. Make sure there is no check mark for Create links to source data. Click OK.

6. Select any cell to deselect the range. Add the standard footer to the Oregon workbook.

7. Save the Oregon workbook as *[your initials]*20-19OR2 in your Lesson 20 folder and print the worksheet.

8. Close the workbooks.

Lesson Applications

EXERCISE 20-20

Copy a worksheet for consolidation. Create a static consolidation.

Monthly expenses for the sales representatives have been entered on two worksheets in a workbook. You need to consolidate the budgeted and actual expense amounts on a new worksheet.

1. Open the file **Expenses**.

2. Copy Sheet2 to the end and name it **Consolidated**.

3. In the Consolidated worksheet, delete column B. Then select the titles in the range B1:B2 and move them to column C.

 NOTE: You cannot consolidate dates.

4. Delete the range B6:C13. Then consolidate the range C6:D13 from Sheet1 and Sheet2 by using SUM. Do not link the source data.

5. In cell D6 in the Consolidated worksheet, key a formula to subtract the amount spent from the budget amount. Copy the formula through row 13.

6. In cell D5, key **Over/Under**. Its format should match the other titles in row 5. Size the column appropriately.

 7. Click the Text Box button on the Drawing toolbar and draw a text box across the range F5:G5. Key **These are consolidated results**.

   REVIEW: Display the Drawing toolbar to use the Text Box tool.

8. Size the text box so that the text fits on one line. Right-click the box and format it so that the text is horizontally and vertically centered in the box. Apply Shadow Style 6 to the text box.

9. Move the text box so that it appears centered between rows 6 and 13, and its left edge starts in column E.

10. Add the standard footer. Edit the file properties to show **Budget Results** as the title, your name as the author, and your school/company.

11. Save the workbook as *[your initials]***20-20** in your Lesson 20 folder.

12. Print the worksheet and close the workbook.

EXERCISE 20-21

Open and edit a workspace.

One of your workspaces has the wrong workbook in it. Instead of the Oregon workbook, it should include the Washington workbook.

 REVIEW: If your computer does not display filename extensions, check the icon to determine the file type.

1. Open the **Yogurt** workspace file.

2. Close the Oregon workbook. Open the file **YogurtWA**. Arrange the windows in a cascade. Size the windows appropriately.

3. Place the Washington workbook on top. Save a workspace file named *[your initials]***20-21** in your Lesson 20 folder.

4. Close all workbooks.

5. Open your workspace file. From the File menu, choose Web Page Preview. Only the active workbook is previewed in a Web page. Close the browser.

6. Close all workbooks.

EXERCISE 20-22

Create a template with external references. Examine links.

A customer order template is to be linked to the price list workbook. With the link established, you simply need to key the quantity for each item and the price is calculated.

1. Open the file **CustOrder**. Add the standard footer. Save the workbook as a template named *[your initials]***20-22** in the Templates folder.

2. Build a formula in cell D4 to compute the total due per item. Copy the formula through row 8. Format the range C4:D8 as currency with two decimals.

TIP: Use the Format Cell dialog box when you format cells with no values to be sure of your choices.

3. Open the file **PriceGroups**. Save it as *[your initials]*20-22PR in your Lesson 20 folder. Arrange the windows vertically.

4. In cell C4 in the template file, key = to start a formula. Then click the appropriate cell in the price list and press (Enter). (This formula just refers to another cell; it does not calculate anything.)

5. Repeat these steps to link the price for each item in the template to the price list.

 NOTE: An absolute reference is acceptable for this worksheet.

6. Click cell B4 in your template file. Save the template, print it, and close it.

7. Close *[your initials]*20-22PR.

8. Create a new workbook based on your template *[your initials]*20-22. Update the links and maximize the workbook.

9. Examine the links to see the name of the source workbook.

 10. Key a quantity for each item. Click the AutoSum button in cell D9.

11. Save the workbook as *[your initials]*20-22 in your Lesson 20 folder.

12. Make a copy of the sheet and display the formulas. AutoFit the columns, and print the worksheet in landscape orientation on one page.

13. Save and close the workbook.

14. Choose File, New from the menu and click On my computer. Click the General tab. Delete *[your initials]*20-22 and close the dialog box.

 NOTE: Make sure you complete the last step of this exercise. Template files remain on the computer until they are deleted.

EXERCISE 20-23 Challenge Yourself

Design worksheets for consolidation. Create a dynamic consolidation.

You have been asked to analyze how many plastic sundae cups were used each quarter this year and last year so that you can determine an average number per quarter. The sundae cups come in three sizes: small, medium, and large.

1. Create a new workbook.

2. Using the information in Figure 20-12, prepare two worksheets. Use the first set of figures for one worksheet and the other set of figures for the second worksheet. Add a main title for each worksheet. As you design the worksheets, keep in mind that they will be consolidated. Name the worksheets accordingly.

 TIP: Group two sheets and key and format common labels.

3. Create a consolidated worksheet by using AVERAGE with links to the source data. Format all sheets with a professional look. No values should show decimal places. Rename the consolidated sheet. Deselect any selected range.

FIGURE 20-12

This Year	Qtr 1	Qtr 2	Qtr 3	Qtr 4
Small	50,000	53,000	58,000	49,000
Medium	65,000	64,500	71,000	68,500
Large	55,000	54,000	62,000	58,000

Last Year	Qtr 1	Qtr 2	Qtr 3	Qtr 4
Small	45,000	51,000	55,000	43,000
Medium	60,000	60,500	69,000	60,500
Large	53,000	52,000	59,000	50,000

4. Group the worksheets and use File, Page Setup to add the standard footer and center the sheets horizontally. Print the entire workbook.

5. Save the workbook as *[your initials]*20-23 in your Lesson 20 folder.

6. Make a copy of the consolidated sheet. Expand the outline, show the formulas, adjust the column widths, and print the formula worksheet in landscape orientation.

7. Save and close the workbook.

On Your Own

In these exercises you work on your own, as you would in a real-life work environment. Use the skills you've learned to accomplish the task—and be creative.

EXERCISE 20-24

Create a new workbook with four worksheets, each one for a week in the month. Name the worksheets accordingly. Group the sheets and key labels in the first column for three daily expenses, activities, or tasks that you have at work or at school. Key the five days of the work week across a row. Insert an appropriate main title. Ungroup the worksheets and enter values for the number of times or amounts spent each day each week. Create a consolidated worksheet for the month. Group the worksheets and add the standard footer to each worksheet. Save the workbook as *[your initials]*20-24 in your Lesson 20 folder. Print and close the workbook.

EXERCISE 20-25

Create two workbooks, one that will be a source and one that will be a dependent on any topic that you like. Build formulas in the dependent workbook that use external references for information in the source workbook. Add your footer and save the workbooks as *[your initials]*20-25A and *[your initials]*20-25B in your Lesson 20 folder. Print both workbooks. Create and print a formula sheet in the dependent workbook. Save and close both workbooks.

EXERCISE 20-26

Create a workspace that uses the three workbooks that you have created in these On Your Own activities or three files from the CD. Arrange the workspace in a way that enables you to easily work with each of the workbooks. While the workspace is displayed, press Print Screen to copy the screen image to the clipboard. Open a new workbook and paste the image. Adjust the size and position as needed. Add the standard footer. Save the workbook with the image as *[your initials]*20-26 in your Lesson 20 folder. Print the worksheet with the image and close all workbooks.

Using Workgroup Features

OBJECTIVES

After completing this lesson, you will be able to:

1. Create a shared workbook.
2. Set change history options.
3. Track changes.
4. Use the Reviewing toolbar.
5. Print a change history worksheet.
6. Compare and merge workbooks.
7. Accept or reject changes.

 Estimated Time: 1½ hours

MICROSOFT OFFICE SPECIALIST ACTIVITIES

In this lesson:
XLO3E-3-3
XLO3E-3-4
XLO3E-3-5

See Appendix.

Users who share workbooks are known as a *workgroup*. Shared workbooks are usually stored on a network drive so that all members of a workgroup have access to it.

For this lesson, you will become a member of a three-person workgroup. The three people in this group are:

- User 1, Keiko Sumara, Sales and Marketing Manager
- User 2, Kim Tamasaki, Contract Sales Representative
- User 3, Juan Sante, Vice President

Your instructor will assign you to a role or ask that you rotate roles. As you complete the lesson, you should complete the steps for your assigned role as well as note what your coworkers are doing.

Creating a Shared Workbook

A *shared workbook* is one that several users can access at the same time. A shared workbook is kept in a single location on a network drive with all users able to access it at the same time. A shared workbook can also be copied so that each user has his or her own copy.

A shared workbook has some limitations. In a shared workbook, you cannot do the following:

- Delete worksheets.
- Insert or delete cell ranges. You can insert or delete rows or columns.
- Merge cells.
- Add or edit charts, images, AutoShapes, or hyperlinks.
- Use conditional formatting.
- Use data validation.
- Create or change passwords.
- Insert automatic subtotals.
- Create or edit macros. You can create a macro in an unshared, open workbook and use the macro in a shared workbook.
- Create or modify scenarios, outlines, PivotTables, and data tables.

EXERCISE 21-1 Create a Shared Workbook

User 1 will create a workbook that will be shared with User 2 and User 3. In order to change the user name, a workbook must be open; a blank workbook is acceptable.

 NOTE: If you are unable to use a network, you can copy and share the workbook by trading disks.

1. **USER 1, Keiko Sumara:** From the Tools menu, choose Options. Click the General tab. Change the User name to **Sumara**. Close the dialog box.
2. **USER 2, Kim Tamasaki:** From the Tools menu, choose Options. Click the General tab. Change the User name to **Tamasaki**. Close the dialog box.
3. **USER 3, Juan Sante:** From the Tools menu, choose Options. Click the General tab. Change the User name to **Sante**. Close the dialog box.

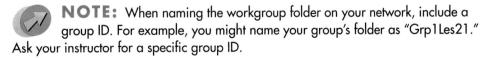 **NOTE:** When naming the workgroup folder on your network, include a group ID. For example, you might name your group's folder as "Grp1Les21." Ask your instructor for a specific group ID.

4. **USER 1:** Open the file **RepQuotas**. Add the standard footer and save the workbook as *[your initials]***21-1Sumara** in a new Lesson 21 folder for your workgroup.

5. **USER 1:** From the Tools menu, choose Share Workbook. The Share Workbook dialog box opens.

6. **USER 1:** On the Editing tab, select Allow changes by more than one user at the same time. The user name for your computer appears in the Who has this workbook open now list.

7. **USER 1:** Click OK. A dialog box alerts you that the workbook will be saved, because you added the shared setting.

FIGURE 21-1
Editing tab in the
Share Workbook
dialog box

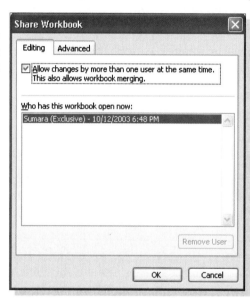

8. **USER 1:** Click OK. The filename shows [Shared] in the title bar.

9. **USER 2:** Open *[your initials]***21-1Sumara** in the Lesson 21 folder for your workgroup. Save the workbook as *[your initials]***21-1Tamasaki** in the Lesson 21 workgroup folder.

10. **USER 3:** Open *[your initials]***21-1Sumara** in the Lesson 21 folder for your workgroup. Save the workbook as *[your initials]***21-1Sante** in the Lesson 21 workgroup folder.

Setting Change History Options

When a workbook is shared, Excel keeps track of changes to the data. It creates a list of changes known as the *change history*. The Advanced tab in the Share Workbook dialog box includes settings for how changes are tracked in a shared workbook.

The change history options on the Advanced tab of the Share Workbook dialog box are as follows:

- The Track changes group activates the change history. When you share a workbook, this setting is automatically enabled. You can turn this setting off or set the number of days for which changes are followed.

- The Update changes group specifies how often you see changes from other users. If you select When file is saved, you see updates from other users when you save your own copy of the workbook. If you select Automatically every and set a time interval, you see others' changes at the specified interval. This setting assumes that workers are sharing one copy of the workbook on a network.

- The Conflicting changes between users group specifies how you handle conflicting changes when you save the shared workbook. If you select Ask me which changes win, you see a dialog box when a conflict occurs and can decide what to do. If you select The changes being saved win, Excel keeps only your changes when you save the workbook.

- The Include in personal view group specifies personal printing and filtering options for the shared workbook. These should be enabled when each user wants to save individual print and filter options.

 NOTE: Excel does not track format changes.

EXERCISE **21-2** **Set Change History Options**

The change history is turned on in the Share Workbook dialog box.

FIGURE 21-2
Advanced tab in the
Share Workbook
dialog box

1. **ALL USERS:** From the Tools menu, choose Share Workbook. Click the Advanced tab.

2. Click the down arrow next to the Keep change history for box until the number of days is 20.

3. Select When file is saved in the Update changes group if it is not already selected.

4. Select Ask me which changes win in the Conflicting changes between users group if it is not already selected.

5. Make sure both Print settings and Filter settings show check marks.

6. Click OK. The change history options are set.

EXERCISE **21-3** **Activate Change Highlighting**

You can have changes to cell contents highlighted in a shared workbook.

1. **ALL USERS:** From the Tools menu, choose Track Changes.

2. Choose <u>H</u>ighlight Changes. The Highlight Changes dialog box opens. The <u>T</u>rack changes while editing option is already selected because User 1 designated this as a shared workbook.

 TIP: If you select <u>T</u>rack changes while editing in an unshared workbook, the workbook automatically becomes a shared workbook.

3. Make sure <u>Wh</u>en is selected.

4. Click the down arrow next to the <u>Wh</u>en text box and choose Not yet reviewed. This setting enables you to accept or reject changes made by others.

FIGURE 21-3
Highlight Changes
dialog box

5. Make sure that the <u>Wh</u>o text box shows Everyone. Your option here is to select <u>Wh</u>o and choose a specific user.

6. Make sure <u>Wh</u>ere is not selected. This sets a specific range of cells for tracking changes. Otherwise, the entire worksheet is tracked.

7. Make sure Highlight changes on screen shows a check mark.

8. Click OK. The dialog box tells you that no changes were found. Click OK.

Tracking Changes

When the tracking feature is in effect, a colored border appears around any cell that is changed and a small, colored revision triangle appears in the upper-left corner of the cell. The row and column headings also change color, showing you where changes have been made. The colors used depend on your workstation settings, and you will see different colors for the other users when all the work is combined. When you place the mouse pointer on the cell, a comment box appears describing who made the change and when.

EXERCISE 21-4 **Track and Highlight Changes**

Excel displays a border around any changed cell.

1. USER 1, Sumara: Change cell B6 to **200000**.

2. USER 1: Change cell B11 to **115000**.

3. USER 1: Position the mouse pointer on cell B6 and then on cell B11 to see the comment boxes for your changes.

4. USER 2, Tamasaki: Change cell C24 to **165000**.

5. USER 2: Change cell C3 to **Rep's Annual Estimate**.

6. USER 2: Position the mouse pointer on cell C24 and then on cell C3 to see the comment boxes for your changes.

7. USER 3, Sante: Change cell C24 to **100000**.

8. USER 3: Change cell B15 to **100000**.

9. USER 3: Position the mouse pointer on cell C24 and then on cell B15 to see the comment boxes for your changes.

Using the Reviewing Toolbar

Comments are added automatically when you make a change to a shared workbook. You can, of course, add your own comments to a shared workbook.

You can insert a comment by using either the Insert command or the shortcut menu. You can also use buttons on the Reviewing toolbar. Some of the buttons on the Reviewing toolbar require that you have a tablet PC or that you have Microsoft Outlook installed as your mail client.

TABLE 21-1 Reviewing Toolbar Buttons

NAME	BUTTON	DESCRIPTION
New Comment		Opens a new comment box for the cell
Edit Comment		Displays the comment box for revision
Previous Comment		Moves the pointer to the previous comment
Next Comment		Moves the pointer to the next comment
Show/Hide Comment		Displays/hides the comment box for the selected cell
Show/Hide All Comments		Displays/hides all comments
Delete Comment		Deletes the comment for the selected cell
Create Microsoft Outlook Task		Creates a task in Microsoft Outlook
Update File		Updates changes made by other users to the shared workbook when one file is used simultaneously
Send to Mail Recipient		Sends the workbook as an attachment to an e-mail message

EXERCISE **21-5** **Add Comments in a Shared Workbook**

Adding comments is a good way to exchange ideas and suggestions in a shared workbook.

1. **ALL USERS:** Right-click the Standard or Formatting toolbar. Choose Reviewing. The Reviewing toolbar can be anchored at the top of the screen, or you can float it.

2. **USER 1, Sumara:** Select cell C8.

3. **USER 1:** Click the New Comment button [icon] on the Reviewing toolbar. Key **Please verify this number; it seems low.** Select another cell to hide the comment.

FIGURE 21-4
New comment added

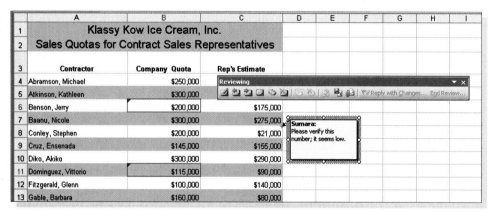

	A	B	C	D	E	F	G	H	I
1		Klassy Kow Ice Cream, Inc.							
2	Sales Quotas for Contract Sales Representatives								
3	Contractor	Company Quota	Rep's Estimate						
4	Abramson, Michael	$250,000							
5	Atkinson, Kathleen	$300,000							
6	Benson, Jerry	$200,000	$175,000						
7	Baanu, Nicole	$300,000	$275,000						
8	Conley, Stephen	$200,000	$21,000						
9	Cruz, Ensenada	$145,000	$155,000						
10	Diko, Akiko	$300,000	$290,000						
11	Dominguez, Vittorio	$115,000	$90,000						
12	Fitzgerald, Glenn	$100,000	$140,000						
13	Gable, Barbara	$160,000	$80,000						

Reviewing toolbar: Reply with Changes... End Review...

Sumara: Please verify this number; it seems low.

 NOTE: If you do not see comment indicators in the cell, choose Tools, Options, and then click the View tab. Select Comment indicator only in the Comments group.

4. **USER 2, Tamasaki:** Select cell B24.

5. **USER 2:** Click the New Comment button [icon]. Key **This number will be difficult to reach.** Select another cell to hide the comment.

6. **USER 3, Sante:** Select cell B17.

7. **USER 3:** Click the New Comment button [icon]. Key **We might need to adjust this number higher.** Select another cell to hide the comment.

8. **ALL USERS:** Save your workbook.

Printing a Change History Worksheet

In addition to showing changes on screen, you can print a history of changes to the worksheet. This separate worksheet, titled History, details each change that was made. The History worksheet is a generated worksheet, similar to a scenario summary report.

EXERCISE   21-6   Display and Print a History Worksheet

You can generate a list of the changes you've made when the tracking option is in effect. The list of changes appears on a separate worksheet.

1. **ALL USERS:** From the Tools menu, choose Track Changes and then Highlight Changes. The Highlight Changes dialog box appears.

2. **ALL USERS:** Select List changes on a new sheet and click OK. The History worksheet is added to the workbook. The History worksheet has AutoFilters so that you can choose which changes to show when several users have been working on the file.

FIGURE 21-5
A History worksheet

	A	B	C	D	E	F	G	H	I	J	K	L
1	Action Number ▾	Date ▾	Time ▾	Who ▾	Change ▾	Sheet ▾	Range ▾	New Value ▾	Old Value ▾	Action Type ▾	Losing Action ▾	
2	1	10/12/2003	7:01 PM	Sumara	Cell Change	Quotas	B6	$200,000.00	$150,000.00			
3	2	10/12/2003	7:01 PM	Sumara	Cell Change	Quotas	B11	$115,000.00	$125,000.00			
4												
5	The history ends with the changes saved on 10/12/2003 at 7:01 PM.											
6												

3. **ALL USERS:** Add the standard footer to the History worksheet and print it.

4. **ALL USERS:** Close the Reviewing toolbar.

5. **USER 1, Sumara:** Save your workbook and leave it open.

6. **USER 2, Tamasaki:** Save and close your workbook.

7. **USER 3, Sante:** Save and close your workbook.

 NOTE: The History worksheet is deleted when you save the workbook.

Comparing and Merging Workbooks

After each workgroup member has saved his or her own copy of a shared workbook, the members' workbooks can be compared and merged into one file. For workbooks to be compared and merged, the following requirements must be met:

- Each copy of the workbook must have been made from the original, have a different filename, and have no passwords.
- The original workbook must have been shared before copies were made.
- The original workbook must have the change history option turned on.
- The merging must occur before the expiration of the change history days.

EXERCISE 21-7 **Compare and Merge Workbooks**

The main copy of the shared workbook is *[your initials]*21-1Sumara. User 1, Sumara, should begin the following exercise, starting with the file *[your initials]*21-1Sumara open.

1. USER 1: From the Tools menu, choose Compare and Merge Workbooks. (Click OK if prompted to save the workbook.) The Select Files to Merge Into Current Workbook dialog box opens. Locate your Lesson 21 workgroup folder.

2. USER 1: Choose *[your initials]*21-1Tamasaki and click OK. Cell C24 and cell C3 show changes. These are the cells that Tamasaki changed, and they are outlined in a different color.

3. USER 1: From the Tools menu, choose Compare and Merge Workbooks. Double-click *[your initials]*21-1Sante. The cells with changes made by Sante (B15 and C24) are outlined in a third color.

4. USER 1: Save the merged workbook as *[your initials]*21-7Sumara in your Lesson 21 workgroup folder.

5. USER 2, Tamasaki: Open *[your initials]*21-7Sumara. Save the workbook as *[your initials]*21-7Tamasaki in your Lesson 21 workgroup folder.

6. USER 3, Sante: Open *[your initials]*21-7Sumara. Save the workbook as *[your initials]*21-7Sante in your Lesson 21 workgroup folder.

EXERCISE 21-8 **Show Comments in a Merged Workbook**

When merging workbooks, it can be helpful to display the comments made by each of the different users.

1. ALL USERS: Display the Reviewing toolbar.

2. ALL USERS: Click the Show All Comments button on the Reviewing toolbar. These are the comments that were keyed by the users. (See Figure 21-6.)

   NOTE: Adjust the Zoom size or scroll the window to see all the comments.

3. ALL USERS: Click the Hide All Comments button 🗔.

4. ALL USERS: Close the Reviewing toolbar.

FIGURE 21-6
Displaying all
comments

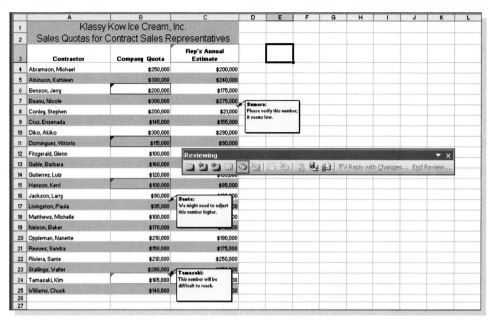

Accepting or Rejecting Changes

After workbooks are merged, you can review the changes and decide whether to accept or reject them. You can review them one at a time or all at once.

EXERCISE **21-9** **Accept or Reject Changes**

All users complete this exercise through step 8 in their own workbook.

1. From the Tools menu, choose Track Changes and then Accept or Reject Changes. The Select Changes to Accept or Reject dialog box opens.

2. Verify that When is selected and that Not yet reviewed appears in the text box.

3. Click OK. The Accept or Reject Changes dialog box opens, and a marquee appears around the first change in cell B6. The dialog box shows who made the change and what it was. (See Figure 21-7 on the next page.)

4. Click Accept. The next change highlighted is in cell B11.

5. Click Accept for the change in cell B11. The next cell with changes (cell C24) has multiple changes. You can choose which one to accept.

FIGURE 21-7
Accepting or
rejecting changes

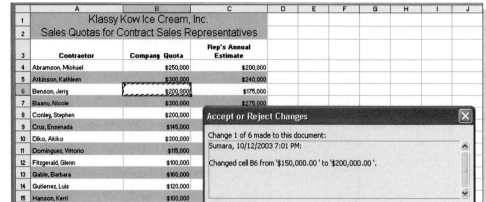

6. Select the original value and click Accept.

7. Click Reject to reject the change to cell C3. The label reverts to the original.

8. Accept the change in cell B15.

9. USER 1: Save the workbook as *[your initials]*21-9Sumara in the workgroup folder.

10. USER 2: Save the workbook as *[your initials]*21-9Tamasaki in the workgroup folder.

11. USER 3: Save the workbook as *[your initials]*21-9Sante in the workgroup folder.

12. ALL USERS: Use Page Setup to print comments at the end of the sheet on a separate page. Change the footer to show your name.

13. Print the worksheet.

14. Save and close the workbook.

15. From the Tools menu, choose Options. Click the General tab.

16. Change the User name to the default name for your computer. Click OK.

 NOTE: Ask your instructor what user name to key for the classroom computer.

USING ONLINE HELP

If you have a tablet computer, you can add written annotations or drawings to a worksheet using the tablet pen. You can then use the Reviewing toolbar to show and delete these annotations.

Use Microsoft Excel Help to learn about using ink.

1. With Internet Explorer and Excel running, look for topics about **using ink**. Look for subtopics that explain how you would use ink with a tablet computer.

2. Read the information. Close the windows.

3. Close Internet Explorer and end your Internet connection.

LESSON 21 Summary

➤ A shared workbook is used by more than one person at a time. Users who share workbooks are a workgroup.

➤ A shared workbook is typically found in a networked computer environment. Shared workbooks have some limitations.

➤ A workbook must be saved before it can be shared.

➤ Excel keeps track of all changes in a shared workbook. It creates a list of changes known as the change history.

➤ In a shared workbook, you can highlight changes on the screen while editing.

➤ Comments are added automatically when you make a change to a shared workbook. You also can add your own comments to a shared workbook.

➤ The Reviewing toolbar has buttons for working with comments.

➤ After making changes to a shared workbook, you can print a list of the changes.

➤ If each user has a separate copy of a shared workbook, the workbooks can be compared and merged.

➤ After workbooks are merged, you can review the changes and either accept or reject the changes.

LESSON 21 Command Summary

FEATURE	BUTTON	MENU	KEYBOARD
Share workbook		Tools, Share Work**b**ook	
Change history options		Tools, Share Work**b**ook	
Highlight changes		Tools, **T**rack Changes, **H**ighlight Changes	
Add comment		Insert, Co**m**ment	
History sheet		Tools, **T**rack Changes, **H**ighlight Changes	
Merge workbooks		**T**ools, Compare and Merge **W**orkbooks	
Accept/reject changes		**T**ools, Track Changes, **A**ccept or Reject Changes	

Concepts Review

TRUE/FALSE QUESTIONS

Each of the following statements is either true or false. Indicate your choice by circling T or F.

T   F   **1.** A workgroup is a set of people who share workbooks.

T   F   **2.** You can insert and delete worksheets in a shared workbook.

T   F   **3.** The list of edits made to a shared workbook is its change history.

T   F   **4.** You can set changes to be highlighted on screen or printed on a separate worksheet.

T   F   **5.** Comment boxes are added to changed cells in a shared workbook.

T   F   **6.** A consolidated workbook is based on individual user copies of a shared workbook.

T   F   **7.** User changes are color-coded in a shared workbook.

T   F   **8.** A cell with a change displays a small triangle in the upper-right corner.

SHORT ANSWER QUESTIONS

Write the correct answer in the space provided.

1. What toolbar can be used to insert, delete, and manage comments?

_____

2. What menu command should you use to print a change history sheet?

_____

3. What is required for three users to work on the same workbook at the same time?

_____

4. What can users do if they want to save their own edits to a shared workbook?

_____

5. What button on the Reviewing toolbar annotates a shared workbook to show changes by other users on the network?

_____

6. What command combines user copies of a workbook into one file?

_____

7. As you review changes in a merged workbook, what can you do about those changes?

_____

8. What is a workgroup?

_____

CRITICAL THINKING

Answer these questions on a separate page. There are no right or wrong answers. Support your answers with examples from your own experience, if possible.

1. If you have a job, what other department do you work with on a regular basis? At your school, what departments or divisions might work together? Explain how work could be shared between the departments.

2. You can share a workbook so that all users are working on it at the same time. Users can also make their own copies and work on them individually. Individual workbooks can later be merged. When might it be better to make separate copies for each user rather than work with one file?

Skills Review

EXERCISE 21-10

Create a shared workbook. Make copies of a shared workbook. Set change history options.

 NOTE: The Skills Review exercises require you to be a member of the same workgroup as in the lesson.

1. USER 1, Sumara: From the <u>T</u>ools menu, choose <u>O</u>ptions. Click the General tab. Set the User <u>n</u>ame to **Sumara**. Click OK.

2. USER 2, Tamasaki: From the <u>T</u>ools menu, choose <u>O</u>ptions. Click the General tab. Set the User <u>n</u>ame to **Tamasaki**. Click OK.

3. USER 3, Sante: From the <u>T</u>ools menu, choose <u>O</u>ptions. Click the General tab. Set the User <u>n</u>ame to **Sante**. Click OK.

4. USER 1: Create a shared workbook by following these steps:

a. Open the file **VendorList**.

b. Save the workbook as *[your initials]*21-10Sumara in the Lesson 21 workgroup folder.

c. Delete Sheet2 and Sheet3.

 REVIEW: You must delete the unused worksheets before you share the workbook because they cannot be deleted in a shared workbook.

d. From the Tools menu, choose Share Workbook.

e. Select Allow changes by more than one user at the same time.

f. Click OK twice.

5. Copy a shared workbook by following these steps:

a. USER 2: Open *[your initials]*21-10Sumara and save the workbook as *[your initials]*21-10Tamasaki in the Lesson 21 workgroup folder.

b. USER 3: Open *[your initials]*21-10Sumara and save the workbook as *[your initials]*21-10Sante in the Lesson 21 workgroup folder.

6. ALL USERS: Set change history options by following these steps:

a. From the Tools menu, choose Share Workbook.

b. Click the Advanced tab.

c. Change the Keep change history for to **10** days.

d. Select When file is saved and Ask me which changes win if they are not already selected.

e. Make sure Print settings and Filter settings are selected.

f. Click OK.

g. From the Tools menu, choose Track Changes and then Highlight Changes.

h. Make sure When is selected.

i. Click the down arrow next to the When text box and choose Not yet reviewed.

j. Make sure that Highlight changes on screen is selected.

k. Click OK twice.

 REVIEW: Unless your instructor tells you differently, add your name in the left footer section, the filename and tab name in the center, and the date in the right section.

7. ALL USERS: Add the standard footer. Save and close the workbook.

NOTE: Restore the default user name for your computer if you are not continuing to the next exercise.

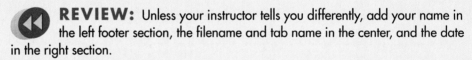

EXERCISE 21-11

Track changes. Make changes to a shared workbook.

1. USER 1: Open *[your initials]*21-10Sumara from Exercise 21-10.

2. USER 2: Open *[your initials]*21-10Tamasaki from Exercise 21-10.

3. USER 3: Open *[your initials]*21-10Sante from Exercise 21-10.

4. ALL USERS: Track changes by following these steps:

 NOTE: If you are continuing from the previous exercise, the user name for your computer is set. If you are starting a new work session, repeat step 1, 2, or 3 from Exercise 21-10 to set the user name for your computer.

   a. From the Tools menu, choose Track Changes and Highlight Changes.
   b. Make sure When is selected. Click the down arrow next to the When text box and choose Not yet reviewed.
   c. Make sure Highlight changes on screen is selected. Click OK twice.

5. Make changes to a shared workbook by following these steps:

   a. USER 1: Starting in cell A19, add a vendor/supplier by keying the following data in row 19:
      2001   Gerrard's   18 Field Lane   Eureka, CA   707-555-3300
   b. USER 2: Starting in cell A20, add a vendor/supplier by keying the following data in row 20:
      2002   RS Inc.   22 Antoine Road   Las Vegas, NV   702-555-0090
   c. USER 3: Starting in cell A21, add a vendor/supplier by keying the following data in row 21:
      2003   Tri-City   1A Ginger Way   Klamath Falls, OR   541-555-0002

   NOTE: You will see revision comments as you key changes.

   d. USER 1: Change the phone number in cell E6 to **707-555-7003**.
   e. USER 2: Change the phone number in cell E6 to **707-555-0003**.
   f. USER 3: Change the phone number in cell E6 to **707-555-1003**.

6. USER 1: Save the workbook as *[your initials]***21-11Sumara** in the Lesson 21 workgroup folder.

7. USER 2: Save the workbook as *[your initials]***21-11Tamasaki** in the Lesson 21 workgroup folder.

8. USER 3: Save the workbook as *[your initials]***21-11Sante** in the Lesson 21 workgroup folder.

9. ALL USERS: Print the worksheet and close the workbook.

EXERCISE 21-12

Use the Reviewing toolbar. Print a change history worksheet.

NOTE: If you are continuing from the previous exercise, the user name for your computer is set. If you are starting a new work session, repeat step 1, 2, or 3 from Exercise 21-10 to set the user name for your computer.

1. USER 1: Open *[your initials]***21-11Sumara** from Exercise 21-11.
2. USER 2: Open *[your initials]***21-11Tamasaki** from Exercise 21-11.

3. **USER 3:** Open *[your initials]***21-11Sante** from Exercise 21-11.

4. **ALL USERS:** From the Tools menu, choose Track Changes and Highlight Changes. Make sure When is selected and that Not yet reviewed appears in the When text box. Make sure that Highlight changes on screen is selected. Click OK.

5. Use the Reviewing toolbar by following these steps:

   a. **ALL USERS:** Right-click the Standard toolbar and choose Reviewing.

   b. **USER 1:** Select cell B4 and click the New Comment button 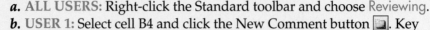. Key **Company will change name within 30 days.** Select another cell.

   c. **USER 2:** Select cell B11 and click the New Comment button . Key **New president on board next month.** Select another cell.

   d. **USER 3:** Select cell D5 and click the New Comment button . Key **Area code to be split within three months.** Select another cell.

6. **ALL USERS:** Close the Reviewing toolbar.

7. **USER 1:** Save the workbook as *[your initials]***21-12Sumara** in the Lesson 21 workgroup folder.

8. **USER 2:** Save the workbook as *[your initials]***21-12Tamasaki** in the Lesson 21 workgroup folder.

9. **USER 3:** Save the workbook as *[your initials]***21-12Sante** in the Lesson 21 workgroup folder.

10. **ALL USERS:** Create a change history worksheet by following these steps:

    a. From the Tools menu, choose Track Changes and then Highlight Changes.

    b. Select List changes on a new sheet. Click OK.

11. **ALL USERS:** Add your standard footer to the History worksheet. Print the History worksheet.

12. **ALL USERS:** Save and close the workbook.

EXERCISE 21-13

Merge shared workbooks. Accept or reject changes.

NOTE: If you are continuing from the previous exercise, the user name for your computer is set. If you are starting a new work session, repeat step 1, 2, or 3 from Exercise 21-10 to set the name for your computer.

1. **USER 1:** Merge shared workbooks by following these steps:

   a. Open *[your initials]***21-12Sumara**.

   b. From the Tools menu, choose Compare and Merge Workbooks. Click OK if prompted to save the workbook.

   c. Double-click *[your initials]***21-12Tamasaki**.

   d. From the Tools menu, choose Compare and Merge Workbooks. Double-click *[your initials]***21-12Sante**.

e. Save the merged workbook as *[your initials]***21-13Sumara** in the Lesson 21 workgroup folder.

2. **USER 2:** Open *[your initials]***21-13Sumara**. Save the workbook as *[your initials]***21-13Tamasaki** in the Lesson 21 workgroup folder.

3. **USER 3:** Open *[your initials]***21-13Sumara**. Save the workbook as *[your initials]***21-13Sante** in the Lesson 21 workgroup folder.

4. **ALL USERS:** Accept or reject changes by following these steps:

a. From the Tools menu, choose Track Changes and then Accept or Reject Changes.

b. Make sure When is selected and displays Not yet reviewed.

c. Click OK.

d. Click Accept to accept the change for cell A19.

e. Click Accept for each change in row 19.

f. Choose the original value for cell E6 and click Accept.

g. Accept all the changes for rows 20 and 21.

 TIP: You can click Accept All to accept all changes from the current change on.

5. **ALL USERS:** Make sure the standard footer includes your name. Print the worksheet.

6. Save and close the workbook.

7. From the Tools menu, choose Options. Click the General tab. Change the User name to the default name for your computer. Click OK.

 NOTE: Ask your instructor what user name to key for the classroom computer.

Lesson Applications

Share a workbook. Edit and track changes. Print a change history.

You have been asked to share the fourth-quarter workbook so that shop managers can make their projections for the first quarter next year.

1. Open the file **ProjShakeMalt**. Save the workbook as *[your initials]***21-14** in a new folder for Lesson 21.
2. Share the workbook and set the change history to 25 days.
3. Turn on tracking so that changes that have not been reviewed are shown on screen.
4. Change the title in cell A2 to show **First Quarter**. Change the worksheet tab name to **1stQtr**.
5. Change the months to **Jan**, **Feb**, and **Mar**.
6. Change the unit values as follows:
   Jan: 12,000   **Feb:** 15,000   **Mar:** 18,000
7. Save the workbook and create a change history worksheet.

 NOTE: You must save changes before creating a change history worksheet.

8. Group the sheets and use File, Page Setup to add your footer. Print the entire workbook.
9. Save and close the workbook.

Use the Reviewing toolbar.

Klassy Kow is thinking about an across-the-board price increase. The price list workbook is used by all shop owners, so it needs comments that clarify what each owner should do to complete and update the list.

1. Open the file **NewPrices**.
2. Display the Reviewing toolbar.
3. Delete the comment in cell A1.
4. Add this comment to cell C3: **Edit these prices to your shop's current prices.**
5. Calculate values in column D according to the information in the comment in cell D4.

6. Show all the comments. Select and move the boxes so that there are no overlapping comments. Boxes should not obscure any text.

7. Add the standard footer. Set the worksheet to print on one page with the comments shown.

 REVIEW: You must use File, Page Setup to print comments.

8. Save the workbook as *[your initials]*21-15 in your Lesson 21 folder and print the worksheet.

9. Close the Reviewing toolbar and close the workbook.

EXERCISE 21-16

Merge copies of shared workbooks. Accept or reject changes.

The third-quarter sales report has been updated by two sales staff members. You now need to merge these workbooks and accept or reject changes.

1. Open the file **ThirdQtr**. Save the workbook as *[your initials]*21-16 in your Lesson 21 folder.

2. Show the changes highlighted on the screen for anything not yet reviewed.

3. Merge **ThirdQtr(2)** and **ThirdQtr(3)**, in this order, into *[your initials]*21-16.

4. Accept or reject the changes that have not yet been reviewed. Accept the change in B4 of $15,000; reject the change in D7, restoring the value of $9,500; accept the change in D4 of $15,000; and reject the change in cell E6, restoring the value of $22,000.

5. Set a print area to exclude the prices at the bottom of the worksheet.

 REVIEW: Select the cells to be printed and choose Print Area from the File menu.

6. Add the standard footer. Set the worksheet to fit on one portrait page.

7. Save the workbook and print the worksheet.

8. Save the worksheet as a Web page named *[your initials]*21-16 in your Lesson 21 folder and use Change Title to key an appropriate title. Preview it in your browser and close the browser.

9. Close the workbook.

EXERCISE 21-17   *Challenge Yourself*

Create a shared workbook and its copies. Track changes. Merge copies of shared workbooks. Accept or reject changes.

Keiko Sumara wants to develop five new ice cream flavors for next summer. She would like to include projections for sales of 1-, 2-, and 3-scoop waffle cones. She has asked for input from Contract Sales Representative Kim Tamasaki and Vice President Juan Sante. These are the three people in your workgroup.

- User 1, Keiko Sumara, Sales and Marketing Manager
- User 2, Kim Tamasaki, Contract Sales Representative
- User 3, Juan Sante, Vice President

 NOTE: All users should set the user name for their computers before starting work.

1. **USER 1:** Create a new workbook. Use a main title and column titles for the 1-, 2-, and 3-scoop cones. Key five ice cream flavor names in column A. Use your imagination to develop new flavor names. For the values in the columns, key numbers that estimate how many of each size you would expect to sell in a week. Format the worksheet in a professional manner. Add your standard footer.

2. **USER 1:** Save the workbook as *[your initials]*21-17Sumara in the Lesson 21 workgroup folder. Print the worksheet and share the workbook. Close the workbook.

3. **USER 2:** Open the shared workbook and save it as *[your initials]*21-17Tamasaki. Track changes that have not yet been reviewed.

4. **USER 3:** Open the shared workbook and save it as *[your initials]*21-17Sante. Track changes that have not yet been reviewed.

5. **USER 2, USER 3:** Change two of the flavor names and one of the values. Change the footer to include your name. Print the worksheet. Save and close your workbook.

6. **USER 1:** Open *[your initials]*21-17Sumara. Compare and merge the workbooks. Save the merged workbook as *[your initials]*21-17SumaraM.

7. **USER 2:** Open the merged workbook and save it as *[your initials]*21-17TamasakiM.

8. **USER 3:** Open the merged workbook and save it as *[your initials]*21-17SanteM.

9. **ALL USERS:** Review the changes. Accept the names and values you think are reasonable and reject those you don't like. Make sure that the worksheet includes the standard footer with your name. Print the worksheet.

10. **ALL USERS:** Save and close your workbook. Restore the default user name for your computer.

NOTE: Ask your instructor what user name to key for the classroom computer.

On Your Own

In these exercises you work on your own, as you would in a real-life work environment. Use the skills you've learned to accomplish the task—and be creative.

EXERCISE 21-18

Create your own workgroup with classmates and develop a workbook. Share the workbook. Name the shared workbook **Shared21-18** and save it in the Lesson 21 workgroup folder. Create a copy of the shared workbook for each person in the group. Make changes to your own copy of the shared workbook and name it *[your initials]*21-18. Have one user merge the original shared workbook. Then make copies of the merged workbook for each member of your group. Each member can highlight the changes and accept or reject them. Save the merged workbook as *[your initials]*21-18M in your Lesson 21 workgroup folder. Add the standard footer and print the workbook. Save and close the workbook.

EXERCISE 21-19

Create your own workgroup and develop a workbook. Name the workbook **Shared21-19** and save it in the Lesson 21 workgroup folder. Each member of the workgroup should open the workbook. Make sure that you will see changes on screen. Each workgroup member should make changes to the data while the other members are doing the same. Decide how to handle conflicts. Have one member save the workbook with all its changes. Create and print a history sheet. Add a footer that includes the names of all members of the workgroup. Print the worksheet. Save and close the workbook.

EXERCISE 21-20

 Create a new workbook with information on a topic that interests you. Save it as *[your initials]*21-20 in your Lesson 21 folder. Display the Reviewing toolbar and add three comments for different cells. Add the standard footer and set the comments to print as displayed. Print the worksheet. If possible, use the Send to Mail Recipient button 📧 to e-mail the workbook as an attachment to your instructor or to your own e-mail account. Save and close the workbook.

Unit 6 Applications

UNIT APPLICATION 6-1

Troubleshoot error messages. Audit and correct errors.

Klassy Kow wants to project sales of ice cream cakes for next year. You first need to audit this year's numbers to correct errors.

1. Open the file **ProjCakeSales**.

2. Display the formulas. This view might make it easier to locate and correct errors. Use whatever method you prefer to correct all errors.

3. Display the Formula Auditing tollbar. Find invalid data and correct those errors. Turn off the formula display when done.

 TIP: The circled data uses a validation list in column P. Choose Data and Validation to see the settings.

4. Copy the range A5:F11 to the range A15:F21. Edit the label in cell A15 to show **Projected Dollar Sales**.

5. Create formulas to project next year's sales for each product. Assume an 8 percent increase in this year's sales for next year. (*Hint:* Use this year's sales values to project next year's sales.) Make sure all formula totals are correct.

6. Copy the range A1:A2 to the range A13:A14. Select the range A13:F14 and center the cells across the selection. Edit the title to show **Next Year Projected Sales of Ice Cream Cakes**. Fix the border to match the titles at the top of the worksheet.

 REVIEW: Center multiple cells across a selection from the Format Cells dialog box.

7. Insert two blank rows at row 15. Make the row heights the same as the row heights in rows 3 and 4.

8. Add your usual footer. Set a print area for the range A1:F23. Set the file properties to show your name as the author and a preview image.

9. Save the workbook as *[your initials]***u6-1** in a new folder for Unit 6 and print the worksheet.

10. Cancel the print area and make a copy of the sheet. Display the formulas on the copied sheet. AutoFit the columns.

11. Do not center the worksheet on the page; use 0.5-inch left and right margins. Set the print area again. Print the formula worksheet on a single landscape page.

12. Save and close the workbook.

UNIT APPLICATION 6-2

Link workbooks. Copy a worksheet.

You are to develop a worksheet that calculates bonuses for this year. The manager receives a bonus if sales show a 10 percent increase over last year.

1. Open the files **NoveltyLastYr** and **NoveltyThisYr.**
2. Create a new workbook while these files are open.
3. Format the range A1:A2 as 16-point Arial. **Key Klassy Kow Ice Cream, Inc.** in cell A1. Key **Sales Manager Bonuses** in cell A2. Key the labels as shown in Figure U6-1, starting in cell A3.

FIGURE U6-1

	A	B	C	D	E
3	Manager	Goal	Actual	Difference	Bonus
4	Holly Maplethorpe (CA)				
5	John Frisbee (NV)				
6	Adrian Needlehoffen (OR)				
7	Jamica Martin (WA)				

4. Widen the columns as needed. Set the height for rows 3 and 4 to 26.25 (35 pixels). Make the labels in row 3 bold and centered.
5. In the Goal column, multiply last year's total dollar sales for each state (cell R19 on each sheet in the **NoveltyLastYr** workbook) by 110%.
6. In the Actual column, link to the total dollar sales for each state for this year (cell R19 on each sheet in the **NoveltyThisYr** workbook).
7. In the Difference column, subtract the Goal amount from the Actual amount.
8. Use an IF expression in the Bonus column. If the difference is greater than 0, the manager receives $5,000. If the difference is equal to or less than 0, show **No Bonus** in the column.
9. Total the bonuses and format the results as bold. Format all values appropriately.
10. Rename the worksheet **Bonuses.** Delete the other worksheets.

11. Add your footer. Center the worksheet horizontally on the page.

12. Make a copy of the **Bonuses** worksheet and name the copy **Formulas**. Display the formulas and AutoFit the columns.

13. Set the Formulas worksheet to show gridlines and row and column headings on one landscape page.

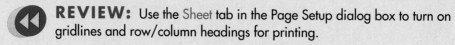

REVIEW: Use the Sheet tab in the Page Setup dialog box to turn on gridlines and row/column headings for printing.

14. Save the workbook as *[your initials]*u6-2 in your Unit 6 folder and print the entire workbook.

15. Close all workbooks.

UNIT APPLICATION 6-3

Predict quarterly sales for next year. Use Goal Seek. Create scenarios.

Klassy Kow wants to set quarterly sales goals for each state based on a growth rate for each state. Nevada is expected to have the highest growth, and the other states' rates are based on Nevada's.

1. Set your workstation macro security to medium. Open the file **ForecastNextYear** and enable the macros.

2. Determine the macro shortcut or run it from the menu.

3. Create range names for the range B4:B7 using the labels in column A. Name cell H8 **Total**.

4. In cells B4, B5, and B7, create formulas that calculate a growth rate based on Nevada's rate. The other states will grow at a percentage of Nevada's rate. California's growth rate is 80% of Nevada's; Oregon's growth rate is 60% of Nevada's; and Washington's is 65% of Nevada's. (*Hint:* Multiply Nevada's rate by the state's percentage.) Format all cells to show percents with two decimals.

5. In the range D4:G7, estimate sales on the basis of the previous quarter's sales and the growth rate for the state. For example, the first quarter formula for California is **C4*(1+B4)**. The second quarter formula is **D4*(1+B4)**.

TIP: You can copy the formula for a particular state. If you copy from one state to another, check the references to see what you need to edit.

6. Total the first through fourth quarters for next year in column H. Do not include the fourth quarter from this year. Then total columns D through H in row 8.

7. Format the values to show commas and no decimals. Format the values in rows 4 and 8 to show a dollar sign. Adjust the column widths.

8. Format the worksheet attractively to highlight its purpose. Rename the sheet **Forecast**. Delete the remaining worksheets.

9. Add your standard footer. Set the page to landscape orientation.

10. Save the workbook as *[your initials]*u6-3 in your Unit 6 folder and print the worksheet.

11. Create a scenario named **Current Estimate** using cell B6 as the changing cell.

12. Use Goal Seek to find the growth rates necessary to achieve $400 million in total sales. Save the results as a scenario named **$400M**. Adjust column widths if necessary. Print the worksheet.

13. Create a scenario summary report using **B4:B7,H8** as Result cells. On the summary sheet, change the title in cell B2 to **Klassy Kow Ice Cream, Inc., Quarterly Growth Rates**. Delete column D (current values), rows 5 and 6 (changing cells), and rows 11:13 (note). Make other adjustments as needed.

14. Add your footer. Print the Scenario Summary worksheet.

15. Save and close the workbook.

UNIT APPLICATION 6-4 *Using the Internet*

Share a workbook. Compare and merge workbooks. Accept and reject changes.

Work with two classmates to form a workgroup. Your task is to find five items each (a total of 15 items) that could be used in a fund-raising contest. These might be prizes such as a new car, a trip to Japan, a large-screen TV, and smaller items. Find items, descriptions, and prices on various Web sites.

1. USER 1: Create a workbook for your workgroup. The worksheet should show the name of your (User 1) five items, Web addresses, brief descriptions, and prices. Include a main title and labels where needed. Format the worksheet attractively. Share the workbook. Save it as **User1u6-4** in a new Unit 6 workgroup folder.

2. USERS 2 and 3: Make a copy of the shared workbook, saving it as **User2u6-4** or **User3u6-4** in the Unit 6 workgroup folder. Then edit the data to show your five items. Save your workbooks.

3. **ALL USERS:** With a copy of each member's workbook, compare and merge the workbooks into your own workbook. Track the changes and decide which items you would use in your contest. Add your footer and print the worksheet. Save your merged workbook as *[your initials]*u6-4 in your workgroup folder.

UNIT 7

Using Data and List Features

Using Data from Other Sources

OBJECTIVES

MICROSOFT OFFICE SPECIALIST ACTIVITIES

In this lesson:
    XLO3E-1-15
    XLO3E-2-1
    XLO3E-4-1
    XLO3E-4-2

See Appendix.

After completing this lesson, you will be able to:

1. **Use Word and text files.**
2. **Import HTML files.**
3. **Import database files.**
4. **Export Excel data.**
5. **View XML code.**
6. **Work with XML maps.**
7. **Save an XML spreadsheet.**

 Estimated Time: 1½ hours

I t is common in the business world to move data back and forth between programs. In this lesson, you'll learn how to incorporate data from various sources into Excel.

Importing data means that information from another program is brought into Excel. *Exporting* data occurs when Excel data is sent to another program.

Using Word and Text Files

You can use data from a Microsoft Word document in an Excel worksheet, with or without formatting. After the data is imported, you can apply formatting in Excel.

A *text file* is unformatted or raw data. Text files make it possible for almost all programs to share data.

There are several methods you can use to bring Word or text data into an Excel worksheet. Three of them are:

- Copy and paste the data using the Clipboard.
- Drag and drop data from Word to Excel.
- Open a text file in Excel.

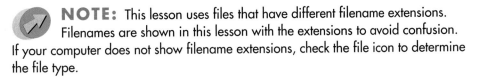

EXERCISE 22-1 **Copy and Paste from Word**

Copy and Paste uses the Windows Clipboard to copy Word data to Excel. In this method, the data is copied with its formatting.

1. Create a new workbook.

 NOTE: This lesson uses files that have different filename extensions. Filenames are shown in this lesson with the extensions to avoid confusion. If your computer does not show filename extensions, check the file icon to determine the file type.

2. Start Word and open **Employees.doc**, a Word table.

3. Press Ctrl+A to select the table.

TIP: You can select parts of the text to be copied instead of all of it.

 4. Click the Copy button ⬚ on the Standard toolbar. The table is copied to the Clipboard.

5. Click the Microsoft Excel button on the taskbar to return to your workbook.

 6. With cell A1 selected, click the Paste button ⬚. The table is copied with most of its formatting, and the data is selected. (See Figure 22-1 on the next page.)

FIGURE 22-1
Word table
pasted into Excel

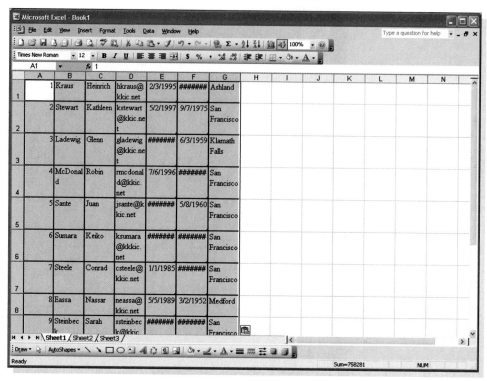

E X E R C I S E 22-2 **Format Data and View Smart Tags**

When you copy data from one program to another, it often needs to be formatted to better fit the application. In this case, the columns are not wide enough and the rows are too high.

Imported data may display smart tags. *Smart tags* are labels that are attached to recognized data in Microsoft Office programs. You can use smart tags to perform actions on the data that you'd usually perform by opening other programs. A purple triangle in the lower-right corner of a cell indicates a smart tag.

1. With the pasted data selected, press Ctrl+1 to open the Format Cells dialog box.

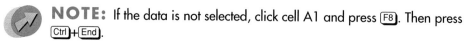

NOTE: If the data is not selected, click cell A1 and press F8. Then press Ctrl+End.

2. Click the Border tab. In the Presets group, click None. Click OK. The border surrounding the imported data is removed.

3. With the pasted data selected, choose Format, Row from the menu and choose Height. Key **16** in the Row height text box and click OK.

REVIEW: Row heights in the dialog box are set using points, not pixels.

4. Widen each column to fit the data. Deselect the cells. Notice that all the cells in the range E1:F13 contain smart tags.

5. Select cell E1. The smart tag button is adjacent to the selected cell.

6. Position the pointer over the smart tag button and click the down arrow. The Smart Tag Actions menu opens. Depending on the type of data, various actions are available. Because this is a date, date-related actions are available, such as showing a calendar in Microsoft Outlook. You can remove a smart tag with the command <u>R</u>emove this Smart Tag.

FIGURE 22-2
Smart Tag
for a date

D	E	F	G
hkraus@kkic.net	2/3/1995	4/17/1957	Ashland
kstewart@kkic.net	5/2/	9/7/1975	San Francisco
gladewig@kkic.net	2/23/		s
rmcdonald@kkic.net	7/6/	Date: 2/3/1995	o
jsante@kkic.net	3/18/	Sh<u>o</u>w my Calendar	o
ksumara@kkkic.net	11/21/		o
csteele@kkic.net	1/1/	Remove this Smart Tag	o
neassa@kkic.net	5/5/	S<u>t</u>op Recognizing "2/3/1995" ▸	o
ssteinbeck@kkic.net	2/15/1999	Smart Tag Options...	San Francisco
tartagnan@kkic.net	5/1/1990	8/3/1981	Anderson
mcalcivechia@kkic.net	6/16/1992	9/14/1961	Red Bluff
talverez@kkic.net	4/15/1999	3/30/1975	San Francisco
lnguyen@kkic.net	6/7/2000	5/23/1978	San Francisco

7. Select cell A1 to close the Smart Tag Actions menu. Smart Tag markers do not print.

EXERCISE   **22-3**   **Create a Custom Format**

You can create your own display features for data, a *custom format*. You create custom formats with formatting codes. In this exercise, you'll create a custom format to show the # symbol with the employee ID numbers in column A.

When you want to display a specific character as a part of the formatting, it must be enclosed in quotation marks. Text, symbols, or numbers enclosed in quotes in a format are known as *literals*.

1. Select the range A1:A13 and press Ctrl+1.

2. Click the Number tab. In the <u>C</u>ategory list, click Custom.

3. In the <u>T</u>ype text box, delete General and then key **"#"0**. The # symbol inside the quotation marks is the literal. It will appear in front of every number to

which this formatting is applied. Notice how Excel shows in the Sample box what the custom format will look like for the first number in your selected range. The 0 means that the value will show as many digits as required with no decimals.

FIGURE 22-3
Creating a
custom format

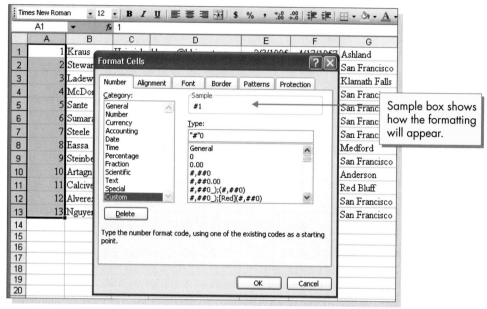

Sample box shows how the formatting will appear.

4. Click OK. The employee numbers are all prefixed with the # symbol.

5. Select cell A1 to deselect the range.

EXERCISE **22-4** **Drag and Drop a Word Document**

With the drag-and-drop method, you drag Word data to a worksheet. You must be able to see the document to be copied and its destination on the screen.

1. Click the Restore Down button ⬜ on the Excel title bar.

2. Click the Word window and click its Restore Down button ⬜. Both windows should now be visible on the screen.

3. Size and position the windows so that you can see cell A15 in the Excel worksheet and any part of the Word table.

4. Click in the Word table and press Ctrl+A to select the entire table. (See Figure 22-4.)

5. Position the pointer anywhere in the text to display a white solid arrow.

6. Press and hold Ctrl and drag the Word table to cell A15 in the Excel window. Release the mouse button first and then Ctrl.

REVIEW: When you drag and drop, hold down Ctrl to copy instead of cut.

FIGURE 22-4
Dragging and dropping a Word table

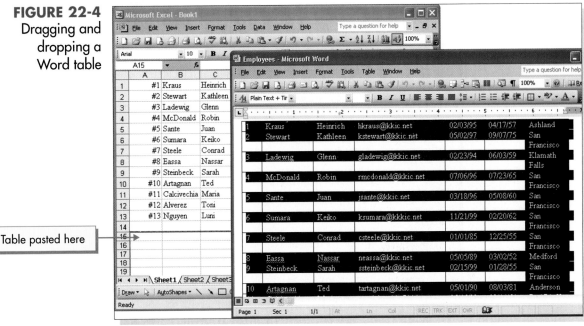

7. Close the Word document but leave Word running.

EXERCISE **22-5** Use Copy and Paste Special

You can use Paste Special to copy a text file into Excel. This method of importing text data is useful when you need only portions of a text file. You can use this method with any program that reads text files.

 1. Start Word if it is not already started and click the Open button 📂.

2. Click the down arrow next to the Files of type text box and select Text Files.

3. Select the text file **Employees.txt** and open it.

 4. Click the Show/Hide ¶ button ¶. You can see line breaks at the end of each employee's data. You can also see tab characters between columns. (See Figure 22-5 on the next page.)

5. Press Ctrl+A and click the Copy button 📋. The data is copied to the Clipboard.

6. Return to your workbook.

7. Press F5 and key **j1**. Press Enter.

 REVIEW: The Go To command uses F5 or Ctrl+G.

FIGURE 22-5
Unformatted text
file in Word

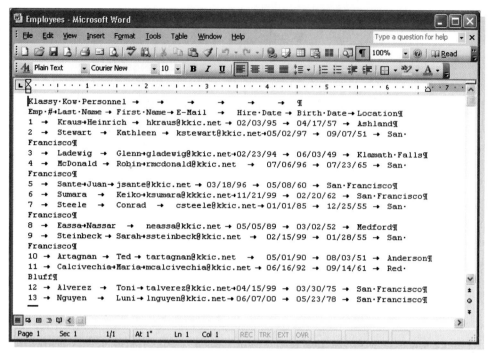

8. Choose <u>E</u>dit, Paste <u>S</u>pecial. The Paste Special dialog box opens.

9. In the <u>A</u>s list, choose Text. You use this option because you are pasting unformatted text from the Word document.

10. Select <u>P</u>aste if it is not already selected and then click OK. The contents of the Clipboard are pasted in the workbook.

11. Adjust the column widths of the imported data so that all the information is visible.

12. Close the text file in Word without saving it. Exit Word.

13. Save the workbook as *[your initials]*22-5 in a new folder for Lesson 22.

14. Add your footer and print the worksheet fit to one landscape page.

EXERCISE **22-6** **Open a Text File in Excel**

When you open a text file in Excel, the Text Import Wizard starts. A *wizard* is a series of dialog boxes that guide you through completing certain tasks.

Text is separated into columns by tabs, commas, or spaces. The *delimiter* is the character that separates the columns. Text files have a .txt filename extension.

1. With *[your initials]*22-5 open, click the Open button .

2. Click the down arrow with the Files of type box and choose Text Files.

TIP: You also can choose All Files in the Files of type box.

3. Double-click the text file **Employees.txt**. The Text Import Wizard dialog box opens. The wizard has determined that the file is delimited and will start the importing with the first line.

4. Click Next. The Text Import Wizard–Step 2 of 3 dialog box shows that the delimiter is a tab. This means that the columns in the text file are separated by tabs.

FIGURE 22-6
Text Import Wizard
dialog box

Text Import Wizard - Step 2 of 3

This screen lets you set the delimiters your data contains. You can see how your text is affected in the preview below.

Delimiters
☑ Tab   ☐ Semicolon   ☐ Comma   ☐ Treat consecutive delimiters as one
☐ Space ☐ Other: Text qualifier: "

Data preview

Klassy Kow Personnel Emp #	Last Name	First Name	E-Mail	Hire
1	Kraus	Heinrich	hkraus@kkic.net	02/03
2	Stewart	Kathleen	kstewart@kkic.net	05/02
3	Ladewig	Glenn	gladewig@kkic.net	02/23

Cancel   < Back   Next >   Finish

5. Click Next. The Text Import Wizard – Step 3 of 3 dialog box allows you to set the type of data in each column. Everything defaults to a General format.

6. Click Finish. The text file is imported into a worksheet in a new workbook. The tab name shows the original text filename.

7. Close the **Employees** workbook without saving, but do not close Excel.

Importing HTML Files

You can import data from a Web page into an Excel workbook. For example, you can import a table on a Web site into your worksheet instead of rekeying the data.

Any data stored in HTML format can be imported into Excel. You can do this in two ways. You can:

- Drag a selected Web page table into Excel.
- Use the Web Query command to get information from a Web page.

 REVIEW: HTML is Hypertext Markup Language, the format used for Web pages.

EXERCISE 22-7 Import from the Web by Dragging

You can import HTML data to a worksheet by dragging the selected data from the browser window to the Excel window. In this exercise, you'll use an existing file to display some Web page data so that you won't have to connect to the Internet.

1. Rename Sheet1 as **Text**. Rename Sheet2 as **Web**.

2. Click the Open button 📂.

3. Click the down arrow with the Files of type text box and select All Web Pages. The file type is set to display HTML files.

4. Select **ThirdQtr.htm**.

5. Click the down arrow with Open and choose Open in Browser. (If a warning box alerts you about hyperlinks, click Yes.) A new window opens, showing the HTML file in your Web browser.

6. Position the pointer just before the beginning of the subtitle, "Product Sales by State."

7. Drag the pointer down to and including "15,600," the last value for the first "Washington" row.

8. Size and position the windows so that you can see the selected data in the browser window and cell A1 in the worksheet.

9. Position the pointer over the highlighted data in the browser window and drag the selected data to cell A1 in the Excel window.

FIGURE 22-7
Dragging data from
the Web to Excel

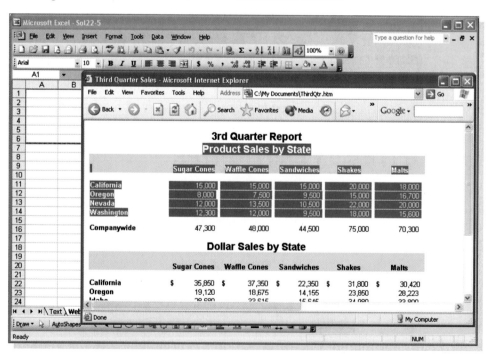

10. Adjust the column widths appropriately.

11. Add your footer. Print the worksheet.

12. Close the browser window.

EXERCISE **22-8** **Create a Web Query**

A *Web query* is a request for data from a Web page. The Web query feature allows you to choose and import tables or preformatted data from a Web page into Excel.

 NOTE: You must establish an Internet connection to complete this exercise.

1. Establish an Internet connection while Excel is running.

2. Return to your workbook.

3. Rename Sheet3 as **WebQuery** and select cell A1.

4. From the Data menu, choose Import External Data and New Web Query. The New Web Query dialog box opens.

5. In the New Web Query Address text box, key **http:// www.moneycentral.msn.com**.

6. Press Enter. Importable tables are flagged with small black arrows in yellow rectangles to mark the tables. Your Internet connection speed affects how quickly you will see the arrows.

  NOTE: If you do not see table markers, click the Show Icons button .

7. When the page displays in the New Web Query dialog box, locate the DOW, NASDAQ, and S&P indexes on the page.

 NOTE: Web sites are updated on a regular basis, so your work may not match the illustrations in this text.

8. Position the pointer over any small, yellow arrow. The table it represents is outlined with a dark border. (See Figure 22-8 on the next page.)

9. Click the arrow to select the DOW, NASDAQ, and S&P stock indexes. It changes to a green check mark.

10. Click Import. The Import Data dialog box opens.

11. Choose Existing worksheet. The cell is A1. (See Figure 22-9 on the next page.)

12. Click OK. You will see a temporary message that Excel is getting the data. After the data is imported, the External Data toolbar might open. Buttons on this toolbar allow you to set options for the data.

13. Insert one row at row 1 and key the title **Klassy Kow Daily Ticker**. Make it 16-point Arial bold.

FIGURE 22-8
Creating a
Web query

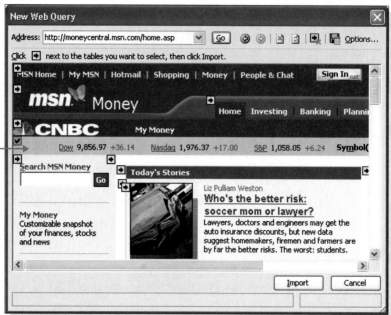

Selected table

FIGURE 22-9
The Import Data
dialog box

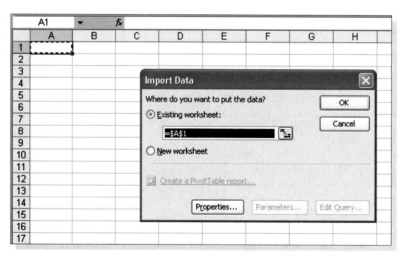

14. Set the height for row 1 to 37.50 (50 pixels).

15. Check the worksheet for unnecessary data or text that was imported with the table and delete it. This may result from the layout and formatting on the original Web page.

16. Select cell A10, and press Ctrl+; to insert the current date.

 NOTE: When you use Ctrl+; to insert the date, it is a value that is nonvolatile and not automatically reset when you open the workbook.

17. Add your footer and print the sheet.

18. Close your Internet connection if required.

Importing Database Files

You can import data from several types of database applications, including FoxPro, dBASE, and Microsoft Access. You can import the data by:

- Dragging and dropping the data from the database application into the Excel worksheet
- Using Microsoft Query

Microsoft Query is a separate program that runs a query on another Excel workbook, an Access database, or one of several other data sources. A *query* is a command that specifies and extracts data from a list.

E X E R C I S E **22-9** **Use Microsoft Query to Import an Access Table**

Klassy Kow has developed a promotional program with Carolina Critters, a company that makes stuffed animals. Carolina Critters uses Microsoft Access, and Klassy Kow needs to use data from the database.

1. Add a new worksheet to your workbook and position it to the right of the WebQuery worksheet. Name it **MSQuery**. Select cell A1.

2. From the Data menu, choose Import External Data and New Database Query. The Choose Data Source dialog box opens. Notice that Excel can read databases from a number of different programs.

3. Select MS Access Database*.

FIGURE 22-10
Creating a
database query

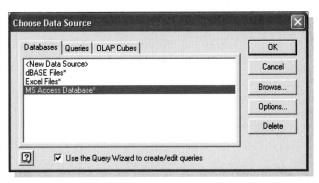

> **TIP:** An OLAP file (Online Analytical Processing) is a type of database.

4. Click OK. The Select Database dialog box opens along with a message that says "Connecting to data source." Next you'll specify the database file.

5. In the Database Name list, select **Carolina.mdb**. (See Figure 22-11 on the next page.)

FIGURE 22-11
Select Database
dialog box

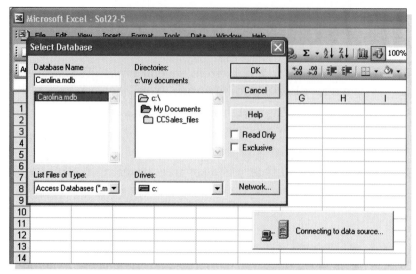

6. Click OK. The Query Wizard – Choose Columns dialog box opens. This wizard shows you the queries and tables in the database.

7. Scroll down the Available tables and columns list and locate tblCustomers.

8. Click the plus (+) symbol next to tblCustomers. The individual fields or columns in the table are listed.

9. Click tblCustomers to highlight it in blue.

10. Click the Move One button [>] to copy all the field names to Columns in your query.

FIGURE 22-12
Query Wizard –
Choose Columns
dialog box

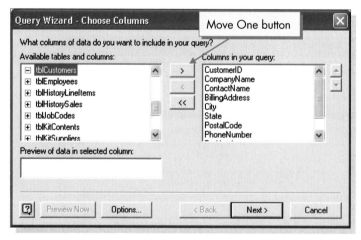

NOTE: You can click individual field names and move them one by one into the Columns in your query list.

11. Click Next. The Query Wizard – Filter Data dialog box opens. You can use this dialog box to filter the data, specifying which rows to choose.

12. Click <u>N</u>ext. The Query Wizard – Sort Order dialog box opens. You can sort the data, too.

13. Click the down arrow next to the Sort by box and select CompanyName. Select Ascending if it is not already selected.

14. Click <u>N</u>ext. The Query Wizard – Finish dialog box opens. You can now choose how to use the imported data.

15. Select <u>R</u>eturn Data to Microsoft Office Excel if it is not already selected, and then click Finish. The Import Data dialog box opens. You use this dialog box to specify where to place the imported data.

16. Select <u>E</u>xisting worksheet if it is not already selected, and then click OK. The Access table is now an Excel list.

 NOTE: The External Data toolbar may open in a worksheet with imported data. You can close it.

Exporting Excel Data

Excel makes it easy to save a workbook in file formats used by other programs. When you save a workbook in one of these formats, you are "exporting" the data to a different program. For example, when you save an Excel workbook as a Web page in HTML format, you are "exporting" the data to HTML. You can also export Excel data to text files, other spreadsheet programs, and dBASE.

 TIP: You cannot save an Excel worksheet in Access format. You can, however, save a worksheet as a text file. Access can read text files.

EXERCISE 22-10 **Copy and Paste Data to Word**

You cannot save a workbook as a Word file with the **.doc** extension. However, you can use the Clipboard to copy and paste a worksheet into Word. The result is a Word table.

1. Display the MSQuery worksheet if it is not already displayed, and select cell A1.

2. Press F8 to turn on Extend mode. Press Ctrl+End to select the cells with data.

3. Click the Copy button 📋.

4. Start Word. (If Word is already running, open a new document.)

5. In the Word window, click the Paste button 📋▾. The Excel data is pasted from the Clipboard. It is formatted as a table in Word.

6. Close the Word document without saving and close Word.

7. Press Esc to turn off the copy marquee.

E X E R C I S E **22-11** **Save a Worksheet as a Text File**

You can save an Excel workbook in a text file format. Saving a workbook in a text file format lets you export Excel data to programs that cannot otherwise read Excel files.

 TIP: If you purchase a mailing list from a commercial source, it is probably in text format.

1. In the MSQuery worksheet, select the range A1:J8 if it is not still selected.

2. From the File menu, choose Save As. The Save As dialog box opens.

3. Click the down arrow next to the Save as type text box and select Text (tab delimited). This will create a text file with tabs to separate the columns/fields.

4. In the File name text box, key *[your initials]***22-11**.

5. Click Save. An information message tells you that the selected file type (text format) cannot save multiple worksheets. It can save only the current worksheet.

6. Click OK. Another message box informs you that there might be some formatting and other features that do not convert to the text format.

 NOTE: Saving an individual worksheet as a text file changes the worksheet's tab name to the filename of the text file.

7. Click Yes. The selected data has been exported to a text format. To see how the exported data appears in a program that reads text files, you'll use Notepad.

8. From the Windows taskbar, click Start. From the All Programs menu, choose Accessories and then choose Notepad. The Notepad window opens.

9. From the Notepad File menu, choose Open.

10. Select the file *[your initials]***22-11.txt**, which you created in step 4. Click Open. The text file opens in the Notepad window. Notice that the bold and the font did not export with the file.

 11. Click the Close button ⊠ in the Notepad window to close the file and Notepad.

12. In the Excel window, change the worksheet's tab name back to **MSQuery**. Select cell A1 to deselect the selected range.

13. Add your standard footer. Set the worksheet to fit on a single page in landscape orientation.

14. Press F12 (or choose File, Save As from the menu).

15. Click the down arrow next to the Save as type text box and select Microsoft Office Excel Workbook.

16. In the File name text box, key *[your initials]***22-11** if it is not already displayed, and then save the workbook in your Lesson 22 folder.

17. Print the worksheet.

18. Close the workbook.

Viewing XML Code

XML, *Extensible Markup Language,* is a file format designed for exchanging data on the Web. An XML file is a text file that can be read and used by many programs.

An XML file includes tags that describe the data. An XML tag such as <Customer Name> describes specific data. Unlike HTML, XML does not include images, backgrounds, or other design elements.

Excel can work with XML data in these ways:

● You can open and save an XML file.

● You can save a workbook as an XML spreadsheet.

● You can build a Web query for XML data sources on the Web.

EXERCISE **22-12** **View XML Code**

When you view an XML file in a Web browser, you can identify tags and determine how the file is built or structured. You open an XML file from Windows Explorer.

1. Right-click Start on the taskbar.

2. From the shortcut menu, choose Explore. Windows Explorer opens.

 NOTE: Do not open the CustCnt.xsd file. This is an XML file with information about the data scheme, but no data.

3. Locate **CustCnt** and double-click it. Your Web browser opens and displays the file. (See Figure 22-13 on the next page.)

4. Look for the XML tag <dataroot> near the beginning of the file. This identifies how and when the XML file was created. There are opening and ending tags for <dataroot>.

5. Scroll to the bottom of the file and look for </dataroot>, the ending tag.

 TIP: Ending XML tags include a forward slash (/) with the name of the tag.

6. Scroll to the top of the file and look for the <City> tag for the first record. XML tags are enclosed in chevron braces like HTML tags. The ending tag includes a forward slash after the left brace.

FIGURE 22-13
XML file in Internet
Explorer

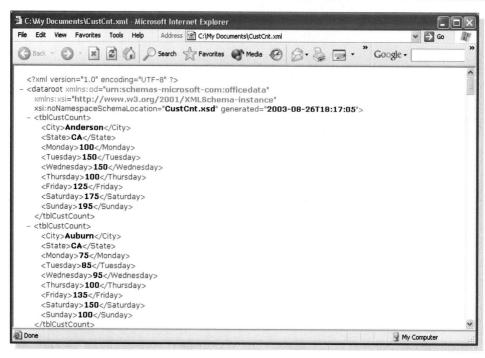

7. Look for the <tblCustCount> tag. This is the name of an Access table that was the original source of the data.

8. Close the browser and close Windows Explorer.

Working with XML Maps

An *XML map* is a tree layout of the tags and other elements in an XML file. An XML map shows the source elements or parts of the file if it has been properly structured and saved.

EXERCISE **22-13** Open an XML File and Remove an Element

You can open or import an XML file into Excel.

1. With no workbook open, click the Open button 📷.

2. Click the down arrow with the Files of type box and choose XML Files.

3. Locate and double-click **CustCnt**. The Open XML dialog box lists three ways that the file can be opened. (See Figure 22-14 on the next page.)

4. Choose As an XML list and click OK. The file opens as a workbook with AutoFilter buttons. The List toolbar may also open.

FIGURE 22-14
Open XML
dialog box

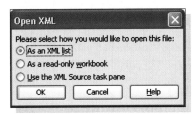

5. From the <u>D</u>ata menu, choose <u>X</u>ML. Choose <u>X</u>ML Source. The XML Source task pane maps the data in the list.

6. In the worksheet, right-click the column J heading. Choose <u>D</u>elete. The Sunday data is removed from the worksheet, but the data is still available in the map.

EXERCISE **22-14** Remap an Element and Refresh Data

An element in the map can be remapped to the list. You simply drag the element to the cell where it should appear.

1. In the XML Source task pane, click to select Sunday.

2. With the solid white arrow, drag Sunday to cell J1. The element is reset in the list, but the data is not. You need to refresh the data.

 NOTE: If the List toolbar is not open, right-click any toolbar and choose it from the list.

 3. Click the Refresh XML button on the List toolbar. The data is updated.

4. Close the workbook without saving.

5. Close the XML Source task pane.

EXERCISE **22-15** Apply a Map and Import Data

You can apply an existing XML map to a new workbook. Then you can map only the elements that you want to use in the workbook and import the data.

1. Create a new workbook.

2. From the <u>D</u>ata menu, choose <u>X</u>ML. Choose <u>X</u>ML Source. The XML Source task pane opens but without any elements.

3. In the XML Source task pane, click XML Maps. The XML Maps dialog box opens.

4. Choose <u>A</u>dd. You can add maps from XML files that have recognizable maps.

5. Choose **CustCnt** and click <u>O</u>pen. The XML Maps dialog box shows the name of the map in the file.

6. Click OK. The XML Source task pane lists the elements.

7. Click City in the task pane and drag it to cell A1. The element is placed in the worksheet without any data. (See Figure 22-15 on the next page.)

FIGURE 22-15
Mapping an
element

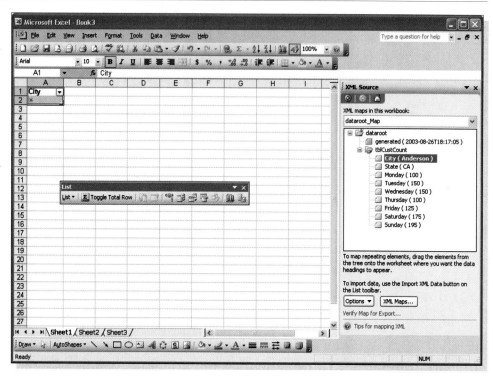

8. Click State in the task pane and drag it to cell B1.

9. Drag Saturday to cell C1 and Sunday to cell D1. You have mapped elements to the worksheet.

10. Click the Import XLM Data button [icon] on the List toolbar.

11. Choose **CustCnt** and click Import. The data is placed in the worksheet.

EXERCISE 22-16 Review Map Properties

Excel stores properties about the map that affect how data is imported and what is stored with the file.

1. From the Data menu, choose XML.

2. Choose XML Map Properties. The XML Map Properties dialog box opens. (See Figure 22-16.)

3. Review the options for how data is formatted, imported, and updated.

4. Click Cancel.

5. Close the XML Source task pane. Close the List toolbar.

6. From the Data menu, choose Filter. Choose AutoFilter to turn off the filter.

7. Make row 1 26.25 (35 pixels) tall.

FIGURE 22-16
XML Map Properties
dialog box

FIGURE 22-16
XML Map Properties
dialog box

Saving an XML Spreadsheet

Each program that reads XML files has its own attributes, maps, elements, or properties. Excel can save a worksheet in XML format for use by other programs that read XML. This allows other programs to use data from the worksheet and lay it out according to specific preferences. When you save an XML spreadsheet, it opens as a regular workbook in Excel and Internet Explorer.

EXERCISE **22-17** **Save an XML Spreadsheet**

1. From the File menu, choose Save As. The Save As dialog box opens.
2. Click the down arrow next to the Save as type text box and select XML Spreadsheet.
3. Save the workbook as *[your initials]*22-17 in your Lesson 22 folder.
4. Click Yes. The workbook is saved in XML format.

 NOTE: You can open and edit an XML workbook like a regular workbook.

5. Close the workbook.

USING ONLINE HELP

Importing data from the Web is a new and expanding task for many workers. Use Help to learn about building Web queries and using the XML format.

Use Help to explore importing Web data.

1. With Internet Explorer and Excel running, look for topics about **web queries**.
2. Read the information. Close the windows.
3. Close Internet Explorer and end your Internet connection.

LESSON 22   Summary

➤ You can import a Word document into a worksheet by performing a copy and paste or by dragging and dropping.

➤ Imported data might display smart tags, which are labels that are attached to recognized data types.

➤ A custom format is a display specification created with Excel's formatting codes. Custom formats can include literals, which are specific symbols, characters, or values that appear as part of the formatting.

➤ You can copy and paste Word data into a worksheet in a text file format by using the Edit, Paste Special command.

➤ When a text file is opened in Excel, the Text Import Wizard opens. A wizard is a series of dialog boxes that guide you through completing certain tasks.

➤ Text files contain unformatted text. Text file data is separated by a delimiter character, usually a space, tab, or comma.

➤ You can select and drag an HTML file from the Web into an Excel worksheet.

➤ A Web query is a request to get table data or preformatted data from a Web page.

➤ Microsoft Query is a utility program that performs queries on other database programs. A query is a command that gets certain data from a list.

➤ You can export Excel data as a text file or an HTML file. You can also export Excel data to other programs such as Word and dBASE.

➤ XML is Extensible Markup Language. It is a text file format designed for exchanging data on the Web.

➤ An XML file includes elements in a map and tags to identify the elements.

➤ Excel can save workbooks in XML format.

LESSON 22   Command Summary

FEATURE	BUTTON	MENU	KEYBOARD
Web query		<u>D</u>ata, Import External <u>D</u>ata, New <u>W</u>eb Query	
Database query		<u>D</u>ata, Import External <u>D</u>ata, New Database Query	
Text Import Wizard		<u>F</u>ile, <u>O</u>pen	Ctrl + O
Save a text file		<u>F</u>ile, Save <u>A</u>s	F12
Save an XML file		<u>F</u>ile, Save <u>A</u>s	F12
XML map		<u>D</u>ata, <u>X</u>ML, <u>X</u>ML Source	
XML map properties		<u>D</u>ata, <u>X</u>ML, XML Map <u>P</u>roperties	

Concepts Review

TRUE/FALSE QUESTIONS

Each of the following statements is either true or false. Indicate your choice by circling T or F.

T   F   **1.** Importing data is similar to sharing a workbook.

T   F   **2.** After data has been imported, it can be formatted like any worksheet data.

T   F   **3.** In a custom format, enclose specific text or values in curly braces so that it appears as part of the format.

T   F   **4.** A drag and drop is a copy if you press and hold (Shift).

T   F   **5.** XML files include tags to describe the data.

T   F   **6.** Text files use a delimiter to separate columns.

T   F   **7.** HTML is a Web file format.

T   F   **8.** A Web query and Microsoft Query work the same way.

SHORT ANSWER QUESTIONS

Write the correct answer in the space provided.

1. What is XML an abbreviation for?

_____

2. What menu command allows you to apply an XML map?

_____

3. What utility enables you to get data from an Access file?

_____

4. The tab character that separates columns in a text file is known as what?

_____

5. What is the menu command to create a Web query?

_____

6. Name two programs that allow you to open, view, and edit a text file.

_____

7. How can you view XML code?

_____

8. What keyboard shortcut inserts the current date?

_____

CRITICAL THINKING

Answer these questions on a separate page. There are no right or wrong answers. Support your answers with examples from your own experience, if possible.

1. Describe types of data or tables that your school or your company might import into Excel from the Web. Describe why it would be helpful to analyze the data in Excel.

2. When you import or link data, it can be static or dynamic. Dynamic data updates when it is changed at the original file or site. Give examples of data that might need to be refreshed repeatedly. Give examples of data that might need to be imported only once.

Skills Review

EXERCISE 22-18

Import a Word document. Format pasted data. Import a text file.

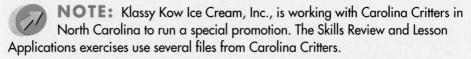 **NOTE:** Klassy Kow Ice Cream, Inc., is working with Carolina Critters in North Carolina to run a special promotion. The Skills Review and Lesson Applications exercises use several files from Carolina Critters.

1. Create a new workbook.

2. Import a Word document into a worksheet by following these steps:

  a. Start Word and open the Word file **StuffedAnimalsCatalog**.

  b. Set the Zoom percentage to 50% in Word.

  c. Position the pointer in the left margin area to the left of the first row in the table, "C001 Dooby Dog."

  d. With the white right-pointing arrow, select all the rows in the table by dragging. Do not include the title.

  e. Click the Copy button [icon].

f. Restore the Zoom setting to 100%. Close the Word document without saving but leave Word open.

g. Select cell A1 in the worksheet if it is not already selected.

h. Click the Paste button 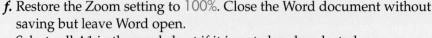.

3. Widen column B so that all animal names fit on a single line in the cell.

4. Select all the row headings between row 1 and row 27 and set a row height of 18.00 (24 pixels).

5. Insert two rows before row 1.

6. Key **Carolina Critters Catalog** in cell A1.

7. Enter the current date in cell A2 by pressing Ctrl+Ⓒ.

8. Format cells A1 and A2 as 22-point Arial. Set the height for rows 1 and 2 to 51.00 (68 pixels).

9. Format the date with a custom format to show the month spelled out, no day, and four digits for the year. Align the date vertically at the top and horizontally at the left.

10. Rename the worksheet **Catalog**. Adjust column widths so that the worksheet fits on a portrait page. Add the standard footer.

11. Rename Sheet2 as **Employees** and delete Sheet3.

12. Add the standard footer to the Employees worksheet.

13. Import a text file by following these steps:

a. From the Data menu, choose Import External Data.

b. Choose Import Data.

c. Navigate to find the text file **Employees.txt** and click to select it. Then click Open. The wizard determines that the file is delimited and will start importing at the first line.

d. Click Next. The delimiter is a tab.

e. Click Next. All columns use a General format.

f. Click Finish. Click OK to place the data in cell A1.

14. Select the labels in row 2 and make them bold italic. Make cell A1 16-point Arial. Make rows 2 and 3 22.50 (30 pixels) tall.

15. Hide column D. Adjust column widths as needed.

16. Save the workbook as *[your initials]*22-18 in your Lesson 22 folder.

17. Print the entire workbook and close the workbook.

EXERCISE 22-19

Import an HTML document. Format imported data. Import a database file.

1. Create a new workbook.

2. Import an HTML document by following these steps:

a. Click the Open button 📷.

    b. Select **CCSales.htm**.

    c. Click the down arrow next to the Open button and select Open in Browser. Click OK. (If you see a warning message about hyperlinks, click Yes.)

    d. Select all the data in the browser by dragging.

    e. Size and position the windows so that you can see the selected data in the browser and cell A1 in the worksheet.

    f. Position the pointer over the highlighted data in the browser window and drag the data to cell A1 in the Excel window.

    g. Close the browser.

3. Format the data by adjusting the alignment of the title, widening columns, and formatting the values for currency with two decimals. Make sure the numbers are right aligned.

4. Delete row 2. Copy the format from cell A2 to A1. Set the height for rows 1 and 2 to 51.00 (68 pixels).

5. Add a top border to cell A1 to match the rest of the data. Set the height of row 3 to 30.00 (40 pixels). Set the range A1:A2 for centered vertical alignment.

6. Rename the worksheet **Overstock**.

7. Add the standard footer. Center the page horizontally.

8. Rename Sheet2 as **SalesReview**.

9. Import database files by following these steps:

    a. With cell A1 in the SalesReview worksheet selected, choose Data, Import External Data from the menu and then choose New Database Query.

    b. Choose MS Access Database* and then click OK.

    c. In the Database Name list, select **Carolina.mdb** and click OK.

    d. Scroll down the Available tables and columns list, locate qryStuffedAnimals, and select it so that it is highlighted in blue.

    e. Click the Move One button ⟩. (Four column names should appear under the Columns in your query list.)

    f. Click Next.

    g. In the Query Wizard – Filter Data dialog box, click Next.

    h. In the Query Wizard – Sort Order dialog box, click Next.

    i. Select Return Data to Microsoft Excel and click Finish.

    j. Select Existing worksheet if it is not already selected and click OK.

10. Add your footer. Center the page horizontally. Delete Sheet3.

11. Save the workbook as *[your initials]***22-19** in your Lesson 22 folder.

12. Print the entire workbook and close it.

EXERCISE 22-20

Export data to Word.

1. Open **CCKitSupplies** in Excel.
2. Export data to Word by following these steps:

   a. Select the range A1:C8.
   b. Click the Copy button 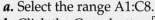.
   c. Start Word if necessary.
   d. In a new document in the Word window, click the Paste button 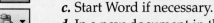.
3. In the Word window, click the Show/Hide ¶ button  to display formatting symbols.
4. Delete extra spaces. They appear as small dots on the screen.
5. Select the values and right-align them. Adjust the column widths as you would do in Excel.
6. Press Ctrl+End to position the insertion point and key *[your name]*.
7. Save the document as a Word document named *[your initials]*22-20 in your Lesson 22 folder.

8. Click the Print button.
9. Close the document and close Word.
10. Close the Excel workbook without saving.

EXERCISE 22-21

Save an XML spreadsheet. Work with XML maps.

1. Save an XML worksheet by following these steps:
   a. Open the Excel file **CCKitSupplies** in Excel.
   b. In cell A10, key **Tallied by** *[your name]*.
   c. From the File menu, choose Save As.
   d. Click the down arrow next to the Save as type text box and select XML Spreadsheet.
   e. Save the file as *[your initials]*22-21 in your Lesson 22 folder.
   f. Close the workbook.
2. Work with XML maps by following these steps:
   a. Create a new workbook.
   b. From the Data menu, choose XML. Then choose XML Source.
   c. In the XML Source task pane, click XML Maps.
   d. Click Add and choose **Customers**. Click Open and then click OK in the message box about a schema.

NOTE: A schema includes additional embedded information about the file that can be used by others.

e. Click OK in the XML Maps dialog box.
f. In the XML Source task pane, click the – symbol with ns2:schema to collapse the element.

NOTE: Your task pane may show ns2 or another number.

g. From the XML Source task pane, drag the Customer ID element to cell A1.
h. Drag the CompanyName element to cell B1.
i. Drag the City element to cell C1 and the TaxStatus element to cell D1.
j. From the Data menu, choose XML. Choose Import.
k. Choose Customers and click Import.

3. Add your footer to the worksheet.

4. Save the file as an Excel workbook named *[your initials]*22-21 in your Lesson 22 folder. Print the worksheet.

5. Close the workbook and the XML Source task pane.

Lesson Applications

EXERCISE 22-22

Copy HTML data into Excel. Import Word data.

Carolina Critters has a Web page displaying closeout items that Klassy Kow might use in their joint promotional campaigns. You need to combine the items on the Web site into a workbook with catalog data imported from a Word document.

1. Create a new workbook.
2. Open the HTML file **CCCloseouts** in your browser. Select and copy all the data to cell A1 in your workbook.
3. Close the browser.
4. Adjust the column widths and format the appropriate values as currency with two decimals.
5. In cell E2, key the column heading **On Hand**. Apply formatting to the cell to match the existing columns.
6. Left-align the label in cell A1 and then center it across columns A through E. Apply the appropriate shading to cell E1. Fix the borders and add a top border to row 1.
7. Start Word and open the document **StuffedAnimalsCatalog**. Save the document as a Word file named *[your initials]*22-22 in your Lesson 22 folder.
8. For the first item in the Word table, "Dooby Dog," copy the value in the rightmost cell of the table to cell E3 of the worksheet. Repeat this step for the remaining values in the "On Hand" cells in the workbook.

    TIP: Check the Item name in the worksheet and find the corresponding name in the Word file.

9. Format the new data so that the font matches existing worksheet data, and fix the border.
10. Close the Word document without saving any changes and close Word.
11. Rename Sheet1 as **Closeouts**. Add your footer. Center the page horizontally.
12. Save the workbook as *[your initials]*22-22 in your Lesson 22 folder.
13. Print the worksheet and close the workbook.

EXERCISE 22-23

Import database information. Export data to a text file format.

Klassy Kow needs a list of suppliers and kits used by Carolina Critters. This information is in the Carolina database and must be imported into a worksheet. The worksheet then needs to be exported to a text file for use by Klassy Kow's own suppliers.

1. Create a new workbook.

2. Create a new database query for the MS Access database file **Carolina.mdb**. For the available tables and columns, use tblKitSuppliers. Include only the SupplierID and the SupplierName columns in your query. (*Hint:* Click the plus (+) symbol next to tblKitSuppliers to expand the list. Then double-click the column name to place it in the query.) Import the data without any filtering or sorting into cell A2 in your workbook.

 NOTE: If you imported the data into cell A1, insert a row.

3. In cell A1, key **Kit Suppliers for Carolina Critters**. Make it 22-point Arial italic. Set the height for row 2 to 36 (48 pixels).

4. In cell A7, key **List of Kits**. Make it 22-point Arial italic. Set the height for row 7 to 51.00 (68 pixels).

5. Select cell A8. Create another query for the MS Access database **Carolina.mdb**. For the available tables and columns, use tblStuffedAnimals and the ProductName and KitNumber columns. Sort by product name in ascending order.

6. Set the height for row 8 to 36.00 (48 pixels). Edit the column labels, inserting spaces between words. Make other formatting adjustments if you think they are necessary.

7. In cell A34, key **Prepared by** *[your name]*. Make it 11-point Arial bold.

8. Add your footer. Delete Sheet2 and Sheet3.

9. Save the workbook as *[your initials]***22-23** in your Lesson 22 folder.

10. Print the worksheet.

11. Export the file to a text file format (tab delimited), saving it as *[your initials]***22-23.txt** in your Lesson 22 folder. Close the workbook.

12. Open Notepad. Open the text file *[your initials]***22-23.txt**.

13. Choose File, Print from the Notepad menu and then close Notepad.

EXERCISE 22-24

Import a text file. Import Word data. Save a workbook in XML format.

Klassy Kow Human Resources has asked for your help in creating a company Web site. They would like to include an employee list. You need to import a text file containing employee names into a worksheet, add some data from a Word file, and then save it in XML format.

1. Open the text file **Employees.txt** in Excel.

2. Move the title in cell A1 to B1, and then delete column A. Delete columns D through F.

3. Make the title 22-point Arial. Set the height for row 2 to 36 (48 pixels), and make the column headings 11-point Arial bold italic. Adjust the column widths appropriately.

4. Start Word and open the document **NewHires**. Select the cells containing the names and e-mail addresses of the two new employees, and drag the data to cell A16 in the Excel worksheet. Remove any smart tags that might appear with the data.

5. Close the Word document without saving and close Word.

6. In the Excel window, format the imported Word data to match the existing data. Add your footer. Center the page horizontally.

7. Save the workbook as a Microsoft Excel Workbook file, as *[your initials]*22-24 in your Lesson 22 folder, and print the worksheet.

8. Save the workbook again, but this time as an XML Spreadsheet named *[your initials]*22-24 in your Lesson 22 folder.

9. Close the workbook.

EXERCISE 22-25 *Challenge Yourself*

Import and export data. Save a workbook in XML format.

Klassy Kow is preparing information for a Web site for employees. They'd like to include employee data, discounted merchandise for sale, and other information. All the information needs to be combined into a single workbook and exported to XML. You've been asked to help out on this project.

1. Open the text file **Employees.txt** in Excel.

2. Make the title 22-point Arial. Set the height for row 2 to 25.50 (34 pixels), and make the column headings 11-point Arial bold italic. Adjust the column widths appropriately.

3. Open a new Word document. Key the title **Current Staff**. Make it 16-point Arial. Press Enter two times.

4. Display the Excel window. Copy and paste the range A2:G15 to the new Word document below the title.

5. In the Word window, position the insertion point under the table, press Enter, and key **Prepared by** *[your name]* in 10-point Arial bold. Save the Word document as *[your initials]*22-25 in your Lesson 22 folder. Print the document, close both Word documents, and close Word.

6. In the Excel window, click any cell to deselect the range, and press Esc to turn off the marquee. Add your footer. Center the page horizontally.

7. Insert a new worksheet, position it after the Employees worksheet, and name it **EmployeeStoreItems**. In cell A1, key **Sale Items**, and make it 22-point Arial.

8. Open the HTML file **CCDiscontinued.htm** in your Web browser. Drag the table starting at "Discontinued Items" to cell A4 in the worksheet. Open the HTML file **CCSales.htm** in your browser. Drag the table starting at "Merchandise Overstocks" to cell A15 in the worksheet. Close the browser.

9. Format the values for currency with two decimal places. Adjust the column widths appropriately. Center the worksheet title in cell A1 across the columns.

10. Add your footer. Center the page horizontally.

11. Save the workbook in Microsoft Excel Workbook format as *[your initials]*22-25.xls in your Lesson 22 folder and print the entire workbook.

12. Save the file in XML Spreadsheet format as *[your initials]*22-25.xml in your Lesson 22 folder and close the workbook.

On Your Own

In these exercises you work on your own, as you would in a real-life work environment. Use the skills you've learned to accomplish the task—and be creative.

EXERCISE 22-26
Log on to the Internet and locate some stock market data. Import the information into a worksheet as a Web query. Format the worksheet attractively, add the standard footer, and then save the workbook as *[your initials]*22-26 in your Lesson 22 folder. Print the workbook and close it.

EXERCISE 22-27
Create a worksheet itemizing all your expenses for a week, formatted attractively. Add the standard footer. Save the workbook as *[your initials]*22-27 in your Lesson 22 folder and then print it. Export the worksheet to Word. Save the Word document as *[your initials]*22-27 in your Lesson 22 folder and then print it. Close the files.

EXERCISE 22-28
Log on to the Internet and locate some statistical data on a topic of interest to you, such as a sports team or weather information. Import the data into a worksheet by dragging. Format it attractively and add the standard footer. Save the workbook as *[your initials]*22-28 in your Lesson 22 folder. Print the workbook.

Using Lists and Database Features

MICROSOFT OFFICE
SPECIALIST
ACTIVITIES

In this lesson:
XLO3E-1-1
XLO3E-1-2
XLO3E-1-3
XLO3E-1-5
XLO3E-1-10
XLO3E-2-2
XLO3E-4-3
XLO3E-5-1

See Appendix.

OBJECTIVES

After completing this lesson, you will be able to:

1. **Prepare a list.**
2. **Sort data.**
3. **Use filters.**
4. **Create advanced filters.**
5. **Add subtotals to a list.**
6. **Use database functions.**
7. **Publish a workbook to the Web.**
8. **Create and edit outlines.**

 Estimated Time: 2 hours

E xcel uses the term *list* to describe tables of information. A list is a series of worksheet rows that contain related information. A list might consist of a set of client names, addresses, and phone numbers or an employee list with similar information.

When data is organized in a list, you can:

- Add data to the list.
- Use filters to display certain rows in the list.
- Sort the rows.
- Show subtotals and outlines.
- Create a special summary table called a PivotTable.

Preparing a List

A list consists of a *header row,* which contains titles or descriptive labels. Immediately after the header row are rows of data.

In a list, a row of data is referred to as a *record.* It includes all the categories of data for that row. A *field* is a single category of information; each column is a field. For example, in a telephone directory list, the column containing the last names is a field. Each column must have a unique *field name,* which is the label in the header row. An individual piece of data in the list is called a *field value.*

When you set up a list, follow these guidelines:

- Key field names or descriptive labels in the first row. This is the header row.
- Do not repeat field names in the header row.
- Field names must start with a letter.
- Do not mix data types in the columns. For example, do not mix currency values and text in the same column.
- Do not leave empty rows within the list.
- Apply a different format to the header row to distinguish it from data rows.
- Keep the list on a worksheet by itself. If you place other information on the worksheet, do not place it below the list.

FIGURE 23-1
Excel list

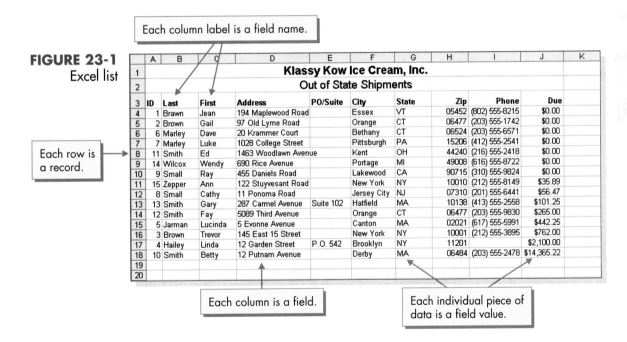

Each column label is a field name.

Each row is a record.

Each column is a field.

Each individual piece of data is a field value.

	A	B	C	D	E	F	G	H	I	J	K
1				Klassy Kow Ice Cream, Inc.							
2				Out of State Shipments							
3	ID	Last	First	Address	PO/Suite	City	State	Zip	Phone	Due	
4	1	Brawn	Jean	194 Maplewood Road		Essex	VT	05452	(802) 555-8215	$0.00	
5	2	Brown	Gail	97 Old Lyme Road		Orange	CT	06477	(203) 555-1742	$0.00	
6	6	Marley	Dave	20 Krammer Court		Bethany	CT	06524	(203) 555-6571	$0.00	
7	7	Marley	Luke	1028 College Street		Pittsburgh	PA	15206	(412) 555-2541	$0.00	
8	11	Smith	Ed	1463 Woodlawn Avenue		Kent	OH	44240	(216) 555-2418	$0.00	
9	14	Wilcox	Wendy	690 Rice Avenue		Portage	MI	49008	(616) 555-8722	$0.00	
10	9	Small	Ray	455 Daniels Road		Lakewood	CA	90715	(310) 555-9824	$0.00	
11	15	Zepper	Ann	122 Stuyvesant Road		New York	NY	10010	(212) 555-8149	$35.89	
12	8	Small	Cathy	11 Ponoma Road		Jersey City	NJ	07310	(201) 555-6441	$56.47	
13	13	Smith	Gary	287 Carmel Avenue	Suite 102	Hatfield	MA	10138	(413) 555-2558	$101.25	
14	12	Smith	Fay	5089 Third Avenue		Orange	CT	06477	(203) 555-9830	$265.00	
15	5	Jarman	Lucinda	5 Evonne Avenue		Canton	MA	02021	(617) 555-5991	$442.25	
16	3	Brown	Trevor	145 East 15 Street		New York	NY	10001	(212) 555-3895	$762.00	
17	4	Hailey	Linda	12 Garden Street	P.O. 542	Brooklyn	NY	11201		$2,100.00	
18	10	Smith	Betty	12 Putnam Avenue		Derby	MA	06484	(203) 555-2478	$14,365.22	
19											
20											

EXERCISE **23-1** **Key Data for a List**

When you create a list, you key the same type of data in each column under the field names. You can use the AutoComplete feature to assist you in keying information that is identical to existing data in the list.

1. Open the file **WenatcheeShakes**.

2. Starting in cell A3, key the following labels for the header row in cells A3 through C3:
   Date   Size   Flavor

3. Make the labels in the header row bold and centered.

4. In cell A11, key **4/5/04**. Press Tab.

5. Key **sm** and press Tab to enter **Small**. Key **v** and press Enter. Notice that AutoComplete helps you enter repetitive data in your list.

 NOTE: When you press Ctrl+' to copy a date field, you first see the serial number for the date to be copied. It is formatted when you press Tab.

6. With cell A12 selected, press Ctrl+' and then press Tab. The same date as in cell A11 is entered in A12. Ctrl+' copies the contents of a cell that is directly above the selected cell.

7. In cell B12, key **m** and press Tab. AutoComplete enters **Medium** in the cell. Key **c** and press Enter to enter **Chocolate** in cell C12.

 TIP: You need not key leading zeros for months and dates.

8. Starting in cell A13, add three additional rows to the list:
4/6/04	Large	Strawberry
4/6/04	Small	Chocolate
4/7/04	Medium	Vanilla

FIGURE 23-2
New data

	A	B	C	D	E
1	*Klassy Kow Ice Cream Shops*				
2	*Wenatchee Shake Sales*				
3	**Date**	**Size**	**Flavor**		
4	1-Apr	Small	Chocolate		
5	2-Apr	Medium	Strawberry		
6	2-Apr	Medium	Chocolate		
7	2-Apr	Large	Strawberry		
8	2-Apr	Small	Chocolate		
9	4-Apr	Medium	Chocolate		
10	4-Apr	Small	Vanilla		
11	5-Apr	Small	Vanilla		
12	5-Apr	Medium	Chocolate		
13	6-Apr	Large	Strawberry		
14	6-Apr	Small	Chocolate		
15	7-Apr	Medium	Vanilla		
16					
17					
18					
19					
20					

EXERCISE   23-2   Apply Conditional Formatting

You can set conditional formatting in a list so that data is formatted as you complete it.

1. Click the column B heading. From the Format menu, choose Conditional Formatting. The Conditional Formatting dialog box opens.

2. Click the down arrow next to the Condition 1 text box and choose Cell Value Is if it is not already selected.

3. Click the down arrow next to the second text box and choose equal to.

4. Key **large** in the third text box.

5. Click Format. The Format Cells dialog box opens. On the Font tab choose Bold Italic. Click OK. The Preview box shows the format for data that meets your condition. (See Figure 23-3 on the next page.)

FIGURE 23-3
Setting a
conditional format
for the list

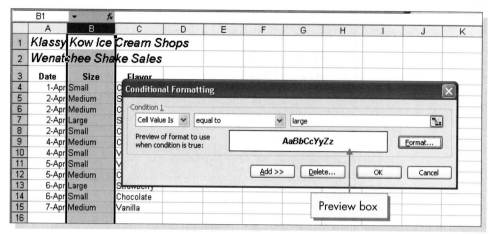

6. Click OK. Conditional formatting is applied to all cells in column B.

EXERCISE 23-3 Create the List

Using a named range for your list makes it easy to accomplish many list-related features that require the cell range of the list. The Create List command includes the header row, all the data rows in the list, and extra blank rows.

 REVIEW: You can name a range from the Name Box on the formula bar, or by using the Insert, Name command.

1. Click cell A4. This is a cell in your list.

2. From the Data menu, choose List and then Create List. The Create List dialog box identifies your header row and additional rows. Make sure there is a check mark for My list has headers.

3. Click OK. The list is highlighted, AutoFilters are applied, and the List toolbar may open. (See Figure 23-4.)

4. Click cell D4, a cell outside the list. The range is no longer shaded, and the toolbar closes.

 NOTE: Your list has been named "Database."

5. Click cell A4. If the List toolbar is not open, right-click any toolbar and choose List.

FIGURE 23-4
List created

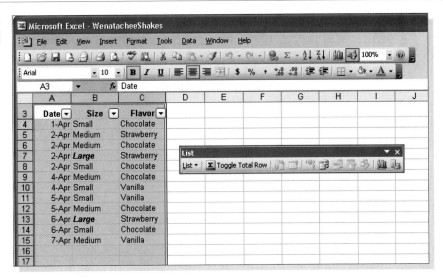

EXERCISE 23-4 **Enter and Edit Records in the Data Form**

You can work with one record at a time in a list by using the data form, adding, deleting, or editing records.

NOTE: The data form can be used when the list has fewer than 32 fields.

The Data Form dialog box has a position indicator in its top-right corner. The position indicator tells you how many records are entered in the list and which record is currently displayed. You can navigate forward or backward, one record at a time.

1. Click the down arrow with the List button <u>List ▾</u> on the List toolbar. Choose Form. The Data Form dialog box opens with the first record displayed. (See Figure 23-5 on the next page.)

2. Click Find Next two times to scroll forward through two records.

3. Click Find Prev to scroll backward one record.

4. Click New. A blank data form opens.

5. In the Date field box, key **4/8/04**.

6. Press [Tab] to move to the Size field box and key **Medium**. Note that you cannot use AutoComplete or Pick from List in the data form.

7. Press [Tab] to move to the Flavor field box and key **Vanilla**.

8. Press [Enter] to add the record to the list. Excel opens another blank data form.

9. Click Find Prev to display the record you just added.

10. Double-click Medium and change it to **Large**.

11. Click Restore. The text reverts to "Medium." If you do not press [Enter] or scroll to a different record, you can revert to the original data.

FIGURE 23-5
Data Form
dialog box

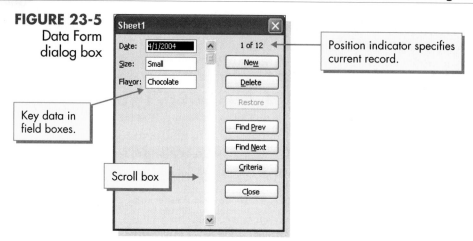

Position indicator specifies current record.

Key data in field boxes.

Scroll box

12. Click Delete. Excel warns that you are about to delete the record permanently.

  NOTE: You cannot use the Undo button to restore a deleted record. You can reenter the record if necessary.

13. Click OK. The record is deleted.

EXERCISE **23-5** **Find Records by Using the Data Form**

You can search in the data form to locate a specific record or group of records. Excel finds records that match the *criteria*, which are conditions you specify for matching in the search.

1. Drag the scroll box in the Data Form dialog box up to return to the first record.

2. Click Criteria. The data form is cleared, and Criteria appears in the top-right corner.

FIGURE 23-6
Adding criteria to
the Data Form
dialog box

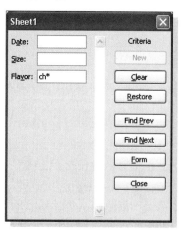

3. Key ch* in the Flavor field.

REVIEW: You can use the question mark (?) as a wildcard to search for any single character and the asterisk (*) to find any number of characters.

4. Click Find Next. The first match is shown in the form.

5. Click Find Next again. Each record is displayed as it is found. Notice that the same cell is still selected within the list. Excel is showing the matched record only in the form.

6. Click Criteria to display the criteria data form.
7. Click Clear and key **large** in the Size field.
8. Click Find Next. One match is found.
9. Click Find Prev. Another match is displayed. You can scroll forward or backward to find matching records.
10. Click Criteria and click Clear. The criteria data form is cleared.
11. Click Form. All the records in the list are now available.
12. Click Close to close the Data Form dialog box.

 TIP: If you have Microsoft Access installed on your computer, you can use it to create a customized data form to enter, find, or delete data in an Excel list.

Sorting Data

Records in a list are often entered in no particular order. Excel allows you to sort a list in a specific order to help you organize your work. For example, you can sort a list of employees by department or by hire date.

In an *ascending* sort, text data is arranged alphabetically from A to Z, and values are arranged from low number to high. In a *descending* sort, text data is arranged in reverse alphabetical order from Z to A, and values are arranged from high to low.

EXERCISE 23-6 Sort by One Column

Since the list range has been named, you can click anywhere in the column to be used for sorting and use the Quick Sort buttons on the Standard toolbar.

1. Click cell C4.

2. Click the Sort Ascending button. The data rows are sorted in alphabetical order by Flavor.
3. Click cell B3. This is the header row.

4. Click the Sort Descending button. The data rows are sorted in reverse alphabetical order by Size.
5. Click the Undo button twice to undo the two sort actions.

EXERCISE 23-7 Sort by Multiple Columns

Sorting by more than one column sorts within a sort. For example, you can sort by the date and then by the flavor. To sort by more than one column, you use the Sort dialog box.

1. Click any cell in the list.

2. Click the down arrow with the List button on the List toolbar. Choose Sort. The Sort dialog box opens. Excel has recognized that your list has a header row.

3. Click the down arrow next to the Sort by text box and choose Date.

4. Choose Descending to the right of the Sort by text box.

5. Click the down arrow next to the Then by text box and choose Flavor.

6. Choose Ascending next to the Then by text box. You're sorting by Date, with the most recent dates first. The secondary sort is by Flavor, alphabetically.

> **NOTE:** Dates are sorted as values, not text. The serial value for a date is larger the more recent the date.

FIGURE 23-7
Sorting by more than one column

7. Click OK. Notice that the most recent date is first. Where there are multiple occurrences of a date, the records are sorted by the flavor.

8. Add your usual footer. Horizontally center the worksheet.

9. Save the workbook as *[your initials]*23-7 in a new folder for Lesson 23.

10. Print the worksheet and close the workbook.

Using Filters

A *filter* is a procedure that creates a subset of data for a list. A filter displays only records that meet specified conditions. Those records that do not meet the conditions are temporarily hidden. AutoFilter is best when your criteria for filtering are simple.

> **NOTE:** Do not begin this exercise unless you can complete Exercise 23-13. You will be changing the Standard toolbar in Exercise 23-8. You will restore the defaults in Exercise 23-13.

EXERCISE | **23-8** | **Add the AutoFilter Button to the Toolbar**

Most Excel menu commands have buttons that you can add to any toolbar. The AutoFilter command has such a button.

1. Open the file **OutOfState**.

2. Select the range A3:J18. Click the Name Box and key **Database**. Press Enter. You have named the list range yourself.

3. Click any cell in the list to deselect the range.

4. Right-click anywhere on the Standard toolbar. Choose Customize. The Customize dialog box opens.

5. Click the Commands tab. Choose Data in the Categories list.

6. In the Commands list on the right, choose AutoFilter. Drag the button and its name to the Standard toolbar between the Sort Ascending button and the Sort Descending button .

7. Click Close. The AutoFilter button is added to the Standard toolbar.

> **NOTE:** If you have difficulty adding the AutoFilter button to the Standard toolbar, ask your instructor for help.

EXERCISE **23-9** **Apply a Filter by Selection**

The AutoFilter button is the quickest way to apply a simple filter. You select the cell in the list that you want to match and then click the button. Excel filters the list and adds drop-down arrows to the labels in the header row.

By clicking the AutoFilter arrows, you can set options for the filter. They include:

- (All)
  Displays all records in the list. Use this to remove the filter.
- (Top 10…)
  Displays ten records from the top of the list. You are not limited to ten. You can set any number of items or a percentage as well as use the top or bottom of the list.
- (Custom…)
  Allows you to use more than one field in the filter.
- (Blanks)
  Displays all rows with no data in the column.
- (NonBlanks)
  Displays all rows that contain data in the column.

1. Select cell G5. Click the AutoFilter button on the Standard toolbar (or choose Data, Filter, AutoFilter from the menu). Only the rows with CT (Connecticut) as the state are shown, and the header row labels have AutoFilter arrows. The filtered row headings are blue, as is the AutoFilter arrow for the State column. (See Figure 23-8 on the next page.)

2. Click the AutoFilter arrow for the State column and choose (All). All the rows are displayed.

3. Select cell B13.

FIGURE 23-8
Filtered list for
Connecticut

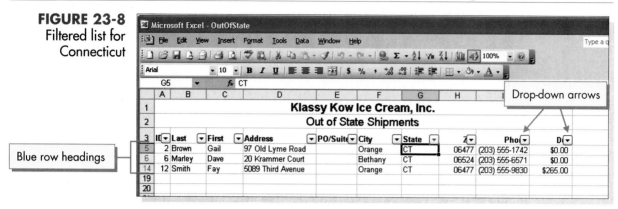

Blue row headings

4. Click the AutoFilter button ▾⯆. Only rows with Smith as the last name are displayed.

5. Click the AutoFilter arrow for the Last field and select (All).

EXERCISE 23-10 Create a Filter within a Filter

You can filter the results of a filter with another filter.

1. Click the AutoFilter arrow for the Last column and choose Smith. All customers whose name is Smith are displayed.

2. Click the AutoFilter arrow for the State column and choose MA. Only the Smith records from Massachusetts (MA) are shown. This is a filter within a filter.

3. Click the AutoFilter arrow for the State column and choose (All). The filter for this column is removed.

4. Click the AutoFilter arrow for the Last column and choose (All). The filter for this column is removed, and all records are shown.

 TIP: You can edit data while the rows are filtered.

EXERCISE 23-11 Create a Top 10 AutoFilter

The Top 10 AutoFilter is a filter for the smallest or largest numbers in a field. You can use a number or a percentage.

1. Click the AutoFilter arrow for the Due field. Choose (Top 10…). The Top 10 AutoFilter dialog box opens.

2. Key 4 in the middle box to show the top (highest) four values in the column.

FIGURE 23-9
Top 10 AutoFilter
dialog box

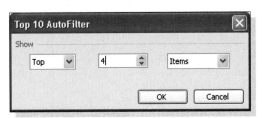

3. If Items does not appear in the rightmost box, click the down arrow for that box and select it.
4. Click OK. The list shows the records with the highest four values in the Due column.

5. Click the AutoFilter arrow for the Due column and choose (All).

EXERCISE 23-12 Create Custom AutoFilters

In a custom AutoFilter, you can use comparison operators, such as greater than (>) or less than (<). You can use "And" and "Or" operators to create multiple conditions. These operators allow you to:

- Display the results of a single criterion, such as >500.
- Display either of two items in a column. For example, you can show rows with either "Smith" or "Jacobs" as last name.
- Display records that fall within a range, such as values between 500 and 1000 (>500 and <1000).

1. Click the AutoFilter arrow for the Due field. Choose (Custom…). The Custom AutoFilter dialog box opens.
2. Click the down arrow next to the upper-left text box. Select is greater than.
3. Click the down arrow next to the upper-right text box. The values in the Due column are shown. You can select a value from this list, or you can key a value.

FIGURE 23-10
Custom AutoFilter
dialog box

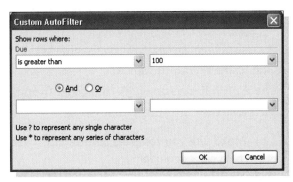

4. Click in the box and key **100**. Click OK. Six records match this criteria of an amount due that is greater than $100.
5. Click the AutoFilter arrow for the Due column and choose (Custom…).
6. Key **300** in the upper-right text box.

7. Choose And if it is not already selected.
8. Click the down arrow next to the lower-left text box and select is less than.
9. Key **800** in the lower-right text box. This filter will find amounts due that are between $300 and $800. (See Figure 23-11 on the next page.)

FIGURE 23-11
An "And" custom
AutoFilter

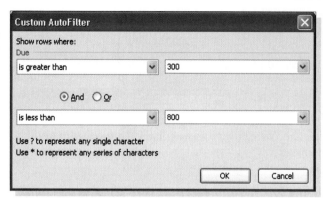

10. Click OK. Two records meet the criteria.

11. Click the AutoFilter arrow for the Due field and choose (All).

12. Click the AutoFilter arrow for the Last field and choose (Custom...).

13. Click the down arrow next to the upper-left text box and choose equals if it is not already selected.

14. Click the down arrow next to the upper-right text box and choose Smith. Choose Or.

15. Click the down arrow next to the lower-left text box and choose equals. Click the down arrow next to the lower-right text box and choose Small. This filter will show customers whose name is either Smith or Small.

16. Click OK. The filtered list shows records for Smith and Small.

17. Display all the rows.

EXERCISE 23-13 Reset the Toolbar

1. From the Data menu, choose Filter and then AutoFilter to turn off the AutoFilter.

2. From the View menu, choose Toolbars and Customize.

3. Click the Toolbars tab. Notice that the Standard toolbar is highlighted in the list.

4. Click Reset. An information box appears asking if you want to reset changes made to the Standard toolbar.

5. Click OK. The AutoFilter button is removed from the toolbar.

6. Click Close to close the Customize dialog box.

> **NOTE:** Make sure you complete this exercise to leave Excel in its default state for the next class or student.

Creating Advanced Filters

If your filtering requirements are more complex than AutoFilter can accommodate, you can use an advanced filter. It is more flexible but does require a bit more work on your part. In an advanced filter, you can:

- Use more complex criteria.
- Use computations in the criteria.
- Extract or copy the filtered results to another location.

E X E R C I S E **23-14** **Set the Criteria Range**

When you use an advanced filter, you must first set up a criteria range. A *criteria range* is a designated area on a worksheet specifying the conditions that filtered data must meet. The criteria range must be at least two rows. The first row of the criteria range must contain some or all of the field names used in the list. In the rows below a field name, you key the conditions or filters for the field.

When creating a criteria range, follow these guidelines:

- If you key criteria for more than one field in the same row, you have created a filter in which the conditions are connected by an "And."
- If you key criteria for more than one field in different rows, you have created a filter in which the conditions are connected by an "Or."

1. Insert a new worksheet and position it to the right of the OutOfState worksheet.
2. Rename Sheet1 as **Criteria**.

 TIP: It is good practice to place criteria on a separate worksheet. If you add or delete records or field names from the list, the criteria range is not affected.

3. Display the OutOfState worksheet. Copy the range A3:J3 to cell A2 in the Criteria worksheet.

 TIP: Copying field names from the list to the criteria range ensures that field names are identical.

4. On the Criteria worksheet, select the range A2:J3.
5. Click the Name Box and key **Criteria**. Press Enter. Note that the criteria range should specify at least two rows.

E X E R C I S E **23-15** **Filter Data in Place**

When you filter in place, the results of the filter are displayed in the existing list, similar to an AutoFilter.

1. Select cell B3 on the Criteria worksheet, key **smith**, and press Enter.
2. Display the OutOfState worksheet and click anywhere in the list.

3. From the Data menu, choose Filter and Advanced Filter. The Advanced Filter dialog box opens with the List range and Criteria range already specified. When you use the name "Database" for your list and "Criteria" for the criteria range, Excel automatically uses these ranges in an advanced filter.

FIGURE 23-12
Creating an
advanced filter

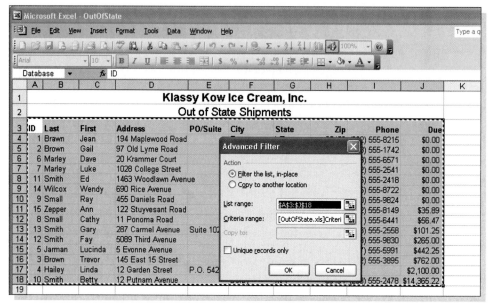

4. Choose Filter the list, in-place if it is not already selected.

5. Click OK. The list is filtered to show customers named Smith.

6. From the Data menu, choose Filter and Show All. The filter is removed.

EXERCISE 23-16 **Create an Output Range**

You can also copy the results of an advanced filter to another location in the worksheet, known as the *output range*. Unlike a filter in place, the rows in the original list are not changed. The output range must be on the same sheet as the list.

1. On the OutOfState worksheet, select the range A3:J3 and copy it to cell M3 on the same sheet.

2. Select the range M3:V3 if it is not already selected.

3. Click the Name Box, key **Output**, and press [Enter]. You need to specify only the header row for an output range. Filtered results will use as many rows as needed under the output header row.

4. Select cell M3 to deselect the range.

NOTE: Normally you would not want to place an output range in the rows below your list. The area below the list should be reserved for new records added to the list.

EXERCISE 23-17 Filter Data to an Output Range

Although your output range includes all the fields of your list, you can create output ranges that contain only selected fields, and the fields can be in any order.

1. Return to the Criteria worksheet. The criteria range still includes Smith in the Last field.

2. Key **ct** in cell G3. This is an "And" filter because both the Last and the State criteria are on the same row.

FIGURE 23-13
Criteria range for an advanced "And" filter

	A	B	C	D	E	F	G	H	I	J
1										
2	ID	Last	First	Address	PO/Suite	City	State	Zip	Phone	Due
3		smith					ct			
4										

OutofState \ Criteria

3. Return to the OutOfState worksheet. Select any cell in the list.

4. From the Data menu, choose Filter and Advanced Filter. The List range and Criteria range are already specified.

5. Choose Copy to another location. The Copy to text box becomes available.

6. In the Copy to text box, key **output**.

7. Click OK. Scroll to cell M3 to see your output. Only one row meets the criteria. Widen columns if necessary.

8. Display the Criteria worksheet.

9. Delete the existing criteria in cells B3 and G3.

10. In cell D3, key ***str*** to find customers whose address includes the word "Street." You need to key only as much of the word as necessary to distinguish it.

11. In cell D4, key ***court*** to find customers whose address includes the word "Court." This is an "Or" filter because the criteria are on separate rows.

12. From the Insert menu, choose Name and Define. The Define Name dialog box opens. You'll need to extend the criteria range to include the new row, because the existing named range is defined as A2:J3.

13. In the Names in workbook list, select Criteria. Edit the range in the Refers to text box to include row 4. (The address should read:=Criteria!$A$2:$J$4.)

14. Click OK. The criteria range has been extended to include the new row.

15. Return to the OutOfState worksheet and select any cell in the list.

16. From the Data menu, choose Filter and Advanced Filter.

17. Select Copy to another location. Notice that Excel uses your last output range in the Copy to text box.

 TIP: When the insertion point is in the Copy to text box, you can press F3 and choose the output range.

18. If the Copy to text box does not show the range $M$3:$V$3, key **output**. Click OK. The new output replaces any existing data.

19. Scroll to see the filtered rows starting in column M. The filter has copied records that include the words "Street" or "Court" in the Address field.

 NOTE: When you copy records in an advanced filter, Excel adds the range named "Extract" to your list of named ranges.

20. Add your standard footer. Set the sheet to landscape orientation.

21. On the Sheet tab, show gridlines and row and column headings.

22. Save the workbook as *[your initials]***23-17** in your Lesson 23 folder.

23. Print the OutOfState worksheet.

24. Select the entire output range and choose Edit, Clear, All.

Adding Subtotals to a List

If your data is organized in a list, you can use the Subtotals command to insert subtotals based on groups of data. When you use this command, Excel creates formulas that calculate values for certain rows in a list. The formulas use statistical functions, such as SUM, AVERAGE, and COUNT.

Excel presents subtotal results in an outline. An *outline* groups worksheet rows into detail and summary rows.

EXERCISE 23-18 Subtotal with COUNT

To add subtotals to a list, you must first sort the rows by the column in which you want to show a subtotal. In this exercise, you'll create subtotals in the State field.

1. Select any cell in the State field in the list.
2. Click the Sort Ascending button ![sort icon]. The rows are arranged in alphabetical order by State.
3. From the <u>D</u>ata menu, choose Su<u>b</u>totals. The Subtotal dialog box opens.
4. Click the down arrow for <u>A</u>t each change in and select State. Every time the state changes, Excel will calculate a subtotal.
5. Click the down arrow for the <u>U</u>se function text box. View the list of available functions. You can use any of these functions to calculate a subtotal.
6. Select Count. Excel will count the number of records for each state.
7. In the A<u>d</u>d subtotal to text box, click to remove the check mark for Due. Scroll up the list and click to place a check mark for State.

FIGURE 23-14
Subtotal dialog box

8. Click OK. The list is grouped by state with a count of the number of records for each state. The outline shows each group expanded so that you see all the records for each state. (See Figure 23-15 on the next page.)

9. Click the first minus symbol (−) at row 5. The detail row for California is hidden, and only the California count is shown.

10. Hide the detail for each of the other states to show only the counts.

11. Click the Level 3 outline symbol. The third level displays all the rows.
12. Click the Level 2 outline symbol. The second level shows only the counts.
13. Click the Level 1 outline symbol. The first level is the grand total only.
14. Click the Level 3 outline symbol. All the rows display.

FIGURE 23-15
Subtotals in the
worksheet

Outline-level symbols

Minus symbols

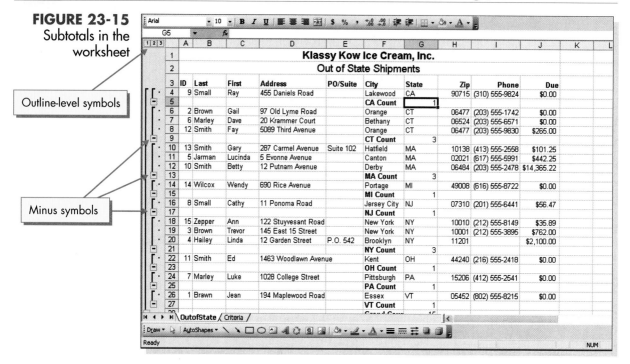

EXERCISE 23-19 Subtotal with AVERAGE

In this exercise, you'll create subtotals that calculate averages. You'll create subtotals for the average amount due by state.

1. From the Data menu, choose Subtotals. The Subtotal dialog box opens.

2. In the At each change in text box, select State if it is not already selected.

3. Click the down arrow for the Use function text box and select Average. The subtotal formula will be an average.

4. In the Add subtotal to text box, remove the check mark for State and place one for Due. Your subtotal will calculate averages in the Due field every time the state changes.

5. Select Replace current subtotals if it is not already selected.

6. Click OK. Scroll to see the Due column if necessary. Subtotals appear in this column. It shows average Due amounts by state.

7. From the Data menu, choose Subtotals. The Subtotal dialog box opens.

8. Click Remove All. All subtotals are removed.

Using Database Functions

Database functions perform statistical calculations on field values that match conditions that you specify. This allows you to control which fields are used in the calculation.

Database functions use the following syntax: *FunctionName(ListName,Field, Criteria)*. The first argument, *ListName*, refers to the list range on the worksheet. You can enter it as a cell range if you have not named the list.

The second argument, *Field,* is the field or column used in the calculation. You can key the field name in quotation marks or key the field's column number in the list. The first column in the list (starting at the left) is 1, the second column is 2, and so on.

The third argument, *Criteria,* is the range that contains the criteria for the records to be included in the calculation. You can enter it by cell address or range name.

TABLE 23-1   Database Functions

FUNCTION	RESULT
DAVERAGE	Averages the values in a field.
DCOUNT	Counts the cells with numbers in a field.
DCOUNTA	Counts the nonblank cells in a field.
DMAX	Displays the largest value in the field.
DMIN	Displays the smallest value in the field.
DSUM	Adds the values in the field.
DGET	Extracts or displays a single record that matches the criteria.

EXERCISE 23-20 Use DMIN

You can use the DMIN function to find the smallest Due amount in the list for amounts greater than zero.

1. Press Shift + F11 to insert a new worksheet. Position the new worksheet to the right of the OutOfState worksheet and rename it **Statistics**.

2. In cell A1, key **Statistics for Out of State Shipments**. Make it 16-point Arial.

3. From the OutOfState worksheet, copy the range A3:J3 to cell A15 in the Statistics worksheet. This part of the worksheet will be a criteria range.

4. In cell J16, key **>0**. With this criterion, the amount due must be greater than 0 for the record to be used in the formula.

5. In cell A2, key **Minimum Amount Due**. Widen column A to accommodate the label.

 6. Select cell B2 and click the Insert Function button .

7. Click the down arrow for the Or select a category text box and select Database. In the Select a function list, select DMIN. Click OK. The Function Arguments dialog box opens.

FIGURE 23-16
The DMIN function and its arguments

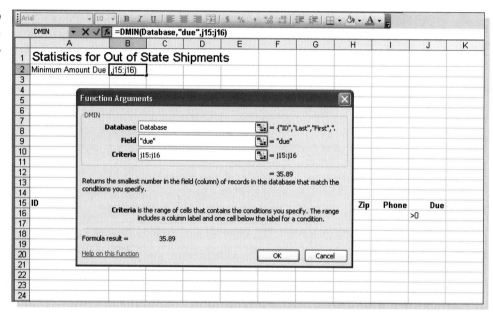

8. With the insertion point in the Database text box, press F3. The Paste Name dialog box opens. Double-click Database, the name of your list.

9. In the Field text box, key **"due"** including the quotation marks. This is the name of the field in your list that is to be used in this calculation.

10. In the Criteria text box, key **j15:j16**, the range which holds your criteria. Click OK. The result is the smallest amount due in the list, excluding the records with 0 amounts.

EXERCISE 23-21 Use DCOUNT

In this exercise, you'll use the DCOUNT database function to count the number of records in the list with Due amounts greater than 0.

1. In cell A3, key **Number of Customers Who Owe**. Widen column A to accommodate the label.

2. Select cell B3 and click the Insert Function button .

3. Select the Database category if it is not already selected and then select DCOUNT in the Select a function list. Click OK. The Function Arguments dialog box opens.

4. With the insertion point in the Database text box, press F3. The Paste Name dialog box opens.

5. Double-click Database. The Function Arguments dialog box is still open. The named range Database appears in the Database text box.

6. Select the Field text box and key **1** for the first column in the list. You can key either the field name in quotes, or the column number, with the leftmost column in the list numbered as 1.

7. Select the Criteria text box and key **j15:j16**. Click OK. The result is the number of records with a Due amount greater than 0.

8. Add your footer. Set the page orientation to landscape.

9. Save the workbook as *[your initials]*23-21 in your Lesson 23 folder.

10. Print the Statistics worksheet.

Publishing a Workbook to the Web

When you save a workbook as a Web page, you can publish it as an interactive workbook. An *interactive workbook* allows users to change the data and the layout while viewing the worksheet on the Web. A noninteractive workbook is an HTML file that can only be viewed.

E X E R C I S E **23-22** **Publish a Worksheet with Interactivity**

When you publish worksheet data, you should name a range that includes all the cells with data that should be visible to the viewer. As a default, Excel publishes the entire worksheet with all empty cells if you do not select a specific range.

1. Click the OutOfState worksheet tab.

2. Select cells A3:J25. This range includes the header row and provides some blank rows for new records.

3. Click the Name box and key **WebData**. Press Enter. Click any cell in the list to deselect the range.

4. From the File menu, choose Save as Web Page.

5. In the Save group, click to place a check mark for Selection: Sheet.

6. Click to place a check mark for Add interactivity.

7. Double "Page" in the File name text box and key *[your initials]*23-22. Verify that the folder is your Lesson 23 folder.

8. Click <u>C</u>hange Title. In the <u>T</u>itle text box, key **New Shipments** and click OK.

9. Click <u>P</u>ublish. The Publish as Web Page dialog box opens.

10. Click the down arrow for <u>C</u>hoose and choose Range of cells. This allows you to specify your named range instead of all the cells.

11. Click in the text box below the Choose box and press [F3]. The Paste Name dialog box opens.

12. Double-click WebData. The name appears with an = sign in the text box.

13. Verify that the Viewing options show <u>A</u>dd interactivity with Spreadsheet functionality.

14. Click to place a check mark for <u>O</u>pen published web page in browser. This will show the page in your browser without establishing an Internet connection.

FIGURE 23-17
Publish as Web
Page dialog box

15. Click <u>P</u>ublish. The worksheet opens in your browser.

EXERCISE 23-23 Edit the Web Page

The Web page includes a toolbar with available commands. Although you can perform several typical tasks, not all commands are available. For a Web page to be truly interactive, of course, it must be published on a Web server that allows authorized users to use its pages.

1. Click the AutoFilter button [img]. The AutoFilter arrows are added to the header row.

2. Click the State AutoFilter arrow. The list is slightly different from a regular worksheet.

3. Click to remove the check mark for (Show All).

4. Click to place a check mark for MA. Click OK. The records are filtered to show customers in Massachusetts.

5. Click the State AutoFilter arrow. Click to place a check mark for (Show All).

6. Click OK. The entire list is shown.

7. Click anywhere in the Last field. Click the Sort Ascending button . The records are sorted in alphabetical order by last name.

8. Select cell A17. Add a record using information about yourself. To key an amount due, you must include the dollar sign and decimal point.

FIGURE 23-18
Changing the
Web page

New Shipments

IC	Last	First	Address	PO/Suite	City	State	Z	Pho	
1	Brawn	Jean	194 Maplewood Road		Essex	VT	05452	(802) 555-8215	
2	Brown	Gail	97 Old Lyme Road		Orange	CT	06477	(203) 555-1742	
3	Brown	Trevor	145 East 15 Street		New York	NY	10001	(212) 555-3895	$:
4	Hailey	Linda	12 Garden Street	P.O. 542	Brooklyn	NY	11201		$2,:
5	Jarman	Lucinda	5 Evonne Avenue		Canton	MA	02021	(617) 555-5991	$4
6	Marley	Dave	20 Krammer Court		Bethany	CT	06524	(203) 555-6571	
7	Marley	Luke	1028 College Street		Pittsburgh	PA	15206	(412) 555-2541	
9	Small	Ray	455 Daniels Road		Lakewood	CA	90715	(310) 555-9824	
8	Small	Cathy	11 Ponoma Road		Jersey City	NJ	07310	(201) 555-6441	!
12	Smith	Fay	5089 Third Avenue		Orange	CT	06477	(203) 555-9830	$:
13	Smith	Gary	287 Carmel Avenue	Suite 102	Hatfield	MA	10138	(413) 555-2558	$
10	Smith	Betty	12 Putnam Avenue		Derby	MA	06484	(203) 555-2478	$14,:
11	Smith	Ed	1463 Woodlawn Avenue		Kent	OH	44240	(216) 555-2418	
14	Wilcox	Wendy	690 Rice Avenue		Portage	MI	49008	(616) 555-8722	
15	Zepper	Ann	122 Stuyvesant Road		New York	NY	10010	(212) 555-8149	!
16	Stewart	Kathleen	4455 West Main Street		Chicago	IL	60601	(312) 555-0000	

OutofState

9. Close the browser and return to Excel.

NOTE: Your Web page is not actually published to a server, so your changes are not saved.

10. Close the workbook without saving.

Creating and Editing Outlines

An outline groups and summarizes data. An outline report can show all details, selected details, or only summary data. Excel creates outlines automatically when you use the Subtotals and Consolidate commands. You can create your own outlines by preparing the data properly for an outline. Outline data is usually a list with subtotals and grand totals. The formulas that calculate the subtotals and grand totals must be in a consistent location on the worksheet.

An outline can be arranged by row or by column. In a row outline, formula rows are either above or below the related data. In a column outline, formula columns are either to the left or the right of related columns.

 TIP: In most row outlines, the summary row is below the data. In most column outlines, the summary column is to the right of the data.

When working with outlines, keep these points in mind.

- A worksheet can have only one outline.
- An outline can include all the data on a worksheet or a selected range of data.
- An outline can have up to eight levels.

EXERCISE 23-24 Use the SUBTOTAL Function

The SUBTOTAL function can be used for intermediate calculations. You can use it for a sum, but you can also you use it for averages, counts, standard deviations, and more.

1. Open **DropCard.** This list shows four states and cities for each of those states. It lists each month for each city, a quarterly summary, and a year-end total.

2. Click cell E5. The Subtotal function creates a subtotal with the calculation that you choose.

3. Click the Insert Function button 🔣. In the Search for a function box, key **subtotal** and press Enter. The SUBTOTAL function is found.

4. Click OK. The Function Arguments dialog box for SUBTOTAL opens. It has two arguments, Function_num and Ref1. The function number is a number that you key from 1 to 11.

5. Click Help on this function. A help window identifies the 11 functions that you can use for a subtotal. For a sum, you use 9. (See Figure 23-19.)

6. Close the Help window.

7. Key **9** in the Function_num box.

8. Click in the Ref1 box. This is the range to be subtotaled.

9. Click cell B5 and drag to select cells B5:D5. The range address appears in the text box.

10. Click OK. The subtotal is 35.

11. Use the Fill handle to copy the formula to cells E6:E18.

FIGURE 23-19
Getting help for
SUBTOTAL

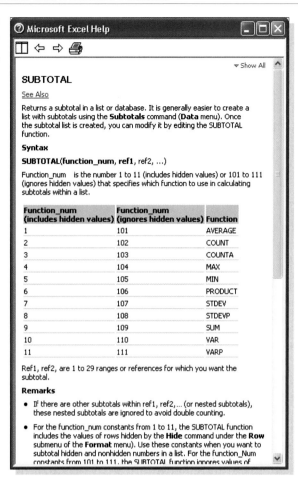

12. Select cells E5:E18. Hold down $\boxed{\text{Ctrl}}$ and drag a copy of the range to cells I5:I18. This copies the formula with a relative reference.

13. Copy the range to cells M5:M18 and Q5:Q18.

14. Click cell E21 to key the Subtotal function.

15. Key **=subtotal(9,** to start the function using SUM as the calculation.

16. Select the range B21:D21 and press $\boxed{\text{Enter}}$.

17. Use the Fill handle to copy the formula for the cities in Oregon. Then copy the formulas for the other quarters.

18. Complete the Subtotal function for Nevada and Washington.

SUBTOTAL

See Also

Returns a subtotal in a list or database. It is generally easier to create a list with subtotals using the **Subtotals** command (**Data** menu). Once the subtotal list is created, you can modify it by editing the SUBTOTAL function.

Syntax

SUBTOTAL(function_num, ref1, ref2, ...)

Function_num   is the number 1 to 11 (includes hidden values) or 101 to 111 (ignores hidden values) that specifies which function to use in calculating subtotals within a list.

Function_num (includes hidden values)	Function_num (ignores hidden values)	Function
1	101	AVERAGE
2	102	COUNT
3	103	COUNTA
4	104	MAX
5	105	MIN
6	106	PRODUCT
7	107	STDEV
8	108	STDEVP
9	109	SUM
10	110	VAR
11	111	VARP

Ref1, ref2, are 1 to 29 ranges or references for which you want the subtotal.

Remarks

● If there are other subtotals within ref1, ref2,... (or nested subtotals), these nested subtotals are ignored to avoid double counting.

● For the function_num constants from 1 to 11, the SUBTOTAL function includes the values of rows hidden by the **Hide** command under the **Row** submenu of the **Format** menu). Use these constants when you want to subtotal hidden and nonhidden numbers in a list. For the function_Num constants from 101 to 111, the SUBTOTAL function ignores values of

EXERCISE **23-25** **Add Grand Totals**

The grand totals include one for each city by year, one for each state by month, and the total for all states.

1. Click cell R5. This formula simply adds the four quarters.

2. Key = and click cell E5. Key + and click cell I5. Key + and click cell M5. Key + and click cell Q5. Press $\boxed{\text{Enter}}$. The total is 135.

3. Use the Fill handle to copy the formula to cells R6:R18.

 TIP: Set your workbook to a Zoom percentage that allows you to work with a minimum of scrolling.

4. Use whatever method you prefer to copy this formula to cells R21:R25, cells R28:R33, and cells R36:R43. Click any copied cell to verify the same formula with a relative cell reference.

5. Select cells B19:R19. Click the AutoSum button Σ ▾.

6. Repeat these steps for rows 26, 34, and 43.

7. Click cell B44. The formula should add each of the monthly state totals.

8. Key = and click cell B19. Key + and click cell B26. Key + and click cell B34. Key + and click cell B43. Press Enter. The total is 505.

9. Use the Fill handle to copy the formula to cells C44:R44.

EXERCISE 23-26 Create an Auto Outline

With a list prepared and formulas in a consistent location, Excel can create an Auto Outline. Using your formulas, it will create the appropriate style and number of levels.

1. Click cell A5. Click any cell in the list to create the outline.

2. From the Data menu, choose Group and Outline and Auto Outline. Excel creates a combination row and column outline. There are three row levels and three column levels.

FIGURE 23-20
Auto Outline

Column-level symbols

Row-level symbols

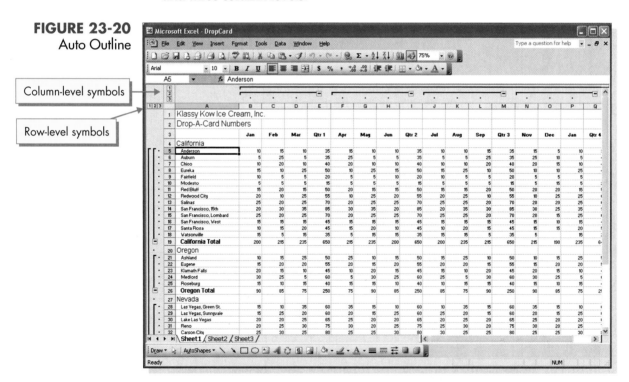

3. Click the Level 1 column symbol. Only the city total is displayed.

4. Click the Level 2 column symbol. The quarters and city total are shown, but not the individual months.

5. Click the Level 3 column symbol. All the column details are displayed.

6. Click the Level 1 row symbol. Only the monthly grand total is displayed.

7. Click the Level 2 row symbol. The state totals are displayed, but not the cities.

8. While the second level is shown, you can expand an individual state.

9. Click the + (Expand) symbol next to row 19, the California Total row. The California group is expanded, and all the cities are shown.

10. Click the – (Collapse) symbol next to row 19. California details are hidden.

11. Click the Level 3 row symbol. All details are displayed.

EXERCISE 23-27 Build a Chart for an Outline

With outlined data, you can build a summary chart. You can hide the details that should not be shown and create a chart as usual.

1. Click the Level 2 row symbol. These are state totals.

2. Click the Level 2 column symbol. These are quarter totals.

3. Click cell A19. Hold down Ctrl and click cell R19. This selects a label and a total for California.

4. Hold down Ctrl and click cell A26. Hold down Ctrl and click cell R26. This selects data for Oregon.

 REVIEW: Use the Ctrl key to add as many noncontiguous cells to the selection as necessary.

5. Hold down Ctrl and click cell A34. Hold down Ctrl and click cell R34 to select data for Nevada.

6. Hold down Ctrl and click cell A43. Hold down Ctrl and click cell R43. This adds Washington to the selection.

 7. Click the Chart Wizard button . Choose the first sub-type for a Column chart and click Finish. A column chart is added to the worksheet.

8. Position and size the chart to be below the data. Deselect the chart.

9. Preview the worksheet. Resize the chart if necessary so that the data and chart will fit on a single landscape page.

10. Add your footer.

11. Save the workbook as *[your initials]*23-27 in your Lesson 23 folder.

12. Print the worksheet and close the workbook.

EXERCISE **23-28** **Create a Row Outline Manually**

Before you can manually create outline groupings in a list without formulas, you need to insert empty rows below each group. Excel uses these empty rows for summary information.

1. Open **OutOfState**.
2. Name cells A3:J18 as **Database**.
3. Click in the State column and sort in ascending order.
4. Insert a blank row at row 5.
5. Click the row 4 heading to select the row.
6. From the <u>Data</u> menu, choose <u>Group</u> and Outline and <u>Group</u>.
7. Locate the outline symbols on the left side of the worksheet. Row 4 is the group for California.
8. Insert a blank row at row 9. Insert a blank row at row 13. Insert a blank row at each of these rows: 15, 17, 21, 23, and 25.
9. Select rows 6 through 8, the CT records.
10. From the <u>Data</u> menu, choose <u>Group</u> and Outline and <u>Group</u>. The three rows are a group.

 TIP: The Repeat command repeats the last command. It is listed in the Edit menu.

11. Select rows 10 through 12, the MA records. Press Ctrl+Y to repeat the <u>Group</u> command.
12. Select row 14 and press Ctrl+Y.
13. Select row 16 and press Ctrl+Y.
14. Select rows 18 through 20 and press Ctrl+Y.
15. Add groups for the remaining three states.

EXERCISE **23-29** **Expand and Hide Details**

After you've manually set up an outline, you can display only those portions of your list that are needed.

1. Click the Level 1 outline symbol. Because there is no data in the totals row, nothing is shown.
2. Click the Level 2 outline symbol. The outline is expanded. You can hide individual groupings by clicking the outline symbols.
3. Click the minus symbol (–) for the CA record. The record is hidden.

4. Click the minus symbols (–) for MI, NJ, OH, PA, and VT. Only the CT, MA, and NY groups should be displayed.

5. Set a print area for the range A1:J20.

 REVIEW: Set and clear a print area from the File menu.

6. Add your footer.

7. Save the file as *[your initials]***23-29** in your Lesson 23 folder.

8. Print the worksheet and close the workbook.

USING ONLINE HELP

Publishing data on the Web is a common but challenging task. Learn more about options for placing your data and what commands are available on the Web.

Use Help to learn about Web publishing:

1. With Internet Explorer and Excel running, look for topics about **publishing**.

2. Read the information. Close the windows.

3. Close Internet Explorer and end your Internet connection if appropriate.

LESSON Summary

➤ A list is a series of rows and columns that contain related information, similar to a database.

➤ Lists have a single header row, followed by rows of data, known as records. Each column is a field. Field names must be unique. Do not leave blank rows within a list.

➤ Name a list to include the header row and all the data rows.

➤ You can use the data form to enter, edit, and find records in a list. Excel finds the records to match criteria you key.

➤ You can sort data in a list in ascending or descending order. Use the buttons on the Standard toolbar to perform quick, one-column sorts on lists. Use the Sort dialog box to sort list data by more than one column.

➤ A filter is a procedure for creating a subset of data in a list, according to specified conditions.

➤ When AutoFilter is active, drop-down arrows display in the header row. Filtering options can be set by choosing from the lists.

➤ The Top 10 AutoFilter can show the top or bottom of the list. Either a number or a percentage can be used to filter the data.

➤ Use a custom AutoFilter to create custom criteria, including comparison operators, such as greater than (>) or less than (<). You can use "And" and "Or" operators for multiple conditions.

➤ Use advanced filters when filtering requirements are more complex than an AutoFilter can accommodate.

➤ Advanced filters use a criteria range, a worksheet area specifying conditions for filtered data.

➤ You can use an advanced filter to copy the results to another location on the same worksheet as the list.

➤ The Subtotals feature automatically inserts subtotal calculations based on groups of data. The results are presented in an outline, which groups data into detail and summary rows and/or columns.

➤ The Database functions are a group of functions for lists. These functions perform calculations on field values that match conditions you specify.

➤ You can save a worksheet as a Web page with interactivity so that users can edit it while viewing it in a browser.

➤ Outlines can be created automatically for some lists if they include properly organized data and formulas.

LESSON 23 Command Summary

FEATURE	BUTTON	MENU	KEYBOARD
Advanced Filter		Data, Filter, Advanced Filter	
AutoFilter	▼≡	Data, Filter, AutoFilter	
Auto Outline		Data, Group and Outline, Auto Outline	
Data Form		Data, Form	
List, Create		Data, List and Create List	Ctrl + L
Outline, Create		Data, Group and Outline, Group	
Outline, Remove		Data, Group and Outline, Clear Outline	
Repeat		Edit, Repeat (task name)	Ctrl + Y
Sort, Ascending	A↓Z	Data, Sort	
Sort, Descending	Z↓A	Data, Sort	
Subtotals		Data, Subtotals	

Concepts Review

TRUE/FALSE QUESTIONS

Each of the following statements is either true or false. Indicate your choice by circling T or F.

T F   **1.** Any worksheet can be used as a list.

T F   **2.** The first row in a list is the header row.

T F   **3.** Outline commands are listed in the Tools menu.

T F   **4.** The range name for a list should include only the data rows.

T F   **5.** A data form shows the columns from the list in a vertical layout.

T F   **6.** The SUBTOTAL function can use SUM, AVERAGE, or others to calculate a value.

T F   **7.** Web pages can be interactive or noninteractive.

T F   **8.** The database functions use the same arguments as Statistical functions.

SHORT ANSWER QUESTIONS

Write the correct answer in the space provided.

1. Which command groups records into detail and summary rows and columns if the formulas are already present?

_____

2. Name two database functions.

_____

3. What should you do if you want users to be able to edit your worksheet on the Web?

_____

4. What term describes a subset of data in a list, based on specific conditions?

_____

5. Name two functions that you can use with the Subtotals command.

_____

6. If you want to display the five youngest workers in a list, which AutoFilter option should you choose?

_____

7. In a data form, how can you move from one field to the next?

_____

8. How can you enter "And" criteria in an advanced filter?

_____

CRITICAL THINKING

Answer these questions on a separate page. There are no right or wrong answers. Support your answers with examples from your own experience, if possible.

1. Suppose that your company keeps all its sales orders in a list. The columns are the date, the customer ID, the ship date, the shipper, the sales representative, the total amount, and the discount. Describe what you might be able to do with AutoFilters in this list.

2. Describe the difference between the statistical function AVERAGE and the database function DAVERAGE.

Skills Review

EXERCISE 23-30

Prepare a list.

1. Open the file **DayCount1**.

2. Prepare a list by following these steps:

    a. Use AutoFill to complete the header row in row 3.

    b. Make the labels in row 3 bold and centered.

    c. Name the range A3:I30 as **Database**. (_Hint:_ Click the first header label, press F8, and then press Ctrl+End to quickly highlight the list.)

3. Format the labels in cells A1:A2 as 16-point Arial. Center these two cells across the list columns. Adjust the row heights and column widths to show these labels as well as those in row 3.

4. Use the data form to enter new records in the list by following these steps:

    a. Select any cell in the list. From the Data menu, choose Form.

    b. Click New.

c. Using the data shown in Figure 23-21, key five new records. Press (Tab) to move from field to field; click New or press (Enter) when a record is finished to start the next record.

FIGURE 23-21

City	State	Monday	Tuesday	Wednesday	Thursday	Friday	Saturday	Sunday
Ashland	OR	100	85	85	125	150	200	125
Eugene	OR	155	90	140	200	135	185	150
Klamath Falls	OR	115	150	125	100	150	145	150
Medford	OR	100	190	170	135	135	185	150
Roseburg	OR	175	135	190	165	150	225	130

d. When the last record is keyed, click Close to close the data form.

5. Add your usual footer. Set the orientation to landscape and horizontally center the worksheet.

6. Save the workbook as *[your initials]*23-30 in your Lesson 23 folder.

7. Print the worksheet and close the workbook.

EXERCISE 23-31

Sort data. Use filters.

1. Open the file **DayCount2**.

2. Name the list, including the header and all the data rows, as **Database**.

3. Sort data by following these steps:

a. Select any cell in the City field.

b. Click the Sort Ascending button on the Standard toolbar.

4. Add your footer. Set the orientation to landscape and horizontally center the worksheet.

5. Save the workbook as *[your initials]*23-31a in your Lesson 23 folder.

6. Print the worksheet.

7. Select any cell in the Sunday field, and click the Sort Descending button on the Standard toolbar.

8. Create a Top 10 AutoFilter by following these steps:

    a. From the Data menu, choose Filter and AutoFilter.
    b. Click the AutoFilter arrow for Sunday and select (Top 10…).
    c. Click OK.

9. Save the workbook as *[your initials]*23-31b in your Lesson 23 folder and print the worksheet.

10. Click the AutoFilter arrow for Sunday and select (All).

11. Create a custom AutoFilter by following these steps:

    a. Click the AutoFilter arrow for Monday and select (Custom…)
    b. Click the down arrow next to the upper-left text box and select is less than.
    c. Click in the upper-right text box and key **100**.
    d. Click OK.

12. Save the workbook as *[your initials]*23-31c in your Lesson 23 folder and print the worksheet.

13. Close the workbook.

EXERCISE 23-32

Create an advanced filter. Add subtotals in a list. Use database functions.

1. Open the file **DayCount2**.
2. Name the list as **Database**.
3. Set up a criteria range by following these steps:

    a. Insert a new worksheet, rename it **Criteria**, and position it to the right of the CustCount worksheet.
    b. Display the CustCount worksheet and copy the range A3:I3 to cell A2 in the Criteria worksheet.
    c. Key **Criteria Sheet** in cell A1 in the Criteria worksheet and make it 14-point Arial italic. Increase the height of row 2 and adjust column widths where necessary.
    d. On the Criteria worksheet, select the range A2:I3. Name the range as **Criteria**.

4. Set up an output range by following these steps:

    a. On the CustCount worksheet, copy the range A3:I3 to cell K3.
    b. Select the range K3:S3 and name the range as **Output**.

5. Create an advanced filter by following these steps:

    a. On the Criteria worksheet, key **nv** in cell B3.
    b. Display the CustCount worksheet and select any cell in the list.
    c. From the Data menu, choose Filter and Advanced Filter.
    d. Select Copy to another location.
    e. Select the Copy to text box and key **output**.
    f. Click OK.

6. Add your footer. Set the orientation to landscape and horizontally center the worksheet.

7. Save the workbook as *[your initials]***23-32a** in your Lesson 23 folder.

8. Set a print area for the extracted records. Adjust column widths as needed and print the area.

9. Clear the print area.

10. Create subtotals by following these steps:

   a. Click anywhere in the list. Sort the list by State in ascending order if it is not already in this order.
   b. From the Data menu, choose Subtotals.
   c. Click the down arrow next to the At each change in text box and select State.
   d. Click the down arrow next to the Use function text box and select Sum if it is not already displayed.
   e. In the Add subtotal to list, click to place a check mark for each of the seven days.
   f. Click OK.

11. Click the Level 2 outline symbol to display only the state totals. Hide column A and adjust the width of the other columns.

12. Set a print area for the range B3:I40.

13. Save the workbook as *[your initials]***23-32b** in your Lesson 23 folder. Print the sheet and close the workbook.

14. Use database functions by following these steps:

   a. Open **Properties**. Name cells A3:I27 as **Database**.
   b. Insert a new worksheet to the right of the Properties sheet and name it **Summary**.
   c. In cell A1, key **Summary of Property Information for Homes Less Than 15 Years Old**. Make it 14-point Times New Roman.
   d. In cell A3, key **Highest Price**. In cell A4, key **Lowest Price**. In cell A5, key **Number of Homes**. Make all three labels 12-point Times New Roman and adjust the width of column A appropriately.
   e. Display the Properties worksheet and copy cells A3:I3 to cell K3.
   f. Key **<15** in cell P4.
   g. Display the Summary worksheet, select cell B3, and click the Insert Function button .
   h. Click the down arrow next to the Or select a category text box and choose Database if it is not already selected.
   i. In the Select a function list, choose DMAX. Click OK.
   j. In the Database text box, press F3, and double-click Database.
   k. In the Field text box key **"price"** with quotation marks.
   l. Click in the Criteria box. Click the Properties tab and select the range P3:P4. Click OK.

NOTE: When you select criteria from another worksheet, Excel includes an identifier with the worksheet name and an exclamation point.

m. Select cell B4 and click the Insert Function button .

n. From the Database category, choose DMIN. Click OK.

o. In the Database text box, press F3, and double-click Database.

p. In the Field text box, key **"price"** with quotation marks.

q. Click in the Criteria box. Click the Properties tab and select the range P3:P4. Click OK.

15. In cell B5, create a DCOUNT database function.

16. Format the range B3:B4 as Currency with no decimals. Change the font for the range B3:B5 to 12-point Times New Roman. Verify that the values are right-aligned.

TIP: If values don't appear right-aligned when choosing formats from the toolbar, reselect the cells and format them from the Format Cells dialog box.

17. Add your footer. Save the workbook as *[your initials]***23-32c** in your Lesson 23 folder and print the Summary worksheet.

18. Make a copy of the Summary worksheet and display the formulas on the copy. Adjust column B so that the formulas are visible, and set the worksheet to landscape orientation. Print the formula sheet.

19. Save and close the workbook.

EXERCISE 23-33

Create and edit an outline. Publish a workbook to the Web.

1. Open the file **Properties**.

2. Make a copy of the Properties sheet and rename it **ByPrice**.

3. In the ByPrice worksheet, name the list as **Database**.

4. Select any cell in the list and sort in descending order by price.

5. Create an outline by following these steps:

a. Right-click the row 7 heading and insert a row. In cell A7, key **Over $200,000**. Make it bold.

b. Insert a blank row at row 14. In cell A14, key **$150,000 to $199,999**. Make it bold.

c. Insert a row at row 22. In cell A22, key **$100,000 to $149,999**. Make it bold.

d. Insert a row at row 29. In cell A29, key **$50,000 to $99,999**. Make it bold.

e. In cell A32, key **Less than $50,000**. Make it bold.

f. Select rows 4 through 6. From the Data menu, choose Group and Outline and Group.

g. Select rows 8 through 13 and press Ctrl+Y.

h. Select rows 15 through 21 and press Ctrl+Y.

     i. Select rows 23 through 28 and press Ctrl+Y.

     j. Select rows 30 and 31 and press Ctrl+Y.

6. Add your footer. Set the orientation to landscape and horizontally center the worksheet.

7. Save the workbook as *[your initials]*23-33 in your Lesson 23 folder and print the sheet.

8. Publish a workbook to the Web by following these steps:

     a. From the File menu, choose Save as Web Page.

     b. In the Save group, click to place a check mark for Selection: Sheet.

     c. Click to place a check mark for Add interactivity.

     d. Double "Page" in the File name text box and key *[your initials]*23-33. Verify that the folder is your Lesson 23 folder.

     e. Click Change Title. In the Title text box, key **Housing Sites** and click OK.

     f. Click Publish.

     g. Click the down arrow for Choose and choose Range of cells. Click in the text box below the Choose box and press F3. Double-click Database.

     h. Check that the Viewing options show Add interactivity with Spreadsheet functionality.

     i. Click to place a check mark for Open published web page in browser. Click Publish.

9. Close the browser and the workbook.

Lesson Applications

EXERCISE 23-34

Enter and edit records in a list. Create a custom AutoFilter.

Klassy Kow adds its accounts payable to an existing worksheet. You need to filter the records by date, make some changes, sort the list, and print the results of an advanced filter.

1. Open the file **AccPay**.
2. Starting in cell A11, add the records shown in Figure 23-22, replacing "xx" with the current year. The Due Date is calculated after the Date Rec'd data is entered. The Late Fee column is either blank or shows "Yes." A Mail-By date is calculated if there is a late fee. These formulas have been copied through row 20.

> **NOTE:** You need not key commas when values are preformatted. You must, however, key decimal points when a significant value follows the decimal point.

FIGURE 23-22

Account	Date Rec'd	Due Date	Amount	Late Fee
Pacific Cable	1/3/xx		975	
Continental Power and Gas	2/4/xx		2456	Yes
Western Telephone	3/8/xx		932.37	
Visa/Mastercard	4/10/xx		1832.77	Yes
US Express	5/15/xx		2458	Yes
Avalon Financial Services	7/10/xx		350	Yes
Federal Shipping	9/7/xx		1200	

3. Format any data that does not match existing records.
4. Name the list **Database** but do not include rows without account data.
5. Create a custom AutoFilter in the Date Rec'd field to show bills received before 12/1/04.
6. Change the name of Pacific Cable to **WestCab**.
7. Add your usual footer.

TIP: You can edit and save data while a filter is applied.

8. Save the workbook as *[your initials]*23-34 in your Lesson 23 folder and print the worksheet.

9. Close the workbook.

EXERCISE 23-35

Sort a list. Use database functions. Create subtotals.

Klassy Kow is planning to purchase and manage a house that serves as temporary shelter for families in need. It has reviewed a list of available properties and wants to see summary information about four-bedroom homes.

1. Open the file **Properties**.

2. Name the list **Database** and sort it by Price in descending order.

3. Insert a new worksheet, name it **Report**, and position it to the right of the Properties worksheet.

4. In cell A1 on the Report worksheet, key **Summary for 4-Bedroom Homes**. Make it 18-point Arial italic.

5. Starting in cell A2, key the following labels in the range A2:A6:
   Lowest Price
   Highest Price
   Largest Lot
   Oldest Home
   Newest Home

6. Create a criteria range for database functions, starting in cell A14 in the Report worksheet, with the condition that properties have 4 bedrooms.

 NOTE: Adjust column widths as needed.

7. In cell B3, compute the price of the most expensive four-bedroom home.

8. In cell B4, compute the largest lot for four-bedroom homes.

 TIP: The criteria are the same for these calculations, but the field changes. Remember to type the field name in quotation marks and spell it exactly as it is in the list.

9. In cell B5, compute the age of the oldest four-bedroom home.

10. In cell B6, compute the age of the newest four-bedroom home.

 TIP: Use the Format Cells dialog box to help solve alignment problems.

11. Format cells B2:B3 for Currency with no decimal places. Fix alignment problems.

12. Add your footer. Save the workbook as *[your initials]*23-35 in your Lesson 23 folder and print the Report worksheet on one portrait page.

13. Create a copy of the Properties worksheet, placing it at the far right. Rename it **Subtotals**.

 REVIEW: Use the Sort dialog box to sort by multiple fields.

14. Sort the Subtotals worksheet by Bedrooms in ascending order, with a secondary sort by Baths in ascending order.

15. Create subtotals for the Bedrooms field using the COUNT function and showing subtotals in the Bedrooms field.

16. Edit the summary label in cell A7 from "1 Count" to **1 Bedroom Total**. Edit the label "2 Count" to **2 Bedroom Total**. Edit the remaining summary labels in the same way.

17. Hide details for all the subtotals except the four-bedroom totals. Your worksheet should show subtotal rows for the one-, two-, three-, and five-bedroom homes but show details for four-bedroom homes. There is also a Grand Count row.

18. Add your footer. Set the orientation to landscape and center the worksheet on the page.

19. Print the worksheet. Save and close the workbook.

EXERCISE 23-36

Use the data form. Create outline groups.

You have received a file from one of the Human Resources managers that must be imported into an employees list. After you import it, you need to match its formatting to the rest of the list, add a record, and sort the data.

1. Open **CurrentEmp** and name the worksheet **Employees**.

2. Select cell A16.

3. Start Word and open **NewEmp.doc**. Copy the entire Word table to cell A16 in the Excel window. Close the Word document and close Word.

 TIP: Use the Format Painter to quickly copy formats from one cell to a range of cells.

4. In the Excel window, apply the formatting of the existing rows to the imported Word data. Set the row height of the imported rows to match the existing rows.

TIP: Be careful not to include blank columns/rows when you name a list.

5. Name the list **Database**. Use the data form to enter the following new record:

Last Name: **Anderson**
First Name: **George**
Hire Date: **3/21/03**
Birth Date: **3/6/73**
Department: **Finance**
Location: **San Francisco**

6. Apply the same row height to the new record. Sort the list by Last Name in ascending order.

7. Add your usual footer and horizontally center the worksheet.

8. Make a copy of the Employees sheet, rename it **Departments**, and position it to the right of the Employees sheet.

9. Sort the Departments worksheet by Department in ascending order. Insert a blank row after each department group.

10. Create outlines for each group except the president. In cell A7, the blank row for the Finance group, key the label **Finance Personnel**. Make it bold. Key similar labels in the blank rows for the other groups. For the Owners group, key the label **Current Owners**. Make the row for the president bold.

11. Hide details for all groups except the Human Resources Personnel and the president.

12. Delete the two blank sheets and save the workbook as *[your initials]*23-36 in your Lesson 23 folder.

13. Print the entire workbook and then close it.

<hr>

EXERCISE 23-37 *Challenge Yourself*

Import Word data for a list. Sort the list. Create advanced filters.

Klassy Kow Human Resources wants a list of employees who have worked at the company five years, ten years, or more than ten years. They will be honored at a dinner next month.

1. Open **CurrentEmp** and name Sheet1 as **Employees**.

2. Open the Word document **NewHires.doc**. The data in this table is not exactly the same as the worksheet data. Copy the data only (no titles) for the two new employees to cell A16 in the worksheet. After the data is copied, delete, shift, and move cells to fit the copied data to the existing data. Assign each new hire to a department of your choice. Close the Word document and close Word.

3. Apply formatting and row heights to the imported data to match the existing data. Remove smart tags with any imported data. Name the list.

4. Sort the list by Last Name in ascending order.

5. Add a new column to the list by keying the field name **Years Employed** in cell G2. Format the label to match the other labels. Adjust the column width as necessary.

◀◀ **REVIEW:** Subtract the date hired from today and divide by 365.25. You must use parentheses to order the formula and format the value to show a number.

6. In cell G3, key a formula that determines years employed as of today. Format the results to show one decimal and increase the indent four times. Copy the formula in cell G3 to G4:G17.

◀◀ **REVIEW:** Choose Insert, Name, and Define to add another column to a named range.

7. Redefine the name of the range list to include this column. Make other format adjustments as needed.

8. Add your usual footer. Set the orientation to landscape and horizontally center the worksheet.

9. Rename Sheet2 **Criteria**. In cell A1, key **Criteria** and make it 16-point Arial.

10. Display the Employees worksheet and copy the range A2:G2 to cell A3 in the Criteria worksheet. Adjust the column widths. In the Criteria worksheet, name the range A3:G4 as **Criteria**.

11. In the Criteria worksheet, key **>10** in cell G4.

12. Copy the header row in the Employees worksheet to cell J2 in the same sheet. Delete column M and then delete column N. Adjust the column widths. Name the range J2:N2 as **Output**.

13. In the Employees worksheet perform an advanced filter, copying the results to the Output range. Copy and paste the filter results, including the field names, to cell A10 in the Criteria worksheet. Make any necessary formatting adjustments.

14. In cell A9 in the Criteria sheet, key **Personnel Employed More Than 10 Years**. Make it 12-point Arial bold.

15. Copy cells G3:G4 to cells H3:H4 so that the Years Employed field appears twice in the criteria range. Redefine the Criteria range name to include these cells.

16. Set new criteria to find personnel employed more than five years but less than ten years. This requires the use of two fields in the criteria range. Perform a second advanced filter, copying the results to the Output range. Copy and paste the new output range to cell A16 in the Criteria worksheet. Apply any necessary formatting to the data.

17. Copy the label in cell A9 to A15 and edit it to show **Personnel Employed Between 5 and 10 Years**.

18. Add your standard footer. Set the orientation to landscape and horizontally center the worksheet. Check and fix the borders.

 NOTE: Decide how to set the borders for consistency.

19. Delete the blank worksheet and save the workbook as *[your initials]*23-37 in your Lesson 23 folder.

20. Print the entire workbook and close the workbook.

On Your Own

In these exercises you work on your own, as you would in a real-life work environment. Use the skills you've learned to accomplish the task—and be creative.

EXERCISE 23-38
Create a list with at least 24 rows of data that can be grouped and outlined. Try to develop several fields that can be subtotaled in some way. Create the groups manually or use formulas to create an Auto Outline. Format the data attractively and add your footer. Save the workbook as *[your initials]*23-38 in your Lesson 23 folder. Print the workbook.

EXERCISE 23-39
Use the Internet to research a dozen companies or mutual funds in which you'd like to invest. Create a list for the data including at least six relevant fields about each field/fund. As you create the list, keep in mind how you might sort and filter it. Format the worksheet attractively and add your footer. Then create an advanced filter in place for your data. While the data is filtered, add an explanation in an available row. Save the workbook as *[your initials]*23-39 in your Lesson 23 folder and print it.

EXERCISE 23-40
Create an inventory listing all your possessions for insurance purposes. Include fields such as Item, Category, Location, Estimated Value, Date Acquired, Description, and other relevant data. Use database functions on another worksheet to show pertinent statistics about your data. Format all data attractively and add footers to both sheets. Save the workbook as *[your initials]*23-40 in your Lesson 23 folder. Print the entire workbook.

Using Data Tables and PivotTables

OBJECTIVES

**MICROSOFT OFFICE
SPECIALIST
ACTIVITIES**

In this lesson:
XLO3E-1-7
XLO3E-1-8

See Appendix.

After completing this lesson, you will be able to:

1. **Build a one-variable data table.**
2. **Build a two-variable data table.**
3. **Analyze data in a PivotTable.**
4. **Create a PivotTable report.**
5. **Use multiple functions, formulas, and custom calculations.**
6. **Create a PivotChart report.**
7. **Create PivotTables for the Web.**

 Estimated Time: 2 hours

A *data table* is a range of cells that displays the results of changing values in a formula. A data table enables you to display multiple versions of a problem on your worksheet. Excel has two types of data tables, a one-variable data table and a two-variable data table.

A *PivotTable report* is a summary table that combines and compares data from a list. The term "pivot" comes from your ability to rotate or move things around in the table. You can "rotate" or rearrange what is in the rows and columns in a PivotTable to see different summaries of the data.

Building a One-Variable Data Table

A one-variable data table shows the results of a formula in which one argument is a variable. You might use a one-variable data table to calculate revenue from beverage sales if the price is changed in ten-cent increments. The price is the variable, and the data table will show the results of the formula as you change the price.

In a one-variable data table, you key *input values,* in either a column or a row. These values are used in place of the variable when the formula calculates. You also designate a single empty cell outside the table range as the input cell. The *input cell* represents the changing values in the data table formula. The input cell is blank on the worksheet; it's like a placeholder.

EXERCISE 24-1 Set Up a Data Table for One Variable

Values for a data table are typically a range of values that increase or decrease incrementally. In this exercise, price is the variable. The values you key are prices, which increase in ten-cent increments.

1. Create a new workbook.
2. In cell A1, key the label **Soda Price Analysis** and make it 16-point Arial.
3. In cell A2, key **Selling Prices** and make it bold.
4. Key **1.19** in cell B3. Key **1.29** in cell C3. Format both cells as Currency with two decimals.
5. Select cells B3 and C3 and use the Fill handle to fill in prices to **$1.69** in cell G3. These are the data table input values.

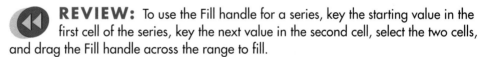 **REVIEW:** To use the Fill handle for a series, key the starting value in the first cell of the series, key the next value in the second cell, select the two cells, and drag the Fill handle across the range to fill.

6. Key **Number Sold** in cell H3 and format it as bold. Adjust the column width to fit the label.
7. Key **200** in cell H4 and format it as a Number with no decimal places.

EXERCISE 24-2 Create a Data Table

The Data, Table command substitutes the values in row 3 into the formula. When the input values are in a row, you must enter the formula one column to the left of the first value and one row below. The *data table range* includes the formula and all the input values. This will be the location of the results.

1. Select cell A4. This is one column to the left of the prices (the input values) and one row down. This will be the location for the data table formula.

2. In cell A4, key **=a10*h4** and press (Enter). This formula multiplies A10 (the input cell and the variable) by the number sold (cell H4). The input cell (A10) is empty, so the result is 0. When you run the Data, Table command, the input cell (A10) is replaced with each of the prices (cells B3:G3).

FIGURE 24-1
Data table formula

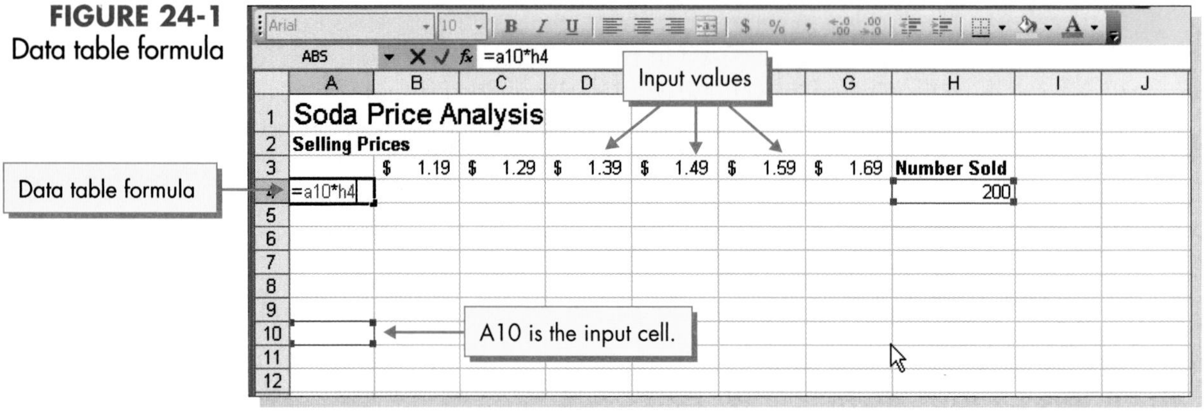

Data table formula

3. Select cells A3:G4. This is the data table range. Excel will show the prices in row 3 multiplied by the value in cell H4.

4. From the Data menu, choose Table. The Table dialog box opens. In this dialog box, you specify the address of the input cell for your formula. Your table has prices in a row, so you'll use the Row input cell text box.

5. In the Row input cell text box, key **a10**. This is the input cell address you keyed in your formula, the one that will be replaced by the values in row 3.

6. Click OK. The range B4:G4 displays the results of multiplying the prices (the input values) by the number sold in cell H4.

7. Format the results as Currency with two decimals.

FIGURE 24-2
Results of the Data, Table command

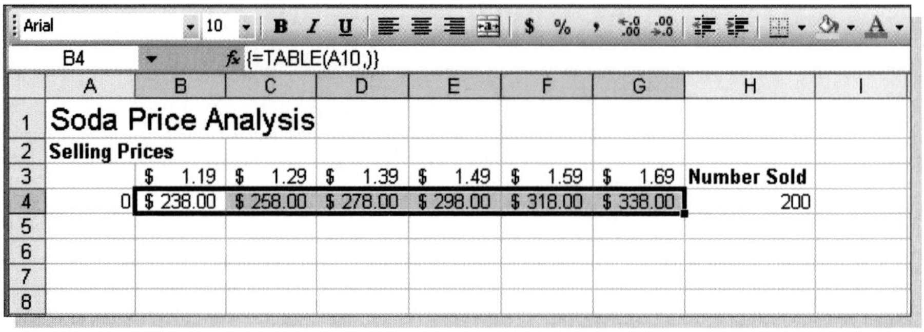

TIP: You can hide the formula result in cell A4 by changing the font color to white. If the result is a negative number, change the format so that negative values are shown in black. Then set the font color to white.

EXERCISE 24-3 Add a Second Formula to a Data Table

A data table can calculate more than one formula. All formulas must refer to the same input cell and must be in the same column. You'll add formulas that show more "Number Sold" values.

1. Key **250** in cell H5 and key **300** in cell H6.

2. Click cell A5, one column to the left of the prices (the input values). In this cell, you'll key a second formula for the Data, Table command.

3. In cell A5, key **=a10*h5** and press [Enter]. The formula uses the same input cell as the first formula but multiplies by cell H5 instead of cell H4. The formula displays 0 because the input cell (A10) is blank.

4. In cell A6, key **=a10*h6** and press [Enter]. This is a third formula.

FIGURE 24-3
Adding formulas to
a data table

Arial	10	B	I	U	≡	≡	≡	≡	$	%	,	‰	‰	≣	≣	⊞ ▾	⬧ ▾	A ▾

ABS ▾ X ✓ ƒx =a10*h6

	A	B	C	D	E	F	G	H	I
1	Soda Price Analysis								
2	Selling Prices								
3		$ 1.19	$ 1.29	$ 1.39	$ 1.49	$ 1.59	$ 1.69	Number Sold	
4	0	$ 238.00	$ 258.00	$ 278.00	$ 298.00	$ 318.00	$ 338.00	200	
5	0							250	
6	=a10*h6							300	
7									
8									
9									
10									
11									
12									

5. Select cells A3:G6. This data table range includes more rows.

 NOTE: You select the entire data table even if some values are already calculated. They are recalculated with the new formulas.

6. From the Data menu, choose Table. Your input values are in a row.

7. In the Row input cell box, key **a10**, the input cell.

8. Click OK. The results of all the formulas appear in the range B4:G6.

9. Format the results to match the first row.

EXERCISE 24-4 Delete, Edit, and Copy a Data Table

Excel uses the TABLE function in a data table. It is an array formula, identified by curly braces in the formula bar. An *array* formula performs multiple calculations that display a single result or multiple results. You cannot delete individual cells in an array formula. You can change the input row values or other arguments in the formula, and the table is recalculated. If you copy a data table, you copy the results, not the formula.

1. Select cell B4. In the formula bar, notice that the TABLE function is enclosed in curly braces. This is an indication that the function is an array formula.

2. Press (Delete). A message box indicates that you cannot change part of a table.

3. Click OK to close the message box.

4. Select cells B4:G6. Press (Delete). The results of the data table are deleted. You can delete the entire table.

 5. Click the Undo button on the Standard toolbar. The table is restored.

6. Select cell H5. Key **225** and press (Enter). Part of the table is recalculated.

7. Select any cell in the table with a result. Press (Ctrl)+(G).

8. Click Special. The Go To Special dialog box opens. You can use this dialog box to quickly highlight a table array.

9. Select Current array and click OK. The data table is highlighted.

 10. Click the Copy button 📋 to copy the values to the clipboard.

11. Display Sheet2 and click the Paste button 📋▾.

12. Select different cells in the table and check the formula bar. The data table values are copied; the formulas are not.

13. Return to Sheet1. Press (Esc) to cancel the marquee and click cell A1.

Building a Two-Variable Data Table

A two-variable table uses two sets of input values. You can use a two-variable data table to calculate results for different prices and different numbers sold.

The two-variable data table uses two input cells. Like the input cell for a single-variable data table, the input cells for a two-variable data table are left blank. The data table formula refers to two input cells, one for the column values and one for the row values.

A two-variable data table has its own layout rules. One set of input values must be in a column. The other set of input values must be in a row. The formula is keyed in the cell above the column values and to the left of the row values.

EXERCISE   **24-5**   **Set Up a Two-Variable Data Table**

In this exercise, the price is one variable, and the number sold is the other variable.

1. Copy cells B3:G3 to cell B12. These are the row input values, the prices.

2. In cell A13, key **350**. In cell A14, key **300**. Select both cells and AutoFill down to **50**. This range represents the column input values, the number sold.

3. In cell A11, key **Prices and Number Sold** and make it bold. You must leave cell A12 available for the data table formula.

 NOTE: You should leave cell A10 empty because it is the input cell for the formulas at the top of the worksheet.

EXERCISE 24-6 Create the Data Table

You use two input cells in this Data, Table command. You'll use cells A25 and A26 as input cells. The formula is entered to the left of the row values and above the column values, cell A12.

1. Select cell A12.

2. In cell A12, key **=a25*a26** and press (Enter). The formula multiplies two input cells, both blank. The input cells will be replaced with the row values and column values when the Data, Table command is run.

FIGURE 24-4
Setting up a two-variable data table

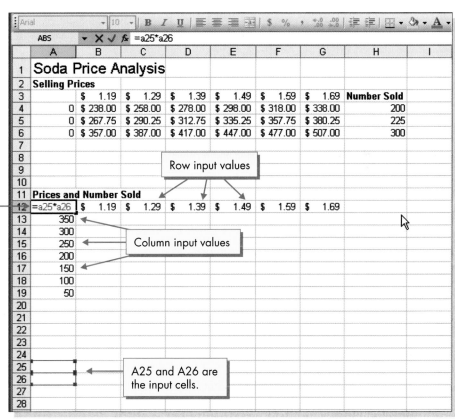

Data table formula

3. Select the range A12:G19. This is the data table range. It includes the formula and all the cells in which results should be shown.

4. From the Data menu, choose Table. The Table dialog box opens. You use both text boxes for a two-variable data table.

5. Key **a25** in the Row input cell text box.

 NOTE: In this formula, use could use either cell A25 or cell A26 as the row or column input cell.

6. Key **a26** in the Column input cell text box.

7. Click OK. The results of multiplying each price (row input value) by each number sold (column input value) are shown.

8. Format the results as Currency with two decimals.

FIGURE 24-5
Results of a two-variable data table

Arial		10	B I U ≡ ≡ ≡ ⊞	$ % , ⁺⁰ ⁰⁰ 增 增 ⊞ ▾ ♦ ▾ A ▾

B13 ▾ ƒₓ {=TABLE(A25,A26)}

	A	B	C	D	E	F	G	H	I
1	Soda Price Analysis								
2	Selling Prices								
3		$ 1.19	$ 1.29	$ 1.39	$ 1.49	$ 1.59	$ 1.69	Number Sold	
4	0	$ 238.00	$ 258.00	$ 278.00	$ 298.00	$ 318.00	$ 338.00	200	
5	0	$ 267.75	$ 290.25	$ 312.75	$ 335.25	$ 357.75	$ 380.25	225	
6	0	$ 357.00	$ 387.00	$ 417.00	$ 447.00	$ 477.00	$ 507.00	300	
7									
8									
9									
10									
11	Prices and Number Sold								
12	0	$ 1.19	$ 1.29	$ 1.39	$ 1.49	$ 1.59	$ 1.69		
13	350	$ 416.50	$ 451.50	$ 486.50	$ 521.50	$ 556.50	$ 591.50		
14	300	$ 357.00	$ 387.00	$ 417.00	$ 447.00	$ 477.00	$ 507.00		
15	250	$ 297.50	$ 322.50	$ 347.50	$ 372.50	$ 397.50	$ 422.50		
16	200	$ 238.00	$ 258.00	$ 278.00	$ 298.00	$ 318.00	$ 338.00		
17	150	$ 178.50	$ 193.50	$ 208.50	$ 223.50	$ 238.50	$ 253.50		
18	100	$ 119.00	$ 129.00	$ 139.00	$ 149.00	$ 159.00	$ 169.00		
19	50	$ 59.50	$ 64.50	$ 69.50	$ 74.50	$ 79.50	$ 84.50		
20									
21									

9. Add your usual footer. Horizontally center the worksheet on the page.

10. Save the workbook as *[your initials]*24-6 in a new folder for Lesson 24.

11. Print the worksheet and close the workbook.

Analyzing Data in a PivotTable

PivotTables let you sort, filter, and generate subtotals. PivotTables are interactive, because you can generate different arrangements of the rows and columns. You can move rows and columns to see various summaries of the data. You can change what is displayed and how it is summarized.

EXERCISE   **24-7**   View Data in a PivotTable

Most PivotTables are created as a separate worksheet in a workbook. In this exercise, you'll learn about PivotTables by examining an existing one.

1. Open the file **SalinasSodas**. The worksheet is a list that tracks the date, the size, and the flavor sold in a particular shop. The data for a PivotTable must be a list.

2. Click the down arrow next to the Name Box and select Database. This is the range name assigned to the list.

3. Click the PivotTable tab. The PivotTable uses the list to show flavors and sizes for each date with related totals.

 NOTE: The PivotTable is set at a 65% view size so that you can see it all at once.

FIGURE 24-6
PivotTable for
soda list

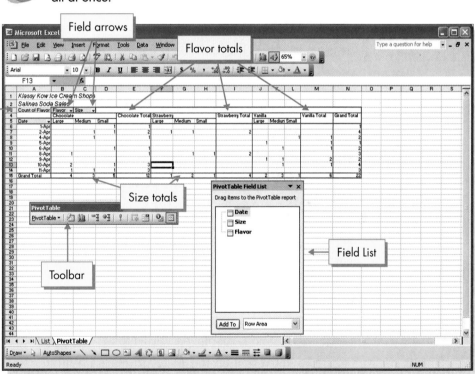

4. Click anywhere within the PivotTable. The PivotTable toolbar and the PivotTable Field List window open.

  NOTE: Right-click an existing toolbar and select PivotTable if the PivotTable toolbar is not displayed. Then click the Show Field List button 🗐 on the PivotTable toolbar to display the PivotTable Field List.

EXERCISE **24-8** **Delete Fields from a PivotTable**

To change the way the information is displayed in the PivotTable, you drag the fields into and out of the layout. It takes some practice learning where to drag items to the PivotTable, but if you don't like the results, you can simply drag them again to a different location.

1. Position the PivotTable Field List and the PivotTable toolbar so that you can see the PivotTable.

2. Position the pointer over "Flavor" in cell B3. The pointer changes to a four-pointed arrow. "Flavor" is a field (a column) from the list.

3. Drag cell B3 down to about row 20. The pointer shows a small field icon and a red X as the field is moved out of the table.

4. Release the mouse button. The field is deleted from the PivotTable, and only the Size field is displayed.

FIGURE 24-7
Field deleted from a
PivotTable

5. Position the pointer on "Size" in cell B3. With the four-pointed arrow displayed, drag down to row 20, and release the mouse button. Now only the Date field is displayed with a total.

6. Position the pointer on "Date" in cell A4. With the four-pointed arrow, drag down to row 20, and release the mouse button. Now the PivotTable shows one grand total with no details.

EXERCISE | **24-9** | **Add and Rotate Fields in a PivotTable**

To place fields in a PivotTable, you drag them from the PivotTable Field List to the desired location in the table. You can drag more than one field to a column or row area. The order of the fields in the column or row determines how the PivotTable is organized.

1. Click Date in the PivotTable Field List and drag it to cell A4. The Date field is displayed in the table.

2. Click Flavor in the PivotTable Field List. Drag it to cell B3. Flavors are now counted in the table.

> **NOTE:** If you see a message about replacing data, click Cancel and try dragging again. If you don't get the table layout as expected, just drag the fields and try to reposition them.

3. Drag Size from the PivotTable Field List to cell C3. The sizes and the flavors are listed for each date.

4. Drag Flavor from cell C3 on top of Size in cell B3. The table is changed to show the flavors first and then each size.

5. Drag Flavor from cell B3 on top of Date in cell A5. The table now shows flavors and dates in rows and the size in columns.

6. Click the Flavor field arrow. The list shows which items are currently displayed.

7. Click to remove the check mark for Strawberry. Click OK. That flavor is no longer shown in the table.

8. Click the Flavor field arrow. Select Strawberry. Click OK.

9. Click the Size arrow. Deselect Large. Click OK. That size is not displayed.

10. Click the Size arrow. Select Large. Click OK. That size is displayed in the list again.

11. Drag Flavor from cell A4 to cell D3 to the right of Size. If you don't get it right the first time, try dragging to rearrange the fields.

12. Close the PivotTable toolbar and the PivotTable Field List.

13. Delete the PivotTable worksheet.

Creating a PivotTable Report

When you create a PivotTable, you use the PivotTable and PivotChart Wizard. In the wizard, you first select the list for the PivotTable. Then you choose the fields and where they should be placed. You can, of course, change the layout after the report is created.

EXERCISE **24-10** **Create a PivotTable Report**

When you choose the PivotTable and PivotChart Report command, the PivotTable and PivotChart Wizard starts. If a list is named "Database," Excel will assume that is the range you want to use in a PivotTable.

1. With **SalinasSodas** open, click any cell in the list.

 NOTE: Excel refers to a PivotTable as a report, but it is just a worksheet in a workbook.

2. From the Data menu, choose PivotTable and PivotChart Report. The PivotTable and PivotChart Wizard – Step 1 of 3 dialog box opens. You can use an Excel list, an external data source (such as Access), ranges from several worksheets, or another PivotTable.

3. Select Microsoft Office Excel list or database if it is not already selected.

4. For the kind of report, choose PivotTable if it is not already selected.

5. Click Next. The PivotTable and PivotChart Wizard – Step 2 of 3 dialog box opens. The Range text box shows the named range Database, and the range is selected in the worksheet.

6. Click Next. The PivotTable and PivotChart Wizard – Step 3 of 3 dialog box opens. You can place the PivotTable in a new worksheet or on the existing worksheet.

7. Select New worksheet if it is not already selected.

8. Click Layout. The PivotTable and PivotChart Wizard – Layout dialog box shows an empty PivotTable form. The fields from the list are buttons on the right.

9. Drag Date to the ROW section in the layout. The dates will be listed as row headings.

 TIP: If you drag a field to the wrong location, drag it out of the layout into unused gray space.

10. Drag Flavor to the COLUMN section.

11. Drag Size next to Flavor in the COLUMN section. The flavors and sizes will be column headings.

12. Drag Flavor to the DATA section. You'll use the Flavor field as the data to be summarized in the report. The flavors will be counted. (See Figure 24-9.)

13. Click OK and then click Finish. Your PivotTable is on a new worksheet. The PivotTable toolbar and PivotTable Field List open.

14. Set the Zoom size to **65%** so that you can see the entire PivotTable.

FIGURE 24-8
Setting the
PivotTable layout

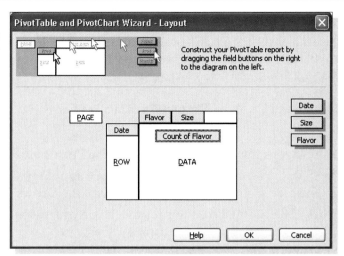

EXERCISE 24-11 Format the PivotTable Report

PivotTables are formatted with an AutoFormat when you create them. You can change the AutoFormat or add your own formatting to specific cells.

1. Double-click the Count of Flavor field in cell A3. The PivotTable Field dialog box opens.

2. In the Name text box, key **Soda Count** to change the name of the field from "Count of Flavor" to "Soda Count." Click OK.

3. Click the Format Report button on the PivotTable toolbar. The PivotTable is highlighted, and the AutoFormat dialog box is displayed.

FIGURE 24-9
AutoFormat
dialog box

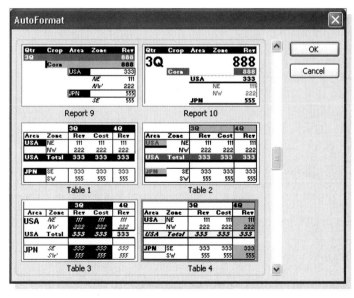

4. Scroll to find the Table 4 AutoFormat.

5. Select it and click OK. Click a cell outside the table to see the format. The PivotTable toolbar becomes inactive when a cell outside the table is selected.

6. Make cell A3 16-point Arial. Widen the column to see the label.

 NOTE: You can change fonts in a PivotTable with the Formatting toolbar.

7. Double-click the Flavor field in cell B3. The PivotTable Field dialog box opens.

8. In the Subtotals group, select None. With this option, you'll be suppressing the display of the Total column for each of the flavors.

9. Click OK. The Total columns for the flavors are no longer displayed.

10. Double-click the Date field in cell A5. Click Advanced. The PivotTable Field Advanced Options dialog box opens.

11. In the AutoSort options group, select Descending. With this option, you'll be changing the order of the dates in the Date field. Click OK to close the PivotTable Field Advanced Options dialog box.

12. Click OK. The dates are arranged with the most current date first.

FIGURE 24-10
Completed
PivotTable

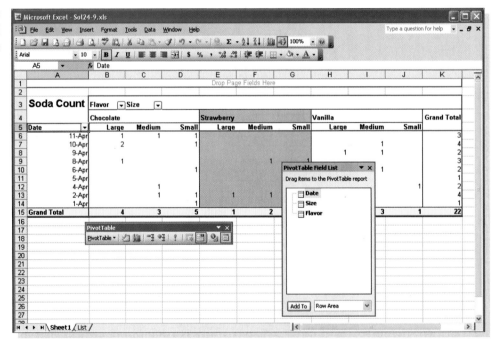

EXERCISE **24-12** **Print the PivotTable Report**

You can print a PivotTable report the same way you print any other worksheet. You'll always want to check the report in print preview to make sure it fits on the page properly.

1. Rename Sheet1 as **PivotTable1**.
2. Add the standard footer.
3. Set the table to print landscape fit to one page.
4. Save the workbook as *[your initials]***24-12** in your Lesson 24 folder.
5. Print the worksheet.

EXERCISE **24-13** **Create a PivotTable from an Existing Table**

You can create another PivotTable from the original list or from the existing PivotTable. Creating a second table from an existing PivotTable uses less memory than creating it from the list. You can do this if the second PivotTable uses the same fields as the first one.

 REVIEW: Press Shift+F11 to insert a new worksheet.

1. Insert a new worksheet and name it **PivotTable2**.
2. From the Data menu, choose PivotTable and PivotChart Report. The PivotTable and PivotChart Wizard – Step 1 of 3 dialog box opens.
3. Select Another PivotTable report or PivotChart report. This option is available because the workbook has an existing PivotTable.
4. For the kind of report, choose PivotTable.
5. Click Next. The PivotTable and PivotChart Wizard – Step 2 of 3 dialog box lists the existing PivotTables in your workbook. The table name appears with complete identifiers, including the workbook name, the type of table, and the worksheet name.

FIGURE 24-11
Choosing another
PivotTable in the
wizard

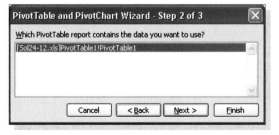

6. Select PivotTable1 if it is not selected and click Next. The PivotTable and PivotChart Wizard – Step 3 of 3 dialog box opens. You can choose where to place the new PivotTable.

7. Choose Existing worksheet if it is not already selected. Click Finish. An empty PivotTable template opens. The PivotTable Field List shows the fields from your first table.

EXERCISE 24-14 Use Multiple Fields in a PivotTable Section

You can analyze sales of flavors and sizes without regard to the date sold. The order in which you drag fields to a PivotTable section determines which field is the major category in the report.

1. Drag Flavor from the PivotTable Field List to cell A4 in the "Drop Row Fields Here" section. This places Flavor as a row heading.

2. Drag Size from the PivotTable Field List to cell A4, the same section, but slightly to the left side of the cell. This inserts Size as a row heading, to the left of Flavor.

 NOTE: When you are adding fields to the same row, the new field will be to the right or left of the existing field, depending on where you release the mouse button.

FIGURE 24-12
Dragging fields to the PivotTable template

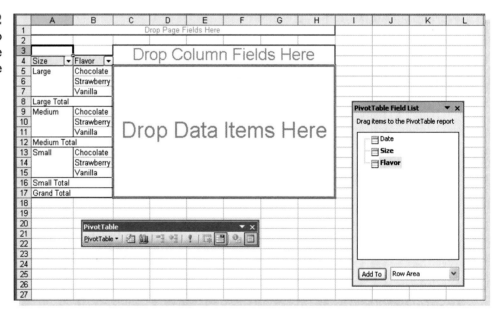

3. Drag Flavor from the field list to the "Drop Data Items Here" section. The flavors are counted, indicated in cell A3. The main category is Size, the leftmost field.

 TIP: You could count either the Size or the Flavor field in this table.

4. Click Count of Flavor in cell A3. Click the Field Settings button on the PivotTable toolbar. The PivotTable Field dialog box opens.

5. Change the Name to **Soda Flavor per Size**. Click OK.

6. Make the label 16-point Arial. Widen the column.

> **NOTE:** The fields in a PivotTable appear shaded, but they are not. Check print preview.

7. Select cell A4 and click the down arrow next to the Fill Color button on the Formatting toolbar. Apply a 25% gray fill, which is the last color in the fourth row.

8. Select cells B4 and C4 and apply the same color. Do the same for the cells in rows 8, 12, and 16.

9. Set the height of row 17 to 18.75 (25 pixels) and make the cells bold.

10. Add your footer. Set the orientation to portrait and horizontally center the worksheet on the page.

11. Save the workbook as *[your initials]***24-14** in your Lesson 24 folder.

12. Print the worksheet.

Using Multiple Functions, Formulas, and Custom Calculations

You've seen how the PivotTable can summarize your data by counting the number of items. You can perform other statistical operations on your data, such as SUM, AVERAGE, MIN, and MAX. You can also create custom calculations or formulas in a PivotTable.

EXERCISE 24-15 Add a Field to the List

Your list needs another field to better illustrate how to use multiple data functions. In this exercise, you'll add a column to show quantities purchased.

1. Display the List worksheet. Key **Quantity** in cell D3.

2. In the range D4:D8, key these values:
   5   10   15   20   25

>
> **REVIEW:** You can use AutoFill to complete this series of values. Key the first two and then use the AutoFill handle.

3. Select the range D4:D8 and click the Copy button .

4. Click cell D9 and click the Paste button . Click cell D14 and click the Paste button . Paste the values in cells D19.

5. Press (Esc) to cancel the Paste function. Key **20** in cell D24 and key **25** in cell D25.

6. From the Insert menu, choose Name and Define. In the Define Name dialog box, select Database under Names in workbook.

7. Edit the Refers to entry to show cell D25 instead of C25. Click OK.

E X E R C I S E **24-16** Use Multiple Functions

Because you will use different fields in your next PivotTable, you should create the table from the list. Excel will display a message reminding you that you can save memory by creating a new PivotTable from an existing one. In this case, however, you need to start with the list because you will use an additional field.

REVIEW: To base a PivotTable on another PivotTable, the tables must use exactly the same fields.

1. Select any cell in the list. From the Data menu, choose PivotTable and PivotChart Report. The PivotTable and PivotChart Wizard – Step 1 of 3 dialog box opens.

2. Select Microsoft Office Excel list or database. Select PivotTable. Click Next. The PivotTable and PivotChart Wizard – Step 2 of 3 dialog box displays.

3. Verify that the Database range will be used. Click Next. A message appears, reminding you that less memory is used by basing the new report on an existing report.

FIGURE 24-13
Message about using the same source data

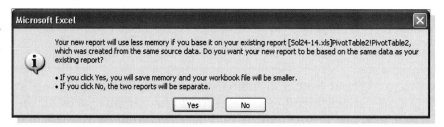

4. Click No to use a separate report for this PivotTable.

5. Select New worksheet. Click Finish. A PivotTable template displays in a new worksheet.

6. Drag Flavor from the PivotTable Field List to cell A4 in the "Drop Row Fields Here" section.

7. Drag Size to cell A5, below the Flavor field.

8. Drag Quantity to the "Drop Data Items Here" section. The quantities are summed for each flavor.

9. Drag Quantity again to cell C5 below the Total label. This is the "Drop Data Items Here" section. There are now two data fields for Quantity, both of them showing the same sum.

10. Select Sum of Quantity2 in cell C5. Click the Field Settings button 🔲 on the PivotTable toolbar.

FIGURE 24-14
Using two functions
for the data

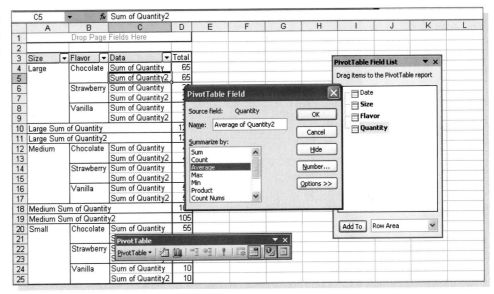

11. Select Average in the Summarize by list. The calculation is changed from a sum to an average.

12. Click Number. The Format Cells dialog box opens.

13. Format the field as a Number with no decimals. Click OK twice.

14. Select Sum of Quantity in cell C4. Click the Field Settings button 🔲.

15. Change the Name to **Total Sold**. Click OK. Notice that this changes all occurrences of the name for this field.

16. Select Average of Quantity2 in cell C5 and click the Field Settings button 🔲.

17. Change the Name to **Average Sold** and click OK.

EXERCISE 24-17 Change Table Options

A PivotTable has options for the entire table as well as individual fields. In this exercise, you'll hide the grand total rows that appear at the bottom of the table.

1. Rename the worksheet **PivotTable3**.

2. Select any cell in the table. Scroll the window so that you can see the last rows with grand totals.

3. Click the PivotTable button [PivotTable ▾] on the PivotTable toolbar and choose Table Options from the drop-down menu. The PivotTable Options dialog box opens.

4. In the Format options group, deselect Grand totals for columns. The grand totals for column D are in rows 28–29.

FIGURE 24-15
PivotTable Options
dialog box

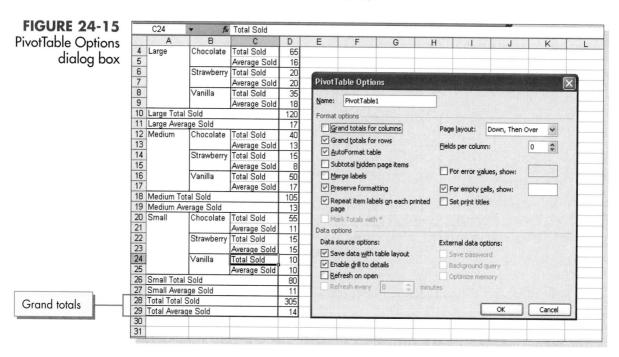

5. Click OK. The grand total rows are hidden.

EXERCISE 24-18 Add a Calculated Field to a PivotTable

You can create a new field in a PivotTable that calculates a result. In your current PivotTable, you can create a field that calculates a cost for each beverage sold if each cup costs three cents.

1. Select any cell in column D. Click the PivotTable button on the PivotTable toolbar.

2. Choose Formulas from the drop-down menu and then choose Calculated Field. The Insert Calculated Field dialog box opens.

3. In the Name text box, key **Cost**.

4. In the Formula text box, delete the zero and the space after the = sign.

5. Double-click Quantity in the Fields list. It is inserted in the formula.

6. Key ***.03** after Quantity in the Formula text box. The formula multiplies the quantity by three cents ($.03).

FIGURE 24-16
Inserting a
calculated field

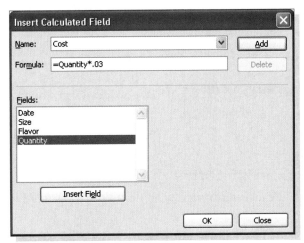

7. Click OK. The calculated field, Sum of Cost, is inserted as a new data item and it is summed.

 NOTE: A calculated field is not a field in your list. You can use only Sum on a calculated field.

8. Select cell C6 and click the Field Settings button 📊.

9. Change the Name to **Cost of Cups**.

10. Click Number. Use Currency with two decimal places. Click OK twice. The new field is renamed Cost of Cups, and the values are formatted.

EXERCISE **24-19** **Use a Custom Calculation**

Excel has several custom functions for PivotTables. One displays a percentage of the total that each data item represents.

1. Scroll to see the bottom of the PivotTable.

2. Click the PivotTable button on the PivotTable toolbar. Choose Table Options from the drop-down menu.

3. Select Grand totals for columns. Click OK. The grand totals are displayed for each item in column D in rows 40–42.

4. Drag Cost from the PivotTable Field List to column D. It is inserted as Sum of Cost again.

5. Select cell C7 and click the Field Settings button 📊.

FIGURE 24-17
Adding a custom
calculation

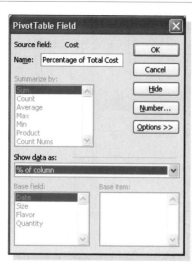

6. Change Na<u>m</u>e to **Percentage of Total Cost**.

7. Click <u>O</u>ptions. The dialog box expands to show more options.

8. Click the down arrow next to the Show d<u>a</u>ta as text box and select % of column.

9. Click OK. The percentage of the total cost of cups for each flavor and size is shown in the Data field. For example, the cost of cups for large chocolate sodas is 18.84% of the total cost of all sodas sold.

10. Add your usual footer. Change the top and bottom margins to **.5** inches. Horizontally center the worksheet.

11. Save the file as *[your initials]*24-19 in your Lesson 24 folder.

12. Print the worksheet.

Creating a PivotChart Report

A PivotChart is associated with a PivotTable in the same workbook. You can create a PivotChart for an existing PivotTable, or you can create a PivotChart as you create a new PivotTable.

When you create a PivotChart for an existing PivotTable, the chart layout follows the table layout. Category fields in the chart (the x-axis in a column chart) are the row fields in the table. The series fields (the values being plotted) are the column fields in the table. After a PivotChart is created, you can use the Chart menu or right-click a chart object to edit it.

EXERCISE **24-20** **Create a PivotChart for an Existing PivotTable**

In this exercise, you'll create a chart for an existing report that will show total sales by beverage size.

1. Display the PivotTable2 worksheet. Click anywhere in the report.

2. Click the Chart Wizard button on the PivotTable toolbar. The PivotChart is placed on a separate worksheet named Chart1.

3. Find the Size field button on the category axis (bottom of chart), and drag it off the chart into the gray background area. The field is removed from the chart. Only flavors are charted now.

4. Drag the Size field from the PivotTable Field List to the left of the Flavor button on the category axis. The chart shows flavors for each size once again.

5. Drag the Size field on the category axis to the right of the Flavor field. The chart is updated to show sizes for each flavor. Sometimes it is helpful to try different arrangements of the fields to see the best way to represent the data.

6. Drag the Size field to the left of Flavor on the category axis.

FIGURE 24-18
Building a
PivotChart report

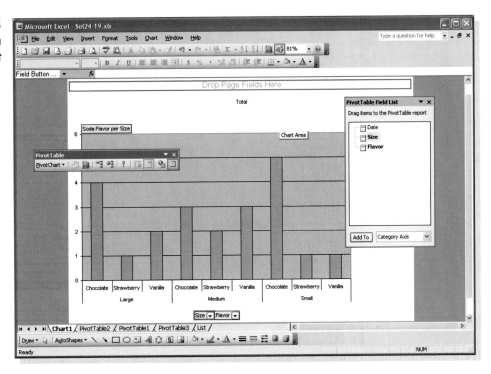

7. Click the down arrow on the Size field on the category axis. You can select which fields you'd like the chart to display.

8. Click Cancel.

9. Click the chart title once to select it. Click again to place an insertion point.

10. Edit the title to **Flavors Sold by Size**. Change the font to 18 points.

11. Rename the worksheet **PivotChart1**. Add your footer.

12. Save the workbook as *[your initials]***24-20** in your Lesson 24 folder.

13. Print the chart.

EXERCISE 24-21 Create a New PivotChart Report

When you create a PivotChart from the list, Excel creates a new PivotTable for the chart.

1. Display the List worksheet and select any cell in the list. From the Data menu, choose PivotTable and PivotChart Report.

2. Select <u>M</u>icrosoft Office Excel list or database. Select PivotCha<u>r</u>t report (with PivotTable report). Click <u>N</u>ext.

3. Verify that the Database range will be used. Click <u>N</u>ext. The memory information box displays.

4. Click <u>N</u>o to use a separate report for this chart.

5. Select <u>N</u>ew worksheet. Click <u>F</u>inish. A blank chart and its associated table, also blank, are inserted.

6. On the Chart2 sheet, drag Date from the PivotTable Field List to the "Drop Category Fields Here" section. Dates appear along the category axis.

7. Drag Quantity to the "Drop Data Items Here" section. Columns display in the chart.

8. Right-click one of the columns and choose Format Data Series from the shortcut menu. The Format Data Series dialog box opens.

 NOTE: You can edit chart objects in a PivotChart as you can in any chart.

9. Click the Options tab. Select <u>V</u>ary colors by point. Click OK. The columns change to different colors.

10. Close the PivotTable Field List. Select and delete the legend.

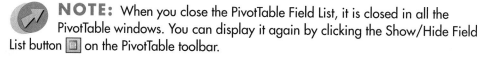 **NOTE:** When you close the PivotTable Field List, it is closed in all the PivotTable windows. You can display it again by clicking the Show/Hide Field List button 🔲 on the PivotTable toolbar.

11. Edit the chart title to **Daily Soda Sales**. Make it 24 points.

12. Double-click the Sum of Quantity field button near the upper-left corner of the chart. The PivotTable Field dialog box opens. You can change the name and calculation illustrated in the chart.

 NOTE: Because the chart is based on an associated PivotTable, if you make the change in the chart, you're also changing its PivotTable.

13. Click Cancel to close the PivotTable Field dialog box.

14. Change the worksheet name to **PivotChart2**. Add your footer.

15. Save the workbook as *[your initials]*24-21 in your Lesson 24 folder.

16. Print the worksheet.

Creating PivotTables for the Web

Noninteractive PivotTables for the Web are like any other Excel worksheet that you save in HTML format and place on the Web. In a noninteractive PivotTable on the Web, you can't change the data or layout of the table.

An interactive PivotTable for the Web enables others to change the data and layout in the Web browser. To create an interactive table, you use a Microsoft Office Web component called PivotTable List.

A PivotTable on the Web has commands and features similar to Excel PivotTable reports. You create a PivotTable List from an existing PivotTable report or from other Excel data.

 NOTE: You must have the Office Web components installed on the computer. The PivotTable List component works with Microsoft Internet Explorer 4.01 or higher.

EXERCISE 24-22 Place a PivotTable Report on the Web

When you create a PivotTable for the Web, you save only the worksheet with the PivotTable. Excel gives you the option of making it interactive or noninteractive. In this exercise, you'll make it interactive.

1. Make the PivotTable2 worksheet the active worksheet.
2. From the File menu, choose Save as Web Page. The Save As dialog box opens with the Save as type set to Web Page.
3. In the Save group, select Selection: Sheet.
4. Click to place a check mark for Add interactivity.
5. In the File name text box, delete the existing filename and key *[your initials]*24-22.
6. Click Change Title. The Set Title dialog box opens. Key **Soda Flavor Sales**. This will be the title of the Web page.
7. Click OK. The Save As dialog box is the active dialog box again.
8. Click Publish. The Publish as Web Page dialog box opens. The default is to publish the entire worksheet, including all empty cells. You'll publish only the PivotTable.
9. In the Choose list, select PivotTable2($A$3:$C$17). Notice in the background that only the PivotTable now is highlighted.
10. Place a check mark for Add interactivity with. The text box should show PivotTable functionality.

 NOTE: The File Name text box in the Publish as Web Page dialog box specifies the drive, folder, Web folder, Web server, or FTP location where your Web page files are stored. Your instructor will inform you if you need to specify this information.

11. Place a check mark for Open published web page in browser. This option will launch your browser and open the PivotTable.

FIGURE 24-19
Publishing an
interactive
PivotTable

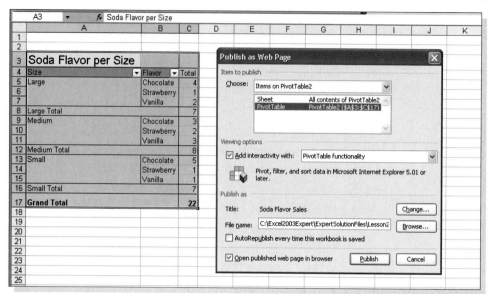

12. Click <u>P</u>ublish. Excel saves the PivotTable report as a Web page and opens it in Internet Explorer.

 NOTE: Some formatting features might not appear on the Web.

EXERCISE 24-23 Edit a PivotTable List on the Web

A PivotTable on the Web is called a PivotTable List. It is slightly different from the original PivotTable but contains essentially the same features found in Excel. You can change the layout and the fields of the table just as you can in an Excel PivotTable report.

1. Maximize the browser window if it is not already maximized.

2. Click the plus (+) or minus (–) symbol for Large, which is located under the Size field. Flavor details for the large size are displayed or hidden.

3. Display the details for Chocolate and Large.

4. Click the minus (–) symbol for Large. Details are hidden.

5. Position the pointer over Flavor in the PivotTable List until the four-pointed arrow appears. (See Figure 24-20.)

6. Drag the Flavor field off the table into white space. The field is removed from the list.

 7. Click the Field List button on the PivotTable List toolbar. The list looks slightly different from the PivotTable Field List in Excel.

FIGURE 24-20
Removing a
field from a
PivotTable List

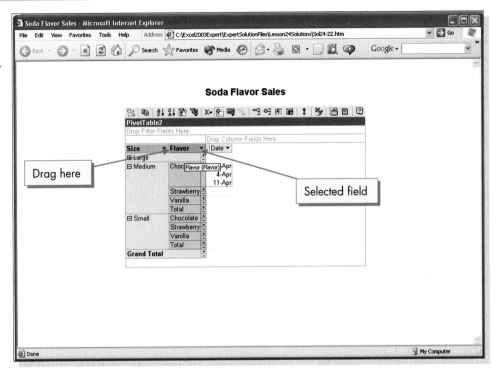

8. Select Flavor in the list and drag it to Size in the PivotTable List, positioning it so that the vertical blue outline appears on the right side of the Size column with the tiny edges facing left. The fields should be positioned with Size to the left of Flavor.

TIP: If the fields are in reverse order compared to Figure 24-20, drag Flavor off the table into the white space and drag it again from the PivotTable Field List.

9. Close the PivotTable Field List. Hide all details except the sizes.

10. From the browser's <u>F</u>ile menu, choose Page Set<u>u</u>p. Edit the header to show your first and last name. Click OK.

11. From the <u>F</u>ile menu, choose <u>P</u>rint and print the list.

12. Close Internet Explorer. Close the workbook without saving.

  NOTE: You can export a PivotTable List from the Web back to Excel. Use the Export to Microsoft Excel button 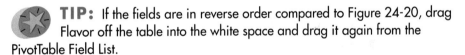 on the PivotTable List toolbar.

USING ONLINE HELP

PivotTables are a powerful tool with many variations. Use Help to learn more about general features of PivotTables and when you might use them.

Use Help to learn more about PivotTables:

1. With Internet Explorer and Excel running, look for topics about **pivottables**.
2. Read the information. Close the windows.
3. Close Internet Explorer and end your Internet connection.

LESSON Summary

➤ A data table is a range of cells that displays the results of different values in a formula. The data table range includes the formula and input values.

➤ In a one-variable data table, input values are substituted for a formula variable. Input values are keyed and usually increase or decrease incrementally.

➤ A one-variable data table can calculate multiple formulas that refer to the same input cell.

➤ Data tables use an array formula. Input values in the table can be edited, but a single result cannot be deleted from a table because it is part of the array.

➤ A two-variable data table uses two sets of input values and two input cells. It has different layout rules than a one-variable data table.

➤ A PivotTable is an interactive table that allows row and column headings to be moved to various positions to show possible layouts of the data.

➤ Fields used in a PivotTable can be inserted, deleted, rotated, and formatted. PivotTables have AutoFormats.

➤ When a second PivotTable is created, it uses less memory when it is based on the first PivotTable.

➤ PivotTables can perform a number of statistical calculations, such as SUM and AVERAGE.

➤ You can use the PivotTable Options dialog box to hide various totals in the PivotTable.

➤ You can add calculated fields and use custom functions in a PivotTable.

➤ A PivotChart report displays the data from a PivotTable with similar interactivity. The chart layout follows the table layout.

➤ A PivotTable on the Web is known as a PivotTable List. You can rotate and edit an interactive PivotTable on the Web just as you can rotate and edit an Excel PivotTable.

LESSON 24   Command Summary

FEATURE	BUTTON	MENU	KEYBOARD
Data table		Data, Table	
PivotTable report		Data, PivotTable and PivotChart Report	
Field settings		PivotTable, Field Settings	
PivotTable AutoFormat		PivotTable, Format Report	
Calculated field		PivotTable, Formulas, Calculated Field	
Custom calculation		PivotTable, Table Options	
PivotChart report		Data, PivotTable and PivotChart Report	
PivotTable List		File, Save as Web Page	

Concepts Review

Each of the following statements is either true or false. Indicate your choice by circling T or F.

T F   **1.** A data table and a PivotTable use the same data.

T F   **2.** A data table uses one or two input cells on the worksheet as placeholders.

T F   **3.** PivotTables summarize information from a list or other database.

T F   **4.** You can format a PivotTable with an AutoFormat.

T F   **5.** Each PivotTable in a workbook must have a separate list as its data source.

T F   **6.** You can use the PivotTable Options dialog box to change a field name in a PivotTable.

T F   **7.** You can create a PivotChart without a PivotTable.

T F   **8.** To delete a field from a PivotTable, click it and press Delete.

Write the correct answer in the space provided.

1. On what menu do the Table and PivotTable commands appear?

2. What name describes the type of formula created by the TABLE function in a Data Table command?

3. What two terms describes types of data tables?

4. How can you delete a field from a PivotTable report?

5. Name two functions that you can use in a PivotTable report.

6. When placed on the Web, what term is used for a PivotTable report?

_____

7. How could you change the font for a field in a PivotTable?

_____

8. If you add your own formula to a PivotTable chart, what type of field is used?

_____

CRITICAL THINKING

Answer these questions on a separate page. There are no right or wrong answers. Support your answers with examples from your own experience, if possible.

1. When you place a PivotTable on the Web, users can edit the table in various ways. What are pros and cons of allowing users to edit your PivotTable report?

2. Determine a situation in your personal life in which a one- or two-variable data table might be helpful. Use "dummy" data and develop your ideas in a worksheet.

Skills Review

EXERCISE 24-24

Create a one-variable data table. Create a two-variable data table.

1. Create a new workbook.

2. In cell A1, key **Sales Rep Commission Comparison** and make it 14-point Arial.

3. Set up a one-variable data table by following these steps:

    a. In cell B2, key **5%**. Key **5.5%** in cell C2. Format both cells as a percent with one decimal and make them bold.

    b. Select both cells and use AutoFill to reach **7.5%** in cell G2.

    c. In cell H2, key **Dollar Sales** and make it bold.

    d. Key **20000** in cell H3. Format it as Currency with no decimals, and adjust the column width.

4. Create a one-variable data table by following these steps:

    a. Key **=a8*h3** in cell A3.

 NOTE: The formula multiplies the row input value (in row 2) by the value in cell H3. Cell A8 is a placeholder in the formula.

    b. Select the range A2:G3. From the Data menu, choose Table.

c. Key **a8** in the Row input cell text box. Click OK.

d. Format the results to show Currency with no decimals.

5. Set up a two-variable data table by following these steps:

   a. Copy the range B2:G2 to cell B10.

 REVIEW: Leave row 8 empty because you have used cell A8 as a placeholder for the formula in cell A3.

   b. Key **20000** in cell A11. Key **25000** in cell A12. Select both cells and AutoFill down to reach **50000** in cell A17. Make these values bold.

   c. Key **Sales versus Commission** in cell A9. Make it bold.

6. Create a two-variable data table by following these steps:

   a. Key **=a20*a21** in cell A10.

   b. Select the range A10:G17. From the Data menu, choose Table.

   c. Key **a20** in the Row input cell text box.

   d. Key **a21** in the Column input cell text box. Click OK.

7. Format all dollar amounts as Currency with no decimals. Hide the formulas in cells A10 and A3 by changing the font color to white.

8. Add your usual footer. Horizontally center the worksheet on the page.

9. Save the workbook as *[your initials]***24-24** in your Lesson 24 folder. Print the worksheet.

10. Make a copy of the worksheet and name the sheet **Formulas**. Display the formulas and fit the columns. Print the worksheet fit to one landscape page. Save and close the workbook.

EXERCISE 24-25

View and edit data in a PivotTable. Create a PivotTable report. Rotate fields in a PivotTable.

1. Open the file **EmpPivot** and display the PivotTable1 worksheet.

2. View and edit data in a PivotTable by following these steps:

   a. Select cell C4 if it is not already selected and click the Field Settings button on the PivotTable toolbar.

   b. Change the Name to **Female Employees**. Click OK.

   c. Select cell C5 and click the Field Settings button .

   d. Change the Name to **Male Employees**. Click OK.

TIP: Use the Ctrl key to select the labels in row 3; you cannot drag to select them because they are fields as well as labels.

   e. Make the row 3 labels bold. Set the width of column D to 7.14 (55 pixels).

   f. Make the data in rows 32 and 33 bold. Do the same for each of the remaining state totals as well as the grand totals at the bottom of the table so that the labels and values in these rows are bold.

REVIEW: Insert a page break by clicking the cell and choosing Insert, Page Break. To repeat this command, press Ctrl+Y.

3. Insert page breaks at cells A34, A48, and A60.

 REVIEW: Choose File and Page Setup to set repeating print rows.

4. Set rows 1 through 3 to repeat at the top of each page. Add your footer. Horizontally center the worksheet.

5. Save the workbook as *[your initials]*24-25a in your Lesson 24 folder and print the worksheet. Each state prints on a separate page.

6. Display the EmpCounts worksheet.

7. Create a PivotTable report by following these steps:

   a. From the Data menu, choose PivotTable and PivotChart Report.
   b. Select Microsoft Office Excel list or database if it is not already selected.
   c. Select PivotTable if it is not already selected and then click Next.
   d. In the Range text box, key **Database** if this range is not already displayed. Click Next.
   e. Click No to use a separate report for this PivotTable.
   f. Select New worksheet and click Finish.

8. Add, edit, and rotate fields in a PivotTable report by following these steps:

   a. Drag the State field from the PivotTable Field List to cell A4 in the "Drop Row Fields Here" section.
   b. Drag the City field to cell A4, the same section, but slightly to the right side of the cell. The City field should be to the right of the State field.
   c. Drag the Students field from the PivotTable Field List to the "Drop Data Items Here" section.
   d. Double-click "Sum of Students" in cell A3. Change the Name to **Employees Who Are Students**. Format the label as 14-point bold. Adjust the column width.

9. Apply a 25% gray fill to the data and blank cells in rows 4, 19, 26, 32, and 40. Make the data in row 41 bold.

10. Center the report horizontally on the page. Add your usual footer.

11. Save the workbook as *[your initials]*24-25b in your Lesson 24 folder.

12. Print the worksheet and close the workbook.

EXERCISE 24-26

Create a PivotTable report. Use multiple functions in a PivotTable. Insert a calculated field. Use a custom calculation. Create a PivotChart report.

1. Open the file **EmpPivot**.

2. Create a new PivotTable report by following these steps:

    a. Select any cell in the list.

    b. From the Data menu, choose PivotTable and PivotChart Report. Select Microsoft Office Excel list or database and PivotTable if they are not already selected. Click Next.

    c. Verify that the Range is Database, click Next, and then click No for a separate report.

    d. Choose New worksheet if it is not already selected. Click Finish.

3. Use multiple functions in a PivotTable by following these steps:

    a. Drag State from the PivotTable Field List to cell A4 in the "Drop Row Fields Here" section in the layout template.

    b. Drag Number of Employees to the "Drop Data Items Here" section.

    c. Drag Females to cell B5 below the Total label.

    d. Drag Males to cell C5 below the Total label.

4. Change field settings by following these steps:

    a. Select cell B5, "Sum of Females." Click the Field Settings button on the PivotTable toolbar.

    b. Change the Name to **Average # of Females**.

    c. In the Summarize by list, select Average.

    d. Click Number. Format the field as a Number with no decimals. Click OK twice.

5. Select cell B6. Format the field as a Number with no decimals. Change the field calculation to Average and the field name to **Average # of Males**.

6. Add a calculated field by following these steps:

    a. Select any cell in column B. Click the PivotTable button PivotTable ▾ on the PivotTable toolbar.

    b. Choose Formulas and Calculated Field.

    c. Key **10% Projection** in the Name text box.

    d. In the Formula text box, delete the zero and the space after the = sign.

> ✎ **NOTE:** The decimal equivalent of 110% is 1.1.

    e. Double-click Number of Employees in the Fields list. Key ***1.1** after Number of Employees in the formula box. Click OK.

    f. Select cell B7 and click the Field Settings button .

    g. Change Name to **Projection Growth**.

    h. Click Number. Format the field as a Number with no decimal places. Click OK twice.

7. Use a custom calculation by following these steps:

    a. Drag Females from the PivotTable Field List to column C.

    b. Select cell C8 and click the Field Settings button .

    c. Change Name to **Female Percentage of Total**.

d. Click <u>O</u>ptions. Click the down arrow next to the Show d<u>a</u>ta as text box and select % of total. Click OK.

8. Edit the field name for cell B4 to **# of Employees**.

9. Change the worksheet name to **MFInfo**. Add your standard footer. Center the page horizontally.

10. Save the workbook as *[your initials]*24-26a in your Lesson 24 folder.

11. Print the worksheet.

12. Create a PivotChart report by following these steps:

a. Select any cell in the PivotTable on the MFInfo worksheet.

b. Click the Chart Wizard button 📊 on the PivotTable toolbar.

c. Click the down arrow for the Data field button on the category axis. Deselect all fields except the two averages. Click OK.

d. Right-click one of the columns and choose Format Data Series. Click the Options tab and select <u>V</u>ary colors by point. Click OK.

e. Close the PivotTable Field List. Select and delete the legend.

f. Change the main chart title to **Average Number of Females/Males Per Store**. Make it 18 points.

13. Change the worksheet name to **MFChart**. Add a footer.

14. Save the workbook as *[your initials]*24-26b in your Lesson 24 folder.

15. Print the chart and close the workbook.

EXERCISE 24-27

Create an interactive PivotTable for the Web.

1. Open the file **SalinasSodas** and display the PivotTable worksheet.

2. Drag the Size field out of the PivotTable.

3. Create a PivotTable List for the Web by following these steps:

a. From the <u>F</u>ile menu, choose Save as Web Page.

b. In the Save group, select S<u>e</u>lection: Sheet.

c. Select <u>A</u>dd interactivity.

d. Navigate to your Lesson 24 folder in the Save <u>i</u>n box. In the File <u>n</u>ame box, delete the existing filename and key *[your initials]*24-27.

e. Click <u>C</u>hange Title and key **April Soda Sales**. Click OK.

f. Click <u>P</u>ublish. In the <u>C</u>hoose list, select the PivotTable.

g. Select <u>A</u>dd interactivity with if it is not already selected. It should show PivotTable functionality.

h. Select <u>O</u>pen published web page in browser if it is not already selected. Click <u>P</u>ublish.

4. In Internet Explorer, choose <u>F</u>ile, Page Set<u>u</u>p from the menu. Change the header to your first and last name. Click OK.

5. Choose <u>F</u>ile, <u>P</u>rint from the menu and print the Web page.

6. Close the browser window, and close the workbook without saving.

Lesson Applications

EXERCISE 24-28

Create one- and two-variable data tables.

Klassy Kow is examining ways to encourage prompt payment from their leading customers. They are considering both late fees and early payment discounts. You need to create a data table that shows discounts of 5% to 10% for the average amount due. You'll need another table showing late fees of 2% to 6% for individual amounts due.

1. Open the file **MarketCust**.

2. Rename Sheet2 as **DiscountData**. In cell A1, key **Discounts On Average Amounts Due**. Make it 16-point Arial.

3. In cell B3, key **5%**. In cell C3, key **6%**. Select both cells and use AutoFill to fill the series to **10%** in cell G3. Format the percentages as bold.

4. In cell H2, key **Avg. Amount Due**. Make it bold.

 REVIEW: Key **=average(** and then select the cells on the appropriate worksheet.

5. In cell H4, key a formula that displays the average of the range F4:F10 in the CustList worksheet. Format the result as Currency with no decimals.

6. In cell A4, key the one-variable data table formula that computes the discount. Use cell A6 as the row input cell and multiply by the Avg. Amount Due in cell H4.

7. Create the data table. Format the results as Currency with no decimals. Change the font color of cell A4 to hide the results of the formula.

8. Add your footer.

9. Rename Sheet3 as **LateFeeData**. Key **Amounts Due and Late Fees** in cell A1. Make it 16-point Arial.

10. Key **2%** in cell B3. Key **3%** in cell C3. Select both cells and use AutoFill to fill the series to **6%** in cell F3. Format the percentages as bold.

11. In the CustList worksheet, copy cells F4:F10 to cell A4 in the LateFeeData worksheet. In the LateFeeData worksheet, format cells A4:A10 as Currency with no decimals and sort these amounts in ascending order.

 REVIEW: Use any two blank cells in the data table formula.

12. In cell A3, key the two-variable data table formula to calculate a late fee for the amounts due at different percentages. Use two input cells, one for the rate (row input) and one for the amount (column input).

13. Create the data table and color the formula cell so that it is invisible. Format the results as Currency with no decimals. Increase the height of row 3. Center the worksheet title across the data.

14. Add your footer. Horizontally center the worksheet.

15. Save the workbook as *[your initials]***24-28** in your Lesson 24 folder.

16. Print the DiscountData and LateFeeData worksheets.

17. Group the DiscountData and LateFeeData worksheets and copy them to the end of the worksheet tabs. Rename them **DiscountDataFormulas** and **LateFeeDataFormulas**.

18. In each formula sheet, change the color for the data table formula cell to black. Display the formulas on each sheet and AutoFit the columns. Set each formula sheet to print in landscape orientation fit to one page. Print both formula sheets.

19. Save and close the workbook.

EXERCISE 24-29

Delete and add fields in an existing PivotTable report. Create a new PivotTable report. Add a custom calculation.

The Marketing Department has asked you to change the PivotTable for second-quarter novelty ice cream sales. They'd like to see sales for only one month instead of the entire quarter's total sales. They'd also like a new PivotTable showing individual monthly sales and a quarterly average.

1. Open the file **NoveltiesQtr2** and display the PivotTable1 worksheet.

 REVIEW: Change the type of calculation in a field through Field Settings.

2. Delete the Sum of Total field from the PivotTable and replace it with the April field from the PivotTable Field List. Change Count of April to Sum of April in cell A3.

3. Change the name of the field from Sum of April to **Total April Sales**. Make cell A3 14-point Arial and widen the column appropriately. Make cell B3 12-point Arial. Notice the blank data in column F.

 NOTE: Lists should not include blank rows because they are then included in any list commands.

4. Return to the NoveltySales sheet. Click the Name box arrow and choose Database. The list includes a blank row 4.

 REVIEW: Right-click a row heading and choose Delete to delete a row.

5. Delete row 4 in the NoveltySales sheet and return to the PivotTable1 sheet. Click anywhere in the table and click the Refresh Data button ☝ on the PivotTable toolbar.

6. Make the labels and values in rows 4 and 8 in the PivotTable bold. Format all values as Currency with no decimals. Widen any columns where necessary.

7. Add your footer and horizontally center the worksheet.

8. Create a new PivotTable report using the range Database but do not base it on the existing PivotTable. Place the report in a new worksheet.

9. Use the Products field as a row field. Use the State field as a column field. Use the April, May, and June fields as data fields. Use the April field as a data field a second time.

10. Change the name of the Sum of April field to **April Totals**. Change the Sum of May to **May Totals**. Change Sum of June to **June Totals**.

TIP: Use Options in the PivotTable Field dialog box and use Show data as to change the calculation.

11. Change Sum of April2 to **April's Percent of Total**. Change the calculation for this field to show the April sum as a percentage of the total.

TIP: Select the field in column B and use Field Settings to change the format for all the values for that field.

12. Format the percentages to show one decimal. Format the remaining values as Currency with no decimals.

13. In cell A1, key the title **Quarterly Novelty Sales by Month**. Make it 16-point Arial and center it across the table.

14. Rename the worksheet **PivotTable2**. Add your footer. Horizontally center the sheet.

15. Save the workbook as *[your initials]*24-29 in your Lesson 24 folder.

16. Print the PivotTable1 and PivotTable2 sheets. Close the workbook.

EXERCISE 24-30

Create a PivotChart report.

You need to create a PivotChart report that shows the average price of the homes that Klassy Kow is considering for its shelter. You also need a PivotChart and PivotTable showing data related to the type of heat.

1. Open **NewProperties** and name the list.

REVIEW: Use the name "Database" so that Excel recognizes it in PivotTable tasks.

2. Create a PivotChart report with its PivotTable on a new worksheet.

3. In the PivotChart, place the Bedrooms field in the Category Fields area. Place the Price field in the Data area.

4. Double-click the Sum of Price field and change the name to **Average Price**. Set the calculation from Sum to Average.

5. Right-click a column in the chart and format the data series to show different colors for each column.

 REVIEW: Click a chart object to make it active. Click somewhere away from the object to deselect it.

6. Edit the chart title to show **Average Price by Number of Bedrooms**. Make it 14-point Arial. Delete the legend. Add your footer.

7. Return to the Properties sheet and create a new PivotTable. Do not base it on the existing report. Place it in a new worksheet.

8. Place the Heat field as a row field. Place the Age and the Address fields as data fields.

9. Change the name of the Sum of Age field to **Average Age**. Set the function to Average, and use a Number format with no decimals. Change the name for Count of Address to **Number** with a Number format with no decimals.

 TIP: Remove the check mark for Grand totals for columns in the PivotTable Options dialog box to hide the totals.

10. Turn off the display of the totals in rows 12 and 13.

11. In cell A1, key **Number of Homes and Average Age by Heat**. Make it 16-point Arial.

12. Use 12-point Arial bold for the labels in row 3 and increase the row height. Adjust the column widths.

13. Insert a blank column at the current column A. Then drag the label from cell B1 to cell A1.

14. Name the worksheet **PivotTable2**. Add your standard footer.

  TIP: Click in the PivotTable and click the Chart Wizard button 📊 to create a chart based on a particular PivotTable.

15. Create a chart based on PivotTable2. Click one of the Number columns two times and format it to color different from the Age color. Then click each one of the other Number columns and press Ctrl+Y to repeat the command.

16. Change the chart title to **Average Age and Number of Homes by Heat Type**. Make it 16-point Arial. Delete the legend.

17. Add your footer. Save the workbook as *[your initials]*24-30 in your Lesson 24 folder.

18. Print the Chart1, Chart2, and PivotTable2 worksheets. Save and close the workbook.

Modify a PivotTable report. Create a PivotTable report with multiple fields and functions. Create a PivotChart report.

Klassy Kow Human Resources needs PivotTable reports showing statistics about its employees. They'd also like a PivotTable created for the Web site so that managers can see employee data when making hiring decisions.

1. Open the file **EmpPivot** and display the PivotTable1 worksheet.

2. In cell A1, edit the title to show **California Part-Time Employees**. Center the title across columns A–D.

3. For the State field, show only data for California.

 TIP: When it's difficult to drag a field to a particular area on a PivotTable, use the PivotTable Field List dialog box to add a field to a specific area.

4. In the PivotTable Field List, click the arrow for the Add To choice at the bottom of the dialog box and choose Data Area. Click Students in the field list and then click Add To.

5. Change Sum of Students to **Total Students**. Change Sum of Females to **Total Females** and Sum of Males to **Total Males**.

 REVIEW: Choose Table Options from the PivotTable choices to hide the totals rows.

6. Turn off the display of totals in rows 49 through 51. Add your footer. Horizontally center the worksheet.

7. Create a new PivotTable report for the EmpCounts sheet. Do not base it on the existing report, but place it in a new worksheet.

8. Place State as a row field and place City, Number of Employees, and Students as Data fields.

9. Change the Count of City field name to **Number of Cities**. Change Sum of Number of Employees to **Avg. # Employees** and the function from Sum to Average. Show the values as Number with no decimals.

10. Change Sum of Students to **Avg. # Students** and the function from Sum to Average. Show the values as Number with no decimals.

11. Turn off the display of totals in rows 16 through 18.

12. In cell A1, key **Employee Statistics by State**. Make it 16-point Arial. Use 12-point Arial bold for the labels in row 3. Adjust column widths.

13. Rename the sheet as **PivotTable2**. Add a footer and horizontally center the page.

14. Create a PivotChart from the PivotTable. Format the data series to show a different color for each column. Delete the legend and change the chart title to **Employee Statistics**. Make the title 16-point Arial. Add your footer.

15. Save the workbook as *[your initials]*24-31 in your Lesson 24 folder.

16. Print the PivotTable1, PivotTable2, and Chart1 worksheets. Save and close the workbook.

On Your Own

In these exercises you work on your own, as you would in a real-life work environment. Use the skills you've learned to accomplish the task—and be creative.

EXERCISE 24-32
Use the Internet to research credit card interest rates for unpaid balances. Set up a two-variable data table that calculates monthly interest charges from interest rates and balances due. Key various interest rates as the row values and a series of balances for the column values. Add a footer. Format the worksheet attractively and save it as *[your initials]*24-32 in your Lesson 24 folder. Print the workbook. Save and close the workbook.

EXERCISE 24-33
Use a local news source or the Internet to develop a list of high and low temperatures for the past 30 days in your city/state. Create and name the list for your data. Create a PivotTable for your list on a separate sheet, deciding how best to show the data. Format the PivotTable attractively. Save the workbook as *[your initials]*24-33 in your Lesson 24 folder. Add footers to both sheets. Print the workbook. Save and close the workbook.

EXERCISE 24-34
Create a list that tracks data of interest to you that can be displayed in a PivotTable and a PivotChart. Build and name the list and experiment creating a meaningful PivotTable and related chart. Format the reports attractively and add footers. Save the workbook as *[your initials]*24-34 in your Lesson 24 folder. Print all sheets. Save and close the workbook.

Unit 7 Applications

UNIT APPLICATION 7-1

Import a text file. Create a list with a formula. Sort and filter a list. Create subtotals.

Klassy Kow wants to analyze their inventory of stuffed animals for promotions. You must import, format, and edit a text file containing this data. Then you'll need to create a list so that you can filter, sort, and subtotal the data.

 REVIEW: When you open a text file in Excel, the Text Import Wizard starts.

1. Open **AnimalsCatalog.txt**, a delimited text file, in Excel. Fix obvious errors.

2. Insert three rows at row 1. In cell A1, key **Stuffed Animal Promotion**. In cell A2, key **Current Value of Inventory**. Choose a font size for these labels.

3. Key the following labels in the range A3:D3 and make them bold.
   Catalog No.   Animal Name   Group   List Price

4. Key these labels in the range E3:G3:
   Promotion   Number   Value

5. In cell G4, key a formula that multiplies the number in stock by the list price. Copy the formula to the range G5:G19. Adjust column widths.

 REVIEW: Include the header row when naming a list.

6. Select and name the list as a range. Sort the list by Value in descending order.

7. Add your footer, and horizontally center the worksheet.

8. Insert a new worksheet and name it **Criteria**. Position it to the right of the AnimalsCatalog sheet.

9. In cell A1, key **Stuffed Animal Promotion Data**. Make the label 16-point Arial.

 REVIEW: Copy the labels from the list for the criteria and output ranges.

10. Set up a criteria range for the list starting in cell A3. Name the criteria range using cells A3:G4.

11. In the AnimalsCatalog sheet, create and name an output range starting in cell I3.

12. Create an advanced filter for all records whose Value is greater than $3,000 and whose Group is D. Copy results to the output range. Cut and paste the entire output range to cell A10 in the Criteria worksheet.

13. In the Criteria sheet, add your footer. Horizontally center the sheet. Fix column widths.

14. Copy the AnimalsCatalog sheet to the end. Name the copied sheet as **Subtotals**.

REVIEW: Use the Sort dialog box for a multiple sort.

15. Sort the Subtotals sheet by Group in ascending order and by Value in descending order. Add subtotals to show the inventory value of each group.

16. Adjust column widths and use a light fill color for each Total row. Make the Grand Total row bold. Adjust row heights and make other formatting changes to make the sheet more attractive and easy to read.

17. Save the workbook as *[your initials]***u7-1** in your Unit 7 folder. Print the entire workbook.

18. Close the workbook.

UNIT APPLICATION 7-2

Query an Access database. Create a PivotTable report.

Klassy Kow has offered to help their promotion partner (Carolina Critters) determine how many times each customer has ordered and which salesperson handled the order. The data is in an Access table and must be imported.

1. Create a new workbook.

2. In cell A1, create a new database query for the MS Access file **Carolina.mdb**. Use all the columns from tblHistorySales. Do not use a filter but sort by OrderID in ascending order.

3. Name the sheet **HistorySales**. Format the Discount data as percent with no decimals. Format the OrderDate and ShipDate data as dates, using the m/dd/yy option. Adjust column widths.

 NOTE: Excel automatically names the imported data "Query_from_MS_Access_Database." You can create your own name for the list that is easier to remember.

4. Name the list. Add your footer, and horizontally center the sheet.

5. Create a PivotTable for your list, and place it in a new worksheet.

6. Place the CustomerID field as a row field and the EmployeeID as a column field. Use OrderID as a data field. Change the Sum of Order field name to **Number of Orders** and change the function to Count.

 NOTE: You can use Merge and Center for a single row.

7. In cell A1, key **Customers and Orders for 2003**. Make it 16-point Arial and center it across the table.

8. Add your footer and horizontally center the sheet. Rename the sheet as **PivotTable**. Delete Sheet2 and Sheet3.

9. Save the workbook as *[your initials]***u7-2** in your Unit 7 folder.

10. Print the entire workbook and close it.

UNIT APPLICATION 7-3

Create two-variable data tables.

Klassy Kow Ice Cream is using the multiplication and division tables again for special school promotions. These are to be built using two-variable data tables.

1. Open **Multiplication**.

 REVIEW: Use any two blank cells as input cells.

2. In cell A2, key a two-variable formula to compute the results in a data table. Use a row input cell and a column input cell.

3. Add borders and shading to the table so that it is easy to follow. Make the formula cell invisible.

4. Add your footer and center the page in a landscape orientation.

5. Make a copy of the sheet, display the formulas, and fit the columns. Delete the text box object. Delete Sheet2 and Sheet3.

6. Save the workbook as *[your initials]***u7-3a** in your Unit 7 folder and print both sheets. Close the workbook.

7. Open **Division** and repeat these steps. In your formula, divide the row values by the column values. Format the results in the data table to show five decimal places.

8. Save the workbook as *[your initials]***u7-3b** in your Unit 7 folder and print both sheets. Close the workbook.

UNIT APPLICATION 7-4 *Using the Internet*

Import data from the Web.

Search the Web site of a local community college or university. Find the current class schedule and course offerings. Use a Web query or other method to import at least ten rows of the schedule into a new workbook.

In the new worksheet, clean up the list to show basic information about the schedule (you decide). Key a new label in the first available column to show credit hours (if that information was not imported). Key logical credit hour values for the courses but make them different (2, 2.5, etc.).

Create a constant for the tuition rate per credit hour. Key a label in the next available column to show total tuition. Key and copy a formula to compute tuition for each course.

Format your schedule so that it is easy to read. Add a footer and save the workbook as *[your initials]***u7-4** in your Unit 7 folder. Print the worksheet and close the workbook.

Appendix

TABLE A-1

Microsoft Office Specialist Standards Related to Lessons

CODE	ACTIVITY	LESSON
XL03S-1	**Creating Data and Content**	
XL03S-1-1	Enter and edit cell content	1, 2, 3, 4, 6, 12
XL03S-1-2	Navigate to specific cell content	1, 3
XL03S-1-3	Locate, select, and insert supporting information	11
XL03S-1-4	Insert, position, and size graphics	10, 11
XL03S-2	**Analyzing Data**	
XL03S-2-1	Filter lists using AutoFilter	13
XL03S-2-2	Sort lists	13
XL03S-2-3	Insert and modify formulas	2, 5, 12
XL03S-2-4	Use statistical, date and time, financial, and logical functions	2, 6, 7, 8, 12, 13
XL03S-2-5	Create, modify, and position diagrams and charts based on worksheet data	9, 11
XL03S-3	**Formatting Data and Content**	
XL03S-3-1	Apply and modify cell formats	2, 3, 4, 5, 6, 11
XL03S-3-2	Apply and modify cell styles	7
XL03S-3-3	Modify row and column formats	2, 4
XL03S-3-4	Format worksheets	2, 5, 11
XL03S-4	**Collaborating**	
XL03S-4-1	Insert, view, and edit comments	10
XL03S-5	**Managing Workbooks**	
XL03S-5-1	Create new workbooks from templates	5
XL03S-5-2	Insert, delete, and move cells	2, 4, 12
XL03S-5-3	Create and modify hyperlinks	8
XL03S-5-4	Organize worksheets	4, 12
XL03S-5-5	Preview data in other views	1, 7, 11
XL03S-5-6	Customize window layout	4, 13, 14
XL03S-5-7	Set up pages for printing	3, 5, 7, 8, 13
XL03S-5-8	Print data	1, 3, 5, 12
XL03S-5-9	Organize workbooks using file folders	1
XL03S-5-10	Save data in appropriate formats for different uses	2, 8, 11, 13

TABLE A-2

Microsoft Office Expert Standards Related to Lessons

CODE	ACTIVITY	LESSON
XL03E-1	**Organizing and Analyzing Data**	
XL03E-1-1	Use subtotals	23
XL03E-1-2	Define and apply advanced filters	23
XL03E-1-3	Group and outline data	23
XL03E-1-4	Use data validation	16
XL03E-1-5	Create and modify list ranges	23
XL03E-1-6	Add, show, close, edit, merge, and summarize scenarios	19
XL03E-1-7	Perform data analysis using automated tools	19, 24
XL03E-1-8	Create PivotTable and PivotChart reports	24
XL03E-1-9	Use Lookup and Reference functions	15
XL03E-1-10	Use Database functions	23
XL03E-1-11	Trace formula precedents, dependents, and errors	15, 18
XL03E-1-12	Locate invalid data and formulas	18
XL03E-1-13	Watch and evaluate formulas	18
XL03E-1-14	Define, modify, and use named ranges	15
XL03E-1-15	Structure workbooks using XML	22
XL03E-2	**Formatting Data and Content**	
XL03E-2-1	Create and modify custom data formats	22
XL03E-2-2	Use conditional formatting	16, 23
XL03E-2-3	Format and resize graphics	11, 16, 17
XL03E-2-4	Format charts and diagrams	9, 11, 19
XL03E-3	**Collaborating**	
XL03E-3-1	Protect cells, worksheets, and workbooks	14, 16
XL03E-3-2	Apply workbook security settings	16, 17, 18, 19
XL03E-3-3	Share workbooks	21
XL03E-3-4	Merge workbooks	21
XL03E-3-5	Track, accept, and reject changes to workbooks	21
XL03E-4	**Managing Data and Workbooks**	
XL03E-4-1	Import data to Excel	22
XL03E-4-2	Export data from Excel	22
XL03E-4-3	Publish and edit Web worksheets and workbooks	23
XL03E-4-4	Create and edit templates	14, 16
XL03E-4-5	Consolidate data	20
XL03E-4-6	Define and modify workbook properties	16
XL03E-5	**Customizing Excel**	
XL03E-5-1	Customize toolbars and menus	17, 23
XL03E-5-2	Create, edit, and run macros	17
XL03E-5-3	Modify Excel default settings	16

TABLE A-3

Lessons Related to Microsoft Office Specialist Standards

LESSON		CODES*
1	Getting Started with Excel	XL03S-1-1, 1-2, 5-5, 5-8, 5-9
2	Creating a Workbook	XL03S-1-1, 2-3, 2-4, 3-1, 3-3, 3-4, 5-2, 5-10
3	Using Editing and Formatting Tools	XL03S-1-1, 1-2, 3-1, 5-7, 5-8
4	Working with Cells, Columns, Rows, and Sheets	XL03S-1-1, 3-1, 3-3, 5-2, 5-4, 5-6
5	Working with Simple Formulas	XL03S-2-3, 3-1, 3-4, 5-1, 5-7, 5-8
6	Working with Math & Trig, Statistical, and Date & Time Functions	XL03S-2-4, 3-1
7	Using Logical and Financial Functions	XL03S-2-4, 3-1, 3-2, 5-5, 5-7
8	Rounding and Nesting Functions	XL03S-2-4, 3-4, 5-3, 5-7, 5-10
9	Building Charts	XL03S-2-4, XL03E2-5
10	Using AutoShapes, WordArt, and Comments	XL03S-1-4, 4-1
11	Using Images, Diagrams, and Research	XL03S-1-3, 1-4, 2-3, 2-4, 2-5, 3-1, 3-4, 5-5, 5-10
12	Working with Multiple Worksheets	XL03S-1-1, 2-3, 2-4, 2-5, 5-2, 5-4, 5-8
13	Working with Lists	XL03S-2-1, 2-2, 2-4, 5-6, 5-7, 5-10
14	Using Worksheet Templates	XL03E-3-1, 4-4, 5-6
15	Working with Ranges and Lookup & Reference Functions	XL03E-1-9, 1-11, 1-14
16	Creating Worksheet and Workbook Templates	XL03E-1-4, 2-2, 2-3, 3-1, 3-2, 4-4, 4-6, 5-3
17	Working with Macros	XL03E-2-3, 3-2, 5-1, 5-2
18	Using Auditing Tools	XL03E-1-11, 1-12, 1-13, 3-2
19	Using What-If Analysis	XL03E-1-6, 1-7, 2-4, 3-2
20	Using Data Consolidation and Linking	XL03E-4-5
21	Using Workgroup Features	XL03E-3-3, 3-4, 3-5
22	Using Data from Other Sources	XL03E-1-15, 2-1, 4-1, 4-2
23	Using Lists and Database Features	XL03E-1-1, 1-2, 1-3, 1-5, 1-10, 2-2, 4-3, 5-1
24	Using Data and Pivot Tables	XL03E-1-7, 1-8

*Microsoft Office Specialist Activity codes are abbreviated in this table.

For more information about the Microsoft Office Specialist program, go to www.microsoft.com/officespecialist.

Glossary

(Numbers in parentheses indicate in the lesson in which the term first appeared or was first defined.)

3-D effect Command that applies a three-dimensional look to an object. (10)

3-D reference A cell address in a formula that refers to cells in another worksheet. (12)

Absolute reference A cell address that does not change when copied in a formula. (5)

Active cell The cell that is ready for data outlined with a thick border. (1)

Add-in Excel function, feature, or command that makes the workbook easier to use. It is installed separately from the main program. (19)

Adjustment handle Yellow diamond handle on an object used to change the shape and design of the object. (10)

Annuity A series of equal payments made at regular intervals for a set period of time. (7)

Argument Values or cell ranges between parentheses in a function or what a function needs to complete its calculation. (6)

Arithmetic mean An average of values calculated by adding the values and then dividing the total by the number of values. (6)

Arithmetic operators Math symbols for calculations (+, −, /, and *). (2)

Array A collection of cells or values that is used as a group in formulas or functions. (15)

Array formula A formula that carries out multiple calculations showing one or more results. (24)

Ascending sort Order in which data is arranged from lowest to highest value or A to Z. (13)

Ascending Text data arranged alphabetically and values arranged low to high. (23)

Assistant Organization chart shape that represents a helper. (11)

Auditing Practice of examining cells and formulas for accuracy. (18)

AutoCalculate Feature that displays sums, averages, counts, maximums, or minimums in the status bar. (2)

AutoComplete Feature that displays a suggested label after the first character is keyed in a cell in the column. (4)

AutoCorrect Excel feature that corrects common spelling errors as you type. (3)

AutoFill Feature that copies or extends data from a cell or range to adjacent cells. (3)

AutoFit To size a column to its longest entry or size a row to the font. (2)

AutoFormat Built-in set of formatting instructions that applies fonts, colors, borders, and other formats to a range. (3)

AutoShape Common, recognized figure, shape, or outline on the Drawing toolbar. (10)

Background An image that displays onscreen for the worksheet. (5)

Backsolve What-if analysis in reverse. It involves knowing the

results and then determining the formula arguments. (19)

Book.xlt Default workbook saved in XLStart folder. (16)

Border Line drawn around a cell or range of cells. (4)

Bounding box Imaginary rectangular box or outline for objects. (10)

Button Control or object on a toolbar. (17)

Callout Descriptive text enclosed in a shape with a pointer or arrow connector. (10)

Category axis What is shown in a chart, created from row or column headings. (9)

Category title Optional label for the axis in a chart. (9)

Cell Intersection of a column and row in a worksheet with an address or reference such as B5. (1)

Cell address Column letter and row number that identifies a location in the worksheet. (1)

Cell alignment Feature that describes and sets how the contents of a cell are positioned within the cell. (4)

Cell protection The ability to set whether cell content can be edited. (14)

Cell reference The cell address or location in the worksheet. (1)

Change history List of changes made to cells in a shared workbook that can be printed. (21)

Character string Sequence of letters, numbers, or other symbols. (3)

Chart Visual display of worksheet data. (9)

Chart area Background of a chart. (9)

Chart title Optional title or name for the chart. (9)

Circular reference A cell address in a formula that refers to itself. (15)

Code Lines written in a programming language. (17)

Code window Part of Visual Basic Editor that displays the macro programming commands. (17)

Column Vertical group of cells in a worksheet identified by an alphabetic letter. (1)

Combination chart Chart with series that use different chart types. (9)

Comment A pop-up cell attachment with descriptive or explanatory text. (10)

Conditional formatting Cell formatting applied only when the cell contents meet the criteria. (16)

Consolidate by category Consolidation in which data in multiple worksheets or workbooks is located in different locations. (20)

Consolidate by position Consolidation in which data in multiple worksheets or workbooks is located in the same locations. (20)

Consolidation Procedure in which data from more than one worksheet or workbook is combined and summarized. (20)

Constant A value used in formulas that does not change. (15)

Constraint A restriction or requirement for a cell value when using Solver. (19)

Control Worksheet object that, when clicked, carries out a task. (17)

Cost The original price of an item or asset. (7)

Coworker Organizational chart shape that represents an employee or colleague. (11)

Criteria Conditions or specifications for matching records. (23)

Criteria range An area on a worksheet that holds conditions for a filter. (23)

Crop Remove parts of an image from view. (11)

Custom format Format created using Excel's codes. (22)

Custom template A workbook model with sample values, labels, formulas, and images. (14)

Data label Optional title for each value in a chart. (9)

Data marker Object that displays individual values, such as a bar or column in a chart. (9)

Data point One value from the data series in a chart. (9)

Data series Collection of related values in the worksheet. (9)

Data table Cell range that displays results from changing values in a formula. (24)

Data table range Cell range that includes data table formula and all input values. (24)

Data validation Feature in which cell entry is checked as it is entered to verify that it matches specified conditions. (16)

DB Financial function that determines the depreciation of an asset. (7)

Delimiter Character in a text file that separates columns. (22)

Dependent A cell that relies on another cell for its value. (18)

Dependent workbook A workbook that has linked formulas (external references) that refer to another workbook. (20)

Descending sort Order in which data is arranged from highest to lowest value or Z to A. (13)

Diagram Object that illustrates an idea or concept. (11)

Digital signature Electronic authentication stamp on a document. (17)

Discussion comment A worksheet attachment that is visible in a browser for online collaboration. (10)

Drag-and-drop pointer Four-headed arrow pointer that appears when the pointer rests on the edge of a cell. It is used to copy or cut a cell or range by dragging. (4)

Draw layer Invisible surface, separate from and on top of the worksheet, that holds drawing objects and images. (10)

Dynamic consolidation A data consolidation that results in a formula. (20)

Dynamic link A formula that refers to another cell. (12)

Electronic spreadsheet software Computer software that produces reports with business and personal calculations, database management, or charts. (1)

Embedded chart Chart that appears on the same sheet as the worksheet data. (9)

End Sub Code that ends a subroutine macro. (17)

Exploded pie chart Pie chart in which one or more slice(s) is detached from the rest of the pie. (9)

Export Sending or saving Excel data for use in another program. (22)

External reference formula Formulas that refer to cells in another workbook. (20)

Field A single category or column in a list. (23)

Field name A label in the first (header) row of a list. (23)

Field value An individual piece of data in a list. (23)

Filename Document name or identifier. (2)

Fill handle Small rectangle at the lower-right corner of a cell or range used for extending a series or copying data. (3)

Filter Criteria that sets a specification for which data will be shown. (13)

Financial function Formula that performs a common business calculation involving money. (7)

Folder Storage location for work files on a disk. (1)

Footer Data that prints at the bottom of each page in a worksheet. (3)

Formula Series of calculations, expressions, numbers, and operators to carry out an arithmetic command. (1)

Function Built-in mathematical formula. (2)

Function Arguments palette Dialog box that displays help and entry areas for completing a function. (6)

FV Financial function argument that specifies the value of the cash at the end of the time period. (7)

Goal Seek Command that backsolves or adjusts the value in a cell value to reach a desired outcome. (19)

Gradient Blend of colors used to fill charts and other objects. (9)

Gridline Horizontal or vertical line in the plot area of a chart to mark values. (9)

Header Data that prints at the top of each page in a worksheet. (3)

Header row First row in a list with unique labels or titles for each column. (23)

HTML Hypertext Markup Language, a widely used format for Web pages. (11)

Hyperlink A clickable text or object that, when clicked, displays another file, another program, or an Internet site/address. (8)

Import Placing data from another program into Excel. (22)

Input cell Placeholder cell used in a data table formula to represent the changing values. (24)

Input values Numbers keyed in either a row or column for a data table. (24)

Integer A whole number or a number with no decimal or fractional parts. (8)

Interactive workbook A workbook saved as a Web page that can be edited in a browser. (23)

Interval Number of steps between values or labels in a series. (3)

Label An entry in a cell that begins with a letter. (2)

Landscape Print orientation that prints a horizontal page that is wider than it is tall. (5)

Leading zero A zero shown as the first digit in a value. (4)

Legend Chart object that explains the colors, patterns, or symbols used in the chart. (9)

Life Number of periods over which an asset is depreciated. (7)

Linking Procedure in which formulas in a worksheet refer to cells in another workbook. (20)

List Table of information with rows of data and a row of labels. (13)

Literal Text, symbol, or values to be shown exactly as is in the format, enclosed in quotation marks in the code. (22)

Lock Property that makes a cell available for editing. (14)

Logical function Formula that determines whether or not something is true. (7)

Macro A sequence of commands and keystrokes that perform a task. (17)

Macro security Computer setting to determine how macros are accepted or reviewed. (17)

Mail-enabled The ability to e-mail a file without closing the application. (8)

Marker Small black rectangle at the location for margin and column edges in Print Preview. (3)

Math hierarchy Alternative term for order of precedence. (5)

Mixed reference A cell address that adjusts either the row or the column when the formula is copied. (5)

Name box Text box in the formula bar that shows current cell address. (1)

Nested function A function inside another function. The second or third functions are used as arguments in the first function. (8)

Nper Financial function argument that specifies the total number of payments or time periods. (7)

Numeric keypad Set of number and symbol keys at the right of the keyboard. (4)

Object Separate element or part of a worksheet. (9)

Office Clipboard Temporary memory area that can hold up to 24 copied elements. (4)

Order of operation Alternative term for order of precedence. (5)

Order of precedence Mathematical rules that determine which part of a formula is calculated first. (5)

Organization chart Object that illustrates hierarchical relationships, usually among company workers. (11)

Outline Worksheet with data that is grouped into detail and summary rows/columns. (23)

Output range An area on a worksheet that holds the results of an advanced filter. (23)

Page break Solid or dashed line to signal where printer will start a new page. (7)

Page orientation Print setting that determines landscape or portrait layout. (5)

Parameter The data or information needed by Solver to determine a solution. (19)

Path File identifier that includes the drive and series of folders to locate a file. (20)

Pattern Cross-hatched, dotted, or other pattern used to fill chart and other objects. (9)

Period The time for which depreciation is calculated. (7)

Pick From List Feature that displays a list of all labels already in a column. (4)

PivotTable List A PivotTable report placed on the Web with interactivity. (24)

PivotTable report Excel table that summarizes data from a list. (24)

Pixel A single screen dot. (2)

Plot area Rectangular bounding area for the category and value axes in a chart. (9)

Portrait Print orientation that prints a page that is taller than it is wide. (5)

Precedent A cell that contributes or provides data to a formula's results. (18)

Preview image Small replica or picture of a workbook for display in the Open and Templates dialog boxes. (14)

Print area Range of cells to be printed. (13)

Property Setting or attribute for a workbook, a cell, or an object. (14)

Protection Worksheet setting that prohibits some edits to cells and objects. (14)

PV Financial function argument that specifies the current cash value of the money transaction. (7)

Query File that specifies and gets certain data from a list. (22)

Range A group of cells that forms a rectangle. (2)

Rate Financial function argument that specifies the interest rate for the time period. (7)

Record A row of data in a list. (23)

Relative reference A cell address that adjusts to the row or column where a copied formula is located. (5)

Replacement string Sequence of characters that is exchanged for existing data in the Replace command. (3)

Rotation handle Green oval handle (circle) on an object used to rotate the shape using the mouse. (10)

Rounding To make a value larger or smaller depending on a specified digit to the left or right of the decimal point. (8)

Row Horizontal group of cells identified by a number in a worksheet. (1)

Salvage The value of an asset after it has been depreciated. (7)

Scale Resize an image by a percentage so that it is proportional. (11)

Scenario A saved set of values for a worksheet. (19)

Scenario summary report A report in outline format that lists changing and results cells for each scenario in a worksheet. (19)

ScreenTip A box on the screen with the name of a button. It appears when you rest the mouse pointer on the button. (1)

Secondary axis Separate set of values for a data series in a chart. (9)

Selection handles Black rectangles surrounding an active object; or, white circles surrounding the bounding box of a drawing object. (9, 10)

Selection pointer White cross-shaped pointer used to select or activate cells. (1)

Serial number Number system assigned to dates, counting from January 1, 1900, as 1. (6)

Series List of labels, numbers, dates, or times that follows a pattern. (3)

Shading Background pattern or color for a cell or range of cells. (4)

Shared workbook Workbook that can be used by several people at the same time. (21)

Sheet.xlt Default worksheet saved in XLStart folder. (16)

Sizing pointer Mouse pointer shaped as a two-headed arrow. (10)

Smart tag Labels with command options for recognized data. (22)

Solver An Excel add-in that backsolves the value for a cell with a formula. (19)

Source workbook A workbook that contains cells used in an external reference in a dependent workbook. (20)

Static consolidation A data consolidation that results in a value. (20)

Style Set of formatting specifications for labels and/or values. (7)

Sub Code that begins a subroutine macro. (17)

Subordinate Organizational chart shape that represents an employee. (11)

Subroutine macro Command sequence than can be run from a workbook or from within another macro. (17)

Superior shape Top shape in an organization chart. (11)

Synchronous scrolling Feature that allows multiple windows to move in the same direction by the same number of rows/columns. (14)

Synonym A word that means the same thing. (11)

Syntax Structure or necessary parts and the order of those parts for a function. (6)

Template Model or sample workbook that can include font types, styles, alignment settings, borders, labels, values, and formulas. It is saved with an **.xlt** extension. (5)

Template Gallery Web site with templates for downloading. (14)

Text box Drawing object with no connector lines for displaying text. (10)

Text file File format that includes unformatted text separated into columns by tabs, commas, or another character. (13)

Texture Grainy or nonsmooth surface appearance used to fill charts and other objects. (9)

Thesaurus Reference book that lists words with the same meaning. (11)

Tick mark Line or marker on an axis to display values. (9)

TIF Tagged Image Format, a popular file format for printed images. (11)

Tiled Object that repeats at a default size across the sheet. (11)

Trace Error button Icon with an exclamation point that notes a problem in a formula. (1)

Trendline A line added to a chart the points out and forecasts future directions and trends in values. (19)

Type Financial function argument that specifies whether the payment/deposit is made at the beginning or end of the period. (7)

User template A template with values, formulas, labels, images, and more for daily use. (16)

Value An entry in a cell that begins with a number or an arithmetic symbol. (2)

Value axis Horizontal or vertical grouping of values from the worksheet. (9)

View Display and print settings that can be saved with a workbook. (13)

Visual Basic Editor Window used to view, edit, or create a macro. (17)

Watch window A window that shows formulas and results while a worksheet is being edited. (18)

Web query A request to get data from a table or preformatted data in a Web page. (22)

What-if analysis Business practice of testing values in a worksheet to forecast and predict future results. (19)

Whole number A value without a fraction or decimal. (6)

Wildcard Character that represents one or more unknown letters or numbers. (3)

Windows Clipboard Temporary memory area that holds cut or copied data. (4)

Wizard Series of dialog boxes for making choices and building a chart. (9)

WordArt Application that inserts shaped and colored text as an object. (10)

WordArt Gallery Collection of 30 styles for text images. (10)

Workbook Excel file that holds worksheets with data. A workbook has an **.xls** filename extension. (1)

Workgroup People who share work. (21)

Worksheet Individual page or sheet in a workbook, shown by a tab at the bottom of the screen. (1)

Workspace A file that specifies workbook names, screen positions, and window sizes. (20)

XML Extensible Markup Language, used to create a text file for exchanging data on the Web. (22)

XML map Tree layout of tags and elements in an XML file. (22)

Zoom size Setting that controls how much of the worksheet appears at once on the screen. (1)

Index

See Glossary for a comprehensive list of terms.